À bord

ABOUT THE AUTHORS

Conrad J. Schmitt

Conrad J. Schmitt received his B.A. degree magna cum laude from Montclair State College, Upper Montclair, NJ. He received his M.A. from Middlebury College, Middlebury, VT. He did additional graduate work at Seton Hall University and New York University.

Mr. Schmitt has taught French and Spanish at the elementary, junior, and senior high school levels. He was Coordinator of Foreign Languages for the Hackensack, New Jersey Public Schools. He also taught French at Upsala College, East Orange, New Jersey; Spanish at Montclair State College; and Methods of Teaching a Foreign Language at the Graduate School of Education, Rutgers University. He was editor-in-chief of Foreign Languages and Bilingual Education for McGraw-Hill Book Company and Director of English Language Materials for McGraw-Hill International Book Company.

Mr. Schmitt has authored or co-authored more than eighty books, all published by Glencoe/McGraw- Hill or by McGraw-Hill. He has addressed teacher groups and given workshops in all states of the U.S. and has lectured and presented seminars throughout the Far East, Europe, Latin America, and Canada. In addition, Mr. Schmitt has travelled extensively throughout France, French-speaking Canada, North Africa, the French Antilles, and Haiti.

Katia Brillié Lutz

Ms. Lutz was Executive Editor of French at Macmillan Publishing Company. Prior to that, she taught French language and literature at Yale University and Southern Connecticut State College. Ms. Lutz also served as a senior editor at Harcourt Brace Jovanovich and Holt, Rinehart and Winston. She was a news translator and announcer for the BBC Overseas Language Services in London.

Ms. Lutz has her *Baccalauréat* in Mathematics and Science from the Lycée Molière in Paris and her *Licence és lettres* in Languages from the Sorbonne. She was a Fulbright Scholar at Mount Holyoke College. Ms. Lutz is author of many foreign language textbooks at all levels of instruction. She presently devotes her time to teaching French at the United Nations and to writing.

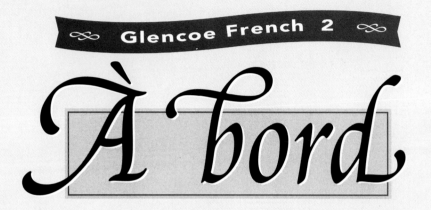

Glencoe French 2

À bord

Conrad J. Schmitt

Katia Brillié Lutz

Glencoe McGraw-Hill

New York, New York   Columbus, Ohio   Woodland Hills, California   Peoria, Illinois

Glencoe/McGraw-Hill

A Division of The **McGraw·Hill** *Companies*

Send all inquiries to:
Glencoe/McGraw-Hill
21600 Oxnard Street, Suite 500
Woodland Hills, CA 91367

ISBN 0-02-636814-5

2 3 4 5 6 7 8 9 027 03 02 01 00 99 98

CONTENTS

INTRODUCTION

Welcome to **Glencoe French**, the junior high and high school French series from Glencoe/McGraw-Hill. Every element in this series has been designed to help you create an atmosphere of challenge, variety, cooperation, and enjoyment for your students. From the moment you begin to use **Glencoe French**, you will notice that not only is it packed with exciting, practical materials and features designed to stimulate young people to work together towards language proficiency, but that it goes beyond by urging students to use their new skills in other areas of the curriculum.

Glencoe French uses an integrated approach to language learning: from the introduction of new material, through reinforcement, evaluation and review, its presentations, exercises and activities are designed to span all four language skills. Another characteristic of this series is that students use and reinforce these new skills while developing a realistic, up-to-date awareness of French culture. **Glencoe French** also incorporates a new feature in which French is used as the medium of instruction for a series of interdisciplinary presentations in the areas of natural sciences, social sciences, and the arts and humanities.

The Teacher's Wraparound Edition you are reading has been developed based on the advice of experienced foreign language educators throughout the United States in order to meet your needs as a teacher both in and out of the foreign language classroom. Here are some of the features and benefits which make **Glencoe French** a powerful set of teaching tools:

- flexible format
- student-centered instruction
- balance among all four language skills
- contextualized vocabulary
- thorough, contextual presentation of grammar
- an integrated approach to culture

FEATURES AND BENEFITS

Flexible Format While we have taken every opportunity to use the latest in pedagogical developments in order to create a learning atmosphere of variety, vitality, communication and challenge, we have also made every effort to make the **Glencoe French** series "teacher-friendly." This is where flexibility comes in.

The Student Textbook and the Teacher's Wraparound Edition provide an instructional method. However, every minute of every class period is not laid out. Plenty of room has been built in for you the teacher to be flexible: to draw on your own education, experience and personality in order to tailor a language program that is suitable and rewarding for the individual "chemistry" of each class.

A closer look at the most basic component, the Student Textbook, serves as an example of this flexibility. Each chapter opens with two sections of vocabulary (*Vocabulaire*: *Mots 1* and *Mots 2*) each with its own set of exercises. *Vocabulaire* is followed by the *Structure* consisting of a series of grammar points, each with accompanying exercises. But, there is nothing which says that the material must be presented in this order. The items of vocabulary and grammar are so well integrated that you will find it easy, and perhaps preferable, to move back and forth between them. You may also wish to select from the third and fourth sections of each chapter (the *Conversation* and *Lecture et culture* sections) at an earlier point than that at which they are presented, as a means of challenging students to identify or use the chapter vocabulary and grammar to which they have already been introduced.

These options are left to you. The only requirement for moving successfully through the Student Textbook is that the vocabulary and grammar of each chapter eventually be presented in their entirety, since each succeeding chapter builds on what has come before.

In the Student Textbook, there is a marked difference between learning exercises (*Exercices*) and communication-based activities (*Activités de communication*), both of which are provided in each chapter. The former serve as their name implies, as exercises for the acquisition and practice of new vocabulary and structures, while the latter are designed to get students communicating in open-ended contexts using the French they have learned. You can be selective among these, depending on the needs of your students.

We have been looking only at the Student Textbook. The abundance of suggestions for techniques, strategies, additional practice, chapter projects, independent (homework) assignments, informal assessment, and more, which are provided in this Teacher's Wraparound Edition—as well as the veritable banquet of resources available in the wide array of ancillary materials provided in the series—are what make **Glencoe French** truly flexible and "teacher-friendly." They guarantee you a great pool of ideas and teaching tools from which to pick and choose in order to create an outstanding course.

Student-Centered Instruction Teaching a foreign language requires coping with different learning styles and special student needs. It

requires the ability to capitalize on the great cultural and economic diversity present in many classrooms and to turn this diversity into an engine for learning by putting students together in goal-oriented groups. It often requires effective techniques for managing large classes.

Glencoe French anticipates these requirements by offering ideas for setting up a cooperative learning environment for students. Useful suggestions to this end accompany each chapter, under the heading Cooperative Learning, in the bottom margin of the Teacher's Wraparound Edition. Additional paired and group activities occur in the Student Textbook (*Activités de communication*), and in headings such as Additional Practice in the Teacher's Wraparound Edition.

Besides cooperative learning strategies, **Glencoe French** contains many other student-centered elements that allow students to expand their learning experiences. Here are a few examples: suggestions are offered in the Teacher's Wraparound Edition for out-of-class projects on topics related to the chapter theme. In Level 1, there is a topic called "For the Younger Student," with activities aimed primarily at stimulating the middle school/junior high student. In the Student Textbook, new grammatical material is divided into "bite-sized" lessons, so as not to be intimidating. The Writing Activities Workbook provides a self-test after every fourth chapter, so that students can prepare alone or in study groups for teacher-administered quizzes and tests. The Audio Cassette Program allows students to work at their own pace, stopping the tape whenever necessary to make directed changes in the language or to refer to their activity sheets in the Student Tape Manual. The Computer Software element consists of not only a Test Generator for the teacher, but also a Practice Generator for students, with which they can practice vocabulary and grammar items at their own pace.

These and other features discussed elsewhere in this Teacher's Manual have been designed with the student in mind. They assure that each individual, regardless of learning style, special need, background, or age, will have the necessary resources for becoming proficient in French.

Balance Among All Four Language Skills

Glencoe French provides a balanced focus on the listening, speaking, reading, and writing skills throughout all phases of instruction. And since it is "teacher-friendly," it gives you leeway if you wish to adjust the integration of these skills to the needs of a particular individual, group or class. Several features of the series lend themselves to this: the overall flexibility of format, the abundance of suggested optional and additional activities and the design of the individual activities themselves. Flexibility was discussed above. Let's look at some sections of a typical chapter as examples of the other two characteristics mentioned.

If the suggested presentation is followed, students are introduced to new words and phrases in *Vocabulaire* by the teacher, and/or by the audio cassette presentation. The focus is on listening and speaking through modeling and repetition. The *Exercices* which accompany the *Vocabulaire* section can be done with books either closed (accentuating listening and speaking) or open (accentuating reading, listening and speaking). However, these *Exercices* can just as well be assigned or reassigned as written work if the teacher wishes to have the whole class or individuals begin to concentrate on reading and writing. Throughout the *Vocabulaire* section, optional and additional reinforcement activities are suggested in the Teacher's Wraparound Edition.

These suggestions address all four language skills. Later in each chapter, students are asked to combine the material learned in *Vocabulaire* with material from the grammar section (*Structure*) using a combination of listening, reading, writing and speaking skills in the process.

Reading and writing activities are brought into play early in the **Glencoe French** series. The authors realize that communication in French includes the use of reading and writing skills and that these skills are indispensable for the assimilation and retention of new language and the organization of thought. Students are launched into writing, for example, as early as Level 1, Chapter 1, through the use of brief assignments such as lists, labeled diagrams, notetaking or short answers. Longer writing activities are added in later chapters. These textbook activities are further reinforced in the Writing Activities Workbook.

Let's take a closer look at how each of the four skills is woven into the Student Textbook, the Teacher's Wraparound Edition and the ancillary materials.

Listening You the teacher are the primary source for listening, as you model new vocabulary, dialogues, structure and pronunciation, share your knowledge of French culture, history and geography, talk to students about their lives and your own, or engage in culturally oriented activities and projects. As always, it is your ability to use French as much as possible with your students, both in and outside of the classroom, which determines how relevant and dynamic their learning experience will be.

Glencoe French offers numerous ways in which to develop the listening skill. There are teacher-focused activities, which provide the consistent modeling that students need. Teachers who use the Audio Program will find that these recordings help students become accustomed to a variety of voices, as well as rates of speech. There are also activities in which students interact with each other to develop listening spontaneity and acuity.

In the Student Textbook, new vocabulary will be modeled by the teacher. Students' attention to the sounds of the new words can be maximized by presenting this material with books closed and using the Vocabulary Transparencies to convey meaning. Following each *Mots* segment are several *Exercices* for practicing the new vocabulary. These can also be done with books closed. After the two *Mots* segments come *Activités de communication*, in which students may work in pairs or groups and must listen to each other in order to find information, take notes or report to others on what was said in their group. In *Structure*, students listen as the teacher models new grammatical material and then are given a chance to practice each structure in several *exercices*. Once again, closing the book will provide increased focus on the listening skill. The next section of each chapter is *Conversation*, in which a real-life dialogue is modeled either by the teacher or by playing the recorded version from the Audio Program. The dialogue is followed by several communication-based activities, where students must listen to and interact with their peers. In *Bienvenue* (Level 1),

Conversation also contains a *Prononciation* segment, covering an aspect of pronunciation related to the chapter material. Here again, students will be listening either to the teacher or recorded models. The last section of each chapter, *Culmination*, offers more listening-intensive *Activités de communication orale*, where students must be able to understand what their partners say in order to play their role.

In addition to the Student Textbook, the Teacher's Wraparound Edition offers several other listening-based activities correlated to the chapters, the most intensive of which occur under the heading "Total Physical Response" (Level 1) and "Pantomime" (Level 2). Here students must perform an action after listening to a spoken command. There are further listening-based activities suggested under the heading "Cooperative Learning" and often under "Additional Practice," both of which occur in the bottom margins in each Teacher's Wraparound Edition chapter.

The Audio Cassette Program has two main listening components. The first is practice-oriented, wherein students further reinforce vocabulary and grammar, following directions and making changes in utterances. They can self-check their work by listening to the correctly modeled utterances, which are supplied after a pause.

The second part of the program places more attention on the receptive listening skills. Students listen to language in the form of dialogues, announcements, or advertisements— language delivered at a faster pace and in greater volume—and then are asked to demonstrate their understanding of the main ideas and important details of what they have heard. The Student Tape Manual contains activity sheets for doing this work, and the Teacher Edition contains the complete transcript of all audio materials to assist you in laying out listening tasks for your class.

More listening practice is offered through the Videocassette Program. This material corresponds to and enriches that in the Student Textbook, and gives students a chance to hear variations of the language elements they have been practicing, as spoken by a variety of native speakers from different parts of France and other francophone countries. Students' listening comprehension can be checked and

augmented by using the corresponding print activities in the Video Activities Booklet.

Speaking Most of the areas of the Student Textbook and the Teacher's Wraparound Edition mentioned above which develop listening skills simultaneously develop the speaking skill. After hearing a model in the *Vocabulaire* or *Structure* sections, students will repeat it, either as a whole class, in small groups, or as individuals. From these modeled cues, they will progress to visual ones, supplied by the Vocabulary Transparencies or the photos and graphics in the textbook. The real thrust in the *Exercices* accompanying these two sections is to get students to produce this new material actively. Then, in the *Activités de communication*, students have the opportunity to adapt what they have learned by asking for and giving information to their classmates on a given topic. Here, and in the *Conversation* sections, students are engaged in meaningful, interesting sessions of sharing information, all designed to make them want to speak and experiment with the language. The Student Textbook regularly enriches this by offering expressions and mannerisms of speech currently popular in French culture, especially among teenagers, so that from the start your students will be accustomed to speaking in a way that is reflective of contemporary French. In Level 1, Chapter 2, for example, popular adjectives of pleasure or displeasure are taught, such as *chouette, moche, extra,* and *terrible.* Previously presented material is constantly recycled in the communication-based activities, so that students' speaking vocabularies and knowledge of structure are always increasing. For this purpose, beginning with Level 1, Chapter 3, there is a *Réintroduction et recombinaison* segment in the *Culmination* section. Another feature of the Student Textbook is that the length of utterances is increased over time, so that when students complete Level 1 (*Bienvenue*) they will have acquired an appreciation of the intonation and inflection of longer streams of language. To assist you in fine-tuning your students' speech patterns, the *Prononciation* section occurs in each chapter of the Level 1 Student Textbook.

The speaking skill is stressed in the first part of each recorded chapter of the Audio Program, where pauses are provided for the student to produce directed, spoken changes in the language. This is an excellent opportunity for those students who are self-conscious about speaking out in class. The Audio Program gives these students a chance to work in isolation, and the format of making a change in the language, uttering the change and then listening for the correct model may improve the speaking skill. Sensitively administered, the Audio Program can serve as a confidence-builder for such students, allowing them to work their way gradually into more spontaneous speech with their classmates.

The packet of Situation Cards provides students with yet another opportunity to produce spoken French. They put the student into a contextualized, real-world situation. Students must ask and/or answer questions in order to perform successfully.

Reading Each chapter of the Student Textbook has a *Lecture et culture* section containing two readings based on the chapter theme. The first reading is accompanied by a comprehension check and an exercise called *Étude de mots*, which focuses on useful strategies for vocabulary-building and recognizing word relationships, which students can carry over into other readings. The second reading, *Découverte culturelle*, is optional and is to be read for more specific and detailed information about the theme of the chapter and as a stimulus for discussion on this theme. In the next section of each chapter, *Réalités*, students again use their reading skills albeit to a lesser degree. While the *Réalités* section is primarily visual in nature, students nevertheless are referred to numbered captions to learn more about the photographs shown in this two-page spread.

After every four chapters of the Student Textbook, **Glencoe French** provides a unique section called *Lettres et sciences*. This presentation is designed to use reading as a means of bridging the gap between French and other areas of the curriculum. Three separate readings are offered, one in each of the three areas of natural sciences, social sciences, arts and humanities. Here students have a chance to stretch their reading abilities in French by reading basic information they may have already learned in other academic subjects. Although the material has been carefully written to include themes (as well as words and structures) which students have learned in

previous chapters, it contains the most challenging readings. The *Lettres et sciences* sections are optional.

The Writing Activities Workbook offers additional readings under the heading *Un Peu Plus*. These selections and the accompanying exercises focus on reading strategies such as cognate recognition, related word forms and the use of context clues.

In addition to the reading development above, students are constantly presented with authentic French texts such as announcements from periodicals, telephone listings, transportation schedules, labeled diagrams, floor plans, travel brochures, school progress reports and many others, as sources of information. Sometimes these documents serve as the bases for language activities, and other times they appear in order to round out a cultural presentation, but, in varying degrees, they all require students to apply their reading skills.

Writing Written work is interwoven throughout the language learning process in **Glencoe French**. The exercises, which occur throughout the *Vocabulaire* and *Structure* sections of each chapter in the Student Textbook, are designed in such a way that they can be completed in written form as well as orally. Frequently, you may wish to reassign (as written homework) exercises which you have gone through orally in class. The Teacher's Wraparound Edition makes special note of this under the topic "Independent Practice." At the end of each chapter of the Student Textbook, direct focus is placed on writing in the *Culmination* section, under the heading *Activités de communication écrite*. Here there are one or more activities that encourage students to use the new vocabulary and structures they have learned in the chapter to create their own writing samples. These are short, and may be descriptive, narrative, argumentative, analytical or in the form of dialogues or interviews. Often a context is set up and then students are asked to develop an appropriate written response.

The Writing Activities Workbook is the component in which writing skills receive the most overt attention. All of the exercises in it are writing-based, and they vary in length from one-word answers to short compositions. They are designed to focus on the same vocabulary and grammar presented in the corresponding chapter of the Student Textbook, but they are all new and all contextualized around fresh visual material or situational vignettes. Since they often have students making lists, adding to charts, and labeling, they provide an excellent means for them to organize the chapter material in their minds and make associations which will help them retain it. As students' knowledge of French increases, longer written pieces are required of them. One workbook section entitled *Mon Autobiographie* has students write installments of their own autobiographies. This is an effective way of stretching student writing skills. It also challenges students to personalize the French they have been studying.

Besides these major sources of writing, students are asked to make implicit use of writing almost everywhere in the series. They are constantly taking notes, listing, categorizing, labeling, summarizing, comparing or contrasting on paper. Even the Audio Program and the Videocassette Program involve students in writing through the use of activity sheets. By choosing among these options, you can be sure that your students will receive the practice they need to develop their writing skills successfully.

Contextualized Vocabulary

From the moment students see new words at the beginning of each chapter in **Glencoe French**, they see them within an identifiable context. So from the start, students learn to group words by association, thereby enhancing their ability to assimilate and store vocabulary for long-term retention. This contextualization remains consistent throughout the practice, testing and recycling phases of learning.

In the *Vocabulaire* section, each of the *Mots* segments contains a short exchange or a few lead-in sentences or phrases which, together with interesting, colorful visuals, establish the context. Other vocabulary items which occur naturally within this context are laid out among additional visuals, often as labels. The result is that students see at a glance the new language set into a real-life situation which provides "something to talk about"—a reason for using it. The accompanying exercises enrich this context. Each *exercice* practice item is related to the others within the set, so that when taken together they form a meaningful

vignette or story. In later sections of the chapter, i.e., *Structure, Conversation, Lecture et culture, Réalités* and *Culmination*, these words and phrases are reintroduced frequently.

Moreover, future chapters build on vocabulary and grammar from previous ones. Chapter themes introduced in Level 1 are reintroduced in Level 2 along with additional related vocabulary. Special attention has been given vocabulary in the reading sections of the series as well. For example, in *Lecture et culture*, students are encouraged to stretch their vocabularies in order to get as much meaning as possible from the selections. In addition to glossed words and frequent use of cognate recognition, the corresponding *Étude de mots* is there to help them with this. Another example is the *Lettres et sciences* section after every four chapters. The selections here include glossaries of the most important new vocabulary items, and the accompanying activities put implicit understanding of vocabulary to the test.

Thorough, Contextual Presentation of Grammar

A quick look through the chapters of *Bienvenue* (Level 1) and *À bord* (Level 2) will show the role grammar plays in the overall approach of the **Glencoe French** series. Although grammar is by no means the driving force behind the series, it is indeed an important aspect. In **Glencoe French**, grammar is presented as one of seven sections in each chapter. What makes this series particularly effective is that, as well as being thorough, the presentation of grammar runs concurrent with, and is embedded in, the chapter-long situational themes. Students are presented with French structure both directly, as grammar, and also as a set of useful functions that will aid them in communication, in expanding and improving their French across the four skills, and in learning about French culture as well as other areas of the school curriculum. Another important series characteristic is that the presentation of grammar has been divided into short, coherent "doses," which prevent grammar from becoming overwhelming to the student.

As you use this series, you will see as you teach the various grammar topics, student interest is kept high due to the presence of meaningful context and the diversity of the tasks that are given. As is the case with the vocabulary exercises, the individual practice items in the grammar section are related to each other contextually, in order to heighten student interest while assimilating and personalizing a new structure.

You will find that it is easy to move in and out of the teaching of grammar, dipping into the other sections of a chapter or other components as you see fit. This is true for several reasons: the grammar segments are short and intelligently divided, each one providing a good sense of closure; language elements (including grammar) taught in one section have been included as much as possible in the others; and again, there is a coherent contextual theme.

Aside from the Student Textbook and Teacher's Wraparound Edition, with their focus on grammar in the *Structure* section of each chapter and in the *Révision* after every four chapters, **Glencoe French** offers students opportunities to practice grammar in other components as well. Chapter by chapter, the Writing Activities Workbook provides ample tasks in which students must put into writing the new structures on which they have been working in class. The Audio Program includes recorded sections in every chapter of the Student Tape Manual which correspond directly to *Structure* in the Student Textbook. The Computer Software Program's Practice Generator contains additional grammar-based exercises. Of course students' knowledge of grammar is evaluated in the Chapter Quizzes and in the Testing Program, and each grammatical structure is practiced in other components, such as the Communication Activities Masters, Situation Cards, and Videocassette Program.

An Integrated Approach to Culture

True competence in a foreign language cannot be attained without simultaneous development of the awareness of the culture in which the language is spoken. That is why **Glencoe French** places such great importance on culture. Accurate, up-to-date information on French culture is present either implicitly or

explicitly throughout every phase of language learning and in every component of the series.

The presentation of French in each chapter of the Student Textbook is embedded in running contextual themes, and these themes richly reflect the culture of France and areas of the world influenced by France. Even in chapter sections which focus primarily on vocabulary or grammar, the presence of culture comes through in the language used as examples or items in exercises, as well as in the content of the accompanying illustrations, photographs, charts, diagrams, maps or other reproductions of authentic, French documents. This constant, implicit inclusion of cultural information creates a format which not only aids in the learning of new words and structures, but piques student interest, invites questions, and stimulates discussion of the people behind the language.

Many culturally oriented questions raised by students may be answered in the two sections per chapter devoted to culture: *Lecture et culture* and *Réalités*. Through readings, captioned visuals and guided activities, these sections provide fundamental knowledge about such topics as French family life, school, restaurants, markets, sports, transportation, food, hotels, offices and hospitals, among others. This information is presented with the idea that culture is a product of people—their

attitudes, desires, preferences, differences, similarities, strengths and weaknesses—and that it is ever changing. Students are always encouraged to compare or contrast what they learn about French culture with their own, thereby learning to think critically and progress towards a more mature vision of the world. In addition to the presence of cultural material in each chapter of the Student Textbook, its importance is particularly apparent in the *Lettres et sciences* section which follows every four chapters. The readings here serve as valuable sources of information on the influence of the French people in the natural and social sciences and the arts and humanities. For more information on this unique feature, see the Teacher's Manual section immediately following, and also the section entitled ORGANIZATION OF THE STUDENT TEXTBOOK.

All of the cultural material described in the Student Textbook can be augmented by following a variety of suggestions in the Teacher's Wraparound Edition. There are guidelines for culturally rich instruction and activities, as well as useful, interesting facts for the teacher under headings such as Chapter Projects, Geography Connection, History Connection, Critical Thinking Activity, Did You Know? and others.

INTERDISCIPLINARY READINGS: LETTRES ET SCIENCES

This distinctive feature of **Glencoe French** allows students to use their French skills to expand their knowledge in other areas of the school curriculum. The interdisciplinary readings, called *Lettres et sciences*, occur in the Student Textbook after Chapters 4, 8, 12, and 16. They consist of three different readings on topics chosen from the Natural Sciences, the Social Sciences, the Arts and Humanities. Each reading topic is accompanied by pre- and post-reading activities. In the *Lettres et sciences* sections, students may read about important French explorers of the New World, for example (Level 1, pages 446 and 447), and begin to make associations between these men, their stories, and well-known names of cities or states in the United States. They may read and talk about the Impressionist movement in painting (Level 1, pages 444 and 445) and a few of the great French artists who created it, as well as learn details which help to put the movement in perspective *vis à vis* other major events in world history. They may learn about the lives of famous French personalities such as Josephine and Napoleon (Level 2, pages 220 and 221), and French scientists responsible for discoveries which are nowadays taken for granted.

Aside from providing basic information about the above topics—*[Pasteur] fonde une nouvelle science, la microbiologie* (Level 1, page 442), for example—the readings have a French perspective. They include insights that students might not receive if they were reading about the same topic in an American textbook: *Au collège, [Pasteur] n'est pas très bon élève… il aime le dessin. On l'appelle «l'artiste»*. By using these interdisciplinary *Lettres et sciences* readings, you can open up two-way avenues of exchange between the French classroom and other subject areas in the school curriculum. These readings will also allow your students to exercise critical thinking skills, draw conclusions, and begin to interrelate in a mature way the knowledge coming to them from fields which they formerly considered unrelated to French. Perhaps the social studies, art, or science teachers in your school will have the pleasure of hearing from your students, "I learned in French class that …" or conversely, students will have outside knowledge about a topic to bring to discussions in your class.

It is hoped that these readings with interdisciplinary content will make this kind of cognitive connection more common in the overall learning process. Of course, while learning about the other subject areas, students are building their French language skills. The selections in *Lettres et sciences* recycle as much as possible the structures and vocabulary from previous chapters. Glossaries contribute to vocabulary building, and the accompanying activities are designed to encourage discussion in French around the topic.

SERIES COMPONENTS

In order to take full advantage of the student-centered, "teacher-friendly" curriculum offered by **Glencoe French**, you may want to refer to this section to familiarize yourself with the various resources the series has to offer. Both Levels 1 and 2 of **Glencoe French** contain the following components:

- Student Edition
- Teacher's Wraparound Edition
- Writing Activities Workbook & Student Tape Manual, Student Edition
- Writing Activities Workbook, Teacher's Annotated Edition
- Student Tape Manual, Teacher's Edition (tapescript)
- Audio Program (Cassette or Compact Disc)
- Overhead Transparencies
- Video Program (Videocassette or Videodisc)
- Video Activities Booklet
- Interactive Conversation Video
- Computer Software: Practice and Test Generator
- Communication Activities Masters
- Lesson Plans with Block Scheduling
- Internet Activities Booklet
- Bell Ringer Review Blackline Masters
- Situation Cards
- Chapter Quizzes with Answer Key
- Testing Program with Answer Key
- Performance Assessment
- CD-ROM Interactive Textbook

À BORD: ORGANIZATION OF THE LEVEL 2 STUDENT TEXTBOOK

Initial Review The Level 2 textbook begins with six review sections, A through F, which together make up the initial *Révision*. These sections review all of the salient grammatical points and vocabulary topics presented in Level 1 (*Bienvenue*). Review sections A, B and C reintroduce content that was presented in Level 1, Chapters 1 through 8. Review sections D, E and F review material that was presented in Level 1, Chapters 9 through 18. The Overview topic in the corresponding Teacher's Wraparound Edition points out more specifically which grammar points and vocabulary are being reviewed in each of these sections. For example, *Révision* section A reviews vocabulary needed to describe people, school and home (Level 1, Chapters 1 through 4). From a grammatical perspective, this section reviews agreement of adjectives, the present tense of the verbs *être* and *aller* and the contractions with *à* and *de* (Level 1, Chapters 1 through 5). Each initial *Révision* section includes practice exercises and activities to help students further internalize these review topics.

Following the initial *Révision*, each chapter of *À bord* is divided into these sections:

- *Vocabulaire (Mots 1* and *Mots 2)*
- *Structure*
- *Conversation*
- *Lecture et Culture*
- *Réalités*
- *Culmination*

After every fourth chapter, the following special sections appear:

- *Révision*
- *Lettres et sciences* (interdisciplinary readings)

Vocabulaire The new vocabulary is laid out in two segments, *Mots 1* and *Mots 2*. Each of these presents new words in a cultural context in keeping with the theme of the chapter. Ample use is made of labeled illustrations to convey meaning and to provide an interesting introduction to the new vocabulary. The contextual vignettes into which the vocabulary items are embedded make use of the same grammatical structures which will be formally addressed later in the chapter, and recycle words and structures from previous chapters. Accompanying each *Mots* segment is a series of *Exercices* requiring students to use the new words in context. These *Exercices* employ techniques such as short answer, matching, multiple choice and labeling. They are always contextual, forming coherent vignettes, and they lend themselves well to any variations you might wish to apply to their delivery (books open, books closed, done as a class, in groups or pairs, written for homework). Wrapping up the *Vocabulaire* section are the *Activités de communication*, a segment consisting of communication-based activities which combine the new words from both *Mots* sections. These are more open-ended activities, requiring students to personalize the new language by performing such tasks as gathering information from

classmates, interviewing, taking notes, making charts or reporting to the class.

Structure This is the grammar section of each chapter. It is conveniently and logically divided into four or five segments to aid in student assimilation of the material. Each segment provides a step-by-step description in English of how the new grammatical structure is used in French, accompanied by examples, tables and other visuals. Each segment's presentation is followed by a series of flexible *Exercices*, designed along the same lines as those which accompany the *Vocabulaire* section, but focusing on the grammar point. As in *Vocabulaire*, the presentation of the new structures and the subsequent exercises is contextualized: examples as well as items in the exercises are never separate and unrelated, but always fit together in vignettes to enhance meaning. These vignettes are always directly related to the overall chapter theme, and the *Structure* section makes regular use of the new vocabulary from *Mots 1* and *Mots 2*, allowing for free interplay between these two sections of the chapter. This thorough yet manageable layout allows you to adapt the teaching of grammar to your students' needs and to your own teaching personality.

Conversation Now that students have had a chance to see and practice the new items of vocabulary and grammar for the chapter, this section provides a recombined version of the new language in the form of an authentic, culturally rich dialogue under the heading *Scènes de la vie*. This can be handled in a variety of ways, depending on the teacher and the class and as suggested by accompanying notes in the Teacher's Wraparound Edition. Teacher modeling, modeling from the recorded version, class or individual repetitions, reading aloud by students, role-playing or adaptation through substitution are some of the strategies suggested. The dialogue is accompanied by one or more exercises which check comprehension and allow for some personalization of the material. Then students are invited once again to recombine and use all the new language in a variety of group and paired activities via the *Activités de communication*. New vocabulary and expressions are sometimes offered here, but only for the sake of richness and variation, and not for

testing purposes. In Level 1, every chapter also contains a *Prononciation* segment, which appears in the *Conversation* section. It provides a guide to the pronunciation of one or more French phonemes, a series of words and phrases containing the key sound(s), and an illustration which cues a key word containing the sound(s). These pronunciation illustrations are part of the Overhead Transparency package accompanying the series. *Prononciation* can serve both as a tool for practice as students perform the chapter tasks, and as a handy speaking-skills reference to be used at any time.

Lecture et culture This is a reading about people and places from France and the francophonic world, offering further cultural input to the theme of the chapter and providing yet another *recombinaison* of the chapter vocabulary and grammar. As is always the case with **Glencoe French**, material from previous chapters is recycled. Following the reading and based on it is *Étude de mots*—an exercise that gives students a chance to experiment with and expand their French vocabularies by using strategies such as searching for synonyms, identifying cognates, completing cloze exercises, matching and others. Next comes a series of comprehension exercises based on the reading (*Compréhension*), and finally the *Découverte culturelle*, where more cultural information is offered in the form of a shorter reading. The *Découverte culturelle* is optional in each chapter.

Réalités These pages are intended as brief but enjoyable visual insights into the French-speaking world. The two pages of this section are filled with photographs that are pertinent to the chapter theme. Each photograph is identified with a caption, thereby providing some additional reading practice. Students are encouraged to formulate questions about what they see, and to compare and contrast elements of French culture with their own. The *Réalités* section is optional in each chapter.

Culmination This wrap-up section requires students to consolidate material from the present as well as from previous chapters in order to complete the tasks successfully. The *Culmination* provides an opportunity for students to assess themselves on their own and to spend

time on areas in which they are weak. You the teacher can pick and choose from them as you see fit. The first segment of *Culmination* consists of *Activités de communication orale,* where students must use the French they have learned to talk about various aspects of themselves: likes, dislikes, favorite activities, hobbies or areas of expertise, among others. This is followed by *Activités de communication écrite,* which encourage students to apply their knowledge of French in written form. The *Réintroduction et recombinaison* segment recalls selected items of vocabulary and grammar from previous chapters. It is short and not meant as a comprehensive review, but rather as a quick reminder of important words, expressions and structures. Finally, the vocabulary words and expressions taught in the current chapter are listed categorically under the heading *Vocabulaire,* serving as a handy reference resource for both the student and the teacher.

Révision This review section, designed to coincide with the more comprehensive Review Tests in the Testing Program, occurs after Chapters 4, 8, 12, and 16 in the Student Textbook. In each *Révision,* the main vocabulary and grammar points from the previous four chapters are recycled through a variety of new exercises, activities and dialogues. While in the individual chapters new grammar was divided into smaller, "bite-sized" portions to aid in the planning of daily lessons and help students assimilate it, now it is reviewed in a more consolidated format. This allows students to see different grammatical points side by side for the first time, to make new connections between the different points, and to progress toward a generative, "whole grammar." For example, in the first *Révision* following Level 2, Chapter 4, the agreement of the past participle with its subject in the *passé composé,* and the *passé composé* and the imperfect are reviewed

together on three pages, accompanied by explanations and various exercises. Previously these concepts were distributed over Chapters 1 through 4 of Level 2. Of course every possible combination of vocabulary and grammar does not reappear in the *Révision.* However, by carefully going through these exercises and activities and referring to the preceding chapters, students will be encouraged to make necessary connections and extrapolations themselves and therefore develop a true working knowledge of the French they have studied. *Révision* is designed to be used by students studying alone, in unguided study groups or as a whole class with teacher guidance.

Lettres et sciences This is a unique, interdisciplinary feature of **Glencoe French** which allows students to use and expand upon the French language skills they have been studying, while at the same time applying them to useful topics in the areas of the natural sciences, social studies, arts and humanities. This material is presented in the form of three readings, one from each of the above areas, accompanied by photos and illustrations. To stimulate discussion and aid in comprehension, there are pre-reading and post-reading activities. The reading selections are more vocabulary intensive than those in the regular chapters, and a French-English glossary is provided for each one. The focus here, however, is on the interdisciplinary content rather than the language itself. By engaging your students in some or all of these readings, you will encourage them to stretch their French reading skills in order to obtain useful, interesting information which will be of great service to them in their other academic courses. Also, you will be giving students the opportunity to judge for themselves the added insight that the study of French offers to their overall education.

SUGGESTIONS FOR TEACHING THE LEVEL 2 STUDENT TEXTBOOK

Teaching the Initial Review Chapter in Level 2

The first day of class, teachers may wish to reiterate the importance of the French language, and suggest reasons for continuing the learning process in the second year. Some suggested activities are:

- Show students a map (the maps located in the back of the Student Textbook can be used) to remind them where French is spoken throughout the world.
- Have students discuss the areas within North America in which there is a high percentage of French speakers. Ask them to name local French-speaking resources including any individuals or groups they may know in their community.
- Make a list of place names such as Baton Rouge, Terre Haute, Des Moines, Vermont, or names in your locality that are of French origin.
- Explain to students that it is possible to use French in numerous careers such as: government, teaching, business, (banking, import/export), tourism, translating.
- The first day, teachers will also want to find out whether their students used a French name in last year's French class. If they didn't, this is a good time to give students a French first name, or to let them take a new French name, if they wish.

The *Révision* sections A through F in *À bord* are designed to give students a concise review of all the essential material taught in *Bienvenue* (Level 1) in a systematic fashion. Each section is designed to take two or three days of instruction. *Révision* sections A, B, and C review material from Level 1, Chapters 1 through 8; sections D, E and F review the content of Chapters 9 through 18. Depending upon the amount of material covered in first year French, student aptitude, and your own teaching preference, you may decide to go over some or all of the *Révision* sections at the beginning of the school year. Many teachers will use the *Révision* sparingly, delving into these sections as required in order to ensure a smooth transition into new material beginning with Chapter 1 of *À bord*. Above all, we would urge you not to spend more than a few weeks on the *Révision* before moving on to Chapter 1. It is always possible to return to these review sections later if necessary.

Teaching Various Sections of the Chapter

One of the major objectives of the **Glencoe French** series is to enable teachers to adapt the material to their own philosophy, teaching style, and students' needs. As a result, a variety of suggestions are offered here for teaching each section of the chapter.

Vocabulaire

The *Vocabulaire* section always contains some words in isolation, accompanied by an illustration that depicts the meaning of the new word. In addition, new words are used in contextualized sentences. These appear in the following

formats: l) one to three sentences accompanying an illustration, 2) a short conversation, 3) a short narrative or paragraph. In addition to teaching the new vocabulary, these contextualized sentences introduce, but do not teach, the new structure point of the chapter.

A vocabulary list appears at the end of each chapter in the Student Textbook.

General Techniques

- The Vocabulary Transparencies contain all illustrations necessary to teach the new words and phrases. With an overhead projector, they can easily be projected as large visuals in the classroom for those teachers who prefer to introduce the vocabulary with books closed. The Vocabulary Transparencies contain no printed words.
- All the vocabulary in each chapter (*Mots 1* and *Mots 2*) is recorded on the Audio Cassette Program. Students are asked to repeat the isolated words after the model.

Specific Techniques

Option 1 Option 1 for the presentation of vocabulary best meets the needs of those teachers who consider the development of oral skills a prime objective.

- While students have their books closed, project the Vocabulary Transparencies. Point to the item being taught and have students repeat the word after you or the audio cassette several times. After presenting several words in this way, project the transparencies again and ask questions such as:
  C'est une enveloppe?
  Qu'est-ce que c'est?
  C'est une employée des postes?
  Qui est-ce? (Level 2, Chapter 1)
- To teach the contextualized segments in the *Mots*, project the Vocabulary Transparency in the same way. Point to the part of the illustration that depicts the meaning of any new word in the sentence, be it an isolated sentence or a sentence from a conversation or narrative. Immediately ask questions about the sentence. For example, the following sentence appears in Level 2, Chapter 2, page 26:
  Nathalie a ouvert le robinet.
  Elle a rincé la vaisselle dans l'évier.

Questions to ask are:
  Est-ce que Nathalie a ouvert le robinet?
  Qui a ouvert le robinet?
  Est-ce que Nathalie a rincé la vaisselle?
  Où est-ce qu'elle a rincé la vaisselle?
- Dramatizations by the teacher, in addition to the illustrations, can also help convey the meaning of many words such as *chanter, danser, etc.*
- After this basic presentation of the *Mots* vocabulary, have students open their books and read the *Mots* section for additional reinforcement.
- Go over the exercises in the *Mots* section orally.
- Assign the exercises in the *Mots* section for homework. Also assign the corresponding vocabulary exercises in the Writing Activities Workbook. If the *Mots* section should take more than one day, assign only those exercises that correspond to the material you have presented.
- The following day, go over the exercises that were assigned for homework.

Option 2 Option 2 will meet the needs of those teachers who wish to teach the oral skills but consider reading and writing equally important.

- Project the Vocabulary Transparencies and have students repeat each word once or twice after you or the audio cassette.
- Have students repeat the contextualized sentences after you or the audio cassette/ compact disc as they look at the illustration.
- Ask students to open their books. Have them read the *Mots* section. Correct pronunciation errors as they are made.
- Go over the exercises in each *Mots* section.
- Assign the exercises of the *Mots* section for homework. Also assign the vocabulary exercises in the Writing Activities Workbook.
- The following day, go over the exercises that were assigned for homework.

Option 3 Option 3 will meet the needs of those teachers who consider the reading and writing skills of utmost importance.

- Have students open their books and read the *Mots* items as they look at the illustrations.

- Give students several minutes to look at the *Mots* words and vocabulary exercises. Then go over the exercises.
- Go over the exercises the following day.

Expansion Activities

Teachers may use any one of the following activities from time to time. These can be done in conjunction with any of the options previously outlined.

- After the vocabulary has been presented, project the Vocabulary Transparencies or have students open their books and make up as many original sentences as they can, using the new words. This can be done orally or in writing.
- Have students work in pairs or small groups. As they look at the illustrations in the textbook, have them make up as many questions as they can. They can direct their questions to their peers. It is often fun to make this a competitive activity. Individuals or teams can compete to make up the most questions in three minutes. This activity provides the students with an excellent opportunity to use interrogative words.
- Call on one student to read to the class one of the vocabulary exercises that tells a story. Then call on a more able student to retell the story in his/her own words.
- With slower groups you can have one student go to the front of the room. Have him or her think of one of the new words. Let classmates give the student the new words from the *Mots* until they guess the word the student in the front of the room has in mind. This is a very easy way to have the students recall the words they have just learned.

Structure

The *Structure* section of the chapter opens with a grammatical explanation in English, accompanied by many examples. With verbs, complete paradigms are given. In the case of other grammar concepts such as the *passé composé* versus the imperfect, many examples are given in order to contrast these two past tenses. Irregular patterns are grouped together to make them appear more regular. For example, *envoyer, employer* and *payer* are taught together in Chapter 1, as are *suivre* and *vivre* in Chapter 6. Whenever the contrast between English and French poses problems for students in the learning process, a contrastive analysis between the two languages is made. Two examples of this are the reflexive construction in Level 1 and the subjunctive in Level 2. Certain structure points are taught more effectively in their entirety and others are more easily acquired if they are taught in segments. An example of the latter is the direct and indirect object pronouns. In Level 1, Chapter 15, *me, te, nous, vous* (as direct object pronouns) are presented, immediately followed by *le, la, l', les* (Chapter 16), followed by *lui, leur* (Chapter 17). Both direct and indirect object pronouns are then consolidated in Level 2 in the initial *Révision*, and are recycled later with affirmative and familiar commands (Chapter 6).

Learning Exercises

The exercises that follow the grammatical explanation are plateaued or phased in to build from simple to more complex. In the case of verbs with an irregular form, for example, emphasis is placed on the irregular form, since it is the one students will most often confuse or forget. However, in all cases, students are given one or more exercises that force them to use all forms at random. The first few exercises that follow the grammatical explanation are considered **learning exercises** because they assist the students in grasping and internalizing the new grammar concept. These learning exercises are immediately followed by test exercises—exercises that make students use all aspects of the grammatical point they have just learned. This format greatly assists teachers in meeting the needs of the various ability levels of students in their classes. Every effort has been made to make the grammatical explanations as succinct and as complete as possible. We have purposely avoided extremely technical grammatical or linguistic terminology that most students would not understand. Nevertheless, it is necessary to use certain basic grammatical terms.

Certain grammar exercises from the Student Textbook are recorded on the Audio Program. Whenever an exercise is recorded, it is noted with a headphones icon ◠ in the Teacher's Wraparound Edition.

The exercises in the Writing Activities Workbook also parallel the order of presentation in the Student Textbook. The Resource boxes and the Independent Practice topics in the Teacher's Wraparound Edition indicate when certain exercises from the Writing Activities Workbook can be assigned.

Specific Techniques for Presenting Grammar

Option 1 Some teachers prefer the deductive approach to the teaching of grammar. When this is the preferred method, teachers can begin the *Structure* section of the chapter by presenting the grammatical rule to students or by having them read the rule in their textbooks. After they have gone over the rule, have them read the examples in their textbooks or write the examples on the chalkboard. Then proceed with the exercises that follow the grammatical explanation.

Option 2 Other teachers prefer the inductive approach to the teaching of grammar. If this is the case, begin the *Structure* section by writing the examples that accompany the rule on the chalkboard or by having students read them in their textbooks. Let us take, for example, the agreement of the past participle with direct objects. The examples the students have in their textbooks (Level 2, page 12) are:

J'ai écrit *une lettre*.	Je *l'*ai écrit**e** ce matin.
	Voici la lettre *que* j'ai écrit**e** ce matin.
Tu as reçu *les lettres*?	Tu *les* as reçu**es**?
	Ce sont les lettres *que* tu as reçu**es**.
Elle a acheté *les timbres*.	Elle *les* a achet**és** hier.
	Voilà les timbres *qu'*elle a achet**és** hier.

In order to teach this concept inductively, teachers can ask students to do or answer the following:

- Have students find the object of each sentence in the first column. Say it or underline the object if it is written on the board.
- Have students notice that these words disappeared in the sentences in the second column. Have students give (or underline) the word that replaced each one.
- Ask students what word replaced *une lettre, les lettres, les timbres*.
- Ask students what variations appear in the past participle in each sentence in the second column. What form of the participle follows a feminine singular pronoun? A feminine plural pronoun, etc.?
- Ask: Where are the direct object pronouns placed in the *passé composé*?

By answering these questions, students have induced, on their own, the rule from the examples. To further reinforce the rule, have students read the grammatical explanation and then continue with the grammar exercises that follow. Further suggestions for the inductive presentation of the grammatical points are given in the Teacher's Wraparound Edition.

Specific Techniques for Teaching Grammar Exercises

In the development of the **Glencoe French** series, we have purposely provided a wide variety of exercises in the *Structure* section so that students can proceed from one exercise to another without becoming bored. The types of exercises they will encounter are: short conversations, answering questions, conducting or taking part in an interview, making up questions, describing an illustration, filling in the blanks, multiple choice, completing a conversation, completing a narrative, etc. In going over the exercises with students, teachers may want to conduct the exercises themselves or they may want students to work in pairs. The *Structure* exercises can be gone over in class before they are assigned for homework or they may be assigned before they are gone over. Many teachers may want to vary their approach.

All the *Exercices* and *Activités de communication* in the Student Textbook can be done with books open. Many of the exercises such as question-answer, interview, and transformation can also be done with books closed.

Types of Exercises

Question Exercises The answers to many question exercises build to tell a complete story. Once you have gone over the exercise by

calling on several students (Student 1 answers items numbered 1,2,3; Student 2 answers items numbered 4,5,6, etc.), you can call on one student to give the answers to the entire exercise. Now the entire class has heard an uninterrupted story. Students can ask one another questions about the story, give an oral synopsis of the story in their own words, or write a short paragraph about the story.

Personal Questions or Interview Exercises Students can easily work in pairs or teachers can call a student moderator to the front of the room to ask questions of various class members. Two students can come to the front of the room and the exercise can be performed—one student takes the role of the interviewer and the other takes the role of the interviewee.

Repetition of a Conversation See Level 2, Chapter 2, page 39 as an example. After students repeat the conversation after you, they can be given time either in class or as an outside assignment to prepare a skit for the class based on the conversation.

Conversation

Specific Techniques Teachers may wish to vary the presentation of the *Conversation* from one chapter to another. In some chapters, the dialogue can be presented thoroughly and in other chapters it may be presented quickly as a reading exercise. Some possible options are:

- Have the class repeat the dialogue after you twice. Then have students work in pairs and present the dialogue to the class. The dialogue does not have to be memorized. If students change it a bit, all the better.
- Have students read the dialogue several times on their own. Then have them work in pairs and read the dialogue as a skit. Try to encourage them to be animated and to use proper intonation. This is a very important aspect of the *Conversation* section of the chapter.
- Rather than read the dialogue, students can work in pairs, having one make up as many questions as possible related to the topic of the dialogue. The other student can answer his/her questions.
- Once students can complete the exercises that accompany the dialogue with relative

ease, they know the dialogue sufficiently well without having to memorize it.
- Students can tell or write a synopsis of the dialogue.

Activités de communication

Specific Techniques The *Activités de communication* presents activities that assist students in working with the language on their own. All the *activités* are optional. In some cases, teachers may want the whole class to do them all. In other cases, teachers can decide which ones the whole class will do. Another possibility is to break the class into groups and have each one work on a different activity.

Lecture

Specific Techniques: Option 1 Just as the presentation of the dialogue can vary from one chapter to the next, the same is true of the *Lecture*. In some chapters teachers may want students to go over the reading selection very thoroughly. In this case all or any combination of the following techniques can be used.

- Give students a brief synopsis of the story in French.
- Ask questions about the brief synopsis.
- Have students open their books and repeat several sentences after you or call on individuals to read.
- Ask questions about what was just read.
- Have students read the story at home and write the answers to the exercises that accompany the *Lecture*.
- Go over the *Étude de mots* and the *Compréhension* in class the next day.
- Call on a student to give a review of the story in his/her own words. If necessary, guide students to make up an oral review. Ask five or six questions, the answers to which review the salient points of the reading selection.
- After the oral review, the more able students can write a synopsis of the *Lecture* in their own words.

It should take from one to two days to present the *Lecture*. Teachers may wish to spend two days on those reading selections they want students to know thoroughly.

Option 2 With those *Lectures* that teachers wish to present less thoroughly, the following techniques may be used:

- Call on an individual to read a paragraph.
- Ask questions about the paragraph read.
- Assign the *Lecture* to be read at home. Have students write the exercises that accompany the *Lecture*.
- Go over the *Étude de mots* and the *Compréhension* the following day.

Option 3 With some reading selections, teachers may wish merely to assign them to be read at home and then go over the exercises the following day. This is possible since the only new material in the *Lecture* consists of a few new vocabulary items that are always footnoted.

Découverte culturelle

The optional *Découverte culturelle* is a reading selection which is designed to give students an in-depth knowledge of many areas of the French-speaking world. You can omit any or all of this reading or they may choose certain selections that they would like the whole class to read. The same suggestions given for the *Lecture* of each chapter can be followed. Teachers may also assign the reading selections to different groups. Students can read the selection outside of class and prepare a report for those students who did not read that particular selection. This activity is very beneficial for slower students. Although they may not read the selection, they learn the material by listening to what their peers say about it. The *Découverte culturelle* can also be done by students on a voluntary basis for extra credit.

Réalités

Specific Techniques The purpose of the *Réalités* section is to permit students to look at photographs of the French-speaking world and to acquaint them with the many areas where French is spoken. The *Réalités* section contains no exercises. The purpose is for students to enjoy the material as if they were browsing through pages of a magazine. Items the students can think about are embedded in the commentary that accompanies the photographs. Teachers can either have students read the extended captions in class or students can read the captions on their own.

ORGANIZATION OF THE TEACHER'S WRAPAROUND EDITION

One important component, which is definitive of **Glencoe French** and adds to the series' flexible, "teacher-friendly" nature, is the Teacher's Wraparound Edition (TWE), of which this Teacher's Manual is a part. Each two-page spread of the TWE "wraps around" a slightly reduced reproduction of the corresponding pages of the Student Textbook and offers in the expanded margins a variety of specific, helpful suggestions for every phase in the learning process. A complete method for the presentation of all the material in the Student Textbook is provided—basically, a complete set of lesson plans—as well as techniques for background-building, additional reinforcement of new language skills, creative and communicative recycling of material from previous chapters and a host of other alternatives from which to choose. This banquet of ideas has been developed and conveniently laid out in order to save valuable teacher preparation time and to aid you in designing the richest, most varied language experience possible for you and your students. A closer look at the kinds of support in the Teacher's Wraparound Edition, and their locations, will help you decide which ones are right for your pace and style of teaching and the differing "chemistries" of your classes.

The notes in the Teacher's Wraparound Edition can be divided into two basic categories:
1. Core notes, appearing in the left- and right-hand margins, are those which most directly correspond to the material in the accompanying two-page spread of the Student Textbook.
2. Enrichment notes, in the bottom margin, are meant to be complementary to the

material in the Student Textbook. They offer a wide range of options aimed at getting students to practice and use the French they are learning in diverse ways, individually and with their classmates, in the classroom and for homework. The enrichment notes also include tips to the teacher on clarifying and interconnecting elements in French language and culture—ideas that have proved useful to other teachers and which are offered for your consideration.

Description of Core Notes in the Teacher's Wraparound Edition

Chapter Overview At the beginning of each chapter a brief description is given of the language functions which students will be able to perform by chapter's end. Mention is made of any closely associated functions presented in other chapters. This allows for effective articulation between chapters and serves as a guide for more successful teaching.

Chapter Objectives This guide immediately follows the Chapter Overview and is closely related to it. Here the focus is on grammatical objectives for the chapter, which are stated in a concise list.

Chapter Resources The beginning of each chapter includes a reference list of all the ancillary components of the series that are applicable to what is being taught in the chapter, including the Writing Activities Workbook and Student Tape Manual, Audio Program, Overhead Transparencies, Communication Activities Masters, Videocassette Program, Computer Software, Practice and Test Generator, Situation Cards, Chapter Quizzes and Test Booklets.

A more precise version of this resource list will be repeated at the beginning of each section within the chapter, so that you always have a handy guide to the specific resources available to you for each and every point in the teaching process. Using these chapter and section resource references will make it easier for you to plan varied, stimulating lessons throughout the year.

Bell Ringer Reviews These short activities recycle vocabulary and grammar from previous chapters and sections. They serve as effective warm-ups, urging students to begin thinking in French, and helping them make the transition from their previous class to French. Minimal direction is required to get the Bell Ringer Review activity started, so students can begin meaningful, independent work in French as soon as the class hour begins, rather than wait for the teacher to finish administrative tasks, such as attendance, etc. Bell Ringer Reviews occur consistently throughout each chapter of Levels 1 and 2.

Presentation Step-by-step suggestions for the presentation of the material in all segments of the six main section headings in each chapter— *Vocabulaire, Structure, Conversation, Lecture et culture, Réalités,* and *Culmination* are presented in the left- and right-hand margins. They offer the teacher suggestions on what to say, whether to have books open or closed, whether to perform tasks individually, in pairs or in small groups, expand the material, reteach, and assign homework. These are indeed suggestions. You may wish to follow them as written or choose a more eclectic approach to suit time constraints, personal teaching style and class "chemistry." Please note however, that the central vocabulary and grammar included in each chapter's *Vocabulaire* and *Structure* sections is intended to be taught in its entirety, since this material is built into that which occurs in succeeding chapters. In addition, answers for all the *Exercices* in each segment are conveniently located near that exercise in the Student Textbook.

Because the answers will vary in the *Activités de communication,* they are usually not provided. However, the Presentation notes do offer other topics for enrichment, expansion and assessment. A brief discussion of these may

help you incorporate them into your lesson plans.

Geography Connection These suggestions encourage students to use the maps provided in the Student Textbook as well as refer them to outside sources in order to familiarize them with the geography of France and the francophone world. These optional activities are another way in which **Glencoe French** crosses boundaries into other areas of the curriculum. Their use will instill in students the awareness that French Class is not just a study of language but an investigation into a powerful culture that has directly or indirectly affected the lives of millions of people all over the globe. Besides studying the geography within France itself, they will be urged to trace the presence of French culture throughout Europe, Africa, the Americas, Asia, and the Pacific. The notes also supply you the teacher with diverse bits of geographical and historical information which you might not have known, and you may decide to pass these on to your students.

Vocabulary Expansion These notes provide the teacher handy access to vocabulary items which are thematically related to those presented within the Student Textbook. They are offered to enrich classroom conversations, allowing students more varied and meaningful responses when talking about themselves, their classmates or the topic in question. Note that none of these items, or for that matter any information, in the Teacher's Wraparound Edition is included in the Chapter Quizzes, or in the Testing Program accompanying **Glencoe French.**

Cognate Recognition Since the lexical relationship between French and English is so rich, these notes have been provided to help you take full advantage of the vocabulary-building strategy of isolating them. The suggestions occur in the *Vocabulaire* section of each chapter and are particularly frequent in Level 1 in order to train students from the very beginning in the valuable strategy of recognizing cognates. Various methods of pointing out cognates are used, involving all four language skills, and the activities frequently encourage students to personalize the new words by using them to talk about things and people they know. Pronunciation differences are stressed

between the two languages. The teacher notes also call attention to false cognates when they occur in other chapter sections.

Informal Assessment Ideas are offered for making quick checks on how well students are assimilating new material. These checks are done in a variety of ways and provide a means whereby both teacher and students can monitor daily progress. By using the Informal Assessment topic, you will be able to ascertain (as you go along) the areas in which students are having trouble, adjust your pace accordingly, or provide extra help for individuals, either by making use of other activities offered in the Teacher's Wraparound Edition or devising your own. The assessment strategies are simple and designed to help you elicit from students the vocabulary word, grammatical structure, or other information you wish to check. Because they occur on the same page as the material to which they correspond, you may want to come back to them again when it is time to prepare students for tests or quizzes.

Reteaching These suggestions provided yet another approach to teaching a specific topic in the chapter. In the event some students were not successful in the initial presentation of the material the reteaching activity offers an alternate strategy. At the same time, they allow other students to further consolidate their learning.

History Connection Following these suggestions can be a very effective springboard from the French classroom into the history and social studies areas of the curriculum. Students are asked to focus their attention on the current world map, or historical ones, then they are invited to discuss the cultural, economic, and political forces which shape the world with an eye on French influence. The notes will assist you in providing this type of information yourself or in creating projects in which students do their own research, perhaps with the aid of a history teacher. By making the history connection, students are encouraged to either import or export learning between the French classroom and the History or Social Studies realms.

Description of Enrichment Notes in the Teacher's Wraparound Edition

The notes in the bottom margin of the Teacher's Wraparound Edition enrich students'

learning experiences by providing additional activities to those in the Student Textbook. These activities will be helpful in meeting each chapter's objectives, as well as in providing students with an atmosphere of variety, cooperation and enjoyment.

Chapter Projects Specific suggestions are given at the start of each chapter for launching individual students or groups into a research project in keeping with the chapter theme. Students are encouraged to gather information by using resources in school and public libraries, visiting local French institutions or interviewing French people or other persons knowledgeable in the area of French culture whom they may know. In Level 2, Chapter 2, for example, they are asked to prepare the menu for a typical American breakfast, lunch and dinner. As they progress through Chapter 2, students note the differences between American and French eating habits. These types of projects may serve as another excellent means for students to make connections between their learning in the French classroom and other areas of the curriculum.

Learning from Photos and Realia Each chapter of **Glencoe French** contains many colorful photographs and reproductions of authentic French documents, filled with valuable cultural information. In order to help you take advantage of this rich source of learning, notes of interesting information have been provided to assist you in highlighting the special features of these up-to-date realia. The questions that appear under this topic have been designed to enhance learners' reading and critical thinking skills.

Total Physical Response (Level 1) At least one Total Physical Response (TPR) activity is provided with each *Mots* segment that makes up the *Vocabulaire* section of the chapter. The Total Physical Response approach to language instruction was developed by James J. Asher. Students must focus their attention on commands spoken by the teacher (or classmates) and demonstrate their comprehension by performing the physical task commanded. This strategy has proven highly successful for concentrating on the listening skill and assimilating new vocabulary. Students are relieved momentarily of the need to speak—by which

some may be intimidated—and yet challenged to show that they understand spoken French. The physical nature of these activities is another of their benefits, providing a favorable change of pace for students, who must move about the room and perhaps handle some props in order to perform the tasks. In addition, Total Physical Response is in keeping with cooperative learning principles, since many of the commands require students to interact and assist each other in accomplishing them. In Level 2, Total Physical Response is replaced by a Role-play or Pantomime activity.

Cooperative Learning At least one cooperative learning activity has been included in each chapter. These activities include guidelines both on the size of groups to be organized and on the tasks the groups will perform. They reflect two basic principles of cooperative learning: (a) that students work together, being responsible for their own learning, and (b) that they do so in an atmosphere of mutual respect and support, where the contributions of each peer are valued. For more information on this topic, please see the section in this Teacher's Manual entitled Cooperative Learning.

Additional Practice There are a variety of Additional Practice activities to complement and follow up the presentation of material in the Student Textbook. Frequently the additional practice focuses on personalization of the new material and employs more than one language skill. Examples of Additional Practice activities include having students give oral or written descriptions of themselves or their classmates; asking students to conduct interviews around a topic and then report their findings to the class; using possessive forms to identify objects in the classroom and their owners. The additional practice will equip you with an ample, organized repertoire from which to pick and choose should you need extra practice beyond the Student Textbook.

Independent Practice Many of the exercises in each chapter lend themselves well to assignment or reassignment as homework. In addition to providing extra practice, reassigning on paper exercises that were performed orally in class makes use of additional language skills

and aids in informal assessment. The suggestions under the Independent Practice heading in the bottom margin of the Teacher's Wraparound Edition will call your attention to exercises that are particularly suited to this. In addition to reassigning exercises in the Student Textbook as independent practice, additional sources are suggested from the various ancillary components, specifically the Writing Activities Workbook and the Communication Activities Masters.

Critical Thinking Activities To broaden the scope of the foreign language classroom, suggestions are given that will encourage students to make inferences and organize their learning into a coherent "big picture" of today's world. These and other topics offered in the enrichment notes provide dynamic content areas to which students can apply their French language skills and their growing knowledge of French culture. The guided discussion suggestions derived from the chapter themes invite students to make connections between what they learn in the French program and other areas of the curriculum.

Did You Know? This is a teacher resource topic where you will find additional details relevant to the chapter theme. You might wish to add the information given under this topic to your own knowledge and share it with your students to spur their interest in research projects, enliven class discussions and round out their awareness of French culture, history or geography.

For the Younger Student (Level 1 only) Because *Bienvenue* is designed for use at the junior high and intermediate level as well as the high school level, this topic pays special attention to the needs of younger students. Each chapter contains suggestions for meaningful language activities and tips to the teacher that cater to the physical and emotional needs of these youngsters. There are ideas for hands-on student projects, such as creating booklets or bringing and using their own props, as well as suggestions for devising games based on speed, using pantomime, show and tell, performing skits, and more.

ADDITIONAL ANCILLARY COMPONENTS

All ancillary components are supplementary to the Student Textbook. Any or all parts of the following ancillaries can be used at the discretion of the teacher.

The Writing Activities Workbook and Student Tape Manual

The Writing Activities Workbook and Student Tape Manual is divided into two parts: all chapters of the Writing Activities Workbook appear in the first half of this ancillary component, followed by all chapters of the Student Tape Manual.

Writing Activities Workbook The consumable workbook offers additional writing practice to reinforce the vocabulary and grammatical structures in each chapter of the Student Textbook. The workbook exercises are presented in the same order as the material in the Student Textbook. The exercises are contextualized, often centering around line art illustrations. Workbook activities employ a variety of elicitation techniques, ranging from short answers, matching columns, and answering personalized questions, to writing paragraphs and brief compositions. To encourage personalized writing, there is a special section in each chapter entitled *Mon Autobiographie*. The workbook provides further reading skills development with the *Un Peu Plus* section, where students are introduced to a number of reading strategies such as scanning for information, distinguishing fact from opinion, drawing inferences and reaching conclusions, for the purpose of improving their reading

comprehension and expanding their vocabulary. The *Un Peu Plus* section also extends the cultural themes presented in the corresponding Student Textbook chapter. The Writing Activities Workbook includes a Self Test after Chapters 4, 8, 12, 16, and 18. The Writing Activities Workbook, Teacher Annotated Edition provides the teacher with all the material in the student edition plus the answers—wherever possible—to the activities.

Student Tape Manual The Student Tape Manual contains the activity sheets which students will use when listening to the audio cassette recordings. The Teacher Edition of the Student Tape Manual contains, in addition, the answers to the recorded activities, plus the complete tapescript of all recorded material.

The Audio Program (Cassette or CD)

The recorded material for each chapter of **Glencoe French**, Levels 1 and 2, is divided into two parts—*Première partie* and *Deuxième partie*. The *Première partie* consists of additional listening and speaking practice for the *Vocabulaire* (*Mots 1 & 2*) and the *Structure* sections of each chapter. There is also a dramatization of the *Conversation* dialogue from the Student Textbook, and a pronunciation section. The *Première partie* concludes with a *dictée*.

The *Deuxième partie* contains more open-ended situations. Students indicate their understanding of brief conversations, advertisements, announcements, et cetera, by making the appropriate response on their activity sheets located in the Student Tape Manual.

Overhead Transparencies

There are five categories in the package of Overhead Transparencies accompanying **Glencoe French**, Level 1, and four for Level 2. Each one has its special purpose. Following is a description:

Vocabulary Transparencies These are full-color transparencies reproduced from each of the *Mots* presentations in the Student Text-book. In converting the *Mots* vocabulary pages to transparency format, all accompanying words and phrases on the *Mots* pages have been deleted to allow for greater flexibility in their use. The Vocabulary Transparencies can be used for initial presentation of new words and phrases in each chapter. They can also be reprojected to review or reteach vocabulary during the course of teaching the chapter, or as a tool for giving quick vocabulary quizzes.

With more able groups, teachers can show the Vocabulary Transparencies from previous chapters and have students make up original sentences using a particular word. These sentences can be given orally or in writing.

Pronunciation Transparencies (Level 1 only) In the *Prononciation* section of each chapter of *Bienvenue* , an illustration has been included to visually cue the key word or phrase containing the sound(s) being taught, e.g., Chapter 3, page 79. Each of these illustrations has been converted to transparency format. These Pronunciation Transparencies may be used to present the key sound(s) for a given chapter, or for periodic pronunciation reviews where several transparencies can be shown to the class in rapid order. Some teachers may wish to convert these Pronunciation Transparencies to black and white paper visuals by making a photocopy of each one. There are no pronunciation transparencies for Level 2. However, the Level 2 teacher may wish to use the Level 1 transparencies from time to time to remind students of the importance of developing good pronunciation habits.

Communication Transparencies For each chapter in Levels 1 and 2 of the series there is one original composite illustration which visually summarizes and reviews the vocabulary and grammar presented in that chapter. These transparencies may be used as cues for additional communicative practice in both oral and written formats. There are 18 Communication Transparencies for Level 1, and 16 for Level 2.

Map Transparencies The full-color maps located at the back of the Student Textbook have been converted to transparency format for the teacher's convenience. These can be used when there is a reference to them in the Student Textbook, or when there is a history or geography map reference in the Teacher's Wraparound Edition. The Map Transparencies can also be used for quiz purposes, or they may be photocopied in order to provide individual students with a black and white version for use with special projects.

Fine Art Transparencies These are full-color reproductions of works by well-known French artists including Matisse, Renoir, and others. Teachers may use these transparencies to reinforce specific culture topics in the *Réalités* sections as well as in the optional *Lettres et sciences* sections of the Student Textbook.

The Video Program (Cassette or Videodisc)

The video component for each level of **Glencoe French** consists of one hour-long video cassette and an accompanying Video Activities Booklet. Together, they are designed to reinforce the vocabulary, structures, and cultural themes presented in the corresponding Student Textbook. The **Glencoe French** Videocassette Program encourages students to be active listeners and viewers by asking them to respond to each video *Scène* through a variety of previewing, viewing and post-viewing activities. Students are asked to view the same video segment multiple times as they are led, via the activities in their Video Activities Booklet, to look and listen for more detailed information in the video segment they are viewing. The Videocassette for each level of **Glencoe French** begins with an Introduction explaining why listening to natural, spoken French can be a difficult task and therefore why multiple viewings of each video *Scène* are required. The Introduction also points out the importance of using the print activities located in the Video Activities Booklet in order to use the Videocassette Program successfully.

Video Activities Booklet

The Video Activities Booklet is the vital companion piece to the hour-long video cassette for each level of **Glencoe French**. It consists of a series of pre-viewing, viewing, and post-viewing activities on Blackline Masters. These activities include specific instructions to students on what to watch and listen for as they view a given *Scène* on the videocassette. In addition to these student activities, the Video Activities Booklet also contains a Teacher's Manual, Culture Notes, and a complete transcript of the video soundtrack.

Computer Software: Practice and Test Generator

Available for Apple II, Macintosh and IBM-compatible machines, this software program provides materials for both students and teacher. The Practice Generator provides students with new, additional practice items for the vocabulary, grammar and culture topics in each chapter of the Student Textbook. All practice items are offered in a multiple choice format. The computer program includes a randomizer, so that each time a student calls up a set of exercises, the items are presented in a different order, thereby discouraging rote memorization of answers. Immediate feedback is given, along with the percent of correct answers, so that with repeated practice, students can track their performance. For vocabulary practice, illustrations from the *Vocabulaire* section of the Student Textbook have been scanned into the software to make practice more interesting and versatile.

The Test Generator allows the teacher to print out ready-made chapter tests, or customize a ready-made test by adding or deleting test items. The computer software comes with a Teacher's Manual as well as a printed transcript of all practice and test items.

Communication Activities Masters with Answer Key

This is a series of Blackline Masters, which provide further opportunities for students to practice their communication skills using the French they have learned. The contextualized, open-ended situations are designed to encourage students to communicate on a given topic, using specific vocabulary and grammatical structures from the corresponding chapter of the Student Textbook. The use of visual cues and interesting contexts will encourage students to ask questions and experiment with personalized responses. In the case of the paired communication activities, students actively work together as they share information provided on each partner's activity sheet.

Situation Cards

This is another component of **Glencoe French** aimed at developing listening and speaking skills through guided conversation. For each chapter of the Student Textbook, there is a corresponding set of guided conversational situations printed on hand-held cards. Working in pairs, students use appropriate vocabulary and grammar from the chapter to converse on the suggested topics. Although they are designed primarily for use in paired activities the Situation Cards may also be used in preparation for the speaking portion of the Testing Program or for informal assessment. Additional uses for the Situation Cards are described in the Situation Cards package, along with specific instructions and tips for their duplication and incorporation into your teaching plans. The cards are in Blackline Master form for easy duplication.

Bell Ringer Reviews on Blackline Masters

These are identical to the Bell Ringer Reviews found in each chapter of the Teacher's Wraparound Edition. For the teacher's convenience, they have been converted to this (optional) Blackline Master format. They may be either photocopied for distribution to students, or the teacher may convert them to overhead transparencies. The latter is accomplished by placing a blank acetate in the paper tray of your photocopy machine, then proceeding to make a copy of your Blackline Master (as though you were making a paper copy).

Interactive Conversation Video
An interactive video allows students to listen to and watch a real-life dramatization of each

Conversation dialogue in the Student Textbook. Students may choose to participate in the video by taking the role of one of the characters.

Lesson Plans with Block Scheduling

Glencoe French offers flexible lesson plans for both 45- and 55-minute schedules. In addition, a separate set of lesson plans has been developed for those schools operating within a block scheduling arrangement.

The various **Glencoe French** support materials are incorporated into these lesson plans at their most logical point of use, depending on the nature of the presentation material on a given day. For example, the Vocabulary Transparencies and the Audio (Cassette or Compact Disc) Program can be used most effectively when presenting the chapter vocabulary. On the other hand, the corresponding Chapter Quiz is recommended for use one or two days after the initial presentation of vocabulary, or following a specific chapter structure point. Because student needs and teacher preferences vary, space has been provided on each lesson plan page for the teacher to write additional notes and comments, adjusting the day's activities as required.

Some Advantages of Block Scheduling This
type of scheduling differs from traditional scheduling in that fewer class sessions are scheduled for larger blocks of time over fewer days. For example, a course might meet for 90 minutes a day for 90 days, or half a school year.

For schools themselves, the greatest advantage of block scheduling is that there is a better use of resources. No additional teachers or classrooms may be needed, and more efficient use is made of those presently available in the school system. The need for summer school is greatly reduced because the students that do not pass a course one term can take it the next term. These advantages are accompanied by an increase in the quality of teacher instruction and student's time on-task.

There are many advantages for teachers who are in schools that use block scheduling. For example, teacher-student relationships are improved. With block scheduling, teachers have responsibility for a smaller number of students at a time, so students and teachers get to know each other better. With more time, teachers are better able to meet the individual needs of their students. Teachers can also be more focused on what they are teaching. Block scheduling may also result in changes in teaching approaches, classrooms that are more student-centered, improved teacher morale, increased teacher effectiveness, and decreased burn-out. Teachers feel free to venture away from discussion and lecture to use more productive models of teaching.

Block scheduling cuts in half the time needed for introducing and closing classes. It also eliminates half of the time needed for class changes, which results in fewer discipline problems. Flexibility is increased because less complex teaching schedules create more opportunities for cooperative teaching strategies such as team teaching and interdisciplinary studies.

Internet Activities Booklet

This booklet of blackline masters serves as a dynamic, real-world connection between cultural themes introduced in **Glencoe French**, and related topics available via the Internet. In addition to serving as an innovative avenue for cultural reinforcement, the activities encourage both students and teachers to view the Internet as an engaging and valuable tool for learning the French language. Through this medium, students are able to further their knowledge of the French language, as well as increase their opportunities for participating in French-speaking communities around the world. The Internet activities encourage students to establish an ongoing keypal/pen pal relationship with French-speaking teenagers abroad.

The Internet Activities Booklet contains directions for the activities, student response sheets, and accompanying background teacher information, all on a chapter-by-chapter basis. Students will find the information required to complete each Internet activity by going to one or more of the websites whose addresses are provided on the Glencoe Foreign Language Home Page.

Performance Assessment

In addition to the tests described earlier, the Performance Assessment tasks provide an alternate approach to measuring student

learning, compared to the more traditional paper and pencil tests. These tasks include individual student assignments, student interviews, and individual and small-group research projects with follow-up presentations. The Performance Assessment tasks can be administered following the completion of every fourth chapter in the Student Textbook.

Chapter Quizzes with Answer Key

This component consists of short (five to ten minute) quizzes, designed to help both students and teachers evaluate quickly how well a specific vocabulary section or grammar topic has been mastered. For both Levels 1 and 2, there is a quiz for each *Mots* section (vocabulary) and one quiz for each grammar topic in the *Structure* section. The quizzes are on Blackline Masters. All answers are provided in an Answer Key at the end of the Chapter Quizzes booklet.

Testing Program with Answer Key

The Testing Program consists of three different types of Chapter Tests, two of which are bound into a testing booklet on Blackline Masters. The third type of test is available as part of the computer software component for **Glencoe French.**

1. The first type of test is discrete-point in nature, and uses evaluation techniques such as fill-in-the-blank, completion, short answers, true/false, matching, and multiple choice. Illustrations are frequently used as visual cues. The discrete-point tests measure vocabulary and grammar concepts via listening, speaking, reading, and writing formats. (As an option to the teacher, the listening section of each test has been recorded on cassette by native French speakers.) For testing cultural information, an optional section is included on each test corresponding to the *Lecture et culture* section of the Student Textbook. For the teacher's convenience, the speaking portion of the tests has been physically separated from the listening, reading, and writing portions, and placed at the back of the testing booklet. These chapter tests can be administered upon the completion of each chapter. The Unit Tests can be administered upon the completion of each *Révision* (after every four chapters).

2. The Blackline Master testing booklet also contains a second type of test, namely the Chapter proficiency tests. These measure students' mastery of each chapter's vocabulary and grammar on a more global, whole-language level. For both types of tests above, there is an Answer Key at the back of the testing booklet.

3. In addition to the two types of tests described above, there is a third type which is part of the Computer Software: Practice and Test Generator Program (Macintosh, IBM, Apple versions). With this software, teachers have the option of simply printing out ready-made chapter tests or customizing a ready-made test by selecting certain items, and/or adding original test items.

GLENCOE FRENCH 2 CD-ROM INTERACTIVE TEXTBOOK

The **Glencoe French 2 CD-ROM Interactive Textbook** is a complete curriculum and instructional system for high school French students. The four-disc CD-ROM program contains all elements of the textbook plus photographs, videos, animations, a student portfolio feature, self-tests and games, all designed to enhance and deepen students' understanding of the French language and culture. Although especially suited for individual or small-group use, it can be connected to a large monitor or LCD panel for whole-class instruction. With this flexible, interactive system, you can introduce, reinforce, or remediate any part of the French 2 curriculum at any time.

The CD-ROM program has four major sections: **Contents**, **Games**, **References**, and **Portfolio**. Of these four sections, the Games, Portfolio, and a special Contents feature, self-tests, are unique to the CD-ROM program.

Contents

The Contents section contains all the components of the French 2 *À bord* textbook. The following selections can be found under Contents:

- **Vocabulaire** Vocabulary is introduced in thematic contexts. New words are introduced, and communication activities based on real-life situations are presented.
- **Structure** Students are given explanations of French structures. They then practice through contextualized exercises. One of the structure points in each chapter is enhanced with an electronic comic strip with which students can interact.

- **Conversation** Interactive videos, which were shot in France, enhance this feature comprised of real-life dialogues. Students may listen to and watch a conversation and then choose to participate as one of the two characters as they record their part of the dialogue.
- **Lecture et culture** Readings give students the opportunity to gain insight into French culture. They are also able to hear the readings in French. The similarities and differences between French and American culture are emphasized.
- **Réalités** In *Réalités*, students see glimpses of everyday life in France. The *Réalités* act as a starting point for discussions about similarities and differences that exist between life in France and in the United States.
- **Culmination** Chapter-end activities require students to integrate the concepts they have learned. There are oral and written activities as well as activities aimed at building skills, and a vocabulary review linked to the glossary.
- **Self-Test** The self-test, *Contrôle de révision*, provides a means for students to evaluate their own progress.

At the end of each four chapters are two features: *Révision* and *Lettres et sciences*. These selections may also be found in the Contents section.

- **Révision** In the *Révision* section, students participate in a variety of review activities.
- **Lettres et sciences** This selection gives students the opportunity to practice their French reading skills through interdisciplinary

readings that provide insights into French culture.

Games

The Games section gives users access to *Chasse au trésor dans le métro* (Discs 1 and 3) and to *Le Tour de France* (Discs 2 and 4). Each game reviews the vocabulary, grammar and culture topics that have been presented in the four chapters contained on that particular CD-ROM disc.

References

Maps, verb charts, and the French-English/ English-French glossaries can be selected from this tab. The maps include France, Paris, and a world map with the French-speaking countries highlighted.

Portfolio

The electronic portfolio feature may be accessed by clicking on this tab. Students can access a photo library, and choose from a variety of "stationery" templates to create original written work, which they can then store in their portfolio document.

For more information see the User's Guide accompanying the **Glencoe French 2 CD-ROM Interactive Textbook.**

COOPERATIVE LEARNING

Cooperative learning provides a structured, natural environment for student communication that is both motivating and meaningful. The affective filter that prevents many students from daring to risk a wrong answer when called upon to speak in front of a whole class can be minimized when students develop friendly relationships in their cooperative groups and when they become accustomed to multiple opportunities to hear and rehearse new communicative tasks. The goal of cooperative learning is not to abandon traditional methods of foreign language teaching, but rather to provide opportunities for learning in an environment where students contribute freely and responsibly to the success of the group. The key is to strike a balance between group goals and individual accountability. Group (team) members plan how to divide the activity among themselves, then each member of the group carries out his or her part of the assignment. Cooperative learning provides each student with a "safe," low-risk environment rather than a whole-class atmosphere. As you implement cooperative learning in your classroom, we urge you to take time to explain to students what will be expected of every group member—listening, participating, and respecting other opinions.

In the Teacher's Wraparound Edition, cooperative learning activities accompany each chapter of the Student Textbook. These activities have been created to assist both the teacher who wants to include cooperative learning for the first time, and for the experienced practitioner of cooperative learning as well.

Classroom Management: implementing cooperative learning activities

Many of the suggested cooperative learning activities are based on a four-member team structure in the classroom. Teams of four are recommended because there is a wide variety of possible interactions. At the same time the group is small enough that students can take turns quickly within the group. Pairs of students as teams may be too limited in terms of possible interactions, and trios frequently work out to be a pair with the third student left out. Teams of five may be unwieldy in that students begin to feel that no one will notice if they don't really participate.

If students sit in rows on a daily basis, desks can be pushed together to form teams of four. Teams of students who work together need to be balanced according to as many variables as possible: academic achievement in the course, personality, ethnicity, gender, attitude, etc. Teams that are as heterogeneous as possible will ensure that the class progresses quickly through the curriculum.

Following are descriptions of some of the most important cooperative learning structures, adapted from Spencer Kagan's Structural Approach to Cooperative Learning, as they apply to the content of *Bienvenue* (Level 1).

Round-robin Each member of the team answers in turn a question, or shares an idea with teammates. Responses should be brief so that students do not have to wait long for their turn.

Example from *Bienvenue*, Chapter 2, Days of the week:

Teams recite the days of the week in a round-robin fashion. Different students begin additional rounds so that everyone ends up needing to know all the names of the days. Variations include starting the list with a different day or using a race format, i.e., teams recite the list three times in a row and raise their hands when they have finished.

Roundtable Each student in turn writes his or her contribution to the group activity on a piece of paper that is passed around the team. If the individual student responses are longer than one or two words, there can be four pieces of paper with each student contributing to each paper as it is passed around the team.

A to Z Roundtable Using vocabulary from *Bienvenue*, Chapters 7 and 8, students take turns adding one word at a time to a list of words associated with plane or train travel in A to Z order. Students may help each other with what to write, and correct spelling. Encourage creativity when it comes to the few letters of the alphabet that don't begin a specific travel word from their chapter lists. Teams can compete in several ways: first to finish all 26 letters; longest word; shortest word; most creative response.

Numbered Heads Together Numbered Heads Together is a structure for review and practice of high consensus information. There are four steps:

Step 1: Students number off in their teams from 1 to 4.
Step 2: The teacher asks a question and gives the teams some time to make sure that everyone on the team knows the answer.
Step 3: The teacher calls a number.
Step 4: The appropriate student from each team is responsible to report the group response.

Answers can be reported simultaneously, i.e., all students with the appropriate number can stand by their seats and recite the answer together, or go to the chalkboard and write the answer at the same time. Answers can also be reported sequentially. Call on the first student to raise his or her hand or have all the students with the appropriate number stand. Select one student to give the answer. If the other students agree, they sit down; if not, they remain standing and offer a different response.

Example from *Bienvenue*, Chapter 2, Telling time:

Step 1: Using a blank clock face on the overhead transparency or chalkboard, the teacher adjusts the hands on the clock.
Step 2: Students put their heads together and answer the question: *Quelle heure est-il?*
Step 3: The teacher calls a number.
Step 4: The appropriate student from each team is responsible to report the group response.

Pantomimes Give each team one card. Have each team decide together how to pantomime for the class the action identified on the card. Each team presents the pantomime for ten seconds while the rest of the teams watch without talking. Then each of the other teams tries to guess the phrase and writes down their choice on a piece of paper. (This is a good way to accommodate kinesthetic learning styles as well as vary classroom activities.)

Example from *Bienvenue*, Chapter 3 vocabulary: The teacher writes the following sentences on slips of paper and places them in an envelope:

1. *Ils parlent.*
2. *Ils parlent au téléphone.*
3. *Ils écoutent des cassettes.*
4. *Ils écoutent des disques compacts.*
5. *Ils écoutent un walkman.*
6. *Ils écoutent la radio.*
7. *Ils regardent la télé.*
8. *Ils dansent.*
9. *Ils chantent.*
10. *Ils rigolent.*

Each team will draw one slip of paper from the envelope and decide together how to pantomime the action for the class. As one team pantomimes their action for 30 seconds, the other teams are silent. Then the students within each team discuss among themselves what sentence was acted out for them. When they have decided on the sentence, each team sends one person to write it on the chalkboard.

Inside/Outside Circle Students form two concentric circles of equal number by counting off 1-2, 1-2 in their teams. The "ones" form a circle shoulder to shoulder and facing out. The

"twos" form a circle outside the "ones" to make pairs. With an odd number of students, there can be one threesome. Students take turns sharing information, quizzing each other, or taking parts of a dialogue. After students finish with their first partners, rotate the inside circle to the left so that the students repeat the process with new partners. For following rounds, alternate rotating the inside and outside circles so that students get to repeat the identified tasks, but with new partners. This is an excellent way to structure 100% student participation combined with extensive practice of communication tasks.

Other suggested activities are similarly easy to follow and to implement in the classroom. Student enthusiasm for cooperative learning activities will reward the enterprising teacher. Teachers who are new to these concepts may want to refer to Dr. Spencer Kagan's book, *Cooperative Learning,* published by Resources for Teachers, Inc., Paseo Espada, Suite 622, San Juan Capistrano, CA 92675.

SUGGESTIONS FOR CORRECTING HOMEWORK

Correcting homework, or any tasks students have done on an independent basis, should be a positive learning experience rather than mechanical "busywork." Following are some suggestions for correcting homework. These ideas may be adapted as the teacher sees fit.

1. Put the answers on an overhead transparency. Have students correct their own answers.

2. Ask one or more of your better students to write their homework answers on the chalkboard at the beginning of the class hour. While the answers are being put on the chalkboard, the teacher involves the rest of the class in a non-related activity. At some point in the class hour, take a few minutes to go over the homework answers that have been written on the board, asking students to check their own work. You may then wish to have students hand in their homework so that they know this independent work is important to you.

3. Go over the homework assignment quickly in class. Write the key word(s) for each answer on the chalkboard so students can see the correct answer.

4. When there is no correct answer, e.g., "Answers will vary," give one or two of the most likely answers. Don't allow students to inquire about all other possibilities, however.

5. Have all students hand in their homework. After class, correct every other (every third, fourth, fifth, etc.) homework paper. Over several days, you will have checked every student's homework at least once.

6. Compile a list of the most common student errors. Then create a worksheet that explains the underlying grammar points and practices on these topics.

STUDENT PORTFOLIOS

The use of student portfolios to represent long-term individual accomplishments in learning French offers several benefits. With portfolios, students can keep a written record of their best work and thereby document their own progress as learners. For teachers, portfolios enable us to include our students in our evaluation and measurement process. For example, the content of any student's portfolio may offer an alternative to the standardized test as a way of measuring student writing achievement. Assessing the contents of a student's portfolio can be an option to testing the writing skill via the traditional writing section of the chapter or unit test.

There are as many kinds of portfolios as there are teachers working with them. Perhaps the most convenient as well as permanent portfolio consists of a three-ring binder which each student will add to over the school year and in which the student will place his or her best written work. In the **Glencoe French** series, selections for the portfolio may come from the Writing Activities Workbook; Communication Activities Masters; the more open-ended activities in the Student Tape Manual and the Video Activities Booklet, as well as from written assignments in the Student Textbook, including the *Activités de communication écrite* sections. The teacher is encouraged to refer actively to students' portfolios so that they are regarded as more than just a storage device. For example, over the course of the school year, the student may be asked to go back to earlier entries in his or her portfolio in order to revise certain assignments, or to develop an assignment further by writing in a new tense, e.g., the *passé composé*. In this way, the student can appreciate the amount of learning that has occurred over several months of time.

Portfolios offer students a multidimensional look at themselves. A "best" paper might be the one with the least errors or one in which the student reached and synthesized a new idea, or went beyond the teacher's assignment. The Student Portfolio topic is included in each chapter of the Teacher's Wraparound Edition as a reminder that this is yet another approach the teacher may wish to use in the French classroom.

CD-ROM Electronic Portfolio

The Student Portfolio topic is a regular feature in each chapter of the Teacher's Wraparound Edition. In addition, the CD-ROM version of the student textbook (see page T35) includes an electronic portfolio feature. Students may access a photo library, and choose from a variety of templates to create original oral and written work, which they can then store as portfolio documents. For more information, see the User's Guide accompanying the **Glencoe French 2 CD-ROM Interactive Textbook**.

PACING

Sample Lesson Plans

Level 2 (*À bord*) has been developed so that it may be completed in one school year. However, it is up to the individual teacher to decide how many chapters will be covered. Although completion of the textbook by the end of the year is recommended, it is not necessary. Most of the important structures of Level 2 are reviewed in a different context in Level 3 (*En voyage*). The establishment of lesson plans helps the teacher visualize how a chapter can

be presented. However, by emphasizing certain aspects of the program and deemphasizing others, the teacher can change the focus and the approach of a chapter to meet students' needs and to suit his or her own teaching style and techniques. Sample lesson plans are provided below. They include some of the suggestions and techniques that have been described earlier in this Teacher's Manual.

STANDARD PACING		
	Days	**Total Days**
(*Révision A–F*)	3 days per section	18
Chapitres 1–14	9 days per chapter	126
Testing	1 day per test	14
Révision (3)	3 days each	9
Lettres et sciences (3 [optional])	2 days each	6

	Class	**Homework**
Day 1	*Mots 1* (with transparencies) exercises (Student Textbook)	*Mots* exercises (written) Writing Activities Workbook: *Mots 1*
Day 2	*Mots 2* (with transparencies) exercises (Student Textbook)	*Mots* exercises (written) exercises from Student Textbook (written) prepare *Activités de communication* Writing Activities Workbook: *Mots 2*
Day 3	present *Activités de communication* one *Structure* topic exercises (Student Textbook)	exercises from Student Textbook (written) Writing Activities Workbook (written)

Day 4	two *Structure* topics	exercises from Student Textbook (written)
	exercises (Student Textbook)	Student Tape Manual exercises
Day 5	one *Structure* topic	exercises from Student Textbook (written)
	exercises (Student Textbook)	Writing Activities Workbook (written)
Day 6	*Conversation* (pronunciation)	read *Lecture*
	Activités de communication	*Étude de mots*
	Audio Program	
Day 7	review *Lecture et culture*	read *Découverte culturelle* and *Réalités*
	Compréhension questions	
	Video Program	
Day 8	review homework	*Activités de communication écrite*
	Activités de communication orale	
	Situation Cards	
Day 9	Communication Activities Masters	review for test
	Communication Transparency	
Day 10	Test	after Chapters 4, 8, 12: *Révision* conversation

Révision (review) and *Lettres et sciences* (optional) sections

Day 1	grammar review	exercises in Student Textbook and Workbook
Day 2	correct homework	review for Test
	Activités de communication	
Day 3	Unit Test	pre-read *Lettres et sciences*, first selection (optional)
Day 4	*Lettres et sciences*, first selection (optional)	*Lettres et sciences*, second selection (optional)
Day 5	*Lettres et sciences,* third selection (optional)	*Lettres et sciences*, second selection in-depth (optional)

ACCELERATED PACING

	Days	Total Days
(Révision A–F)	3 days per section	18
Chapters 1–8	8 days per chapter	64*
Chapters 9–16	7 days per chapter	56
Test	1 day per test	16
Révision (4)	2 days each	8
Lettres et sciences (4 [optional])	2 days each	8

	Class	Homework
Day 1	Mots 1 (with transparencies) exercises (Student Textbook)	Mots exercises (written) Writing Activities Workbook: Mots 1
Day 2	Mots 2 (with transparencies) exercises (Student Textbook)	Mots exercises (written) exercises from Student Textbook (written) prepare Activités de communication Writing Activities Workbook: Mots 2
Day 3	present Activités de communication two Structure topics	exercises from Student Textbook (written) Writing Activities Workbook (written)
Day 4	two Structure topics	exercises from Student Textbook (written) Writing Activities Workbook (written)
Day 5	Conversation present Activités de communication Audio Program	read Lecture Étude de mots and Compréhension
Day 6	Découverte culturelle (optional) Réalités (optional) Videocassette Program Communication Activities Masters	Culmination
Day 7	review Culmination Situation Cards Communication Transparency	review for test
Day 8	Test	After Chapters 4, 8, 12, 16: Révision

*Note: After Chapter 8, the teacher may choose among the Culmination activities on Days 6 and 7, thereby eliminating one day.

Révision (review) and Lettres et sciences (optional) sections

Day 1	Révision exercises	review for test
Day 2	Unit Test	
Day 3	Lettres et sciences, first selection (optional)	Lettres et sciences, second selection (optional)
Day 4	Lettres et sciences, third selection (optional)	

USEFUL CLASSROOM WORDS AND EXPRESSIONS

Below is a list of the most frequently used words and expressions needed in conducting a French class.

Words

le papier	paper
la feuille de papier	sheet of paper
le cahier	notebook
le cahier d'exercices	workbook
le stylo	pen
le stylo-bille	ballpoint pen
le crayon	pencil
la gomme	(pencil) eraser
la craie	chalk
le tableau noir	blackboard
la brosse	blackboard eraser
la corbeille	waste basket
le pupitre	desk
le rang	row
la chaise	chair
l'écran (m.)	screen
le projecteur	projector
la cassette	cassette
le livre	book
la règle	ruler

Commands

Both the singular and the plural command forms are provided.

Viens.	Venez.	Come.
Va.	Allez.	Go.
Entre.	Entrez.	Enter.
Sors.	Sortez.	Leave.
Attends.	Attendez.	Wait.

Mets.	Mettez.	Put.
Donne-moi.	Donnez-moi.	Give me.
Dis-moi.	Dites-moi.	Tell me.
Apporte-moi.	Apportez-moi.	Bring me.
Répète.	Répétez.	Repeat.
Pratique.	Pratiquez.	Practice.
Étudie.	Étudiez.	Study.
Réponds.	Répondez.	Answer.
Apprends.	Apprenez.	Learn.
Choisis.	Choisissez.	Choose.
Prépare.	Préparez.	Prepare.
Regarde.	Regardez.	Look at.
Décris.	Décrivez.	Describe.
Commence.	Commencez.	Begin.
Prononce.	Prononcez.	Pronounce.
Écoute.	Écoutez.	Listen.
Parle.	Parlez.	Speak.
Lis.	Lisez.	Read.
Écris.	Écrivez.	Write.
Demande.	Demandez.	Ask.
Suis le modèle.	Suivez le modèle.	Follow the model.
Joue le rôle de…	Jouez le rôle de…	Take the part of…
Prends.	Prenez.	Take.
Ouvre.	Ouvrez.	Open.
Ferme.	Fermez.	Close.
Tourne la page.	Tournez la page.	Turn the page.
Efface.	Effacez.	Erase.
Continue.	Continuez.	Continue.
Assieds-toi.	Asseyez-vous.	Sit down.
Lève-toi.	Levez-vous.	Get up.
Lève la main.	Levez la main.	Raise your hand.
Tais-toi.	Taisez-vous.	Be quiet.
Fais attention.	Faites attention.	Pay attention.
Attention.		Attention.
Attention, s'il vous plaît.		Your attention, please.
Silence.		Quiet.
Fais attention.	Faites attention.	Careful.
Encore.		Again.
Encore une fois.		Once again.
Un à un.		One at a time.
Tous ensemble.		All together.
À haute voix.		Out loud.
Plus haut, s'il vous plaît.		Louder, please.
En français.		In French.
En anglais.		In English.

ADDITIONAL FRENCH RESOURCES

Pen pal sources Following is a list of French and American organizations that assist in finding French pen pals:

1. American Association of Teachers of French
    Bureau de Correspondance Scolaire
    Mailcode 4510
    Southern Illinois University
    Carbondale, IL 62901-4510
    tel: (618) 453-5731
2. Fédération Internationale des Organisations de Correspondance et d'Échanges Scolaires (FIOCES)
    29, rue d'Ulm
    75230 Paris CEDEX 05
    France
3. Contacts
    55, rue Nationale
    37000 Tours
    France
4. Office National de la Coopération à l'École
    101 bis, rue du Ranelagh
    75016 Paris
    France
5. Mairie
    Maison des Sociétés
    Square Weingarten
    69500 Bron
    France

French Embassy and Consulates in the United States

French Embassy
Press and Information Service
4101 Reservoir Road, N.W.
Washington, DC 20007
tel: (202) 944-6060

French Consulates
Atlanta: (404) 522-4226
Boston: (617) 542-7374
Chicago: (312) 787-5359
Honolulu: (808) 599-4458
Houston: (713) 528-2181
Los Angeles: (310) 235-3200
Miami: (305) 372-9799
New York: (212) 606-3688
New Orleans: (504) 523-5772
San Francisco: (415) 397-4330
San Juan, Puerto Rico: (809) 753-1700

The Embassy of France distributes neither French flags nor posters. To purchase a flag contact one of the following manufacturers:

U.N. Association
Capital Area Division
1319 18th St. N.W.
Washington, DC 20036-1802
(202) 785-2640

Abacrome
I-B Quaker Ridge Rd.
New Rochelle, NY 10804
(914) 235-8152

NOTES

À bord

Glencoe French 2

À bord

Conrad J. Schmitt

Katia Brillié Lutz

**Glencoe
McGraw-Hill**

New York, New York   Columbus, Ohio   Woodland Hills, California   Peoria, Illinois

About the Cover

The Château de Sully is a magnificent 14th-century castle in the Loire Valley. The castle is set in a moat created from the diverted Sange River.

Glencoe/McGraw-Hill

A Division of The McGraw-Hill Companies

Copyright ©1998 by Glencoe/McGraw-Hill. All rights reserved. Except as permitted under the United States Copyright Act, no part of this publication may be reproduced or distributed in any form or by any means, or stored in a database or retrieval system, without prior permission of the publisher.

Printed in the United States of America.

Send all inquiries to:
Glencoe/McGraw-Hill
21600 Oxnard Street, Suite 500
Woodland Hills, CA 91367

ISBN 0-02-636813-7 (Student Edition)

ISBN 0-02-636814-5 (Teacher's Wraparound Edition)

2 3 4 5 6 7 8 9 0   003   03 02 01 00 99 98

Acknowledgments

We wish to express our deep appreciation to the numerous individuals throughout the United States and France who have advised us in the development of these teaching materials. Special thanks are extended to the people whose names appear below.

Esther Bennett
Notre Dame High School
Sherman Oaks, California

Brillié Family
Paris, France

Kathryn Bryers
French teacher
Berlin, Connecticut

G. Gail Castaldo
The Pingry School
Martinsville, New Jersey

Veronica Dewey
Brother Rice High School
Birmingham, Massachusetts

Lyne Flaherty
Hingham High School
Hingham, Massachusetts

Marie-Jo Hoffmann
Poudre School District
Fort Collins, Colorado

Marcia Brown Karper
Fayetteville-Manlius Central Schools
Manlius, New York

Annette Lowry
Ft. Worth Independent School District
Ft. Worth, Texas

Fabienne Raab
Paris, France

Sally Schneider
Plano Independent School District
Plano, Texas

Faith Weldon
Schalmont Central School District
Schenectady, New York

TABLE DES MATIÈRES

RÉVISION

CHAPITRE 1

LA POSTE ET LA CORRESPONDANCE

vii

CHAPITRE 2

FAMILLES

CHAPITRE 3

LE TÉLÉPHONE

CHAPITRE 6

UN ACCIDENT ET L'HÔPITAL

CHAPITRE 7

DE LA MARTINIQUE À PARIS EN AVION

CHAPITRE 8

EN ROUTE

CHAPITRE 9

LA TEINTURERIE ET LA LAVERIE AUTOMATIQUE

CHAPITRE 10

LES TRANSPORTS EN COMMUN

CHAPITRE 11

LES FÊTES

CHAPITRE 12

AU LYCÉE

CHAPITRE 13

LE SAVOIR-VIVRE EN FRANCE

LE MAGHREB

LES AGRICULTEURS EN FRANCE

LES PROFESSIONS ET LES MÉTIERS

APPENDICES

XV

RÉVISION A

OVERVIEW

The review chapters A–F review all the key structure points and vocabulary topics presented in *Bienvenue*. Additional review of Level 1 material can be found in the *Réintroduction et recombinaison* section of each chapter of *À bord*. The presentation of new material begins in Chapter 1. As in *Bienvenue*, there is a review section after each four chapters of *À bord*.

Révision A covers vocabulary needed to describe people, school, and home. These topics were first presented in *Bienvenue*, Chapters 1–4.

The agreement of adjectives, the present tense of the verbs *être* and *aller*, and the contractions with *à* and *de* are also reviewed.

RÉVISION
A
LES COPAINS ET LES COURS

R 1

REVIEW RESOURCES

1. Bell Ringer Review Blackline Masters
2. Workbook
3. Lesson Plans
4. Testing Program
5. CD-ROM Interactive Textbook

Pacing

This review chapter should take two to three days depending on the length of the class and the age and aptitude of your students.

Note The Lesson Plans offer guidelines for 45- and 55-minute classes and **Block Scheduling.**

Exercices vs. *Activités*

The exercises and activities are color-coded. Exercises, which provide guided practice to prepare students for independent communication, are coded in blue. Communicative activities, which give students opportunities for creative, open-ended expression, are coded in red.

LEARNING FROM PHOTOS

You may wish to give students the following information and ask them some questions about the photo: *C'est la cour du Collège du Pays d'Aigues à Pertuis, une petite ville près d'Aix-en-Provence. Décrivez les élèves. Comment sont-ils? Qu'est-ce qu'ils portent? Que font-ils?*

Bell Ringer Review

Put the following on the board or use BRR Blackline Master R-1: Make a list of expressions used for greeting people and saying goodbye to them.

Une Française

PRESENTATION *(page R2)*

A. Have students open their books and repeat the sentences about Nathalie after you.

B. Ask the questions that follow.

Note Students may listen to recorded versions of the sentences and the conversation below on the CD-ROM.

ANSWERS

Exercice A

1. C'est Nathalie.
2. Elle est française.
3. Elle est de Paris.
4. Elle est très intelligente.
5. Elle va au lycée Henri IV.

Deux Français

PRESENTATION *(page R2)*

A. Review the expressions used for greeting people and saying goodbye to them that the students listed in the Bell Ringer Review. Have the class repeat the conversation after you.

B. Call on two students to read the conversation to the class.

C. **Extension** Call on pairs to change the conversation in any way that makes sense.

Une Française

Voici Nathalie.
Elle est française.
Nathalie est de Paris, la capitale.
Nathalie est très intelligente.
Elle est élève au lycée.
Elle va au lycée Henri IV.

 A **Nathalie.** Répondez.

1. Qui est la fille?
2. Elle est de quelle nationalité?
3. Elle est de quelle ville?
4. Nathalie est intelligente ou pas?
5. Elle va à quel lycée?

Deux Français

ÉRIC: Salut, Paul.
PAUL: Salut, Éric. Ça va?
ÉRIC: Oui, ça va bien, et toi?
PAUL: Pas mal.
ÉRIC: Où vas-tu maintenant?
PAUL: Je vais au cours de français.
ÉRIC: Qui est le prof?
PAUL: M. Guillemette. Il est très chouette.

B **Salut, Paul!** Répondez d'après la conversation.

1. Éric va bien ou pas?
2. Où est-ce que Paul va maintenant?
3. Qui est le professeur de français?
4. Comment est-il?

ADDITIONAL PRACTICE

1. Have students make up questions about Nathalie to ask you or their classmates.
2. Have students make up false statements about Éric and Paul. Their classmates will correct these statements.

C Les deux copains. Répondez d'après la photo.

1. Qui sont les deux garçons?
2. Où sont-ils maintenant?
3. D'où sont les deux garçons?
4. Ils sont de quelle nationalité?
5. Comment sont les deux garçons?

Peter et Steve sont de New York.

D Personnellement. Donnez des réponses personnelles.

1. Salut!
2. Comment ça va?
3. Qui est ton (ta) prof de français?
4. Comment est-il (elle)?
5. Comment est le cours de français?

R 3

Exercice B *(page R2)*

1. Oui, il va bien.
2. Il va au cours de français.
3. M. Guillemette est le professeur de français.
4. Il est très chouette.

PRESENTATION *(page R3)*

Exercices C and D

These exercises can be done with books open or closed.

Extension of *Exercice C*

After completing Exercise C, have a student retell the story in his/her own words.

ANSWERS

Exercice C

1. Ce sont Peter et Steve.
2. Ils sont à New York. (Ils sont dans le parc.)
3. Ils sont de New York.
4. Ils sont américains.
5. Answers will vary but may include: Ils sont grands, intelligents et sympathiques.

Exercice D

Answers will vary.

LEARNING FROM PHOTOS

1. Ask students where they think the boys in the photo might be going.
2. Have students give as thorough a description of the boys as possible.

INDEPENDENT PRACTICE

Assign any of the following:
1. Exercises, pages R2–R3
2. Workbook, *Mots et Conversation: A–C,* page R1
3. CD-ROM, Disc 1, pages R2–R3

Structure Teaching Resources

1. Bell Ringer Review Blackline Master: R-2, page 1
2. Workbook, *Structure: A–H*, pages R2–R5
3. CD-ROM, Disc 1, pages R4–R6

L'accord des adjectifs

PRESENTATION *(page R4)*

A. Read step 1 to the class.
B. Write the adjectives in the chart on the board. Cross out the *-e* at the end of *intelligente* and remind students that the pronunciation changes. Have them repeat *intelligente/intelligent* after you. Then ask them what the difference is in pronunciation.
C. Explain to students that adjectives that end in a consonant have four forms and those that end in *-e* have two forms.

Exercices

PRESENTATION *(page R4)*

Exercices A and B

Encourage students to say as much as they can when doing these exercises. After students do them orally, you may wish to have them write them.

ANSWERS

Exercices A and B

Answers will vary.

Les verbes être *et* aller

PRESENTATION *(page R4)*

A. Have the students repeat the verb forms after you.
B. Remind them to make the liaison in *vous êtes, nous allons, vous allez.*
C. Have them read the model sentences after you.

L'accord des adjectifs

1. Adjectives agree with the nouns they describe. If the noun is feminine, the adjective must be in the feminine form. If the noun is plural, the adjective must be in the plural form. Review the following.

	FÉMININ	MASCULIN
SINGULIER	une fille intelligente une amie sincère	un garçon intelligent un ami sincère
PLURIEL	des filles intelligentes des amies sincères	des garçons intelligents des amis sincères

2. Note that adjectives that end in a consonant in the masculine form (*intelligent*) change pronunciation in the feminine form. Adjectives that end in *-e* (*sincère*) do not change pronunciation.

A **Qui est-ce?** Décrivez un ami.

B **Les amies.** Décrivez les filles.

Les verbes être et aller

1. Review the forms of the important irregular verbs *être*, "to be," and *aller*, "to go."

ÊTRE	
je suis	nous sommes
tu es	vous êtes
il/elle/on est	ils/elles sont

ALLER	
je vais	nous allons
tu vas	vous allez
il/elle/on va	ils/elles vont

ADDITIONAL PRACTICE

Read the following to the class or write it on the board or on a transparency: *Faites une liste des caractéristiques que vous cherchez dans un(e) ami(e) et que vous considérez comme importantes.*

PAIRED ACTIVITY

Have students work in pairs. One student describes a famous person and the other tries to guess who it is.

2. Note that to make a sentence negative, you put *ne... pas* (or *n'... pas*) around the verb.

   Je suis française.   **Je *ne* suis *pas* américaine.**
   Jeanne est sympathique.   **Elle *n'*est *pas* antipathique.**

3. Remember that you also use *aller* to express how someone feels.

   Comment vas-tu?
   Comment allez-vous?   **Je vais bien, merci.**

C **Charles est de New York.**   Répétez la conversation.

ANNICK: Bonjour, Charles. Ça va?
CHARLES: Oui, ça va bien, et toi?
ANNICK: Bien, merci. Tu es francais, Charles, n'est-ce pas?
CHARLES: Mais non, je ne suis pas français. Je suis américain.
ANNICK: Sans blague! Tu es de quelle ville?
CHARLES: Je suis de New York.
ANNICK: Tu vas à l'université à New York?
CHARLES: Non, non. Je ne vais pas à l'université. Je vais à l'école secondaire.

Répondez d'après la conversation.

1. Charles est français?
2. Il est de quelle nationalité?
3. Il est de quelle ville?
4. Il va à l'université?
5. Où est-ce qu'il va à l'école?

D **Moi!**   Donnez des réponses personnelles.

1. Qui es-tu?
2. D'où es-tu?
3. Tu es de quelle nationalité?
4. Tu vas à quelle école?
5. Tu vas à l'école avec des copains?
6. Tes copains et toi, vous allez à l'école à pied ou en bus?
7. Où est l'école?
8. Comment sont les professeurs?

E **Au restaurant.**   Complétez avec «être» ou «aller».

1. C'___ un petit restaurant. Il ___ vraiment très bon.
2. Tous les serveurs ___ vietnamiens.
3. La cuisine vietnamienne ___ délicieuse.
4. Le copain de Françoise y ___ aussi.
5. Au restaurant, qui ___ demander l'addition?
6. Qui ___ payer?
7. Vous ___ laisser un pourboire?

R 5

Exercices

PRESENTATION   *(page R5)*

Exercice C
Call on two students with good pronunciation to read the conversation in this exercise to the class.

Extension of *Exercice C*
Call on a student to retell the story of the conversation in his/her own words.

Exercice D
It is recommended that you do Exercise D once orally with books closed.

Extension of *Exercice D*
Call on a student to say as much as possible about his/her school.

Exercice E
This exercise is more difficult than Exercises C and D because students must determine which verb to use in addition to using the correct form.

ANSWERS
Exercice C
1. Non, il n'est pas français. (Non, il est américain.)
2. Il est américain.
3. Il est de New York.
4. Non, il ne va pas à l'université.
5. Il va à l'école secondaire à New York.

Exercice D
Answers will vary.

Exercice E
1. est, est
2. sont
3. est
4. va
5. va
6. va
7. allez

LEARNING FROM PHOTOS

1. Have students describe the people in the photo.
2. Have them make up a conversation between the two people.

Write the following on the board or use BRR Blackline Master R-2: Match each adjective in Column A with its opposite in Column B.

A	B
blond	facile
patient	petit
moche	brun
jeune	impatient
grand	antipathique
difficile	vieux
sympathique	beau

Les contractions avec à et de

PRESENTATION *(page R6)*

A. Write the contractions on the board.

B. Have the students read the model sentences aloud.

C. Since the *au* and *du* forms present the greatest problem, you may wish to start by asking the following simple questions: *Tu vas au parc? Tu vas au restaurant? Tu vas au lycée? Tu vas au magasin? Tu vas au marché? Tu habites près du parc? Tu habites près du restaurant? Tu habites près du lycée? Tu habites près du magasin? Tu habites près du marché?*

Exercices

PRESENTATION *(page R6)*

Exercices F and G

It is recommended that you go over the exercises in class before assigning them for homework.

ANSWERS

Exercice F

1. au	5. à l'
2. au	6. au
3. à la	7. au
4. à la	8. aux

Exercice G

Answers will vary.

Les contractions avec *à* et *de*

1. The preposition *à* can mean "to," "in," or "at." It remains unchanged with the articles *la* and *l'*, but it contracts with *le* to form one word, *au*, and with *les* to form one word, *aux*. Note the liaison with *aux* and a word that begins with a vowel or silent *h*. The *x* is pronounced like a *z*. Review the following.

à + la = à la	Je vais *à la* boulangerie.
à + l' = à l'	Je vais *à l'*école.
à + le = au	Je vais *au* restaurant.
à + les = aux	Je parle *aux* élèves.

2. The preposition *de*, meaning "of" or "from," also contracts with *le* and *les* to form one word, *du* or *des*. Note that *de* is also a part of many longer prepositions such as *près de, loin de*, etc.

de + la = de la	Il habite près *de la* cathédrale.
de + l' = de l'	Il habite près *de l'*école.
de + le = du	Elle habite loin *du* parc.
de + les = des	Elle habite loin *des* magasins.

F **On y va ou pas?** Complétez.

Aujourd'hui on ne va pas ___₁ parc, on ne va pas ___₂ restaurant, on ne va pas ___₃ maison, on ne va pas ___₄ pâtisserie. Où est-ce qu'on va alors? On va ___₅ école. On va ___₆ cours de français. On va parler ___₇ professeur et ___₈ élèves.

G **Où habites-tu?** Donnez des réponses personnelles.

1. Tu habites près ou loin de l'aéroport?
2. Tu vas souvent à l'aéroport?
3. Tu habites près ou loin de la gare?
4. Tu vas souvent à la gare?
5. Tu habites près ou loin de l'école?
6. Tu quittes l'école à quelle heure?
7. Tu habites près ou loin des magasins?
8. Tu vas souvent au magasin?

R 6

Activités de communication orale

A **L'ami(e) idéal(e).** Make a list of qualities you look for in a friend. Then ask your partner if he or she likes the same things in a friend.

> Élève 1: Pour moi, l'ami(e) idéal(e) est très sympathique. Tu es d'accord?
> Élève 2: Oui, je suis d'accord. Pour moi, l'ami(e) idéal(e) est aussi très patient(e).

B **Au restaurant.** With a classmate, make up a conversation between a waiter or waitress and a customer at a restaurant. You may want to use some of the following words and expressions.

le menu	une pizza	à point
le service	un coca-cola	bien cuit
un hamburger	saignant	l'addition

C **On fait les courses.** You and two classmates are planning a picnic in Évian-les-Bains, a town on Lake Geneva. First, make a list of what you need. Then take turns asking one another where you would buy these items.

> du pain
> Élève 1: Où est-ce qu'on achète du pain?
> Élève 2: On achète du pain à la boulangerie.

La carte pomme de pain :

Les sandwichs

LE LYONNAIS ROSETTE DE LYON *450 CALORIES*	**LE COMTE** COMTÉ DU JURA *430 CALORIES*	**LE PARISIE** JAMBON AU TORCH *333 CALORIES*
LE SAVOYARD JAMBON CRU *347 CALORIES*	**LE SPECIAL** JAMBON/CRUDITÉS *400 CALORIES*	**LE PROVEN** OLIVES/CRUDITÉS *400 CALORIES*
LE CORDON BLEU JAMBON AU TORCHON COMTÉ *530 CALORIES*	**LE VILLAGEOIS** VOLAILLE/CRUDITÉS *360 CALORIES*	**LE NICO** THON/CRUDI *420 CALORIES*

- bière de luxe pression
- bordeaux A.O.C.
- cidre normand
- boisson à l'orange
- coca-cola
- chocolat - café - thé

- eau minérale
- la salade fraicheur
- la salade pomme de pain
- la quiche lorraine
- le feuilleté volaille

- le croissant
- le pain au cho
- le chausson a
- la tarte aux p
- les glaces et

R 7

Activités de communication orale
PRESENTATION (page R7)

These activities encourage students to use the language on their own. You may wish to let them choose the activities they would like to do.

Note Activity A recycles material from *Bienvenue,* Chapters 1 and 2; Activity B, from Chapter 5; and Activity C, from Chapter 6.

Extension of *Activité B*
After the students complete Activity B, have them present their conversation to the class.

ANSWERS
Activités A, B, and C
Answers will vary.

LEARNING FROM REALIA

Have students make up a conversation between a waiter and a customer using the menu from Le Restaurant Pomme de Pain.

INDEPENDENT PRACTICE

Assign any of the following:
1. Exercises and activities, pages R4–R7
2. Workbook, *Structure: A–H,* pages R2–R5
3. CD-ROM, Disc 1, pages R2–R5

OVERVIEW

This chapter reviews vocabulary related to home and family activities, after-school activities, dining out, and shopping at a market. These topics were presented in *Bienvenue,* Chapters 3–6.

The structures reviewed are the present tense of regular *-er* verbs, the infinitive, the irregular verbs *avoir* and *faire,* the partitive, and possessive adjectives.

RÉVISION
B
DES ACTIVITÉS AMUSANTES

MUSIQUE DU MONDE

R 9

REVIEW RESOURCES

1. Bell Ringer Review Blackline Masters
2. Workbook
3. Lesson Plans
4. Testing Program
5. CD-ROM Interactive Textbook

Pacing

This review chapter should take two to three days depending on the length of the class and the age and aptitude of your students.

Note The Lesson Plans offer guidelines for 45- and 55-minute classes and **Block Scheduling**.

Exercices vs. *Activités*

The exercises and activities are color-coded. Exercises, which provide guided practice to prepare students for independent communication, are coded in blue. Communicative activities, which give students opportunities for creative, open-ended expression, are coded in red.

LEARNING FROM PHOTOS

You may wish to ask students the following questions about the photo and about themselves: *Où sont les deux filles? Qu'est-ce qu'elles regardent? Allez-vous souvent au magasin de disques? Aimez-vous la musique? Avez-vous beaucoup de compact discs (de cassettes)? Quelle sorte de musique préférez-vous? Quelle sorte de musique détestez-vous?*

MOTS ET CONVERSATION

Vocabulary Teaching Resources

1. Bell Ringer Review Blackline Masters: R-3 & R-4, page 2
2. Workbook, *Mots et Conversation: A–C*, pages R7–R8
3. CD-ROM, Disc 1: *Mots et Conversation*, pages R10–R11

Bell Ringer Review

Put the following on the board or use BRR Blackline Master R-3: Make a list of party activities. Follow the model: Dans une fête, on...

La fête de Caroline

PRESENTATION *(page R10)*

Have the students repeat the sentences after you. Intersperse your presentation with questions from Exercises A and B.

Note Students may listen to a recorded version of the sentences on the CD-ROM.

Exercices

PRESENTATION *(page R10)*

Go over the exercises orally first with books closed. Have students write the exercises for homework and go over them the next day with books open.

ANSWERS

Exercice A

1. Oui, elle donne une fête.
2. Oui, elle invite des copains.
3. Oui, ils arrivent chez Caroline à sept heures.
4. Oui, ils parlent à Caroline. Ils parlent français.
5. Oui, ils dansent pendant la fête.
6. Oui, ils écoutent des cassettes.

La fête de Caroline

Caroline donne une fête.
Elle invite des copains.

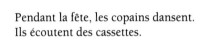

Les copains arrivent chez Caroline à sept heures.
Ils parlent à Caroline.

Pendant la fête, les copains dansent.
Ils écoutent des cassettes.

A Chez Caroline. Répondez.

1. Caroline donne une fête?
2. Elle invite des copains?
3. Les copains arrivent chez Caroline à sept heures?
4. Ils parlent à Caroline? Ils parlent français ou anglais?
5. Pendant la fête, les copains dansent?
6. Ils écoutent des cassettes?

B Qui? Répondez.

1. Qui donne la fête?
2. Qui arrive chez Caroline?
3. Quand est-ce qu'ils arrivent?
4. Qui parle?
5. À qui est-ce qu'ils parlent?
6. Qui écoute des cassettes?
7. Qui danse?

ADDITIONAL PRACTICE

To reinforce the lesson, you may wish to ask students the following questions: *Donnez-vous souvent des fêtes? Qui invitez-vous? À quelle heure arrivent-ils? Qu'est-ce que vous faites dans une fête? Vous dansez? Vous écoutez des compact discs ou des cassettes? Vous chantez?*

C La maison de Caroline. Lisez le paragraphe.

La maison de Caroline est jolie.
Au rez-de-chaussée il y a quatre pièces.
Au premier étage il y a les chambres à coucher.
Caroline a une très jolie chambre à coucher.
Elle fait ses devoirs dans sa chambre à coucher.

D Comment est sa maison? Décrivez la maison de Caroline.

E Qu'est-ce que les amis de Caroline font? Choisissez la bonne réponse.

1. Les amis écoutent des cassettes?
   a. Oui, ils détestent la musique.
   b. Oui, ils adorent le rock.
   c. Oui, ils vont au théâtre.
2. Quand est-ce qu'ils dansent?
   a. Le samedi soir à la fête.
   b. Quand je vais à l'école.
   c. Quand nous réservons une table au restaurant.
3. Ils parlent français à Caroline?
   a. Oui, je téléphone à mon amie.
   b. Oui, ils sont français.
   c. Oui, nous parlons français.
4. La maison de Caroline est grande?
   a. Oui, il y a deux étages.
   b. Oui, il y a trois pièces.
   c. Oui, il y a deux immeubles.

R 11

Exercice B
1. Caroline donne la fête.
2. Les copains arrivent chez Caroline.
3. Ils arrivent à sept heures.
4. Les copains parlent.
5. Ils parlent à Caroline.
6. Les copains écoutent des cassettes.
7. Les copains dansent.

Bell Ringer Review
Put the following on the board or use BRR Blackline Master R-4: Make a list of the rooms of a house.

PRESENTATION (*page R11*)
Exercice C
Call on a student to read the sentences in Exercise C.

Exercice D
Call on another student to say as much as possible about the photo in Exercise D.

ANSWERS
Exercice C
Students read the paragraph in the text.

Exercice D
Answers will vary but may include: **La maison est grande et jolie. Il y a un grand jardin avec une table et des chaises. Dans la maison il y a quatre pièces au rez-de-chaussée et il y a des chambres à coucher au premier étage.**

Exercice E
1. b
2. a
3. b
4. a

ADDITIONAL PRACTICE

You may wish to ask the following questions about the information in Exercise C in order to review question words. Students can respond with a brief answer. *Comment est la maison de Caroline? Il y a combien de pièces au rez-de-chaussée? Où sont les chambres à coucher? Qui a une très jolie chambre à coucher? Qu'est-ce qu'elle fait dans sa chambre à coucher?*

LEARNING FROM REALIA

You may wish to have the students suggest different times and dates for the party invitation. Then briefly review time and dates.

Structure Teaching Resources

1. Bell Ringer Review Blackline Masters: R-5 & R-6, page 2
2. Workbook, *Structure: A–N*, pages R9–R12
3. CD-ROM, Disc 1, pages R12–R16

Les verbes réguliers en -er

PRESENTATION *(page R12)*

A. Write the forms of *parler* and *aimer* on the board and underline the endings.
B. Have the students read the forms aloud. Point to the ones that are pronounced the same even though they are written differently.

Exercices

PRESENTATION *(page R12)*

Exercices A, B, and C

Exercises A and B can be done with books open or closed. Exercise C can be done with books open. Upon completion of each of these exercises, call on a student to give the information in the exercise in his/her own words.

ANSWERS

Exercices A and B
Answers will vary.

Exercice C
1. prépare
2. décide
3. téléphone

Les verbes réguliers en -er

The infinitive of many regular French verbs ends in *-er.* Review the following present-tense forms of regular *-er* verbs.

INFINITIVE	PARLER	AIMER	
STEM	parl-	aim-	ENDINGS
	je parle	j'aime	-e
	tu parles	tu aimes	-es
	il/elle/on parle	il/elle/on aime	-e
	nous parlons	nous aimons	-ons
	vous parlez	vous aimez	-ez
	ils/elles parlent	ils/elles aiment	-ent

A Moi!   Donnez des réponses personnelles.

1. Tu habites quelle ville?
2. Tu habites une petite ville ou une grande ville?
3. Tu arrives à l'école à quelle heure le matin?
4. Tu parles à tes copains?
5. Tes copains et toi, vous étudiez le français?
6. Vous aimez le cours de français?
7. Vous chantez en français?

B Une fête.   Donnez des réponses personnelles.

1. Tu aimes donner des fêtes?
2. Tu donnes des fêtes?
3. Qui invites-tu?
4. Tu téléphones à tes copains?
5. Ils acceptent toujours ton invitation?
6. Quel soir est-ce que tu donnes la fête?
7. Tes amis arrivent à quelle heure?
8. Tes copains et toi, vous dansez pendant la fête?

C On dîne au restaurant.   Complétez.

1. Ce soir Angélique ne ___ pas le dîner. (préparer)
2. Elle ___ d'aller dîner au restaurant. (décider)
3. Elle ___ à sa copine. (téléphoner)

R 12

---

4. Elle ___ sa copine au restaurant. (inviter)
5. Elles ___ dans un restaurant italien. (aller)
6. Les deux amies ___ au restaurant à sept heures. (arriver)
7. Le serveur ___ à leur table. (arriver)
8. Les deux amies ___ une pizza. (commander)
9. Angélique ___ l'addition. (demander)
10. Tu ___ la pizza? (aimer)
11. Quand tes copains et toi ___ dans un restaurant italien,
    qu'est-ce que vous ___? (aller, commander)

L'infinitif

1. The infinitive form follows verbs such as *aimer, détester, adorer,* and
   préférer.

   > J'aime danser mais je déteste chanter.
   > Je n'aime pas du tout chanter.

2. You also use the infinitive after the verb *aller* to tell what you or others are
   going to do.

   > Ce soir je vais regarder la télé.
   > Je ne vais pas écouter la radio.
   > Demain nous allons donner une fête.

D **Mes préférences.** Donnez des réponses personnelles.

1. Tu aimes manger?
2. Tu préfères manger dans un restaurant italien ou
   dans un restaurant chinois?
3. Tu vas dîner au restaurant ce soir?
4. Tu aimes donner des fêtes?
5. Tu vas inviter tes amis à la fête?
6. Tu préfères donner des fêtes ou aller à des fêtes?

E **Pas maintenant.** Répondez d'après le modèle.

> Tu regardes la télé maintenant?
> *Non, mais je vais regarder la télé ce soir.*

1. Tu écoutes la radio maintenant?
2. Tu étudies maintenant?
3. Tu travailles maintenant?
4. Ton copain téléphone maintenant?
5. Ton copain arrive maintenant?

R 13

4. invite
5. vont
6. arrivent
7. arrive
8. commandent
9. demande
10. aimes
11. allez, commandez

L'infinitif
PRESENTATION *(page R13)*
Have students read the model
sentences.

Exercices
ANSWERS
Exercice D
1. Oui, j'aime manger. (Non, je
   n'aime pas manger.)
2. Je préfère manger dans un
   restaurant italien (chinois).
3. Oui, je vais dîner au restaurant
   ce soir. (Non, je ne vais pas
   dîner...)
4. Oui, j'aime donner des fêtes.
   (Non, je n'aime pas donner
   de...)
5. Oui, je vais inviter mes amis à
   la fête. (Non, je ne vais pas
   inviter...)
6. Je préfère donner des fêtes. (Je
   préfère aller à des fêtes.)

Exercice E
1. Non, mais je vais écouter la
   radio ce soir.
2. Non, mais je vais étudier ce
   soir.
3. Non, mais je vais travailler ce
   soir.
4. Non, mais il va téléphoner ce
   soir.
5. Non, mais il va arriver ce soir.

Les verbes avoir et faire

PRESENTATION *(page R14)*

A. Write verb forms on the board and have the class repeat them after you.

B. Call on an individual to read the model sentences.

Exercices

PRESENTATION *(page R14)*

Exercice F

Go over Exercise F and have students fill in the correct verb forms. You may wish to write the answers on the board.

ANSWERS

Exercice F

1. a
2. a
3. ont
4. a, a
5. ont
6. avez
7. avons, avons

Exercice G

Answers will vary.

Les verbes *avoir* et *faire*

1. Review the forms of the irregular verbs *avoir*, "to have," and *faire*, "to do," "to make."

AVOIR	
j' ai	nous avons
tu as	vous avez
il/elle/on a	ils/elles ont

FAIRE	
je fais	nous faisons
tu fais	vous faites
il/elle/on fait	ils/elles font

2. You use the verb *avoir* to express age.

   Tu as quel âge? Moi, j'ai quatorze ans.

3. The verb *faire* is used in many expressions: *faire du français, faire la cuisine, faire de la gymnastique, faire un pique-nique, faire les courses.*

4. Remember that in negative sentences *un, une,* and *des* change to *de (d')*.

J'ai un frère.	Je n'ai pas de sœur.
Elle fait du français.	Elle ne fait pas d'espagnol.
Tu as des livres.	Tu n'as pas de cahiers.

F **Les Dejarnac.** Complétez avec «avoir».

1. La famille Dejarnac ___ une maison dans la banlieue parisienne.
2. Le pavillon des Dejarnac ___ sept pièces.
3. M. et Mme Dejarnac ___ deux enfants.
4. Pierre ___ quatorze ans et Michèle ___ seize ans.
5. Les Dejarnac ___ un chien?
6. Vous ___ un chien?
7. Non, nous n'___ pas de chien mais nous ___ un chat.

G **Moi!** Donnez des réponses personnelles.

1. Tu as une grande ou une petite famille?
2. Tu as combien de frères?
3. Tu as combien de sœurs?
4. Ta famille et toi, vous avez un chat ou un chien?
5. Tu as une voiture?

R 14

H **On fait les courses.** Répétez la conversation.

CHRISTINE: Salut, Michèle. Comment vas-tu?
MICHÈLE: Bien, merci. Et toi?
CHRISTINE: Pas mal. Où vas-tu maintenant?
MICHÈLE: Je vais faire les courses.
CHRISTINE: Tu fais les courses où?
MICHÈLE: Au marché de la rue Mouffetard.
Et aujourd'hui j'ai beaucoup de choses à acheter.

Répondez d'après la conversation.

1. Michèle va bien?
2. Est-ce qu'elle va faire les courses?
3. Elle va au marché de la rue Mouffetard?
4. Elle a beaucoup de choses à acheter?

Le partitif

1. In French, you use the definite article when talking about a specific item.

   La salade est sur *la* table dans *la* cuisine.

2. You also use the definite article when talking about a noun in the general sense.

   Moi, j'aime beaucoup *le* chocolat.

3. However, when you refer to only a part or a certain quantity of an item, the partitive construction is used. The partitive is expressed in French by *de* + the definite article.

de + le = du	J'ai *du* pain.
de + la = de la	J'ai *de la* crème.
de + l' = de l'	J'ai *de l'*argent.
de + les = des	J'ai *des* gâteaux.

4. When the partitive follows a verb in the negative, all forms change to *de*.

J'ai du pain.	Je n'ai pas *de* pain.
J'ai de la viande.	Je n'ai pas *de* viande.
J'ai de l'argent.	Je n'ai pas *d'*argent.
J'ai des fruits.	Je n'ai pas *de* fruits.

R 15

INDEPENDENT PRACTICE

Assign any of the following:
1. Exercises, pages R10–R15
2. Bell Ringer Review Blackline Masters:
   R-5 & R-6, page 2
3. Workbook, *Structure: A–I,* pages R9–R11
4. CD-ROM, Disc 1, pages R12–R15

Exercices
PRESENTATION *(page R15)*
Exercice H
    Have two students read the conversation to the class. After completing the comprehension questions that follow, have a student retell the story of the conversation in his/her own words.

ANSWERS
Exercice H
1. Oui, elle va bien.
2. Oui, elle va faire les courses.
3. Oui, elle va au marché de la rue Mouffetard.
4. Oui, elle a beaucoup de choses à acheter.

Bell Ringer Review
    Put the following on the board or use BRR Blackline Master R-6: Make a list of the words or expressions you would need for shopping for food at a market.

Le partitif
PRESENTATION *(page R15)*
A. When explaining step 1, you may wish to point to some specific items in class: *Le livre est sur la table. Le crayon est sur le livre.*
B. When going over step 2, mention some other things people may like: *J'aime le lait. J'aime les légumes. J'aime les sports.*
C. When going over step 3, put some objects on a table and point to them from a distance. To demonstrate the use of the partitive, say, for example: *Il y a des livres sur la table. Il y a des crayons sur la table. Il y a de l'argent.*
D. Then take the items off the table to demonstrate the negative: *Il n'y a pas de livres sur la table. Il n'y a pas de crayons sur la table. Il n'y a pas d'argent.*

Les adjectifs possessifs

PRESENTATION *(page R16)*

A. Explain to students that the adjectives *mon*, *ton*, and *son* have three forms. The adjectives *notre*, *votre*, and *leur* have two forms.

B. Call students to the front of the room. Have them point to indicate the meaning of the possessive adjectives: to themselves *(mon)*, to someone they are talking to *(ton)*, to a boy or girl in the distance *(son)*.

Exercice

ANSWERS

Exercice J
  Answers will vary.

I **Georges fait les courses.** Complétez.

Georges fait les courses. Il va à la boulangerie où il achète ⎯ pain. Georges
achète ⎯ pain tous les jours. Mais il n'achète pas toujours ⎯ viande.
Aujourd'hui il n'achète pas ⎯ viande. Il ne va pas à la boucherie. Il achète
⎯ poisson. Pour acheter ⎯ poisson il va à la poissonnerie. Ensuite il va à
l'épicerie du coin où il achète ⎯ eau minérale et ⎯ boîtes de conserve. Il
n'achète pas ⎯ lait aujourd'hui.

Les adjectifs possessifs

1. Like all other French adjectives, the possessive adjectives must agree with the noun they modify. Remember that *son*, *sa*, and *ses* can mean either "his" or "her."

MASCULIN SINGULIER	FÉMININ SINGULIER	PLURIEL
mon père ton père son père	ma mère ta mère sa mère	mes parents tes parents ses parents

2. Remember that the masculine singular form is used before feminine singular nouns that begin with a vowel and that there is a liaison.

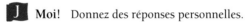

mon amie   ton amie   son amie

3. The adjectives *notre*, *votre*, and *leur* have only two forms, singular and plural.

MASCULIN SINGULIER	FÉMININ SINGULIER	PLURIEL
notre cousin votre cousin leur cousin	notre cousine votre cousine leur cousine	nos cousin(e)s vos cousin(e)s leurs cousin(e)s

J **Moi!** Donnez des réponses personnelles.

1. Tes parents ont une voiture?
2. Leur voiture est dans le garage le soir?
3. Ta mère travaille?
4. Ton père travaille?
5. Où est votre maison ou appartement?
6. Votre maison ou appartement a combien de pièces?

Activités de communication orale et écrite

A **Ma famille.**   Imagine that you're a new student at your school. Your classmate wants to find out about you and your family. Answer his or her questions.

> Où est-ce que tu habites?
> Comment est ta maison ou ton appartement?
> Il y a combien de personnes dans ta famille?
> Tu as combien de frères et combien de sœurs?
> Tu as quel âge?
> Tu vas à quelle école?
> Tu aimes quels cours?
> Qu'est-ce que tu fais après les cours?

B **Ma maison et ma chambre.**   Write a short paragraph describing your house or apartment and your room.

C **Aujourd'hui.**   Work with a classmate. Find out the following information from him or her.

1. what day it is
2. what the date is today
3. what time it is
4. what time his or her English class is
5. what time he or she is leaving school today

R 17

PRESENTATION *(page R17)*

These activities recycle material from *Bienvenue,* Chapters 2, 3, and 4.

Extension of *Activité A*

After completing Activity A, call on volunteers to give a brief autobiography of themselves.

ANSWERS

Activités A, B,* and *C

Answers will vary.

LEARNING FROM PHOTOS

1. Have students say as much about the photo of the family on page R16 as they can. Then ask individuals to say as much about their own families as they can.
2. Have students identify as many items as they can in the photos on page R17. You may wish to teach them the words: *une trousse, une lampe, un feutre, un bloc-notes.*

INDEPENDENT PRACTICE

Assign any of the following:
1. Exercises and activities, pages R16–R17
2. Workbook, *Structure: J–N,* pages R11–R12
3. CD-ROM, Disc 1, pages R15–R17

RÉVISION C

OVERVIEW

This chapter reviews vocabulary dealing with train and plane travel that was presented in *Bienvenue*, Chapters 7 and 8.

The structure points reviewed are the present tense of regular *-ir* and *-re* verbs, verbs like *partir* and *dormir*, and the verbs *pouvoir* and *vouloir*.

RÉVISION
C

ON VOYAGE

R 19

Pacing

This review chapter should take two to three days depending on the length of the class and the age and aptitude of your students.

Note The Lesson Plans offer guidelines for 45- and 55-minute classes and **Block Scheduling.**

Exercices vs. *Activités*

The exercises and activities are color-coded. Exercises, which provide guided practice to prepare students for independent communication, are coded in blue. Communicative activities, which give students opportunities for creative, open-ended expression, are coded in red.

LEARNING FROM PHOTOS

You may wish to give students some information about the photo and ask them the following questions about the photo and themselves: *C'est une photo de Villefranche, un joli port près de Nice sur la Côte d'Azur. Qu'est-ce que vous voyez sur la photo? C'est un TGV ou un vieux train? Aimez-vous voyager en train? Prenez-vous souvent le train? Faites-vous souvent des voyages? Où allez-vous?*

MOTS ET CONVERSATION

Vocabulary Teaching Resources

1. Bell Ringer Review Blackline Masters: R-7 & R-8, page 3
2. Workbook, *Mots et Conversation: A–C*, page R14
3. CD-ROM, Disc 1: *Mots et Conversation*, pages R20–R21

Bell Ringer Review

Put the following on the board or use BRR Blackline Master R-7: Write down as many words and expressions as you can think of having to do with airports.

À l'aéroport

PRESENTATION *(page R20)*

A. Have students share the words they wrote down for the Bell Ringer Review.
B. Have students repeat each sentence of the conversation once after you.
C. Call on a pair of students to read the conversation with as much expression as possible.

Note Students may listen to a recorded version of the conversation on the CD-ROM.

Exercices

PRESENTATION *(page R20)*

Extension of *Exercice A*

After completing Exercise A, have one student retell the story of the conversation in his/her own words.

ANSWERS

Exercice A

1. Elle est à l'aéroport.
2. Elle va au Sénégal.
3. Ahmed parle à Thérèse.
4. Il part pour Dakar.
5. Elle part pour le Sénégal.

À l'aéroport

AHMED: Salut, Thérèse. Qu'est-ce que tu fais ici à l'aéroport?
THÉRÈSE: Je vais au Sénégal.
AHMED: Pas possible! Moi aussi, je pars pour Dakar. Tu as ta carte d'embarquement?
THÉRÈSE: Bien sûr.
AHMED: Tu as quelle place?
THÉRÈSE: 22A. On annonce le départ d'un avion. C'est quel numéro de vol?
AHMED: Le 214. C'est notre vol. L'avion part de quelle porte?
THÉRÈSE: De la porte vingt-cinq.

A **On part pour Dakar.** Répondez d'après la conversation.

1. Où est Thérèse?
2. Où va-t-elle?
3. Qui parle à Thérèse à l'aéroport?
4. Ahmed part pour quelle ville?
5. Et Thérèse part pour quel pays?
6. Elle a sa carte d'embarquement?
7. Thérèse a quelle place?
8. Qu'est-ce qu'ils entendent?
9. Quel est le numéro de leur vol?
10. Leur avion part de quelle porte?

R 20

PAIRED ACTIVITY

Have students work in pairs and make up a conversation about a trip to a French-speaking destination that interests them. Then ask for volunteers to present their conversations to the class.

À la gare

Alain est dans la gare à Deauville. Il a de la chance. Il n'y a pas de queue devant le guichet. Il va au guichet. Il achète un billet aller-retour en deuxième classe pour Paris. Il composte le billet et va sur le quai où il attend le train. Le train part exactement à 14h10. Alain monte dans une voiture non-fumeurs.

B **Un voyage en train.** Répondez par «oui» ou «non».

1. Alain est dans la salle d'attente de la gare?
2. Il est dans la gare à Paris?
3. Il y a une queue devant le guichet?
4. Alain achète un aller simple?
5. Il voyage en première classe?
6. Alain va sur le quai?
7. Le train part en retard?
8. Alain choisit une voiture fumeurs?

R 21

---

6. Oui, elle a sa carte d'embarquement.
7. Elle a la place 22A.
8. Ils entendent l'annonce du départ d'un avion.
9. C'est le 214.
10. Il part de la porte 25.

À la gare

PRESENTATION *(page R21)*

Call on a student with good pronunciation to read the paragraph to the class.

Note Students may listen to a recorded version of the paragraph on the CD-ROM.

Exercices

PRESENTATION *(page R21)*

Exercice B

Do Exercise B orally with books closed.

ANSWERS

Exercice B

1. Non, il n'est pas dans la salle d'attente de la gare.
2. Non, il est dans la gare à Deauville.
3. Non, il n'y a pas de queue devant le guichet.
4. Non, il achète un (billet) aller-retour.
5. Non, il voyage en deuxième classe (en seconde).
6. Oui, il va sur le quai.
7. Non, il part à l'heure.
8. Non, il choisit une voiture non-fumeurs.

STRUCTURE

Structure Teaching Resources

1. Workbook, *Structure: A–K*, pages R15–R17
2. CD-ROM, Disc 1, pages R22–R24

Les verbes en -ir et -re

PRESENTATION *(page R22)*

Write the verb forms on the board and have the students repeat them aloud.

Note Other common *-ir* verbs the students know are *choisir, obéir à, réussir à, atterrir.* Other *-re* verbs the students know are *entendre, répondre, perdre, descendre, vendre.*

Exercices

PRESENTATION *(pages R22–R23)*

Exercice A

Go over the exercise once in class before assigning it for homework.

ANSWERS

Exercice A

Answers will vary but may include the following:

1. Oui, je choisis un vol Air France.
2. Je choisis une place côté fenêtre.
3. Oui, beaucoup de passagers choisissent des places côté couloir.
4. Oui, je réussis à avoir toujours les places que je désire.
5. Oui, mon avion atterrit généralement à l'heure.
6. Il atterrit à l'aéroport (*JFK*).

Les verbes en *-ir* et *-re*

Review the following forms of regular *-ir* and *-re* verbs in French.

INFINITIVE	FINIR	
STEM	fin-	ENDINGS
	je finis	-is
	tu finis	-is
	il/elle/on finit	-it
	nous finissons	-issons
	vous finissez	-issez
	ils/elles finissent	-issent

INFINITIVE	ATTENDRE	
STEM	attend-	ENDINGS
	j'attends	-s
	tu attends	-s
	il/elle/on attend	–
	nous attendons	-ons
	vous attendez	-ez
	ils/elles attendent	-ent

A **Un voyage en avion.** Répondez.

1. Quand tu voyages tu choisis un vol Air France?
2. Tu choisis une place côté fenêtre ou côté couloir?
3. Beaucoup de passagers choisissent des places côté couloir?
4. Vous réussissez à avoir toujours les places que vous désirez?
5. Votre avion atterrit généralement à l'heure?
6. Il atterrit à quel aéroport?

INDEPENDENT PRACTICE

Assign any of the following:

1. Exercises, pages R22–R23
2. Workbook, *Structure: A–H,* pages R15–R17
3. CD-ROM, Disc 1, pages R22–R23

B Un voyage en train. Complétez.

1. On ___ les billets au guichet. (vendre)
2. On ___ des magazines et des journaux au kiosque. (vendre)
3. Les voyageurs ___ le train. (attendre)
4. Nous aussi, nous ___. (attendre)
5. Vous ___ le train dans la salle d'attente. (attendre)
6. J'___ l'annonce du départ de notre train. (entendre)
7. Marie aussi ___ l'annonce au haut-parleur. (entendre)

Les verbes *partir, sortir, servir* et *dormir*

Study the following *-ir* verbs that have shortened forms in the singular.

PARTIR	SORTIR	SERVIR	DORMIR
je pars	je sors	je sers	je dors
tu pars	tu sors	tu sers	tu dors
il/elle/on part	il/elle/on sort	il/elle/on sert	il/elle/on dort
nous partons	nous sortons	nous servons	nous dormons
vous partez	vous sortez	vous servez	vous dormez
ils/elles partent	ils/elles sortent	ils/elles servent	ils/elles dorment

C En voiture! Répondez d'après les indications.

1. Le train part de quelle voie? (numéro deux)
2. Il part à quelle heure? (18h16)
3. On sert des repas dans le train? (oui)
4. Qui sert les repas? (les serveurs)
5. Les voyageurs dorment? (oui, dans une voiture-lit)
6. Le contrôleur arrive. Tu sors ton billet? (oui)

D Carole fait un voyage. Complétez.

Carole est à la Gare du Nord. Où est-ce qu'on ___ (vendre) les billets? Ah,
voilà le guichet. Carole achète son billet. Elle ___ (sortir) de l'argent de son
sac à dos et paie. Son train ___ (partir) de la voie numéro quatre. Tous les
trains ___ (partir) à l'heure. Beaucoup de voyageurs ___ (dormir) dans le train.
Mais Carole ne ___ (dormir) pas. Elle aime bien voyager en train.

R 23

PRESENTATION *(page R24)*

A. Have the students read the verb forms and the model sentences aloud.

B. **Extension** Call on students to tell what they can do this weekend: *Ce week-end je peux...*

Exercice

ANSWERS

Exercice E

1. Oui, elle veut aller à Nice.
2. Oui, elle peut partir demain.
3. Oui, il veut aller à Nice aussi.
4. Oui, ils peuvent faire le voyage ensemble.
5. Oui, ils veulent aller à Nice en train.
6. Oui, ils peuvent aller à Nice en train. Ils peuvent aller à Nice en avion aussi.
7. Oui, ils veulent regarder la mer Méditerranée.
8. Oui, je veux regarder la mer Méditerranée.
9. Oui, je peux regarder la mer Méditerranée.

Les verbes *pouvoir* et *vouloir*

1. Review the forms of the verbs *pouvoir,* "to be able to," "can," and *vouloir,* "to want."

POUVOIR	VOULOIR
je peux	je veux
tu peux	tu veux
il/elle/on peut	il/elle/on veut
nous pouvons	nous voulons
vous pouvez	vous voulez
ils/elles peuvent	ils/elles veulent

2. These verbs are frequently followed by the infinitive.

> Je peux sortir et je veux sortir.
> Tu veux sortir avec moi?
> Elle ne veut pas sortir avec Gilles.

E **Un petit voyage à Nice.** Répondez par «oui».

1. Marie-Claire veut aller à Nice?
2. Elle peut partir demain?
3. Son frère veut aller à Nice aussi?
4. Ils peuvent faire le voyage ensemble?
5. Ils veulent aller à Nice en train?
6. Ils peuvent aller à Nice en train? En avion?
7. Ils veulent regarder la mer Méditerranée?
8. Tu veux regarder la mer Méditerranée?
9. Tu peux regarder la mer Méditerranée?

Vues de la côte et de la mer Méditerranée

PAIRED ACTIVITY

Have students work in pairs. One student makes a statement about what he/she wants to do tomorrow but can't. The other reports to the class about what his/her partner has just said. For example:

É1: Je veux aller au cinéma, mais je ne peux pas.

É2: Kelly veut aller au cinéma demain, mais elle ne peut pas.

Activités de communication orale et écrite

A En avion. Make a list of words associated with airline travel. Write a short paragraph using these words to describe a plane trip you'd like to take.

B À la gare. Working with a classmate, make up a conversation between a passenger who wants to buy a ticket and a ticket agent in a train station. You may want to use some of the following words and expressions.

un aller-retour   en première/en seconde
un aller simple   à quelle heure
un billet   le quai
combien   la voie
fumeurs/non-fumeurs

C La gare. Describe the illustration in your own words.

R 25

Activités de communication orale et écrite

PRESENTATION (page R25)

These activities recycle material from *Bienvenue,* Chapters 7 and 8.

Extension of Activité B

After completing Activity B, you may wish to have the students present the conversation to the class.

Extension of Activité C

You may wish to have the students write Activity C.

ANSWERS

Activités A, B, and C

Answers will vary.

OVERVIEW

This chapter reviews vocabulary related to seasons and both individual and team sports taught in *Bienvenue,* Chapters 9, 13, and 14.

The structure points reviewed are the *passé composé* of regular and irregular verbs conjugated with *avoir,* and irregular past participles.

RÉVISION

D

LES SPORTS ET LES SAISONS

R 27

1. Bell Ringer Review Blackline Masters
2. Workbook
3. Lesson Plans
4. Testing Program
5. CD-ROM Interactive Textbook
6. Map Transparencies

Pacing

This review chapter should take two to three days depending on the length of the class and the age and aptitude of your students.

Note The Lesson Plans offer guidelines for 45- and 55-minute classes and **Block Scheduling.**

Exercices vs. *Activités*

The exercises and activities are color-coded. Exercises, which provide guided practice to prepare students for independent communication, are coded in blue. Communicative activities, which give students opportunities for creative, open-ended expression, are coded in red.

LEARNING FROM PHOTOS

You may wish to ask students the following questions about the photo: *C'est une course? Quelle sorte de course? Les coureurs cyclistes sont à vélo? Ils sont sur une route ou sur une piste? Est-ce que les coureurs cyclistes portent des lunettes de soleil? Ils roulent vite?*

MOTS ET CONVERSATION

Qu'est-ce qu'ils ont fait?

L'été dernier Jennifer a nagé.
Elle a beaucoup nagé pendant ses vacances.
Elle a fait du ski nautique.
Elle a joué au tennis.
Elle a pris des bains de soleil.
Elle a mis de la crème solaire.
Elle a bronzé.

L'hiver dernier Nicolas a appris à faire du ski.
Il a descendu la piste verte.
Mélanie a fait du patin à glace.
Elle a eu un petit accident.

Samedi dernier notre équipe a joué au foot.
Julien a donné un coup de pied dans le ballon.
Il a marqué un but.
Notre équipe a gagné 6 à 0.
Nous avons joué contre les Ours.

Un match de football

Au bord de la mer

LISE: Jennifer, qu'est-ce que tu as fait pendant les vacances?
JENNIFER: J'ai passé un mois au bord de la mer.
LISE: C'est chouette ça! Tu as de la chance.
JENNIFER: J'ai passé tout mon temps à la plage. J'ai beaucoup nagé et j'ai appris à faire de la planche à voile.
LISE: Et je vois que tu as bien bronzé.

Cet homme fait de la planche à voile dans la mer des Caraïbes.

R 28

Vocabulary Teaching Resources

1. Bell Ringer Review Blackline Master: R-9, page 4
2. Workbook, *Mots et Conversation: A–F*, pages R19–R21
3. CD-ROM, Disc 1: *Mots et Conversation*, pages R28–R29

Bell Ringer Review

Put the following on the board or use BRR Blackline Master R-9: You are preparing the weather report for your French class. Sketch the following:

1. **Il fait chaud.**
2. **Il fait du vent.**
3. **Il fait du soleil.**
4. **Il pleut.**
5. **Il y a des nuages.**

Note Paragraph 1 of *Qu'est-ce qu'ils ont fait?* and the conversation *Au bord de la mer* recycle material from *Bienvenue*, Chapter 9; paragraphs 2 and 3, from Chapters 13 and 14.

Qu'est-ce qu'ils ont fait?

PRESENTATION *(page R28)*

A. Use gestures to reinforce the meaning of: *nager, faire du ski nautique, jouer au tennis, prendre des bains de soleil, mettre de la crème solaire, faire du ski, faire du patin à glace, jouer au foot, donner un coup de pied dans le ballon.*
B. Have students repeat the sentences after you.

Note Students may listen to recorded versions of the sentences and the conversation below on the CD-ROM.

Au bord de la mer

PRESENTATION *(page R28)*

Call on a pair of students to read the conversation with as much expression as possible.

R 28

LEARNING FROM PHOTOS

1. Ask the following questions about the top photo: *Il y a combien de joueurs sur la photo? Ils jouent au foot? Il y a combien d'équipes? Il y a des gradins?*
2. Ask the following questions about the bottom photo: *Qu'est-ce que cet homme fait? Aimez-vous faire de la planche à voile?*

PAIRED ACTIVITY

Have students work in pairs to prepare a conversation based on the stories in Exercises A, B, and D on page R29. Assign several pairs to each exercise. You may wish to have volunteers present their conversations to the class.

A Les vacances de Jennifer. Répondez.

1. Jennifer a passé ses vacances au bord de la mer ou à la montagne?
2. Elle a beaucoup nagé?
3. Elle a nagé dans la mer ou dans une piscine?
4. Elle a fait du ski nautique?
5. Elle a appris à faire de la planche à voile?
6. Elle a pris des bains de soleil?
7. Elle a mis de la crème solaire?
8. Elle a bronzé?

B Un voyage à la montagne.
Répondez d'après les indications.

1. Quand est-ce que Nicolas a fait un voyage à la montagne? (au mois de février)
2. Qu'est-ce qu'il a pris? (des leçons de ski)
3. Il a eu un moniteur? (Oui)
4. Il a beaucoup appris? (Oui)
5. Il a descendu quelle piste? (la piste verte)
6. Il est tombé? (jamais)
7. Il a eu de la chance? (beaucoup)
8. Où a-t-il fait du patin? (à la patinoire)

C En quelle saison?
Choisissez.

	EN ÉTÉ	EN HIVER	LES DEUX

1. Il fait beau.
2. Il fait froid.
3. Il fait chaud.
4. Il neige.
5. Il pleut.
6. Il y a beaucoup de soleil.
7. Il y a beaucoup de vent.
8. Il fait deux degrés.

D Un match de foot. Répondez d'après les indications.

1. Dans un match de foot, il y a combien d'équipes? (deux)
2. Chaque équipe a combien de joueurs? (onze)
3. Il y a combien de joueurs sur le terrain? (vingt-deux)
4. Dans un match il y a combien de camps? (deux)
5. Le match est divisé en quoi? (mi-temps)
6. Il y a combien de mi-temps? (deux)
7. Chaque mi-temps dure combien de minutes? (quarante-cinq)
8. Qui garde le but? (le gardien de but)
9. Qu'est-ce que chaque équipe veut faire? (marquer un but)
10. Qui bloque ou arrête le ballon? (le gardien de but)

R 29

INDEPENDENT PRACTICE

Assign any of the following:
1. Exercises, pages R29
2. Workbook, *Mots et Conversation: A–F,* pages R19–R21
3. CD-ROM, Disc 1, pages R28–R29

Exercices

PRESENTATION (*page R29*)

Extension of *Exercices A, B,* and *D*

After completing Exercises A, B, and D, call on a student to retell the story in each exercise in his/her own words.

ANSWERS

Exercice A

1. Jennifer a passé ses vacances au bord de la mer.
2. Oui, elle a beaucoup nagé.
3. Elle a nagé dans la mer.
4. Oui, elle a fait du ski nautique. (Non, elle n'a pas fait de ski nautique.)
5. Oui, elle a appris à faire de la planche à voile.
6. Oui, elle a pris des bains de soleil.
7. Oui, elle a mis de la crème solaire.
8. Oui, elle a bronzé.

Exercice B

1. Nicolas a fait un voyage à la montagne au mois de février.
2. Il a pris des leçons de ski.
3. Oui, il a eu un moniteur.
4. Oui, il a beaucoup appris.
5. Il a descendu la piste verte.
6. Non, il n'est jamais tombé.
7. Oui, il a eu beaucoup de chance.
8. Il a fait du patin à la patinoire.

Exercice C

1. les deux	5. les deux
2. en hiver	6. en été
3. en été	7. les deux
4. en hiver	8. en hiver

Exercice D

1. ... il y a deux équipes.
2. Chaque équipe a onze joueurs.
3. Il y a vingt-deux joueurs...
4. ... il y a deux camps.
5. Le match est divisé en mi-temps.
6. Il y a deux mi-temps.
7. Chaque mi-temps dure quarante-cinq minutes.
8. Le gardien de but garde...
9. Chaque équipe veut marquer un but.
10. Le gardien de but bloque...

Structure Teaching Resources

1. Bell Ringer Review Blackline Master: R-10, page 4
2. Workbook, *Structure: A–D,* pages R22–R23
3. CD-ROM, Disc 1, pages R30–R33

Bell Ringer Review

Put the following on the board or use BRR Blackline Master R-10: Make a list of as many items of clothing as you can think of.

Le passé composé des verbes réguliers avec avoir

PRESENTATION (page R30)

A. Have the students repeat the past participles in step 1 of the structure explanation after you.

B. Write the forms of the verb *avoir* on the board.

C. Put the past participles on the board with *avoir* and have the students repeat aloud the forms of the *passé composé.*

Le passé composé des verbes réguliers avec *avoir*

1. You use the *passé composé* in French to express an action completed in the past. The *passé composé* of most French verbs is formed by using the present tense of the verb *avoir* and the past participle of the verb. Review the formation of the past participle of regular verbs.

INFINITIF	PARTICIPE PASSÉ	INFINITIF	PARTICIPE PASSÉ	INFINITIF	PARTICIPE PASSÉ
-er → -é		-ir → -i		-re → -u	
regarder	regardé	choisir	choisi	perdre	perdu
parler	parlé	réussir	réussi	vendre	vendu

2. Now review the *passé composé* of regular French verbs.

PARLER	FINIR	PERDRE
j'ai parlé	j'ai fini	j'ai perdu
tu as parlé	tu as fini	tu as perdu
il/elle/on a parlé	il/elle/on a fini	il/elle/on a perdu
nous avons parlé	nous avons fini	nous avons perdu
vous avez parlé	vous avez fini	vous avez perdu
ils/elles ont parlé	ils/elles ont fini	ils/elles ont perdu

3. In the negative, *ne... pas* goes around the verb *avoir.*

Je n'ai pas parlé aux joueurs.
Je n'ai pas choisi cette équipe.
Ils n'ont pas perdu le match.

R 30

A Marseille contre Rennes. Répondez.

1. Marseille a joué contre Rennes?
2. Vous avez regardé le match?
3. Garros a donné un coup de pied dans le ballon?
4. Desnos a passé le ballon à Garros?
5. Garros a renvoyé le ballon?
6. Les Marseillais ont marqué un but?
7. Le gardien n'a pas arrêté le ballon?
8. Les Rennois ont égalisé le score?
9. L'arbitre a sifflé?
10. Il a déclaré un penalty contre Marseille?
11. Marseille a perdu le match?
12. Vous avez applaudi les gagnants?

B Au grand magasin.
Complétez au passé composé.

1. Hier j'___ avec ma sœur. (parler)
2. Nous ___ d'acheter un cadeau pour mon père. (décider)
3. Nous ___ la maison à midi pour aller au grand magasin. (quitter)
4. J'___ une chemise. (acheter)
5. J'___ le prix au vendeur. (demander)
6. Le vendeur ___ à ma question. (répondre)
7. J'___ une chemise blanche pour mon père. (choisir)
8. Mon père ___ son anniversaire. (célébrer)
9. Ma sœur et moi, nous n'___ pas ___ la même chose pour lui. (acheter)
10. Elle ___ des tennis. (choisir)
11. Nous ___ à la caisse. (payer)

R 31

PRESENTATION *(page R31)*

Exercice A

Do Exercise A orally first. Then have students write the answers.

ANSWERS

Exercice A

1. Oui (Non), Marseille (n') a (pas) joué contre Rennes.
2. Oui (Non), j'ai (je n'ai pas) regardé le match.
3. Oui (Non), Garros (n') a (pas) donné un (de) coup de pied dans le ballon.
4. Oui (Non), Desnos (n') a (pas) passé le ballon à Garros.
5. Oui (Non), Garros (n') a (pas) renvoyé le ballon.
6. Oui (Non), les Marseillais (n') ont (pas) marqué un (de) but.
7. Non, le gardien n'a pas arrêté le ballon.
8. Oui (Non), les Rennois (n') ont (pas) égalisé le score.
9. Oui (Non), l'arbitre (n') a (pas) sifflé.
10. Oui (Non), il (n') a (pas) déclaré un (de) penalty contre Marseille.
11. Oui (Non), Marseille (n') a (pas) perdu le match.
12. Oui (Non), j'ai (je n'ai pas) applaudi les gagnants.

Exercice B

1. ai parlé
2. avons décidé
3. avons quitté
4. ai acheté
5. ai demandé
6. a répondu
7. ai choisi
8. a célébré
9. avons... acheté
10. a choisi
11. avons payé

ADDITIONAL PRACTICE

1. After completing Exercise A on page R31, have a student retell the story in his/her own words.
2. After completing Exercise B on page R31, have pairs of students make up a conversation about shopping for something in a department store.

INDEPENDENT PRACTICE

Assign any of the following:
1. Exercises, page R31
2. Workbook, *Structure: A–B*, page R22
3. CD-ROM, Disc 1, pages R30–R31

Les participes passés irréguliers

PRESENTATION *(page R32)*

A. Have the students pay particular attention to the spelling of the participles that end in the /i/ sound.
B. Have the students read the past participles in the chart aloud.
C. Write the *passé composé* of two verbs on the board in paradigm order.
D. Have students repeat the paradigms.
E. Have them read the model sentences aloud.

Exercices

PRESENTATION *(pages R32–R33)*

Exercice C

Go over Exercise C the first time by calling on individuals to do two items each. Do the exercise a second time. Have two students complete the entire exercise.

ANSWERS

Exercice C

1. Oui, Nathalie et ses copines ont été à la plage.
2. Oui, Nathalie a pris sa voiture.
3. Oui, c'est elle qui a conduit.
4. Oui, Nathalie a pris des bains de soleil.
5. Oui, elle a mis de la crème solaire.
6. Oui, toutes les copines ont mis leur maillot.
7. Oui, elles ont fait du ski nautique.
8. Oui, elles ont appris à faire de la planche à voile.
9. Oui, elles ont pris des leçons.
10. Oui, elles ont eu une bonne monitrice.
11. Oui, elles ont pu faire de la plongée sous-marine.

Les participes passés irréguliers

The past participles of regular verbs end in the sounds /é/, /i/, or /ü/. Note that many irregular past participles also end in the sound /i/ or /ü/ even though their spelling may change.

INFINITIF →	PARTICIPE PASSÉ
mettre	mis
permettre	permis
prendre	pris
comprendre	compris
apprendre	appris
dire	dit
écrire	écrit
conduire	conduit
avoir	eu
croire	cru
voir	vu
pouvoir	pu
vouloir	voulu
lire	lu
être	été
faire	fait

J'ai pris des leçons de ski nautique.
J'ai appris à faire du ski nautique.
J'ai voulu aller très vite.
J'ai fait beaucoup de progrès.

C À la plage. Répondez par «oui».

1. Nathalie et ses copines ont été à la plage?
2. Nathalie a pris sa voiture?
3. C'est elle qui a conduit?
4. Nathalie a pris des bains de soleil?
5. Elle a mis de la crème solaire?
6. Toutes les copines ont mis leur maillot?
7. Elles ont fait du ski nautique?
8. Elles ont appris à faire de la planche à voile?
9. Elles ont pris des leçons?
10. Elles ont eu une bonne monitrice?
11. Elles ont pu faire de la plongée sous-marine?

Ce jeune homme fait de la plongée sous-marine à Tahiti.

STUDENT PORTFOLIO

Written assignments which may be included in students' portfolios are *Activités de communication écrite A–B* on page R24 of the Workbook.

Note Students may create and save both oral and written work using the Electronic Portfolio feature on the CD-ROM.

D **En route!**   Complétez au passé composé.

Mon ami Nicolas ____ (dire) que Chamonix est une belle station de sports
d'hiver. Il ____ (lire) le Guide Michelin et il ____ (voir) que Chamonix est loin
de Paris. Mais il ____ (vouloir) y aller. Ses parents ____ (permettre) à Nicolas de
prendre leur voiture. Il ____ (prendre) leur voiture et c'est lui qui ____
(conduire) pendant tout le chemin. Il ____ (faire) le voyage avec son copain
Alain. Ils ____ (mettre) leurs skis sur la voiture. Ils ____ (prendre) l'autoroute.
Ils n'____ pas ____ (avoir) de problème.

E **L'été dernier.**   Donnez des réponses personnelles.

1. Tu as nagé?
2. Tu as nagé où?
3. Tu as pris des leçons de planche à voile?
4. Tu as eu un bon moniteur (une bonne monitrice)?
5. Tu as beaucoup appris?
6. Tu as joué au tennis?
7. Tu as pris des leçons?
8. Tu as compris tout ce que le moniteur (la monitrice) a dit?
9. Tu as vu la Coupe Davis à la télé?
10. Tu as lu un article sur le tennis?

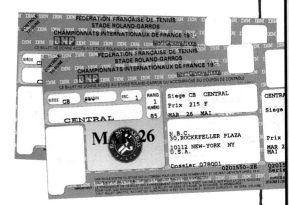

Activités de communication orale

A **L'été dernier.**   Tell your partner what you did last summer and find out
if he or she did the same things.

> Élève 1: J'ai pris des leçons de tennis et je suis allé(e) à la plage avec
> mes copains. Et toi?
> Élève 2: Moi, j'ai travaillé en juillet. En août j'ai passé quinze jours
> au bord de la mer.

B **Les sports.**   Divide into small groups. Take turns describing a sport
without mentioning its name. The others have to guess what sport is being
described.

R 33

INDEPENDENT PRACTICE

Assign any of the following:
1. Exercises and activities, pages R32–R33
2. Workbook, *Structure: C–D,* page R23
3. CD-ROM, Disc 1, pages R32–R33

Exercice D
1. a dit
2. a lu
3. a vu
4. a voulu
5. ont permis
6. a pris
7. a conduit
8. a fait
9. ont mis
10. ont pris
11. ont... eu

Exercice E
Answers will vary.

*Activités de
communication orale*

PRESENTATION *(page R33)*

These activities recycle material
from *Bienvenue,* Chapters 9 and 13.

Activité A

Have students take notes on
what their partners say in Activity
A and then report to the class.

ANSWERS

Activités A and B
Answers will vary.

OVERVIEW

This chapter reviews vocabulary related to physical fitness, personal hygiene, and medicine that was presented in *Bienvenue,* Chapters 11 and 15. It also reviews vocabulary needed to discuss the symptoms of some minor illnesses.

The structure points reviewed are the *passé composé* of verbs conjugated with *être* and the present tense of reflexive verbs.

RÉVISION

E

LA FORME ET LA MÉDECINE

REVIEW RESOURCES

1. Bell Ringer Review Blackline Masters
2. Workbook
3. Lesson Plans
4. Testing Program
5. CD-ROM Interactive Textbook

Pacing

This review chapter should take two to three days depending on the length of the class and the age and aptitude of your students.

Note The Lesson Plans offer guidelines for 45- and 55-minute classes and **Block Scheduling.**

Exercices vs. *Activités*

The exercises and activities are color-coded. Exercises, which provide guided practice to prepare students for independent communication, are coded in blue. Communicative activities, which give students opportunities for creative, open-ended expression, are coded in red.

LEARNING FROM PHOTOS

Tell students the following about the photo: *On s'entraîne sur ce mur d'escalade au Complexe sportif du Val de l'Arc tout près d'Aix-en-Provence.*

Vocabulary Teaching Resources

1. Bell Ringer Review Blackline Master: R-11, page 5
2. Workbook, *Mots et Conversation: A–B*, page R25
3. CD-ROM, Disc 1: *Mots et Conversation*, pages R36–R37

Bell Ringer Review

Put the following on the board or use BRR Blackline Master R-11: Divide this list of words into three categories: **fruits/légumes/viandes**

une banane	du bœuf
une carotte	une pomme
une orange	du saucisson
du poulet	des haricots
un oignon	verts
une laitue	une pomme
une tomate	de terre

Émilie et Sébastien

PRESENTATION (page R36)

Note The sentences in the first paragraph review material from *Bienvenue*, Chapter 11; the second paragraph, from Chapter 15.

A. Have students repeat after you.
B. Call on a student to read all the sentences as a story.

Note Students may listen to recorded versions of the sentences and the conversation below on the CD-ROM.

Chez le médecin

PRESENTATION (page R36)

A. Call on two students with good pronunciation to read the conversation to the class.
B. Have the class repeat each line of the conversation after you.

Émilie et Sébastien

Émilie se réveille.
Elle se lève tout de suite.
Ce matin, comme tous les matins, elle est allée au gymnase.
Elle veut rester en forme.
Elle est arrivée au gymnase avec ses copines.
Elles sont entrées dans le gymnase ensemble.
Elles ont fait de la gymnastique.

Voilà le pauvre Sébastien.
Il ne se sent pas très bien.
Il a mal au ventre.
Sébastien est allé chez le médecin.

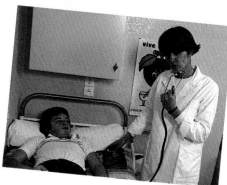

Chez le médecin

PATRICK: Ah, docteur. Je suis bien malade.
LE MÉDECIN: Qu'est-ce que vous avez? Quels sont vos symptômes?
PATRICK: C'est terrible. Je tousse. J'éternue. J'ai les yeux qui piquent. J'ai mal à la gorge.
LE MÉDECIN: Vous avez de la fièvre?
PATRICK: Je ne sais pas.
LE MÉDECIN: Je crois que vous avez un rhume. Ce n'est pas grave. Je vais vous faire une ordonnance.
PATRICK: Et moi qui suis toujours en bonne forme...
LE MÉDECIN: Il n'y a pas de quoi vous inquiéter. *(Il lui donne l'ordonnance.)* Allez avec ça à la pharmacie. Le pharmacien va vous donner des médicaments. Vous allez vite vous sentir mieux.

ADDITIONAL PRACTICE

After practicing the sentences and conversation from *Mots et Conversation*, reinforce the lesson by asking the following questions.

Émilie et Sébastien
1. Qui se réveille?
2. Elle se lève tout de suite?
3. Où est-elle allée?
4. Pourquoi est-elle allée au gymnase?
5. Avec qui est-elle allée au gymnase?
6. Qu'est-ce qu'elles ont fait au gymnase?

Chez le médecin
1. Qui ne se sent pas très bien?
2. Où a-t-il mal?
3. Il est allé chez le médecin?
4. Le médecin l'examine?

A L'horaire d'Émilie.   Répondez d'après les indications.

1. Émilie se réveille à quelle heure le matin? (six heures et demie)
2. Quand est-ce qu'elle se lève? (tout de suite)
3. Qu'est-ce qu'elle se lave? (la figure et les mains)
4. Où prend-elle son petit déjeuner? (dans la cuisine)
5. Quand est-ce qu'elle se brosse les dents? (après le petit déjeuner)

B Pour hommes, pour femmes ou les deux?   Choisissez.

HOMMES	FEMMES	LES DEUX

1. un peigne
2. une brosse
3. le déodorant
4. le parfum
5. une brosse à dents
6. le dentifrice
7. une glace
8. le savon

C Qu'est-ce qu'ils font?   Répondez par «oui» ou «non» d'après le dessin.

1. Les copains font du jogging?
2. Ils se promènent?
3. Ils font du volley-ball?
4. Ils pratiquent un sport?
5. Ils font de la gymnastique?

D La même idée.   Choisissez les phrases qui vont ensemble.

1. Guillaume a un rhume.
2. Il n'est pas en bonne santé.
3. Il a la gorge qui gratte.
4. Il a de la fièvre.
5. Il a mal au ventre.

a. Il a mal à la gorge.
b. Guillaume est enrhumé.
c. Il a mal à l'estomac.
d. Il est malade.
e. Il a de la température.

R 37

Exercices

PRESENTATION (page R37)

Exercices A, B, C, and D

These exercises are to be done with books open.

Extension of Exercice A

After completing Exercise A, extend it by repeating the questions in random order and supplying additional answer cues.

Extension of Exercice C

After completing Exercise C, have students sketch their own scenes of physical fitness activities and write several questions about them to ask their classmates.

ANSWERS

Exercice A

1. Émilie se réveille à six heures et demie le matin.
2. Elle se lève tout de suite.
3. Elle se lave la figure et les mains.
4. Elle prend son petit déjeuner dans la cuisine.
5. Elle se brosse les dents après le petit déjeuner.

Exercice B

1. les deux	5. les deux
2. les deux	6. les deux
3. les deux	7. les deux
4. femmes	8. les deux

Exercice C

1. Non, les copains ne font pas de jogging.
2. Non, ils ne se promènent pas.
3. Oui, ils font du volley-ball.
4. Oui, ils pratiquent un sport.
5. Non, ils ne font pas de gymnastique.

Exercice D

1. b
2. d
3. a
4. e
5. c

PANTOMIME

Call on a student to act out the following.
____, venez ici. Vous êtes Émilie.
Réveillez-vous. Levez-vous.
Faites de la gymnastique.
Pauvre Émilie, vous avez mal à la gorge.
Toussez. Éternuez.
Vous avez les yeux qui piquent.
Lisez une ordonnance. Prenez des comprimés.

INDEPENDENT PRACTICE

Assign any of the following:
1. Exercises, page R37
2. Workbook, *Mots et Conversation: A–B,* page R25
3. CD-ROM, Disc 1, pages R36–R37

R 37

Structure Teaching Resources

1. Bell Ringer Review Blackline Master: R-12, page 5
2. Workbook, *Structure: A–F,* pages R26–R28
3. CD-ROM, Disc 1, pages R38–R41

Le passé composé avec être

PRESENTATION *(page R38)*

A. Have the students pronounce the past participles in step 1.
B. Write the forms of the verb *être* on the board.
C. Add a past participle after each of the forms of the verb *être* in order to form the *passé composé.* Then have the students repeat them after you.
D. Underline the endings of the past participle.
E. Have the students repeat the model sentences.
F. **Extension** You may wish to write a verb conjugated with *avoir* on the board to contrast it with the *passé composé* formed with *être.* Point out the difference in agreement.

Le passé composé avec *être*

1. With certain verbs, you use *être* as the helping verb rather than *avoir*. Many verbs that are conjugated with *être* express motion to or from a place.

arriver	Il est arrivé.	descendre	Il est descendu.
partir	Il est parti.	aller	Il est allé en ville.
entrer	Il est entré.	venir	Il est venu.
sortir	Il est sorti.	revenir	Il est revenu.
monter	Il est monté.	rentrer	Il est rentré.

2. The past participle of verbs conjugated with *être* must agree with the subject in number (singular or plural) and gender (masculine or feminine). Study the following forms.

MASCULIN	FÉMININ
Je suis sorti. Tu es sorti. Il est sorti.	Je suis sortie. Tu es sortie. Elle est sortie.
Nous sommes sortis. Vous êtes sorti(s). Ils sont sortis.	Nous sommes sorties. Vous êtes sortie(s). Elles sont sorties.

3. Although the following verbs do not express motion to or from a place, they are also conjugated with *être*.

rester	Il est resté huit jours.	*He stayed a week.*
tomber	Il est tombé.	*He fell.*
devenir	Il est devenu malade.	*He became sick.*
naître	Elle est née en France.	*She was born in France.*
mourir	Elle est morte en 1991.	*She died in 1991.*

R 38

A Moi. Donnez des réponses personnelles.

1. Tu es né(e) quel jour?
2. Tu es né(e) où?
3. Tu es allé(e) à quelle école primaire?
4. Tu es sorti(e) de la maison à quelle heure ce matin?
5. Comment es-tu allé(e) à l'école?
6. Tu es arrivé(e) à l'école à quelle heure?

B Où est-ce qu'elle est allée? Complétez au passé composé.

1. Monique ___ de la maison. (sortir)
2. Je ___ avec elle. (sortir)
3. Nous ___ au gymnase. (aller)
4. Nous ___ au deuxième étage. (monter)
5. Tu ___ au gymnase aussi? (aller)
6. Tu y ___ avec un copain? (aller)
7. Vous ___ au gymnase à quelle heure? (arriver)
8. Monique a fait de l'aérobic et ensuite elle ___ à la piscine. (descendre)
9. Monique et moi, nous ___ du gymnase vers six heures. (sortir)
10. Elle ___ à la maison à six heures et demie et moi, je ___ à sept heures moins le quart. (rentrer)

INDEPENDENT PRACTICE

1. Exercises, page R39
2. Workbook, *Structure: A–C,* pages R26–R27
3. CD-ROM, Disc 1, pages R38–R39

Exercices

PRESENTATION (*page R39*)

Exercices A and B

A. Exercise A can be done with books either open or closed. Exercise B is to be done with books open.

B. After students complete the exercises, you may wish to have them write their answers and check for agreement of the past participles.

Extension of *Exercice A:* Speaking

After completing Exercise A, have students give as much additional information about themselves as they can.

Extension of *Exercice B*

After completing Exercise B, call on a student to retell the story in his/her own words.

ANSWERS

Exercice A

Answers will vary.

Exercice B

1. est sortie
2. suis sorti(e)
3. sommes allé(e)s
4. sommes monté(e)s
5. es allé(e)
6. es allé(e)
7. êtes arrivés
8. est descendue
9. sommes sorti(e)s
10. est rentrée, suis rentré(e)

Les verbes réfléchis

PRESENTATION *(page R40)*

A. Circle the reflexive pronoun. Underline the subject pronoun and draw a line from the reflexive pronoun to the subject to show that it is the same person.

B. Practice word order by giving many model sentences and having students change them to the negative.

Exercices

PRESENTATION *(pages R40–R41)*

Extension of *Exercice C*

Exercise C can be done in pairs. Students first practice the conversation, then ask and answer the questions.

ANSWERS

Exercice C

1. Charles se lève à six heures et demie.
2. Oui, il se lave.
3. Oui, il se brosse les dents dans la salle de bains.
4. Oui, il se rase.
5. Il quitte la maison à sept heures.
6. Bien sûr qu'il s'habille!

Les verbes réfléchis

1. A verb is reflexive when the subject both performs and receives the action of the verb. Since the subject also receives the action, an additional pronoun is needed. This is called the reflexive pronoun. Review the following.

SE LEVER	S'HABILLER
je me lève	je m' habille
tu te lèves	tu t' habilles
il/elle/on se lève	il/elle/on s' habille
nous nous levons	nous nous habillons
vous vous levez	vous vous habillez
ils/elles se lèvent	ils/elles s' habillent

Note that *me, te,* and *se* become *m', t',* and *s'* before a vowel or a silent *h.*

2. In the negative, *ne* comes before the reflexive pronoun. *Pas* follows the verb.

> **Je me réveille mais je *ne* me lève *pas* tout de suite.**
> **Il se couche mais il *ne* s'endort *pas* tout de suite.**

C **L'horaire de Charles.** Répétez la conversation.

PAUL: Tu te lèves à quelle heure, Charles?
CHARLES: À quelle heure est-ce que je me lève ou je me réveille?
PAUL: Tu te lèves.
CHARLES: Je me lève à six heures et demie.
PAUL: Et tu quittes la maison à quelle heure?
CHARLES: À sept heures. Je me lave, je me brosse les dents, je me rase et je prends mon petit déjeuner en une demi-heure.
PAUL: Et tu t'habilles aussi?
CHARLES: Bien sûr que je m'habille!

Répondez d'après la conversation.

1. Charles se lève à quelle heure?
2. Il se lave?
3. Il se brosse les dents dans la salle de bains?
4. Il se rase?
5. Il quitte la maison à quelle heure?
6. Il s'habille?

R 40

D Mon horaire. Donnez des réponses personnelles.

1. Comment t'appelles-tu?
2. Tu te réveilles à quelle heure le matin?
3. Tu te lèves tout de suite?
4. Tu t'habilles avant ou après le petit déjeuner?
5. Quand est-ce que tu te brosses les dents?
6. Tu te brosses les cheveux ou tu te peignes?
7. Tu te couches à quelle heure le soir?
8. Tu t'endors tout de suite?

E La matinée de Julie. Complétez.

Bonjour! Je ___ (s'appeler) Julie et mon frère ___ (s'appeler) Stéphane. Lui et
₁ ₂

moi, nous ___ (se lever) à sept heures du matin. Quand je ___ (se lever), je
₃ ₄

vais tout de suite à la salle de bains. Dans la salle de bains, je ___ (se laver), je
₅

___ (se brosser) les dents et je ___ (se peigner). Le matin, je ___ (se dépêcher),
₆ ₇ ₈

je n'ai pas de temps à perdre. Je ne reste pas longtemps dans la salle de bains.

Je sors, et tout de suite après, mon frère entre dans la salle de bains. Il ___
₉

(se laver), ___ (se brosser) les dents et ___ (se raser).
₁₀ ₁₁

À quelle heure est-ce que tu ___ (se lever) le matin? Tu as le même problème
₁₂

que nous? Tu ___ (se dépêcher) pour ne pas être en retard à l'école?
₁₃

Activités de communication orale et écrite

A Pour rester en forme. Work with a classmate. Tell him or her what
you do to stay in shape. He or she asks you if you did the same thing yesterday.
Answer, then reverse roles.

B Chez le médecin. Imagine that you went to the doctor's. Write a short
paragraph describing your visit.

R 41

PRESENTATION *(continued)*
Extension of *Exercice D*
Have students work in pairs
and ask each other the questions
in Exercise D.

Exercice E
When doing Exercise E, first
call on individuals. Then have one
student read the entire exercise to
the class.

ANSWERS
Exercice D
Answers will vary.

Exercice E
1. m'appelle
2. s'appelle
3. nous levons
4. me lève
5. me lave
6. me brosse
7. me peigne
8. me dépêche
9. se lave
10. se brosse
11. se rase
12. te lèves
13. te dépêches

Activités de communication orale et écrite

PRESENTATION *(page R41)*
These activities recycle material
from *Bienvenue,* Chapters 11
and 15.

ANSWERS
Activités A* and *B
Answers will vary.

OVERVIEW

This chapter reviews vocabulary related to travel: checking into a hotel, changing money, shopping for clothing and souvenirs, and attending cultural events. These topics were presented in *Bienvenue,* Chapters 10, 16, 17, and 18.

The structure points reviewed are direct object pronouns and the indirect object pronouns *lui* and *leur.*

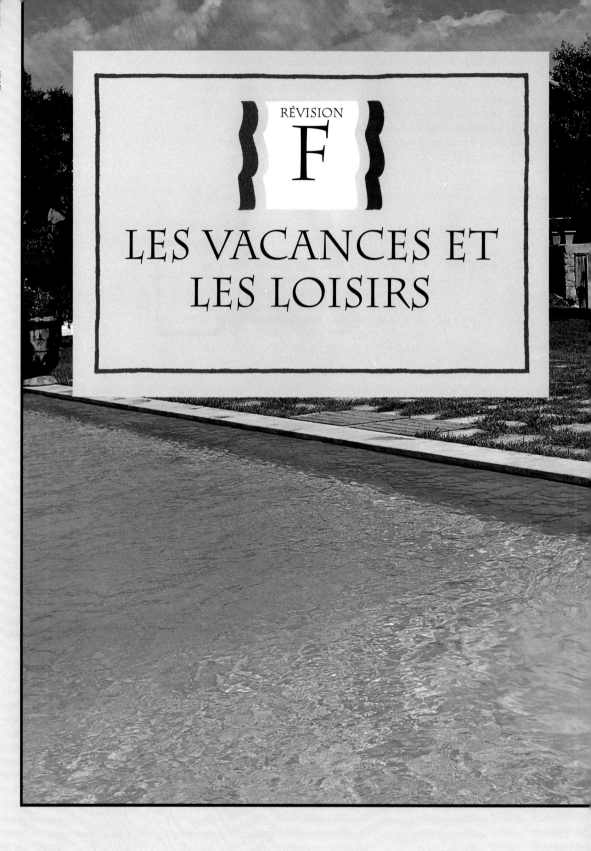

RÉVISION

F

LES VACANCES ET LES LOISIRS

R 43

Pacing

This review chapter should take two to three days depending on the length of the class and the age and aptitude of your students.

Note The Lesson Plans offer guidelines for 45- and 55-minute classes and **Block Scheduling.**

Exercices vs. *Activités*

The exercises and activities are color-coded. Exercises, which provide guided practice to prepare students for independent communication, are coded in blue. Communicative activities, which give students opportunities for creative, open-ended expression, are coded in red.

LEARNING FROM PHOTOS

Have students say as much as they can about the photo.

Un voyage en France

Les élèves de Madame Leroux ont fait un voyage en France.
Ils sont arrivés à l'hôtel.
Ils sont allés à la réception.

Daniel est au bureau de change.
Il veut changer de l'argent.
Il change 50 dollars.
Il a un chèque de voyage.
Il le signe.
Il donne le chèque à l'agent de change.
L'agent le regarde.
L'agent lui donne 250 francs.
Le dollar est à 5 francs.

Tous les élèves sont allés aux Galeries Lafayette.
Les Galeries Lafayette, c'est le nom d'un grand magasin.
Les élèves sont maintenant au rayon prêt-à-porter.
Ils paient à la caisse.

Les copains vont au cinéma.
Ils prennent leurs billets.
Ils les prennent au guichet.
La séance commence à 18h.
Ils voient un film.
Ils le voient en V.O. (version originale).
Ils le voient en français.
Ils sont contents. Ils le comprennent sans problème.
Les acteurs sont superbes.

A À l'hôtel. Répondez par «oui».

1. Les élèves de Madame Leroux sont arrivés à l'hôtel?
2. Ils sont entrés dans le hall?
3. Ils sont allés à la réception?
4. Le réceptionniste leur a donné leurs clés?
5. Ils ont pris l'ascenseur?
6. Ils ont monté leurs bagages?
7. Ils ont tous des chambres à deux lits?
8. Ils sortent tout de suite?
9. Ils visitent la ville?
10. Ils rentrent à l'hôtel pour le dîner?

R 44

MOTS ET CONVERSATION

Un voyage en France

PRESENTATION *(page R44)*

Note The first paragraph of *Un voyage en France* recycles material from Chapter 17 of *Bienvenue;* the second, from Chapter 18; the third, from Chapter 10; and the fourth, from Chapter 16.

A. Have a student read a sentence.
B. Ask questions such as the following about each sentence: *Qui est allé au bureau de change? Qu'est-ce qu'il veut changer? Il veut changer combien d'argent? Qu'est-ce qu'il signe? À qui est-ce qu'il donne le chèque? Qu'est-ce que l'agent fait avec le chèque? Il donne combien de francs à Daniel? Le dollar est à combien?*

Note Students may listen to a recorded version of the sentences on the CD-ROM.

Exercices

ANSWERS

Exercice A

1. Oui, ils sont arrivés à l'hôtel.
2. Oui, ils sont entrés dans le hall.
3. Oui, ils sont allés à la réception.
4. Oui, il leur a donné leurs clés.
5. Oui, ils ont pris l'ascenseur.
6. Oui, ils ont monté leurs bagages.
7. Oui, ils ont tous des chambres à deux lits.
8. Oui, ils sortent tout de suite.
9. Oui, ils visitent la ville.
10. Oui, ils rentrent à l'hôtel pour le dîner.

ADDITIONAL PRACTICE

1. After students complete Exercise A, have them do it again, this time responding with *Non* in order to practice negative constructions.
2. Call on a student to retell the story of Exercise A in his/her own words.

LEARNING FROM PHOTOS

You may wish to ask the following questions about the photo: *C'est une chambre pour combien de personnes? C'est une chambre à un lit ou à deux lits? C'est une chambre confortable? Il y a une télé? Et un téléphone?*

B Au bureau de change. Répondez.

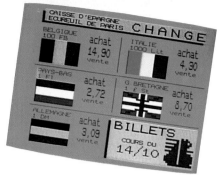

1. Où est-ce que Daniel est allé?
2. Il a de l'argent américain ou français?
3. Il a changé de l'argent?
4. Il a changé combien de dollars?
5. À combien est le dollar aujourd'hui?
6. Il a reçu combien de francs?
7. Il a signé son chèque de voyage?

C Des vêtements sport ou pas? Indiquez si les vêtements suivants sont des vêtements sport ou habillés.

	SPORT	HABILLÉ
1. des tennis		
2. une chemise blanche		
3. une cravate		
4. un survêtement		
5. un tailleur		
6. un pull		
7. un blouson		
8. un maillot		
9. des chaussures à talon haut		
10. un jean		

D Fana de cinéma ou pas? Donnez des réponses personnelles.

1. Tu es fana de cinéma? C'est-à-dire, tu aimes beaucoup voir des films?
2. Tu vas souvent au cinéma?
3. Il y a un cinéma près de chez toi?
4. La première séance est à quelle heure?
5. Il y a toujours un dessin animé avant le film?
6. Tu fais la queue devant le cinéma? Quels soirs en général?
7. Où est-ce que tu achètes les billets?
8. Dans la salle de cinéma, tu préfères une place près de l'écran ou loin de l'écran?
9. Quelle est la vedette de ton film préféré?
10. Si tu vois un film étranger, tu préfères le voir en version originale avec des sous-titres, ou doublé?

R 45

PRESENTATION (page R45)

Exercices B, C, and D

Exercise B deals with changing money, Exercise C with clothing, and Exercise D with cultural activities. The questions in Exercise B refer to the second paragraph of *Un voyage en France*, page 44.

Extension of *Exercice C*

After completing Exercise C, have students write sentences telling where they or someone else wears each article of clothing. For example: *Au bureau ma mère porte un tailleur.*

ANSWERS

Exercice B

1. Daniel est allé au bureau de change.
2. Il a de l'argent américain.
3. Oui, il a changé de l'argent.
4. Il a changé cinquante dollars.
5. Le dollar est à cinq francs aujourd'hui.
6. Il a reçu 250 francs.
7. Oui, il a signé son chèque de voyage.

Exercice C

1. sport
2. habillé
3. habillé
4. sport
5. habillé
6. sport
7. sport
8. sport
9. habillé
10. sport

Exercice D

Answers will vary.

LEARNING FROM REALIA

You may wish to ask students the following questions about the exchange rates listed on the screen: *Quel est le cours du change du franc belge? de la livre anglaise? du mark allemand? Ce sont les cours du change pour quelle date? Comment s'appelle le bureau de change ou la banque?*

INDEPENDENT PRACTICE

Assign any of the following:
1. Exercises, pages R44–R45
2. Workbook, *Mots et Conversation: A–C,* page R30
3. CD-ROM, Disc 1, pages R44–R45

STRUCTURE

Les pronoms *le, la, les, me, te, nous* et *vous*

1. *Le, la, les, me, te, nous* and *vous* are direct object pronouns. A direct object receives the action of the verb. These pronouns can replace people or things. Review the following.

Marie regarde *le* livre.	Elle ne *le* lit pas.	Elle *le* regarde.
Marie regarde *la* carte.	Elle ne *la* lit pas.	Elle *la* regarde.
Marie regarde *les* livres.	Elle ne *les* lit pas.	Elle *les* regarde.
Marie regarde *les* cartes.	Elle ne *les* lit pas.	Elle *les* regarde.

Note that the direct object pronoun comes immediately before the conjugated form of the verb.

2. In a sentence with a verb + an infinitive, the pronoun comes before the infinitive.

   Marie regarde le livre. Elle va *l'*acheter.
   Marie regarde la carte. Elle va *l'*acheter.
   Marie ne regarde pas les livres. Elle ne va pas *les* acheter.
   Marie ne regarde pas les cartes. Elle ne va pas *les* acheter.

   Note that *le* and *la* become *l'* before a vowel or a silent *h*.

3. The pronouns *me, te, nous* and *vous* can be used as either direct or indirect object pronouns. An indirect object pronoun is the indirect receiver of the action of the verb.

   Richard *te* regarde? Oui, il *me* regarde mais il ne *me* parle pas.
   Il *vous* donne le livre? Oui, il *nous* donne le livre.

A **Tu aimes ou tu détestes?** Donnez des réponses personnelles d'après le modèle.

les pommes de terre
Les pommes de terre? Je les aime beaucoup.
(Je ne les aime pas. Je les déteste.)

1. les gâteaux
2. l'eau minérale
3. la viande
4. le bœuf
5. le poisson
6. la glace
7. les fruits
8. les crevettes
9. le poulet
10. les haricots verts

Structure Teaching Resources

1. Workbook, *Structure: A–D,* pages R31–R32
2. CD-ROM, Disc 1, pages R46–R47

Les pronoms le, la, les, me, te, nous *et* vous

PRESENTATION *(page R46)*

A. As you go over the structure explanation, draw a box around the direct objects in the sentences on the left.
B. Circle the direct object pronouns in the sentences on the right.
C. Then draw a line from the noun to the pronoun to show that they represent the same person or thing.
D. Have the students read the model sentences aloud.

Exercices

ANSWERS

Exercice A

1. Les gâteaux? Je les aime beaucoup. (Je ne les aime pas. Je les déteste.)
2. ... Je l'aime beaucoup. (Je ne l'aime pas. Je la déteste.)
3. ... Je l'aime beaucoup. (Je ne l'aime pas. Je la déteste.)
4. ... Je l'aime beaucoup. (Je ne l'aime pas. Je le déteste.)
5. ... Je l'aime beaucoup. (Je ne l'aime pas. Je le déteste.)
6. ... Je l'aime beaucoup. (Je ne l'aime pas. Je la déteste.)
7. ... Je les aime. (Je ne les aime pas. Je les déteste.)
8. ... Je les aime. (Je ne les aime pas. Je les déteste.)
9. ... Je l'aime. (Je ne l'aime pas. Je le déteste.)
10. ... Je les aime beaucoup. (Je ne les aime pas. Je les déteste.)

B Un petit problème. Complétez en utilisant un pronom.

JEAN: Mélanie, Guillaume ___ cherche.

MÉLANIE: Guillaume ___ cherche? Qu'est-ce qu'il veut?

JEAN: Il veut ___ dire quelque chose.

MÉLANIE: Qu'est-ce qu'il veut ___ dire? Tu sais, je suis furieuse contre Guillaume. Je ne veux pas lui parler.

JEAN: Oui, je sais. Mais il ___ adore et je sais que toi aussi, tu ___ adores.

MÉLANIE: Ah, oui, oui. Il est plutôt adorable!

Les pronoms *lui, leur*

The pronouns *lui* and *leur* are indirect object pronouns. They refer to people. Review the following.

Je donne un cadeau *à Jérémie*	Je *lui* donne un cadeau.
Je donne un cadeau *à Mélanie*.	Je *lui* donne un cadeau.
Je donne un cadeau *à mes amis*.	Je *leur* donne un cadeau.
Je donne un cadeau *à mes amies*.	Je *leur* donne un cadeau.

C Qu'est-ce que tu as fait? Répondez en utilisant *lui* ou *leur.*

1. Hier soir, tu as parlé à Jean?
2. Tu as parlé à Marie aussi?
3. Tu leur as parlé au téléphone?
4. Tu as donné un cadeau à Jean et à Marie?
5. Tu as donné une chemise à Jean?
6. Tu as donné un chemisier à Marie?
7. Tu as donné le même cadeau à Jean et à Marie?

Activités de communication orale

A Nos loisirs. Tell a classmate what you do when you have free time. Find out if he or she likes to do the same things.

> Élève 1: J'aime jouer au basket-ball quand j'ai du temps libre. Toi aussi, tu aimes jouer au basket?
> Élève 2: Non, moi je préfère lire ou parler au téléphone avec mes copines.

B Des vacances formidables. Work with a classmate. Ask your partner questions about his or her vacation using the following expressions. Then reverse roles.

1. où 2. quand 3. avec qui 4. combien 5. quelles activités

R 47

Exercice B
te, me, te, me, t', l'

Les pronoms lui, leur
PRESENTATION (*page R47*)

A. Go over the structure explanation, drawing a box around the indirect objects (*à* + noun) in the sentences on the left and a circle around the pronouns in the sentences on the right.
B. Then draw a line from the nouns to the pronouns, showing students that they represent the same people. Emphasize that *lui* and *leur* refer to people.
C. Have the students read the model sentences aloud.

Exercice
PRESENTATION (*page R47*)

Exercise C is to be done with books closed. You may wish to have students give additional examples by talking about their families or classmates.

ANSWERS
Exercice C

1. Oui, hier soir, je lui ai parlé. (Non, hier soir, je ne lui ai pas parlé.)
2. Oui, je lui ai parlé aussi. (Non, je ne lui ai pas parlé.)
3. Oui, je leur ai parlé au téléphone. (Non, je ne leur ai pas parlé au téléphone.)
4. Oui, je leur ai donné un cadeau. (Non, je ne leur ai pas donné de cadeau.)
5. Oui, je lui ai donné une chemise. (Non, je ne lui ai pas donné de chemise.)
6. Oui, je lui ai donné un chemisier. (Non, je ne lui ai pas donné de chemisier.)
7. Oui, je leur ai donné le même cadeau. (Non, je ne leur ai pas donné le même cadeau.)

Activités de communication orale

ANSWERS
Activités A and B
Answers will vary.

R 47

CHAPTER OVERVIEW

Students will learn to communicate with postal clerks, write letters, and address an envelope in French. Structure points are the pronouns *qui* and *que,* the agreement of the past participle, and verbs like *envoyer.* The cultural focus is on the French postal system and letter-writing etiquette.

CHAPTER OBJECTIVES

By the end of this chapter, students will know:

1. vocabulary associated with the postal service and letter writing
2. the use of the relative pronouns *qui* and *que*
3. the agreement of the past participle with a preceding direct object
4. the present indicative forms and past participles of verbs with spelling changes, such as *envoyer, employer,* and *payer*

CHAPTER 1 RESOURCES

1. Workbook
2. Student Tape Manual
3. Audio Cassette 2A/CD-1
4. Bell Ringer Review Blackline Masters
5. Vocabulary Transparencies
6. Communication Transparency C-1
7. Communication Activities Masters
8. Situation Cards
9. Conversation Video
10. Videocassette/Videodisc, Unit 1
11. Video Activities Booklet, Unit 1
12. Lesson Plans
13. Computer Software: Practice/Test Generator
14. Chapter Quizzes
15. Testing Program
16. Internet Activities Booklet
17. CD-ROM Interactive Textbook
18. Map Transparencies

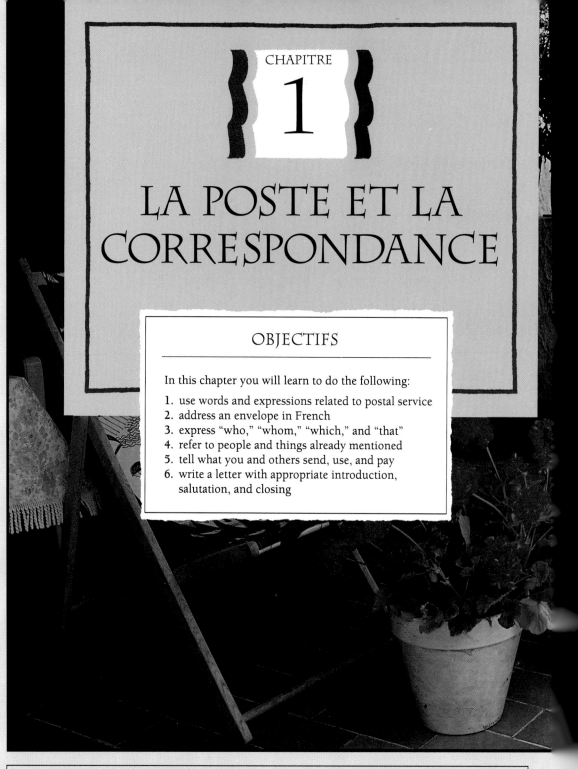

CHAPITRE

1

LA POSTE ET LA CORRESPONDANCE

OBJECTIFS

In this chapter you will learn to do the following:

1. use words and expressions related to postal service
2. address an envelope in French
3. express "who," "whom," "which," and "that"
4. refer to people and things already mentioned
5. tell what you and others send, use, and pay
6. write a letter with appropriate introduction, salutation, and closing

CHAPTER PROJECTS

(optional)

Have students make a list of services offered by the U.S. Postal Service and ask them to explain them in French.

COMMUNITIES

If you live in an area where foreign language materials are available, have students look for French greeting cards. Prepare a bulletin board using these cards.

1

Pacing

This chapter will require eight to ten class sessions. Pacing will depend on the length of the class and the age and aptitude of the students.

For more information on planning your class, see the Lesson Plans, which offer guidelines for 45- and 55-minute classes and **Block Scheduling**.

NOTE ON INTERROGATIVES

1. In conversational French the most common way to ask a question is to raise one's voice at the end of the sentence. This rising intonation can be used with yes/no questions and many question words: *Guy va à Paris? Il part quand?*

2. Another common way to ask a question is to begin a statement with *est-ce que* or with a question word + *est-ce que*: *Est-ce que Marie est française? Où est-ce qu'elle habite?*

3. Simple inversion can also be used: *Où va Jean?*

4. *À bord* makes occasional use of the more formal inversion: *À qui Marie parle-t-elle?*

In *À bord*, the rising intonation pattern is used most often since this is the case in colloquial French conversation. You may wish to review the four ways to form questions outlined above. (See *Bienvenue*, Chapter 12, page 316 for a summary of the first three.)

Exercices vs. *Activités*

The exercises and activities are color-coded. Exercises, which provide guided practice to prepare students for independent communication, are coded in blue. Communicative activities, which give students the opportunities for creative, open-ended expression, are coded in red.

INTERNET ACTIVITIES

(optional)

These activities, student worksheets, and related teacher information are in the *À bord* Internet Activities Booklet and on the Glencoe Foreign Language Home Page at **http://www.glencoe.com/secondary/fl**

LEARNING FROM PHOTOS

After presenting the *Mots 1* vocabulary, ask these questions about the photo: *Est-ce que le facteur distribue le courrier ou livre un paquet? Est-ce que le facteur vend des timbres?*

MOTS 1

Vocabulary Teaching Resources

1. Vocabulary Transparencies 1.1 (A & B)
2. Audio Cassette 2A/CD-1
3. Student Tape Manual, Teacher's Edition, *Mots 1: A-C*, pages 1–3
4. Workbook, *Mots 1: A–B*, page 1
5. Communication Activities Masters, *Mots 1: A–B*, page 1
6. Chapter Quizzes, *Mots 1: Quiz 1*, page 1
7. CD-ROM, Disc 1, *Mots 1: pages 2–5*

Bell Ringer Review

Write the following on the board or use BRR Blackline Master 1-1: Write five sentences about what you did during the summer. Be sure to use the *passé composé.*

PRESENTATION (*pages 2–3*)

A. Have students close their books. Present the new words and phrases using Vocabulary Transparencies 1.1 (A & B). Have students repeat each word after you or Cassette 2A/CD-1.
B. Present one word or phrase at a time. Then build to a complete sentence.

VOCABULAIRE

MOTS 1

À LA POSTE

un bureau de poste = la poste

un guichet

une employée des postes

un employé des postes

un aérogramme

une enveloppe

un distributeur automatique

un timbre

une lettre

une carte postale

ROLE-PLAY

(Student 1) et (Student 2), **venez ici, s'il vous plaît.**

(Student 1), **vous êtes un(e) employé(e) des postes.**

(Student 2), **vous avez quelque chose à envoyer. Allez à la poste. Dites «bonjour» à l'employé(e).**

(Student 1), **répondez-lui. Demandez-lui ce qu'il/elle veut.**

(Student 2), **dites-lui ce que vous voulez envoyer. Dites-lui où vous voulez l'envoyer.**

(Student 1), **dites-lui combien ça va coûter.**

(Student 2), **payez l'employé(e). Donnez-lui de l'argent.**

(Student 1), **donnez-lui des timbres.**

(Student 2), **regardez bien les timbres. Il y a un problème. L'employé(e) ne vous a pas donné assez de timbres. Expliquez le problème à l'employé(e).**

C'est combien, une carte postale pour les États-Unis?

une boîte aux lettres

Daniel a mis une lettre à la poste.
Il l'a mise dans la boîte aux lettres.
Il l'a envoyée ce matin.
Il ne l'a pas envoyée hier.

un facteur

Le facteur a distribué le courrier.
Il l'a distribué ce matin.
Il ne l'a pas distribué cet après-midi.

Teaching Tip When introducing material, proceed from the easiest to the most difficult type of question. Begin with yes/no or either/or questions. (*C'est une enveloppe? C'est une enveloppe ou un aérogramme?*) Save information questions (*Qu'est-ce que c'est?*) until students have had a chance to produce or at least hear the new vocabulary several times.

C. Have students open their books and read the new words and sentences aloud.

COGNATE RECOGNITION
Note the following cognates.
un aérogramme
automatique
distribuer
une enveloppe
une lettre
postal (postaux)

Vocabulary Expansion

Some additional words you may wish to give students are:
un télégramme
par avion
la poste aérienne
une lettre recommandée

ADDITIONAL PRACTICE

1. The following are additional questions you may ask after presenting the *Mots 1* vocabulary: *Daniel a mis la lettre à la poste? Il l'a mise dans la boîte aux lettres? Qui a mis la lettre dans la boîte aux lettres? Où l'a-t-il mise? Quand est-ce qu'il a envoyé la lettre? Il l'a envoyée hier?*

2. For these next questions, it may be helpful to give the woman in the illustration on the bottom of the page a name: *Madame Leblanc. Qui a donné le courrier à Madame Leblanc? Qu'est-ce que Madame Leblanc a reçu? Le facteur a un vélo ou un vélomoteur? Quand est-ce que le facteur a distribué le courrier?*

Exercices

PRESENTATION (pages 4–5)

Exercices A and C

Exercises A and C can be done with books open.

Exercice B

Exercise B can be done with books either open or closed.

Extension of Exercice B: Speaking

After completing Exercise B, call on one student to retell the story in his/her own words.

Extension of Exercice C

After a student gives the correct answer to each item in Exercise C, have students make up additional sentences using the alternate choices. For example: *Nicole a mis un timbre sur l'enveloppe. Nicole a envoyé un aérogramme.*

ANSWERS

Exercice A

1. C'est un aérogramme.
2. C'est un timbre.
3. C'est une carte postale.
4. C'est une boîte aux lettres.
5. C'est un distributeur automatique.
6. C'est un facteur.

Exercice B

1. Oui, Paul a écrit une lettre.
2. Oui, il l'a mise dans une enveloppe.
3. Oui, il l'a envoyée.
4. Oui, il est allé au bureau de poste.
5. Oui, il a mis sa lettre à la poste.
6. Oui, il l'a mise dans la boîte aux lettres.
7. Oui, le facteur a distribué le courrier.
8. Oui, il a distribué le courrier le matin.

Exercices

A Qu'est-ce que c'est? Identifiez.

1. C'est une carte postale ou un aérogramme?

2. C'est un timbre ou une lettre?

3. C'est une enveloppe ou une carte postale?

4. C'est une boîte aux lettres ou la poste?

5. C'est un guichet ou un distributeur automatique?

6. C'est un facteur ou un employé des postes?

B Au bureau de poste. Répondez par «oui».

1. Paul a écrit une lettre?
2. Il l'a mise dans une enveloppe?
3. Il l'a envoyée?
4. Il est allé au bureau de poste?
5. Il a mis sa lettre à la poste?
6. Il l'a mise dans la boîte aux lettres?
7. Le facteur a distribué le courrier?
8. Il a distribué le courrier le matin?

4   CHAPITRE 1

PAIRED ACTIVITY

Students role-play in pairs. The first partner plays the role of a person waiting excitedly for the letter carrier to arrive. The second partner wants to find out what the other is waiting for. Allow partners time to prepare the skit, then have them present it to the class.

INDEPENDENT PRACTICE

Assign any of the following:
1. Exercises, pages 4–5
2. Workbook, *Mots 1: A–B*, page 1
3. Communication Activities Masters, *Mots 1: A–B*, page 1
4. CD-ROM, Disc 1, pages 2–5
   (See suggestions for homework correction in the Teacher's Manual.)

C Elle a envoyé la lettre. *Choisissez.*

1. Nicole a mis la lettre dans ___.
   a. une enveloppe
   b. un timbre
   c. un aérogramme

2. Elle a acheté des timbres ___.
   a. au distributeur automatique
   b. à la boîte aux lettres
   c. au facteur

3. Elle a mis des ___ sur l'enveloppe.
   a. aérogrammes
   b. facteurs
   c. timbres

4. Nicole a mis la lettre ___.
   a. au guichet
   b. dans la boîte aux lettres
   c. dans le distributeur automatique

5. ___ a distribué le courrier.
   a. L'employée des postes
   b. Le distributeur automatique
   c. Le facteur

Vocabulary Teaching Resources

1. Vocabulary Transparencies 1.2 (A & B)
2. Audio Cassette 2A/CD-1
3. Student Tape Manual, Teacher's Edition, *Mots 2: D–F*, pages 4–5
4. Workbook, *Mots 2: C–E*, pages 2–3
5. Communication Activities Masters, *Mots 2: C–D*, pages 2–4
6. Computer Software, *Vocabulaire*
7. Chapter Quizzes, *Mots 2: Quiz 2*, page 2
8. CD-ROM, Disc 1, *Mots 2*: pages 6–9

Bell Ringer Review

Write the following on the board or use BRR Blackline Master 1-2: Write all the words you can think of related to letter-writing or the post office.

PRESENTATION (*pages 6–7*)

A. Have students close their books. Use Vocabulary Transparencies 1.2 (A & B) to introduce the new words and expressions.

B. Model each new word or phrase and have students repeat after you or Cassette 2A/CD-1.

C. As you present the new vocabulary, ask questions such as the following: *Qui a écrit des lettres? Quand est-ce qu'elle les a écrites? Elle a écrit l'adresse de qui? Qu'est-ce qu'elle a écrit sur l'enveloppe?*

VOCABULAIRE

MOTS 2

DES LETTRES ET DES COLIS

Madame Lanoux a écrit des lettres.
Elles les a écrites ce matin.
Elle a écrit l'adresse du destinataire.
Elle l'a écrite sur l'enveloppe.

6   CHAPITRE 1

ADDITIONAL PRACTICE

Create additional "sample" envelopes using a blank overhead transparency. Then ask students questions about them. For example: *Qui est l'expéditrice/l'expéditeur? Qui est le/la destinataire? Comment s'appelle la rue? Quel est le code postal?*, etc.

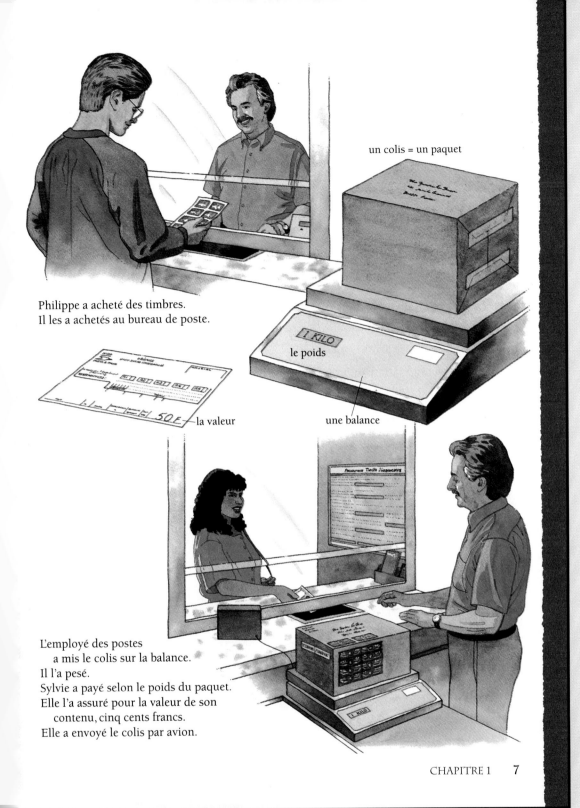

un colis = un paquet

Philippe a acheté des timbres.
Il les a achetés au bureau de poste.

le poids

la valeur

une balance

L'employé des postes
   a mis le colis sur la balance.
Il l'a pesé.
Sylvie a payé selon le poids du paquet.
Elle l'a assuré pour la valeur de son
   contenu, cinq cents francs.
Elle a envoyé le colis par avion.

PRESENTATION *(page 8)*

A. Go over the exercises in class before assigning them for homework.

B. Exercise A is designed to be done with books open. Exercises B and C can be done with books either open or closed.

Extension of *Exercise A*

After completing Exercise A, have students make up additional sentences using the alternate choice from each sentence. For example: *L'expéditeur ne reçoit pas la lettre. Il envoie la lettre.*

ANSWERS

Exercice A

1. b
2. a
3. a
4. b
5. b

Exercice B

1. Stéphane a écrit une lettre.
2. Oui, il l'a mise dans une enveloppe.
3. Il a écrit le nom et l'adresse du destinataire.
4. Oui, il a indiqué le code postal sur l'enveloppe.
5. Oui, il a mis des timbres sur l'enveloppe.
6. Oui, il a envoyé la lettre.
7. Oui, il l'a mise dans la boîte aux lettres.

Exercice C

1. Marianne est allée au bureau de poste.
2. Elle a mis le colis sur la balance.
3. L'employé des postes l'a pesé.
4. Marianne a assuré le paquet.
5. Oui, Marianne a payé selon le poids du paquet.
6. Oui, Marianne l'a assuré pour sa valeur.
7. Elle l'a envoyé par avion.

Exercices

A **Qui ou quoi?** Choisissez.

1. ___ reçoit la lettre.
   a. L'expéditeur / L'expéditrice   b. Le / La destinataire

2. ___ envoie la lettre.
   a. L'expéditeur / L'expéditrice   b. Le / La destinataire

3. ___ indique le numéro, la rue et la ville du destinataire.
   a. L'adresse   b. Le code postal

4. ___ indique seulement la ville du destinataire.
   a. L'adresse   b. Le code postal

5. Le facteur distribue ___.
   a. les timbres   b. le courrier

B **Une lettre ou une carte postale?** Répondez d'après les photos.

1. Stéphane a écrit une lettre ou une carte postale?
2. Il l'a mise dans une enveloppe?
3. Il a écrit le nom et l'adresse du destinataire ou de l'expéditeur?
4. Il a indiqué le code postal sur l'enveloppe?
5. Il a mis des timbres sur l'enveloppe?
6. Il a envoyé la lettre?
7. Il l'a mise dans la boîte aux lettres?

C **Marianne a envoyé un colis.**
Répondez d'après les indications.

1. Où est-ce que Marianne est allée? (au bureau de poste)
2. Où est-ce qu'elle a mis le colis? (sur la balance)
3. Qui l'a pesé? (l'employé des postes)
4. Qu'est-ce que Marianne a assuré? (le paquet)
5. Marianne a payé selon le poids du paquet? (Oui)
6. Marianne l'a assuré pour sa valeur? (Oui)
7. Comment l'a-t-elle envoyé? (par avion)

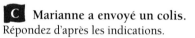

Camille Bailly
14 rue de Vaugirard
91370 Verrières

8   CHAPITRE 1

Activités de communication orale
Mots 1 et 2

A **À la poste.**   You're visiting Grenoble in southeastern France and you want to mail a letter to a friend in the U.S. Find out from the post office clerk (your partner) whether they sell airgrams and how much they cost. Then ask where there's a mailbox in the post office.

B **La correspondance.**   You're an exchange student in France. Your French host (your partner) wants to know what you usually send to each person listed below for the following occasions.

1. tes parents (pour demander de l'argent)
2. ton (ta) meilleur(e) ami(e) (pour son anniversaire)
3. un copain ou une copine (pour dire bonjour)
4. tes grands-parents (quand tu es en vacances)
5. ton professeur de français (pour lui parler de la France)

> Élève 1: Qu'est-ce que tu envoies à ta mère pour la Fête des Mères?
> Élève 2: Je lui envoie un colis.

C **Des timbres.**   Bring in cancelled stamps from francophone countries around the world. Work in groups and classify the stamps according to topic—art, history, literature, science, current events, etc. Choose an interesting stamp and prepare an oral report on its subject and present it to the class. Then share the information with your art (history, science, etc.) class.

Activités de communication orale
Mots 1 et 2

PRESENTATION *(page 9)*
   These activities allow students to use the chapter vocabulary in open-ended situations. It is not necessary to do all the activities. Select those you consider most appropriate.

ANSWERS
Activité A
   Answers will vary.
Activité B
   É1 questions should follow the model. É2 answers will vary.
Activité C
   Answers will vary.

INFORMAL ASSESSMENT
(Mots 1 and 2)
   Have individuals say anything they can about mailing a letter or a parcel.

LEARNING FROM REALIA

1. Have students read the front of the brochure and explain what it is advertising.
2. Have students explain in French what the stickers *(les autocollants)* shown on the bottom of the page are for.

INDEPENDENT PRACTICE

Assign any of the following:
1. Exercises and activities, pages 8–9
2. Workbook, *Mots 2: C–E*, pages 2–3
3. Communication Activities Masters, *Mots 2: C–D*, pages 2–4
4. Computer Software, *Vocabulaire*
5. CD-ROM, Disc 1, pages 6–9

STRUCTURE

1. Workbook, *Structure: A–H*, pages 4–6
2. Student Tape Manual, Teacher's Edition, *Structure: A–C*, pages 6–7
3. Audio Cassette 2A/CD-1
4. Communication Activities Masters, *Structure: A–D*, pages 5–7
5. Computer Software, *Structure*
6. Chapter Quizzes, *Structure*: Quizzes 3–5, pages 3–5
7. CD-ROM, Disc 1, pages 10–13

Bell Ringer Review

Write the following on the board or use BRR Blackline Master 1-3: Rewrite the sentences in Column A, replacing the underlined word or phrase with the correct pronoun from Column B.

A	B
Je vois <u>Pierre.</u>	leur
Je parle <u>à Pierre.</u>	le
J'habite <u>à Paris.</u>	les
J'aime <u>les films.</u>	y
Je téléphone <u>à mes amis.</u>	en
J'ai besoin <u>d'argent.</u>	lui

Les pronoms relatifs qui et que

PRESENTATION *(pages 10–11)*

A. Write the sentences from step 1 on the board. Tell students that the first example in each pair consists of two separate sentences, each with a separate subject. The second example in each pair combines these two sentences into one, using a relative pronoun.

B. Circle the pronoun, draw a box around its antecedent, and connect the two with a line to

---

Les pronoms relatifs *qui* et *que*

Expressing "Who," "Whom," "Which," and "That"

Qui and *que* are called relative pronouns. A relative pronoun replaces a noun or a pronoun. You use a relative pronoun to combine two short sentences into one.

1. *Qui* replaces the subject of a sentence. It is followed by a verb.

QUI		
Je parle à un employé.	**Il**	travaille à la poste.
Je parle à un employé	**qui**	travaille à la poste.
Je parle à une employée.	**Elle**	travaille à la poste.
Je parle à une employée	**qui**	travaille à la poste.
Je parle à des employés.	**Ils**	travaillent à la poste.
Je parle à des employés	**qui**	travaillent à la poste.
Je parle à des employées.	**Elles**	travaillent à la poste.
Je parle à des employées	**qui**	travaillent à la poste.

2. *Que* replaces a direct object. It is followed by a *subject* and a verb.

QUE		
Je parle à un employé. Vous	**le**	connaissez.
Je parle à un employé	**que**	vous connaissez.
Je parle à une employée. Vous	**la**	connaissez.
Je parle à une employée	**que**	vous connaissez.
Je parle à des employés. Vous	**les**	connaissez.
Je parle à des employés	**que**	vous connaissez.
Je parle à des employées. Vous	**les**	connaissez.
Je parle à des employées	**que**	vous connaissez.

3. The relative pronouns *qui* and *que* are also used to refer to things.

> J'ai lu la lettre *qui* est sur la table.
> Voilà le colis *que* le facteur a apporté.

ADDITIONAL PRACTICE

1. After completing Exercises A, B, C, and D, reinforce the lesson with the following: Give two cards (or slips of paper) to each student, one with the word *qui*, the other with *que*. On the board or overhead, show sample complex sentences with the relative pronoun missing. Students hold up the card showing the appropriate pronoun. After some practice, try cueing the model sentences orally instead of visually.

2. Have students create a few original sentences using *qui* and *que*.

4. Note that *que* becomes *qu'* before a vowel. *Qui* is never shortened.

> **La femme *qu'*il voit est l'employée des postes.**
> **Voilà une employée *qui* est très compétente.**

Exercices

A **C'est la même fille qui lit et qui écrit.** Répondez par «oui».

1. La fille qui parle maintenant est très intelligente?
2. Tu aimes le poème qu'elle lit?
3. Le poème qu'elle lit est intéressant ou pas?
4. C'est le poème de Sylvie qui est sur la table?
5. Tu as lu le poème qu'elle a écrit et qui est là sur la table?

B **C'est Martin.** Faites une seule phrase en utilisant «qui» ou «que».

> **C'est Martin. Martin aime écrire.**
> *C'est Martin qui aime écrire.*

1. C'est Martin. Martin m'écrit.
2. Il m'écrit des lettres. Les lettres sont très intéressantes.
3. Le facteur me donne les lettres. Martin m'envoie des lettres.
4. Martin m'envoie aussi des photos. Les photos sont très jolies.
5. J'aime regarder les photos. Martin m'envoie les photos.

C *Qui ou que?* Complétez.

1. Robert a écrit la lettre ___ vous lisez.
2. La personne ___ distribue le courrier est le facteur.
3. L'enveloppe ___ est sur la table est trop petite.
4. Les cartes postales ___ vous voulez envoyer n'ont pas assez de timbres.
5. C'est l'expéditeur ___ envoie une lettre et c'est le destinataire ___ la reçoit.

D **Du courrier pour moi?** Faites une phrase en utilisant «qui» ou «que».

1. Je vois le facteur. Il distribue le courrier dans notre quartier.
2. Aujourd'hui j'ai reçu une carte postale. Elle est très jolie.
3. Mon meilleur ami m'a envoyé la carte. Il est en vacances en Bretagne.
4. La Bretagne est une jolie province. Elle est au nord-ouest de la France.

Le port de Sainte-Marine en Bretagne

demonstrate their relationship. After a few examples, ask a student whether the relative pronoun in each sentence functions as the subject or the object of the clause.
C. Do the step 2 examples the same way. Ask students which relative pronoun functions as the subject and which one functions as the object.
D. Give additional examples for step 3. *J'ai vu la photo qui est sur la table. J'ai pris la photo que vous regardez,* etc.

Note In the CD-ROM version, this structure point is presented via an interactive electronic comic strip.

Exercices

ANSWERS

Exercice A

1. Oui, la fille qui parle...
2. Oui, j'aime le poème qu'elle lit.
3. Oui, le poème qu'elle lit...
4. Oui, c'est le poème de Sylvie qui est...
5. Oui, j'ai lu le poème qu'elle a écrit...

Exercice B

1. C'est Martin qui m'écrit.
2. Il m'écrit des lettres qui sont très intéressantes.
3. Le facteur me donne les lettres que Martin m'envoie.
4. Martin m'envoie aussi des photos qui sont très jolies.
5. J'aime regarder les photos que Martin m'envoie.

Exercice C

1. que   3. qui   5. qui, qui
2. qui   4. que

Exercice D

1. Je vois le facteur qui distribue le courrier dans notre quartier.
2. Aujourd'hui j'ai reçu une carte postale qui est très jolie.
3. Mon meilleur ami, qui est en vacances en Bretagne, m'a envoyé la carte.
4. La Bretagne est une jolie province qui est au nord-ouest de la France.

LEARNING FROM PHOTOS

1. Ask these questions about the top photo: *C'est Jean-Claude? Où est-il? Qu'est-ce qu'il écrit? Il a combien de feuilles de papier? D'après vous, il écrit une lettre sérieuse ou pas sérieuse? Pourquoi?*
2. Have students describe Jean-Claude in their own words.

DID YOU KNOW?

Have students say a few things they remember about *la Bretagne,* then read the following to them: *La Bretagne se trouve dans le nord-ouest de la France. Cherchez-la sur la carte. L'océan Atlantique est au sud de la Bretagne et la Manche est au nord. Tout le long de la côte bretonne, il y a de très jolis ports de pêche. Le port de Sainte-Marine n'est pas très loin de Quimper.*

L'accord du participe passé

PRESENTATION *(page 12)*

We suggest that you not spend a great deal of time explaining this structure point now. As students write more and more French, it will be necessary to remind them frequently to make the past participle agree with the preceding direct object.

Exercices

PRESENTATION *(page 12)*

Since participle agreement is a written concern, have students write the exercises first and then read their responses. As the student says the past participle, write it on the board. Underline the ending when applicable.

ANSWERS

Exercice A

1. Oui, j'ai écrit une lettre. (Non, je n'ai pas écrit de...)
2. Oui, je l'ai écrite hier. (Non, je ne l'ai pas écrite hier.)
3. Oui, je l'ai lue. (Non, je ne l'ai pas lue.)
4. Oui, j'ai lu la lettre que j'ai écrite. (Non, je n'ai pas lu la lettre que j'ai écrite.)
5. Oui, j'ai mis la lettre dans une enveloppe. (Non, je n'ai pas mis la lettre...)
6. Oui, je l'ai mise dans une grande enveloppe. (Non, je ne l'ai pas mise...)
7. Oui, j'ai écrit l'adresse sur l'enveloppe. (Non, je n'ai pas écrit l'adresse...)
8. Oui, je l'ai écrite clairement. (Non, je ne l'ai pas écrite...)
9. Oui, j'ai envoyé la lettre. (Non, je n'ai pas envoyé la lettre.)
10. Oui, je l'ai envoyée du bureau de poste. (Non, je ne l'ai pas envoyée du bureau de poste.)

Exercice B

1. —	6. —	11. e
2. —	7. e	12. e
3. es	8. —	13. es
4. es	9. —	14. es
5. es	10. —	

L'accord du participe passé

Referring to People and Things Already Mentioned

1. In French, the past participles of verbs conjugated with *avoir* must agree in number (singular or plural) and gender (masculine or feminine) with the direct object of the verb when the direct object *comes before* the participle. Study the following sentences.

NO AGREEMENT	AGREEMENT
J'ai écrit *une lettre*.	Je l'ai écrite ce matin.
	Voici la lettre *que* j'ai écrite ce matin.
Tu as reçu *les lettres*?	Tu *les* as reçues?
	Ce sont les lettres *que* tu as reçues?
Elle a acheté *les timbres*.	Elle *les* a achetés hier.
	Voilà les timbres *qu'*elle a achetés hier.

2. Note that the problem of agreement of the past participle is more a written concern than an oral one. The agreement is only heard with the feminine forms of past participles that end in a consonant: écrit, écrite.

Exercices

A **La lettre que j'ai écrite.** Répondez.

1. Tu as écrit une lettre?
2. Tu l'as écrite hier?
3. Tu l'as lue?
4. Tu as lu la lettre que tu as écrite?
5. Tu as mis la lettre dans une enveloppe?
6. Tu l'as mise dans une grande enveloppe?
7. Tu as écrit l'adresse sur l'enveloppe?
8. Tu l'as écrite clairement?
9. Tu as envoyé la lettre?
10. Tu l'as envoyée du bureau de poste?

B **Les photos que j'ai prises.** Complétez.

J'ai pris___ des photos. J'ai envoyé___ les photos que j'ai pris___ à mon amie
Catherine. Je les ai envoyé___ la semaine dernière. Je les ai mis___ dans une
grande enveloppe. J'ai écrit___ l'adresse de Catherine sur l'enveloppe. Je sais
que je l'ai écrit___ clairement. Mais, zut! Je ne sais pas si j'ai mis___ le code
postal. Je crois que je l'ai mis___ mais je n'en suis pas sûr. Je vais téléphoner à
Catherine pour savoir.

MARC: Catherine, tu as reçu___ l'enveloppe que je t'ai envoyé___ ?
CATHÉRINE: Oui, je l'ai reçu___. Et je crois que les photos que tu as pris___ sont
extra. Je les ai regardé___ deux fois.

12   CHAPITRE 1

Les changements d'orthographe avec les verbes comme *envoyer*, *employer* et *payer*

Telling What You or Others Send, Use, and Pay

1. Note the spelling of the verbs *envoyer*, "to send," *employer*, "to use," and *payer*, "to pay." The *y* changes to *i* in all forms but the infinitive, *nous*, and *vous*.

ENVOYER	EMPLOYER	PAYER
j'envoie	j'emploie	je paie
tu envoies	tu emploies	tu paies
il/elle/on envoie	il/elle/on emploie	il/elle/on paie
nous envoyons	nous employons	nous payons
vous envoyez	vous employez	vous payez
ils/elles envoient	ils/elles emploient	ils/elles paient

2. Verbs with infinitives ending in *-ayer* can be spelled with either a *y* or an *i* in all forms except *nous*, *vous*, and the infinitive.

3. The past participles of these verbs are regular: *envoyé*, *employé*, *payé*.

Exercices

A **Qu'est-ce que tu envoies?** Complétez au présent avec «envoyer».

1. J' ___ une lettre.
2. Tu l' ___ du bureau de poste?
3. Oui, toute ma famille, nous ___ toutes nos lettres du bureau de poste.
4. Vous les ___ de la poste? Pourquoi? Ce n'est pas nécessaire.
5. Nos voisins aussi ___ leurs lettres de la poste.

B **Le courrier.** Répondez.

1. Tu paies combien pour envoyer une carte postale?
2. Tu envoies combien de cartes postales?
3. À qui est-ce que tu les envoies?
4. Tu emploies toujours le code postal?
5. Tu as envoyé une lettre ou un colis récemment?
6. Pour écrire ta lettre tu as employé un stylo ou un crayon?
7. Quand tu as acheté les timbres, tu les as payés combien?

CONVERSATION

PRESENTATION *(page 14)*

A. Tell students that the conversation takes place at *la poste.* Tell them to listen carefully to find out what someone forgot to do.

B. Have students close their books. Play the Conversation Video or have them listen as you read the conversation or play the recorded audio version on Cassette 2A/CD-1.

C. Have them open their books and read along the second time the conversation is read or played. You may wish to repeat it another time and have students repeat after you. (Use *Activité E* in the Student Tape Manual to check oral comprehension.)

D. Allow a few minutes for pairs to practice the conversation several times. Then call on volunteers to present it to the class as a skit.

Note In the CD-ROM version, students can play the role of either one of the characters and record the conversation.

Exercice

PRESENTATION *(page 14)*

A. Go over the comprehension exercise, calling on different

CONVERSATION

Scènes de la vie   *Au bureau de poste*

> GUILLAUME: C'est combien, une carte postale pour les États-Unis?
> L'EMPLOYÉE: Quatre francs soixante.
> GUILLAUME: Je voudrais dix timbres à 4,60 F, s'il vous plaît.
> L'EMPLOYÉE: Ça fait quarante-six francs.
> GUILLAUME: Où est la boîte aux lettres, s'il vous plaît?
> L'EMPLOYÉE: À gauche de l'entrée.
> GUILLAUME: Merci, Madame.
> L'EMPLOYÉE: Vous avez bien mis le code postal?
> GUILLAUME: Ah, zut! J'ai oublié. Merci, Madame, vous êtes très aimable.

A **Dix timbres, s'il vous plaît.**
Répondez d'après la conversation.

1. Où est allé Guillaume?
2. Il parle à qui?
3. C'est combien, une carte postale pour les États-Unis?
4. Guillaume a besoin de combien de timbres?
5. Il les paie combien?
6. Il envoie combien de cartes postales?
7. Où est la boîte aux lettres?
8. Qu'est-ce que Guillaume a oublié?

14   CHAPITRE 1

CRITICAL THINKING ACTIVITY

(Thinking skills: making inferences; drawing conclusions)

Read the following to the class or write it on the board or on a transparency:
Mon Dieu! Il est deux heures de l'après-midi. D'habitude, le facteur distribue le courrier à dix heures du matin, mais il n'est pas encore passé. Quel peut être le problème?

Activités de communication orale

A **Une photo de famille.** Working with a partner, describe one of the people in the picture. Ask your partner to say who the person might be. Reverse roles.

> Élève 1: À ton avis, qui est la personne qui porte un complet gris?
> Élève 2: C'est le grand-père du petit garçon.

B **Tout disparaît.** Make a list with a classmate of things you usually need to write a letter or mail a package (pen, paper, envelopes, etc.). Of course, none of these things can ever be found when you need them. Take turns asking each other where the missing items are.

> Élève 1: Paul, qu'est-ce que tu as fait des enveloppes?
> Élève 2: Je les ai laissées sur mon bureau. Et toi, qu'est-ce que tu as fait de mon stylo?
> Élève 1: Je ne sais pas. Ce n'est pas moi qui l'ai pris!

CHAPITRE 1   **15**

students to answer each question.

B. Do the exercise a second time and have one student answer all the questions.

ANSWERS
Exercice A
1. Guillaume est allé au bureau de poste.
2. Il parle à l'employée.
3. Une carte postale pour les États-Unis est quatre francs soixante.
4. Guillaume a besoin de dix timbres.
5. Il les paie quarante-six francs.
6. Il envoie dix cartes postales.
7. La boîte aux lettres est à gauche de l'entrée du bureau de poste.
8. Guillaume a oublié (de mettre) le code postal.

INFORMAL ASSESSMENT
After going through the exercise, call on volunteers to retell the story of the conversation in their own words.

Activités de communication orale
PRESENTATION *(page 15)*
It is not necessary to do both activities. Select the one you consider most appropriate or have the students choose the activity they would prefer to do.

ANSWERS
Activités A and B
Questions and answers will vary. Follow the models provided.

LECTURE ET CULTURE

READING STRATEGIES
(page 16)

Pre-reading
This reading selection is not typical of most of the reading selections in *À bord* since it explains how to address an envelope and how to write standard salutations and closings for letters in French.

Reading
A. Have the class read along with you or call on a volunteer with good pronunciation to read aloud.

B. As each piece of information is given, write an example of it on the board. For instance:
le nom: Sophie Dubois
l'adresse: 792, rue de Grenelle

Post-reading
After completing the reading, have students tell what salutations and closings they would use for letters to the following people: *leur meilleur(e) ami(e), leur professeur de français, le directeur ou le proviseur du lycée, leur tante.*

Note Students may listen to a recorded version of the *Lecture* on the CD-ROM.

ON VA ÉCRIRE UNE LETTRE

SUR L'ENVELOPPE

Sur l'enveloppe on écrit clairement...

le nom et l'adresse de l'expéditeur ou de l'expéditrice (vous);

le nom du destinataire (c'est la personne à qui vous envoyez la lettre);

l'adresse du destinataire, c'est-à-dire, le numéro et la rue; le code postal d'abord et ensuite le nom de la ville (en France le code postal précède le nom de la ville).

LA LETTRE MÊME[1]

En haut de la page on écrit...

le lieu et la date: *Paris, le 25 septembre 19__.*

Pour saluer on écrit...

Madame / Mademoiselle / Monsieur à quelqu'un qu'on ne connaît pas;

(Ma) chère Michèle / (Mon) cher Maurice à quelqu'un qu'on connaît.

Pour commencer la lettre on peut écrire...

J'ai bien reçu votre (ta) lettre.
En réponse à votre lettre...

Pour finir on écrit...

Veuillez agréer[2], Madame, (Mademoiselle, Monsieur), l'expression de mes sentiments distingués à quelqu'un qu'on ne connaît pas;

Meilleurs souvenirs[3] à quelqu'un qu'on connaît mais pas très bien;

Amitiés (Grosses bises[4], Je t'embrasse[5]) à quelqu'un qu'on connaît bien.

[1] même *itself*
[2] Veuillez agréer *Sincerely yours*
[3] Meilleurs souvenirs *Yours*
[4] Grosses bises *Love and kisses*
[5] Je t'embrasse *Love*

Nice, le 25 septembre

Chère Camille,

J'ai bien reçu ta lettre...

Grosses bises

Benoît

JACQUES BANCEL
3 RUE DE LA PAIX
37000 TOURS

Galerie Mirabeau
43 rue Montpensier
86000 Poitiers

Tours, le 11 octobre
Monsieur,

En réponse a votre lettre du 20 septembre...

Veuillez agréer, Monsieur, l'expression de mes sentiments distingués.

Jacques Bancel
Jacques Bancel

16   CHAPITRE 1

COOPERATIVE LEARNING

Have individuals write French salutations and closings on separate cards (or pieces of paper). Each student should make about three cards. Students form groups of four and mix their cards together in a pile. They take turns drawing one card at a time. The person who draws the card decides whether the phrase on the card is for a letter to *quelqu'un* que je connais très bien or *quelqu'un que je ne connais pas très bien.*

Étude de mots

A Noms et verbes. Choisissez le nom qui correspond au verbe.

1. envelopper
2. saluer
3. connaître
4. répondre
5. expédier

a. un expéditeur
b. une réponse
c. une enveloppe
d. une connaissance
e. une salutation

B Définitions. Choisissez la bonne réponse.

1. le contraire de «en bas de»
2. la personne qui reçoit la lettre
3. la personne qui envoie la lettre
4. le numéro, la rue et la ville
5. dire «bonjour»
6. terminer
7. le contraire de «finir»
8. accepter

a. commencer
b. le / la destinataire
c. agréer
d. saluer
e. finir
f. en haut de
g. l'expéditeur, l'expéditrice
h. l'adresse

Compréhension

C Correspondance à la française.

1. Écrivez votre adresse sur une enveloppe comme on l'écrit en France.
2. Écrivez une salutation à un(e) ami(e).
3. Écrivez la dernière phrase d'une lettre à un(e) ami(e).
4. Écrivez la première phrase d'une lettre à quelqu'un que vous ne connaissez pas bien.
5. Écrivez la dernière phrase d'une lettre à quelqu'un que vous ne connaissez pas bien.

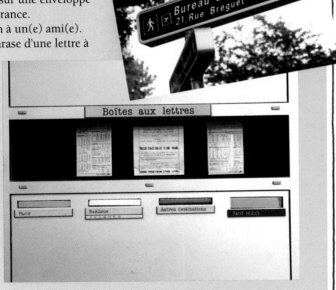

Étude de mots

PRESENTATION *(page 17)*

It is suggested that you go over the exercises quickly in class with books open.

ANSWERS

Exercice A

1. c
2. e
3. d
4. b
5. a

Exercice B

1. f   5. d
2. b   6. e
3. g   7. a
4. h   8. c

Compréhension

PRESENTATION *(page 17)*

You may wish to have students write the information asked for in this exercise at home first and then share it with the class the following day.

ANSWERS

Exercice C

Answers will vary.

RECYCLING

Ask students to look at the informal letter on page 16 and say where Benoît is from. Have students write or say as much as they can about Nice. Remind them that Nice is on the Mediterranean. They can review all of the vocabulary they learned in *Bienvenue* about the beach and summer activities.

GEOGRAPHY CONNECTION

Ask students to look at the business letter on page 16 and say where M. Bancel is from. Have students locate Tours on the map of France on page 435 or use the France Map Transparency. Tell them that very soon they will learn about the fabulous *châteaux* of the Loire Valley. Many people who tour the *château* country begin their trip in Tours.

LEARNING FROM PHOTOS

Have students read the words under each mail slot in the photo of the *boîtes aux lettres* at the bottom of this page. Explain in French what each slot is for.

INDEPENDENT PRACTICE

Assign any of the following:
1. *Étude de mots* and *Compréhension* exercises, page 17
2. Workbook, *Un Peu Plus*, pages 7–11
3. CD-ROM, Disc 1, pages 16–17

Découverte culturelle

PRESENTATION *(pages 18–19)*

A. You may wish to have students read this selection, or parts of it, aloud in class and answer questions about it afterwards.

B. You may, however, just have students read the selection silently and give a brief summary of it.

Note Students may listen to a recorded version of the *Découverte culturelle* on the CD-ROM.

DÉCOUVERTE CULTURELLE

LA POSTE

Comme aux États-Unis, en France la Poste est une administration publique qui assure le service de distribution du courrier. Du bureau de poste on peut envoyer des lettres, des colis et des télégrammes.

En France, la Poste se charge aussi d'un grand nombre d'opérations bancaires. Le Compte-Chèques Postal[1], par exemple, est très populaire. Beaucoup de Français paient leurs achats avec des chèques postaux et pas avec des chèques bancaires. Les chèques postaux ne coûtent presque rien et ils offrent un autre avantage. On reçoit un relevé de compte après chaque chèque. On n'est pas obligé d'attendre le relevé mensuel[2] de la banque pour vérifier le solde[3]. On peut vérifier le solde après chaque chèque. On a toujours un solde courant.

LE CODE POSTAL

La France est divisée en 95 départements. Chaque département a un numéro. Le numéro du département fait partie du code postal et se trouve aussi sur la plaque d'immatriculation de la voiture.

Aux États-Unis on écrit toujours sur une enveloppe l'état où habite le destinataire. En France on n'a pas besoin de mettre le nom du département, on écrit seulement le nom de la ville, précédé du code postal.

Le code postal de Paris commence par 75 suivi du numéro de l'arrondissement. Le code postal d'une personne qui habite dans le septième est 75007. Quel est le code postal d'une personne qui habite dans le seizième?

[1] le Compte-Chèques Postal *French postal checking account*
[2] mensuel *monthly*
[3] le solde *the balance*

18 CHAPITRE 1

CRITICAL THINKING ACTIVITY

(Thinking skills: making inferences; drawing conclusions)

Read the following to the class or write it on the board or on a transparency:

De nos jours, les gens des pays industrialisés écrivent de moins en moins de lettres. Pourquoi? Donnez plusieurs raisons.

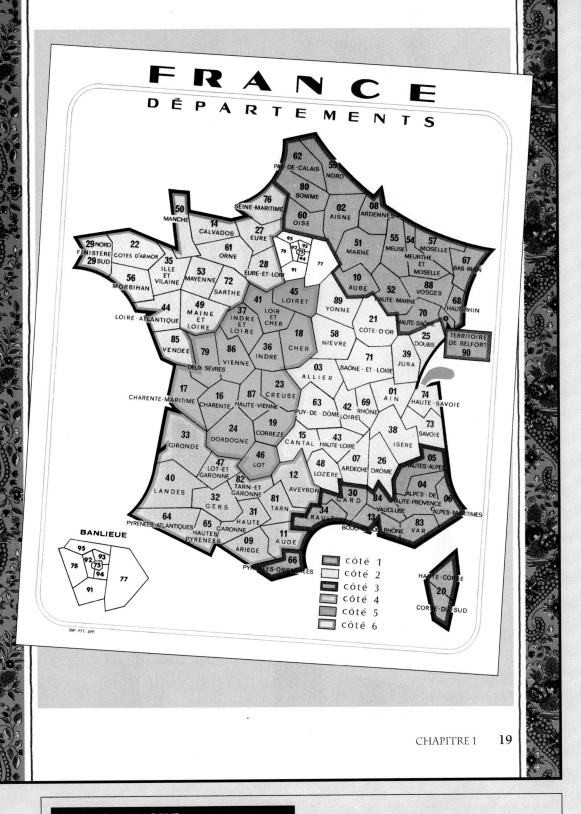

FRANCE
DÉPARTEMENTS

62 PAS-DE-CALAIS
59 NORD
80 SOMME
76 SEINE-MARITIME
50 MANCHE
60 OISE
02 AISNE
08 ARDENNES
14 CALVADOS
27 EURE
95
93
92
75
94
51 MARNE
55 MEUSE
54 MEURTHE ET MOSELLE
57 MOSELLE
67 BAS-RHIN
29 NORD FINISTERE
29 SUD
22 COTES D'ARMOR
35 ILLE ET VILAINE
61 ORNE
28 EURE-ET-LOIR
91
77
56 MORBIHAN
53 MAYENNE
72 SARTHE
45 LOIRET
10 AUBE
52 HAUTE-MARNE
88 VOSGES
68 HAUT-RHIN
44 LOIRE-ATLANTIQUE
49 MAINE ET LOIRE
41 LOIR-ET-CHER
89 YONNE
70 HAUTE-SAÔNE
85 VENDEE
37 INDRE-ET-LOIRE
18 CHER
58 NIEVRE
21 CÔTE-D'OR
25 DOUBS
TERRITOIRE DE BELFORT 90
79 DEUX-SEVRES
86 VIENNE
36 INDRE
03 ALLIER
71 SAÔNE-ET-LOIRE
39 JURA
17 CHARENTE-MARITIME
16 CHARENTE
87 HAUTE-VIENNE
23 CREUSE
63 PUY-DE-DÔME
42 LOIRE
69 RHÔNE
01 AIN
74 HAUTE-SAVOIE
33 GIRONDE
24 DORDOGNE
19 CORREZE
15 CANTAL
43 HAUTE-LOIRE
38 ISERE
73 SAVOIE
47 LOT-ET-GARONNE
46 LOT
48 LOZERE
07 ARDECHE
26 DRÔME
05 HAUTES-ALPES
40 LANDES
82 TARN-ET-GARONNE
12 AVEYRON
30 GARD
84 VAUCLUSE
04 ALPES-DE-HAUTE-PROVENCE
06 ALPES-MARITIMES
32 GERS
81 TARN
34 HERAULT
13 BOUCHES-DU-RHÔNE
83 VAR
64 PYRENEES-ATLANTIQUES
65 HAUTES-PYRENEES
31 HAUTE-GARONNE
11 AUDE
09 ARIEGE
66 PYRENEES-ORIENTALES

BANLIEUE
95
93
92
75
94
78
91
77

côté 1
côté 2
côté 3
côté 4
côté 5
côté 6

2B HAUTE-CORSE
20
2A CORSE-DU-SUD

IMP. PTT. DPP.

La France est divisée en 95 départements. Les États-Unis sont divisés en 50 états. Chaque état est divisé en comtés.

1. Vous habitez dans quel état?
2. Votre état est divisé en combien de comtés?
3. Quel est votre code postal?
4. De quelle(s) couleur(s) sont les plaques d'immatriculation de votre état?
5. Sur la plaque d'immatriculation, il y a un numéro?
6. Il y a aussi des lettres?
7. Est-ce qu'il y a quelque chose sur la plaque qui indique votre comté? Par exemple, est-ce que les numéros indiquent le comté?

THE FRANCOPHONE WORLD

France is divided into 95 administrative metropolitan *départements* and has nine overseas possessions, called either *départements d'outre-mer* (D.O.M.) or *territoires d'outre-mer* (T.O.M.). *La Martinique, la Guadeloupe, la Réunion* and *la Guyane* are *départements* and *la Nouvelle-Calédonie, la Polynésie française, Wallis et Futuna, Mayotte,* and *Saint-Pierre-et-Miquelon* are *territoires*. These possessions are considered part of France. Their citizens vote in French presidential elections and send representatives to both houses of the French parliament.

(For photos of Martinique and Guadeloupe, see *À bord*, Chapter 7, page 162. For additional photos and information about other French-speaking countries, see *Le Monde francophone* in *Bienvenue*, pages 110–113, 220–223, 326–329, and 434–437.)

DID YOU KNOW?

The *départements* are numbered from 1 to 95 in accordance with the alphabetical order of their names. Thus, the *département* bearing the number 01 is Ain, number 02 is Aisne, 03 is Allier, and so on. Paris is in the *département* of Seine-et-Marne, whose number is 75.

RÉALITÉS

Bell Ringer Review

Write the following on the board or use BRR Blackline Master 1-6: Match each expression in Column A with its opposite in Column B. Then choose one expression from each column and use it in a sentence about yourself.

A	B
quelque chose	jamais
toujours	personne
quelqu'un	rien
souvent	jamais

OPTIONAL MATERIAL

PRESENTATION (pages 20–21)

The purpose of this section is to allow students to enjoy the photographs that bring to life the content of the chapter. Students may read the information that accompanies each photo aloud or silently.

Note In the CD-ROM version, students can listen to the recorded captions and discover a hidden video behind one of the photos.

Voici un bureau de poste à Paris **1**. Qu'est-ce qu'il y a dans le mur à gauche de l'entrée de la poste? À quelle heure est-ce que cet homme met sa lettre à la poste?

Voici Madame Déveraux **2**. Elle est facteur. Est-ce qu'elle distribue le courrier maintenant?

Voici un chèque postal **3**. Il y a une différence entre ce chèque postal et les chèques de tes parents? Il y a des chèques postaux aux États-Unis?

Voici la Vidéoposte **4**. Cet ordinateur permet aux clients d'effectuer toutes sortes d'opérations postales et bancaires. Est-ce qu'on a des Vidéopostes dans les bureaux de poste aux États-Unis?

Voici un grand bureau de poste à Lyon **5**. Il est très beau, n'est-ce pas? Est-ce qu'il y a beaucoup de monde? Ce bureau de poste ressemble aux bureaux de poste américains?

PAIRED ACTIVITY

Have students work in pairs to create questions for each photo that appears in the *Réalités* section. Then have several pairs of students read their questions aloud. They can call on other students to respond.

ADDITIONAL PRACTICE

Assign any of the following:
1. Student Tape Manual, Teacher's Edition, *Deuxième Partie*, pages 8–11
2. Situation Cards, Chapter 1

COOPERATIVE LEARNING

Display Communication Transparency C-1. Have students work in groups to make up as many questions as they can about the illustration. Have groups take turns asking and answering the questions.

RECYCLING

The *Activités de communication orale* and *écrite* allow students to use the vocabulary and grammar from this chapter in open-ended situations. They also provide an opportunity to recycle vocabulary and structures from *Bienvenue*.

INFORMAL ASSESSMENT

Oral Activities A, B, and C may be used to evaluate the speaking skill informally. You may assign a grade based on students' ability to communicate in French. Following are some grading suggestions:

5 (A): Complete message conveyed, precise structural and vocabulary control.

4-3 (B–C): Complete message conveyed, some structural or vocabulary control errors.

2-1 (D): Message partially conveyed, frequent errors.

0 (F): No message conveyed.

Activités de communication orale

PRESENTATION (page 22)

Activité B

In the CD-ROM version of this activity, students can interact with an on-screen native speaker.

ANSWERS

Activités A, B, and C
Answers will vary.

Activité de communication écrite

ANSWERS

Activité A
Answers will vary.

Activités de communication orale

A **Des cartes postales.** You're in the post office in a French city. You want to send some postcards to friends in France. Find out from the post office clerk (your partner) how much it costs to mail a postcard, then tell him or her how many stamps you want. Find out if you have to put the zip code and the name of the *département* on the card.

B **Je voudrais envoyer des lettres.** Alain Lacroix, un élève qui passe l'année dans votre école, veut envoyer des lettres en France. Il vous pose des questions parce qu'il ne sait pas comment faire. Répondez à ses questions.

1. Où est-ce qu'on peut acheter des timbres?
2. Il y a des distributeurs automatiques dans les bureaux de poste aux États-Unis?
3. Pour envoyer une lettre, il faut aller à la poste?

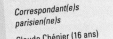

Alain Lacroix

C **Où habite-t-il?** Before choosing a French pen pal from the list on the right, you'd like to find out more about where each of the teenagers lives in Paris. Give a classmate the postal code of each of them. Your partner can then use the map on p. 436 to tell you which *arrondissement* the pen pal lives in and what the nearest Parisian monument is.

> Élève 1: Le code postal de Claude Chénier est 75007.
> Élève 2: Claude habite dans le 7ᵉ arrondissement. Il habite près de la tour Eiffel.

PEN PALS INTERNATIONAL

Correspondant(e)s parisien(ne)s

Claude Chénier (16 ans)
10, rue Saint-Dominique
75007 Paris

Jacques Christian (17 ans)
109, avenue Foch
75016 Paris

Marie-Christine Perrault (14 ans)
23, boulevard de Rochechouart
75009 Paris

Fabienne Édouard (16 ans)
54, rue de Rivioli
75001 Paris

Activité de communication écrite

A **Le concours du nouveau timbre.** The French Postmaster General has asked for suggestions from the public for a new airmail stamp. Using the proper format, write him or her a letter with your idea. Tell who or what you'd like to see featured on the stamp and why. The class then votes on the various suggestions and chooses the best one.

COMMUNITIES

For information on how to find electronic pen pals (keypals) for interested students, refer to the *Bienvenue* Internet Activities Booklet, Chapter 2 or the Glencoe Foreign Language Home Page on the World Wide Web (**http://www.glencoe.com/secondary/fl**)

Réintroduction et recombinaison

A **Au bureau de poste.** Complétez avec «y» ou «en».

1. Robert va au bureau de poste? Oui, il ___ va.
2. Quand il ___ arrive, le bureau est fermé?
3. Oui, il attend devant la porte. Il ___ attend cinq minutes.
4. Quand il entre dans la poste, il va au guichet. Il ___ va tout de suite. Il n'y a personne. Il n'y a pas de queue.
5. Il veut des timbres? Oui, il ___ veut.
6. Il a des cartes postales à envoyer? Oui, il ___ a.
7. Il ___ a combien?
8. Il ___ a dix.
9. Alors, il va acheter combien de timbres? Il va ___ acheter dix.

B **Une lettre.** Récrivez au présent.

1. J'ai écrit une lettre à un ami.
2. Je suis allé(e) au bureau de poste.
3. J'ai acheté des timbres.
4. J'ai mis les timbres sur l'enveloppe.
5. J'ai envoyé la lettre.
6. Je l'ai mise dans la boîte aux lettres.
7. Mon ami a reçu la lettre.
8. Il a ouvert la lettre.
9. Il a sorti la lettre de l'enveloppe.
10. Il l'a lue.

C **Ma journée.** Répondez en utilisant «qui» ou «que».

1. Tous les matins c'est mon père ___ se lève le premier à six heures.
2. Ma mère, ___ aime rester un peu au lit, se lève à six heures et demie.
3. À sept heures je prends mon petit déjeuner ___ je prépare moi-même.
4. Je donne à manger à notre chat, Minou, ___ j'aime beaucoup et ___ a toujours très faim le matin.
5. Pour aller à l'école je prends le bus ___ passe juste devant la maison.
6. Dans le bus je révise les leçons ___ j'ai apprises le soir d'avant.
7. Quand j'arrive au lycée, je vais à mon cours de maths ___ est très difficile.

Vocabulaire

NOMS
la poste
le bureau de poste
le guichet
l'employé(e) des postes
le colis
le paquet
le contenu
la balance
le poids
la valeur

le timbre
le distributeur automatique
la carte postale
l'aérogramme (m.)
la lettre
l'enveloppe (f.)
le nom
l'expéditeur (m.)
l'expéditrice (f.)
le / la destinataire

l'adresse (f.)
la rue
le numéro
la ville
le code postal
la boîte aux lettres
le courrier
le facteur

VERBES
employer
payer

envoyer
peser
assurer
distribuer

AUTRES MOTS ET EXPRESSIONS
mettre une lettre à la poste
par avion
selon

Réintroduction et recombinaison

PRESENTATION (*page 23*)

These exercises review material learned in *Bienvenue*, recombining it with vocabulary and structures from this chapter. Exercise C reviews material learned in this chapter.

ANSWERS

Exercice A

1. y	4. y	7. en
2. y	5. en	8. en
3. y	6. en	9. en

Exercice B

1. J'écris...	6. Je la mets...
2. Je vais...	7. ... reçoit...
3. J'achète...	8. Il ouvre...
4. Je mets...	9. Il sort...
5. J'envoie...	10. Il la lit.

Exercice C

1. qui	4. que,	6. que
2. qui	qui	7. qui
3. que	5. qui	

ASSESSMENT RESOURCES

1. Chapter Quizzes
2. Testing Program
3. Situation Cards
4. Communication Transparency C-1
5. Computer Software: Practice/Test Generator

VIDEO PROGRAM

INTRODUCTION À LA VIDÉO (00:43)

INTRODUCTION (06:51)

À LA POSTE (07:31)

STUDENT PORTFOLIO

You may wish to have students keep a notebook containing their best written work from the textbook, the Workbook, and the Communication Activities Masters. (See the Teacher's Manual for additional information regarding the Student Portfolio topic.)

Note Students may create and save both oral and written work using the Electronic Portfolio feature on the CD-ROM.

INDEPENDENT PRACTICE

Assign any of the following:
1. Exercises and activities, pages 22–23
2. Communication Activities Masters, pages 1–7
3. CD-ROM, Disc 1, pages 22–23

CHAPTER OVERVIEW

In this chapter students will learn to talk about the daily activities of a typical suburban family in France. They will learn the vocabulary needed to discuss household appliances and typical home-oriented family activities. They will also learn the verb *s'asseoir*, reciprocal verbs, and the *passé composé* of reflexive verbs.

The cultural focus of the chapter is on life in the suburbs of Paris.

CHAPTER OBJECTIVES

By the end of this chapter, students will know:

1. vocabulary associated with a typical day in the life of suburban families, including morning and evening routines during the week
2. vocabulary associated with the breakfast, lunch, and dinner habits of such families
3. the present indicative forms and the past participle of the verb *s'asseoir*
4. the use of reflexive pronouns in reciprocal constructions
5. the formation of the *passé composé* of reflexive verbs
6. reciprocal constructions in the *passé composé*
7. the use of various negative constructions in the *passé composé*, including *ne... pas, ne... jamais, ne... plus, ne... rien, ne... personne,* and *ne... que*
8. the placement of object pronouns in negative constructions in the *passé composé*

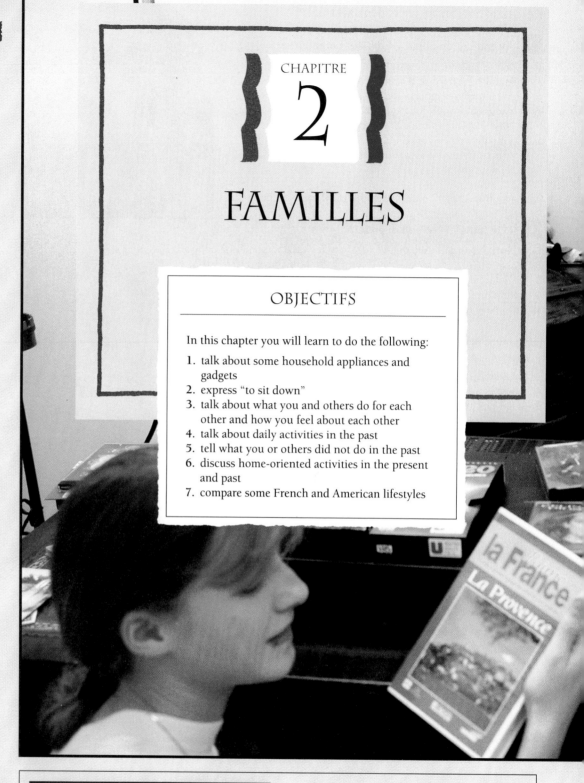

CHAPITRE

2

FAMILLES

OBJECTIFS

In this chapter you will learn to do the following:

1. talk about some household appliances and gadgets
2. express "to sit down"
3. talk about what you and others do for each other and how you feel about each other
4. talk about daily activities in the past
5. tell what you or others did not do in the past
6. discuss home-oriented activities in the present and past
7. compare some French and American lifestyles

CHAPTER PROJECTS

(optional)

1. Have students prepare a menu for a typical American breakfast, lunch, and dinner. As they proceed through the chapter, have them observe some differences between American and French eating habits.
2. With more sophisticated groups, you may wish to have students prepare a report on demographic trends in the United States.

Which groups tend to live in the suburbs? Do Americans of the middle class usually live in our large cities? After completing the chapter, have students compare American demographics with what they have learned about France.

3. Make a *pot-au-feu* with the students using the recipe on page 43 or, if your class is in the morning, prepare a typical French breakfast with them.

25

CHAPTER 2 RESOURCES

1. Workbook
2. Student Tape Manual
3. Audio Cassette 2B/CD-1
4. Bell Ringer Review Blackline Masters
5. Vocabulary Transparencies
6. Communication Transparency C-2
7. Communication Activities Masters
8. Situation Cards
9. Conversation Video
10. Videocassette/Videodisc, Unit 1
11. Video Activities Booklet, Unit 1
12. Lesson Plans
13. Computer Software: Practice/Test Generator
14. Chapter Quizzes
15. Testing Program
16. Internet Activities Booklet
17. CD-ROM Interactive Textbook

Pacing

This chapter will require eight to ten class sessions. Pacing will depend on the length of the class, the age of the students, and student aptitude.

For more information on planning your class, see the Lesson Plans, which offer guidelines for 45- and 55-minute classes and **Block Scheduling**.

Exercices vs. *Activités*

The exercises and activities are color-coded. Exercises, which provide guided practice to prepare students for independent communication, are coded in blue. Communicative activities, which give students the opportunities for creative, open-ended expression, are coded in red.

INTERNET ACTIVITIES

(optional)

These activities, student worksheets, and related teacher information are in the *À bord* Internet Activities Booklet and on the Glencoe Foreign Language Home Page at: http://www.glencoe.com/secondary/fl

LEARNING FROM PHOTOS

After teaching the vocabulary in this chapter, have students say as much about this French family as they can.

Bell Ringer Review

Write the following on the board or use BRR Blackline Master 2-1: Write three sentences telling about things you would like to do now but can't because of what you must do in class. For example: *Je voudrais regarder la télé, mais je dois écouter le prof.*

PRESENTATION (pages 26–27)

A. Have students close their books. Present the new words and phrases by using Vocabulary Transparencies 2.1 (A & B) or props such as a table, a plate, silverware, a *baguette*, a TV remote, etc. You may also wish to use magazine photos of a kitchen and living room.

B. Present one word or phrase and have students repeat after you or Cassette 2B/CD-1. Intersperse the presentation with simple questions.

C. After you have gone over the vocabulary orally with books closed, have students open

VOCABULAIRE

MOTS 1

CHEZ LES DELORME

la cuisine
un robinet
un lave-vaisselle
une machine à laver
un évier

mettre le couvert

Avant le dîner Pierre a mis le couvert.

un pot-au-feu

une tartine

débarrasser la table

Après le dîner M. Delorme a débarrassé la table.

un repas

La famille s'est assise.
La famille s'est mise à table.
Au petit déjeuner les Delorme ont mangé des tartines.
Au dîner ils ont mangé un pot-au-feu.

faire la vaisselle

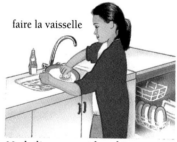

Nathalie a ouvert le robinet.
Elle a rincé la vaisselle dans l'évier.
Elle a mis la vaisselle dans le lave-vaisselle.

26   CHAPITRE 2

un téléphone sans fil

une cassette

un répondeur automatique

un magnétophone

une chaîne stéréo

M. Delorme a mis (allumé) la télé.

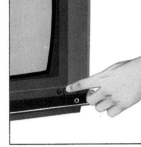
Il a éteint la télé.

un magnétoscope
une vidéocassette

Nathalie est sortie ce soir. Elle n'a pas regardé le film à la télé. Elle l'a enregistré.

une télécommande = un zappeur

la salle de séjour

une chaîne

un poste de télévision = un téléviseur

Les Delorme ont seulement un téléviseur. Ils n'ont qu'un poste de télévision.

M. Delorme a changé de chaîne avec le zappeur. Il a regardé son émission préférée.

CHAPITRE 2   **27**

---

their books and read the new words and sentences.

D. Ask students to give the opposite:
rester à la maison
éteindre la télé
allumer la télé
débarrasser la table

Note You may wish to tell students that the verb *débarrasser* is frequently used without *la table*. For example: *Il a débarrassé. Débarrasse!*

Vocabulary Expansion

You may wish to give students the following additional vocabulary so that they may talk about a typical American breakfast. It is important that students learn the vocabulary necessary to discuss American customs because this is exactly what people in foreign countries are likely to ask about. They are curious about our customs.

du jus d'orange
du lait (un verre de lait)
du chocolat
des céréales
des œufs sur le plat (fried)
des œufs pochés (poached)
des œufs brouillés (scrambled)
des œufs à la coque
    (soft-boiled)
du pain grillé
de la marmelade

PAIRED ACTIVITIES

1. Have students work in pairs. One student writes down five items typically found in a kitchen. The second student lists five items typically found in a living room. They exchange papers. Each student then writes a sentence using the items on his/her sheet of paper. They then read their sentences to each other and decide if they are correct.

2. Have students work in pairs. They each make a list of all the appliances, household items, and gadgets taught in *Mots 1*. They take turns saying whether they have a given item on their list and asking if their partner has it. If possible, they should say how they use each item.

Exercices

PRESENTATION (pages 28–29)

Exercice A

Exercise A can be done with books closed, open, or once each way.

Exercice B

Exercise B can be done with books closed, open, or once each way.

Extension of Exercice B

After going over Exercise B, you may wish to call on two students. Each student will do one half of the exercise. Then call on a third student to retell the story in his/her own words.

ANSWERS

Exercice A

1. C'est un lave-vaisselle.
2. C'est un robinet.
3. C'est un téléphone sans fil.
4. C'est un magnétoscope.
5. C'est un répondeur automatique.
6. C'est une machine à laver.
7. C'est une chaîne stéréo.

Exercice B

1. Oui, la famille Delorme est à la maison.
2. Oui, Pierre a mis le couvert.
3. Oui, la famille s'est mise à table.
4. Oui, Mme Delorme a servi le repas.
5. Oui, elle a servi un pot-au-feu.
6. Oui, après le dîner M. Delorme a débarrassé la table.
7. Oui, Nathalie a rincé la vaisselle.
8. Oui, elle a mis la vaisselle dans le lave-vaisselle.
9. Oui, Nathalie est sortie. Oui, elle a enregistré le film à la télé.
10. Oui, les Delorme n'ont qu'un poste de télévision.
11. Oui, la famille s'est assise dans la salle de séjour.
12. Oui, M. Delorme a mis la télé.
13. Oui, il a regardé son émission préférée.
14. Oui, ensuite il a éteint la télévision.

Exercices

A Qu'est-ce que c'est? Identifiez.

1. C'est un évier ou un lave-vaisselle?
2. C'est un robinet ou une cuisine?
3. C'est un téléviseur ou un téléphone sans fil?
4. C'est un magnétoscope ou un magnétophone?
5. C'est un répondeur automatique ou un distributeur automatique?
6. C'est une machine à laver ou un lave-vaisselle?
7. C'est une télécommande ou une chaîne stéréo?

B À la maison. Répondez par «oui».

1. La famille Delorme est à la maison?
2. Pierre a mis le couvert?
3. La famille s'est mise à table?
4. Mme Delorme a servi le repas?
5. Elle a servi un pot-au-feu?
6. Après le dîner M. Delorme a débarrassé la table?
7. Nathalie a rincé la vaisselle?
8. Elle a mis la vaisselle dans le lave-vaisselle?
9. Nathalie est sortie? Elle a enregistré le film à la télé?
10. Les Delorme n'ont qu'un poste de télévision?
11. La famille s'est assise dans la salle de séjour?
12. M. Delorme a mis la télé? `
13. Il a regardé son émission préférée?
14. Ensuite il a éteint la télévision?

LEARNING FROM PHOTOS

Have students find the following items on the table in the top photo on page 29. The starred words will be new to them. Allow volunteers to guess at these words.

des tomates	un artichaut*
des carottes	des radis*
des assiettes	un poivron rouge*
des serviettes	du café

Now say: *Regardez la photo et dites ce que chaque personne fait.*

C Quel est le mot? Complétez.

1. Mme Delorme est ___ de M. Delorme et M. Delorme est ___ de Mme Delorme.
2. On prépare le repas dans ___. Au petit déjeuner on mange ___.
3. Avant le dîner on ___ le couvert.
4. Et après le dîner on ___ la table.
5. Après le dîner il faut faire ___.
6. On rince les assiettes dans ___ et ensuite on les met dans ___.
7. Je ne veux pas répondre au téléphone. Alors je mets ___ et j'écoute les messages plus tard.
8. Je ne peux pas regarder mon émission préférée ce soir. Alors je vais l' ___.
9. Je change de chaîne avec ___.
10. Les cassettes sont pour ___ et les vidéocassettes sont pour ___.

D Non, non. Ce n'est pas ça. Choisissez le contraire.

1. Pierre s'est assis.
2. François a débarrassé la table.
3. Maman a allumé la télé.
4. Carole a ouvert le robinet.

a. Elle a éteint la télé.
b. Il s'est levé.
c. Elle l'a fermé.
d. Il a mis le couvert.

PRESENTATION *(page 29)*

Exercices C and D

It is suggested that you go over each exercise once in class before assigning it for homework.

ANSWERS

Exercice C

1. la femme, le mari
2. la cuisine, des tartines
3. met
4. débarrasse
5. la vaisselle
6. l'évier, le lave-vaisselle
7. le répondeur automatique
8. enregistrer
9. le zappeur (la télécommande)
10. le magnétophone, le magnétoscope

Exercice D

1. b
2. d
3. a
4. c

INDEPENDENT PRACTICE

Assign any of the following:
1. Exercises, pages 28–29
2. Workbook, *Mots 1: A–D*, pages 13–14
3. Communication Activities Masters, *Mots 1: A–B*, pages 8–9
4. CD-ROM, Disc 1, pages 26–29

VOCABULAIRE

MOTS 2

Vocabulary Teaching Resources

1. Vocabulary Transparencies 2.2 (A & B)
2. Audio Cassette 2B/CD-1
3. Student Tape Manual Teacher's Edition, *Mots 2: D–F*, pages 14–16
4. Workbook, *Mots 2: E–H*, pages 14–15
5. Communication Activities Masters, *Mots 2: C–D*, pages 10–12
6. Computer Software, *Vocabulaire*
7. Chapter Quizzes, *Mots 2: Quiz 2*, page 7
8. CD-ROM, Disc 1, *Mots 2: pages 30–33*

PRESENTATION *(pages 30–31)*

A. Have students repeat each word after you or Cassette 2B/CD-1. Use Vocabulary Transparencies 2.2 (A & B).

B. Break the sentences into logical segments and have students repeat after you. For example: *La mère de Lisette/travaille/dans un bureau.*

C. Intersperse the presentation with simple *oui/non* questions, followed by either/or choices, and then interrogative-word questions. For example: *Le père de Lisette travaille dans une usine? Il travaille dans une usine ou dans un magasin? Où est-ce que son père travaille?*

Note A colloquial way to ask the last question above is: *Il travaille où, son père?* This type of construction is used by French people of all ages and educational levels. It is recommended that students hear this type of wording from time to time. It does not, however, appear in this textbook.

VOCABULAIRE

MOTS 2

AU TRAVAIL

une contremaîtresse

une ouvrière

une usine = une fabrique

un ouvrier

un contremaître

Le père de Lisette travaille dans une usine.
Il est contremaître.
Il parle à une ouvrière.
Dans cette usine on fabrique des jouets.

un jouet

un bureau

La mère de Lisette travaille dans un bureau.
Elle se sert souvent du téléphone.
Elle emploie souvent le téléphone.
Un client lui a téléphoné à deux heures.
Elle l'a rappelé à deux heures et demie.

PANTOMIME

___, venez ici, s'il vous plaît. Vous allez être Lisette.
Allez à la cuisine.
Mettez le couvert.
Préparez un pot-au-feu.
Asseyez-vous. Mangez.
Levez-vous. Débarrassez la table.
Ouvrez le robinet.
Rincez la vaisselle.
Mettez la vaisselle dans le lave-vaisselle.
Allez dans la salle de séjour.
Mettez la télé.
Changez de chaîne avec le zappeur.
Éteignez la télé.
Allez dans la salle de bains.
Lavez-vous la figure et les mains.
Brossez-vous les dents.
Allez dans la chambre à coucher.
Couchez-vous.
Merci. Retournez à votre place.

LA MATINÉE DE LISETTE

Lisette s'est réveillée à sept heures.
Elle s'est réveillée de bonne heure.
Elle s'est levée tout de suite.

Elle s'est lavé la figure et les mains.
Elle s'est brossé les dents.

Elle n'a pas pris son temps.
Elle s'est dépêchée.
Elle s'est habillée rapidement.

Elle a couru à l'école.

CHAPITRE 2   **31**

RECYCLING

The meaning of most of the reflexive verbs in *Mots 2* was taught in *Bienvenue*, Chapter 11. What is new here is the use of these verbs in the *passé composé*. Note that only third-person *passé composé* forms are introduced at this point. The remaining forms will be taught in the *Structure* section of this chapter.

D. To vary the presentation of the vocabulary, you may wish to dramatize the meaning of the following: *se réveiller, se lever, se laver, se brosser, se dépêcher, courir*

E. After going over the vocabulary orally, have students open their books and read the new material. If their pronunciation is satisfactory, call on individuals to read immediately. If, however, their pronunciation is weak, you may wish to have them repeat once after you.

INFORMAL ASSESSMENT
(*Mots 2*)

After going over all the vocabulary, let students look at Vocabulary Transparencies 2.2 (A & B) and say anything they can about the illustrations.

ADDITIONAL PRACTICE

Student Tape Manual, Teacher's Edition, *Activités E–F,* pages 15–16

PRESENTATION *(page 32)*

Exercice A

Exercise A can be done with books closed, open, or once each way.

Extension of *Exercice A*

After completing Exercise A, call on a student to retell the story in his/her own words.

Exercices B and C

Exercises B and C can be done with books open.

Extension of *Exercice B*

Upon completion of Exercise B, call on a student to retell the story in his/her own words.

ANSWERS

Exercice A

1. Oui, Lisette s'est réveillée à sept heures du matin.
2. Oui...
3. Oui...
4. Oui...
5. Oui...
6. Oui...
7. Oui...
8. Oui...
9. Oui...
10. Oui...
11. Oui...
12. Oui...
13. Oui...
14. Oui...

Exercice B

1. usine	5. emploie
2. bureau	6. client
3. bureau	7. client
4. sert	8. rappelé

Exercice C

1. Il a débarrassé la table.
2. Il s'est levé.
3. Il s'est réveillé.
4. Il s'est habillé.
5. Il s'est dépêché.

RETEACHING *(Mots 2)*

Have students redo the sentences in Exercise C in the present tense.

32

Exercices

A **Ce matin.** Répondez par «oui».

1. Lisette s'est réveillée à sept heures du matin?
2. Lisette s'est réveillée de bonne heure?
3. Elle s'est levée tout de suite?
4. Elle s'est vite lavée?
5. Elle s'est lavé la figure et les mains?
6. Après le petit déjeuner, elle s'est brossé les dents?
7. Elle s'est habillée rapidement?
8. Elle s'est dépêchée?
9. Elle est partie pour l'école à sept heures et demie?
10. Elle a couru à l'école?
11. Le père de Lisette travaille dans une usine?
12. Son père parle à une ouvrière?
13. On fabrique des jouets dans cette usine?
14. Le père de Lisette est contremaître?

B **La mère de Lisette.** Complétez.

La mère de Lisette ne travaille pas dans une ___. Elle travaille dans un ___. Au ___ elle se ___ souvent du téléphone, c'est-à-dire, elle ___ souvent le téléphone. En ce moment elle parle au téléphone. Elle parle à une amie? Mais non! Elle parle à un ___. Le ___ lui a téléphoné à deux heures et elle l'a ___ à deux heures et demie.

C **Non, au contraire.** Donnez le contraire.

1. Il a mis le couvert.
2. Il s'est couché.
3. Il s'est endormi.
4. Il s'est déshabillé.
5. Il a pris son temps.

32   CHAPITRE 2

Activités de communication orale
Mots 1 et 2

A **Tu as besoin de…** You're visiting a French family. You need to use some gadgets and household appliances but can't remember the words for them in French. Tell your French friend (your partner) what you'd like to do, and he or she tells you what you need.

> Élève 1: Je voudrais laver mes vêtements ce soir.
> Élève 2: Tu as besoin d'une machine à laver.

B **Le dîner.** Work with a classmate. Take turns finding out about each other's dinner last night: who prepared it, who set the table, what was served, who cleaned up after dinner, etc.

> Élève 1: Qui a préparé le dîner?
> Élève 2: C'est mon père qui a préparé le dîner.
> Élève 1: Qu'est-ce qu'il a préparé? (Qui a mis le couvert?…)

Bell Ringer Review

Write the following on the board or use BRR Blackline Master 2-2: Make a list of foods you might eat for dinner.

Activités de communication orale
Mots 1 et 2

PRESENTATION *(page 33)*

These activities allow students to use the chapter vocabulary in open-ended situations. It is not necessary to do all the activities. Select those you consider most appropriate.

ANSWERS

Activités A and B

Answers will vary.

STRUCTURE

Structure Teaching Resources

1. Workbook, *Structure: A–I*, pages 16–19
2. Student Tape Manual, Teacher's Edition, *Structure: A–F*, pages 16–18
3. Audio Cassette 2B/CD-1
4. Communication Activities Masters, *Structure: A–E*, pages 13–16
5. Computer Software, *Structure*
6. Chapter Quizzes, *Structure: Quizzes 3–7*, pages 8–12
7. CD-ROM, Disc 1, pages 34–39

Le verbe s'asseoir

PRESENTATION *(page 34)*

Go over the explanation. Write the verb forms on the board and have students repeat them.

ANSWERS

Exercice A

Answers will vary.

Les actions réciproques au présent

PRESENTATION *(page 34)*

A. Call two boys to the front of the room. Have them look at each other. Point from one to the other and say: *Jean voit Luc. Et Luc voit Jean.* Then wave your hand back and forth between them as you say: *Luc et Jean se voient. Ils se voient.*

B. Now bring an outgoing boy and girl up front. The boy looks at the girl and says: *Je t'aime.* The girl says: *Moi aussi je t'aime.* Then they hold hands and say: *Nous nous aimons.*

Note In the CD-ROM version, this structure point is presented via an interactive electronic comic strip.

Le verbe *s'asseoir*

Expressing "To Sit" or "To Sit Down"

1. The verb *s'asseoir*, "to sit down," is irregular in the present tense. Study the following forms.

S'ASSEOIR	
je m'assieds	nous nous asseyons
tu t'assieds	vous vous asseyez
il/elle/on s'assied	ils/elles s'asseyent

2. The past participle of the verb *s'asseoir* is *assis*.

Voici des élèves assis au premier rang.

Exercice

A **Au cours de français.** Donnez des réponses personnelles.

1. Tu t'assieds dans la classe de français?
2. Tu t'assieds devant qui?
3. Qui s'assied devant toi?
4. Qui s'assied derrière toi?
5. Tes copains et toi, vous vous asseyez près du professeur?
6. Tous les élèves s'asseyent au même rang?
7. Qui s'assied toujours au premier rang?
8. Et qui s'assied toujours au dernier rang?

Les actions réciproques au présent

Telling What You and Others Do For Each Other and How You Feel About Each Other

Reflexive pronouns can also express a reciprocal action or interaction between two or more people. Study the following.

Jean voit son ami. ⎫
Son ami voit Jean. ⎭ Jean et son ami se voient.
                        Ils se voient.

Je t'aime. ⎫
Tu m'aimes. ⎭ Nous nous aimons.

Tu téléphones souvent à Marie. ⎫
Et Marie te téléphone souvent. ⎭ Vous vous téléphonez souvent.

34 CHAPITRE 2

LEARNING FROM PHOTOS

You may wish to ask the students the following questions about the photo: *Où sont les élèves? Quel âge ont-ils, à votre avis? Ils sont à l'école primaire ou au collège? Il y a combien de garçons et combien de filles au premier rang? Que portent-ils?*

Exercice

 A **Les amis.** Faites une seule phrase d'après le modèle.

Tu adores Isabelle. Isabelle t'adore.
Vous vous adorez.

1. Jacques parle à Suzanne. Suzanne parle à Jacques.
2. Jacques aime Suzanne. Suzanne aime Jacques.
3. Je t'aime. Tu m'aimes.
4. Je te vois. Et tu me vois.
5. Marie-France regarde Daniel. Daniel regarde Marie-France.
6. J'écris à Daniel. Daniel m'écrit.
7. Daniel écrit à Corinne. Corinne écrit à Daniel.
8. Tu téléphones à Pierre. Pierre te téléphone.

Le passé composé des verbes réfléchis

Telling What You or Others Did at One Point in the Past

1. You form the *passé composé* of reflexive verbs with the verb *être*.

MASCULIN	FÉMININ
je me suis levé	je me suis levée
tu t'es levé	tu t'es levée
il s'est levé	elle s'est levée
nous nous sommes levés	nous nous sommes levées
vous vous êtes levé(s)	vous vous êtes levée(s)
ils se sont levés	elles se sont levées

2. A reflexive pronoun can be either a direct object or an indirect object.

DIRECT OBJECT **Marie s'habille.**
INDIRECT OBJECT **Marie s'achète une robe.**

3. Although the *passé composé* of reflexive verbs is always formed with *être*, the agreement of the past participle actually follows the pattern of verbs that use *avoir*:

  • If the reflexive pronoun is the direct object, the past participle agrees with it: **Marie s'est habillée.**
  • If the reflexive pronoun is the indirect object, the past participle does not agree with it: **Marie s'est acheté une robe.**

4. In negative sentences, you put the negative words around the reflexive pronoun and the form of the verb *être*. Study the following.

Nous *ne* nous sommes *pas* bien amusés à la fête.

CHAPITRE 2   35

INDEPENDENT PRACTICE

Assign any of the following:
1. Exercises, pages 34–35
2. Workbook, *Structure: A–E*, pages 16–18
3. Communication Activities Masters, *Structure: A–C,* pages 13–15
4. CD-ROM, Disc 1, pages 34–35

Exercices

ANSWERS

Exercice A

1. Mais il s'est déjà lavé.
2. Mais il s'est déjà peigné.
3. Mais il s'est déjà habillé.
4. Mais il s'est déjà mis à table.

Exercice B

1. Mais elle s'est déjà lavée.
2. ... peignée.
3. ... habillée.
4. ... mise à table.

Exercice C

Answers will vary.

Exercice D

1. nous sommes réveillé(e)s, vous êtes réveillé(e)(s)
2. nous sommes rendormi(e)s, vous êtes rendormi(e)(s)
3. nous sommes levé(e)s, vous êtes levé(e)(s)
4. nous sommes dépêché(e)s, vous êtes dépêché(e)(s)
5. nous sommes... mis(es) à table, vous êtes... mis(e)(s) à table
6. nous sommes... peigné(e)s, vous êtes... peigné(e)(s)

Exercice E

1. Ils se sont levés.
2. Ils se sont lavés.
3. Ils se sont rasés.
4. Ils se sont habillés.
5. Ils se sont mis à table.
6. Ils ont pris le petit déjeuner.
7. Elles se sont levées tard.
8. Elles ne se sont pas rasées bien sûr.
9. Elles se sont habillées rapidement.
10. Elles ne se sont pas mises à table.
11. Elles se sont dépêchées.

Exercices

A **Papa s'est déjà endormi.** Répondez d'après le modèle.

> **Papa va s'endormir?**
> *Mais il s'est déjà endormi.*

1. Papa va se laver?
2. Papa va se peigner?
3. Papa va s'habiller?
4. Papa va se mettre à table?

B **Maman.** Refaites l'Exercice A en remplaçant «Papa» par «Maman».

> **Maman va s'endormir?**
> *Mais elle s'est déjà endormie.*

C **Je me suis réveillé(e) de bonne heure.** Donnez des réponses personnelles.

1. Tu t'es réveillé(e) de bonne heure ce matin?
2. Tu t'es levé(e) tout de suite ou tu t'es rendormi(e)?
3. Tu as pris un bain ou tu t'es lavé(e) seulement?
4. Tu t'es habillé(e) avant ou après le petit déjeuner?
5. Tu t'es assis(e) dans la cuisine ou dans la salle à manger?
6. Tu t'es dépêché(e) ou tu as pris ton temps?
7. Tu t'es amusé(e) à l'école?
8. Tu t'es couché(e) à quelle heure hier soir?

D **Nous et vous.** Complétez au passé composé.

1. Ce matin ma sœur et moi, nous ___ à sept heures. Vous ___ à quelle heure? (se réveiller)
2. Malheureusement nous ___. Vous ___ ou pas? (se rendormir)
3. Par conséquent, nous ___ tard. Vous ___ tard? (se lever)
4. Nous ___. Vous ___ aussi? (se dépêcher)
5. Nous ne ___ pas ___. Vous ne ___ pas ___? (se mettre à table)
6. Nous ne ___ pas ___ ce matin. Vous ne ___ pas ___? (se peigner)

E **Les deux cousins et les deux cousines.** Mettez au pluriel.

1. Il s'est levé.
2. Il s'est lavé.
3. Il s'est rasé.
4. Il s'est habillé.
5. Il s'est mis à table.
6. Il a pris le petit déjeuner.
7. Elle s'est levée tard.
8. Elle ne s'est pas rasée bien sûr.
9. Elle s'est habillée rapidement.
10. Elle ne s'est pas mise à table.
11. Elle s'est dépêchée.

LEARNING FROM PHOTOS

Have students answer the following questions about the photo: *Où est la famille? Qu'est-ce que la famille mange? C'est quel repas? C'est une famille française ou américaine? Qu'est-ce qu'il y a sur la table?*

CRITICAL THINKING ACTIVITY

(Thinking skills: drawing conclusions)
Read the following to the students or write it on the board or on a transparency:
Expliquez comment vous savez que la famille sur la photo est une famille française et pas une famille américaine.

F **Oui, c'est Claudine.** Répondez par «oui» ou «non».

1. Claudine s'est lavée?
2. Elle s'est lavé la figure?
3. Elle s'est lavé les mains?
4. Elle s'est peignée?
5. Elle s'est brossé les cheveux?
6. Elle s'est habillée?
7. Elle s'est acheté une nouvelle robe?
8. Elle s'est acheté un petit cadeau?

Les actions réciproques au passé

Telling What You or Others Did To or For Each Other

In the case of reciprocal constructions, the reflexive pronoun can also be either a direct or an indirect object. Study the following.

OBJET DIRECT

Jean a vu *son ami.* ⎫
Son ami a vu *Jean.* ⎭ **Ils se sont vus.**

OBJET INDIRECT

Jean a parlé *à son ami.* ⎫
Son ami a parlé *à Jean.* ⎭ **Ils se sont parlé.**

Exercices

A **Les deux copains.** Répondez par «oui» ou «non».

1. Les deux copains se sont vus souvent?
2. Ils se sont salués à l'école?
3. Ils se sont parlé?
4. Ils se sont téléphoné régulièrement?
5. Ils se sont écrit de temps en temps?

B **Ce matin.** Complétez.

Ce matin je me suis levé__ de bonne heure. Je me suis lavé__
                         1   2
les mains et la figure, je me suis brossé__ les dents et je me suis
                                          3
peigné__. Je me suis dépêché__. À l'école je me suis amusé__.
       4   5   6
À l'école mes copains et moi, nous nous sommes vu__,
                                                 7
nous nous sommes salué__, nous nous sommes dit__ «bonjour»,
                        8   9
nous nous sommes parlé__. Comme nous nous sommes vu__
                         10   11
et nous nous sommes parlé__, nous ne nous sommes pas
                            12
écrit__ et nous ne nous sommes pas téléphoné__.
     13   14

Exercice F

1. Oui (Non), elle (ne) s'est (pas) lavée.
2. ... lavé la figure.
3. ... lavé les mains.
4. ... peignée.
5. ... brossé les cheveux.
6. ... habillée.
7. ... acheté...
8. ... acheté...

Les actions réciproques au passé

PRESENTATION *(page 37)*

Use the technique suggested on page 34 to teach reciprocal actions in the past.

Note The agreement of the past participle will need a great deal of reinforcement. Recycling the concept frequently will be more beneficial than intensive, short-term scrutiny.

Exercices

ANSWERS

Exercice A

1. Oui (Non), ils (ne) se sont (pas) vus souvent.
2. Oui (Non), ils (ne) se sont (pas) salués à l'école.
3. Oui (Non), ils (ne) se sont (pas) parlé.
4. Oui (Non), ils (ne) se sont (pas) téléphoné régulièrement.
5. Oui (Non), ils (ne) se sont (pas) écrit de temps en temps.

Exercice B

1. (e)	8. s
2. —	9. —
3. —	10. —
4. (e)	11. s
5. (e)	12. —
6. (e)	13. —
7. s	14. —

ADDITIONAL PRACTICE

1. Have individuals tell three things they did this morning using the *passé composé.*
2. Student Tape Manual, Teacher's Edition, *Activités A–B,* pages 16–17

PAIRED ACTIVITY

Have students work in pairs (a boy and a girl, if possible) to create the telephone conversation in the photos on page 37. Have several pairs present their conversation to the class.

A. You may want to introduce the negative words by contrasting the following statements. Indicate each negative statement with a gesture, such as a nod of the head, or empty hands.

Je parle.
Je ne parle pas.

Je parle toujours.
Je ne parle jamais.

Je parle.
Je ne parle plus.

Je vois quelque chose.
Je ne vois rien.

Je vois quelqu'un.
Je ne vois personne.

B. When going over step 2, write examples on the board and circle the negative words.

C. When going over step 3, give the following contrasting examples.

Je n'ai rien vu.
Je n'ai vu personne.

Je n'ai rien compris.
Je n'ai compris personne.

Je n'ai rien cherché.
Je n'ai cherché personne.

Expressions négatives au passé composé

Telling What You or Others Did Not Do in the Past

1. The most commonly used negative expressions are *ne...pas, ne...rien, ne...personne, ne...jamais,* and *ne...plus* ("no longer"). In the present tense you put the negative expressions around the verb.

Je	*ne* parle	*pas.*
Je	*ne* parle	*jamais.*
Je	*ne* parle	*plus.*
Je	*ne* vois	*rien.*
Je	*ne* vois	*personne.*

2. In the *passé composé,* the negative expressions *ne...pas, ne...rien, ne...jamais,* and *ne...plus* go around the helping verb *avoir* or *être.*

Je	*n'* ai	*pas*	parlé.
Je	*n'* ai	*rien*	compris.
Je	*n'* ai	*plus*	parlé.
Je	*ne* suis	*jamais*	allé(e) en France.

3. Note that *personne,* however, goes after the past participle.

Je *n'*ai vu *personne.*
Je *n'*ai parlé à *personne.*

4. Although *ne...que,* which means "only," is not actually a negative expression, it functions the same way as *ne...personne. Que* comes after the past participle.

Il *n'*a vu *que* trois pièces de théâtre.
Il *n'*a parlé *qu'*à ses amis.

5. If there is an object pronoun in the sentence, *ne* always comes before the pronoun.

Je *ne* le vois plus.
Je *ne* lui ai pas parlé.
Vous *ne* vous dépêchez jamais.

ADDITIONAL PRACTICE

1. Have students prepare three columns on a sheet of paper and label them *Personne, Jamais,* and *Rien.* Then read out prepared sentences while students check the appropriate column. For example: *Qui arrive en retard à l'école? Quand vas-tu à l'opéra? Quel est le problème?*

2. Student Tape Manual, Teacher's Edition, *Activités D–E,* pages 17–18

LEARNING FROM REALIA

Ask students the following about the ticket: *C'est un billet pour quel théâtre? Où est le théâtre? La représentation (la pièce) est à quelle heure? C'est le matin ou le soir? Le billet est pour quel jour? Combien coûte le billet?*

Exercices

A **Tu n'as rien fait, toi?** Répétez la petite conversation.

OLIVIER: Marc, tu as vu maman?
MARC: Non, je ne l'ai pas vue. Je n'ai vu personne.
OLIVIER: Tu as téléphoné à Paul?
MARC: Non plus! Je n'ai téléphoné à personne.
OLIVIER: Qu'est-ce que tu as fait alors?
MARC: C'est pas tes oignons! Je n'ai rien fait.

C'est pas tes oignons!

Répondez d'après la conversation.

1. Marc a vu sa mère?
2. Il a vu quelqu'un?
3. Il a téléphoné à Paul?
4. Il a téléphoné à quelqu'un?
5. Il a fait quelque chose?

B **Pas vraiment.** Donnez le contraire.

1. J'ai invité tout le monde à la fête.
2. J'ai vu beaucoup de choses.
3. J'y suis souvent allé(e).
4. J'ai écrit à mes copains.
5. J'ai entendu quelque chose.
6. Je lui ai téléphoné régulièrement.

C **Je n'ai que trois billets.** Répondez d'après le modèle.

    Tu as cinq billets à vendre? (trois)
    Non, je n'ai que trois billets à vendre.

1. Tu as vingt dollars à me prêter? (deux)
2. Tu as trois éclairs au chocolat? (un)
3. Il a beaucoup de cassettes à vendre? (dix)
4. Elles ont passé quelques semaines au bord de la mer? (une)
5. Ton frère et toi, vous avez gagné cinquante dollars? (vingt-cinq)
6. Elle a téléphoné à ses parents? (sa grand-mère)

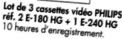

Lot de 3 cassettes vidéo PHILIPS réf. 2 E-180 HG + 1 E-240 HG 10 heures d'enregistrement.

Lot de 3 cassettes vidéo SCOTCH réf. E 240 EG+ 12 heures d'enregistrement. (l'unité: 43F)

CHAPITRE 2   **39**

Exercices

PRESENTATION *(page 39)*

Exercice A

Have students repeat the conversation after you. Use the proper annoyed intonation to indicate the meaning of *C'est pas tes oignons.* ("It's none of your business.") Then ask pairs of students to present the conversation to the class.

Exercice B

Use the recorded version of this exercise to reinforce the structure point.

Note In spoken French most people today omit *ne* in the negative. We have not done this in the exercises, readings, etc. of *À bord,* but it is nevertheless true that in certain popular expressions, such as *C'est pas tes oignons,* the *ne* would never be used. Students will notice that the *ne* is sometimes missing in the realia in this book.

ANSWERS

Exercice A

1. Non, Marc ne l'a pas vue.
2. Non, il n'a vu personne.
3. Non, il n'a pas téléphoné à Paul.
4. Non, il n'a téléphoné à personne.
5. Non, il n'a rien fait.

Exercice B

1. Je n'ai invité personne à la fête.
2. Je n'ai rien vu.
3. Je n'y suis jamais allé(e).
4. Je n'ai écrit à personne.
5. Je n'ai rien entendu.
6. Je ne lui ai plus téléphoné.

Exercice C

1. Non, je n'ai que deux dollars.
2. Non, je n'ai qu'un éclair au chocolat.
3. Non, il n'a que dix cassettes à vendre.
4. Non, elles n'ont passé qu'une semaine au bord de la mer.
5. Non, nous n'avons gagné que vingt-cinq dollars.
6. Non, elle n'a téléphoné qu'à sa grand-mère.

CONVERSATION

PRESENTATION (page 40)

A. Play the conversation video, or have students repeat the conversation once or twice after you or Cassette 2B/CD-1.

B. Call on two individuals to read the conversation to the class. (Use *Activité H* in the Student Tape Manual to check oral comprehension.)

C. Call on one or more pairs of students to dramatize the conversation in front of the class. They can improvise in any way they wish.

Note In the CD-ROM version, students can play the role of either one of the characters and record the conversation.

ANSWERS

Exercice A

1. Oui, Étienne s'est réveillé à l'heure ce matin.
2. Non, il s'est levé tard, parce qu'il s'est rendormi.
3. Non, il n'est pas arrivé à l'école en retard.
4. Cette année, il n'est jamais arrivé en retard.
5. Oui, il s'est dépêché pour arriver à l'heure.
6. Il ne sait pas.

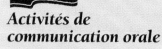

Activités de communication orale

ANSWERS

Activité A
    Answers will vary.

Scènes de la vie   *Tu t'es dépêché*

STÉPHANIE: Étienne, tu t'es levé à quelle heure ce matin?
ÉTIENNE: Comme toujours, je me suis levé tard. Je me suis réveillé à l'heure mais je me suis rendormi.
STÉPHANIE: Tu es arrivé à l'école en retard?
ÉTIENNE: Franchement, c'est pas tes oignons! Mais non. Cette année je ne suis jamais arrivé en retard. Mais qu'est-ce que je me suis dépêché, j'ai couru comme un fou!
STÉPHANIE: Qu'est-ce que tu penses faire après les cours?
ÉTIENNE: Oh, moi je ne sais pas. Aucune idée! Qu'est-ce que tu suggères?

A **Étienne s'est dépêché.** Répondez d'après la conversation.

1. Étienne s'est réveillé à l'heure ce matin?
2. Il s'est levé à l'heure? Pourquoi pas?
3. Il est arrivé à l'école en retard?
4. Cette année, il est arrivé combien de fois en retard?
5. Il s'est dépêché pour arriver à l'heure?
6. Qu'est-ce qu'Étienne pense faire après les cours?

Activités de communication orale

A **Le jeu des cinq questions.** Choose an item from the list below. A classmate has to try and guess which one you're thinking of. Then reverse roles and take several turns each.

une cassette
une chaîne stéréo
un lave-vaisselle
une machine à laver
un magnétophone
un magnétoscope

un poste de télévision
une radio
un répondeur automatique
un téléphone sans fil
une vidéocassette
un zappeur

Élève 1: On l'emploie pour enregistrer.
Élève 2: C'est un magnétophone.

LEARNING FROM PHOTOS

Have students look at the picture of *Téléstar* magazine. You may wish to tell them that Patrick Bruel is a singer who is currently making movies and is quite popular in France. Point out that when the English word "star" is used in French, it is always feminine: *la star.* The same is true of the French word *vedette: la vedette.*

B **Tes préférences.** Divide into small groups and choose a leader. Using the list below, the leader finds out where everyone in the group likes to sit. He or she takes notes and reports to the class.

à la cafétéria	au concert
au cinéma	au cours de français
	dans une voiture

Élève 1: Où est-ce que tu t'assieds au cinéma?
Élève 2: Je m'assieds souvent près de l'écran.
Élève 1 (*à la classe*): Dans mon groupe, il y a deux personnes qui s'asseyent près de l'écran au cinéma et trois personnes qui s'asseyent loin de l'écran. Au concert…

C **Devine ma matinée!** With a classmate, take turns trying to guess each other's routine this morning: what time you woke up, got up, got dressed, whether you hurried, ate breakfast, etc.

Élève 1: À mon avis, tu t'es réveillé à 6 heures et quart.
Élève 2: Non, je me suis réveillé à 7 heures moins le quart. À mon avis tu t'es réveillée à 7 heures et demie…

D **Une journée ennuyeuse.** Think about the most boring day you ever had at home. One of your classmates wants to know if you invited any friends over, saw anyone, called anyone, read anything, studied anything, watched anything on TV, or did anything at all.

Élève 1: Tu as invité des copains chez toi?
Élève 2: Non, je n'ai invité personne.

CHAPITRE 2   41

Activités B, C, and D
Answers will vary.

Vocabulary Expansion

You may wish to have students say something about the photos on this page. To do so, they will need the following words:
un camionneur
    truck driver
un poids-lourd
    tractor-trailer, big rig
un ouvrier en construction
    construction worker
un chantier
    construction site
un casque
    hard-hat

INDEPENDENT PRACTICE

Assign any of the following:
1. Exercise and activities, pages 40–41
2. Workbook, *Un Peu Plus*, pages 20–23
3. CD-ROM, Disc 1, pages 40–41

LECTURE ET CULTURE

Bell Ringer Review

Write the following on the board or use BRR Blackline Master 2-4: Make three columns on a piece of paper and head them: *envoyer/ employer/payer.* Write each word from the following list in the appropriate column.

un aérogramme	une lettre
une facture	un timbre
le code postal	un colis
un stylo	

READING STRATEGIES
(page 42)

Pre-reading
Briefly summarize the story in French. Then ask questions about it.

Reading
Have students open their books. Then have them repeat several sentences after you, or call on individuals to read. Ask questions about what was just read.

Post-reading
A. Have students read the story at home and write the answers to the exercises that accompany the *Lecture.*

B. Go over the exercises in class the next day.

C. Call on a student to give a summary of the story in his/her own words. If necessary, ask five or six questions which review the key points of the reading selection.

D. Then have the more able students write a summary of the *Lecture* in their own words.

E. If you wish to vary the procedure, you may break the selection into parts. Do some paragraphs thoroughly as suggested and assign others for silent reading.

Note Students may listen to a recorded version of the *Lecture* on the CD-ROM.

42

LECTURE ET CULTURE

LA FAMILLE VERDIER

*D*ans la famille Verdier il y a quatre personnes: Madame Verdier et son mari, Monsieur Verdier, et leurs deux enfants, Alain, qui a seize ans, et Michèle, qui a onze ans—et leur petit chien Milou!

Les Verdier habitent à Aubervilliers, dans la banlieue de Paris. Ils y ont un petit pavillon[1] confortable. Comment se passe une journée typique[2] chez les Verdier? Allons voir!

Ce matin, comme d'habitude, tout le monde s'est levé entre six heures et six heures et demie. Ils ont fait leur toilette et ils ont pris leur petit déjeuner ensemble—du café au lait ou du chocolat et des tartines. Vers sept heures et quart ils ont quitté la maison.

M. Verdier est allé à l'usine où il travaille comme contremaître. Mme Verdier a pris le RER, un train de banlieue relié[3] au métro parisien, pour aller à son travail. Elle est caissière dans une banque à Paris. Comme beaucoup de femmes françaises aujourd'hui, Mme Verdier travaille à l'extérieur. Tout est assez cher et la famille a besoin de deux salaires. Alain et sa sœur sont allés à l'école. Alain est élève dans une école technique et Michèle va au collège.

Aubervilliers, dans la banlieue de Paris

Les Verdier sont rentrés déjeuner? Non, les Verdier, comme beaucoup de familles aujourd'hui, ne rentrent pas chez eux pour le déjeuner. Mme Verdier a des tickets-restaurant que la banque lui donne. Elle déjeune au restaurant avec ses collègues. Si elle commande quelque chose qui coûte plus cher que le montant[4] de son ticket, elle paie la différence (un supplément). M. Verdier déjeune au restaurant de l'entreprise (la compagnie) et les jeunes déjeunent à la cantine de l'école—ou, pour être plus moderne, disons «la cafétéria».

Vers six heures du soir tout le monde est rentré à la maison. Ils se sont dirigés[5] vers la cuisine. Alain a mis le couvert.

---

[1] un petit pavillon   *a suburban-type house*
[2] une journée typique   *a typical day*
[3] relié   *connected*
[4] le montant   *amount*
[5] ils se sont dirigés   *they headed towards*

42   CHAPITRE 2

ADDITIONAL PRACTICE

After reading the *Lecture* and completing the *Étude de mots,* reinforce the lesson with the following: *Dans la lecture, trouvez les renseignements suivants:*
1. la ville où habitent les Verdier
2. le métier de M. Verdier
3. ce qu'est le RER
4. le métier de Mme Verdier
5. la marque de la voiture des Verdier

DID YOU KNOW?

Aubervilliers was a very poor working-class suburb in 1946 when the poet Jacques Prévert wrote the lyrics of a song for a movie made about it. The song was entitled "Aubervilliers" and contained the lines:

Gentils enfants d'Aubervilliers
Gentils enfants des prolétaires
Gentils enfants de la misère
Gentils enfants du monde entier

Vers sept heures et demie Mme Verdier a servi le dîner. Ce soir elle a servi un pot-au-feu, une salade, du fromage et des fruits. Hier soir ils ont mangé une omelette au fromage. Après le dîner M. Verdier a débarrassé la table et Michèle a fait la vaisselle, c'est-à-dire, elle a rincé les assiettes et puis elle les a mises dans le lave-vaisselle.

Ensuite M. et Mme Verdier sont passés dans la salle de séjour. Ils ont regardé le journal télévisé. Après le journal télévisé M. Verdier a mis la six. Il s'est levé pour changer de chaîne? Absolument pas! Il l'a changée avec son zappeur. Une minute après, Alain est entré dans la salle de séjour, un téléphone sans fil à la main. «Papa, j'ai écouté le répondeur automatique. Il y a un message pour toi. Rappelle ton copain Guy.»

Oui, les Verdier ont beaucoup de gadgets. Mais la France est un pays vraiment moderne. La France est un vieux pays, mais ses habitants ont tout le confort moderne. Les Verdier ont une voiture? Oui, ils ont une Renault, une R21. Et ils vont faire un grand voyage en voiture cet été. Ils vont aller au bord de la mer où ils vont passer tout le mois d'août. Les Verdier, comme tous les salariés[6] en France, ont cinq semaines de vacances par an.

[6] salariés   *full-time employees*

POT-AU-FEU

1 kg. de viande, os non compris
2 carottes moyenne
un navet
2 beaux poireaux
un gros oignon piqué d'un clou de girofle
un petit quartier de panais

une branche de céleri
un bouquet garni
2 litres et demi d'eau
une cuillérée rase de sel
Préparation: 3 à 4 heures après écumage terminé.

Étude de mots

A Quel est le mot? Choisissez.

1. un pavillon
2. faire sa toilette
3. une usine
4. un ouvrier
5. à l'extérieur de
6. le montant
7. la cantine
8. le couvert

a. une fabrique
b. la somme
c. une petite maison dans la banlieue
d. pas à la maison
e. un travailleur
f. se laver, se peigner, se brosser les dents, etc.
g. l'assiette, le couteau, la fourchette, la cuillère
h. la cafétéria

Étude de mots

ANSWERS

Exercice A

1. c	5. d
2. f	6. b
3. a	7. h
4. e	8. g

COGNATE RECOGNITION

The following cognates appear in this reading selection:

la famille	le train
le restaurant	la personne
la banque	le/la collègue
la toilette	le salaire
la différence	le chocolat
le ticket	le supplément
la compagnie	les fruits
le message	la cafétéria
une omelette	le gadget
le dîner	la table
le confort	la salade
le téléphone	les vacances
confortable	servir
typique	rincer
technique	changer
automatique	moderne

CROSS-CULTURAL COMPARISON

En ce moment plus de huit millions de femmes en France travaillent à l'extérieur (du foyer). Elles représentent à peu près 40% de la population active. Plus de 75% des Françaises estiment préférable que la femme exerce un métier.

La loi française exige depuis 1946 qu'une femme reçoive le même salaire qu'un homme qui fait le même travail. (À travail égal, salaire égal.)

INDEPENDENT PRACTICE

Assign any of the following:
1. *Étude de mots* exercise, page 43
2. CD-ROM, Disc 1, pages 42–43

Compréhension

Exercice B

1. Il y a quatre personnes dans la famille Verdier.
2. Les Verdier habitent en banlieue.
3. Ils habitent dans un pavillon.
4. Ils ont un chien.
5. M. Verdier travaille dans une usine.
6. Alain est élève dans une école technique.
7. Michèle va au collège.

Exercice C

1. Oui, les Verdier se sont levés de bonne heure.
2. Oui, tout le monde est parti au travail ou à l'école.
3. M. Verdier travaille dans une usine.
4. Mme Verdier travaille dans une banque à Paris.
5. Mme Verdier a pris le train pour aller au travail.
6. Non, les Verdier ne sont pas rentrés déjeuner.
7. Oui, ils sont rentrés dîner.

Exercice D

1. M. Verdier a déjeuné au restaurant de l'entreprise. Mme Verdier a déjeuné au restaurant. Les jeunes ont déjeuné à la cantine de l'école.
2. Alain a mis le couvert. Après le dîner M. Verdier a débarrassé la table. Michèle a fait la vaisselle.

Exercice E

1. Ils ont pris du café au lait ou du chocolat et des tartines.
2. Ils ont mangé un pot-au-feu, une salade, du fromage et des fruits.

Exercice F

Answers will vary.

Compréhension

B   Vous avez compris?   Choisissez.

1. Il y a quatre / six personnes dans la famille Verdier.
2. Les Verdier habitent en banlieue / en ville.
3. Ils habitent dans un appartement / un pavillon.
4. Ils ont un chat / un chien.
5. M. Verdier travaille dans une banque / une usine.
6. Alain est élève dans un lycée / une école technique.
7. Michèle va au lycée / au collège.

C   La journée des Verdier.   Répondez.

1. Les Verdier se sont levés de bonne heure?
2. Tout le monde est parti au travail ou à l'école?
3. M. Verdier travaille où?
4. Mme Verdier travaille où?
5. Qui a pris le train pour aller au travail?
6. Les Verdier sont rentrés déjeuner?
7. Ils sont rentrés dîner?

D   À vous de dire.   Répondez par des phrases complètes.

1. Où est-ce que chaque membre de la famille Verdier a déjeuné?
2. Le soir, qu'est-ce que chaque membre de la famille a fait pour aider Mme Verdier?

E   Qu'est-ce qu'ils ont mangé?
Décrivez.

1. le petit déjeuner des Verdier
2. le dîner des Verdier

F   La vie moderne.   Expliquez.

Aujourd'hui, dans beaucoup de familles françaises, les deux parents travaillent à l'extérieur. Pourquoi?

INDEPENDENT PRACTICE

Assign any of the following:
1. *Compréhension* exercises, page 44
2. CD-ROM, Disc 1, page 44

DÉCOUVERTE CULTURELLE

LES APPAREILS MODERNES

Vous avez remarqué que les Verdier, comme beaucoup de familles qui ne sont pas nécessairement très aisées[1] en France, ont une voiture. Ils ont aussi des appareils ménagers (comme, par exemple, une machine à laver ou un lave-vaisselle) et plusieurs autres appareils modernes: un poste de télévision, un téléphone sans fil, un magnétoscope, etc. Mais en France les jeunes n'ont pas de téléviseur dans leur chambre à coucher. C'est très rare. Il n'y a qu'un seul poste pour toute la famille, dans la salle de séjour ou la salle à manger.

Tout le monde a le téléphone. Certaines familles en ont même deux ou trois. Mais les jeunes Français ne passent pas des heures au téléphone. Ils utilisent le téléphone moins que les jeunes Américains.

LE DÉJEUNER EN FRANCE

Comme les Français travaillent de plus en plus loin de leur domicile[2], ils ne rentrent pas déjeuner chez eux. Mais le déjeuner continue à être le repas principal. Il est vrai que la restauration rapide ou le fast-food devient de plus en plus populaire en France. Mais les Français aiment un bon déjeuner et le dîner est souvent un repas assez léger — un pot-au-feu ou une omelette, par exemple.

LE RER

Le RER (Réseau Express Régional) est un réseau[3] de trains qui desservent[4] la banlieue parisienne. Le RER est relié au réseau du métro en ville.

[1] aisées *well-off*
[2] domicile *home*
[3] réseau *system*
[4] desservent *serve*

PRESENTATION (*pages 46–47*)

A. The purpose of this section is to allow students to enjoy the photographs that bring to life the content of the chapter. You may wish to have students read, either aloud or silently, the information that accompanies each photo.

B. Using the photos on pages 46–47, have students look for the following:

1. un plan
2. une cantine
3. un bureau
4. un pavillon
5. une usine

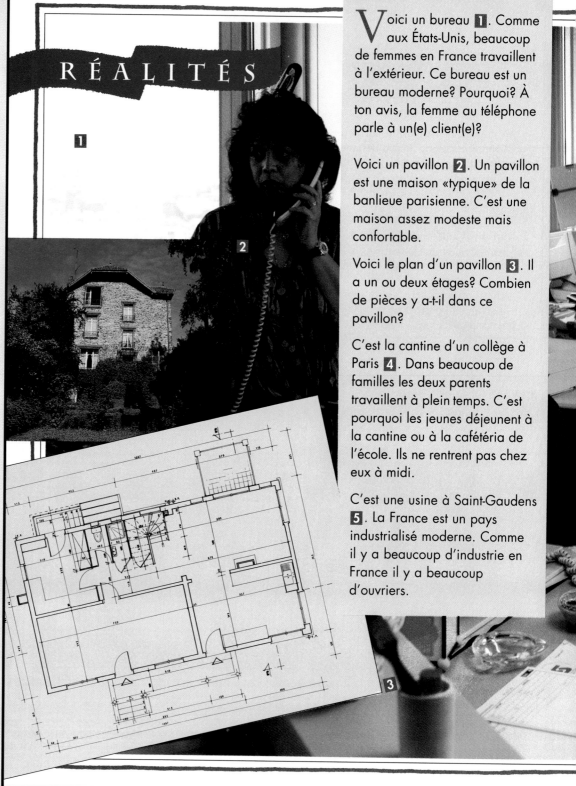

RÉALITÉS

V oici un bureau **1**. Comme aux États-Unis, beaucoup de femmes en France travaillent à l'extérieur. Ce bureau est un bureau moderne? Pourquoi? À ton avis, la femme au téléphone parle à un(e) client(e)?

Voici un pavillon **2**. Un pavillon est une maison «typique» de la banlieue parisienne. C'est une maison assez modeste mais confortable.

Voici le plan d'un pavillon **3**. Il a un ou deux étages? Combien de pièces y a-t-il dans ce pavillon?

C'est la cantine d'un collège à Paris **4**. Dans beaucoup de familles les deux parents travaillent à plein temps. C'est pourquoi les jeunes déjeunent à la cantine ou à la cafétéria de l'école. Ils ne rentrent pas chez eux à midi.

C'est une usine à Saint-Gaudens **5**. La France est un pays industrialisé moderne. Comme il y a beaucoup d'industrie en France il y a beaucoup d'ouvriers.

COOPERATIVE LEARNING

Have students work in groups to make up as many questions as they can about the photos. Then have the groups take turns asking other groups the questions.

C. Have the students look at photo #4 on page 47 and ask the following questions: *D'après vous, c'est la cantine (la cafétéria) d'une école primaire ou secondaire? Pourquoi? Voyons si vous vous rappelez bien ce que vous avez appris l'année dernière! Qu'est-ce qu'un collège en France? Et qu'est-ce qu'un lycée?*

Note In the CD-ROM version, students can listen to the recorded captions and discover a hidden video behind one of the photos.

ADDITIONAL PRACTICE

1. Student Tape Manual, Teacher's Edition, *Deuxième Partie*, pages 20–24
2. Communication Transparency C-2

INDEPENDENT PRACTICE

Assign either of the following:
1. CD-ROM, Disc 1, pages 46–47
2. Situation Cards, Chapter 2

CULMINATION

INFORMAL ASSESSMENT

The *Activités de communication orale* lend themselves to assessing speaking and listening abilities. Use the evaluation criteria given on page 22 of this Teacher's Wraparound Edition.

Activités de communication orale

PRESENTATION *(page 48)*

Activité A

In the CD-ROM version of this activity, students can interact with an on-screen native speaker.

ANSWERS

Activités A and B

Answers will vary.

Activités de communication écrite

ANSWERS

Activités A and B

Answers will vary.

OPTIONAL MATERIAL

Réintroduction et recombinaison

RECYCLING

Exercise A reviews vocabulary taught in Chapter 4 of *Bienvenue*; Exercises B, C, and D, Chapter 5. Exercise C also reviews vocabulary from Chapter 6.

Exercices

ANSWERS

Exercice A

Answers will vary.

Exercice B

Answers will vary but may include the following:
Il faut mettre des assiettes, des fourchettes, etc.

Exercice C

Answers will vary.

48

CULMINATION

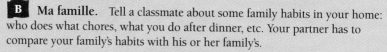

Activités de communication orale

A **Une soirée chez un(e) ami(e).** Votre copine française Sophie vous pose des questions sur le dîner que vous avez eu chez un(e) de vos ami(e)s. Répondez à ses questions.

1. Qui a préparé le dîner?
2. Qui a mis le couvert?
3. Qu'est-ce qu'on a servi?
4. Ton ami(e) et toi, vous avez aidé à débarrasser la table et à faire la vaisselle?
5. Qu'est-ce que vous avez fait après le dîner?

B **Ma famille.** Tell a classmate about some family habits in your home: who does what chores, what you do after dinner, etc. Your partner has to compare your family's habits with his or her family's.

Sophie

Activités de communication écrite

A **Lundi et samedi.** Write two schedules, one for Monday and one for Saturday of last week. List everything you did from morning till night, giving the times. Exchange schedules with a classmate. He or she tells the class the differences between your weekday and weekend activities. Then you do the same for your partner.

Lundi Jean s'est levé à 6 h 30. Samedi matin il s'est levé à 11 h...

B **Mes meilleurs amis.** Write a note to your French pen pal describing some of the things you and your friends do together. Be sure to use the appropriate French salutation and closing.

Réintroduction et recombinaison

A **Une maison.** Décrivez votre maison ou appartement.

B **À table.** On va se mettre à table. Avant le repas, qu'est-ce qu'il faut mettre sur la table?

C **La nourriture.** Faites une liste des choses qu'on peut manger en France et aux États-Unis aux repas suivants: le petit déjeuner, le déjeuner et le dîner.

48 CHAPITRE 2

STUDENT PORTFOLIO

Written assignments which may be included in students' portfolios are *Activité de communication écrite B* on page 48 and any writing activities from the *Un Peu Plus* section in the Workbook.

Note Students may create and save both oral and written work using the Electronic Portfolio feature on the CD-ROM.

D **Au restaurant.** Préparez une liste des mots qu'on peut employer au restaurant. Écrivez des phrases avec ces mots.

E **Nous le faisons.** Récrivez en utilisant «nous».

1. J'ai seize ans.
2. Je sais son adresse.
3. Je connais ses parents.
4. Je les vois souvent.
5. Je veux les revoir.
6. Je peux aller chez eux.
7. Quand je ne peux pas aller chez eux, je leur écris une lettre.
8. Je mets la lettre dans la boîte aux lettres.
9. J'envoie la lettre.
10. Je ne la reçois pas.

Vocabulaire

NOMS
la cuisine
l'évier (m.)
le robinet
le lave-vaisselle
la vaisselle
la machine à laver
le repas
le petit déjeuner
le déjeuner
le dîner
la tartine
le pot-au-feu

la femme
le mari

la salle de séjour
la télévision
le poste de télévision
le téléviseur
la télécommande
le zappeur
la chaîne
l'émission (f.)
le film
le magnétoscope
la vidéocassette
le magnétophone
la cassette
la chaîne stéréo
le téléphone (sans fil)
le répondeur
   automatique
le jouet

l'usine (f.)
la fabrique
l'ouvrier (m.)
l'ouvrière (f.)
le contremaître
la contremaîtresse
le bureau
le client
la cliente

ADJECTIF
préféré(e)

VERBES
se réveiller
se laver
se lever
se brosser les
   dents
s'habiller
se dépêcher
se servir de
s'asseoir

rincer
enregistrer
courir
allumer
éteindre
rappeler

ADVERBES
ensuite
rapidement
seulement

AUTRES MOTS ET EXPRESSIONS
mettre le couvert
se mettre à table
débarrasser la table
faire la vaisselle
changer de chaîne

prendre son temps
de bonne heure
tout de suite
ne...que
ne...plus

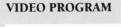

INDEPENDENT PRACTICE

Assign any of the following:
1. Activities and exercises, pages 48–49
2. Communication Activities Masters, pages 8–16
3. CD-ROM, Disc 1, pages 48–49

Note The *imparfait* will be introduced in the next chapter. The sentences in Exercise E review the *nous* form of important irregular verbs in the present tense. This will help prepare students for the introduction to the formation of the imperfect, whose root is derived from the *nous* form of the present tense.

Exercice D
   Answers will vary.

Exercice E
1. Nous avons seize ans.
2. Nous savons son adresse.
3. Nous connaissons ses parents.
4. Nous les voyons souvent.
5. Nous voulons les revoir.
6. Nous pouvons aller chez eux.
7. Quand nous ne pouvons pas aller chez eux, nous leur écrivons une lettre.
8. Nous mettons la lettre dans la boîte aux lettres.
9. Nous envoyons la lettre.
10. Nous ne la recevons pas.

CHAPITRE 3

CHAPTER OVERVIEW

In this chapter students will learn to make a telephone call in a French-speaking country and to communicate with an operator when necessary. They will also learn the proper expressions for beginning and ending a telephone conversation. The formation and basic uses of the imperfect tense are presented in this chapter.

The cultural focus of Chapter 3 is on French telephone etiquette and telephone service of yesterday and today in France.

CHAPTER OBJECTIVES

By the end of this chapter, students will know:

1. vocabulary associated with making and receiving telephone calls
2. vocabulary associated with various types of phones, both older and modern
3. the formation of the imperfect
4. the uses of the imperfect and some verbs that are often used in the imperfect
5. the use of infinitives of reflexive verbs

CHAPITRE

3

LE TÉLÉPHONE

OBJECTIFS

In this chapter you will learn to do the following:

1. make calls from a public phone in France
2. use proper phone etiquette
3. describe people, things, and events in the past
4. use certain verbs to express routine actions
5. talk about telephone service in France

CHAPTER PROJECTS

(*optional*)

Have students prepare advertisements for *les pages jaunes* of a French phone book using the ads on page 134 as a model.

COMMUNITIES

Have students prepare a pamphlet in French for French-speaking visitors to the U.S. that explains how to make calls from a public telephone. Send it to your local Chamber of Commerce or the nearest foreign exchange student organization.

51

CHAPTER 3 RESOURCES

1. Workbook
2. Student Tape Manual
3. Audio Cassette 3A/CD-2
4. Bell Ringer Review
   Blackline Masters
5. Vocabulary Transparencies
6. Communication
   Transparency C-3
7. Communication Activities
   Masters
8. Situation Cards
9. Conversation Video
10. Videocassette/Videodisc,
    Unit 1
11. Video Activities Booklet,
    Unit 1
12. Lesson Plans
13. Computer Software:
    Practice/Test Generator
14. Chapter Quizzes
15. Testing Program
16. Internet Activities Booklet
17. CD-ROM Interactive
    Textbook

Pacing

This chapter will require eight to ten class sessions. Pacing will depend on the length of the class, the age of the students, and student aptitude.

For more information on planning your class, see the Lesson Plans, which offer guidelines for 45- and 55-minute classes and **Block Scheduling.**

Exercices vs. *Activités*

The exercises and activities are color-coded. Exercises, which provide guided practice to prepare students for independent communication, are coded in blue. Communicative activities, which give students opportunities for creative, open-ended expression, are coded in red.

INTERNET ACTIVITIES

(optional)

These activities, student worksheets, and related teacher information are in the *À bord* Internet Activities Booklet and on the Glencoe Foreign Language Home Page at: **http://www.glencoe.com/secondary/fl**

LEARNING FROM PHOTOS

After presenting the vocabulary in this chapter, ask the following questions about the photograph. *Qui fait un appel téléphonique? Elle téléphone d'un téléphone public ou privé? Qu'est-ce qu'elle introduit dans le téléphone? C'est un téléphone à cadran ou à touches?*

VOCABULAIRE

MOTS 1

un numéro de téléphone

l'indicatif du pays ⟶ **(44)** **71** 499 9192

l'indicatif de la ville

un annuaire

un téléphone à cadran

un téléphone à touches

une cabine téléphonique

une télécarte

FRANCE 600 AGENCES PARTOUT EN FRANCE — TÉLÉCARTE 50

44 23 86 55

le bon numéro

~~44 22 86 54~~

le mauvais numéro

un standardiste

un téléphone public

Vocabulary Teaching Resources

1. Vocabulary Transparencies 3.1(A & B)
2. Audio Cassette 3A/CD-2
3. Student Tape Manual, Teacher's Edition, *Mots 1: A–C*, pages 25–27
4. Workbook, *Mots 1: A–D*, pages 24–25
5. Communication Activities Masters, *Mots 1: A–B*, pages 17–18
6. Chapter Quizzes, *Mots 1: Quiz 1*, page 13
7. CD-ROM, Disc 1, *Mots 1:* pages 52–55

Bell Ringer Review

Write the following on the board or use BRR Blackline Master 3-1: Write the following sentences in the *passé composé*:

1. **Je ne vais jamais au théâtre.**
2. **Il ne voit rien.**
3. **Elle ne parle à personne.**
4. **Nous ne voyons personne.**

PRESENTATION *(pages 52–53)*

A. Have students close their books. Introduce the *Mots 1* vocabulary using Vocabulary Transparencies 3.1 (A & B). Have students repeat the words after you or Cassette 3A/CD-2 as you point to the appropriate illustration on transparency.

B. If possible, use props such as a telephone, a telephone book, coins, a telephone card, etc. to help teach the new vocabulary.

C. Ask yes/no or either/or questions to elicit the new vocabulary. For example: *Je décroche ou je raccroche? C'est un annuaire ou un standardiste? Ce téléphone a des touches?*

PANTOMIME

___, venez ici, s'il vous plaît.
Prenez l'annuaire.
Ouvrez l'annuaire.
Regardez dedans.
Cherchez un numéro.
Allez au téléphone.
Ouvrez la porte de la cabine téléphonique.
Entrez.
Mettez votre télécarte dans le téléphone.

Décrochez.
Attendez la tonalité.
Faites le numéro que vous voulez.
Parlez.
Raccrochez.
Merci, ___. Retournez à votre place et asseyez-vous.

téléphoner = donner un coup de fil

décrocher

attendre la tonalité

une fente

composer (faire) le numéro

raccrocher

introduire (mettre) une pièce

Ah, zut! J'ai oublié le numéro. Je ne me souviens pas du numéro. Où est l'annuaire?

Ah, zut! Ça sonne occupé. La ligne n'est pas libre.

J'ai envie de parler à Léo. Je vais l'appeler.

un appel interurbain = un appel entre deux villes

Pour faire un appel international, il n'est pas nécessaire de passer par le standardiste.
On peut composer le numéro directement.

CHAPITRE 3   **53**

D. Have students open their books. Ask them to read the new words and sentences aloud. Model the correct pronunciation as necessary. Have students repeat the mini-conversations with as much expression as possible.

Vocabulary Expansion

You may wish to give students additional vocabulary for the following types of calls:
une communication urbaine
   local call
une communication interurbaine
   toll call, long-distance call
une communication internationale
   international call
une communication avec préavis
   person-to-person call

CROSS-CULTURAL COMPARISON

Public coin phones are becoming increasingly hard to find in France. Most public phones only accept *télécartes. Télécartes* contain various amounts of time units that are priced accordingly. The more time units on a card, the more it costs. The *télécarte* can be used for local, long-distance, and international calls. An international call takes many more time units per second than a local call. The number of units used for each call is automatically calculated and deducted from the *télécarte*. The card is good until all the units have been used. Then it is thrown away—or saved, if the owner happens to be a collector of *télécartes*, which have a variety of colorful pictures on them. (See the photo of the *télécarte* on page 54 and those on page 73.)

ADDITIONAL PRACTICE

1. You may wish to ask students the following additional questions to practice the *Mots 1* vocabulary: *Quel est votre numéro de téléphone? Quel est l'indicatif de notre (votre) ville? Pourquoi regarde-t-on dans l'annuaire? Quand vous oubliez un numéro, vous regardez dans l'annuaire ou vous téléphonez aux Renseignements? Vous avez un téléphone à touches ou à cadran? On a des télécartes aux États-Unis?*

2. Ask the following questions about the boy and the girl on page 53. *Jonathan a oublié quelque chose. Qu'est-ce qu'il a oublié? Il veut l'annuaire. Pourquoi? À qui est-ce qu'il a envie de parler? A qui téléphone-t-il? Isabelle a un petit problème. Quel est son problème?*

Exercices

PRESENTATION *(page 54)*

Exercice A

Exercise A must be done with books open.

Exercice B

Exercise B can be done with books open, closed, or once each way.

Extension of *Exercice B*

After completing Exercise B, call on a student to summarize what he/she has said in the exercise.

ANSWERS

Exercice A

1. C'est un téléphone à touches.
2. C'est une standardiste.
3. C'est un téléphone public.
4. C'est un répondeur automatique.
5. C'est une télécarte.
6. Ce téléphone public est au café.

Exercice B

Answers will vary.

Exercices

A Qu'est-ce que c'est? Identifiez.

1. C'est un téléphone à touches ou à cadran?

2. C'est une standardiste ou une vendeuse?

3. C'est un téléphone public ou un téléphone privé?

4. C'est un téléphone sans fil ou un répondeur automatique?

5. C'est une télécarte ou une pièce?

6. Ce téléphone public est à la maison ou au café?

B Des coups de fil. Donnez des réponses personnelles.

1. Tu téléphones souvent?
2. À qui donnes-tu des coups de fil?
3. Quel est ton numéro de téléphone?
4. Quel est l'indicatif de ta ville?
5. Tu as un téléphone sans fil?
6. Ton téléphone a un cadran ou des touches?

7. Tu as un répondeur automatique?
8. Tu mets le répondeur quand tu n'es pas chez toi?
9. Il faut passer par le (la) standardiste pour faire un appel international?
10. Tu fais souvent de mauvais numéros?
11. Il y a des cabines téléphoniques à ton école? Où?

54 CHAPITRE 3

ADDITIONAL PRACTICE

Student Tape Manual, Teacher's Edition, *Activité C*, page 27

C Quel est le mot? Complétez.

1. Allô, Marc? Ah, je suis désolé, Madame. J'ai le ___ numéro.
2. Si on n'est pas sûr d'avoir le bon numéro, on doit le vérifier dans l' ___.
3. Les téléphones les plus modernes ont des ___, pas de cadran.
4. Ah, zut!! J'ai ___ le numéro. Je ne me ___ pas du numéro.
5. Un téléphone public a une ___ où on met une pièce ou une télécarte. Un téléphone privé n'a pas de ___.
6. Tu téléphones à ton copain? Oui, je lui donne un ___.
7. Ève veut parler à son ami. Elle a ___ de lui parler. Elle va l'___.
8. La ligne n'est pas libre. Ça sonne ___.
9. Un appel entre deux villes est un appel ___.
10. Pour faire un appel international, il n'est pas nécessaire de passer par le ou la ___.
11. Pour faire un appel international, il faut savoir l'___ du pays et l'___ de la ville.

D Comment faire un appel téléphonique? Mettez les phrases suivantes en ordre.

À la fin de la conversation, on raccroche.
On compose le numéro.
On commence à parler.
Si c'est un téléphone public, on introduit une pièce dans la fente.
On attend la tonalité.
L'interlocuteur (la personne à qui on téléphone) répond.
On décroche.

Exercices C and D
Exercises C and D can be done with books open.

ANSWERS
Exercice C
1. mauvais
2. annuaire
3. touches
4. oublié, souviens
5. fente, fente
6. coup de fil
7. envie, appeler
8. occupé
9. interurbain
10. standardiste
11. indicatif, indicatif

Exercice D
1. On décroche.
2. On attend la tonalité.
3. Si c'est un téléphone public, on introduit une pièce dans la fente.
4. On compose le numéro.
5. L'interlocuteur (la personne à qui on téléphone) répond.
6. On commence à parler.
7. À la fin de la conversation, on raccroche.

INFORMAL ASSESSMENT
(Mots 1)
Have individuals give simple instructions in their own words for making a telephone call.

LEARNING FROM PHOTOS

Call the young man in the photo on page 55 Marc, for example, and ask the following questions: *C'est Marc qui téléphone? Où est Marc? Qu'est-ce qu'il porte? Qu'est-ce qu'il regarde? Il habite dans un immeuble ou dans une maison? Cette pièce est au rez-de-chaussée ou pas? Il se sert d'un téléphone à cadran ou à touches?*

INDEPENDENT PRACTICE

Assign any of the following:
1. Exercises, pages 54–55
2. Workbook, *Mots 1: A–D*, pages 24–25
3. Communication Activities Masters, *Mots 1: A–B*, pages 17–18
4. CD-ROM, Disc 1, pages 52–55

Vocabulary Teaching Resources

1. Vocabulary Transparencies 3.2 (A & B)
2. Audio Cassette 3A/CD-2
3. Student Tape Manual, Teacher's Edition, *Mots 2: D–H*, pages 27–29
4. Workbook, *Mots 2: E*, page 25
5. Communication Activities Masters, *Mots 2: C–D*, pages 18–20
6. Computer Software, *Vocabulaire*
7. Chapter Quizzes, *Mots 2: Quiz 2*, page 14
8. CD-ROM, Disc 1, *Mots 2:* pages 56–59

Bell Ringer Review

Write the following on the board or use BRR Blackline Master 3-2: Sketch the inside of a French post office. Label at least seven features or people.

PRESENTATION *(pages 56–57)*

A. Have students repeat the conversation after you or Cassette 3A/CD-2.
B. Now call on several pairs of students to read the conversation with as much expression as possible.
C. Call on two students who can improvise and present the conversation to the class in their own words.

Allô, Madame Duval?

Je regrette mais c'est une erreur. Vous n'avez pas le bon numéro.

LE TÉLÉPHONE DE MA JEUNESSE

un jeton

Quand j'étais jeune, j'aimais me servir du téléphone.
J'aimais surtout téléphoner des téléphones publics.

Papa me donnait un jeton.
Il me soulevait.
Je mettais (introduisais) le jeton dans la fente.
Le téléphone sonnait.

CHAPITRE 3   57

Exercices

PRESENTATION *(page 58)*

Exercice B

You may wish to have students close their books first. Read each cue to them, followed by the three choices. Call on volunteers to give the correct answer.

Extension of *Exercice B*: Paired Activity

You may also do Exercise B as a paired activity. One student reads the cue and the other supplies the correct answer.

Extension of *Exercice C*

After completing Exercise C, have one student retell the story in his/her own words.

ANSWERS

Exercice A

1. Allô, oui!
2. C'est de la part de qui?
3. Je peux lui laisser un message?
4. Mon numéro de téléphone est...

Exercice B

1. a	5. a
2. b	6. a
3. b	7. b
4. c	8. b

Exercice C

1. Oui, quand Paul était jeune, il aimait utiliser le téléphone.
2. Oui, il aimait surtout se servir des téléphones publics.
3. Son père le soulevait.
4. Son père lui donnait un jeton.
5. Il mettait le jeton dans la fente.
6. Oui, il composait le numéro.
7. Oui, le téléphone sonnait.

58

Exercices

A **Une communication téléphonique.** Répondez.

1. Allô?
2. Pourrais-je parler à Monsieur Caso, s'il vous plaît?
3. Je suis désolé(e). Il n'est pas là.
4. Quel est votre numéro de téléphone, s'il vous plaît? Monsieur Caso va vous rappeler.

B **On va parler au téléphone.** Choisissez.

1. Allô?
   a. Allô, oui!
   b. C'est de la part de qui?
   c. Il est là?
2. Monsieur Delacroix, s'il vous plaît.
   a. Je suis désolé. Il est là.
   b. C'est de la part de qui, s'il vous plaît?
   c. Raccrochez, s'il vous plaît.
3. Monsieur Delacroix est là, s'il vous plaît?
   a. Oui, je suis désolé. Il est là.
   b. Non, je suis désolé. Il n'est pas là.
   c. Non. Ne quittez pas!
4. C'est de la part de qui, s'il vous plaît?
   a. Il part?
   b. Ça sonne occupé?
   c. De Gilbert Caso.
5. Pourrais-je parler à M. Baud, s'il vous plaît?
   a. Un moment. Ne quittez pas.
   b. Allô?
   c. De Gilbert Caso.

6. Allô, Marc?
   a. Je regrette, mais c'est une erreur.
   b. Pourrais-je parler à Marc?
   c. Ça sonne occupé.
7. Vous avez fait un mauvais numéro, Monsieur.
   a. Je veux laisser un message.
   b. Je suis désolé, Madame.
   c. C'est de la part de qui?
8. Zut! Ça sonne occupé.
   a. Un moment. Ne quittez pas.
   b. Tu as le bon numéro?
   c. Il n'y a personne?

C **Quand Paul était tout jeune.** Répondez.

1. Quand Paul était jeune, il aimait utiliser le téléphone?
2. Il aimait surtout se servir des téléphones publics?
3. Qui le soulevait?
4. Qu'est-ce que son père lui donnait?
5. Où mettait-il le jeton?
6. Il composait le numéro?
7. Le téléphone sonnait?

58 CHAPITRE 3

D **J'ai envie d'inviter Corinne.** Répétez la conversation.

CHRISTOPHE: Je vais inviter Corinne. Je vais l'appeler… Ah, zut! Ça sonne occupé.
JEAN-CLAUDE: Tu as le bon numéro?
CHRISTOPHE: Je crois, mais regarde dans l'annuaire, on ne sait jamais.
JEAN-CLAUDE: Simonet… Son père s'appelle Serge, n'est-ce pas?
CHRISTOPHE: Oui.
JEAN-CLAUDE: Simonet, Serge, c'est le 43.55.66.72.
CHRISTOPHE: Oui, c'est ça. Je vais refaire le numéro.
(Il compose le numéro.)
Ça y est! Ça sonne… Ah zut!!
JEAN-CLAUDE: Qu'est-ce qu'il y a?
CHRISTOPHE: C'est le répondeur.

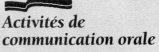

Répondez d'après la conversation.

1. Qui est-ce que Christophe appelle?
2. Pourquoi?
3. La ligne est libre?
4. Il a le bon numéro ou le mauvais numéro?
5. Il se souvient du numéro ou il l'a oublié?
6. Qui le vérifie?
7. Où est-ce qu'il le vérifie?
8. Ça sonne? Corinne répond?

Activités de communication orale
Mots 1 et 2

A **Comment faire?** Vous êtes dans une rue d'une ville des États-Unis. Vous voyez un(e) touriste français(e) (votre camarade de classe) qui essaie de faire un appel téléphonique.

1. Le/La touriste vous demande comment utiliser le téléphone public.
2. Vous lui dites ce qu'il faut faire.
3. Vous lui demandez de répéter les instructions.

B **Tu veux… ?** Vous êtes en France et vous avez rencontré un garçon ou une fille que vous voulez inviter à une fête, au cinéma, etc. Vous lui téléphonez pour voir s'il/si elle est libre. Avec un(e) autre élève préparez votre conversation téléphonique.

C **Bonjour, c'est le répondeur!** You work for a Canadian company that creates pre-recorded messages for answering machines. Make up personalized messages for the people below and present them to the class.

ton (ta) meilleur(e) ami(e)   ton frère ou ta sœur
quelqu'un dans la classe   une personne célèbre

Bonjour! C'est Jean-Pierre. Je ne peux pas répondre au téléphone. Laissez votre nom, votre numéro de téléphone et votre message après le bip sonore.

CHAPITRE 3   **59**

Structure Teaching Resources

1. Workbook, *Structure: A–H,* pages 26–29
2. Student Tape Manual, Teacher's Edition, *Structure: A–D,* pages 30–31
3. Audio Cassette 3A/CD-2
4. Communication Activities Masters, *Structure: A–C,* pages 21–24
5. Computer Software, *Structure*
6. Chapter Quizzes, *Structure:* Quizzes 3–5, pages 15–17
7. CD-ROM, Disc 1, pages 60–65

L'imparfait

PRESENTATION *(pages 60–61)*

A. Read steps 1 and 2 to the students.
B. In step 2, write the infinitives on the board. Beneath them, write the *nous* form. Then cross out the *-ons* ending, leaving just the stem.
C. Now pronounce the *je, tu, il/elle, ils/elles* forms of the verb.
D. Write these four forms on the board in paradigm order, leaving space for the *nous* and *vous* forms. Indicate that the pronunciation remains the same even though the spelling changes.
E. Now add the *nous* and *vous* forms.
F. Alongside the paradigms, write the endings (see chart, page 60). Have students repeat all the forms after you.

L' imparfait
Narrating in the Past

1. In French several tenses are used to express past actions. You have already learned the *passé composé*. The *passé composé* is used to express past actions that started and ended at a specific time in the past. You are now going to learn the imperfect tense.

2. First let's look at how the imperfect tense is formed. To get the stem or root for the imperfect, you drop the *-ons* ending from the *nous* form of the present tense. You add the imperfect endings to this stem. Study the following.

INFINITIVE	parler	finir	vendre	ENDINGS
STEM	nous *parl-*	nous *finiss-*	nous *vend-*	
IMPERFECT	je parlais	je finissais	je vendais	-ais
	tu parlais	tu finissais	tu vendais	-ais
	il/elle/on parlait	il/elle/on finissait	il/elle/on vendait	-ait
	nous parlions	nous finissions	nous vendions	-ions
	vous parliez	vous finissiez	vous vendiez	-iez
	ils/elles parlaient	ils/elles finissaient	ils/elles vendaient	-aient

3. Note that in the imperfect you pronounce the *je, tu, il/elle/on,* and *ils/elles* forms of the verb the same way. They are, however, spelled differently.

Une rue commerçante à Guérande en Bretagne

4. Except for the verb *être,* the imperfect of all verbs, regular or irregular, is formed the same way. As you have just seen, you drop the *-ons* from the *nous* form of the present tense and add the endings.

INFINITIVE	STEM	IMPERFECT
avoir	nous *av-*	j'avais
savoir	nous *sav-*	je savais
voir	nous *voy-*	je voyais
croire	nous *croy-*	je croyais
vouloir	nous *voul-*	je voulais
pouvoir	nous *pouv-*	je pouvais
dire	nous *dis-*	je disais
lire	nous *lis-*	je lisais
faire	nous *fais-*	je faisais
écrire	nous *écriv-*	j'écrivais
devoir	nous *dev-*	je devais
recevoir	nous *recev-*	je recevais
mettre	nous *mett-*	je mettais
appeler	nous *appel-*	j'appelais
acheter	nous *achet-*	j'achetais
préférer	nous *préfér-*	je préférais
commencer	nous *commenç-*	je commençais
manger	nous *mange-*	je mangeais

5. The only verb that does not follow this rule for the formation of the imperfect is the important verb *être.* Study its forms.

ÊTRE	
j' étais	nous étions
tu étais	vous étiez
il/elle/on était	ils/elles étaient

Des costumes folkloriques en Bretagne

6. In French, you use the imperfect to express habitual, repeated actions or to describe an emotional or physical state in the past. The time at which they began or ended is not important.

Madame Benoît était le professeur de français.
Elle parlait toujours français en classe.
Elle chantait souvent.
De temps en temps elle dansait des danses folkloriques.
Toute la classe regardait et applaudissait.

CHAPITRE 3 **61**

Exercices

PRESENTATION (*page 62*)

Exercice A

A. Have students repeat the conversation after you. Then call on a pair of students to read it.

B. Go over the comprehension questions that follow.

Note This exercise deals only with the third-person forms.

Exercice B

Exercise B can be done with books closed, open, or once each way. It contrasts the *tu/je* forms and reincorporates the third-person forms.

Extension of *Exercice C*

After completing Exercise C, call on one student to do the entire exercise and retell the story in his/her own words.

ANSWERS

Exercice A

1. On parlait anglais chez Sophie.
2. Ses grands-parents parlaient français.
3. Ils habitaient à Québec.
4. Oui, elle parlait français quand elle allait au Canada.
5. Oui, elle parlait français quand elle rendait visite à ses grands-parents au Canada.

Exercice B

Answers will vary.

Exercice C

1. était
2. habitait
3. habitait
4. adorait
5. adorait
6. aimait
7. téléphonait
8. téléphonait
9. était
10. donnait
11. sonnait
12. entendait
13. répondait

Exercices

A   Elle parlait français, n'est-ce pas?

Répétez la petite conversation.

YANN: Sophie, tu parlais français quand tu étais petite, n'est-ce pas?

SOPHIE: Non, pas vraiment. On parlait anglais chez nous. Mes grands-parents parlaient français mais ils habitaient à Québec.

YANN: Alors tu parlais français quand tu allais au Canada, c'est-à-dire quand tu rendais visite à tes grands-parents.

SOPHIE: Oui, un peu.

Répondez d'après la conversation.

1. On parlait anglais ou français chez Sophie?
2. Qui parlait français?
3. Où habitaient ses grands-parents?
4. Sophie parlait français quand elle allait au Canada?
5. Elle parlait français quand elle rendait visite à ses grands-parents au Canada?

Notre-Dame-des-Victoires, place Royale à Québec

B   Quand j'étais jeune.   Donnez des réponses personnelles.

1. Quand tu étais jeune, tu téléphonais souvent à tes grands-parents?
2. Tu leur écrivais de temps en temps?
3. Tu les voyais souvent?
4. Tu leur achetais de petits cadeaux?
5. C'était toi qui choisissais les cadeaux pour ta grand-mère?
6. Tu choisissais les cadeaux pour ton grand-père ou c'était ton frère ou ta sœur qui les choisissait?
7. Tes grands-parents t'invitaient souvent chez eux?

C   Gilbert adorait sa grand-mère.   Complétez.

Quand Gilbert ___ (être) jeune, il ___ (habiter) à Paris. Sa grand-mère ___ (habiter) dans un petit village breton. Gilbert ___ (adorer) sa grand-mère et sa grand-mère l' ___ (adorer) aussi. Il ___ (aimer) téléphoner à sa grand-mère. Il lui ___ (téléphoner) presque toujours de la maison, mais de temps en temps, il lui ___ (téléphoner) d'une cabine téléphonique. Sa grand-mère ___ (être) toujours contente quand Gilbert lui ___ (donner) un coup de fil. Quand le téléphone ___ (sonner), elle ___ (entendre) la sonnerie et y ___ (répondre) tout de suite.

62   CHAPITRE 3

DID YOU KNOW?

You may wish to tell the students that when they speak of the province of Quebec in French they must always use the article with it: *le Québec*. The city of Québec, however, does not require an article. Compare: *Je vais au Québec* and *Je vais à Québec*. The first sentence refers to the province, the second, to the city. Ask them which they think Sophie is talking about in Exercise A above.

CRITICAL THINKING ACTIVITY

(*Thinking skill: making inferences*)

After completing Exercise A, ask: **D'après vous, est-ce que Sophie préfère parler français ou anglais? Pourquoi?**

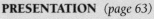

D On va parler au prof. Posez des questions à votre professeur d'après le modèle.

> aller à quelle école
> *Quand vous étiez jeune, vous alliez à quelle école?*

1. aller à quelle école
2. parler quelle langue
3. aimer vos cours
4. faire du français
5. passer des examens
6. réussir toujours
7. recevoir de bonnes notes
8. lire beaucoup
9. écrire beaucoup
10. s'amuser

E Les loisirs. Donnez des réponses personnelles.

1. Quand tu étais jeune, tu allais à la plage, à la piscine, à la montagne ou tu restais chez toi?
2. Tu faisais du ski ou de la natation?
3. Tu aimais mieux les sports d'hiver ou les sports d'été?
4. Tu partais en vacances en voiture?
5. Qui conduisait?
6. Tu prenais quelquefois le train ou l'avion?
7. Ta famille et toi, vous faisiez souvent des pique-niques?
8. Vous faisiez du sport ensemble?
9. Vous vous amusiez bien?

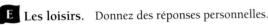

Les emplois de l'imparfait — *Uses of the Imperfect*

1. As you have already learned, the imperfect is used to express continuous, repeated, or habitual actions in the past.

> **Quand j'étais très jeune, je me couchais toujours de bonne heure. Je partais pour l'école à sept heures et demie.**

2. You also use the imperfect to describe persons, places, and things in the past.

Jean habitait Paris.	Location
Il avait trente ans.	Age
Il était grand.	Appearance
Il était fatigué.	Physical condition
Il était triste.	Emotional state of being
Il avait envie de dormir.	Attitudes
Il voulait rentrer chez lui.	Desires
Il était dix heures du soir.	Time
Il faisait froid.	Weather

3. Verbs that describe mental or emotional states in the past are very often used in the imperfect. The following are some of the most common:

aimer	croire	préférer
avoir envie de	désirer	pouvoir
vouloir	penser	savoir

CHAPITRE 3   **63**

PRESENTATION *(page 63)*

Exercice D

Exercise D gives students practice using questions with the *vous* form.

ANSWERS

Exercice D

1. Quand vous étiez jeune, vous alliez à quelle école?
2. ... vous parliez quelle langue?
3. ... vous aimiez vos cours?
4. ... vous faisiez du français?
5. ... vous passiez des examens?
6. ... vous réussissiez toujours?
7. ... vous receviez de bonnes notes?
8. ... vous lisiez beaucoup?
9. ... vous écriviez beaucoup?
10. ... vous vous amusiez?

Exercice E

Answers will vary but should use the imperfect.

Les emplois de l'imparfait

PRESENTATION *(page 63)*

Emphasize the fact that the imperfect is used for description in the past. Read the sentences from step 2 as if they were part of an ongoing story in the past.

> **THE FRANCOPHONE WORLD**
>
> La jolie ville de Québec, qui se trouve au confluent du fleuve Saint-Laurent et de la rivière Saint-Charles, est la capitale de la province du même nom. Elle a une population de 177.000 habitants (550.000 avec la banlieue). La grande majorité des Québécois, les habitants de Québec, sont francophones. (Montréal, la plus grande ville du Québec, est la deuxième ville francophone du monde après Paris.) La célèbre université Laval se trouve à Québec. Québec a été fondé par le Français, Champlain, en 1608. La ville a été prise par les Anglais en 1759.

ADDITIONAL PRACTICE

Student Tape Manual, Teacher's Edition, *Activités A, C, D*, pages 30–31

INDEPENDENT PRACTICE

Assign any of the following:

1. Exercises, pages 62–63
2. Workbook, *Structure: A–B*, page 26
3. Communication Activities Masters, *Structure: A*, page 21
4. CD-ROM, Disc 1, 60–63

Exercices

PRESENTATION (page 64)

Exercice B

A. Have students close their books. Read the story to them, filling in the correct verb forms yourself as you go along. When you get to *Mais qui était ce garçon?*, ask if anyone knows who the story is about.

B. Then call on students to read and fill in the verb forms. Have each individual do two or three sentences until the exercise is completed.

C. Call on a student to retell the life of Braille in his/her own words.

ANSWERS

Exercice A

1. Il était minuit.
2. Il faisait très mauvais.
3. Le jeune homme était dans un désert.
4. Il s'appelait Michel.
5. Il avait dix-neuf ans.
6. Il était malade et triste.
7. Il voulait rentrer chez lui.
8. Il ne pouvait pas parce qu'il était à l'armée.

Exercice B

1. avait	14. savait
2. était	15. allait
3. habitait	16. allait
4. avait	17. travaillait
5. était	18. croyaient
6. voulait	19. voulait
7. pouvait	20. faisait
8. était	21. continuait
9. était	22. était
10. pouvait	23. s'appelait
11. pouvait	24. était
12. était	25. saviez
13. avait	26. habitait

Exercices

A **Le pauvre jeune homme.** Répondez d'après les indications.

1. Il était quelle heure? (minuit)
2. Il faisait quel temps? (très mauvais)
3. Où était le jeune homme? (dans un désert)
4. Comment s'appelait-il? (Michel)
5. Il avait quel âge? (dix-neuf ans)
6. Il était comment, le pauvre? (malade et triste)
7. Qu'est-ce qu'il voulait faire? (rentrer chez lui)
8. Il ne pouvait pas. Pourquoi? (il était à l'armée)

B **Il était bien triste, le pauvre garçon.** Complétez à l'imparfait.

Quel âge ___ (avoir) le petit garçon? Vous savez? Non, je ne sais pas
₁
mais je sais qu'il ___ (être) très jeune. Il ___ (habiter) tout près de
₂ ₃
Paris. Je crois que sa famille ___ (avoir) une maison en banlieue.
₄
Mais le pauvre garçon n' ___ (être) presque jamais vraiment
₅
heureux. Il ___ (vouloir) bien apprendre à lire. Mais il ne ___
₆ ₇
(pouvoir) pas. Pourquoi? Il n' ___ (être) pas intelligent?
₈
Tout au contraire! Il ___ (être) vraiment très intelligent.
₉
Mais il ne ___(pouvoir) pas lire car il ne ___ (pouvoir)
₁₀ ₁₁
pas voir. Il ___ (être) aveugle. Il ___ (avoir) très envie
₁₂ ₁₃
d'apprendre à lire comme les autres enfants de son âge. Il ___
₁₄
(savoir) ce qu'il ___ (aller) faire. Il ___ (aller) inventer un
₁₅ ₁₆
système d'écriture (un alphabet) pour les aveugles. Il ___
₁₇
(travailler) jour et nuit pour développer et perfectionner son
alphabet. Tous ses camarades de classe ___ (croire) qu'il
₁₈
___ (vouloir) faire quelque chose d'impossible. Mais le petit
₁₉
garçon ne ___ (faire) pas attention à ses camarades. Il ___
₂₀ ₂₁
(continuer) son travail.

Mais qui ___ (être) ce garçon? Vous voulez savoir? Il ___
₂₂ ₂₃
(s'appeler) Louis Braille. C'___ (être) Louis Braille, un
₂₄
jeune Français, qui a créé et développé un système
d'écriture pour les aveugles. Le système porte son nom—
le système Braille. Vous ne ___ (savoir) pas que Braille
₂₅
est un nom français et que Louis Braille ___ (habiter)
₂₆
tout près de Paris?

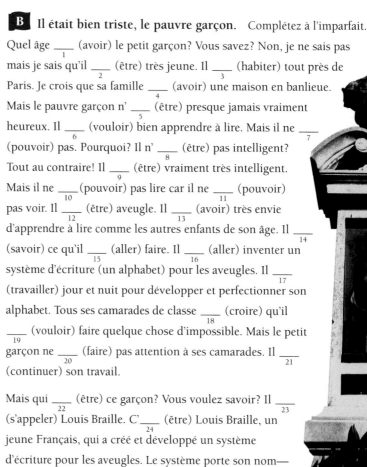

Le monument Braille à Coupvray,
le village natal de Louis Braille

64 CHAPITRE 3

ADDITIONAL PRACTICE

Have students bring in vacation photos or use transparencies from previous chapters to elicit descriptions of the weather, places, times, or things using the imperfect.

C On était comment? Répondez.

1. Quand ça sonnait occupé tu étais triste ou content(e)?
2. Quand ton père n'était pas là tu étais content(e) ou désolé(e)?
3. Le garçon avait quatre ans. Il était vieux ou jeune?
4. Il avait envie de dormir. Il était fatigué?
5. Il était au lit. Il était malade?
6. Il ne voulait pas manger. Il n'avait pas d'appétit?
7. Qu'est-ce qu'il prenait quand il avait soif?

D Je ne voulais pas. Dites ce que vous ne vouliez pas manger quand vous étiez petit(e).

E Qu'est-ce que tu aimais faire? Demandez à un copain ou une copine ce qu'il ou elle aimait faire quand il/elle était petit(e).

> Élève 1: Tu aimais jouer avec tes jouets?
> Élève 2: Oui, j'aimais jouer avec mes jouets.

F Ce que je savais faire. Dites des choses que vous ne saviez pas faire quand vous étiez petit(e).

L'infinitif des verbes réfléchis

Using Certain Verbs to Express Routine Actions

When a reflexive verb follows a helping verb, the reflexive pronoun agrees with the subject.

> **Robert** ne veut pas *se* lever tôt demain matin.
> Mais *moi*, je vais *me* lever très tôt.
> *Tu* vas *te* lever à cinq heures? Pourquoi?

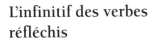

Exercice

A Demain. Donnez des réponses personnelles.

1. Tu vas te lever à quelle heure demain?
2. Tu vas t'habiller avant de prendre le petit déjeuner?
3. Tu préfères te laver les cheveux le matin ou le soir?
4. Tu veux te coucher de bonne heure ce soir?
5. Tu vas voir ton ami(e) demain? Où est-ce que vous allez vous voir?
6. Ton ami(e) et toi, vous aimez vous parler au téléphone?

PRESENTATION *(page 66)*

A. Have students close their books. Play the Conversation Video or have them listen as you read the conversation aloud, or play Cassette 3A/CD-2.

B. Have students read along as you model the conversation a second time. (Use *Activité F* in the Student Tape Manual to check oral comprehension.)

C. Allow time for pairs of students to practice the conversation. Then call on one or two pairs to read it to the class in as realistic a manner as possible. You may wish to use toy telephones as props.

D. After several pairs of students have presented the conversation, ask the comprehension questions. Then call on an individual to retell the story in his/her own words.

Note In the CD-ROM version, students can play the role of either one of the characters and record the conversation.

ANSWERS

Exercice A

1. M. Berger téléphone.
2. M. Berger veut parler à Maurice Haddad.
3. Non, M. Haddad ne répond pas au téléphone.
4. Oui, Mme Haddad va voir s'il est là.
5. Non, M. Haddad n'est pas là.
6. Oui, il est parti.
7. Oui, M. Berger lui laisse un message.
8. Non, il ne laisse pas son numéro de téléphone.
9. Il ne le laisse pas parce que M. Haddad l'a déjà.
10. M. Haddad peut le rappeler cet après-midi.

Scènes de la vie *Un coup de fil*

M. BERGER: Allô!
MME HADDAD: Allô, oui?
M. BERGER: Maurice Haddad est là, s'il vous plaît?
MME HADDAD: C'est de la part de qui?
M. BERGER: Paul Berger.
MME HADDAD: Je vais voir s'il est là. Ne quittez pas, Monsieur. *(Elle revient.)* Je suis désolée mais il est parti. Vous voulez lui laisser un message?
M. BERGER: Oui, il peut me rappeler cet après-midi. Il a mon numéro de téléphone.

A **Au téléphone.** Répondez d'après la conversation.

1. Qui téléphone, M. Berger ou M. Haddad?
2. À qui est-ce que M. Berger veut parler?
3. M. Haddad répond au téléphone?
4. Mme Haddad va voir s'il est là?
5. M. Haddad est là?
6. Il est parti?
7. M. Berger lui laisse un message?
8. Il laisse son numéro de téléphone?
9. Pourquoi pas?
10. Quand est-ce que M. Haddad peut le rappeler?

Chéri,
Rappelle M. Berger
cet après-midi.
Sophie

66   CHAPITRE 3

CRITICAL THINKING ACTIVITY

(Thinking skills: problem-solving)
   Read the following to the class or write it on the board or on a transparency:
M. Berger croit que M. Haddad a son numéro de téléphone. Si M. Haddad n'a pas le numéro de M. Berger, qu'est-ce que M. Haddad peut faire pour rappeler M. Berger?

Activités de communication orale

A **Les Renseignements.** Vous n'avez pas de Minitel et vous voulez savoir le numéro de téléphone de plusieurs personnes. Vous téléphonez au 12, le Service des Renseignements.

> Élève 1: Les Renseignements, bonjour.
> Élève 2: Bonjour (Madame). Je voudrais le numéro de téléphone de Monsieur Derain, 13 rue Lévis…
> Élève 1: Vous pouvez épeler le nom, s'il vous plaît?
> Élève 2: D comme Denise, E comme Ernani, R comme Raoul, A comme Anatole, I comme Isidore, N comme Noël.
> Élève 1: Alors, c'est le 45.67.89.34.

B **Je ne suis pas là.** Vous voulez inviter un(e) ami(e) chez vous mais quand vous lui téléphonez, c'est le répondeur automatique (votre camarade) qui répond. Laissez un message. Votre camarade va l'écrire, puis il/elle va vous relire votre message.

1. Laissez votre nom.
2. Donnez la date et l'heure.
3. Dites pourquoi vous téléphonez.
4. Donnez votre numéro de téléphone.

C **Le jeu du téléphone.** Divide into teams by row. Using the imperfect, the last person in each row whispers to the person in front of him or her one sentence about what he or she used to do in the past. Each person whispers the sentence to the next person until the message reaches the front of the row. The first person in each row says the sentence to the class. The team whose final sentence most closely resembles the original wins!

> Élève 1: Quand j'avais six ans, je me levais toujours de bonne heure.
> Élève 2: Quand j'avais dix ans…

Activités de communication orale

PRESENTATION *(page 67)*

These activities enable students to use the vocabulary and structures learned in the chapter in open-ended exchanges. You may wish to assign different activities to different groups or allow the students to choose the activities they wish to do.

Activité B

 In the CD-ROM version of this activity, students can record their message on an answering machine.

ANSWERS

Activités A, B, and C

Answers will vary.

LEARNING FROM PHOTOS

Tell students that these screens are from the *annuaire électronique* of the Minitel. Then ask: *On cherche le numéro de téléphone de qui?*

INDEPENDENT PRACTICE

Assign any of the following:
1. Exercise and activities, pages 66–67
2. CD-ROM, Disc 1, pages 66–67

LECTURE ET CULTURE

READING STRATEGIES

(pages 68–69)

Pre-reading

Give students a brief oral summary in French of the reading.

Reading

A. Call on an individual to read two or three sentences.
B. Then ask questions about the sentences the student just read. Call on other students to answer these questions.
C. Continue in this way until the entire selection has been completed.

Post-reading

Assign the reading selection and the exercises that follow for homework. Go over the exercises the following day.

Teaching Tip Call on students other than the reader to answer your comprehension questions. Most students have difficulty comprehending what they are reading when reading aloud. They concentrate more on pronunciation than comprehension.

Note Students may listen to a recorded version of the *Lecture* on the CD-ROM.

LE TÉLÉPHONE D'HIER ET D'AUJOURD'HUI

Je m'appelle Jean-Pierre Coluche. Je vais vous parler du téléphone. Quand j'étais très jeune, j'aimais bien utiliser le téléphone. Ça m'amusait beaucoup. Maman me permettait de téléphoner à Grand-mère. Je composais le numéro moi-même. Mais Maman m'aidait un peu car (parce que) de temps en temps je composais un mauvais numéro. Notre téléphone était un appareil à cadran et pas mal de fois, c'est-à-dire assez souvent, mon petit doigt[1] glissait dans le mauvais trou[2].

Pas souvent, mais de temps en temps, je téléphonais à Grand-mère d'un téléphone public. Je m'en souviens bien. Maman allait dans le bureau de tabac où elle achetait un jeton. Papa me prenait dans ses bras et me soulevait car je n'arrivais pas à la fente du téléphone et je voulais toujours mettre le jeton moi-même. Papa décrochait et me donnait le combiné[3]. C'était lui qui faisait le numéro et moi, j'attendais la réponse de Grand-mère. Quand elle répondait, j'appuyais sur[4] un bouton. Si je n'appuyais pas sur le bouton, je pouvais entendre ce que Grand-mère me disait mais elle ne pouvait pas entendre ce que je lui disais.

Que la vie a changé! Et moi, je ne suis pas vieux, vous savez! Aujourd'hui je suis étudiant à l'université. Quand je parle des coups de fil que je donnais à Grand-mère, il n'y a pas très longtemps de cela[5]. Et aujourd'hui acheter un jeton pour faire un appel? Appuyer sur un bouton pour permettre à votre interlocuteur (la personne à qui vous parlez) de vous entendre? Absolument

---

[1] doigt   *finger*
[2] trou   *hole*
[3] le combiné   *receiver*
[4] j'appuyais sur   *I would push*
[5] il n'y a pas très longtemps de cela   *it wasn't very long ago*

ADDITIONAL PRACTICE

After reading and discussing the *Lecture* and completing the exercises, have students summarize in their own words the steps Jean-Pierre took to place a phone call.

CRITICAL THINKING ACTIVITY

(Thinking skill: drawing conclusions from facts)

Ask students the following question: **Pourquoi est-ce qu'il y a une photo d'un bureau de tabac sur cette page?**

pas! On peut acheter une télécarte pour faire des appels d'une cabine téléphonique, mais plus de jetons. Et notre nouveau téléphone, il n'a pas de cadran. C'est un téléphone à touches. Il a un clavier, pas de cadran. Et il a une carte à mémoire pour les numéros qu'on appelle souvent. Et moi j'ai un téléphone sans fil.

Me voici avec mon téléphone sans fil dans la cour de mon immeuble. Je crois que je vais donner un coup de fil à Grand-mère. Je l'adorais et je l'adore toujours. «Allô, Grand-mère! Ici ton Jean-Pierre.»

Étude de mots

A Quelle est la définition?

1. utiliser	a. je ne l'oublie pas
2. pas mal de fois	b. un appel téléphonique
3. je m'en souviens	c. employer
4. vieux	d. âgé
5. un coup de fil	e. assez souvent
6. se procurer	f. obtenir, acheter
7. le combiné	g. le récepteur

B Quel est le nom? Trouvez le nom qui correspond au verbe.

1. permettre	a. l'utilisation
2. téléphoner	b. la permission
3. utiliser	c. l'aide
4. aider	d. le téléphone
5. se souvenir de	e. le souvenir
6. changer	f. le changement

Étude de mots

ANSWERS

Exercice A

1. c
2. e
3. a
4. d
5. b
6. f
7. g

Exercice B

1. b
2. d
3. a
4. c
5. e
6. f

PAIRED ACTIVITY

Have students work in pairs. One student plays the role of a small child. The other plays the grandparent. Have them make up a telephone conversation.

INDEPENDENT PRACTICE

Assign any of the following:
1. *Étude de mots* exercises, page 69
2. CD-ROM, Disc 1, pages 68–69

Compréhension

ANSWERS

Exercice C

1. Jean-Pierre Coluche nous parle.
2. Il aimait utiliser le téléphone...
3. Il téléphonait souvent à sa grand-mère.
4. ... parce que de temps en temps il composait le mauvais numéro.
5. Sa mère achetait un jeton...
6. ... parce qu'il n'arrivait pas à la fente du téléphone.
7. Il voulait toujours mettre le jeton lui-même.
8. Le père de Jean-Pierre lui donnait le combiné...
9. ... quand sa grand-mère répondait.
10. ... sa grand-mère ne pouvait pas entendre la conversation.

Exercice D

Answers will vary but may include the following:

1. Je *téléphonais* à ma grand-mère.
2. Maman *me permettait* de lui téléphoner.
3. Je *faisais* le numéro moi-même.
4. Je voulais *mettre* le jeton moi-même dans la fente.
5. Aujourd'hui je ne suis pas très *vieux*.

Exercice E

1. Non.
2. Oui.
3. Non.
4. Non.
5. Oui.

Exercice F

Answers will vary.

Compréhension

C **Avez-vous compris?** Répondez d'après la lecture.

1. Qui vous parle?
2. Qu'est-ce qu'il aimait utiliser quand il était jeune?
3. À qui est-ce qu'il téléphonait souvent?
4. Sa mère l'aidait à composer le numéro. Pourquoi?
5. Qu'est-ce que sa mère achetait au bureau de tabac?
6. Le père de Jean-Pierre le soulevait. Pourquoi?
7. Qu'est-ce que Jean-Pierre voulait toujours faire?
8. Qu'est-ce que le père de Jean-Pierre lui donnait quand il décrochait?
9. Quand est-ce que Jean-Pierre appuyait sur un bouton?
10. S'il n'appuyait pas sur le bouton, qui ne pouvait pas entendre la conversation?

D **Autrement dit.** Dites d'une autre façon.

1. Je *faisais des appels téléphoniques* à ma grand-mère.
2. Maman *me donnait la permission* de lui téléphoner.
3. Je *composais* le numéro moi-même.
4. Je voulais *introduire* le jeton moi-même dans la fente.
5. Aujourd'hui je ne suis pas très *âgé*.

E **Vrai ou faux?** Répondez par «oui» ou «non».

1. Aujourd'hui, on achète des jetons pour utiliser les téléphones publics en France?
2. On peut utiliser une télécarte pour téléphoner de la plupart des téléphones publics?
3. Les nouveaux téléphones ont des cadrans?
4. Un téléphone à touches a un cadran?
5. Jean-Pierre peut téléphoner à Grand-mère de la cour de son immeuble parce qu'il a un téléphone sans fil?

F **Des comparaisons.** Comparez les choses suivantes.

1. Un vieux téléphone public en France et un nouveau téléphone public.
2. Un téléphone à cadran et un téléphone à touches.

1. You may wish to ask students: What is the message in the top photo on page 70? Have them explain it in their own words.
2. Ask students to say as much as they can about the second photo. Have students make up an imaginary conversation between the two women.

DÉCOUVERTE CULTURELLE

Les vieux téléphones publics en France étaient «pittoresques» avec leur fente pour les jetons qu'on achetait dans un bureau de tabac et leur petit bouton sur lequel on appuyait quand l'interlocuteur répondait au téléphone. Mais tout cela a changé.

Aujourd'hui on va souvent au bureau de tabac avant d'appeler d'un téléphone public. Mais pas pour acheter des jetons. On y va pour obtenir une télécarte. On demande la quantité d'unités qu'on désire. Pour téléphoner on introduit la télécarte dans une fente. On peut utiliser la télécarte pour des appels urbains, interurbains et internationaux. Les unités utilisées pour l'appel sont prélevées[1] automatiquement. On peut acheter une télécarte au bureau de poste aussi.

Aujourd'hui beaucoup de familles françaises et surtout[2] beaucoup de commerces français ont des téléphones avec carte à mémoire connectables sur télécopieurs[3], ordinateurs, etc.

Les téléphones sans fil de longue portée[4] sont très populaires en France aussi. Ils fonctionnent mains libres, c'est-à-dire qu'on parle sans avoir le combiné à la main.

[1] prélevées *deducted*
[2] surtout *especially*
[3] télécopieurs *fax machines*
[4] de longue portée *long-range*

Conversation à Trois.
Pour converser avec deux correspondants en même temps sur votre ligne.

Aria.
Le téléphone sans fil qui vous suit partout.

Guide pratique Carte Pastel
Votre passeport pour téléphoner.

CARTE PASTEL
internationale
FRANCE TELECOM

CHAPITRE 3   71

Bell Ringer Review

Write the following on the board or use BRR Blackline Master 3-5: For each phrase in Column A, choose a logical ending from Column B. Draw lines to connect your matches.

mettre	son temps
faire	le couvert
prendre	la vaisselle
se mettre	à table
débarrasser	la table

OPTIONAL MATERIAL

Découverte culturelle

PRESENTATION *(page 71)*

You may present the information in the *Découverte culturelle* the same way you would present any other reading selection, or you may wish to assign it as a silent reading exercise.

Note Students may listen to a recorded version of the *Découverte culturelle* on the CD-ROM.

LEARNING FROM REALIA

Have students look at the realia on page 71. Tell students that the telephone service in France is nationalized. Its name is *France Télécom.* Ask students to tell in their own words the message conveyed in each brochure.

INDEPENDENT PRACTICE

Assign any of the following:
1. *Compréhension* exercises, page 70
2. Workbook, *Un Peu Plus*, pages 30–34
3. CD-ROM, Disc 1, pages 70–71

RÉALITÉS

Bell Ringer Review

Write the following on the board or use BRR Blackline Master 3-6: Which items would you tell your friend to take on a trip to the mountains?

une écharpe
un pull
un bonnet
un complet
an anorak
un chemisier à manches longues
des skis
un chemisier à manches courtes
des gants
des lunettes
une cravate
des bâtons

OPTIONAL MATERIAL

PRESENTATION *(pages 72–73)*

A. Allow students to enjoy the photos and talk about them. You may wish to explain that one of the beauties of France that impresses many Americans is its wonderful contrast of past and present. These photos nicely illustrate that contrast: the old apartment building and antique furniture in Photo #2 alongside up-to-date, computerized equipment and more modern buildings glimpsed through the window.

B. Call on volunteers to read the captions aloud. Then have the class discuss the information.

RÉALITÉS

C'est un vieux téléphone **1**. Où est-ce qu'on mettait les pièces? Et pourquoi est-ce qu'on appuyait sur le bouton?

Ce poste moderne est un mini-bureau **2**. Tout est là—un ordinateur, un télécopieur, un téléphone avec répondeur et, bien sûr, le Minitel.

Voici une sélection de télécartes **3**. On utilise la télécarte dans les téléphones publics en France aujourd'hui pour faire des appels urbains, interurbains et internationaux. Ces cartes sont très jolies, n'est-ce pas? Beaucoup de gens aiment les collectionner.

Voici le Minitel à la poste **4**. Aujourd'hui, quand on oublie un numéro de téléphone, on peut utiliser l'annuaire électronique du Minitel.

C'est un nouveau téléphone public **5**. C'est un téléphone à cadran ou à touches? On peut utiliser des pièces dans ce téléphone?

ADDITIONAL PRACTICE

Assign any of the following:
1. Student Tape Manual, Teacher's Edition, *Deuxième Partie*, pages 32–34
2. Situation Cards, Chapter 3

Note In the CD-ROM version, students can listen to the re-corded captions and discover a hidden video behind one of the photos.

INDEPENDENT PRACTICE

Assign the following:
CD-ROM, Disc 1, pages 72–73

RECYCLING

The *Activités de communication orale* and *écrite* allow students to use the vocabulary and grammar from this chapter in open-ended situations. They also provide an opportunity to recycle vocabulary and structures from earlier chapters, and from *Bienvenue*. Have students do as many of the *Activités* as you wish.

INFORMAL ASSESSMENT

The *Activités de communication orale* are an excellent way to assess speaking and listening abilities. Use the evaluation criteria given on page 22 of this Teacher's Wraparound Edition.

Activités de communication orale

ANSWERS

Activité A and B
Answers will vary.

Activités de communication écrite

ANSWERS

Activités A and B
Answers will vary.

Activités de communication orale

A **L'indicatif régional.** Vous êtes en France et vous voulez faire un appel international. Appelez le/la standardiste (votre camarade). Demandez-lui l'indicatif du pays et l'indicatif de la ville où vous voulez téléphoner.

B **Les étés de mon enfance.** Demandez à un(e) camarade ce qu'il/elle faisait d'habitude en été quand il/elle était petit(e). Demandez-lui où il/elle allait, avec qui, ce qu'il/elle faisait, etc. Changez ensuite de rôles.

Activités de communication écrite

A **Souvenirs d'enfance.** Quand vous étiez petit(e) est-ce que vous alliez quelquefois chez vos grands-parents ou chez un(e) ami(e)? En un paragraphe, décrivez chez qui vous alliez, comment étaient les gens et leur maison, et ce que vous faisiez d'habitude chez eux.

B **Un travail collectif.** Work in groups and make up a story sentence by sentence in the past. The first person writes a sentence for Category 1 (below) on a piece of paper and passes it to the next person. The second person reads the sentence and continues the story by writing a sentence for Category 2, and so on. When the story is completed, a student reads it to the class.

1. Date
2. Temps
3. Personnages et lieu
4. Description physique ou émotionnelle des personnages
5. Attitudes
6. Désirs
7. Actions habituelles

> Élève 1: C'était le 3 janvier.
> Élève 2: Il faisait très froid.
> Élève 3: J'étais à San Francisco avec mes amis.

74   CHAPITRE 3

COMMENT OBTENIR VOTRE CORRESPONDA

Automatique

décrochez   tonalité   19   tonalité

indicatif du pays	indicatif de la ville	numéro demandé

COMMUNICATIONS:ETRANGER
Indicatifs des pays et indicatifs des villes les plus demandées

Australie indicatif du pays **61**
Melbourne
Sydney 3

Canada indicatif du pays **1**
Montréal 2
Québec 514
Toronto 418

États-Unis indicatif du pays **1** 416
Boston
Chicago 617
Dallas 312
Houston 214
Los Angeles 713
New York 213
San Francisco 212
Washington, D.C. 415

Espagne indicatif du pays **34** 202
Barcelona
Granada 3
Madrid 58
Sevilla 1

Mexique indicatif du pays **52** 54
Guadalajara
Mexico 36

Royaume-Uni indicatif du pays **44** 5
Belfast
Liverpool
Edimbourg

Réintroduction et recombinaison

A **J'écrivais à mes grands-parents.** Complétez à l'imparfait.

1. Quand j' ____ jeune, j' ____ souvent à mes grands-parents. (être, écrire)
2. Moi, j' ____ à Paris et eux, ils ____ à Lyon. (habiter, habiter)
3. Maman ____ au bureau de poste où elle ____ des timbres. (aller, acheter)
4. Moi, je ne ____ pas très bien écrire et Maman m' ____. (savoir, aider)
5. Elle ____ ou ____ l'adresse sur l'enveloppe. (mettre, écrire)
6. Je ____ les timbres. (mettre)

B **La communication.** Dites si c'est une lettre ou un coup de fil.

1. l'indicatif régional
2. le code postal
3. l'adresse
4. le numéro de téléphone
5. le destinataire
6. l'interlocuteur
7. le timbre
8. la pièce
9. le distributeur automatique
10. le répondeur automatique

C **Pas maintenant, hier.** Récrivez au passé composé.

1. Il y va maintenant.
2. Il part maintenant.
3. Il arrive à l'aéroport.
4. Il prend l'avion.
5. Il fait enregistrer ses bagages.
6. Il entend l'annonce du départ de son avion.
7. Il va à la porte d'embarquement.
8. Il prend sa place.
9. Il lit le magazine de la ligne aérienne.
10. Il voit un film.

L'horloge parlante

Vivez à l'heure exacte
Appelez le 36 99

Vocabulaire

NOMS
le téléphone
 à cadran
 à touches
l'appel (m.)
le numéro de téléphone
l'indicatif (m.)
 de la ville
 du pays
l'annuaire (m.)
la cabine téléphonique
le/la standardiste
le cadran
la touche
la tonalité
la fente

le jeton
la télécarte
la ligne
le message
le bureau de tabac

ADJECTIFS
libre
occupé(e)
interurbain(e)
public, publique

ADVERBE
directement

VERBES
téléphoner

appeler
décrocher
sonner
raccrocher
soulever
oublier
se souvenir de
introduire (une pièce)

AUTRES MOTS ET
EXPRESSIONS
donner un coup de fil
composer (faire) le
 numéro
attendre la tonalité
sonner occupé
laisser un message

le bon numéro
le mauvais numéro
C'est une erreur.
Allô.
Pourrais-je parler à… ?
C'est de la part de qui?
Un moment, s'il vous plaît.
Ne quittez pas.
Je regrette.
être désolé(e)
avoir envie de
il est nécessaire de
surtout

Réintroduction et recombinaison

ANSWERS

Exercice A

1. étais, écrivais
2. habitais, habitaient
3. allait, achetait
4. savais, aidait
5. mettait, écrivait
6. mettais

Exercice B

1. un coup de fil
2. une lettre
3. une lettre
4. un coup de fil
5. une lettre
6. un coup de fil
7. une lettre
8. un coup de fil
9. une lettre
10. un coup de fil

Exercice C

1. Il y est allé (hier).
2. Il est parti (hier).
3. Il est arrivé à l'aéroport.
4. Il a pris l'avion.
5. Il a fait enregistrer ses…
6. Il a entendu l'annonce…
7. Il est allé à la porte…
8. Il a pris sa place.
9. Il a lu le magazine de…
10. Il a vu un film.

ASSESSMENT RESOURCES

1. Chapter Quizzes
2. Testing Program
3. Situation Cards
4. Communication Transparency C-3
5. Computer Software: Practice/Test Generator

VIDEO PROGRAM

INTRODUCTION (13:31)

LE MINITEL (14:17)

STUDENT PORTFOLIO

Written assignments which may be included in students' portfolios are *Activité de communication écrite A* on page 74 and any writing activities from the *Un Peu Plus* section in the Workbook.

Note Students may create and save both oral and written work using the Electronic Portfolio feature on the CD-ROM.

INDEPENDENT PRACTICE

Assign any of the following:
1. Activities and exercises, pages 74–75
2. Communication Activities Masters, pages 17–24
3. CD-ROM, Disc 1, pages 74–75

CHAPTER OVERVIEW

In this chapter students will increase their ability to communicate in situations involving travel by train. They will be able to cope with complications such as a missed train, special reservations, changing trains, etc. They will learn some additional negative expressions and the difference between the imperfect and the *passé composé*.

The cultural focus of Chapter 4 is on modern train service in France and on the differences between trains of the past and those of today.

CHAPTER OBJECTIVES

By the end of this chapter, students will know:

1. vocabulary associated with travel in various types of trains
2. vocabulary associated with rail travel procedures, including booking reservations and checking baggage
3. the contrasting uses of the *passé composé* and the imperfect
4. the use of the *passé composé* and the imperfect in the same sentence
5. the use of *Personne ne...* or *Rien ne...* as the subject of a sentence

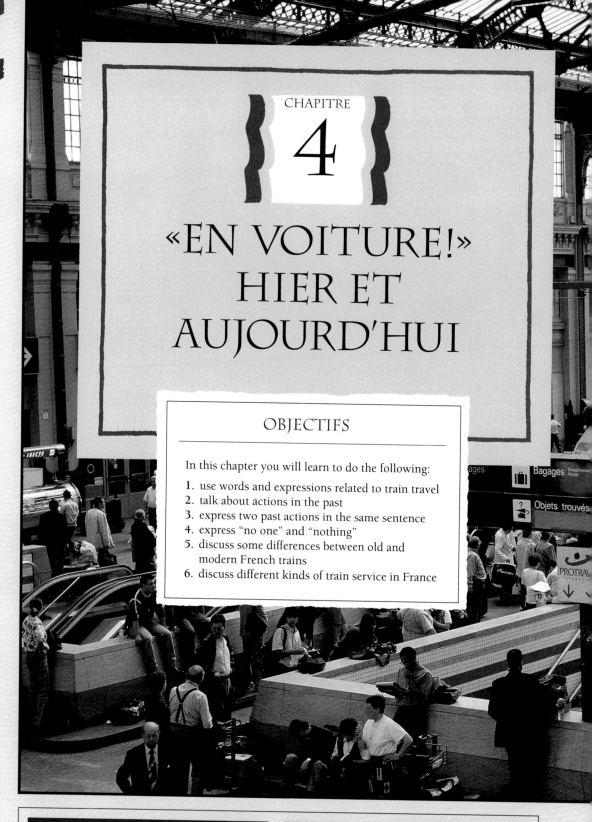

«EN VOITURE!» HIER ET AUJOURD'HUI

OBJECTIFS

In this chapter you will learn to do the following:

1. use words and expressions related to train travel
2. talk about actions in the past
3. express two past actions in the same sentence
4. express "no one" and "nothing"
5. discuss some differences between old and modern French trains
6. discuss different kinds of train service in France

CHAPTER PROJECT

(optional)

Bring brochures from a local travel agency about American and French rail service to class. Ask students to compare and contrast the rail service available in the two countries.

COMMUNITIES

Have students create a huge poster of a cutaway train filled with passengers (self-portraits). All parts of the train should be labeled in French. Hang the poster in the main hallway of the school for National Foreign Language Week (the first full week in March).

CHAPTER 4 RESOURCES

1. Workbook
2. Student Tape Manual
3. Audio Cassette 3B/CD-2
4. Vocabulary Transparencies
5. Bell Ringer Review Blackline Masters
6. Communication Transparency C-4
7. Communication Activities Masters
8. Situation Cards
9. Conversation Video
10. Videocassette/Videodisc, Unit 1
11. Video Activities Booklet, Unit 1
12. Computer Software: Practice/Test Generator
13. Chapter Quizzes
14. Testing Program
15. Lesson Plans
16. Internet Activities Booklet
17. CD-ROM Interactive Textbook
18. Map Transparencies
19. Fine Art Transparency F-1
20. Performance Assessment

Pacing

This chapter will require eight to ten class sessions. Pacing will depend on the length of the class, the age of the students, and student aptitude.

For more information on planning your class, see the Lesson Plans, which offer guidelines for 45- and 55-minute classes and **Block Scheduling**.

Exercices vs. *Activités*

The exercises and activities are color-coded. Exercises, which provide guided practice to prepare students for independent communication, are coded in blue. Communicative activities, which give students opportunities for creative, open-ended expression, are coded in red.

INTERNET ACTIVITIES

(optional)

These activities, student worksheets, and related teacher information are in the *À bord* Internet Activities Booklet and on the Glencoe Foreign Language Home Page at: **http://www.glencoe.com/secondary/fl**

DID YOU KNOW?

The Gare de Lyon in Paris was built between 1895–1900 in time for the *Exposition Universelle* of 1900 in the Belle Époque style of architecture popular between 1871 and 1914. "Le Train Bleu" restaurant, situated above the main entry, opened in 1901 and was listed as a historic monument in 1972. The station has been modernized to accommodate the TGV.

VOCABULAIRE

MOTS 1

Vocabulary Teaching Resources

1. Vocabulary Transparencies 4.1(A & B)
2. Audio Cassette 3B/CD-2
3. Student Tape Manual, Teacher's Edition, *Mots 1: A–E*, pages 35–37
4. Workbook, *Mots 1: A–C*, page 35
5. Communication Activities Masters, *Mots 1: A–B*, page 25
6. Chapter Quizzes, *Mots 1: Quiz 1*, page 18
7. CD-ROM, Disc 1, *Mots 1*: pages 78–81

Bell Ringer Review

Write the following on the board or use BRR Blackline Master 4-1: List five activities you used to do when you were five years old but don't do anymore.

RECYCLING

Some of the vocabulary dealing with rail travel was taught in *Bienvenue,* Chapter 8. In this chapter it is recycled, expanded upon, and used in the imperfect and *passé composé.*

PRESENTATION *(pages 78–79)*

A. Have students close their books. Use Vocabulary Transparencies 4.1 (A & B) to introduce the new words and phrases. Have students repeat each word several times after you or Cassette 3B/CD-2.
B. Now ask *Qu'est-ce que c'est?* as you point to the item on the transparency and have students come up with the new words themselves.

À LA GARE DE DÉPART

une nouvelle voiture à couloir central

une voiture-restaurant

un vieux wagon à compartiments (à couloir latéral)

Marc a réservé sa place.

ADDITIONAL PRACTICE

Using props, pictures and various areas of the classroom, guide students with TPR techniques in acting out as many of the vocabulary phrases as possible. For example: *Indiquez un voyageur assis. Indiquez un voyageur debout. Indiquez une place libre. Vous êtes le contrôleur: Entrez dans la voiture. Vérifiez les billets,* etc.

debout

assis

Les compartiments étaient complets.
Il n'y avait plus de places disponibles.
Il y avait de nombreux voyageurs debout.
Les voyageurs n'étaient pas tous assis.

Vous permettez, Mademoiselle?

Julien est entré dans le dernier compartiment.
Il y avait une place en face d'une jeune fille.

À LA GARE D'ARRIVÉE

Le contrôleur est entré dans la voiture.
Il a vérifié les billets.
Il a ramassé les billets.
Il les a poinçonnés.

L'ami de Camille est venu la chercher à la gare.
Personne n'est venu chercher Julien.

CHAPITRE 4   79

79

C. Have students open books. Ask them to role-play and read the mini-conversations with as much expression as possible.

Extension Have students repeat the mini-conversations, changing their expression and intonation to indicate the following: anger, pleasantness, nastiness, and shyness.

D. Have students close their books again. Ask someone in the classroom to stand up. Point to the person and say *debout*. Now point to a student who is seated and say *assis(e)*.

E. Ask for individual repetitions of the words and phrases. Intersperse the repetitions with yes/no, either/or, or interrogative-word questions. For example: *Tous les compartiments étaient complets? Il y avait des places libres? Tous les passagers étaient assis ou debout? Où est-ce que les voyageurs étaient debout?*

F. After you have introduced the *Mots 1* vocabulary using the Vocabulary Transparencies, have students open their books and read the words and sentences on these pages.

CRITICAL THINKING ACTIVITIES

(Thinking skills: making inferences, problem-solving)
    Read the following to the class or write it on the board or on a transparency:

1. Quand Julien entre dans la voiture, pourquoi dit-il: «Vous permettez, Mademoiselle?» Qu'est-ce qu'il veut?

2. Chantal a loué une place dans le train pour Nice. Elle a pris sa place et quelqu'un d'autre est entré dans la voiture. Cette personne a la même place que Chantal. Que faire?

Exercices

PRESENTATION (pages 80–81)

Exercice A

You may wish to use the recorded version of this exercise.

Extension of Exercice A

After completing Exercise A, have students bring in magazine pictures of interiors or exteriors of trains. You could also supply them with these or have them sketch their own. They then create yes/no questions about their pictures similar to those in the exercise and ask them of a partner or of the class.

Exercice B

Have students read the conversation with different types of intonation and expression to convey different moods and reactions.

ANSWERS

Exercice A

1. C'est un train moderne.
2. Non, ce n'est pas un wagon à compartiments.
3. C'est une voiture à couloir central.
4. Il y a deux sièges de chaque côté du couloir.
5. Oui, les sièges sont réglables.
6. Oui, les places sont numérotées.
7. Non, la voiture n'est pas complète.
8. Non, il n'y a personne debout.
9. Oui, les voyageurs sont tous assis.
10. Oui, il y a des places disponibles.
11. Oui, chaque siège a une tablette rabattable.

Exercices

A Le train.   Répondez d'après le dessin.

1. C'est un vieux train ou un train moderne?
2. C'est un wagon à compartiments?
3. C'est une voiture à couloir latéral ou central?
4. Il y a combien de sièges de chaque côté du couloir?
5. Les sièges sont réglables?
6. Les places sont numérotées?
7. La voiture est complète ou pas?
8. Il y a de nombreux voyageurs debout?
9. Les voyageurs sont tous assis?
10. Il y a des places disponibles?
11. Chaque siège a une tablette rabattable?

ADDITIONAL PRACTICE

Student Tape Manual, Teacher's Edition, *Activités D–E,* page 37

B Pardon. Il y a un petit problème. Répétez la conversation.

DAVID: Excusez-moi, Madame, mais je crois que vous avez ma place.

MME BRUNET: Je suis désolée, jeune homme, mais vous vous trompez. Je sais que c'est ma place. Regardez bien votre billet.

DAVID: J'ai la place numéro 15, voiture numéro 30.

MME BRUNET: Voilà le problème! Ici c'est la voiture numéro 31.

DAVID: Ah, excusez-moi, Madame.

MME BRUNET: Ce n'est pas grave. La voiture numéro 30 est par là.

Répondez d'après la conversation.

1. Où est le jeune homme?
2. Qui a la place numéro 15?
3. Qui a pris la place de David?
4. David s'est trompé?
5. Sa place est dans quelle voiture?
6. Il est dans quelle voiture maintenant?
7. Qu'est-ce qu'il dit pour s'excuser?
8. Que répond Mme Brunet?

C Le voyage de Julien. Répondez par «oui».

1. Les compartiments étaient complets?
2. Il n'y avait plus de places disponibles?
3. Les voyageurs étaient tous assis?
4. Julien est entré dans le dernier compartiment?
5. Il y avait une place en face d'une jeune fille?
6. Julien a dit, «Vous permettez, Mademoiselle?»
7. Le contrôleur est entré dans le compartiment pour vérifier les billets?
8. Le contrôleur a ramassé et poinçonné les billets?
9. L'ami de Camille est venu la chercher à la gare?
10. Personne n'est venu chercher Julien?

D Un voyage en train. Complétez.

1. Je pars en voyage. Je prends le train à la ___.
2. Avant le départ du train les voyageurs entendent l'annonce: «___!»
3. Mon Dieu! Il n'y a plus de places ___. Le train est complet.
4. Un autre voyageur est debout devant ma place. Je ne peux pas m'asseoir. Alors je dis: «___.»
5. J'ai faim. Je vais aller prendre quelque chose à manger à la ___.
6. Ce soir on va dîner dans la ___ du train.
7. Tu préfères t'asseoir à côté de moi ou ___ moi?
8. Le voyage est fini. Le train arrive dans la ___.
9. Ton ami vient te ___ à la gare?
10. Non. ___ ne vient me chercher.
11. Mon ami m'a dit, « ___, mais je ne peux pas venir te chercher.»

ANSWERS

Exercice B

1. Le jeune homme est dans le train.
2. David a la place numéro 15.
3. David pense que Mme Brunet a pris sa place.
4. Oui, David s'est trompé.
5. Sa place est dans la voiture numéro 30.
6. Il est dans la voiture numéro 31 maintenant.
7. Il dit: «Ah, excusez-moi, Madame.»
8. Mme Brunet répond: «Ce n'est pas grave.»

Exercice C

1. Oui, les compartiments étaient complets.
2. Oui, il n'y avait plus de places disponibles.
3. Oui, les voyageurs étaient tous assis.
4. Oui, Julien est entré dans le dernier compartiment.
5. Oui, il y avait une place en face d'une jeune fille.
6. Oui, Julien a dit: «Vous permettez, Mademoiselle?»
7. Oui, le contrôleur est entré dans le compartiment pour vérifier les billets.
8. Oui, le contrôleur a ramassé et poinçonné les billets.
9. Oui, l'ami de Camille est venu la chercher à la gare.
10. Oui, personne n'est venu chercher Julien.

Exercice D

1. gare de départ
2. Attention à la fermeture des portes! Attention au départ!
3. disponibles
4. Vous permettez, Monsieur?
5. voiture gril-express
6. voiture-restaurant
7. en face de
8. gare d'arrivée
9. chercher
10. Personne
11. Je suis désolé

Vocabulary Teaching Resources

1. Vocabulary Transparencies 4.2 (A & B)
2. Audio Cassette 3B/CD-2
3. Student Tape Manual, Teacher's Edition, *Mots 2: F–H*, pages 38–40
4. Workbook, *Mots 2: D–G*, pages 36–37
5. Communication Activities Masters, *Mots 2: C–D*, page 26
6. Computer Software, *Vocabulaire*
7. Chapter Quizzes, *Mots 2: Quiz 2*, page 19
8. CD-ROM, Disc 1, *Mots 2:* pages 82–85

Bell Ringer Review

Write the following on the board or use BRR Blackline Master 4-2: Complete the following telephone conversation with the appropriate words:
«Âllo!»
«_____, oui!»
«Pourrais-_____ parler à M. Brun, s'il _____ _____?»
«C'est de la _____ de _____?»
«De Mme Le Jeune.»
«Un _____, ne _____ pas.»

PRESENTATION (pages 82–83)

A. Have students close their books. Use Vocabulary Transparencies 4.2 (A & B) to introduce the new words and expressions. Have students repeat each word after you or Cassette 3B/CD-2. Point to each item and give the individual word—*la queue, les voyageurs,* etc. Build to complete sentences. For example, *Les voyageurs font la queue.*

VOCABULAIRE

MOTS 2

le tableau des départs		le tableau des arrivées	
les grandes lignes		les lignes (f.) de banlieue	
Départs	**Départs**	**Arrivées**	**Arrivées**
Grandes Lignes	Lignes de Banlieue	Grandes Lignes	Lignes de Banlieue
Londres			Roissy
Lille			Mitry-Claye
Bruxelles			Les Noues

Les lignes de banlieue sont les trains qui desservent les villes de banlieue.
Les grandes lignes sont les trains qui desservent les grandes villes de France et des autres pays d'Europe.

le bureau de location

Les voyageurs font la queue.
Ils veulent louer (réserver) des places à l'avance.

Ils louent (réservent) leurs places au bureau de location.

PANTOMIME

Have a student or students pantomime the following.

Allez à la gare.
Attendez le train sur le quai.
Mettez votre vélo dans le fourgon à bagages.
Montez en voiture.
Trouvez votre compartiment.

Ouvrez la porte du compartiment.
Entrez dans le compartiment.
Trouvez votre place.
Prenez votre place. Asseyez-vous.
Voilà une femme âgée qui cherche une place. Levez-vous.
Offrez-lui votre place.
Allez dans le couloir. Restez debout.
Le train arrive à la gare. Descendez.

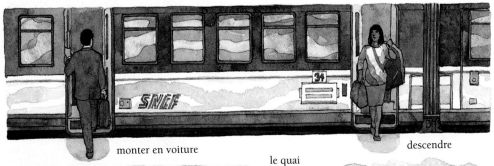

monter en voiture

le quai

descendre

Ah, zut!
J'ai raté le train.

Le train s'est arrêté.
Les voyageurs ont changé de train.
Ils ont pris la correspondance.

Le train est déjà parti.
Le prochain train part à quelle heure?

un fourgon à bagages

un château

un vélo

Les jeunes gens vont visiter les châteaux de
    la Loire.
Ils ont emporté leur vélo.

Ils ont mis leur vélo dans le fourgon à
    bagages.

CHAPITRE 4   **83**

B. Now have students open their
   books and read the words and
   sentences.
C. Reinforce the *Mots 2* presentation with the following questions: *Quelles villes les lignes de
   banlieue desservent-elles? Et les
   grandes lignes? Où est-ce que les
   voyageurs font la queue? Qu'est-
   ce qu'ils veulent louer? Où est-ce
   qu'ils louent leur place? Quand
   le train s'est arrêté, qu'est-ce que
   les voyageurs ont fait? Qu'est-ce
   que les jeunes gens vont visiter?
   Qu'est-ce qu'ils ont emporté? Où
   est-ce qu'ils ont mis leur vélo?*

**CRITICAL THINKING
ACTIVITIES**

(Thinking skills: problem-solving)
    Read the following to the class or write it
on the board or on a transparency:
1. **Robert a perdu sa montre. Il ne sait pas
    l'heure. Il doit prendre un train qui part à
    14h30. Qu'est-ce qu'il va faire?**
2. **Carole a raté son train. Qu'est-ce qu'elle
    peut faire?**

ADDITIONAL PRACTICE

    Student Tape Manual, Teacher's Edition,
Activité G, page 39

Exercices

PRESENTATION (page 84)

Exercice A

🎧 You may wish to use the recorded version of this exercise.

ANSWERS

Exercice A

1. Oui, le train est arrivé en gare.
2. Oui, il est arrivé à l'heure.
3. Oui, le train s'est arrêté.
4. Oui, les voyageurs sont descendus.
5. Oui, ils ont changé de train.
6. Oui, il y avait d'autres voyageurs qui attendaient le train.
7. Oui, ils l'attendaient sur le quai.
8. Oui, les voyageurs sont montés en voiture.
9. Oui, les voyageurs qui étaient en retard ont raté le train.
10. Oui, ils ont dit «Zut!» quand le train est parti sans eux.

Exercice B

1. Le train va à Tours.
2. Non, il n'est pas direct.
3. Oui, il faut changer de train.
4. Il faut prendre la correspondance à Saint-Pierre-des-Corps.
5. Les voyageurs qui vont à Tours descendent du train à Saint-Pierre-des-Corps.
6. Oui, les jeunes gens ont emporté leur vélo.
7. Ils ont mis leur vélo dans le fourgon à bagages.
8. Oui, ils vont visiter les châteaux de la Loire.

Exercice C

1. c   3. b   5. e
2. d   4. a

Exercice D

1. C'est le tableau des arrivées.
2. C'est le tableau des départs.
3. Les lignes de banlieue desservent les villes de banlieue.
4. Les grandes lignes desservent les grandes villes de France et des autres pays d'Europe.
5. On va au bureau de location pour louer une place à l'avance.
6. Oui, quand on rate le train il faut attendre le prochain train.

Exercices

A **Le train est arrivé.** Répondez par «oui».

1. Le train est arrivé en gare?
2. Il est arrivé à l'heure?
3. Le train s'est arrêté?
4. Les voyageurs sont descendus?
5. Ils ont changé de train?
6. Il y avait d'autres voyageurs qui attendaient le train?
7. Ils l'attendaient sur le quai?
8. Les voyageurs sont montés en voiture?
9. Les voyageurs qui étaient en retard ont raté le train?
10. Ils ont dit «Zut!» quand le train est parti sans eux?

Le château de Chambord

B **Le train n'est pas direct.** Répondez d'après les indications.

1. Où va le train? (à Tours)
2. Il est direct? (non)
3. Il faut changer de train? (oui)
4. Où est-ce qu'il faut prendre la correspondance? (à Saint-Pierre-des-Corps)
5. Où les voyageurs qui vont à Tours descendent-ils du train? (à Saint-Pierre-des-Corps)
6. Les jeunes gens ont emporté leur vélo? (oui)
7. Où est-ce qu'ils ont mis leur vélo? (dans le fourgon à bagages)
8. Ils vont visiter les châteaux de la Loire? (oui)

C **Guide du train: SNCF.** Lisez le document. Cherchez le contraire.

1. emporter   a. interdit
2. de petits parcours b. le déchargement
3. le chargement   c. laisser à la maison
4. autorisé   d. de longs parcours
5. disponible   e. pris

D **À la gare.** Répondez.

1. Quel est le tableau qui indique les arrivées?
2. Et quel est le tableau qui indique les départs?
3. Quelles villes les lignes de banlieue desservent-elles?
4. Quelles villes les grandes lignes desservent-elles?
5. Où va-t-on pour louer une place à l'avance?
6. Quand on rate le train il faut attendre le prochain train?

Guide du train et du vélo

SNCF

PRENEZ LE TRAIN SANS VOUS PRIVER DE VOTRE VELO !

■ **VOUS POUVEZ EMPORTER GRATUITEMENT VOTRE BICYCLETTE EN BAGAGE A MAIN.**

Dans plus de 2000 trains de petits parcours, vous pouvez emporter, tous les jours, votre vélo comme un bagage à main. Vous assurez vous-même le chargement de votre vélo dans le fourgon à bagages, et son déchargement.
Attention, le chargement est autorisé dans le fourgon dans la limite de la place disponible. Dans certains types d'autorails, la capacité du fourgon est limitée à 3 bicyclettes.
Les trains sont repérés dans les documents horaires par le pictogramme :

A noter : la SNCF n'est pas responsable des vélos transportés en bagages à main.

Activités de communication orale
Mots 1 et 2

A **C'est qui ou quoi?** Choisissez une personne ou une chose dans la liste qui suit. Décrivez-la à un(e) camarade. Votre camarade doit deviner de qui ou de quoi vous parlez. Ensuite changez de rôles.

un fourgon à bagages
un tableau des départs
une tablette rabattable
un train à compartiments
un train moderne
une valise

une voiture-restaurant
un contrôleur
un porteur
un voyageur
une voyageuse
un billet

Élève 1: Le contrôleur le poinçonne.
Élève 2: C'est un billet.

B **Quelle catastrophe!** Your train trip to Strasbourg is a disaster: everything goes wrong! Take turns acting out the following situations with a classmate. Remember to answer with the appropriate remark or apology and say what you'll do to correct your mistake.

1. Another passenger says you're in the wrong seat.
2. The conductor says you're in the wrong class of car.
3. The conductor says you're on the wrong train.
4. The waiter in the *voiture-restaurant* says you're at the wrong table and that you didn't make a reservation.

Élève 1: Excusez-moi, Mademoiselle. Je crois que vous vous êtes trompée de place. J'ai la place 15.
Élève 2: Oh, là, là! Je suis désolée, Monsieur. Je vais regarder mon billet. (Je vais changer de place.)

C **Le train est déjà parti!** Vous arrivez en retard à la Gare de Lyon. Vous avez raté votre train pour Dijon et maintenant vous ne savez pas quoi faire. Un autre voyageur dans la gare veut vous aider. Répondez à ses questions.

1. Je peux vous aider? Vous avez raté votre train?
2. Où alliez-vous?
3. Il y a beaucoup de trains pour Dijon. Regardez le tableau des départs dans le hall. Voulez-vous que je vous le montre?

Un autre voyageur

CRITICAL THINKING ACTIVITIES

(Thinking skills: problem-solving)
    Read the following to the class or write it on the board or on a transparency:

1. Julie a un rendez-vous à Lyon qui est très important. Elle pensait aller à Lyon en train. Malheureusement il y a eu an accident ferroviaire (de train) et il n'y a plus de trains pour Lyon. Qu'est-ce que Julie doit faire?
2. Olivier a pris le mauvais train. Qu'est-ce qu'il doit faire?

(Mots 2)
    Make incorrect statements about the *Mots 2* Vocabulary Transparencies and have students correct you. For example: *Les employés font la queue. Les jeunes gens mettent leur vélo dans la voiture-restaurant. Les voyageurs louent leur place au tableau des arrivées,* etc.

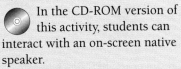

Activités de communication orale
Mots 1 et 2
PRESENTATION *(page 85)*
    You may wish to assign different activities to different groups or pairs. You may also wish to have students select the activities they wish to do.

Activité C
    In the CD-ROM version of this activity, students can interact with an on-screen native speaker.

ANSWERS
Activités A, B, and C
    Answers will vary.

GEOGRAPHY CONNECTION
    Have students look at the photo at the top of page 84 as you say: **Trouvez Tours et Orléans sur la carte de France à la page 435. Le château de Chambord est tout près de Blois, une jolie ville sur la Loire qui se trouve entre ces deux villes.**

HISTORY CONNECTION
    Have students look at the photo at the top of page 84. Read or paraphrase the following information to them:
    Le château de Chambord est l'un des plus grands châteaux de la vallée de la Loire. Construit entre 1519 et 1530, ce château fabuleux était la résidence favorite de François Ier. Le château de Chambord lui servait de pavillon de chasse.

Structure Teaching Resources

1. Workbook, *Structure: A–H*, pages 38–40
2. Student Tape Manual, Teacher's Edition, *Structure: A–D*, pages 40–43
3. Audio Cassette 3B/CD-2
4. Communication Activities Masters, *Structure: A–C* pages 27–30
5. Computer Software, *Structure*
6. Chapter Quizzes, *Structure: Quizzes 3–5*, pages 20–22
7. CD-ROM, Disc 1, pages 86–91

Bell Ringer Review

Write the following on the board or use BRR Blackline Master 4-3: Write all the words or expressions you can think of related to the following words: un annuaire/une cabine téléphonique/un mauvais numéro.

L'imparfait et le passé composé

PRESENTATION *(page 86)*

A. Lead students through steps 1–5 on page 86.
B. For step 2, draw a timeline on the board. Each time you give a verb in the *passé composé*, write an abrupt slash through the timeline to indicate termination or completion.
C. As you go over the sentences in step 4, put another timeline on the board. Each time you give a verb in the imperfect, draw a long shaded box on the timeline to indicate duration.

L'imparfait et le passé composé

Talking About Actions in the Past

1. The choice of whether to use the *passé composé* or the imperfect tense depends upon whether the speaker is describing an action completed in the past or a continuous, recurring action in the past.

2. You use the *passé composé* to express actions or events that began and ended at a specific time in the past.

> J'ai passé l'été dernier en Bretagne.
> Un jour je suis allé à Cancale.
> À Cancale j'ai acheté des fruits de mer.

3. The following time expressions are often used with the *passé composé*.

hier	à huit heures
hier soir	l'année dernière
ce matin	vendredi dernier
un jour	

4. The imperfect, in contrast to the *passé composé*, is used to express a continuous, habitual, or repeated action in the past. The moment when the action began or ended is unimportant.

> Je passais tous les étés en Bretagne quand j'étais jeune.
> J'allais tous les jours à Cancale où je faisais les courses.
> De temps en temps j'achetais des fruits de mer.

5. The following time expressions are often used with the imperfect.

de temps en temps	tous les jours
fréquemment	tous les mois
souvent	toutes les semaines
toujours	

Cancale, en Bretagne, est connu pour ses huîtres.

LEARNING FROM PHOTOS

Have students look at the photos on page 86. Read the following information to them: *Cancale est un port de pêche et une station balnéaire sur la côte nord de la Bretagne entre Saint-Malo et le Mont-Saint-Michel. Cancale est connu pour ses huîtres. Dans la baie de Cancale il y a de très grands parcs à huîtres.*

Exercices

A On le faisait souvent ou on l'a fait une fois? Répondez.

1. Le train est arrivé à l'heure hier?
   Quand est-ce que le train est arrivé à l'heure?
   Le train arrivait toujours à l'heure?
   Quand est-ce que le train arrivait à l'heure?
2. Le train est parti ce matin du quai onze?
   Quand est-ce que le train est parti du quai onze?
   Le train partait tous les jours du quai onze?
   Quand est-ce que le train partait du quai onze?
3. Tu es allé(e) au cinéma vendredi soir?
   Quand est-ce que tu es allé(e) au cinéma?
   Tu allais au cinéma tous les vendredis soirs?
   Quand est-ce que tu allais au cinéma?
4. Madame Benoît est allée en France l'été dernier?
   Quand est-ce que Madame Benoît est allée en France?
   Madame Benoît allait en France tous les étés?
   Quand est-ce que Madame Benoît allait en France?
5. Tu as regardé la télé hier soir?
   Quand est-ce que tu as regardé la télé?
   Tu regardais la télé tous les soirs?
   Quand est-ce que tu regardais la télé?
6. Tu as reçu une lettre hier?
   Quand est-ce que tu as reçu une lettre?
   Tu recevais des lettres souvent?
   Quand est-ce que tu recevais des lettres?

B Mes vacances. Donnez des réponses personnelles.

Pendant les vacances d'été quand tu étais petit(e)...

1. Tu allais toujours au bord de la mer?
2. Tu prenais le train?
3. Tu écrivais des cartes postales?
4. Tu allais à quelle plage?
5. Tu faisais du ski nautique?
6. Tu bronzais?
7. Tu mangeais des glaces?
8. Tu t'amusais bien?

Et l'été dernier...

1. Tu es allé(e) au bord de la mer?
2. Tu as pris le train?
3. Tu as écrit des lettres?
4. Tu es allé(e) à quelle plage?
5. Tu as nagé?
6. Tu as fait du ski nautique?
7. Tu as bronzé?
8. Tu as mangé des glaces?
9. Tu t'es bien amusé(e)?

CHAPITRE 4   87

Exercices

PRESENTATION (page 87)

Exercices A and B

A. Exercises A and B can be done with books closed, open, or once each way.
B. While doing Exercises A and B, gesture with a slash of the hand to indicate completion with the *passé composé*. Wave your hand back and forth to indicate duration with the imperfect.
C. Exercise A uses the question word *quand* to force students to focus their attention on the time element.

ANSWERS

Exercice A

1. Oui, le train est arrivé à l'heure hier. (Non, le train n'est pas arrivé...)
   Le train est arrivé à l'heure (ce matin).
   Oui, le train arrivait toujours à l'heure. (Non, le train n'arrivait pas toujours...)
   Le train arrivait à l'heure (toutes les semaines).
2. Oui, le train est parti ce matin du quai onze. (Non, le train n'est pas parti...)
   Le train est parti du quai onze (vendredi dernier).
   Oui, le train partait tous les jours du quai onze. (Non, le train ne partait pas...)
   Le train partait (souvent) du quai onze.
3. Oui, je suis allé(e) au cinéma vendredi soir. (Non, je ne suis pas allé[e]...)
   Je suis allé(e) au cinéma (samedi soir).
   Oui, j'allais au cinéma tous les vendredis soirs. (Non, je n'allais pas...)
   J'allais au cinéma (tous les samedis soirs).
4.–6. Answers follow the same pattern as 1.–3.

Exercice B

Answers will vary.

Exercices

Exercices D and E

Have the students prepare Exercises D and E before going over them in class.

Extension of *Exercices C, D,* and *E*

After completing these exercises, have students make up a question about each sentence. They will use *tu* in Exercise C, *ils* in Exercise D, and *Maman* in Exercise E.

ANSWERS

Exercice C

Students read the paragraph.

Exercice D

Hier ils se sont levés de bonne heure. Ils ont fait leur toilette, ils se sont habillés, ils ont pris leur petit déjeuner et ils ont quitté la maison. Ils sont allés à la gare où ils ont attendu le train. Ils sont descendus sur le quai. Le train est arrivé et ils sont montés en voiture. Ils sont arrivés en ville une demi-heure plus tard. Ils sont entrés dans leur bureau à neuf heures précises.

Exercice E

Tous les jours Maman se levait de bonne heure. Elle faisait sa toilette, elle s'habillait, elle prenait son petit déjeuner et elle quittait la maison. Maman allait à la gare où elle attendait le train. Elle descendait sur le quai. Le train arrivait et elle montait en voiture. Elle arrivait en ville une demi-heure plus tard. Elle entrait dans son bureau à neuf heures précises.

Exercice F

1. voyageait, a voyagé
2. allais, es allé(e)
3. passait, a passé
4. dînions, avons dîné
5. recevaient, ont reçu

C **Hier.** Lisez.

Hier je me suis levé(e) de bonne heure. J'ai fait ma toilette, je me suis habillé(e), j'ai pris mon petit déjeuner et j'ai quitté la maison. Je suis allé(e) à la gare où j'ai attendu le train. Je suis descendu(e) sur le quai. Le train est arrivé et je suis monté(e) en voiture. Je suis arrivé(e) en ville une demi-heure plus tard. Je suis entré(e) dans mon bureau à neuf heures précises.

D **Hier encore.** Dans l'Exercice C, remplacez «je» par «ils» et faites tous les changements nécessaires d'après le modèle.

> **Hier ils se sont levés de bonne heure...**

E **Tous les jours.** Dans l'Exercice C, remplacez «hier» par «tous les jours» et «je» par «Maman». Faites tous les changements nécessaires d'après le modèle.

> **Tous les jours Maman se levait de bonne heure...**

F **Toujours ou pas?** Mettez les verbes à l'imparfait ou au passé composé d'après le modèle.

> arriver
> Quand Julie avait 12 ans le train <u>arrivait</u> toujours en retard.
> Mais hier le train <u>est arrivé</u> en avance.

1. voyager
   On ___ souvent en train quand on allait en vacances.
   Mais l'été dernier on ___ en avion.

2. aller
   Tu ___ au cinéma tous les vendredis quand tu étais au lycée.
   Mais vendredi dernier tu ___ au théâtre.

3. passer
   De temps en temps Madame Napier ___ ses vacances en Provence.
   Mais l'été dernier Madame Napier ___ ses vacances en Bretagne.

4. dîner
   En 1990 nous ___ fréquemment à la voiture-restaurant.
   Mais l'année dernière nous ___ rarement à la voiture-restaurant.

5. recevoir
   Anne et Solange ___ des lettres toutes les semaines quand elles étaient à l'école.
   Mais l'année dernière elles ___ des lettres en septembre seulement.

LE BON MOMENT
la Restauration du Voyage

MENU DU DÉJEUNER

200 F
Eau minérale 14 cl et Vin 25 cl compris

Flan de Saint-Jacques
Spaghettis de Légumes aux Herbes

Assiette Froide Festive
(Cœur de Rumsteck, Blanc de Pintade aux Fines Herbes, Jambon d'Aoste, Céleri-Rave aux Champignons Chinois)
ou
Délice de Veau au Poivre
Fonds d'Artichauts et Champignons
ou
Noisette d'Agneau Grillée
Pommes de Terre au Thym, Haricots Verts

Dôme Cendré

Dessert

Café, thé ou infusion

TAXES ET SERVICE 15 % COMPRIS

LEARNING FROM REALIA	INDEPENDENT PRACTICE
Tell students that the lunch menu is from the dining car on the train. Ask them to find all the foods they know on the menu. Explain all the new words to them. Now have pairs of students make up a conversation between a waiter and a customer in the dining car. Have different pairs present their conversations to the class.	Assign any of the following: 1. Exercises, pages 87–88 2. Workbook, *Structure: A–D,* pages 38–39 3. Communication Activities Masters, *Structure: A,* page 27 4. CD-ROM, Disc 1, pages 86–88

Deux actions au passé dans la même phrase

Expressing Two Past Actions in the Same Sentence

1. Many sentences that relate past actions or events have two verbs that are either in the same tense or in two different tenses. Study the following sentences.

   > **Jean** *est sorti* **et Hélène** *est entrée*.
   > **Quand elle** *est entrée*, **j'**ai servi **le dîner.**

   In each of the above sentences both verbs are in the *passé composé* because they express two simple actions or events that began and ended at a specific time in the past.

2. Study the following sentences.

   > **Pendant les vacances Charles** *allait* **à la plage et moi je** *travaillais*.
   > **Quand j'**avais **soif, je** prenais **de l'eau minérale.**

   In each of the above sentences the two verbs are in the imperfect because they both describe a habitual or continuous action in the past. The time at which the action began or ended is unimportant.

3. Study the following sentences.

   > **Quand je** *suis arrivé(e)*, **Jean-Claude** *dormait*.
   > **Ma sœur** *jouait* **du piano quand Pierre** *est entré*.

   In each of the above sentences one verb is in the imperfect and the other is in the *passé composé*. The verb in the imperfect describes the background, what was going on. The verb in the *passé composé* expresses the action or event that interrupted what was going on. Study the diagram below.

   > **Ma sœur jouait du piano quand Pierre est entré.**

PASSÉ	PRÉSENT	FUTUR
est jouait entré		

ADDITIONAL PRACTICE

Student Tape Manual, Teacher's Edition,
Activités A–C, pages 40–42

Bell Ringer Review

Write the following on the board or use BRR Blackline Master 4-4: Rewrite the sentences making the subjects and verbs plural.

1. Il me paie chaque semaine.
2. Elle emploie toujours un stylo.
3. Tu envoies beaucoup de cartes postales?
4. J'emploie souvent le téléphone de ma sœur.

Deux actions au passé dans la même phrase

PRESENTATION *(page 89)*

A. When explaining the difference between the *passé composé* and the imperfect, you may wish to have students think of a play. Explain to them that all the stage background, the description, the sets, the scenery are in the imperfect. What the actors and actresses actually do on stage is in the *passé composé*.

B. Give some examples to illustrate the difference between background and acting. Background: *Il faisait très beau. Il y avait une fête. Tout le monde s'amusait. Marie jouait de l'accordéon. Charles et Julie dansaient.* Acting: *Et alors Jean est entré. Il a dit bonjour à tout le monde.*

C. Use two verbs in one sentence to contrast the background activities with the actors' or actresses' performances. *Charles et Julie dansaient quand Jean est entré.*

Note In the CD-ROM version, this structure point is presented via an interactive electronic comic strip.

Exercices

ANSWERS

Exercice A

Answers will vary.

Exercice B

1. Papa n'a pas répondu. Il travaillait dans le jardin.
2. Maman n'a pas répondu. Elle faisait la cuisine.
3. Suzanne n'a pas répondu. Elle lisait le journal.
4. Paul n'a pas répondu. Il écrivait une composition.
5. Le bébé n'a pas répondu. Il dormait.
6. Anne et Sylvie n'ont pas répondu. Elles s'habillaient.
7. Je n'ai pas répondu. Je prenais une douche.
8. Tu n'as pas répondu. Tu dormais comme un bébé.

Exercice C

1. Oui, Jean regardait la télé quand le téléphone a sonné. Oui, il a répondu au téléphone.
2. Oui, sa mère lisait le journal quand Jean l'a appelée au téléphone. Oui, elle est allée au téléphone.
3. Oui, sa mère parlait au téléphone quand Jean est sorti. Oui, il est allé au café.
4. Oui, il allait au café quand il a vu sa copine Brigitte. Oui, ils sont allés au café ensemble.
5. Oui, Jean et Brigitte se parlaient quand deux autres copains sont arrivés. Oui, les deux copains se sont assis à leur table.
6. Oui, ils se parlaient quand le serveur est arrivé à leur table. Oui, ils ont commandé quelque chose à manger.

Exercices

A **Quand j'étais jeune.** Donnez des réponses personnelles.

1. Quand tu étais jeune, tu allais à quelle école primaire?
2. Quand la maîtresse parlait, tu écoutais?
3. Tu faisais toujours attention quand la maîtresse parlait?
4. Tu parlais quand elle parlait?
5. Et maintenant tu es élève dans une école secondaire. Tu n'as plus de maîtresse. Tu as un professeur. Hier, ton professeur t'a posé une question difficile? Tu lui as donné la bonne réponse?
6. Tu as levé la main quand le professeur a posé la question?
7. Tu as répondu aux autres questions que le professeur t'a posées?
8. Tu as dit «au revoir» au professeur quand tu as quitté la classe?

B **Le téléphone a sonné. Qui a répondu? Personne! Pourquoi?** Répondez d'après le modèle.

> **Papa / travailler**
> *Papa n'a pas répondu. Il travaillait.*

1. Papa / travailler dans le jardin
2. Maman / faire la cuisine
3. Suzanne / lire le journal
4. Paul / écrire une composition
5. Le bébé / dormir
6. Anne et Sylvie / s'habiller
7. Je / prendre une douche
8. Tu / dormir comme un bébé

C **Les interruptions.** Répondez par «oui».

1. Jean regardait la télé quand le téléphone a sonné? Il a répondu au téléphone?
2. Sa mère lisait le journal quand Jean l'a appelée au téléphone? Elle est allée au téléphone?
3. Sa mère parlait au téléphone quand Jean est sorti? Il est allé au café?
4. Il allait au café quand il a vu sa copine Brigitte? Ils sont allés au café ensemble?
5. Jean et Brigitte se parlaient quand deux autres copains sont arrivés? Les deux copains se sont assis à leur table?
6. Ils se parlaient quand le serveur est arrivé à la table? Ils ont commandé quelque chose à manger?

D Ils attendaient le train. Complétez à l'imparfait et au passé composé.

1. Les voyageurs ___ assis dans la salle d'attente quand ils ___ l'annonce du départ de leur train. (être, entendre)
2. Ils ___ sur le quai quand le train ___. (attendre, arriver)
3. Pendant que le train ___ en gare, quelques voyageurs ___ du train et d'autres voyageurs ___ en voiture. (être, descendre, monter)
4. Quelques voyageurs ___ debout quand le train ___. (être, partir)
5. Marie et Paul ___ leurs places quand ils ___ le contrôleur. (chercher, voir)
6. Ils ___ quand le contrôleur ___ dans le compartiment. (se parler, entrer)

Personne ne... et Rien ne... Expressing "No one" and "Nothing"

1. You use the negative expressions *Personne ne...* and *Rien ne...* as the subject of a sentence. Note that you do not use *pas* after the verb.

   Personne ne répond au téléphone.
   *Rien n'*a changé ici.

2. *Rien ne...* is often used with the verbs *se passer* and *arriver,* which both mean "to happen." *Qu'est-ce qui se passe?* and *Qu'est-ce qui arrive?* mean "What's happening?," "What's going on?"

   Qu'est-ce qui se passe?   Qu'est-ce qui est arrivé?
   Rien ne se passe.   Rien n'est arrivé.

Exercice

A Personne. Répondez d'après le modèle en utilisant «Personne ne» ou «Rien ne».

   Quelqu'un est là?
   Personne n'est là.

1. Quelqu'un est venu?
2. Quelqu'un a téléphoné au bureau de location?
3. Quelqu'un est allé à la gare?
4. Quelqu'un a loué une place dans le train?
5. Quelque chose a intéressé Laurent?
6. Quelque chose était différent aujourd'hui?
7. Qu'est-ce qui est arrivé?
8. Et qu'est-ce qui s'est passé?

CHAPITRE 4   **91**

CONVERSATION

CONVERSATION

CAROLINE: Pardon, c'est le train pour aller
à Tours?
UN HOMME: Oui, mais il n'est pas direct.
CAROLINE: Pas direct?
UN HOMME: Non, il faut prendre la
correspondance à Saint-Pierre-des-
Corps.
CAROLINE: Prendre la correspondance?
UN HOMME: Oui, il faut changer de train
à Saint-Pierre-des-Corps.
CAROLINE: À Saint-Pierre-des-Corps?
UN HOMME: Oui, vous descendez à la
prochaine.
CAROLINE: Merci. Vous êtes très aimable.
UN HOMME: Je vous en prie.

A **Caroline prend le train.** Répondez d'après la conversation.

1. À ton avis, Caroline est française ou pas?
2. Où est-ce qu'elle va?
3. Elle y va comment?
4. Le train est direct?
5. Il faut changer de train?
6. Où faut-il prendre la correspondance?
7. Saint-Pierre-des-Corps est la prochaine gare?

Activités de communication orale

A **Ta jeunesse.** Vous parlez à un(e) camarade français(e) de ce que vous faisiez tou(te)s les deux quand vous étiez petit(e)s. Faites d'abord une liste de plusieurs activités: aller en vacances, jouer après les cours, passer la nuit chez des copains, etc.

> Élève 1: Comment est-ce que vous alliez en vacances?
> Élève 2: On allait en vacances en train.
> Élève 1: Nous, on partait toujours en voiture et j'étais toujours malade.

Bell Ringer Review

Write the following on the board or use BRR Blackline Master 4-5: Write the opposite of the following words or phrases.
la gare d'arrivée
monter en voiture
prendre un train direct
debout

PRESENTATION (page 92)

A. Tell students they are going to hear a conversation between Caroline and a man at the train station.
B. Have students close their books. Play the Conversation Video or ask them to listen as you read the conversation or play Cassette 3B/CD-2.
C. Have students repeat the conversation once or twice after you.
D. Now have students read the conversation aloud. (Use *Activité F* in the Student Tape Manual to check for oral comprehension.)
E. Have students practice the conversation in pairs. Ask for volunteers to present an improvised version of the conversation to the class.

Note Be sure students understand that *à la prochaine* means *à la prochaine gare.*

Note In the CD-ROM version, students can play the role of either one of the characters and record the conversation.

ANSWERS

Exercice A

1. À mon avis, Caroline n'est pas française.
2. Elle va à Tours.
3. Elle y va en train.
4. Non, le train n'est pas direct.

DID YOU KNOW?

Travelers on most trains to Tours must get off the train at Saint-Pierre-des-Corps and take a shuttle train to the town center, about ten minutes away.

B **Tu te souviens?** Choisissez une des situations suivantes et demandez à un(e) camarade ce qu'il/elle faisait à ce moment-là.

> M. Un Tel a gagné la médaille d'or aux Jeux Olympiques.
> Mlle Une Telle a gagné la médaille d'argent…
> On a appris la mort de…
> On a appris l'élection de M. Un Tel à la présidence, etc.

> Élève 1: Qu'est-ce que tu faisais quand tu as appris l'élection de M. Un Tel?
> Élève 2: Je dînais.

C **Une excursion à vélo.** You and some friends (your group) are planning a bicycle excursion to the Loire Valley. Using the map below, decide your departure date, how many days you'll need, and how you'll get yourselves and your bikes from Paris to your starting point.

5. Oui, il faut changer de train.
6. Il faut prendre la correspondance à Saint-Pierre-des-Corps.
7. Oui, Saint-Pierre-des-Corps est la prochaine gare.

Activités de communication orale

PRESENTATION *(pages 92–93)*

These activities enable students to use the vocabulary and structures learned in the chapter in open-ended exchanges. You may assign different activities to different groups or allow the students to choose the activities they wish to do.

ANSWERS
Activités A, B, and C
Answers will vary.

INDEPENDENT PRACTICE

Assign any of the following:
1. Exercise and activities, pages 92–93
2. CD-ROM, Disc 1, pages 92–93

LECTURE ET CULTURE

Bell Ringer Review

Write the following on the board or use BRR Blackline Master 4-6: Write the heads la cuisine *and* la salle de séjour *on a piece of paper. Decide where you would find the following objects and write their names under the appropriate head.*

un évier
un magnétoscope
un robinet
un pot-au-feu
une chaîne stéréo
un poste de télévision
un zappeur
une tartine
un lave-vaisselle
un repas
un répondeur automatique

READING STRATEGIES
(*pages 94–95*)

Pre-reading

Focus on the topic of the reading by asking students who among them has traveled by train. Ask them to tell the class a few details in French about their trip. Share your own train experiences in the same way.

Reading

A. To vary the presentation, you may wish to read the *Lecture* to students. Use as much expression as you can.

B. Call on an individual to read several sentences. Then ask other students questions about the sentences the student has just read.

C. You may wish to select several paragraphs that students will read silently.

Post-reading

After going over the *Lecture* in class, have the students read it for homework and write the exercises that follow it.

Note Students may listen to a recorded version of the *Lecture* on the CD-ROM.

LES TRAINS D'HIER ET D'AUJOURD'HUI

L'été dernier Carole est allée en France avec d'autres élèves qui faisaient du français avec Mademoiselle Gautier. Ils y ont passé trois semaines fabuleuses et Carole s'est très bien amusée. Ils sont allés à Avignon, une ville très animée à 683 kilomètres au sud-est de Paris et où il règne une certaine atmosphère de joie de vivre. Naturellement, ils ont visité le Palais des Papes[1] et ils sont allés voir les remparts qui entourent[2] la ville et le célèbre pont[3] d'Avignon qui traversait le Rhône. Avez-vous jamais chanté «Sur le pont d'Avignon»? C'est une chanson bien connue. Il faut l'apprendre si vous ne la connaissez pas! À Avignon il y a aussi un grand festival artistique qui a lieu[4] tous les ans. Ce festival réunit des acteurs, des danseurs et des musiciens de tous les pays du monde.

Le Palais des Papes à Avignon

Carole et ses copains sont allés à Avignon en train? Oui, ils ont pris le train. Mais quel train? Ils ont pris le TGV—le Train à Grande Vitesse. Ce train français est l'un des plus rapides du monde. Il roule à plus de 300 kilomètres à l'heure. Le voyage en TGV coûte cher. Il faut payer un supplément pour une réservation. La réservation est obligatoire. Le TGV est un train moderne, sans compartiments, à couloir central.

Pendant le voyage le contrôleur est entré dans la voiture pour vérifier les billets. Chaque élève avait sa place numérotée louée à l'avance. Pendant le voyage on a servi un repas à prix fixe. Ils sont allés à la voiture-restaurant pour dîner? Mais non, pas dans le TGV! Le serveur a servi le dîner sur place, dans leur voiture. Quel service splendide, n'est-ce pas? Mais c'était en première classe. Pour avoir l'expérience de prendre le TGV, les élèves ont payé plus pour voyager en

---

[1] Papes *popes*
[2] entourent *surround*
[3] pont *bridge*
[4] a lieu *takes place*

94   CHAPITRE 4

ADDITIONAL PRACTICE

After reading the *Lecture*, you may wish to ask the following questions to elicit a guided oral summary of the story.

1. Où est-ce que Carole est allée? Quand? Avec qui?
2. Comment sont-ils allés à Avignon?
3. Où ont-ils dîné?
4. Qui voyageait souvent en train en France?
5. Comment étaient les trains quand Mlle Gautier était étudiante?

première classe parce qu'il n'y avait plus de places en seconde. Dans le TGV en première classe il y a une tablette rabattable à chaque siège et les sièges sont réglables. Quel confort!

Ce n'était pas la première fois que Mademoiselle Gautier, la prof de Carole et des autres élèves, voyageait en France. Quand elle était étudiante, elle allait en France tous les étés. Elle voyageait souvent en train. Mais les vieux trains étaient bien différents du TGV. D'abord, ils n'avaient pas de couloir central avec deux sièges de chaque côté. Les vieux trains avaient des compartiments. Dans un compartiment de première classe il y avait six places et dans un compartiment de seconde il y en avait huit.

Mademoiselle Gautier voyageait toujours en seconde. Elle trouvait ça plus sympathique. Pourquoi? Parce que tout le monde montait en voiture muni de provisions[5]: un filet (ou deux) plein de fromage, de jambon, de pâté, de fruits et un litre de vin rouge. Tous les voyageurs du même compartiment se parlaient et faisaient connaissance[6]. Si quelqu'un n'avait rien à manger, on partageait[7]. C'était vraiment sympa. De temps en temps on sortait dans le couloir pour se dégourdir les jambes[8] et bavarder avec les voyageurs des autres compartiments.

Ces vieux trains existent toujours? Ah oui. Il y en a beaucoup. Mais les TGV deviennent de plus en plus nombreux et desservent de plus en plus de villes. Tout le monde adore la vitesse. Vive la vitesse!

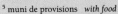

[5] muni de provisions *with food*
[6] faisaient connaissance *got acquainted with one another*
[7] partageait *shared*
[8] se dégourdir les jambes *stretch one's legs*

Étude de mots

A **Quelle est la définition?**
Choisissez les mots qui correspondent.

1. rapide
2. cher
3. sympa
4. debout
5. bavarder

a. agréable
b. sur ses pieds
c. qui coûte beaucoup
d. vite
e. parler

B **Quel est le contraire?**
Trouvez le contraire.

1. dernier
2. le sud
3. cher
4. monter
5. quelque chose

a. descendre
b. le nord
c. prochain
d. bon marché
e. rien

Étude de mots

ANSWERS

Exercice A

1. d	4. b
2. c	5. e
3. a	

Exercice B

1. c	4. a
2. b	5. e
3. d	

LEARNING FROM PHOTOS

C'est une vieille photo ou pas? Que font les garçons? Où sont-ils?

Compréhension (page 96)

ANSWERS

Exercice C

1. Carole est allée en France l'été dernier.
2. Elle y est allée avec d'autres élèves et Mademoiselle Gautier.
3. Avignon est à 683 kilomètres au sud-est de Paris.
4. Le festival d'Avignon a lieu tous les ans.
5. Carole a pris le TGV pour aller à Avignon.
6. C'est le Train à Grande Vitesse.
7. Oui, le contrôleur est entré dans la voiture pour vérifier les billets.
8. Oui, on a servi un repas pendant le voyage.
9. On l'a servi sur place, dans leur voiture.
10. Il y a une tablette rabattable à chaque siège en première classe.
11. Oui, Mademoiselle Gautier prenait souvent le train.
12. Elle voyageait toujours en seconde parce qu'elle trouvait ça plus sympathique.
13. Tous les voyageurs montaient en voiture munis de provisions.
14. On partageait ses provisions.
15. Les voyageurs faisaient connaissance quand ils parlaient avec les autres dans le même compartiment ou quand ils sortaient dans le couloir pour se dégourdir les jambes.

Exercice D

1. Mademoiselle Gautier
2. Avignon
3. le Rhône
4. le Palais des Papes
5. «Sur le Pont d'Avignon»

Exercice E

1. vieux
2. central
3. en première
4. en première
5. huit
6. le couloir
7. de pain

Exercice F

Answers will vary.

96

Compréhension

C Avez-vous compris?   Répondez d'après la lecture.

1. Quand est-ce que Carole est allée en France?
2. Avec qui est-ce qu'elle y est allée?
3. Où est Avignon?
4. Quand est-ce que le festival d'Avignon a lieu?
5. Quel train est-ce que Carole a pris pour aller à Avignon?
6. Le TGV, qu'est-ce que c'est?
7. Le contrôleur est entré dans la voiture? Pourquoi?
8. On a servi un repas pendant le voyage?
9. Où est-ce qu'on l'a servi?
10. Qu'est-ce qu'il y a à chaque siège en première classe?
11. Mademoiselle Gautier prenait souvent le train?
12. Elle voyageait en quelle classe? Pourquoi?
13. Tous les voyageurs montaient en voiture munis de quoi?
14. Qu'est-ce qu'on partageait?
15. Comment est-ce que les voyageurs faisaient connaissance?

D Savez-vous la réponse?   Donnez les renseignements suivants.

1. le nom du professeur de Carole
2. le nom de la ville que le groupe a visitée
3. le fleuve qui passe par cette ville
4. le nom d'un palais historique célèbre situé dans cette ville
5. le nom d'une chanson française bien connue

E Les trains.   Choisissez.

1. Les vieux / nouveaux trains ont des compartiments.
2. Le TGV a un couloir central / latéral.
3. Dans le TGV le repas est servi sur place en première / en seconde.
4. Dans le TGV les sièges sont réglables en première / en seconde.
5. Il y a six / huit places dans un compartiment de seconde.
6. Les voyageurs sortaient dans le compartiment / le couloir.
7. Une baguette est une sorte de pain / de vin.

F Le TGV.   Décrivez le TGV. Dites tout ce que vous savez sur ce train.

96   CHAPITRE 4

INDEPENDENT PRACTICE

Assign any of the following:
1. Workbook, *Un Peu Plus*, pages 41–43
2. *Étude de mots* and *Compréhension* exercises, pages 95–96
3. CD-ROM, Disc 1, pages 94–96

DÉCOUVERTE CULTURELLE

*L*e train est un moyen de transport très populaire et très confortable en France. Le service est excellent.

En France les trains, ou les chemins de fer, appartiennent en partie à[1] l'État. C'est-à-dire que le gouvernement exerce un certain contrôle sur les trains. La compagnie des trains s'appelle la SNCF—la Société Nationale des Chemins de Fer Français.

Comme vous le savez, le TGV est le Train à Grande Vitesse, un train extrêmement moderne et rapide—et assez cher. Il faut

La Gare Saint-Lazare à Paris

Les T.E.R. (Trains Express Régionaux): les omnibus qui desservent les villes de province et leurs environs[2]—par exemple, Rennes et ses environs.

Le R.E.R. (Réseau Express Régional): les trains qui desservent la banlieue parisienne. Ces trains sont reliés[3] au système de métro en ville.

[1] appartiennent en partie à   *are partly owned by, belong partly to*
[2] leurs environs   *the surrounding areas*
[3] reliés   *connected*

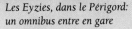

Les Eyzies, dans le Périgord: un omnibus entre en gare

réserver ses places à l'avance. Le nouveau TGV est plus rapide que le célèbre «bullet train» japonais.

Voici d'autres sortes de trains français.

Trains-rapides-express: les trains qui desservent l'ensemble de la France— les grandes villes du pays, c'est-à-dire «la France radiale».

Guide pratique du voyageur à mobilité réduite

SNCF

INFORMAL ASSESSMENT

After completing the exercises, have students say as much as they can about:

1. les trains en France aujourd'hui
2. les trains du passé
3. la ville d'Avignon

Bell Ringer Review

Write the following on the board or use BRR Blackline Master 4-7: In the following sentences, some of the verbs are missing. Fill in the blanks with a verb which makes sense using either the imperfect or the *passé composé.*

1. Quand j'étais petit(e) je rendais souvent visite à ma tante qui ____ à Pittsburgh.
2. Ma tante et moi, nous ____ souvent au cinéma ensemble.
3. Je ____ le journal quand le téléphone a sonné.
4. Quand je ____ à la maison après la fête, mes parents dormaient.

OPTIONAL MATERIAL

Découverte culturelle

PRESENTATION (page 97)

You may wish to have students read the *Découverte* silently.

Note Students may listen to a recorded version of the *Découverte culturelle* on the CD-ROM.

GEOGRAPHY CONNECTION

Le Périgord forme la majeure partie du département de la Dordogne. Le Périgord est formé de plateaux arides et peu peuplés. Dans cette région il y a aussi beaucoup de vallées fertiles. L'agriculture y est importante. La ville de Sarlat est la capitale du foie gras.

LEARNING FROM REALIA AND PHOTOS

1. Have students look at the center photo on page 97 and say: *Cherchez le Périgord sur une carte. Cherchez la ville de Périgueux, la capitale du Périgord.*
2. Refer students to the brochure and ask them to find another term for *le voyageur handicapé.*

RÉALITÉS

C'est le TGV **1**. Il faut réserver ses places à l'avance? Tu veux prendre le TGV?

Ce tableau du peintre impressionniste Claude Monet est intitulé *Gare Saint-Lazare* **2**. Monet a peint ce tableau en 1877. Est-ce que la Gare Saint-Lazare existe encore aujourd'hui? Où est-elle?

Voici l'écran du Minitel **3**. Beaucoup de Français ont cet ordinateur chez eux. En France tu peux réserver par Minitel tes places dans le train. Si tu n'aimes pas faire la queue devant le guichet le Minitel est très pratique!

C'est le tableau des départs de la Gare du Nord à Paris **4**. Les trains qui partent de cette gare vont dans quelles villes? Ils vont dans quelle direction?

Bell Ringer Review

Write the following on the board or use BRR Blackline Master 4-8: Match the words in Column A with a suitable ending in Column B.

A	B
une tablette	numérotée
une voiture	gril-express
un siège	réglable
une place	des portes
la fermeture	rabattable

OPTIONAL MATERIAL

PRESENTATION *(pages 98–99)*

A. The purpose of this section is to allow students to enjoy the photographs that bring to life the content of the chapter. You may wish to have students read the information that accompanies each photo aloud or silently.

B. You may wish to ask the questions in the caption text, but this is not necessary.

Note In the CD-ROM version, students can listen to the recorded captions and discover a hidden video behind one of the photos.

ART CONNECTION

For more information on *La Gare Saint-Lazare,* Claude Monet, Impressionism, and student activities related to this painting, please refer to *À bord* Fine Art Transparency F-1.

DID YOU KNOW?

During the winter of 1876–1877, Claude Monet used the Gare Saint-Lazare as the subject of many paintings. He had first arrived in Paris via this major terminus some twenty years earlier and now lived in a studio nearby. Monet's interest in the station was not as a vehicle for social commentary, but as an end in itself. He was drawn to the physical building of glass and steel, the steam caught by the roof, the network of tracks, and the constant movement of trains and passengers. He wanted to capture the essence of its activity while it constantly changed around him. This study marked an important development in his working method: the tendency to create multiple views of a single theme. He showed seven paintings from the series in the Impressionist exhibition of 1877.

DEPART GRANDES LIGNES

train n.	nature	départ	voie	destination et principales gares d'arrêt
3105	RAPIDE 1ère et 2ème CL "CORAIL"	10h40	5	AMIENS BOULOGNE CALAIS LONDON VICTORIA
70737		10h55	12	ORRY CHANTILLY CREIL CLERMONT AMIENS
28817		11h24		DAMMARTIN LE MESNIL DAMMY CREPY EN V.
72969		11h30		PERSAN BEAUMONT CHAMBLY MERU BEAUVAIS
403	RAPIDE 1ère 2ème CL "CORAIL"	12h02		FEG CATAMARAN BOULOGNE MARITIME LONDON
32321	EXPRESS 1ère 2ème CL "CORAIL"	12h10		NOYON CHAUNY ST-QUENTIN MAUBEUGE
76823		12h37		ORRY CHANTILLY CREIL PONT COMPIEGNE
77825		13h00		VILLERS SOISSONS ANIZY PINON LAON
70057		13h05		PERSAN BEAUMONT CHAMBLY MERU BEAUVAIS
239	RAPIDE 1ère 2ème CL "CORAIL"	13h39		AULNOYE BRUXELLES LIEGE AACHEN KOLN
76725		13h60		CHANTILLY CREIL LIANCOURT CLERMONT
405	RAPIDE 1ère 2ème CL "CORAIL"	13h55		AMIENS BOULOGNE-M. CALAIS-M. LONDON-VICT
2227	RAPIDE 1ère 2ème CL "CORAIL"	14h09		ARRAS DOUAI LILLE ROUBAIX TOURCOING
2027	EXPRESS 1ère 2ème CL "CORAIL"	14h22		AMIENS ABBEVILLE BOULOGNE CALAIS-VILLE
285	RAPIDE 1ère 2ème CL "CORAIL"	14h38		ST-QUENTIN MONS BRUXELLES AMSTERDAM

LE N DE LA VOIE EST AFFICHE ENVIRON 20min AVANT LE DEPART DU TRAIN

99

ADDITIONAL PRACTICE

Assign any of the following:
1. Student Tape Manual, Teacher's Edition, *Deuxième Partie*, pages 44–46
2. Situation Cards, Chapter 4

RECYCLING

The *Activités de communication orale* and *écrite* allow students to use the vocabulary and grammar from this chapter in open-ended situations. They also provide an opportunity to recycle vocabulary and structure from earlier chapters and from *Bienvenue*.

Have students do as many of the *Activités* as you wish.

INFORMAL ASSESSMENT

The *Activités de communication orale* lend themselves to assessing speaking and listening abilities. Use the evaluation criteria given on page 22 of this Teacher's Wrap-around Edition.

Activité de communication orale

ANSWERS

Activité A

Answers will vary but may include the following:

1. Él: Il y a des TGV qui partent pour Irun?
   É2: Oui, il y en a deux.
2. Él: À quelle heure partent-ils?
   É2: Le premier part à 6h55, le deuxième à 10h.
3. Él: On sert des repas dans le train?
   É2: Oui, il y a un service restauration.
4. Él: À quelle heure est-ce que les trains arrivent à Irun?
   É2: Le premier arrive à 12h47, le deuxième à 15h14.

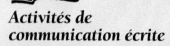

Activités de communication écrite

ANSWERS

Activités A and B

Answers will vary.

Activité de communication orale

A **En Espagne!** You'd like to buy a ticket on the TGV from Paris to Irun, on the Spanish border. Ask the agent (your partner) the following questions about the trip. He or she can use the train schedule on the right to answer your questions.

1. if there are TGV's leaving for Irun
2. what time the trains leave
3. if meals are served on the train
4. what time the trains arrive in Irun

Service restauration à la place en 1ʳᵉ classe, en réservation : tous les jours de circulation, sauf pour les TGV 8501, 8515, 8519, 8549, 8565, 8469, où ce service est assuré certains jours.

Espaces "Carré" réservables, en priorité, par les voyageurs "Kiwi" et les voyageurs accompagnés d'enfants.

(*) Le service bar n'est pas offert dans ce TGV.

N° du TGV		8501	8505	8407	8407	8515	8519
Particularités							
Restauration		▣	▣			▣	▣
Paris-Montparnasse 1-2	D	6.55	8.10	8.15	8.15	10.00	10.45
Massy TGV	D	7.05					11.41
Saint-Pierre-des-Corps	A	7.56					
Châtellerault	A	8.26					12.21
Poitiers	A	8.43		9.44	9.44		
Angoulême	A	9.29		10.29	10.29		13.06
Libourne	A			11.10	11.10		13.48
Bordeaux	A	10.25	11.08	11.29	11.29	12.57	14.08
Facture	A	b	a	a	11.53	a	a
Arcachon	A	b	a	a	12.09	b	a
Dax	A	11.34	12.17			a	a
Bayonne	A	12.04				14.33	a
Biarritz	A	12.14				14.43	a
Saint-Jean de Luz	A	12.27				14.55	a
Hendaye	A	12.40				15.07	a
Irun	A	12.47				15.14	a

HORAIRES

Activités de communication écrite

A **En voyage.** Faites une liste des mots qui concernent le train. Faites des phrases en employant ces mots. Ensuite écrivez un paragraphe.

B **Qu'est-ce qui s'est passé?** You're on the Orient-Express when a mysterious woman in black enters your train car. At the Swiss border the police get on the train looking for the woman, who has disappeared. Work in groups of three and make up a story sentence by sentence. Write down the story as you create it. The first person gives some background information. The second person tells what the woman did when she got on the train. The third person, the passenger, tells what he/she was doing when the woman got on. Continue until you have a complete story to tell the police.

Élève 1: Il était minuit.
Élève 2: Une femme en noir est entrée dans le compartiment.
Élève 3: Je dormais quand elle est entrée.
Élève 1: Il y avait une place disponible...

100   CHAPITRE 4

LEARNING FROM REALIA

Have students make up questions about the train schedule. Call on volunteers to ask their questions of classmates.

COOPERATIVE LEARNING

Display Communication Transparency C-4. Have students work in groups of six to create the conversation between the six people in the illustration. Have them use props to show which role they have taken. Have the various groups present their conversation to the class.

Réintroduction et recombinaison

A En voiture! Complétez au présent.

1. Les voyageurs ___ le train. (attendre)
2. Le train ___ à onze heures. (partir)
3. On ___ l'annonce du départ du train. (entendre)
4. Les voyageurs ___ sur le quai dans beaucoup de gares aux États-Unis. (descendre)
5. Le train ___ beaucoup de petites villes. (desservir)
6. Il ___ dans toutes les gares. (s'arrêter)

B Bill est perdu! Complétez avec «ce» ou «quel».

BILL JOHNSON: Excusez-moi, Monsieur, le train pour Marseille part à ___ heure? Et de ___ quai?
UN VOYAGEUR: Regardons ___ horaire... voilà! Il part à 14h20 de ___ quai.
BILL JOHNSON: Il part de ___ quai, mais de ___ voie?
LE VOYAGEUR: De ___ voie.
BILL JOHNSON: Excusez-moi, Monsieur, ___ voitures sont non-fumeurs?
LE CONTRÔLEUR: Les voitures numéros 36 et 37 sont non-fumeurs.
BILL JOHNSON: Est-ce qu'il y a des places disponibles dans ___ voitures?
LE CONTRÔLEUR: Non, Monsieur, dans les trains qui vont à Marseille il y a toujours beaucoup de monde. Il y a rarement de places disponibles dans ___ trains.

SNCF
GARE MONTPARNASSE

Vocabulaire

NOMS
la gare de départ
la gare d'arrivée
le tableau des départs
le tableau des arrivées
la ligne de banlieue
le quai
le bureau de location
le couloir
le compartiment
la place numérotée
le siège réglable
la tablette rabattable
le wagon à compartiments
  (à couloir latéral)
la voiture à couloir central
la voiture-restaurant
la voiture gril-express

le fourgon à bagages
le château

ADJECTIFS
assis(e)
complet, complète
disponible
prochain(e)
nombreux, nombreuse

VERBES
louer
réserver
chercher
emporter
vérifier
ramasser
poinçonner

s'arrêter
descendre
desservir

AUTRES MOTS ET
EXPRESSIONS
faire la queue
monter en voiture
changer de train
prendre la
  correspondance
rater le train
Attention à la fermeture
  des portes!
Attention au départ!
Excusez-moi.
Vous vous trompez.
Ce n'est pas grave.

Vous permettez?
à l'avance
en face de
debout
de temps en temps
fréquemment

CHAPITRE 4   101

OPTIONAL MATERIAL

Réintroduction et recombinaison

PRESENTATION (page 101)

Extension of Exercice A

You may wish to have students rewrite the sentences in Exercise A in the passé composé.

Extension of Exercice B

After completing Exercise B, call on pairs of volunteers to present the conversation to the class as a skit.

ANSWERS

Exercice A

1. attendent   4. descendent
2. part   5. dessert
3. entend   6. s'arrête

Exercice B
quelle, quel
cet, ce
ce, quelle
cette
quelles
ces
ces

ASSESSMENT RESOURCES

1. Chapter Quizzes
2. Testing Program
3. Situation Cards
4. Communication Transparency C-4
5. Performance Assessment
6. Computer Software: Practice/Test Generator

VIDEO PROGRAM

INTRODUCTION   (17:18)

DESTINATION: DIJON   (17:52)

STUDENT PORTFOLIO

Written assignments which may be included in students' portfolios are the *Activités de communication écrite* on page 100 and any writing activities from the *Un Peu Plus* section in the Workbook.

Note Students may create and save both oral and written work using the Electronic Portfolio feature on the CD-ROM.

INDEPENDENT PRACTICE

Assign any of the following:
1. Activities and exercises, pages 100–101
2. Communication Activities Masters, pages 25–30
3. CD-ROM, Disc 1, pages 100–101

RÉVISION

CHAPITRES 1-4

Conversation *Un appel à l'agence de voyages*

L'EMPLOYÉE:	Bonjour, Agence France Tours.
MME ROY:	Bonjour, Madame. Monsieur Boileau est là, s'il vous plaît?
L'EMPLOYÉE:	C'est de la part de qui?
MME ROY:	De Madame Roy.
L'EMPLOYÉE:	Ne quittez pas, Madame.
M. BOILEAU:	Bonjour, Madame. Quelle surprise! Vous pensez peut-être faire un autre voyage?
MME ROY:	C'est ça. Voilà: l'année dernière mon mari et moi, nous sommes allés en Grèce. C'était formidable. Il faisait très beau et on s'est bien amusés. Mais maintenant on voudrait quelque chose de plus aventureux.
M. BOILEAU:	Eh bien, un safari au Kenya! Ça vous intéresse?
MME ROY:	Ah oui! Ça me tente. Nos voisins en ont fait un il y a deux ans. Ils ont pris des photos magnifiques. Et la nature intéresse beaucoup mon mari. Mais un safari, ça coûte cher, n'est-ce pas?
M. BOILEAU:	Non, pas tellement. Je peux vous envoyer des brochures, si vous voulez.
MME ROY:	D'accord! Je crois que c'est une très bonne idée, ça—un safari!

A **Un voyage aventureux.**   Répondez d'après la conversation.

1. À qui Mme Roy a-t-elle téléphoné?
2. Il a répondu au téléphone?
3. Il était là?
4. Qu'est-ce que Mme Roy pense faire? Avec qui?
5. Où sont-ils allés l'année dernière?
6. Comment était le voyage?
7. Quel temps faisait-il?
8. Pour le prochain voyage, qu'est-ce que M. Boileau suggère?
9. Pourquoi suggère-t-il un safari?
10. Un safari intéresse Mme Roy? Et son mari?
11. Qui a fait un safari? Quand?
12. Qu'est-ce qu'ils ont pris?
13. Qu'est-ce que M. Boileau va envoyer à Mme Roy?

SAFARI KENYA

9 JOURS/7 NUITS
AVEC CHAUFFEUR-GUIDE LOCAL PARLANT FRANÇAIS

8 990 F

(EXEMPLE DE PRIX LE 5/12/1992 EN CHAMBRE DOUBLE)

TOUT COMPRIS
(VOLS, PENSION COMPLÈTE ET ASSURANCES)

Les grands troupeaux de zèbres, de gnous et de buffles, les lions, les guépards, les girafes et les éléphants d'Amboseli et de Masaï Mara, les flamants roses et les pélicans du lac Nakuru, Nairobi : c'est l'Afrique des grands espaces sauvages, des plus belles et des plus célèbres réserves d'animaux que vous découvrirez au cours de ce safari proposé par les Voyages Diffusion. Avec la possibilité de prolonger vos vacances à Mombasa au bord de l'océan Indien.

DE PARIS

OVERVIEW

This section recycles key grammatical structures and vocabulary from Chapters 1–4. The topics were first presented on the following pages: past participle agreement, page 12; the imperfect and the *passé composé,* pages 60–61, 63, 86, and 89.

REVIEW RESOURCES

1. Workbook, Self-Test 1, pages 44–48
2. Videocassette/Videodisc, Unit 1
3. Video Activities Booklet, Unit 1: Chapters 1–4, pages 1–16
4. Computer Software, Chapters 1–4
5. Testing Program, Unit Test: Chapters 1–4, pages 27–31
6. Performance Assessment
7. CD-ROM, Disc 1, *Révision:* pages 102–105
8. CD-ROM, Disc 1, Self-Tests 1–4
9. CD-ROM, Disc 1, Game: *Chasse au trésor dans le métro*
10. Lesson Plans

Conversation

PRESENTATION *(page 102)*

A. Have students close their books and listen as you read the conversation.
B. Call on volunteers to read the conversation aloud.
C. Have one student summarize the conversation in his/her own words.

ANSWERS

Exercice A

1. Elle a téléphoné à M. Boileau.
2. Non, il n'a pas répondu au téléphone.

102

LEARNING FROM REALIA

1. Have students look at the safari ad as you ask: *Ce sont des lions? Les lions sont des animaux sauvages ou domestiques? D'après vous, ce sont des lions ou des lionnes? C'est peut-être la mère lionne avec son bébé?*
2. Have students look for the following information in the ad: *Cette publicité est pour un safari dans quel pays? C'est pour combien de jours? Et pour combien de nuits? Combien coûte le safari? Qu'est-ce qui est compris dans le prix? Quels animaux sont mentionnés dans cette publicité?*

Structure

L'accord du participe passé au passé composé

1. When *être* is the helping verb in the *passé composé*, the past participle agrees with the subject.

   Paul est allé à Paris.   *Paul et Georges* sont allés à Paris.
   Marie est allée à Paris.   *Marie et Claire* sont allées à Paris.

   The past participle also agrees when the subjects are *je*, *tu*, *nous*, or *vous*.

	UNE FILLE	UN GARÇON	2 FILLES	2 GARÇONS	MIXTE
Je suis	restée	resté			
Tu es	restée	resté			
Nous sommes			restées	restés	restés
Vous êtes	restée	resté	restées	restés	restés

2. When the helping verb is *avoir* in the *passé composé*, the past participle agrees only when there is a preceding direct object.

   J'ai acheté ma voiture hier. (No agreement.)
   but
   Ma voiture? Je l'ai achetée hier.
   C'est *la voiture* que j'ai achetée hier.

3. Even though all reflexive verbs are conjugated with *être* in the *passé composé*, the rule for agreement is that of *avoir*: the past participle agrees with the reflexive pronoun when the reflexive pronoun is the direct object.

   Elle s'est lavée.   Ils *se* sont rencontrés.
   but   *but*
   Elle s'est lavé les cheveux. Ils se sont parlé.

A **L'anniversaire de Maman.** Faites l'accord si nécessaire.

Hier Isabelle s'est levé____ très tôt. C'était l'anniversaire de sa mère. Alors, elle
l'a laissé____ dormir et lui a fait____ une surprise. D'abord elle est sorti____ et
elle est allé____ acheter des croissants tout chauds et une baguette toute
chaude aussi. Puis elle est rentré____. Elle a sorti____ les croissants du filet et
les a mis____ sur une assiette. Avec la baguette, elle a fait____ des tartines. Elle
les a fait____ avec du beurre et de la confiture (*jam*) de fraises, la confiture
préférée de sa mère. Puis elle a fait____ du café au lait. Ensuite elle a
réveillé____ son frère Olivier. Olivier l'a aidé____ à monter le petit déjeuner à
leur mère. Leur mère a été____ très surprise et les a embrassé____.

---

3. Oui, il était là.
4. Mme Roy pense faire un autre voyage avec son mari.
5. Ils sont allés en Grèce l'année dernière.
6. Le voyage était formidable.
7. Il faisait très beau.
8. M. Boileau suggère un safari au Kenya pour le prochain voyage.
9. Il suggère un safari parce que c'est un peu plus aventureux.
10. Oui, un safari intéresse Mme Roy et son mari. (parce que la nature intéresse son mari.)
11. Leurs voisins ont fait un safari il y a deux ans.
12. Ils ont pris des photos magnifiques.
13. M. Boileau va envoyer des brochures à Mme Roy.

Structure

L'accord du participe passé au passé composé

PRESENTATION *(page 103)*

A. Write the model sentences from steps 1–3 on the board. Underline the participle endings.
B. Provide or elicit additional examples for each step. Discuss the difference between direct and indirect objects.
C. Do not spend a great deal of time on this point. Students will need constant reinforcement of agreement on all their written work.

Exercice

PRESENTATION *(page 103)*

Call on volunteers to read the exercise aloud as a story. Have students ready at the board to write down the past participles as they hear them and underline the endings, if any.

ANSWERS

1. e	9. —
2. e	10. es
3. —	11. —
4. e	12. —
5. e	13. e
6. e	14. —
7. —	15. s
8. —	

PAIRED ACTIVITY

Have pairs of students prepare and present conversations about taking the safari advertised on page 102 or another trip they wish to take.

INDEPENDENT PRACTICE

Assign any of the following:
1. Exercises, pages 102–103
2. CD-ROM, Disc 1, pages 102–103

L'imparfait et le passé composé

PRESENTATION (page 104)

A. As you go through steps 1–3, remind students to think of a play (or movie), as suggested on page 89 of this Teachers Wraparound Edition.

B. In step 2, use an abrupt, chopping motion of the hand to indicate *passé composé* constructions and a sweeping horizontal motion for the imperfect.

Exercices

PRESENTATION (pages 104–105)

Exercice B

In Exercise B, you may wish to discuss with students why the first verb is in the *passé composé* and the second in the imperfect. One way to demonstrate the difference is to ask students which activity began first and continued for some time, and which was more sudden, with a clear start and finish.

Exercice C

In Exercise C, emphasize that both actions were short and separate and independent, with clear starting and ending points. They are cause and effect actions.

ANSWERS

Exercice B

1. Quand il a entendu l'explosion, il travaillait.
2. ... il regardait la télévision.
3. ... il était au téléphone.
4. ... il faisait une promenade à vélo.
5. ... il écrivait une lettre.
6. ... il prenait un bain.
7. ... il mettait le couvert.
8. ... il dormait.

Exercice C

1. Quand j'ai entendu l'explosion, je me suis levé(e).
2. ... j'ai téléphoné à la police.
3. ... je suis sorti(e) dehors.
4. ... j'ai regardé par la fenêtre.
5. ... je me suis réveillé(e).

104

L'imparfait et le passé composé

1. The use of the *imperfect* or the *passé composé* depends on whether the speaker sees the past action as an event or action with a beginning and an end, or as an action in progress, a state, a situation with no real beginning or end. Compare the following sentences.

> **Quand j'ai entendu l'explosion, je lisais.**
> **Quand j'ai entendu l'explosion, j'ai couru à la fenêtre.**

In the first sentence, the *passé composé* is used to indicate an event or action, and the *imperfect,* a situation. In the second sentence, the *passé composé* is used to indicate two successive events or actions.

2. The following time expressions will generally be used with the indicated tenses.

PASSÉ COMPOSÉ	IMPARFAIT
hier (lundi, l'an) dernier pendant une heure à trois heures	souvent tous les ans (jours, mois) de temps en temps toujours

3. The difference between the *imperfect* and the *passé composé* is best shown in context. The more you are exposed to examples in context, the more you will get a feel for when to use one tense or the other.

B **Que faisait-il?** Répondez d'après le modèle.

> **Quand il a entendu l'explosion, il... (lire)**
> *Quand il a entendu l'explosion, il lisait.*

1. ...(travailler)
2. ...(regarder la télévision)
3. ...(être au téléphone)
4. ...(faire une promenade à vélo)
5. ...(écrire une lettre)
6. ...(prendre un bain)
7. ...(mettre le couvert)
8. ...(dormir)

C **Qu'avez-vous fait?** Répondez d'après le modèle.

> **Quand j'ai entendu l'explosion, je... (courir à la fenêtre)**
> *Quand j'ai entendu l'explosion, j'ai couru à la fenêtre.*

1. ...(se lever)
2. ...(téléphoner à la police)
3. ...(sortir dehors)
4. ...(regarder par la fenêtre)
5. ...(se réveiller)

Une promenade à vélo en Bretagne

COOPERATIVE LEARNING

Each team member writes five sentences beginning with *Quand j'étais petit(e)...* + an imperfect verb, and five beginning with *L'autre jour...* + the *passé composé.* Members take turns reading one sentence at a time, to which the others respond with their own statements.

LEARNING FROM PHOTOS

Have students say as much as they can about the photos.

D **Une rencontre à Paris.** Complétez en utilisant le passé composé ou l'imparfait.

Karl ___ (rencontrer) Mary à Paris. Quand il l'___ (rencontrer), elle ___
    1   2   3
(porter) une robe rouge. Ils ___ (se regarder) et ils ___ (se sourire). C'est
                             4   5
Karl qui ___ (parler) le premier. Il ___ (dire):
        6   7

KARL: Je crois que nous nous ___ déjà ___ (rencontrer).
                               8

MARY: Ah non, je ne crois pas, je ne ___ jamais ___ (venir) ici avant. Vous
                                   9
    ___ (voir) quelqu'un qui me ___ (ressembler), peut-être.
    10   11

KARL: Non, je crois que je vous ___ (voir) quelque part. Mais ce n'est pas
                                 12
    forcément (nécessairement) ici que je vous ___ (voir) la première fois.
                                        13
    Voyons, vous ___ déjà ___ (aller) à la tour Eiffel?
                    14

MARY: Oui, nous y ___ (aller), ma sœur et moi, hier.
                15

KARL: Alors, vous voyez, j'___ (avoir) raison! Je vous ___ déjà ___ (voir)!
                          16   17
    Moi aussi, je ___ (être) à la tour Eiffel hier avec mon frère. Nous
                  18
    ___ (passer) toute la matinée à regarder Paris du haut du deuxième
    19
    étage. Le temps ___ (être) magnifique. Il ne ___ (faire) pas trop froid...
                      20   21
    Mais vous le savez, vous y ___ (être) aussi. Vous êtes américaine?
                              22

MARY: Oui, et vous allemand?

KARL: Non, suisse.

MARY: Ah vraiment? Quelle coïncidence! Nous ___ (passer) la semaine
                                 23
    dernière en Suisse.

KARL: Et vous ___ (aimer)?
            24

MARY: Beaucoup. Nous ___ (aller) à Genève, Lausanne, Neuchâtel et aussi à
                25
    Zermatt. Que c'est beau!

KARL: Oui, mais il faut venir en hiver. C'est là où c'est bien. Vous faites du ski?

MARY: Oui, j'adore le ski. Quand je ___ (être) petite, nous ___ (habiter) dans
                              26   27
    le Vermont, alors je ___ (faire) du ski tout le temps.
                      28

Activité de communication orale

A **Un voyage super.** Vous invitez des amis à regarder les photos ou les diapositives (*slides*) que vous avez prises pendant un voyage. Vous expliquez à vos camarades où vous étiez, avec qui, ce que vous avez fait, etc.

INDEPENDENT PRACTICE

Assign any of the following:
1. Exercises and activity, pages 104–105
2. Workbook, Self-Test 1, pages 44–48
3. Computer Software, Chapters 1–4
4. CD-ROM, Disc 1, pages 104–105
5. CD-ROM, Disc 1, Self-Tests 1–4
6. CD-ROM, Disc 1, Game: *Chasse au trésor dans le métro*

PRESENTATION (*page 105*)

Exercice D

Allow students time to prepare Exercise D before working together on it. Then have each student read 2–3 sentences as you write the verb forms on the board.

Extension of *Exercice D*

After completing Exercise D, assign the roles to individuals and have them read the finished exercise.

ANSWERS

Exercice D

1. a rencontré
2. a rencontrée
3. portait
4. se sont regardés
5. se sont souri
6. a parlé
7. a dit
8. sommes... rencontrés
9. suis... venue
10. avez vu
11. ressemblait
12. ai vue
13. ai vue
14. êtes... allée
15. sommes allées
16. avais
17. ai... vue
18. étais
19. avons passé
20. était
21. faisait
22. étiez
23. avons passé
24. avez aimé
25. sommes allées
26. étais
27. habitions
28. faisais

Activité de communication orale

PRESENTATION (*page 105*)

Activité A

For this activity, you may wish to have students bring in actual slides or photos of past trips.

ANSWERS

Activité A

Answers will vary.

OPTIONAL MATERIAL

Littérature: Victor Hugo

OVERVIEW

The three reading selections in each *Lettres et sciences* section are all optional. They deal with course content in the areas of social sciences, natural sciences, and arts and letters. The content of the reading selections is related topically to material presented in the previous four lessons.

It is recommended that you allow students to choose the selection or selections they wish to read based on their own personal interests or preferences.

Each reading may be presented at different levels of intensity:

1. The least intensive treatment would be to assign the selection as independent reading and the post-reading exercises as homework. This requires no class time and minimal teacher involvement.
2. For a more intensive treatment, the reading and post-reading exercises can be assigned for homework, which will be gone over orally in class the next day.
3. The most intensive treatment includes a pre-reading presentation of the text by the teacher, an in-class reading and discussion of the passage, the assignment of the exercises for homework, and a discussion of the assignment in class the following day.

Avant la lecture

PRESENTATION *(page 106)*

A. Explain to students that cognates will greatly facilitate their reading comprehension. Have them scan the reading for cognates. There are approximately 20.
B. Have the students read the *Avant la lecture* section.

LITTÉRATURE: VICTOR HUGO (1802-1885)

Avant la lecture

In the following poem, Victor Hugo recalls happy times when Léopoldine, her sister Adèle, and her brothers Charles and François were children. The Hugo family was living in a lovely wooded region, just outside of Paris.

1. The poet uses images referring to birds. What words convey such images?
2. Can you find the words that convey happiness?

Lecture

Victor Hugo est un personnage très impressionnant dans l'histoire de la littérature française. C'est non seulement un grand poète romantique, mais aussi un écrivain[1] de pièces de théâtre et de romans[2] (c'est lui qui a écrit le roman *Les Misérables* dont on a fait une célèbre comédie musicale).

Victor Hugo pensait que le poète avait pour mission d'être «l'écho sonore» de son époque[3], et c'est pour cela qu'il a également eu une vie politique très active. Son œuvre est une œuvre humanitaire: elle célèbre la famille, l'amour[4], la générosité, la grandeur de tous les êtres humains.

La mort de sa fille Léopoldine en 1843 l'a profondément marqué et a interrompu pendant quelque temps son activité de poète.

[1] écrivain *writer*
[2] romans *novels*
[3] époque *time*
[4] l'amour *love*

Victor Hugo en 1880. Les enfants de Victor Hugo dessinés par Madame Hugo en 1833.

DID YOU KNOW?

Have students locate the Pantheon on the map of Paris on page 436. Many famous Frenchmen are buried in its crypt, including Victor Hugo.

S C I E N C E S

Ô SOUVENIRS!

Ô souvenirs! printemps! aurore°!   dawn
Doux rayon° triste et réchauffant!   soft ray of light
— Lorsqu'°elle était petite   when
   encore,
Que sa sœur était tout enfant... —
Connaissez-vous sur la colline°   hill
Qui joint Montlignon à Saint-Leu*
Une terrasse qui s'incline°   slopes
Entre un bois° sombre et le ciel bleu?   wood
C'est là que nous vivions°. — Pénètre,   lived
Mon cœur°, dans ce passé   heart
   charmant! —
Je l'entendais sous ma fenêtre
Jouer le matin doucement.
Elle courait dans la rosée°,   dew
Sans bruit°, de peur de° m'éveiller;   noise, for fear of
Moi, je n'ouvrais pas ma
   croisée°,   window
De peur de la faire envoler°.   fly away
Ses frères riaient°... — Aube°   were laughing; dawn
   pure!
Tout chantait sous ces frais
   berceaux°,   arbors
Ma famille avec la nature,
Mes enfants avec les oiseaux°!   birds

*Montlignon and Saint-Leu are two villages in the Montmorency Forest, northwest of Paris.

Léopoldine Hugo, par
Auguste de Châtillon

Trois scènes du film «Les Misérables»

Après la lecture

A **Un bon souvenir.** Racontez un moment heureux de votre vie.

B **Poète.** Écrivez un petit poème en français pour célébrer ce souvenir.

Lecture

PRESENTATION (pages 106–107)

A. Read the biographical information about Victor Hugo with the students.
B. Now have them close their books and listen as you read the poem to them.
C. Now have them open their books and follow along as you read the poem again.
D. Have the students read the poem silently.

Après la lecture

PRESENTATION (page 107)

Have students explain to you the general idea of the poem. What feelings did it evoke in them? See if they can answer the two questions from *Avant la lecture.*

Exercices

ANSWERS

Exercices A and B
   Answers will vary.

CRITICAL THINKING ACTIVITY

(Thinking skill: making inferences)
   Read the following to the class or write it on the board or on a transparency:
Why does the poet mention birds in this poem about his daughter who has died?
What do the birds symbolize?

Biologie: *Le sommeil*

Note Although all the reading selections in *Lettres et sciences* are optional, this one can be a lot of fun, and you may want to have most, if not all, of your students read it.

Avant la lecture

PRESENTATION *(page 108)*

A. Have the students consider the questions in the *Avant la lecture* section.

B. Have the students scan the reading selection for cognates.

C. Have the students scan the reading again and make a list of the following:
1. body parts
2. body functions
3. personality traits

Lecture

PRESENTATION *(pages 108–109)*

A. You may have the students read the selection aloud or silently.

B. **Reading strategies** Explain to students that they have to use different techniques and strategies to guess the meaning of words they are not familiar with. In the first sentence on this page, the word *matelas* is new. What does it mean? Explain to students that they have to guess the meaning based on the message in the rest of the sentence: *Bien dormir, c'est d'abord avoir un bon lit avec un bon matelas.* What's the most important thing on a bed? What does *matelas* mean?

BIOLOGIE: LE SOMMEIL[1]

Avant la lecture

1. Many people cannot sleep; they suffer from insomnia. What do you think some of the causes are?
2. Think about your sleeping habits. Do you have a regular schedule for going to bed and getting up? Do you go to bed early or late? What are your room and your bed like?

Lecture

Les besoins en sommeil[2] varient d'une personne à une autre. Pour certains, six heures de sommeil suffisent. D'autres ont besoin de neuf heures de sommeil ou même plus. Il y a des gens qui se couchent tôt, d'autres qui se couchent tard. Mais la qualité du sommeil est très importante. Par exemple, on peut dormir dans un environnement plein de bruit[3], mais on dort mal même si on dort pendant dix heures ou plus.

Les rythmes du sommeil

Pendant une nuit, nous avons quatre ou cinq cycles d'une heure et demie ou deux heures. Chaque cycle a cinq stades (degrés) différents. Il y a d'abord un sommeil très léger[4], puis un sommeil léger, un sommeil normal, un sommeil profond[5] et un sommeil agité appelé «le sommeil paradoxal». Pendant les quatre premiers stades, c'est un «sommeil lent»: le corps se repose. Les yeux ne bougent pas, la respiration est régulière et le cœur ralentit (va moins vite). Puis, au cinquième stade, la respiration et le cœur s'accélèrent. Les yeux bougent et la pression artérielle[6]

monte. C'est le stade du «sommeil paradoxal». C'est pendant cette période que nous rêvons[7]. Les rêves sont essentiels pour notre équilibre mental. Les mauvais rêves, ou cauchemars, sont importants aussi. Ils nous aident à intégrer les éléments nouveaux de notre vie.

La vie pendant la nuit

Pendant que nous dormons, notre corps est très actif. La nuit, certaines glandes fonctionnent plus vite: l'estomac se remplit d'acide, les cheveux poussent[8] plus vite et c'est essentiellement la nuit que les enfants grandissent (deviennent plus grands). Beaucoup d'hormones sont fabriquées la nuit.

DID YOU KNOW?

You may wish to point out to students that this is the type of information that appears in many teen magazines in France.

SCIENCES

Comment dormez-vous?

Comment bien dormir

Bien dormir, c'est d'abord avoir un bon lit avec un bon matelas. Il est préférable de dormir sans oreiller. Votre chambre ne doit être ni trop chaude, ni trop froide. Et enfin tout le monde a sa position préférée: si vous dormez en boule, vous êtes probablement timide. Si vous dormez sur le ventre, vous avez tendance à être anxieux. Si vous dormez sur le dos, ou le côté, vous êtes content de vous. Savez-vous que 75% des gens dorment sur le côté, ce qui semble dire qu'ils sont contents dans la vie? En tout cas, c'est ce qu'on dit, mais ça n'a jamais été vérifié.

[1] le sommeil *sleep*
[2] les besoins en sommeil *the amount of sleep needed*
[3] bruit *noise*
[4] léger *light*
[5] profond *deep*
[6] la pression artérielle *blood pressure*
[7] nous rêvons *we dream*
[8] poussent *grow*

Après la lecture

A **Les rythmes du sommeil.**
Remettez dans l'ordre.

le sommeil normal
le sommeil paradoxal
le sommeil très léger
le sommeil léger
le sommeil profond

B **Dormez-vous bien?** Dites quelle est la meilleure manière de dormir pour la santé.

1. Dormir avec ou sans oreiller
2. Dormir sur le ventre ou sur le côté
3. Avoir une chambre chaude ou froide
4. Dormir dans le bruit ou le calme
5. Rêver ou ne pas rêver

C **Enquête.** Demandez à vos camarades comment ils dorment: pendant combien d'heures, avec ou sans oreiller, sur le ventre ou sur le côté, etc. Comparez les résultats.

Après la lecture

PRESENTATION *(page 109)*

A. You may wish to do the following vocabulary exercises. Write them on the board or on a transparency.

Trouvez la définition.
1. un stade   a. changer,
2. varier   modifier
3. ralentir   b. un mauvais
4. un   rêve
   cauchemar   c. devenir plus
5. essentiel   grand
6. grandir   d. l'estomac
7. le ventre   e. nécessaire
                     f. aller moins vite
                     g. un degré

Trouvez le contraire.
1. actif   a. rapide
2. normal   b. léger
3. profond   c. accélérer
4. lent   d. physique
5. ralentir   e. anormal
6. mental   f. inactif

B. You may wish to ask the following questions: *Vous avez besoin de combien d'heures de sommeil? En général, vous dormez combien d'heures par nuit? Vous dormez avec un oreiller ou pas? Vous dormez avec combien d'oreillers? Votre matelas est dur ou pas? Vous rêvez? Vous faites toujours de bons rêves? Vous avez des cauchemars de temps en temps? Les cauchemars vous font peur?*

Exercices

ANSWERS

Exercice A
le sommeil très léger
le sommeil léger
le sommeil normal
le sommeil profond
le sommeil paradoxal

Exercice B
1. Dormir sans oreiller
2. Tout le monde a sa position préférée.
3. La chambre doit être ni trop chaude ni trop froide.
4. Dormir dans le calme
5. Rêver

Exercice C
   Answers will vary.

INDEPENDENT PRACTICE

1. Have students write about a pleasant dream (*un bon rêve*).
2. Have students write about a nightmare (*un cauchemar*).

Architecture: Versailles et la Grande Arche
Avant la lecture

PRESENTATION *(page 110)*

A. Give students a few moments to look at the photos of the buildings they are going to read about.

B. Have the students scan the reading to look for cognates. You may wish to have them list the cognates.

Lecture

PRESENTATION *(pages 110–111)*

You may wish to have three students or three groups of students work on this selection. One student reads the introduction, one reads about *le château de Versailles*, and one reads about *la Grande Arche*. They then report to one another about what they read.

ARCHITECTURE: VERSAILLES ET LA GRANDE ARCHE

Avant la lecture

Which do you prefer, old or modern architecture? Why? Use the photos below to help explain your answers.

Le château de Chenonceau

Lecture

La France est bien connue[1] pour la beauté de son architecture. Les châteaux de France sont célèbres dans le monde entier. La pureté des châteaux de la Loire et la splendeur de Versailles sont vraiment légendaires. Mais l'architecture a aussi sa place dans la France moderne. Le centre Pompidou (Beaubourg), la pyramide du Louvre et la Grande Arche en sont la preuve[2].

Le centre Pompidou

La pyramide du Louvre

Le château de Versailles

Louis XIV, le Roi-Soleil, n'aime pas Paris. Il décide de faire construire un château magnifique en dehors de[3] Paris. Il choisit Versailles et fait de Versailles la capitale de la France. C'est en 1682. Et Versailles reste la capitale jusqu'à la Révolution en 1789. La construction de ce château magnifique a duré[4] 50 ans. En 1684, 22 000 ouvriers[5] et 6 000 chevaux[6] travaillent à Versailles. Il y a 3 000 personnes qui habitent dans le château. C'est l'architecte Mansart qui dirige la construction du château.

Pendant tout le règne de Louis XIV, de grandes fêtes magnifiques se succèdent à l'intérieur du château et dans les jardins. Les fêtes sont toujours accompagnées de spectacles splendides de danse et de musique.

Le château de Versailles et ses jardins

DID YOU KNOW?

The Pompidou Center or Beaubourg, as it is often called, is a futuristic building designed by architects Richard Rogers (British) and Renzo Piano (Italian) to house the *Musée National d'Art Moderne*. The construction of this multi-purpose cultural center was part of the redevelopment project of the *Les Halles* quarter initiated by Georges Pompidou in 1969.

SCIENCES

L'arche de la Défense

La Grande Arche

À Paris, l'axe qui part de l'arc de triomphe du Carrousel et passe par l'obélisque de la place de la Concorde, les Champs-Élysées et l'arc de triomphe de l'Étoile va maintenant jusqu'à la Défense, le quartier moderne des affaires (commercial). En effet cet axe se termine maintenant par la Grande Arche. En 1982, un grand concours[7] international est organisé pour choisir un architecte. C'est le Danois Johan Otto von Spreckelsen qui gagne.

La Grande Arche est un grand cube de marbre blanc. Elle a 112 m de haut et pèse 300 000 tonnes. Il y a 87 000 m^2 de surface de bureaux. L'espace vide[8] à l'intérieur du cube est large comme les Champs-Élysées. Et incroyable mais vrai, dans cet espace la Grande Arche pourrait abriter[9] Notre-Dame!

Si vous voulez avoir une vue splendide sur tout Paris, prenez un des ascenseurs panoramiques jusqu'au toit-terrasse de la Grande Arche.

[1] connue *known*
[2] la preuve *the proof*
[3] en dehors de *outside*
[4] a duré *lasted*
[5] ouvriers *workers*
[6] chevaux *horses*
[7] concours *competition*
[8] vide *empty*
[9] abriter *house*

La Grande Arche pourrait abriter Notre-Dame

Après la lecture

A **L'architecture française.** Associez les mots suivants avec Versailles ou la Grande Arche.

1. Mansart
2. 6 000 chevaux
3. un architecte danois
4. l'axe célèbre
5. de grandes fêtes magnifiques
6. 112 mètres de haut
7. une vue splendide sur tout Paris
8. en construction pendant 50 ans

B **Le plan de Paris.** Regardez le plan de Paris à la page 436 et trouvez les endroits mentionnés dans le texte.

C **Les architectes américains.** Connaissez-vous des architectes américains célèbres? Qu'est-ce qu'ils ont construit? Où?

D **Louis XIV.** Appelé le Roi-Soleil, Louis XIV a eu une très longue vie et un très long règne. Lisez son histoire et écrivez un paragraphe dessus.

LETTRES ET SCIENCES **111**

Après la lecture

PRESENTATION *(page 111)*

You may wish to have the students do the following additional activity:

Indiquez si les bâtiments suivants sont des exemples d'architecture moderne ou ancienne.

1. le palais de Versailles
2. Notre-Dame de Paris
3. la Grande Arche
4. le Louvre
5. la pyramide du Louvre
6. le centre Pompidou
7. le château de Chenonceau

Exercices

ANSWERS

Exercice A

1. Versailles
2. Versailles
3. la Grande Arche
4. la Grande Arche
5. Versailles
6. la Grande Arche
7. la Grande Arche
8. Versailles

Exercice B

Students must locate places on the map of Paris.

Exercice C

I.M. Pei (National Gallery, Washington, D.C.); Frank Lloyd Wright (Guggenheim Museum, New York); Louis Sullivan (Wainright Building, Saint Louis)

Exercice D

Answers will vary.

DID YOU KNOW?

Ask students if they know what a mansard roof is. Explain that many of the roofs they see in photos of Paris are mansard roofs. This type of roof is named after the architect who popularized them, François Mansart. If the students don't know what a mansard roof looks like, have them look it up in a dictionary or encyclopedia.

CHAPITRE 5

CHAPTER OVERVIEW

In this chapter students will learn the vocabulary associated with various hairstyles and the words or expressions they would need at a barber shop or beauty salon. Vocabulary associated with cosmetics is presented as well. Students will also learn the pronouns *celui* and *lequel*, some irregular nouns and adjectives, and the time expression *depuis*.

The cultural focus of this chapter is on hairstyles, cosmetics, and French perfume.

CHAPTER OBJECTIVES

By the end of this chapter, students will know:

1. vocabulary associated with hairstyles for both sexes and features of the head and face
2. vocabulary associated with hairstyling equipment and procedures, cosmetics, and perfume
3. demonstrative and interrogative pronouns
4. nouns and adjectives that form their plurals with *-x*
5. the time expression *depuis*

CHAPITRE 5

LA COIFFURE

OBJECTIFS

In this chapter you will learn to do the following:

1. use words and expressions related to hairstyles and cosmetics
2. express "which one(s)" and "this one," "that one," "these," and "those"
3. express the plural of certain nouns and adjectives
4. express "how long," "since," and "for"
5. discuss French and American hairstyles

CHAPTER PROJECTS

(optional)
1. Have students look for ads for cosmetics and perfume in American magazines. Have them make a list of any French words they find. Ask them why they think French is being used.
2. Have students bring in a photo of a celebrity and talk about his/her hairstyle.

COMMUNITIES

Have students write a letter to a French-speaking pen pal describing hairstyles that are currently in fashion. Have students find out what hairstyles are popular in their pen pal's country.

CHAPTER 5 RESOURCES

1. Workbook
2. Student Tape Manual
3. Audio Cassette 4A/CD-3
4. Bell Ringer Review Blackline Masters
5. Vocabulary Transparencies
6. Communication Transparency C-5
7. Communication Activities Masters
8. Situation Cards
9. Conversation Video
10. Videocassette/Videodisc, Unit 2
11. Video Activities Booklet, Unit 2
12. Lesson Plans
13. Computer Software: Practice/Test Generator
14. Chapter Quizzes
15. Testing Program
16. Internet Activities Booklet
17. CD-ROM Interactive Textbook
18. Map Transparencies

Pacing

This chapter will require eight to ten class sessions. Pacing will depend on the length of the class, the age of the students, and student aptitude.

For more information on planning your class, see the Lesson Plans, which offer guidelines for 45- and 55-minute classes and **Block Scheduling.**

Exercices vs. *Activités*

The exercises and activities are color-coded. Exercises, which provide guided practice to prepare students for independent communication, are coded in blue. Communicative activities, which give students opportunities for creative, open-ended expression, are coded in red.

INTERNET ACTIVITIES

(optional)
These activities, student worksheets, and related teacher information are in the *À bord* Internet Activities Booklet and on the Glencoe Foreign Language Home Page at: http://www.glencoe.com/secondary/fl

LEARNING FROM PHOTOS

After presenting the vocabulary in this chapter, have students come back to this photo and say as much as they can about it. You may want to give them the word for curling iron: *le fer à friser (le fer à coiffer).*

Vocabulary Teaching Resources

1. Vocabulary Transparencies 5.1 (A & B)
2. Audio Cassette 4A/CD-3
3. Student Tape Manual, Teacher's Edition, *Mots 1: A–C*, pages 47–49
4. Workbook, *Mots 1: A–C*, pages 49–50
5. Communication Activities Masters, *Mots 1: A–B*, page 31
6. Chapter Quizzes, *Mots 1:* Quiz 1, page 23
7. CD-ROM, Disc 2, *Mots 1:* pages 114–116

Bell Ringer Review

Write the following on the board or use BRR Blackline Master 5-1: A new student is coming to your school and wants your advice. Write five things no one in your school does. Follow this model: Personne ne porte de vêtements habillés.

PRESENTATION (pages 114–115)

A. Have students close their books. Present the *Mots 1* vocabulary by pointing to the items on Vocabulary Transparencies 5.1 (A & B) and having students repeat after you or Cassette 4A/CD-3.
B. You may wish to use student models for the different hairstyles mentioned.

Note You may wish to point out to students that the adjective *châtain* derives from the noun *une châtaigne*, which means "chestnut." *Châtain* is invariable after a feminine noun: for example, *une femme châtain* (a woman with chestnut-brown hair).

114

LA COIFFURE

une coiffure

les cheveux raides

les cheveux frisés

les cheveux bouclés

les pattes (f.)

la raie

les cheveux longs

les cheveux mi-longs

les cheveux courts

les cheveux blonds

les cheveux roux

les cheveux châtains

PAIRED ACTIVITY

Have students work in pairs. Each one draws a person with an unusual hairdo. They exchange drawings and describe what they see.

Lequel de ces styles préfères-tu?

Je préfère celui-là.

Comment est-ce que tu te coiffes?
J'ai…

une frange

un chignon

une natte

une queue de cheval

une mèche sur le front

les cheveux en brosse

le haut de la tête

le côté

la nuque

une mise-en-plis

une permanente

CHAPITRE 5   115

C. Mention several hairstyle features and have students raise their hands if they have the feature. For example: *Levez la main si vous avez une frange. Une queue de cheval,* etc.

INFORMAL ASSESSMENT
(*Mots 1*)
   Have individuals describe the style, length, and color of their own hair.

ADDITIONAL PRACTICE

1. After going over the *Mots 1* vocabulary, you may wish to ask students the following additional questions: *Quand vous étiez jeune, vous aviez les cheveux longs? Vous aviez une frange? Une natte? Une mèche sur le front? Comment est-ce que vous aviez les cheveux quand vous étiez jeune? Qu'est-ce que vous préférez pour les garçons—les cheveux blonds, noirs, bruns, châtains ou roux? Et pour les filles?*

2. Student Tape Manual, Teacher's Edition, *Activités B–C,* pages 48–49

Exercices A, B, and C

Exercises A and B can be done with books either open or closed. Exercise C is to be done with books open.

ANSWERS

Exercices A, B, and C

Answers will vary.

Exercices

A **Les cheveux.** Donnez des réponses personnelles.

1. Tu as les cheveux blonds, noirs, bruns, châtains ou roux?
2. Tu as les cheveux raides, bouclés ou frisés?
3. Tu as les cheveux longs, mi-longs ou courts?
4. Tu as une queue de cheval?
5. Tu as une mèche sur le front?
6. Si tu es un garçon, tu as des pattes?
7. Tu as des pattes longues ou courtes?
8. Tu as les cheveux en brosse?
9. Si tu es une fille, tu préfères une mise-en-plis, une permanente ou rien du tout?
10. Tu as une frange?
11. Quelles coiffures aimes-tu pour les filles? Et pour les garçons?
12. Quelles sont celles que tu n'aimes pas pour les filles? Et pour les garçons?

B **Dans la classe.** Répondez.

1. Dans la classe, qui a les cheveux longs? Les cheveux courts?
2. Qui a les pattes longues? Les pattes courtes?
3. Qui a une mèche sur le front?
4. Qui a la raie à droite? À gauche?
5. Qui a les cheveux roux? Les cheveux blonds?
6. Qui a les cheveux châtains? Les cheveux noirs?
7. Qui a une permanente?
8. Qui a les cheveux courts sur les côtés?
9. Qui a les cheveux longs sur la nuque?
10. Qui a les cheveux très courts sur le haut de la tête?

C **Lequel préfères-tu?** Regardez les photos et dites à un(e) camarade lequel des styles (masculins ou féminins) vous préférez. Décrivez le style de coiffure que vous avez choisi.

> Élève 1: Lequel de ces styles est-ce que tu préfères?
> Élève 2: Je préfère celui-là. La fille a les cheveux courts sur les côtés...

LEARNING FROM PHOTOS

Have students give as complete a description as possible of the color, length, and style of hair of each teen in the photos.

INDEPENDENT PRACTICE

Assign any of the following:
1. Exercises, page 116
2. Workbook, *Mots 1: A–C*, pages 49–50
3. Communication Activities Masters, *Mots 1: A–B*, page 31
4. CD-ROM, Disc 2, pages 114–116

VOCABULAIRE

MOTS 2

LES PRODUITS DE BEAUTÉ

le shampooing

le shampooing-crème

le talc

la crème
pour le visage

l'eau (f.)
de toilette

le parfum

le gel

la laque

le maquillage

les cils (m.)

le mascara

le rouge
à lèvres

les
lèvres (f.)

les ongles (m.)

le vernis à ongles

CHAPITRE 5   **117**

ADDITIONAL PRACTICE

1. Have students describe the hair (color, length, style) of the girls in the illustrations on this page.
2. To reinforce the vocabulary ask questions such as: *Est-ce que la fille aux cheveux bouclés met du mascara ou du vernis à ongles? Qui met du vernis à ongles? Qu'est-ce que la fille aux cheveux blonds met?*, etc.

VOCABULAIRE

MOTS 2

Vocabulary Teaching Resources

1. Vocabulary Transparencies 5.2, (A & B)
2. Audio Cassette 4A/CD-3
3. Student Tape Manual, Teacher's Edition, *Mots 2: D–F*, pages 49–51
4. Workbook, *Mots 2: D–G*, pages 50–51
5. Communication Activities Masters, *Mots 2: C–D*, pages 32–33
6. Computer Software, *Vocabulaire*
7. Chapter Quizzes, *Mots 2: Quiz 2*, page 24
8. CD-ROM, Disc 2, *Mots 2:* pages 117–120

Bell Ringer Review

Write the following on the board or use BRR Blackline Master 5-2: Write the following time expressions under the appropriate heading: *passé composé* or *imparfait.*
hier matin/toujours/un jour/ fréquemment/souvent/mercredi dernier/de temps en temps/à sept heures et quart/ toutes les semaines/l'année dernière

PRESENTATION *(pages 117–118)*

A. Have students close their books. Using Vocabulary Transparencies 5.2 (A & B), have students repeat the words, phrases, and sentences after you or Cassette 4A/CD-3.
B. Ask questions about the new material. For example: *C'est de l'eau de toilette? C'est de l'eau de toilette ou du parfum? Qu'est-ce que c'est?*
C. Have students open their books and read the new words.

Have individuals describe each illustration on page 118 as completely as possible.

RETEACHING (Mots 2)

Ask students the following questions, which use the vocabulary presented on this page: *Tu te fais un shampooing tous les jours (tous les deux jours)? Quand tu quittes la maison le matin, est-ce que tu as les cheveux secs ou mouillés? Tu les sèches avec un séchoir ou une serviette? Tu vas souvent chez le coiffeur/la coiffeuse? Qu'est-ce qu'il/elle te fait?*

CHEZ LE COIFFEUR

les cheveux mouillés

les cheveux secs

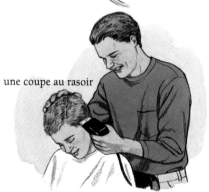

des rouleaux (m.) chauffants

un séchoir

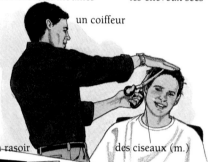

un coiffeur

un rasoir

des ciseaux (m.)

Le coiffeur lui coupe les cheveux.
Le coiffeur lui fait une coupe
    aux ciseaux.

une coupe au rasoir

une coiffeuse

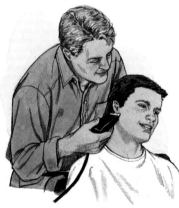

Le coiffeur lui taille les pattes.

La coiffeuse lui fait un shampooing.
Elle lui fait un brushing.
Elle lui donne un coup de peigne.

118 CHAPITRE 5

PANTOMIME GAME

Write the actions below on index cards. Give the cards to individuals to mime. As each student presents the action, call on another student to say in French what his/her classmate is doing.

mettre du rouge à lèvres
mettre du vernis à ongles
mettre du mascara

faire un shampooing à quelqu'un
se sécher les cheveux avec une serviette
se sécher les cheveux avec un séchoir
faire un brushing à quelqu'un
se donner un coup de peigne
se brosser les cheveux
faire une coupe aux ciseaux à quelqu'un
tailler les pattes à quelqu'un

Exercices

A **Quelle horreur!** Regardez le dessin et identifiez chacune des choses numérotées.

B **Chez le coiffeur.** Donnez des réponses personnelles.

1. Quand tu vas chez le coiffeur, le coiffeur ou la coiffeuse te fait un shampooing?
2. Il/Elle te coupe les cheveux mouillés ou secs?
3. Il/Elle te sèche les cheveux avec un séchoir ou il/elle les laisse sécher tout seuls?
4. Il/Elle te fait une coupe au rasoir ou aux ciseaux?
5. Il/Elle te fait un brushing?
6. Décris tout ce qu'il/elle te fait.

C **Question de goût.** Répondez.

1. Tu emploies des produits de beauté?
2. Tu aimes le maquillage pour les filles?
3. Tu aimes le vernis à ongles? Le mascara? Le rouge à lèvres?
4. En ce moment, le maquillage est à la mode pour les jeunes filles américaines?
5. Les permanentes sont à la mode ou pas?
6. Les cheveux longs, mi-longs ou courts sont à la mode?
7. Tu te donnes un coup de peigne le matin?
8. Tu te peignes avec un peigne ou tu te brosses les cheveux avec une brosse?

D **C'est pour qui?** Choisissez.

pour hommes   pour femmes   unisexe

1. le mascara
2. le shampooing-crème
3. le gel pour les cheveux
4. le parfum
5. l'eau de toilette
6. la crème pour le visage
7. le talc
8. la laque
9. le vernis à ongles

CHAPITRE 5   **119**

COOPERATIVE LEARNING

1. Have groups of boys discuss and report on whether they prefer girls to wear a lot of makeup or a little makeup.
2. Have groups of girls discuss whether they like to wear makeup or not and why.

ADDITIONAL PRACTICE

1. Call on individual girls to tell which of the cosmetics in *Mots 2* they use or don't use.
2. Student Tape Manual, Teacher's Edition, *Activités E–F*, pages 50–51

Exercices

PRESENTATION *(page 119)*

Exercices A, B, C, and D

Exercise A is to be done with books open. Exercises B, C, and D can be done with books either open or closed.

ANSWERS

Exercice A

1. des rouleaux chauffants
2. les cils
3. la figure (le visage)
4. les ongles (le vernis à ongles)
5. les lèvres (le rouge à lèvres)

Exercice B

Answers will vary but may include the following:

1. Oui, il/elle me fait un shampooing. (Non, il/elle ne me fait pas de shampooing.)
2. Il/Elle me coupe les cheveux mouillés (secs).
3. Il/Elle me sèche les cheveux avec un séchoir. (Il/Elle les laisse sécher tout seuls.)
4. Il/Elle me fait une coupe aux ciseaux (au rasoir).
5. Oui, il/elle me fait un brushing. (Non, il/elle ne me fait pas de brushing.)
6. Answers will vary.

Exercice C

Answers will vary.

Exercice D

1. pour femmes
2. unisexe
3. unisexe
4. pour femmes
5. pour femmes
6. pour femmes
7. unisexe
8. unisexe
9. pour femmes

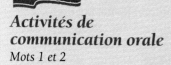

Bell Ringer Review

Write the following on the board or use BRR Blackline Master 5-3: Answer the following questions:

1. Qu'est-ce que vous faisiez quand votre mère ou votre père est rentré(e) hier?
2. Qu'est-ce que votre meilleur(e) ami(e) faisait quand vous l'avez appelé(e) hier?
3. Qu'est-ce que le professeur de français faisait quand les élèves sont entrés dans la classe?

Activités de communication orale

Mots 1 et 2

PRESENTATION *(page 120)*

These activities encourage students to use the new vocabulary on their own. You may wish to allow students to select the activities they wish to do.

Activité A

In the CD-ROM version of this activity, students can interact with an on-screen native speaker.

ANSWERS

Activités A, B, and C
Answers will vary.

Activités de communication orale

Mots 1 et 2

Anne Delon

A **Quels beaux cheveux tu as!** Votre amie française Anne Delon veut savoir comment vous vous coiffez. Répondez à ses questions.

1. Tu mets combien de temps pour te coiffer le matin?
2. Qu'est-ce que tu mets sur tes cheveux?
3. Est-ce que tu vas quelquefois chez le coiffeur? Chez quel coiffeur?

B **Qui est-ce?** Décrivez les cheveux (style, longueur et couleur) d'un(e) de vos camarades. Un(e) autre élève va deviner qui vous décrivez.

> Élève 1: Elle a les cheveux longs, bruns et frisés. Elle met beaucoup de gel.
> Élève 2: Est-ce que c'est Martine?

C **C'est quoi?** Choose several products from the list below and give a classmate clues about each of them—who uses the item, when, and why. Your partner has to guess which item you're describing.

> Élève 1: Les femmes en mettent sur les ongles.
> Élève 2: C'est du vernis à ongles.

du mascara	du dentifrice
du rouge à lèvres	du parfum
du vernis à ongles	du maquillage
de la laque	de la crème pour
du gel	le visage
	du shampooing

GEFF COIFFURE
FEMININ - MASCULIN

Fermé le Lundi
R.C. PARIS B 324 342 237

49 rue Lacépède
75005 PARIS
Tél. : 45 35 16

Les pronoms interrogatifs et démonstratifs

Expressing "Which One(s)" and "This One," "That One," "These," or "Those"

1. Review the forms of the interrogative adjectives.

MASCULIN	Tu aimes quel livre? Tu aimes quels livres?
FÉMININ	Tu as écouté quelle cassette? Tu as écouté quelles cassettes?

2. In French you use a form of the interrogative pronoun *lequel* to ask "which one(s)."

MASCULIN	J'ai lu un livre super. J'ai lu des livres super.	Ah, oui? Lequel? Ah, oui? Lesquels?
FÉMININ	J'ai entendu une cassette super. J'ai entendu des cassettes super.	Ah, oui? Laquelle? Ah, oui? Lesquelles?

CHAPITRE 5 **121**

Structure Teaching Resources

1. Workbook, *Structure: A–E,* pages 52–53
2. Student Tape Manual, Teacher's Edition, *Structure: A–C,* pages 51–52
3. Audio Cassette 4A/CD-3
4. Communication Activities Masters, *Structure: A–C,* pages 34–36
5. Computer Software, *Structure*
6. Chapter Quizzes, *Structure:* Quizzes 3–5, pages 25–27
7. CD-ROM, Disc 2, pages 121–125

LITERATURE CONNECTION

Students already have some information about Victor Hugo, if they read *Lettres et sciences,* pages 106–107. Here is some information about Daudet:

Alphonse Daudet est né à Nîmes en 1840. Il a fait ses études au lycée de Lyon. Ses parents ont perdu leur argent quand Daudet était très jeune et il est allé vivre avec son frère aîné (plus âgé) à Paris. Son frère l'a beaucoup aidé dans sa carrière.

Daudet a écrit des contes. Il est devenu célèbre avec un recueil (une collection) de contes: *Lettres de Mon Moulin.* Daudet a eu beaucoup de succès. Il encourageait toujours les jeunes écrivains (auteurs) qu'il accueillait dans sa villa de Champrosay où il est mort en 1897.

LEARNING FROM REALIA

Ask students to give the English titles of the works pictured. Ask them to name other works by Dumas (*Les Trois Mousquetaires, L'Homme au Masque de Fer*).

ADDITIONAL PRACTICE

Student Tape Manual, Teacher's Edition, *Activité A,* page 51

PRESENTATION (*pages 121–122*)

A. Go over the explanation with the students as they follow along in their books.

B. Write the forms of *quel* and *lequel* on the board.

C. Write the forms of the demonstrative pronouns on the board and go over the explanation with the students.

Note In the CD-ROM version, this structure point is presented via an interactive electronic comic strip.

Exercices

PRESENTATION (*pages 122–123*)

Exercice A

Exercise A can be done with books either open or closed.

ANSWERS

Exercice A

1. Je préfère celui-là.
2. Je préfère celui-là.
3. Je préfère celle-là.
4. Je préfère celle-là.
5. Je préfère ceux-là.
6. Je préfère ceux-là.
7. Je préfère celles-là.
8. Je préfère celles-là.

---

3. When the question "which one(s)" is asked, one often answers with "this one," "that one," "these," or "those." These are called demonstrative pronouns. Study the following forms of the demonstrative pronouns in French.

MASCULIN	Quel livre préfères-tu? Quels livres préfères-tu?	Celui-là. Ceux-là.
FÉMININ	Quelle cassette préfères-tu? Quelles cassettes préfères-tu?	Celle-là. Celles-là.

4. The demonstrative pronouns are never used alone. They are followed by:

- *-là* to single out
  Lequel de ces stylos aimes-tu? J'aime bien *celui-là*.

- *de* to indicate possession
  C'est ton livre? Non, c'est *celui de* Jean.

- the relative pronouns *qui* and *que* to identify
  Laquelle de ces filles est ta sœur? C'est *celle qui* parle avec Jean.

5. Note that *-ci* is used to refer to a person or object that is nearer the speaker and *-là* to a person or object farther away.

Veux-tu ce livre-ci ou ce livre-là?

Exercices

A **Tu préfères lequel?** Répondez d'après le modèle.

> Élève 1: **Voici deux shampooings. Tu préfères lequel?**
> Élève 2: **Je préfère celui-là.**

1. Voici deux gels pour les cheveux. Tu préfères lequel?
2. Voilà deux parfums. Tu préfères lequel?
3. Voici deux eaux de toilette. Tu préfères laquelle?
4. Voici deux crèmes solaires. Tu préfères laquelle?
5. De tous les parfums tu préfères lesquels?
6. De tous les rouges à lèvres tu préfères lesquels?
7. De toutes les crèmes pour le visage tu préfères lesquelles?
8. De toutes les laques pour les cheveux tu préfères lesquelles?

ADDITIONAL PRACTICE

1. You may wish to give students the following exercise to practice the use of *de* after a demonstrative pronoun. Model: *C'est ton livre? Non, c'est celui de mon frère.*
   a. C'est ton magazine?
   b. C'est ta voiture?
   c. Ce sont tes livres?
   d. Ce sont tes cassettes?

2. To practice the use of the relative pronoun *qui* after a demonstrative pronoun, you may wish to give students the following exercise. Tell them to answer according to the model: *Laquelle de ces filles est ta sœur? Ma sœur? C'est celle qui parle à Jean.*
   a. Lequel de ces garçons est ton frère?
   b. Laquelle de ces femmes est ta mère?
   c. Lesquels de ces élèves sont tes cousins?
   d. Lesquelles de ces actrices sont tes tantes?

B Il n'y a pas de différence entre le «look» de Serge et celui de son copain. Répondez d'après le modèle.

> Élève 1: Le «look» de Serge est à la mode. Et celui de son copain?
> Élève 2: Celui de son copain est à la mode aussi.

1. La coiffure de Serge est formidable. Et celle de son copain?
2. Les cheveux de Serge sont mouillés. Et ceux de son copain?
3. Les pattes de Serge sont très longues. Et celles de son copain?
4. Le shampooing de Serge coûte cher. Et celui de son copain?
5. La raie de Serge est à gauche. Et celle de son copain?

C Le shampooing de mes rêves. Complétez avec une forme de *celui de* ou *celui qui/que*.

Je n'aime plus le shampooing que j'utilise depuis un an. Je vais acheter ___ Michel utilise, ___ s'appele «Ultra». C'est un produit excellent. Et la laque Ultra est excellente aussi. C'est ___ on voit toujours à la télévision. Une actrice célèbre dit que ses cheveux et ___ son mari sont fantastiques parce qu'ils utilisent Ultra. J'aime beaucoup la coiffure de l'actrice mais je déteste ___ son mari. Je préfère les «looks» élégants mais pas ___ sont artificiels. De tous les «looks» à la mode en ce moment, ___ j'aime le mieux sont les «looks» très chic mais naturels.

Modèles de coiffures chez un coiffeur en Guinée

INDEPENDENT PRACTICE

Assign any of the following:
1. Exercises, pages 122–123
2. Workbook, *Structure: A–B*, page 52
3. Communication Activities Masters, *Structure: A*, page 34
4. CD-ROM, Disc 2, pages 121–123

PAIRED ACTIVITY

Have students come to the front of the room in pairs. One student asks a question about something or someone in the class using a form of *lequel*. The other answers with a form of *celui-là*. For example, É1 *(pointing to two chairs): Laquelle de ces chaises est plus confortable? É2 (pointing to one of the chairs): Celle-là est plus confortable.*

PRESENTATION *(continued)*

Exercices B and C

These exercises can be done with books open. You may wish to present Exercise C by reading it to the students as a story.

ANSWERS

Exercice B

1. Celle de son copain est formidable aussi.
2. Ceux de son copain sont mouillés aussi.
3. Celles de son copain sont très longues aussi.
4. Celui de son copain coûte cher aussi.
5. Celle de son copain est à gauche aussi.

Exercice C

1. celui que
2. celui qui
3. celle qu'
4. ceux de
5. celle de
6. ceux qui
7. ceux que

Le pluriel en -x

PRESENTATION *(page 124)*

A. Ask students to name some nouns and adjectives that end in *-eau, -eu, -ou, -al* or *-ail*. (For a complete list of words of this type that they are familiar with, see ADDITIONAL PRACTICE below.) Write the words on the board, using them as examples of how the plural is formed. Then have the students repeat the singular-plural pairs after you.

B. Now guide students through steps 1–3 on page 124.

Exercices

PRESENTATION *(pages 124–125)*

Exercice A

You may wish to use the recorded version of this exercise.

Exercices A and B

Since Exercises A and B deal with spelling changes, assign them for homework after going over them in class.

ANSWERS

Exercice A

1. les petits rouleaux
2. les beaux châteaux
3. les eaux de toilette
4. les cheveux longs
5. les journaux locaux
6. les animaux brutaux
7. les travaux publics
8. les hôpitaux régionaux

124

Le pluriel en -x   *More About the Plural*

1. Nouns ending in *-eau, -eu,* and *-ou* usually form their plural with *-x* rather than *-s*. Study the following.

SINGULIER	PLURIEL
le ciseau	les ciseaux
le rouleau	les rouleaux
le cheveu	les cheveux

2. Most nouns ending in *-al* or *-ail* change to *-aux* in the plural.

SINGULIER	PLURIEL
le journal	les journaux
le travail	les travaux

3. Remember that most adjectives ending in *-al* in the masculine singular also change to *-aux* in the plural.

MASCULIN SINGULIER	MASCULIN PLURIEL
local	locaux
national	nationaux

Exercices

A Le pluriel, s'il vous plaît.
Mettez au pluriel.

   le bel animal
   les beaux animaux

1. le petit rouleau
2. le beau château
3. l'eau de toilette
4. le cheveu long
5. le journal local
6. l'animal brutal
7. le travail public
8. l'hôpital régional

Le château d'Azay-le-Rideau

124   CHAPITRE 5

B Vos préférences. Donnez des réponses personnelles.

1. Tu aimes les animaux?
2. Tu aimes visiter les châteaux?
3. Tu connais les châteaux de la Loire?
4. Tu préfères les cheveux longs ou courts?
5. Pour les garçons, ce sont les cheveux longs ou les cheveux courts qui sont à la mode maintenant?
6. Tu préfères les coupes au rasoir ou aux ciseaux?
7. Tu lis des journaux français ou américains?

Les expressions de temps *Expressing Time*

1. You use the expression *depuis* with the present tense to describe an action that began at some time in the past and continues into the present.

Vous travaillez ici depuis combien de temps?	Je travaille ici depuis cinq ans.
Depuis quand est-ce qu'elle habite ici?	Elle habite ici depuis 1990.

2. The following are expressions that mean the same thing as *depuis*.

Il y a cinq ans que je travaille ici.
Voilà cinq ans que je travaille ici.
Ça fait cinq ans que je travaille ici.

Exercice

A Depuis quand? Donnez des réponses personnelles.

1. Tu habites dans la même ville ou dans le même village depuis quand?
2. Tu habites dans la même maison depuis quand?
3. Depuis quand vas-tu à la même école?
4. Depuis quand est-ce que tu fais du français?
5. Tu études avec le même prof depuis quand?
6. Depuis combien de temps est-ce que tu as les cheveux longs ou les cheveux courts?
7. Tu vas chez le même coiffeur depuis quand?

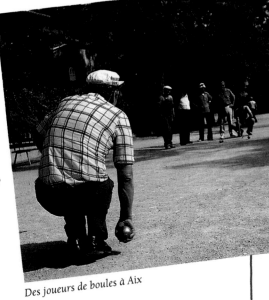

Des joueurs de boules à Aix

Exercice B
Answers will vary but should include:

1. les animaux
2. les châteaux
3. les châteaux
4. les cheveux
5. les cheveux
6. les coupes aux ciseaux (au rasoir)
7. des journaux

Les expressions de temps
PRESENTATION (*page 125*)

A. It is recommended that you not translate these time expressions. Students tend to become confused when they think in terms of the present perfect progressive construction ("have been … ing"). Stress that actions that began in the past but are still going on in the present are considered present-tense actions by French speakers.

B. The three expressions in step 2 are presented for passive recognition only. Students are not required to produce them actively.

Exercices
ANSWERS
Exercice A
Answers will vary but should all include a verb in the present tense and *depuis*.

HISTORY CONNECTION
Azay-le-Rideau, qui se trouve près de Tours, est l'un des plus petits des châteaux de la Loire, mais c'est un vrai bijou du point de vue architecture de la Renaissance. Le château, construit sur une petite île, se reflète dans l'Indre, la rivière qui l'entoure.

LEARNING FROM PHOTOS
You may wish to give students the following information about the photo on this page: *Partout en Provence, on voit des gens qui jouent aux boules sur la place. C'est un jeu très populaire chez les Provençaux. Ce jeu est d'origine italienne. En italien il s'appelle «bocci».*

INDEPENDENT PRACTICE
Assign any of the following:
1. Exercises, pages 124–125
2. Workbook, *Structure: C–E*, page 53
3. Communication Activities Masters, *Structure: B–C*, pages 35–36
4. Computer Software, *Structure*
5. CD-ROM, Disc 2, pages 124–125

Bell Ringer Review

Write the following on the board or use BRR Blackline Master 5-5: Write sentences with the following subjects, telling what each person used to do as a child.

Mon ami(e)...

Je...

Ma grand-mère...

Ma mère/Mon père...

PRESENTATION *(page 126)*

A. Tell students they will hear a conversation between Dominique and a hairdresser.

B. Have students close their books. Play the Conversation Video or have them listen as you read the conversation or play Cassette 4A/CD-3.

C. Have students open their books. Ask pairs to practice the conversation aloud. Model correct pronunciation as necessary. (Use *Activité E* in the Student Tape Manual to check oral comprehension.)

D. Now, call on a student to summarize the story of the conversation in his/her own words.

Note In the CD-ROM version, students can play the role of either one of the characters and record the conversation.

ANSWERS

Exercice A

1. C'est un garçon qui parle à la coiffeuse.

2. Il préfère les cheveux longs sur la nuque, mais plus courts sur les côtés.

3. Oui, il veut un shampooing.

4. Oui, elle a coupé les cheveux assez courts.

5. Non, il ne veut pas de gel.

6. Non, il n'aime pas «le wet look».

Scènes de la vie   *Une coupe*

LA COIFFEUSE: Qu'est-ce que je vous fais aujourd'hui?
DOMINIQUE: Une coupe, s'il vous plaît. Longs sur la nuque, plus courts sur les côtés.
LA COIFFEUSE: Je vous fais un shampooing?
DOMINIQUE: Oui, s'il vous plaît. *(Plus tard.)*
LA COIFFEUSE: C'est assez court comme ça?
DOMINIQUE: Oui, ça va bien.
LA COIFFEUSE: Vous voulez un gel «Wet Look»?
DOMINIQUE: Non, merci. Je n'aime pas le «look» gominé[1]. Je sais que c'est très «in», mais ce n'est pas mon genre.

[1] gominé   *plastered down*

A **Chez le coiffeur.** Répondez d'après la conversation.

1. C'est une fille ou un garçon qui parle à la coiffeuse?

2. Quel genre de coiffure est-ce que Dominique préfère?

3. Dominique veut un shampooing?

4. La coiffeuse a coupé les cheveux assez courts?

5. Dominique veut un gel?

6. Dominique aime «le wet look»?

126   CHAPITRE 5

COOPERATIVE LEARNING

Have students work in groups of three to make up a conversation between a hairstylist, a client, and the client's friend, who has another opinion about how his/her friend's hair should be styled. Call on volunteers to present their conversations to the class.

Activités de communication orale

A Lequel préfères-tu? Avec un(e) camarade, discutez de vos stars, groupes de rock, films, etc. préférés.

> Élève 1: J'aime bien Nirvana et Pearl Jam. Lequel préfères-tu?
> Élève 2: Moi, je préfère Pearl Jam.

B Depuis combien de temps? Demandez à un(e) camarade depuis combien de temps il/elle a les oreilles percées, les cheveux courts (longs), les cheveux en brosse, une queue de cheval, les cheveux verts, une permanente, etc. Demandez-lui aussi depuis quand il/elle s'habille de cette façon, utilise des produits de beauté, etc.

> Élève 1: Tu as les oreilles percées depuis combien de temps?
> Élève 2: Depuis trois ans.

C Quelle transformation! Compare the "before" and "after" pictures of one of the two models below. Ask a classmate questions about the differences between the two pictures regarding the model's hair (length, color, and style), nails, eyelashes, lips, and makeup.

> Élève 1: Quelles différences y a-t-il entre la coiffure de Chantal sur la première photo et la deuxième?
> Élève 2: Sur la première photo Chantal a les cheveux très raides. Sur la deuxième, elle a les cheveux très frisés! On lui a fait une permanente!

Chantal Dubois

Sylvie Fragnière

Activités de communication orale

PRESENTATION *(page 127)*

You may wish to allow students to select the activities they would like to do.

Extension of *Activité C*

Have students bring in "before" and "after" photos from fashion magazines for this activity.

ANSWERS

Activités A, B, and C

Answers will vary.

LECTURE ET CULTURE

READING STRATEGIES
(*pages 128–129*)

Pre-reading
You may wish to have two students present the reading as a TV interview. Select students who have good pronunciation and have them practice the conversation together a day prior to their classroom presentation. Ask all the students to bring in pictures of themselves with different hairstyles.

Teacher Tip If a student has a video camera at home, have him or her tape the interview prior to, or during, class.

Reading
A. Have the two students present the TV interview. Then open the discussion of changing styles to the whole class, who have brought their pictures.

Note Explain to the class that *dingue* ("crazy," "nuts") is used a great deal, especially by young people. See if they can guess the Disney cartoon character whose name is translated into French as *Dingo*. (Goofy)

B. Ask comprehension questions of the other students in the class.

Post-reading
Ask students to describe the hairstyles that were "in" last year in the United States. What kinds of hairstyles are "in" this year?

Note Students may listen to a recorded version of the *Lecture* on the CD-ROM.

Étude de mots

ANSWERS
Exercice A
1. b
2. e
3. a
4. c
5. d

NOUVELLES COUPES, NOUVELLES COIFFURES

CLAIRE: Michel, en France en ce moment, quel «look» est «in» au point de vue coiffure?

MICHEL: Eh bien, j'hésite à répondre à cette question. C'est difficile, tu sais. Le style change très vite. C'est dingue![1] Cette année, le court domine. Le «look» est très naturel, décontracté[2].

CLAIRE: C'est incroyable. Le court domine depuis quand? L'année dernière j'étais en France et tout le monde avait les cheveux longs.

MICHEL: Exactement. Comme je t'ai dit, le style change très vite. Aujourd'hui c'est le court, un peu de gel peut-être, mais on ne met plus de laque. Et demain, le long? Je ne sais pas.

Mon coiffeur mise sur[3] le retour des cheveux longs. Peut-être! Mais c'est la même chose aux États-Unis, n'est-ce pas?

CLAIRE: Ah, oui. Les coiffures changent tout le temps.

MICHEL: Quel est le «look» «in» maintenant?

CLAIRE: Franchement je ne sais pas.

MICHEL: Tu vois?

[1] dingue *crazy*
[2] décontracté *relaxed, informal*
[3] mise sur *is betting on*

Étude de mots

A Des correspondances. Trouvez le nom qui correspond au verbe.

1. hésiter
2. répondre
3. se coiffer
4. retourner
5. changer

a. une coiffure
b. une hésitation
c. un retour
d. un changement
e. une réponse

A DEUX PAS DE CHEZ VOUS UN GRAND COIFFEUR
Jean Louis David

128 CHAPITRE 5

Compréhension

ANSWERS

Exercice B

1. Non, les styles de coiffure changent très vite en France.
2. Non, le court domine quelque-fois et le long domine quel-quefois.
3. Non, le «look» décontracté n'est pas très élégant. (Il est naturel.)
4. Non, d'après Michel, on ne met plus de laque maintenant.
5. Non, le coiffeur de Michel mise sur le retour des cheveux longs.

Exercice C

b. Les styles de coiffure changent très vite en France et aux États-Unis.

Le kaléidoscoupe est la manière la plus efficace et la plus astucieuse de choisir la coupe qui vous va. L'une de ces formes mondialement connues signées JEAN LOUIS DAVID s'adaptera forcément à votre personnalité ou à votre problème spécifique de cheveux. Passez le kaléidoscoupe au peigne fin, et montrez à notre coiffeur le modèle qui vous plaît. Il sera alors réalisé par des équipes maîtrisant parfaitement la technique de l'un des modèles griffés JEAN LOUIS DAVID. Plus besoin de savoir parler de sa coupe, il suffit de la montrer. Contrat-coiffure : venez vite l'essayer !

LES BEST-SELLERS

Compréhension

B   Vous avez compris?   Répondez par «oui» ou «non» d'après la lecture.

1. Les styles de coiffure ne changent presque jamais en France.
2. Le court domine toujours.
3. Un «look» décontracté est très élégant et distingué, sophistiqué.
4. D'après Michel, la laque est très «in» en France en ce moment.
5. Le coiffeur de Michel dit que les cheveux longs, c'est fini.

C   L'idée principale.   Choisissez l'idée principale de la lecture.

a. Le «look» décontracté est presque toujours «in» en France.
b. Les styles de coiffure changent très vite en France et aux États-Unis.
c. Le «look» n'est jamais le même en France et aux États-Unis.

CHAPITRE 5   **129**

OPTIONAL MATERIAL

Découverte culturelle

PRESENTATION *(pages 130–131)*

A. Survey the class to see how many students go to *un coiffeur unisexe* and how many go to *un coiffeur pour hommes ou pour femmes.*

B. Have students locate Nice on the Map Transparency of France or on the map of France on page 435. Tell them that Grasse is a hillside town located about 19 miles northwest of Nice.

C. Have students read the selection silently.

Note Students may listen to a recorded version of the *Découverte culturelle* on the CD-ROM.

DÉCOUVERTE CULTURELLE

LES COIFFURES

En France, comme aux États-Unis, les coiffures changent fréquemment. De temps en temps le style qui est à la mode aux États-Unis est «in» en France aussi. Mais ce n'est pas toujours le cas. Les cheveux sont longs ici et courts en France.

Dans les villes de France surtout et dans celles d'autres pays européens, il y a beaucoup de coiffures unisexe. À l'heure actuelle[1] les coiffures unisexe existent aux États-Unis et deviennent de plus en plus populaires. Mais les changements fréquents de coiffures chez les hommes américains sont plus récents que chez les Français. Aux États-Unis, jusqu'à récemment, le coiffeur coupait les cheveux toujours de la même manière. Il se servait d'une tondeuse[2] pour couper les cheveux et raser la nuque. Il utilisait rarement des ciseaux. En France ça fait longtemps que le coiffeur demande à ses clients, «Vous désirez une coupe aux ciseaux ou au rasoir?» Le shampooing et une coupe avec un certain style, «look» ou allure est assez nouveau pour les hommes américains.

LES PARFUMS

Guerlain, Dior, Nina Ricci, Yves Saint-Laurent, et Chanel sont des marques françaises de parfum célèbres. Plus de 75% des extraits de parfums vendus

[1] à l'heure actuelle *now, currently*
[2] une tondeuse *clipper*

Grasse, la ville des parfums

DID YOU KNOW?

Grasse, an old and picturesque hillside town about 19 miles northwest of Nice, was a thriving town in the 12th century. Distillation of the essences of flowers began here as early as the 16th century. The cultivation of jasmine in the 17th century, and the later addition of lavender, mint, roses, and orange, brought Grasse its reputation as the world's leading center for the production of scents, a reputation it has never lost.

Some of the major *parfumeurs,* such as Molinard and Fragonard, give tours of their factories.

Une fabrique de parfums à Grasse

dans le monde sont produits à Grasse, une vieille ville de Haute-Provence. Tout autour de[3] la ville il y a des champs de lavande, de roses, de jasmin, d'orangers et de mimosas qui servent à la fabrication des parfums. Les belles fleurs mauves de la lavande embaument l'air d'été au mois de juillet. Et les femmes de tous les coins du monde apprécient un joli flacon[4] de parfum français.

[3] tout autour de   *all around*
[4] flacon   *bottle*

Parfum de Pénélope Zagoras
Paris

Leïda

INDEPENDENT PRACTICE

1. If the topic of cosmetology or the perfume industry is of particular interest to an individual, have him/her prepare a special report.
2. Workbook, *Un Peu Plus*, pages 54–56

RÉALITÉS

Bell Ringer Review

Write the following on the board or use BRR Blackline Master 5-8: Think of the last phone call you made. Tell where you were, who you called, and what you talked about.

OPTIONAL MATERIAL

PRESENTATION
(pages 132–133)

Allow students to look at the photos for enjoyment. Then have them read the captions that go with the photos and discuss the information.

Note In the CD-ROM version, students can listen to the recorded captions and discover a hidden video behind one of the photos.

Voici un beau champ de lavande en Provence **1**. On utilise la lavande dans la fabrication des savons et des parfums.

Regardez cette coiffure extraordinaire du dix-huitième siècle **2**.

Voici le salon de coiffure «Au Figaro des Treize Coins» à Marseille **3**. Les femmes peuvent se faire couper les cheveux ici?

Cette jeune femme choisit un parfum dans une parfumerie à La Rochelle **4**. Quel est ton parfum préféré?

C'est la salle des parfumeurs chez Roger & Gallet **5**. On y teste les parfums. Il faut avoir un nez très sensible pour faire ce travail. C'est un travail qui t'intéresse?

Voici un flacon de parfum **6**. À ton avis la forme est belle? C'est un parfum de quel grand couturier?

DID YOU KNOW?

Write *le nez* on the board. Have students look at Photo #5, then ask them who or what *le nez* might be in the perfume industry. (A very highly paid research chemist who discovers, creates, and modifies perfume fragrances.)

COOPERATIVE LEARNING

Display Communication Transparency C-5. Have students work in groups to make up as many questions as they can about the illustration. Then have the groups take turns asking and answering each other's questions.

HISTORY CONNECTION

Lavender, a small purple-flowered herb, is the most characteristic scent of Provence. Approximately 70% of France's crop grows in an area referred to as the "mauve triangle" between Sault, Banon and Séderon. There are different varieties of lavender, but all are used in two ways. Oil of lavender is derived from the flower and used in the manufacture of perfumes, toilet water, and aromatic vinegar. The flowers can also be dried and used for sachets for linen and clothing.

The Romans added lavender to their baths for its soothing qualities. The name *lavender* is derived from the Latin *lavare*, which means "to wash." The first distillery for extracting oil from lavender was founded in 1880. After World War I, lavender fields were systematically cultivated to meet the demands of the *parfumeurs* in Grasse.

ADDITIONAL PRACTICE

Assign any of the following:
1. Student Tape Manual, Teacher's Edition, *Deuxième Partie*, pages 54–56
2. Situation Cards, Chapter 5

CULMINATION

RECYCLING

These activities encourage students to use all the language they have learned in the chapter and to recombine it with previously learned material. It is not necessary to do all the activities with all students. You may select the ones you consider most appropriate or permit students to choose the ones they would like to do.

INFORMAL ASSESSMENT

The *Activités de communication orale* lend themselves to assessing speaking and listening abilities. Use the evaluation criteria given on page 22 of this Teacher's Wraparound Edition.

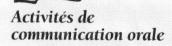

Activités de communication orale

ANSWERS

Activités A, B, and C
Answers will vary.

Activités de communication écrite

ANSWERS

Activités A and B
Answers will vary.

Activités de communication orale

A Au théâtre. Vous avez décidé de monter une pièce de théâtre. Avec un(e) camarade, choisissez une pièce qui vous plaît (*West Side Story*, par exemple) et décidez comment vont être les personnages:

> Quelle coiffure
> Quel costume
>
> Élève 1: Comment vont être Tony et Maria?
> Élève 2: Je ne sais pas, moi. Il va avoir le look gominé. Elle va avoir les cheveux raides.
> Élève 1: Il peut porter un blouson noir. Elle peut porter une robe blanche.

B Les Best-sellers. Working with a classmate, look at the hairstyle poster on page 129. You choose one of the models and describe his or her hair in as much detail as possible. Your partner has to guess who you're describing. You may each take several turns describing and guessing.

C Qu'est-ce que je suis beau (belle)! Vous êtes invité(e) à une fête. Mais avant d'y aller, vous allez chez le coiffeur pour une coupe de cheveux. Décrivez ce que le coiffeur ou la coiffeuse vous fait.

Activités de communication écrite

A Chez le coiffeur. Using the ads on the right as a guide, write an ad for a real or imaginary French hair salon. Be sure to include the following information.

1. who the salon caters to
2. what kinds of haircuts and services are available
3. a price list
4. a catchy phrase to interest clients in the salon

B À la mode. Décrivez les styles de coiffure pour hommes et femmes qui sont à la mode en ce moment aux États-Unis.

ADDITIONAL PRACTICE

Ask students: *C'est nécessaire pour l'hygiène ou pas?*

une brosse à dents	du mascara
du gel	du déodorant
du savon	du parfum
du dentifrice	du shampooing
de la laque	du maquillage
du rince-bouche	

COOPERATIVE LEARNING

Have students work in groups of three to prepare a conversation between a sales clerk at a cosmetics counter and two customers who want to buy a gift together for someone. Call on volunteers to present their conversations to the class.

Réintroduction et recombinaison

A **Ma journée.** Donnez des réponses personnelles.

1. Tu te lèves à quelle heure le matin?
2. Ton frère ou ta sœur se lève à la même heure que toi?
3. Tu te laves la figure et les mains?
4. Tu te laves les cheveux tous les matins?
5. Tu te brosses les dents combien de fois par jour?
6. Tu emploies quelle marque de dentifrice?
7. Ton copain et toi, vous restez en forme?
8. Vous faites de la gymnastique?
9. Tu fais du sport? Quel sport?
10. Tu rentres chez toi à quelle heure l'après-midi?

B **On fait sa toilette.** Choisissez le mot.

du rince-bouche	du savon	une serviette
du dentifrice	du déodorant	du shampooing

1. On se lave avec ___.
2. On se sèche avec ___.
3. On se rince la bouche avec ___.
4. On se brosse les dents avec ___.
5. On se lave les cheveux avec ___.
6. On met ___ quand on fait de l'exercice.

C **L'école primaire.** Donnez des réponses personnelles.

1. Tu allais à quelle école primaire?
2. Qui était ta maîtresse préférée ou ton maître préféré?
3. Tu allais à l'école à pied ou tu prenais le bus?
4. Tu déjeunais à la cantine ou tu rentrais chez toi?

Vocabulaire

NOMS
le coiffeur
la coiffeuse
la coiffure
les cheveux (m.)
la coupe
  au rasoir
  aux ciseaux
le shampooing
la mise-en-plis
la permanente
le peigne
les ciseaux (m.)
le rasoir
le rouleau (chauffant)
le séchoir
le style
les cheveux en brosse

le chignon
la frange
la mèche
la queue de cheval
la natte
la raie
les pattes (f.)
le côté
le haut
la nuque
le front
les cils (m.)
la lèvre
l'ongle (m.)
le produit de beauté
la crème pour le visage
le shampooing-crème

le gel
la laque
le talc
le parfum
l'eau (f.) de toilette
le maquillage
le rouge à lèvres
le vernis à ongles
le mascara

ADJECTIFS
bouclé(e)
raide
frisé(e)
court(e)
mi-long(ue)
long(ue)
mouillé(e)

sec, sèche
châtain
roux, rousse
unisexe

VERBES
se coiffer
couper
tailler

AUTRES MOTS ET
EXPRESSIONS
faire un shampooing
faire une coupe
faire un brushing
donner un coup de
  peigne

Réintroduction et recombinaison

PRESENTATION *(page 135)*

Exercices A, B, and C

Exercise A recycles the present tense of reflexive verbs taught in *Bienvenue*. Exercises A and B both recycle some of the vocabulary associated with health and hygiene presented in *Bienvenue*. Exercise C recycles the imperfect.

ANSWERS

Exercice A
  Answers will vary.

Exercice B
1. du savon
2. une serviette
3. du rince-bouche
4. du dentifrice
5. du shampooing
6. du déodorant

Exercice C
  Answers will vary.

ASSESSMENT RESOURCES

1. Chapter Quizzes
2. Testing Program
3. Situation Cards
4. Communication Transparency C-5
5. Computer Software: Practice/Test Generator

VIDEO PROGRAM

INTRODUCTION   (21:22)

MÉLANIE VA CHEZ   (22:02)
LE COIFFEUR

STUDENT PORTFOLIO

Written assignments which may be included in students' portfolios are the *Activités de communication écrite A and B* on page 134 and any writing activities from the *Un Peu Plus* section in the Workbook.

 Note Students may create and save both oral and written work using the Electronic Portfolio feature on the CD-ROM.

INDEPENDENT PRACTICE

Assign any of the following:
1. Activities and exercises, pages 134–135
2. Communication Activities Masters, pages 31–36
3. CD-ROM, Disc 2, pages 134–135

CHAPTER OVERVIEW

In this chapter students will learn vocabulary needed to report and describe certain accidents and talk about minor injuries. They will also learn vocabulary associated with emergency hospital treatment. Students will learn to form questions using *qu'est-ce que* and *qu'est-ce qui*. They will also learn to use *ce qui* and *ce que*, the verbs *suivre* and *vivre*, the expressions *meilleur* and *mieux*, and the imperative form of the verb with an object pronoun.

The cultural focus of Chapter 6 is on health services in France.

CHAPTER OBJECTIVES

By the end of this chapter, students will know:

1. vocabulary associated with minor accidents, injuries, and visits to a doctor
2. vocabulary associated with more serious accidents, illnesses, and emergency hospital care
3. the direct interrogative expressions *Qu'est-ce qui* and *Qu'est-ce que*
4. the relative pronouns *ce qui* and *ce que*
5. the present indicative forms and past participles of *suivre* and *vivre*
6. the use of object pronouns with the imperative
7. the comparatives and superlatives *mieux* and *meilleur*

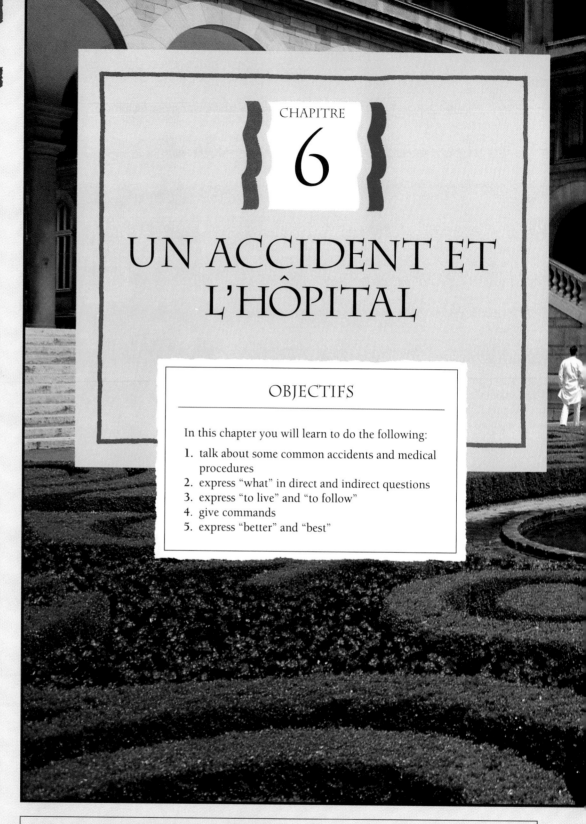

UN ACCIDENT ET L'HÔPITAL

OBJECTIFS

In this chapter you will learn to do the following:

1. talk about some common accidents and medical procedures
2. express "what" in direct and indirect questions
3. express "to live" and "to follow"
4. give commands
5. express "better" and "best"

CHAPTER PROJECTS

(optional)

1. Have students select a health problem or injury they learn about in this chapter and write a paragraph about it.
2. In *Bienvenue,* some students read about Louis Pasteur and the Pasteur Institute on pages 442–443 in the *Lettres et sciences* section. Have those students interested in medicine do a report on this famous person and institute.

1. Workbook
2. Student Tape Manual
3. Audio Cassette 4B/CD-3
4. Bell Ringer Review Blackline Masters
5. Vocabulary Transparencies
6. Communication Transparency C-6
7. Communication Activities Masters
8. Situation Cards
9. Conversation Video
10. Videocassette/Videodisc, Unit 2
11. Video Activities Booklet, Unit 2
12. Lesson Plans
13. Computer Software: Practice/Test Generator
14. Chapter Quizzes
15. Testing Program
16. Internet Activities Booklet
17. CD-ROM Interactive Textbook
18. Map Transparencies

Pacing

This chapter will require eight to ten class sessions. Pacing will depend on the length of the class, the age of the students, and student aptitude.

For more information on planning your class, see the Lesson Plans, which offer guidelines for 45- and 55-minute classes and **Block Scheduling.**

Exercices vs. *Activités*

The exercises and activities are color-coded. Exercises, which provide guided practice to prepare students for independent communication, are coded in blue. Communicative activities, which give students opportunities for creative, open-ended expression, are coded in red.

INTERNET ACTIVITIES

(optional)

These activities, student worksheets, and related teacher information are in the *À bord* Internet Activities Booklet and on the Glencoe Foreign Language Home Page at: **http://www.glencoe.com/secondary/fl**

CRITICAL THINKING ACTIVITY

(Thinking skills: making inferences; supporting statements with reasons)

Read the following to the class or write it on the board or on a transparency:

Sur la photo, on voit deux étudiants en médecine qui font leur stage dans un hôpital à Paris. De quoi parlent-ils? De leurs études, de la médecine, d'un malade ou de quelque chose d'autre? Justifiez votre réponse.

UN ACCIDENT

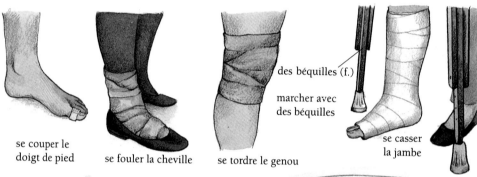

le bras

le genou

la jambe

le doigt

la cheville

glisser

tomber

le doigt de pied

se couper le
doigt de pied

se fouler la cheville

se tordre le genou

des béquilles (f.)

marcher avec
des béquilles

se casser
la jambe

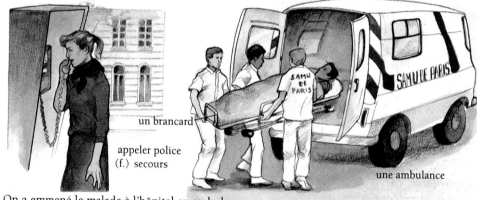

un brancard

appeler police
(f.) secours

une ambulance

On a emmené le malade à l'hôpital en ambulance.

Vocabulary Teaching Resources

1. Vocabulary Transparencies 6.1 (A & B)
2. Audio Cassette 4B/CD-3
3. Student Tape Manual, Teacher's Edition, *Mots 1: A–C,* pages 57–59
4. Workbook, *Mots 1: A–F,* pages 57–59
5. Communication Activities Masters, *Mots 1: A–B,* page 37
6. Chapter Quizzes, *Mots 1: Quiz 1,* page 28
7. CD-ROM, Disc 2, *Mots 1:* pages 138–141

Bell Ringer Review

Write the following on the board or use BRR Blackline Master 6-1: Write as many words as you can remember related to health or health care.

PRESENTATION
(pages 138–139)

A. In addition to Vocabulary Transparencies 6.1 (A & B), you may wish to use gestures or dramatizations to introduce many of these terms. Those which lend themselves to easy dramatization are: *glisser, tomber, se couper le doigt, se fouler la cheville, se tordre le genou, se casser la jambe,* and *marcher avec des béquilles.*

B. Refer to yourself or a student model to demonstrate *le genou, la jambe, le doigt, la cheville,* and *le doigt de pied.*

Note Ask students if they remember from French 1 what SAMU stands for (*Service d'aide médicale d'urgence*).

PANTOMIME 1

_____ , venez ici, s'il vous plaît.
Montrez-moi le bras.
Montrez-moi le doigt.
Montrez-moi le pied.
Montrez-moi le genou.
Montrez-moi la cheville.
Montrez-moi la jambe.
Montrez-moi le ventre.
Montrez-moi les lèvres.
Montrez-moi les yeux.
Merci, _____ .

À LA SALLE DES URGENCES

Qu'est-ce qui est arrivé?

Un accident.

un fauteuil roulant

Vous avez mal? Où? Montrez-moi.

J'ai mal à la jambe.

des points (m.) de suture

CHEZ LE MÉDECIN

C'est une petite blessure.
Qu'est-ce qui lui est arrivé?
Elle s'est coupé le doigt.

un infirmier

un pansement

Maryse s'est blessée.
L'infirmière la soigne.
Elle lui met un pansement.

CHAPITRE 6   139

C. Have students repeat the vocabulary after you or Cassette 4B/CD-3. Have pairs read the mini-conversations with as much natural expression as possible.

Note You may wish to have students supply additional answers to the questions: *Qu'est-ce qui est arrivé? Vous avez mal? Où? Montrez-moi.*

D. Ask questions to elicit the vocabulary. For example: *C'est le genou ou la jambe? Le garçon s'est cassé le bras? La jeune fille a une petite blessure? Qu'est-ce qui lui est arrivé? Est-ce que l'infirmière va lui faire des points de suture? Elle va lui mettre un pansement?*

PANTOMIME 2

____, venez ici, s'il vous plaît.
Allez au téléphone.
Vous allez appeler police secours.
Décrochez.
Composez le numéro.
Parlez. Dites ce qui est arrivé.
Merci, ____.

PANTOMIME 3

Et maintenant ____, venez ici, s'il vous plaît.
Mimez ce qui vous est arrivé:
Vous avez glissé.
Vous êtes tombé(e).
Vous vous êtes foulé la cheville.
Vous marchez avec des béquilles.
Merci, ____.

Exercices

PRESENTATION
(pages 140–141)

Exercice A
🎧 Exercise A can be done with books open as students refer to the illustrations.

Exercice B
Exercise B can be done with books either open or closed.

Extension of *Exercice B*: Speaking
After completing Exercise B, call on a student to retell the story in his/her own words.

Extension of *Exercice B*: Writing
After completing Exercise B, have students reconstruct the story in writing.

ANSWERS

Exercice A
1. C'est une infirmière.
2. C'est une ambulance.
3. C'est un brancard.
4. C'est un fauteuil roulant.
5. C'est la salle des urgences.
6. C'est le genou.
7. C'est un pansement.
8. C'est le doigt de pied.
9. C'est la cheville.

Exercice B
1. François a eu un accident.
2. Oui, il est tombé.
3. Il est tombé en face de l'école.
4. Il a glissé sur la glace.
5. Oui, il a eu une blessure.
6. Oui, il a pu se relever.
7. Non, on n'a pas appelé police secours.
8. Il est allé à l'hôpital.
9. Son copain l'a emmené à l'hôpital.
10. Il l'a emmené à la salle des urgences.

Exercices

A Qu'est-ce que c'est? Identifiez d'après les dessins.

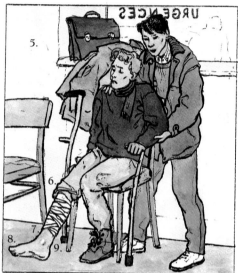

1. C'est un médecin ou une infirmière?
2. C'est une ambulance ou une voiture?
3. C'est un brancard ou un fauteuil roulant?
4. Ce sont des béquilles ou un fauteuil roulant?
5. C'est la salle d'opération ou la salle des urgences?
6. C'est le bras ou le genou?
7. C'est un pansement ou un point de suture?
8. C'est le doigt ou le doigt de pied?
9. C'est la jambe ou la cheville?

B Un petit accident. Répondez.

1. Qui a eu un accident? (François)
2. Il est tombé? (oui)
3. Où est-ce qu'il est tombé? (en face de l'école)
4. Il a glissé sur quoi? (la glace)
5. Il a eu une blessure? (oui)
6. Il a pu se relever? (oui)
7. On a appelé police secours? (non)
8. Où est-il allé? (à l'hôpital)
9. Qui l'a emmené à l'hôpital? (son copain)
10. Où à l'hôpital? (à la salle des urgences)

ADDITIONAL PRACTICE

1. You may wish to reinforce the lesson by asking students the following questions: *Vous avez déjà eu un petit accident? Qu'est-ce qui est arrivé? Vous avez eu mal? Vous vous êtes blessé(e)?*
2. Student Tape Manual, Teacher's Edition, *Activité C,* page 59

INDEPENDENT PRACTICE

Assign any of the following:
1. Exercises, pages 140–141
2. Workbook, *Mots 1: A–F,* pages 57–59
3. Communication Activities Masters, *Mots 1: A–B,* page 37
4. CD-ROM, Disc 2, pages 138–141

C **Tu as déjà eu un accident?** Donnez des réponses personnelles.

1. Tu es déjà tombé(e)?
2. Où est-ce que tu es tombé(e)?
3. Qu'est-ce qui t'est arrivé? Tu as glissé?
4. Tu as eu mal? Où?
5. Tu t'es cassé la jambe? le bras? le doigt?
6. Tu t'es foulé la cheville?
7. Tu t'es tordu le genou?
8. On t'a transporté(e) sur un brancard?
9. On t'a emmené(e) à l'hôpital en ambulance?
10. Tu es allé(e) à la salle des urgences?
11. Qui t'a soigné(e)?
12. Tu as dû marcher avec des béquilles?
13. Tu t'es déjà blessé(e)?
14. Tu t'es coupé le doigt?
15. Tu as eu des points de suture?

141

PRESENTATION (continued)
Exercice C

Exercise C can be done with books open or closed. It is recommended that you go over the exercise in class before assigning it for homework.

ANSWERS
Exercice C

Answers will vary but may include the following:

1. Oui, je suis déjà tombé(e). (Non, je ne suis jamais tombé[e].)
2. Je suis tombé(e)...
3. Oui, j'ai glissé. (Non, je n'ai pas glissé. J'ai...)
4. Oui, j'ai eu mal à... (au, à la, aux)... (Non, je n'ai pas eu mal.)
5. Oui, je me suis cassé la jambe (le bras/le doigt). (Non, je ne me suis rien cassé.)
6. Oui, je me suis foulé la cheville. (Non, je ne me suis pas foulé...)
7. Oui, je me suis tordu le genou. (Non, je ne me suis pas tordu...)
8. Oui, on m'a transporté(e) sur un brancard. (Non, on ne m'a pas transporté[e]...)
9. Oui, on m'a emmené(e) à l'hôpital en ambulance. (Non, on ne m'a pas emmené[e]...)
10. Oui, je suis allé(e) à la salle des urgences. (Non, je ne suis pas allé[e]...)
11. Un médecin m'a soigné(e).
12. Oui, j'ai dû marcher avec des béquilles. (Non, je n'ai pas dû marcher...)
13. Oui, je me suis déjà blessé(e). (Non, je ne me suis jamais blessé[e].)
14. Oui, je me suis coupé le doigt. (Non, je ne me suis pas coupé...)
15. Oui, j'ai eu des points de suture. (Non, je n'ai pas eu de...)

LEARNING FROM PHOTOS

Have students identify as many items as they can in the first aid kit (*la trousse de secours*). You may also wish to teach them the words for tweezers (*des pinces*) and safety pin (*une épingle de sûreté*).

LEARNING FROM REALIA

Have students glance at the brochure and decide what it is about.

VOCABULAIRE

MOTS 2

Vocabulary Teaching Resources

1. Vocabulary Transparencies 6.2 (A & B)
2. Audio Cassette 4B/CD-3
3. Student Tape Manual, Teacher's Edition, *Mots 2: D–F*, pages 59–61
4. Workbook, *Mots 2: G*, page 59
5. Communication Activities Masters, *Mots 2: C–D*, pages 38–39
6. Chapter Quizzes, *Mots 2: Quiz 2*, page 29
7. Computer Software, *Vocabulaire*
8. CD-ROM, Disc 2, *Mots 2*: pages 142–145

Bell Ringer Review

Write the following on the board or use BRR Blackline Master 6-2: Write answers to the following questions: **Depuis quand...**

1. faites-vous du français?
2. connaissez-vous votre meilleur(e) ami(e)?
3. habitez-vous à la même adresse?
4. avez-vous le même numéro de téléphone?

PRESENTATION (*pages 142–143*)

A. Pointing to Vocabulary Transparencies 6.2 (A & B), have students repeat the words, phrases, and sentences after you or Cassette 4B/CD-3.

B. Practice some of the expressions by putting them into short sentences. For example: *Faire une piqûre: Le médecin lui a fait une piqûre. Faire une radio: Le médecin lui a fait une radio. Prendre la tension artérielle: Le médecin lui a pris la tension artérielle, etc.*

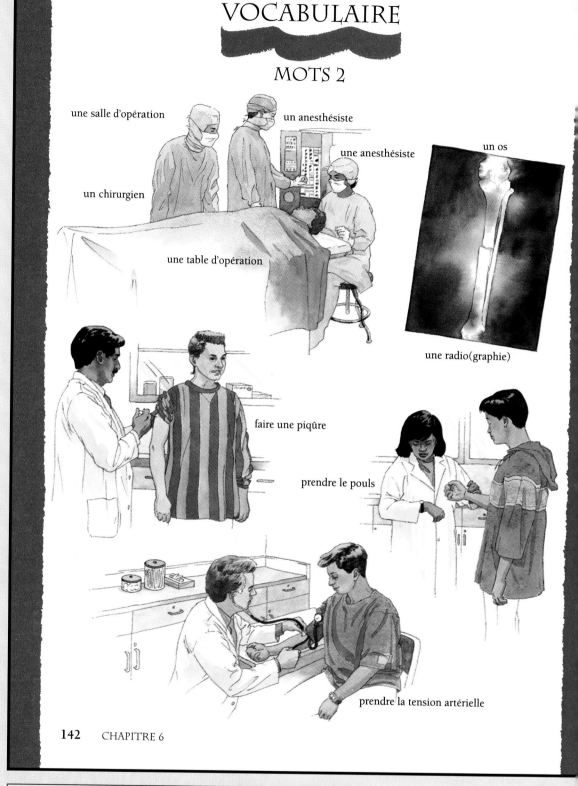

une salle d'opération

un anesthésiste

une anesthésiste

un chirurgien

un os

une table d'opération

une radio(graphie)

faire une piqûre

prendre le pouls

prendre la tension artérielle

142   CHAPITRE 6

ADDITIONAL PRACTICE

1. You may wish to reinforce the vocabulary by asking the following questions about the illustrations. *Où est le malade? Et où est la table d'opération? Le chirurgien regarde le malade? Qui va lui faire une anesthésie? Qu'est-ce qu'on peut voir sur la radio? Qui fait une piqûre au garçon? Qui lui prend le pouls? Qui lui prend la tension artérielle?*

2. Student Tape Manual, Teacher's Edition, *Activité F*, page 61

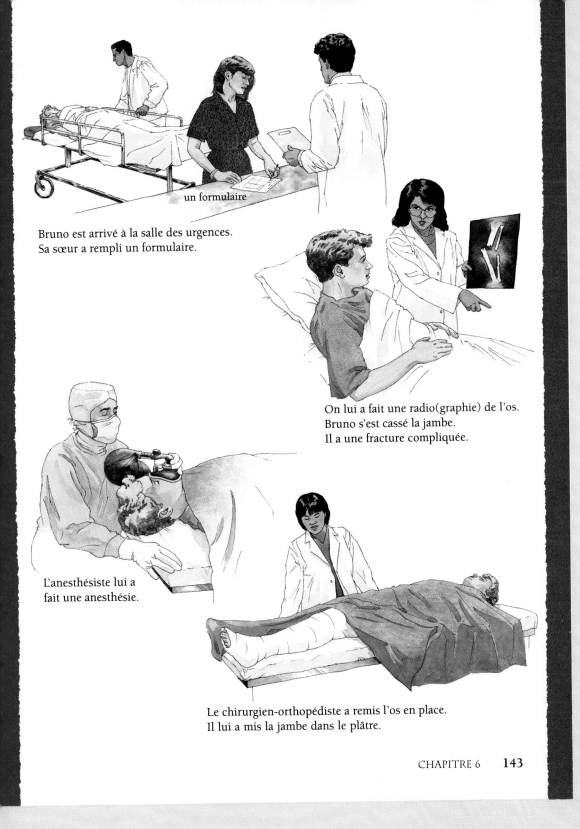

un formulaire

Bruno est arrivé à la salle des urgences.
Sa sœur a rempli un formulaire.

On lui a fait une radio(graphie) de l'os.
Bruno s'est cassé la jambe.
Il a une fracture compliquée.

L'anesthésiste lui a
fait une anesthésie.

Le chirurgien-orthopédiste a remis l'os en place.
Il lui a mis la jambe dans le plâtre.

CHAPITRE 6 **143**

C. You may wish to ask the following questions during your
presentation: *Où est-ce que
Bruno est arrivé? Qui a rempli le
formulaire? On lui a fait une
radio de l'os? Qu'est-ce qui
lui est arrivé? Qu'est-ce que
l'anesthésiste lui a fait? Et le
chirurgien-orthopédiste?*

Pronunciation Note Point out
the difference in pronunciation
between the singular and plural
forms of *os: un os*, the final *s* is
pronounced; *des os*, the final *s* is
silent.

Exercices

PRESENTATION (page 144)

Exercices A and C

Exercises A and C can be done with books either open or closed.

Exercice B

Exercise B can be done with books either open or closed.

Extension of Exercice B: Reading

After completing Exercise B, have one student read aloud all the items with the correct answers in the form of a story.

Exercice C

Students should not be held responsible for the new words in this exercise. They should be able to use the French they know to determine the word being defined.

ANSWERS

Exercice A

1. Oui, le médecin l'a ausculté.
2. Oui, le médecin lui a dit: «Respirez à fond».
3. Oui, le médecin lui a pris le pouls.
4. Oui, le médecin lui a pris sa tension artérielle.
5. Oui (Non), le médecin (ne) lui a (pas) fait une (de) piqûre.
6. Oui (Non), le médecin (ne) lui a (pas) fait une (de) radio.

Exercice B

1. c
2. c
3. a
4. c
5. a
6. b
7. b
8. c

Exercice C

1. le chirurgien
2. les infirmiers (infirmières)
3. des os
4. une radio(graphie)
5. faire une piqûre
6. un formulaire
7. l'orthopédiste

Exercices

A **Une visite médicale.** Jean-Claude est allé chez le médecin parce qu'il veut jouer dans l'équipe de football cette année. Qu'est-ce que le médecin lui a fait? Répondez.

1. Le médecin l'a ausculté?
2. Le médecin lui a dit: «Respirez à fond»?
3. Le médecin lui a pris le pouls?
4. Le médecin lui a pris sa tension artérielle?
5. Le médecin lui a fait une piqûre?
6. Le médecin lui a fait une radio?

B **À l'hôpital.** Choisissez.

1. On a emmené Bruno à l'hôpital en ___.
   a. voiture
   b. fauteuil roulant
   c. ambulance

2. Il est allé tout de suite ___.
   a. à la salle d'opération
   b. chez le médecin
   c. à la salle des urgences

3. Quand Bruno est arrivé à l'hôpital, sa sœur a rempli ___ pour lui.
   a. un formulaire
   b. une piqûre
   c. un os

4. Bruno croit qu'il s'est cassé ___ .
   a. les cils
   b. les lèvres
   c. la jambe

5. On lui a fait une ___ de l'os.
   a. radio
   b. fracture compliquée
   c. piqûre

6. ___ lui a fait une anesthésie.
   a. L'infirmière
   b. L'anesthésiste
   c. Le chirurgien

7. ___ a remis l'os en place.
   a. L'infirmier
   b. Le chirurgien-orthopédiste
   c. Le radiologue

8. Le chirurgien-orthopédiste lui a mis la jambe dans ___.
   a. les béquilles
   b. le brancard
   c. le plâtre

C **C'est quel mot?** Pour chaque définition, donnez le mot exact.

1. Celui qui opère, qui fait des interventions chirurgicales, qui fait des opérations
2. Ceux qui aident les médecins et soignent les malades dans un hôpital
3. Le squelette humain en a beaucoup.
4. Le négatif d'une photo d'un os, d'un organe, etc.
5. Ce que l'anesthésiste fait au malade avant et pendant une opération (ou une intervention chirurgicale)
6. Ce qu'il faut remplir quand on est admis à l'hôpital
7. Le médecin qui est spécialiste des os

144   CHAPITRE 6

Activités de communication orale

Mots 1 et 2

Guy Favet

A **Qu'est-ce qui est arrivé?** Vous avez eu un accident. Votre ami français Guy Favet vous pose des questions au sujet de cet accident. Répondez-lui.

1. Quel accident est-ce que tu as eu?
2. Comment est-ce que c'est arrivé?
3. Tu es allé(e) à l'hôpital?
4. Qu'est-ce que les médecins et les infirmières ont fait pour te soigner?

B **Qui est-ce?** Travaillez avec un(e) camarade. Vous allez décrire un traitement médical. Votre camarade va décider si ce traitement est administré par un infirmier, un médecin généraliste, un chirurgien ou un orthopédiste.

> Élève 1: Cette personne fait des piqûres.
> Élève 2: C'est l'infirmière ou l'infirmier.

C **Tu t'es déjà cassé le bras?** Make a chart like the one below and interview a classmate to find out which of the following have happened to him or her. Then reverse roles.

	OUI	NON
1. se fouler la cheville		
2. se tordre le genou		
3. se couper le doigt ou le doigt de pied		
4. avoir la jambe ou le bras dans le plâtre		
5. marcher avec des béquilles		
6. être dans un fauteuil roulant		

CHAPITRE 6 **145**

Activités de communication orale

Mots 1 et 2

PRESENTATION *(page 145)*

You may allow students to select the activities they wish to do.

Activité B

 In the CD-ROM version of this activity, students can interact with an on-screen native speaker.

ANSWERS

Activités A, B, and C

Answers will vary.

COGNATE RECOGNITION

Have students scan pages 138–145 and identify cognates.

RETEACHING *(Mots 1 and 2)*

Quickly review the vocabulary from *Bienvenue*, Chapter 15 (*La Santé et la Médecine*), whose context is similar to that of this chapter.

STRUCTURE

Structure Teaching Resources

1. Workbook, *Structure: A–M,* pages 60–64
2. Student Tape Manual, Teacher's Edition, *Structure: A–D,* pages 61–63
3. Audio Cassette 4B/CD-3
4. Communication Activities Masters, *Structure: A–E,* pages 40–42
5. Computer Software, *Structure*
6. Chapter Quizzes, *Structure:* Quizzes 3–6, pages 30–33
7. CD-ROM, Disc 2, pages 146–151

Des pronoms interrogatifs et relatifs

PRESENTATION *(page 146)*

Students may find this point difficult. Go over it thoroughly, but do not strive for mastery at this point. Differentiating between *ce qui* and *ce que* takes a great deal of ear training. For this reason, these expressions will be reintroduced often.

Exercices

PRESENTATION
(pages 146–147)

Exercice A

It is recommended that you let students prepare Exercise A before going over it in class.

ANSWERS

Exercice A

1. Qu'est-ce qui est sur la table?
2. Qu'est-ce que le malade a eu?
3. Qu'est-ce qu'il s'est blessé?
4. Qu'est-ce que le frère de Jean s'est coupé?
5. Qu'est-ce que l'infirmière a mis sur la blessure?
6. Qu'est-ce qui intéresse beaucoup ta sœur?

Des pronoms interrogatifs et relatifs

Expressing "What" in Direct and Indirect Questions

1. To ask a direct question with "what" in French, you use the interrogative expressions *Qu'est-ce qui* and *Qu'est-ce que. Qu'est-ce qui* is used as the subject and *Qu'est-ce que* is used as the object of the sentence.

> *Qu'est-ce qui* intéresse Pierre?
> *Qu'est-ce que* vous voulez faire aujourd'hui?

2. To introduce an indirect question with "what" in French, you use *ce qui* and *ce que.* Note that *ce qui,* like *Qu'est-ce qui,* is used as the subject of the indirect question and *ce que,* like *Qu'est-ce que,* is used as the object.

> Elle demande *ce qui* intéresse Pierre.
> Elle demande *ce que* vous voulez faire aujourd'hui.

3. Compare the following forms.

	QUESTION DIRECTE	QUESTION INDIRECTE
SUJET	*Qu'est-ce qui* se passe?	Je ne sais pas *ce qui* se passe.
OBJET	*Qu'est-ce que* Luc a dit?	Je ne sais pas *ce que* Luc a dit.

Note that *ce qui* is usually followed by a verb and *ce que* is usually followed by a subject and a verb.

Exercices

A **Je n'ai pas entendu.** Répondez par «qu'est-ce qui» ou «qu'est-ce que» d'après le modèle.

> *La science-fiction* intéresse Jean-Luc.
> *Qu'est-ce qui intéresse Jean-Luc?*

1. *Ton livre de biologie* est sur la table.
2. Le malade a eu *un accident.*
3. Il s'est blessé *le genou.*
4. Le frère de Jean s'est coupé *le doigt.*
5. L'infirmière a mis *un pansement* sur la blessure.
6. *La médecine* intéresse beaucoup ma sœur.

B Dis donc! Tu sais ce qui est arrivé?
Répondez par «oui».

1. Tu sais ce qui est arrivé?
2. Tu sais ce qui se passe maintenant?
3. Tu sais ce que le médecin a dit à Carole?
4. Tu sais ce qu'il a fait?
5. Tu sais ce que le médecin a prescrit?
6. Tu sais ce qu'il a écrit sur l'ordonnance?
7. Tu comprends ce que le pharmacien a dit?

C Des bêtises! Tu es furax. Complétez
avec «ce qui» ou «ce que».

1. Je crois ___ je vois.
2. Je sais ___ se passe.
3. Je comprends ___ je lis.
4. Je ne suis pas d'accord avec ___ tu dis.
5. ___ tu dis n'est pas vrai, je t'assure.
6. ___ je fais, c'est pas tes oignons!

Les verbes *suivre* et *vivre*   *Expressing "To Live" and "To Follow"*

1. The verbs *suivre*, "to follow," and *vivre*, "to live," are irregular in the present tense.

SUIVRE	VIVRE
je suis	je vis
tu suis	tu vis
il/elle/on suit	il/elle/on vit
nous suivons	nous vivons
vous suivez	vous vivez
ils/elles suivent	ils/elles vivent

L'automne suit l'été.
En été nous vivons à la montagne.

2. The verb *suivre* is also used to mean "to take a course."

   Je suis un cours de biologie. Mon amie suit un cours de maths.

3. *Vivre* can be used to express "to live" in all its different meanings.

   Il vit à Genève.   **Il vit bien.**

   Habiter means "to live" in the sense of "to dwell."

   Il habite à Paris.

4. The past participles of *suivre* and *vivre* are *suivi* and *vécu*.

CHAPITRE 6   **147**

PRESENTATION *(page 148)*

Exercices A and B

It is recommended that you go over the exercises in class before assigning them for homework. Exercise A can be done with books either open or closed. Exercise B is to be done with books open.

ANSWERS

Exercice A

Answers will vary.

Exercice B

1. suit   5. suivent
2. suit   6. suivent
3. suis   7. suivez
4. suivons

Les pronoms avec l'impératif

PRESENTATION
(pages 148–149)

A. Guide students through steps 1–5.
B. Provide students with this summary of pronoun use.
  1. The pronoun always precedes the verb except in the affirmative command. There it follows the verb.
  2. *Me* and *te* become *moi* and *toi* when they follow the verb.

Exercices

A   **Personnellement.**   Donnez des réponses personnelles.

1. Si tu veux maigrir, tu suis un régime?
2. Tu suis un régime pour rester en forme?
3. Tu suis un cours de français?
4. Tu as suivi un cours de français l'année dernière?
5. Tu as bien suivi les explications du professeur?
6. Toi et tes copains, vous voulez vivre jusqu'à l'âge de 100 ans?
7. Tu veux vivre jusqu'à quel âge?
8. Qu'est-ce que tu en penses? On vit bien aux États-Unis ou pas?
9. As-tu vécu dans un autre pays? Lequel?

B   **Tout le monde va être médecin.**
Complétez avec «suivre».

1. Carole va être médecin. Elle ____ un cours de biologie.
2. Et son frère va être médecin. Il ____ un cours de microbiologie.
3. Moi aussi, je pense être médecin. Je ____ un cours d'anatomie.
4. Tous les trois nous ____ un cours de chimie organique.
5. Nos deux copains, David et Thérèse, ____ un cours de physiologie.
6. Les étudiants qui vont être médecins ____ des cours de sciences.
7. Tes amis et toi, vous allez être médecins? Vous ____ aussi des cours de sciences?

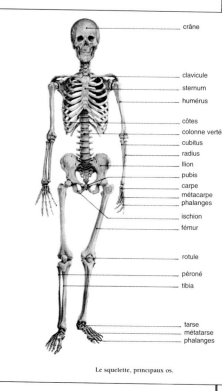

Le squelette, principaux os.

Les pronoms avec l'impératif   *More About Commands*

1. As you have already learned, object pronouns come directly before the verb.

> **La piqûre? Je *la* fais tout de suite.**
> **Les radios? Je *les* regarde maintenant.**
> **Je *lui* prends sa température.**

2. In the case of the affirmative commands, however, the object pronoun follows the verb and is attached to it by a hyphen.

> **La piqûre? Faites-*la* tout de suite.**
> **Les radios? Regardez-*les* maintenant.**
> **Prends-*lui* sa température.**

LEARNING FROM REALIA

Have students look at the skeleton and tell you what part of the body the following bones belong to: *le crâne? l'humérus? les phalanges? le fémur? la rotule? le tarse, le métatarse et les phalanges?*

INDEPENDENT PRACTICE

Assign any of the following:
1. Exercises, pages 146–148
2. Workbook, *Structure: A–E,* pages 60–61
3. Communication Activities Masters, *Structure: A–C,* pages 40–41
4. CD-ROM, Disc 2, pages 146–148

3. Note that in negative commands the order is the usual one. The object pronoun comes before the verb.

> **La piqûre? Ne *la* faites pas tout de suite.**
> **Les radios? Ne *les* regardez pas maintenant.**
> **Ne *lui* prends pas sa température.**

4. In affirmative commands you use *moi* instead of *me* and *toi* instead of *te*.

> **Ne *me* dites pas ce qui est arrivé.**
> *but*
> **Dites-*moi* ce qui est arrivé.**

5. With reflexive verbs in the command form, the position of the pronouns is the same as with any other verb. In the negative command the pronoun comes before and in the affirmative command it comes after. Note, too, that *te* changes to *toi* after the verb.

NÉGATIF	AFFIRMATIF
Ne *te* couche pas.	Couche-*toi*.
Ne *te* lève pas.	Lève-*toi*.
Ne *vous* levez pas.	Levez-*vous*.
Ne *nous* dépêchons pas.	Dépêchons-*nous*.

Exercices

A **Bon! Fais-le si tu veux.** Répondez d'après le modèle.

> **Je vais regarder la télé.**
> *Bon! Regarde-la si tu veux.*

1. Je vais regarder le film.
2. Je vais écouter la cassette.
3. Je vais lire le magazine.
4. Je vais écrire la lettre.
5. Je vais acheter les billets.
6. Je vais mettre le couvert.
7. Je vais faire la vaisselle.
8. Je vais aider Maman.

B **Non, tu ne peux pas. Ne le fais pas.** Répondez d'après le modèle.

> **Je veux regarder la télé.**
> *Non, tu ne peux pas. Ne la regarde pas.*

1. Je veux regarder le film.
2. Je veux écouter la cassette.
3. Je veux lire le magazine.
4. Je veux écrire la lettre.
5. Je veux acheter les billets.
6. Je veux mettre le couvert.
7. Je veux faire la vaisselle.
8. Je veux aider Maman.

C. You may wish to have students do the following easy exercises before beginning the exercises in the text. Tell them to follow the model: *Ne la regardez pas.→ Regardez-la.*
Ne la touchez pas.
Ne le dites pas.
Ne le faites pas.
Now tell them to follow this model: *Regardez-la.→ Non, ne la regardez pas.*
Touchez-la.
Dites-le.
Faites-le.
Finally, have them follow this model: *Ne me regarde pas.→ Regarde-moi.*
Ne m'écoute pas.
Ne me parle pas.
Ne me donne pas ça.

Note In the CD-ROM version, this structure point is presented via an interactive electronic comic strip.

Exercices

PRESENTATION *(pages 149–150)*

Exercice A
Exercise A can be done with books either open or closed.

Exercice B
Exercise B can be done with books either open or closed.

ANSWERS
Exercice A
1. Bon! Regarde-le si tu veux.
2. Bon! Écoute-la si tu veux.
3. Bon! Lis-le si tu veux.
4. Bon! Écris-la si tu veux.
5. Bon! Achète-les si tu veux.
6. Bon! Mets-le si tu veux.
7. Bon! Fais-la si tu veux.
8. Bon! Aide-la si tu veux.

Exercice B
1. Non, tu ne peux pas. Ne le regarde pas.
2. ... Ne l'écoute pas.
3. ... Ne le lis pas.
4. ... Ne l'écris pas.
5. ... Ne les achète pas.
6. ... Ne le mets pas.
7. ... Ne la fais pas.
8. ... Ne l'aide pas.

PRESENTATION (continued)

Exercice C

Exercise C can be done with books either open or closed.

Exercices D, E, and F

Exercises D and E can be done with books either open or closed. Exercise F is to be done with books open.

ANSWERS

Exercice C

1. C'est très bien. Téléphonez-leur!
2. ... Parlez-lui!
3. ... Écrivez-lui!
4. ... Obéissez-leur!
5. ... Dites-lui bonjour!

Exercice D

1. Alors, lève-toi.
2. Alors, lave-toi.
3. Alors, sèche-toi.
4. Alors, rase-toi.
5. Alors, peigne-toi.
6. Alors, habille-toi.
7. Alors, assieds-toi.
8. Alors, couche-toi.

Exercice E

1. Non, ne te lève pas.
2. Non, ne te lave pas.
3. Non, ne te sèche pas.
4. Non, ne te rase pas.
5. Non, ne te peigne pas.
6. Non, ne t'habille pas.
7. Non, ne t'assieds pas.
8. Non, ne te couche pas.

Exercice F

1. moi	6. vous
2. moi, moi	7. moi
3. me	8. moi
4. vous	9. moi
5. vous	

C **C'est très bien. Écrivez-lui!** Répondez d'après le modèle.

> Je voudrais écrire à Michel.
> *C'est très bien. Écrivez-lui!*

1. Je voudrais téléphoner à mes grands-parents.
2. Je voudrais parler à Simone.
3. Je voudrais écrire à mon copain.
4. Je voudrais obéir à mes parents.
5. Je voudrais dire bonjour au professeur de français.

D **Alors, fais-le!** Répondez d'après le modèle.

> Je vais me maquiller.
> *Alors, maquille-toi.*

1. Je vais me lever.	5. Je vais me peigner.
2. Je vais me laver.	6. Je vais m'habiller.
3. Je vais me sécher.	7. Je vais m'asseoir.
4. Je vais me raser.	8. Je vais me coucher.

E **Non, ne le fais pas.** Refaites l'Exercice D d'après le modèle.

> Je vais me maquiller.
> *Non, ne te maquille pas.*

F **Le médecin vous parle.** Complétez avec «me», «moi» ou «vous».

1. Dites-___ vos symptômes.
2. Montrez-___ ou indiquez- ___ où ça vous fait mal.
3. Ne ___ donnez pas votre radio. Je ne peux pas la regarder maintenant.
4. Asseyez-___, s'il vous plaît.
5. Ne ___ asseyez pas sur cette chaise.
6. Et maintenant, levez- ___.
7. Docteur, je ne peux pas. Aidez- ___, s'il vous plaît.
8. D'accord. Donnez- ___ votre main.
9. Dites- ___ où vous avez mal.

Ampoules petites blessures oubliées...

Mieux/Meilleur — *Expressing "Better" and "Best"*

1. Study the forms of the comparative and superlative of the adverb *bien*.

> Il le fait *bien*.
> Mais moi, je le fais *mieux*.
> Et toi, tu le fais *le mieux*.

2. Note the comparative and superlative forms of the adverb *mal: pis, le pis*. Although you will not have to use these forms frequently, you should be able to recognize them.

3. The adjective *bon* is also irregular in the comparative and superlative: *meilleur(e)(s); le (la)(les) meilleur(e)(s)*. Note that since *meilleur* is an adjective it must agree with the noun it modifies in number and gender.

> Robert est *bon* en maths.   Carole est *bonne* en maths.
> Mais Pierre est *meilleur* en   Mais Julie est *meilleure* en
>   maths que Robert.   maths que Carole.
> Et Jonathan est *le meilleur* en   Et Camille est *la meilleure* en
>   maths de tous.   maths de toutes.
> Qui sont *les meilleurs* en   Qui sont *les meilleures* en
>   maths de votre école?   maths de votre école?

4. Note that the comparative and superlative forms of the adjective *mauvais* are: *pire* and *le (la) pire*.

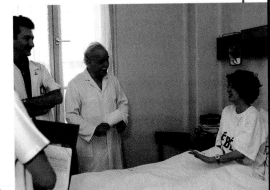

Exercices

A   **Comment va-t-elle?**   Répondez d'après les indications.

1. Julie va bien? (non)
2. Comment est elle? (malade)
3. Qu'est-ce qu'elle a? (des crampes)
4. Elle se sent mieux aujourd'hui? (oui, un peu)
5. Elle va se sentir mieux demain? (oui, sans doute)

B   **Toi ou quelqu'un d'autre?**   Donnez des réponses personnelles.

1. Tu skies bien?
2. Qui skie mieux que toi?
3. Qui est un meilleur skieur ou une meilleure skieuse que toi?
4. De tous tes amis, qui skie le mieux?
5. Qui est le meilleur skieur ou la meilleure skieuse?
6. Tu nages bien?
7. Qui nage mieux que toi?
8. Qui est un meilleur nageur ou une meilleure nageuse que toi?
9. De tous tes amis, qui nage le mieux?
10. Qui est le meilleur nageur ou la meilleure nageuse?

Mieux/Meilleur
PRESENTATION (*page 151*)
  Guide students through steps 1–4.

Exercices
PRESENTATION (*page 151*)
  Exercises A and B can be done with books either open or closed.

ANSWERS
Exercice A
1. Non, Julie ne va pas bien.
2. Elle est malade.
3. Elle a des crampes.
4. Oui, elle se sent un peu mieux aujourd'hui.
5. Oui, sans doute elle va se sentir mieux demain.

Exercice B
1. Oui, je skie bien. (Non, je ne skie pas bien.)
2. ____ skie mieux que moi.
3. ____ est un meilleur skieur (une meilleure skieuse) que moi.
4. De tous mes amis, ____ skie le mieux.
5. ____ est le meilleur skieur (la meilleure skieuse).
6. Oui, je nage bien. (Non, je ne nage pas bien.)
7. ____ nage mieux que moi.
8. ____ est un meilleur nageur (une meilleure nageuse) que moi.
9. De tous mes amis, ____ nage le mieux.
10. ____ est le meilleur nageur (la meilleure nageuse).

CONVERSATION

Bell Ringer Review

Write the following on the board or use BRR Blackline Master 6-6: Write the following words under the correct heading: La cuisine or La salle de séjour.

la chaîne stéréo/le robinet/le magnétoscope/l'évier/le lave-vaisselle/le zappeur/la table/ le poste de télévision/le pot-au-feu/la vidéocassette

PRESENTATION *(page 152)*

A. Have students close their books. Play the Conversation Video or have them listen as you read the conversation or play Cassette 4B/CD-3.

B. Have students repeat the conversation after you or the cassette. (Use *Activité F* in the Student Tape Manual to check oral comprehension.)

C. Call on volunteers to read the conversation with as much expression as possible.

D. Call on a student to retell the story in his/her own words.

Note In the CD-ROM version, students can play the role of either one of the characters and record the conversation.

ANSWERS

Exercice A

1. Annie veut savoir ce qui est arrivé à Éric.
2. Non, elle ne savait rien de son accident.
3. Il a eu son accident à l'école.
4. Il l'a eu il y a trois jours.
5. Il est tombé.
6. Non, il ne s'est pas cassé la jambe.

CONVERSATION

Scènes de la vie   *Éric est tombé*

ANNIE: Qu'est-ce qui t'est arrivé?
ÉRIC: Quoi?
ANNIE: Je te demande ce qui t'est arrivé.
ÉRIC: J'ai eu un accident. Tu ne le savais pas?
ANNIE: Absolument pas! Personne ne m'a rien dit. Tu as eu un accident? Quand? Et où?
ÉRIC: Je suis tombé à l'école il y a trois jours.
ANNIE: Tu t'es cassé la jambe?
ÉRIC: Non, je me suis simplement foulé la cheville. C'est pour ça que le médecin ne m'a pas mis la jambe dans le plâtre.

A **Il est tombé.** Répondez d'après la conversation.

1. Qu'est-ce qu'Annie veut savoir?
2. Elle ne savait rien de son accident?
3. Où est-ce qu'il a eu son accident?
4. Quand est-ce qu'il l'a eu?
5. Qu'est-ce qu'il a fait?
6. Il s'est cassé la jambe?
7. Il s'est tordu le genou?
8. Le médecin lui a mis la jambe dans le plâtre? Pourquoi pas?

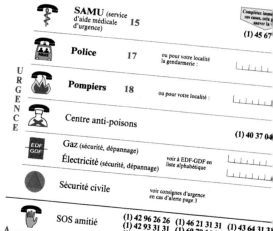

152 CHAPITRE 6

LEARNING FROM REALIA

Have the students look at the page from a phone book as you ask: *À qui allez-vous téléphoner dans les situations suivantes?*

1. Il y a un incendie. Vous voyez des flammes.
2. Il y a eu un accident sur la route et quelqu'un est blessé.
3. Vous sentez une odeur étrange. Vous croyez que c'est du gaz. Vous voulez éviter une explosion.
4. Vous voulez savoir quel temps il va faire demain.
5. Vous avez un problème personnel et vous voulez parler à quelqu'un.
6. Vous voulez savoir s'il y a beaucoup de circulation sur l'autoroute.
7. Quelqu'un a eu une crise cardiaque.
8. Vous avez perdu votre carte de crédit.

Activités de communication orale

A **Marc attire les accidents!** Le pauvre Marc, il a toujours de petits accidents. Regardez les dessins suivants et dites à Marc pourquoi il faut faire très attention. Dites-lui ce qui peut arriver s'il ne fait pas attention. Votre camarade va vous dire quel dessin vous décrivez.

> Élève 1: Attention, Marc! Tu vas te fouler la cheville!
> Élève 2: C'est le dessin numéro 1.

1.

2.

B **Quels cours avez-vous suivis?** Posez des questions à un(e) camarade sur sa vie scolaire de l'année dernière. Changez ensuite de rôles. Comparez vos réponses pour voir si vous êtes d'accord ou pas.

1. Quels cours as-tu suivis l'année dernière?
2. Quels cours as-tu aimés le mieux?
3. Qui était le meilleur prof de tous tes profs? Pourquoi?

C **Au lycée.** Demandez à un(e) camarade ce qu'il/elle considère comme très important dans la vie d'un(e) élève. Changez ensuite de rôles et comparez vos réponses. Préparez un exposé basé sur vos réponses et présentez-le à la classe.

> Élève 1: Qu'est-ce qui compte le plus pour toi dans la vie d'un élève?
> Élève 2: Ce qui compte le plus pour moi, c'est…

D **Un peu de révision.** You and a classmate have finished your training class for the local first aid squad and are reviewing for the exam. Suggest a typical emergency situation to your partner and ask him or her what to do. Then reverse roles.

> Élève 1: Le malade s'est cassé la jambe. Qu'est-ce que je dois faire?
> Élève 2: Fais une radio et mets-lui la jambe dans le plâtre.

LECTURE ET CULTURE

READING STRATEGIES
(*pages 154–155*)

Note This *Lecture* provides many examples of the contrast between the *passé composé* and the imperfect.

Pre-reading

A. Find out if any students in the class have ever had a broken bone. Ask how the injury was treated.

B. Have students look at the map of Paris on page 436 or use the Map Transparency. Say: *L'Hôtel-Dieu se trouve à Paris sur l'Île de la Cité tout près de Notre-Dame.*

Reading

A. You may wish to divide the *Lecture* into two or three segments.

B. Call on individuals to read aloud about three sentences at a time.

C. After each student reads, ask a few comprehension questions.

D. Have students scan the reading and make a list of things that were done to Marc before his leg was set.

Post-reading

Assign the reading and the exercises that follow for homework.

Note Students may listen to a recorded version of the *Lecture* on the CD-ROM.

HÔTEL-DIEU, J'ARRIVE!

L'autre jour j'étais avec Marc quand il a eu un petit accident. Je dis un «petit» accident mais c'était assez grave. Nous étions en ville et il ne faisait pas très attention où il marchait. Il y avait des travaux[1] et il y avait donc un trou[2] dans le trottoir. Marc ne l'a pas vu et il est tombé dedans. Il s'est fait très mal et il ne pouvait pas se relever[3]. J'ai tout de suite compris qu'il était blessé.

Je suis allé appeler police secours. J'ai composé le 18. L'ambulance est arrivée en quelques minutes. Les secouristes ont allongé Marc sur un brancard et l'ont emmené à l'Hôtel-Dieu, un grand hôpital en face de Notre-Dame. Je suis allé chercher ma moto qui était garée tout près. J'ai suivi l'ambulance à l'hôpital.

J'ai aidé Marc à remplir les formulaires dans la salle des urgences. Il était un peu inquiet[4]. Un médecin l'a examiné et a ordonné une radiographie. La radiographie a indiqué une fracture compliquée. On a emmené Marc à la salle d'opération où le chirurgien-

---

[1] des travaux   *construction work*
[2] un trou   *hole*
[3] se relever   *get up*
[4] inquiet   *worried*

Hôtel-Dieu à Paris

CRITICAL THINKING ACTIVITY

(*Thinking skill: identifying consequences*)
Have the students look at the left-hand photo. Read the following to them or write it on the board or on a transparency:
Ce panneau indique qu'il y a des travaux. Il indique un chantier. Est-ce qu'il faut faire attention quand on marche dans la rue devant un chantier? Pourquoi?

orthopédiste l'attendait. Les infirmiers lui ont pris la tension artérielle et le pouls. L'anesthésiste a administré une anesthésie et l'orthopédiste a remis l'os en place. Il lui a mis la jambe dans le plâtre et Marc a pu quitter l'hôpital. Le chirurgien lui a fait une ordonnance pour des comprimés pour soulager la douleur[5].

Deux heures plus tard Marc et moi, nous étions devant l'hôpital. Marc était assis dans un fauteuil roulant, la jambe dans le plâtre, et moi avec ma moto. Je savais que je ne pouvais pas le mettre sur la selle[6] de ma moto. Que faire? J'ai téléphoné à son père et heureusement il était là. Je lui ai expliqué que Marc avait eu un petit accident, que ce n'était pas trop grave, et que nous l'attendions devant l'Hôtel-Dieu.

[5] soulager la douleur   relieve the pain
[6] la selle   seat

Étude de mots

A   Quel est un autre mot?   Trouvez le mot ou l'expression qui correspond.

1. grave
2. essayer
3. garer
4. une opération
5. des comprimés

a. faire des efforts
b. des pilules
c. sérieux
d. stationner
e. une intervention chirurgicale

B   On peut le dire autrement?   Dites d'une autre façon.

1. Il *ne regardait pas* où il marchait.
2. J'ai *fait* le 18.
3. Ils *ont mis* Marc sur un brancard.
4. Ils l'*ont transporté* à l'hôpital.
5. La radiographie *a montré* une fracture compliquée.
6. L'anesthésiste lui *a fait* une anesthésie.

HISTORY CONNECTION

The first Hôtel-Dieu (18th *arrondissement*) was built in 660 by Saint Landry, Bishop of Paris. He opened the doors to all, without regard to the patient's sex, race, creed, age, nationality, or ability to pay—a philosophy way ahead of its time. The hospital grew and expanded into two buildings spanning across a bridge. The bridge itself housed a 100-bed annex. By the 18th century, the hospital had expanded to 9,000 beds. The hospital only lost about one-fifth of its patients, a low rate considering the state of medicine at that time. The original hospital was demolished in 1878, and the present hospital near Notre-Dame Cathedral was constructed.

LEARNING FROM PHOTOS

You may wish to ask the following questions about the bottom photo: *Ce sont des médecins? Ils sont dans la salle d'opération? Où sont-ils? Qu'est-ce qu'ils font? Le médecin qui porte des lunettes regarde une radio?*

Compréhension

PRESENTATION (page 156)

Exercises F and G require some imagination.

ANSWERS

Exercice C

1. Marc a eu un «petit» accident.
2. Il ne faisait pas très attention où il marchait.
3. Il n'a pas vu un trou dans le trottoir.
4. L'ami de Marc a appelé police secours parce qu'il savait que son ami était blessé.
5. Marc est allé à l'hôpital en ambulance. Son ami y est allé à moto.
6. Les deux copains ont rempli des formulaires dans la salle des urgences.
7. La radiographie a indiqué une fracture compliquée.
8. Le chirurgien-orthopédiste l'attendait dans la salle d'opération.
9. Oui, le chirurgien-orthopédiste a mis la jambe dans le plâtre parce qu'il y avait une fracture compliquée.

Exercice D

1. une radiographie
2. la tension artérielle et le pouls
3. une anesthésie
4. l'os

Exercice E

Possible answer: Son père est venu le chercher.

Exercice F

Answers will vary.

Exercice G

Answers will vary.

Compréhension

C **Vous avez compris?** Répondez d'après la lecture.

1. Qui a eu un «petit» accident?
2. Comment est arrivé son «petit» accident?
3. Qu'est-ce qu'il n'a pas vu?
4. L'ami de Marc a appelé police secours. Pourquoi?
5. Comment est-ce que Marc est allé à l'hôpital? Et son ami?
6. Où est-ce que les deux copains ont rempli des formulaires?
7. Qu'est-ce que la radiographie a indiqué?
8. Qui attendait Marc dans la salle d'opération?
9. Le chirurgien-orthopédiste a mis la jambe de Marc dans le plâtre? Pourquoi?

D **Marc a eu un accident.** Complétez.

1. Le médecin a ordonné ___.
2. Les infirmiers lui ont pris ___.
3. L'anesthésiste lui a fait ___.
4. L'orthopédiste a remis ___ en place.

E **Après l'accident.** Expliquez comment Marc est rentré chez lui.

F **Et son ami?** On ne sait pas ce que l'ami de Marc a fait quand le père de Marc est arrivé à l'hôpital. Imaginez ce qu'il a fait.

G **Des conséquences.** Comment Marc a-t-il passé son temps après son «petit» accident?

Laboratoire Conseil Oberlin

DÉCOUVERTE CULTURELLE

En France les hôpitaux dépendent du Ministère de la Santé Publique. Il y a de très grands établissements de soins polyvalents[1]. Il y a certains hôpitaux qui sont spécialisés: l'Hôpital Saint-Louis à Paris, par exemple, est pour les maladies de la peau[2]. Ces grands centres hospitaliers sont équipés d'installations techniques très modernes.

Hôpital Saint-Louis à Paris

Il existe en France des cliniques. Mais ce mot ne veut pas dire la même chose en français qu'en anglais. Une clinique en France est un hôpital privé. Les cliniques sont plus petites que les grands centres hospitaliers universitaires (C.H.U.) ou les centres hospitaliers régionaux (C.H.R.).

Les dispensaires sont des établissements de soins médicaux et de petite chirurgie pour les malades qui ne sont pas hospitalisés. Beaucoup de dispensaires offrent des services de médecine préventive. Il y a des dispensaires pour la lutte contre les fléaux[3] sociaux comme l'alcoolisme, la toxicomanie[4], les m.s.t. (les maladies sexuellement transmissibles) et le SIDA.

Les frais médicaux en France sont remboursés à 80% par la Sécurité Sociale.

Beaucoup de Français vont «faire une cure». Qu'est-ce qu'une cure? On traite certaines maladies chroniques dans une station thermale[5]. Le malade qui fait une cure boit des eaux minérales, prend des bains, etc. Il y a même des stations thermales qui ont un casino.

[1] établissements de soins polyvalents   *multi-care centers*
[2] peau   *skin*
[3] les fléaux   *plagues, evils*
[4] la toxicomanie   *drug addiction*
[5] une station thermale   *spa*

Bell Ringer Review

Write the following on the board or use BRR Blackline Master 6-9: Write each of the following words or expressions in a sentence.

rater le train
le fourgon à bagages
le quai
faire la queue

OPTIONAL MATERIAL

PRESENTATION
(*pages 158–159*)

Read and discuss the captions in groups or as a class. Allow students time to enjoy the photos.

Note In the CD-ROM version, students can listen to the recorded captions and discover a hidden video behind one of the photos.

RÉALITÉS

Depuis le temps des Romains, Aix-en-Provence est une ville d'eau (*spa*) célèbre pour ses eaux minérales et curatives **1**. La Fontaine de la Rotonde se trouve au bout du Cours Mirabeau, la rue principale de cette station thermale.

C'est le Docteur Luc Montagnier **2**. C'est lui qui a été l'un des premiers à isoler le virus du SIDA. Il travaille dans son laboratoire à l'Institut Pasteur de Paris.

C'est l'Hôpital de la Pitié-Salpêtrière à Paris **3**. Autrefois, on y traitait les maladies nerveuses et mentales. Tu vois la belle cour intérieure? Derrière ces bâtiments, il y a des jardins à la française.

Voici un petit hôpital dans le village de Houdan, pas très loin de Paris **4**. Si tu étais de passage à Houdan et si tu te sentais malade, est-ce que tu voudrais te faire soigner dans cet hôpital?

DID YOU KNOW?

In 122 B.C. the Roman consul Caïus Sextius Calvinus founded the thermal baths *Aquae Sextiae* on the site of what is now Aix-en-Provence.

CROSS-CULTURAL COMPARISON

Ask students if they are surprised by the appearance of some French hospitals. If they are, ask them why. Many of the older hospitals in France look like beautiful *châteaux.* However, many of them have the same modern equipment as newer ones. The newer, large medical centers look more like the hospitals in the United States.

ADDITIONAL PRACTICE

Assign any of the following:
1. Student Tape Manual, Teacher's Edition, *Deuxième Partie,* pages 64–66
2. Situation Cards, Chapter 6

COOPERATIVE LEARNING

Display Communication Transparency C-6. Have students work in groups of three to make up the conversation that the people in the illustration could be having.

CULMINATION

These activities encourage students to use all the language they have learned in the chapter and to recombine it with previously learned material. It is not necessary to do all the activities with all students. You may select the ones you consider most appropriate or permit students to choose the ones they would like to do.

INFORMAL ASSESSMENT

The *Activités de communication orale* lend themselves to assessing speaking and listening abilities. Use the evaluation criteria given on page 22 of this Teacher's Wraparound Edition.

Activités de communication orale

ANSWERS

Activités A and B
Answers will vary.

Activités de communication écrite

ANSWERS

Activités A and B
Answers will vary.

Activités de communication orale

A   Au commissariat de police.   Beaucoup de gens téléphonent à la police quand ils sont en difficulté. Vous êtes en difficulté et un policier au commissariat (votre camarade) vous dit ce qu'il faut faire.

> Élève 1: Mon frère s'est coupé le doigt.
> Élève 2: Faites-lui un pansement.

B   Au secours!   Imaginez que vous êtes journaliste en France. Regardez le dessin de l'accident. Téléphonez à votre bureau et donnez tous les détails à votre collègue (votre camarade). Il/Elle va écrire tout ce que vous lui dites. Ensuite votre camarade va vous relire tous les détails sur:

1. qui a été blessé
2. ce qui est arrivé
3. le lieu et l'heure de l'accident
4. les soins médicaux nécessaires

Activités de communication écrite

A   Un accident.   Décrivez, en un paragraphe, un accident que vous avez eu, ou qu'un autre membre de votre famille a eu. Écrivez ce qui est arrivé, comment, quand, etc. Écrivez tout ce que le médecin, l'infirmière ou les secouristes ont dit et fait.

B   Une visite désastreuse à l'hôpital.   Imaginez que vous avez eu un petit accident qui est devenu un vrai cauchemar *(nightmare)*. Du moment où vous avez appelé police secours jusqu'au *(until)* moment où vous avez quitté l'hôpital, tout s'est très mal passé. Dans une lettre, décrivez votre expérience horrible à un(e) ami(e).

> Chère Sophie,
>   La semaine dernière je me suis foulé la cheville.
> Je marchais sur le trottoir et je suis tombé dans un trou.
> Quand j'ai appelé police secours, ça sonnait occupé...

Réintroduction et recombinaison

A **Un rhume, c'est ennuyeux.** Donnez des réponses personnelles.

1. Quand tu as un rhume, tu as le nez qui coule?
2. Tu as les yeux qui piquent?
3. Tu as la gorge qui gratte?
4. Tu éternues?
5. Tu as mal à la tête?
6. Tu tousses?
7. Tu vas chez le médecin?
8. Il t'examine, fait un diagnostic et te fait une ordonnance?

B **Chez le médecin.** Complétez avec «le», «la», «l'» ou «lui».

1. Le médecin parle au malade. Il ___ parle.
2. Il examine le malade. Il ___ examine.
3. Le malade ouvre la bouche. Il ___ ouvre.
4. Le médecin regarde la gorge du malade. Il ___ regarde.
5. Le médecin fait l'ordonnance. Il ___ fait.
6. Le médecin donne l'ordonnance au malade. Il ___ donne l'ordonnance.

C **Je suis allé(e) voir le médecin.** Complétez avec le passé composé ou l'imparfait.

1. Quand je ___ au cabinet du médecin, il y ___ beaucoup de monde qui ___. (arriver, avoir, attendre)
2. Quand je ___ dans le cabinet du médecin, le médecin ___ à l'infirmière. (entrer, parler)
3. Il m'___ de m'asseoir. (dire)
4. Je ___. (s'asseoir)
5. J'___ au médecin que je ___ toujours et que j'___ mal à la gorge. (expliquer, tousser, avoir)

Une affiche de l'Institut Pasteur au Cameroun

Vocabulaire

NOMS
le bras
le doigt
la jambe
le genou
la cheville
le doigt de pied
l'os (m.)
l'accident (m.)
la blessure
la fracture
    (compliquée)
la police secours

l'ambulance (f.)
le brancard
le fauteuil roulant
l'hôpital (m.)
le formulaire
la salle des urgences
la radio(graphie)
la salle d'opération
la table d'opération
le chirurgien(-orthopédiste)
l'anesthésiste (m. et f.)
la piqûre
l'infirmier

l'infirmière
le point de suture
le pansement
le plâtre
les béquilles (f.)

VERBES
emmener
transporter
marcher
montrer
soigner
se casser
se fouler

se tordre
se blesser
vivre
suivre

AUTRES MOTS ET EXPRESSIONS
avoir mal (à)
faire une radiographie
faire une piqûre
faire une anesthésie
faire un point de suture
remettre en place
prendre la tension artérielle
prendre le pouls

Réintroduction et recombinaison

PRESENTATION *(page 161)*

These exercises recycle the health vocabulary from *Bienvenue*, Chapter 15. Exercise C recycles the imperfect and the *passé composé.*

ANSWERS

Exercice A
    Answers will vary.

Exercice B

1. lui	4. la
2. l'	5. la
3. l'	6. lui

Exercice C

1. suis arrivé(e), avait, attendait
2. suis entré(e), parlait
3. a dit
4. me suis assis(e)
5. ai expliqué, toussais, avais

ASSESSMENT RESOURCES

1. Chapter Quizzes
2. Testing Program
3. Situation Cards
4. Communication Transparency C-6
5. Computer Software: Practice/Test Generator

VIDEO PROGRAM

INTRODUCTION   (24:19)

OLIVIER SE FAIT MAL   (25:15)

LEARNING FROM REALIA

This poster is from the Institut Pasteur in Cameroun. Ask students what the poster is about. See how many childhood diseases students can identify: *diphtérie,* diphtheria; *tétanos,* tetanus; *poliomyélite,* polio; *tuberculose,* tuberculosis; *coqueluche,* whooping cough; *rougeole,* measles; *rage,* rabies. (These diseases were discussed in *Bienvenue, Lettres et sciences,* pages 442–443.)

INDEPENDENT PRACTICE

Assign any of the following:
1. Activities and exercises, pages 160–161
2. Communication Activities Masters, pages 37–42
3. CD-ROM, Disc 2, pages 160–161

CHAPTER OVERVIEW

In this chapter students will expand their ability to talk about air travel, including boarding, in-flight services, and disembarking. They will learn to plan for these and other situations in the future tense. Students will also learn to use a direct object pronoun in the same sentence with *me, te, nous,* or *vous.*

The cultural focus of Chapter 7 is on a typical flight from Martinique to Paris, the relationship between France and the Antilles, and life in the French-speaking islands of the Caribbean.

CHAPTER OBJECTIVES

By the end of this chapter, students will know:

1. vocabulary associated with equipment, services, personnel, and procedures aboard a modern commercial airliner
2. vocabulary associated with departure, arrival, baggage claim and arranging ground transportation when traveling by air
3. the future tense of regular verbs
4. the future tense of the irregular verbs *être, faire,* and *aller*
5. the use of indirect and direct object pronouns in the same sentence, both in the present and the *passé composé*

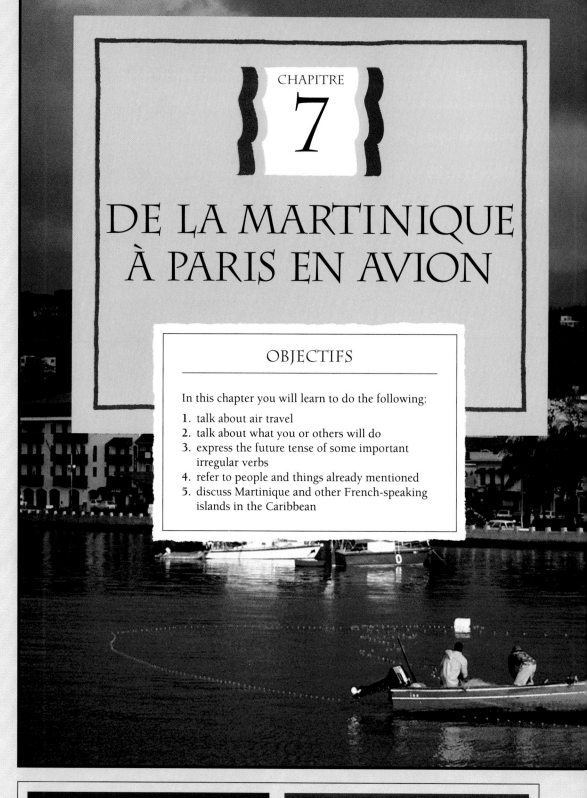

CHAPITRE

7

DE LA MARTINIQUE À PARIS EN AVION

OBJECTIFS

In this chapter you will learn to do the following:

1. talk about air travel
2. talk about what you or others will do
3. express the future tense of some important irregular verbs
4. refer to people and things already mentioned
5. discuss Martinique and other French-speaking islands in the Caribbean

CHAPTER PROJECTS

1. Have groups prepare reports on the history of France in the Caribbean.
2. Have students prepare a biography of Josephine Bonaparte. (There is a reading selection about her in the *Lettres et sciences* section following Chapter 8.)
3. Have students prepare a brief report on the history of Haiti.

COMMUNITIES

1. Have students visit a travel agency and obtain brochures on Martinique, Guadeloupe, or Saint-Barthélemy. Have them write captions for the brochures in French and make a bulletin board display.
2. Have students obtain information on the Club Med resorts in Martinique and Guadeloupe and write several paragraphs describing a Club Med vacation.

163

CHAPTER 7 RESOURCES

1. Workbook
2. Student Tape Manual
3. Audio Cassette 5A/CD-4
4. Vocabulary Transparencies
5. Bell Ringer Review Blackline Masters
6. Communication Transparency C-7
7. Communication Activities Masters
8. Situation Cards
9. Conversation Video
10. Videocassette/Videodisc, Unit 2
11. Video Activities Booklet, Unit 2
12. Lesson Plans
13. Computer Software: Practice/Test Generator
14. Chapter Quizzes
15. Testing Program
16. Internet Activities Booklet
17. CD-ROM Interactive Textbook
18. Map Transparencies

Pacing

This chapter will require eight to ten class sessions. Pacing will depend on the length of the class, the age of the students, and student aptitude.

For more information on planning your class, see the Lesson Plans, which offer guidelines for 45- and 55-minute classes and **Block Scheduling**.

Exercices vs. *Activités*

The exercises and activities are color-coded. Exercises, which provide guided practice to prepare students for independent communication, are coded in blue. Communicative activities, which give students opportunities for creative, open-ended expression, are coded in red.

INTERNET ACTIVITIES

(optional)

These activities, student worksheets, and related teacher information are in the *À bord* Internet Activities Booklet and on the Glencoe Foreign Language Home Page at: http://www.glencoe.com/secondary/fl

LEARNING FROM PHOTOS

Have students say as much as they can about this photo of Fort-de-France, Martinique. (This is the heart of the downtown section of the capital.)

VOCABULAIRE

MOTS 1

Vocabulary Teaching Resources

1. Vocabulary Transparencies 7.1 (A & B)
2. Audio Cassette 5A/CD-4
3. Student Tape Manual, Teacher's Edition, *Mots 1: A–D*, pages 67–70
4. Workbook, *Mots 1: A–D*, pages 69–70
5. Communication Activities Masters, *Mots 1: A–B*, pages 43–45
6. Chapter Quizzes, *Mots 1*: Quiz 1, page 34
7. CD-ROM, Disc 2, *Mots 1*: pages 164–167

Bell Ringer Review

Write the following on the board or use BRR Blackline Master 7-1: List all the words you can remember that have to do with air travel.

PRESENTATION (*pages 164–165*)

Note All new verbs in the future tense in the *Vocabulaire* section are in the third person in order to limit the structural changes students must make when they use them. Students will learn the complete formation of the future tense in the *Structure* section.

A. Point to the items on Vocabulary Transparencies 7.1 (A & B) and have students repeat the new words after you or Cassette 5A/CD-4 at least twice.

B. Call on students to point out the correct item on the transparency as you say the new word or expression.

164

VOCABULAIRE

MOTS 1

l'équipage (m.)

le pilote = le commandant de bord

le personnel de bord
une hôtesse de l'air   un steward

une aile

le décollage

l'atterrissage (m.)

la cabine

une sortie de secours = une issue de secours

première classe   classe affaires   classe économique

Il y a deux sorties (issues) de secours sur les ailes.

le poste de pilotage

piloter

Le commandant de bord pilote l'avion du poste de pilotage.
Il est interdit d'entrer dans le poste de pilotage pendant le vol.

un coffre à bagages

le dossier du siège

un siège réglable

une tablette rabattable

Les passagers mettront leurs bagages à main dans les coffres.

164   CHAPITRE 7

ADDITIONAL PRACTICE

After introducing the *Mots 1* vocabulary, write the following on the board or on a transparency: *Match the verb with the corresponding noun.*

1. décoller
2. atterrir
3. piloter
4. sortir
5. écouter
6. couvrir
7. distribuer
8. sauver
9. secourir
10. boire

a. la sortie
b. la boisson
c. le décollage
d. l'atterrissage
e. les écouteurs
f. le secours
g. le pilote, le pilotage
h. la distribution
i. le sauvetage
j. la couverture

un masque à oxygène

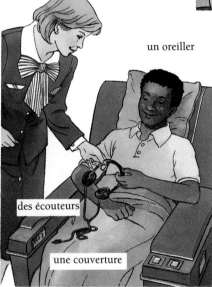

un gilet de sauvetage

une ceinture de sécurité

J'ai faim. J'espère que le personnel de bord servira un repas. J'espère que les stewards et les hôtesses de l'air serviront aussi des boissons.

un repas

une boisson

une collation

un plateau

un oreiller

des écouteurs

une couverture

Le personnel de bord distribuera des écouteurs.
Raoul mettra les écouteurs.
Il écoutera de la musique.
Il y aura plusieurs chaînes de musique en stéréo.

On passera un film.
Les passagers regarderont le film.

CHAPITRE 7   **165**

C. As you present the sentences on page 165, intersperse your presentation with questions. For example: *Que servira le personnel de bord pendant le vol? Qu'est-ce qu'on distribuera? Il y aura plusieurs chaînes en stéréo? Qu'est-ce que les passagers écouteront? Qu'est-ce qu'on passera pendant le vol?*

ADDITIONAL PRACTICE

   After practicing the *Mots 1* vocabulary, have students write sentences using an appropriate direct object with each verb. Some possible answers are in parentheses.
1. attacher (la ceinture de sécurité)
2. mettre (les écouteurs, le gilet de sauvetage, le masque à oxygène)
3. servir (un repas, une boisson, une collation)
4. écouter (de la musique en stéréo)
5. regarder (un film)
6. passer (un film)

Exercices

PRESENTATION (*pages 166–167*)

Exercice A

🎧 Exercise A is to be done with books open.

Exercice B

Exercise B can be done with books either open or closed. When doing Exercise B, you may wish to have students repeat the sentence as a question and then give the appropriate reaction. For example: *On débarquera par une issue de secours? J'espère que non.*

Teaching Tip If students have trouble with the meaning of *amerrissage* in Exercise C, say: *la terre—un atterrissage; la mer— un amerrissage.*

ANSWERS

Exercice A

1. C'est un coffre à bagages.
2. C'est la cabine des passagers.
3. C'est un masque à oxygène.
4. C'est un oreiller.
5. C'est la sortie.
6. C'est une hôtesse de l'air.
7. C'est un repas.

Exercice B

1. J'espère que non.
2. Absolument!
3. J'espère que non.
4. J'espère que non.
5. J'espère que non.
6. Absolument!
7. Absolument!
8. J'espère que non.
9. J'espère que non.

Exercices

A **Qu'est-ce que c'est?** Identifiez.

1. C'est un siège réglable ou un coffre à bagages?
2. C'est la cabine des passagers ou le poste de pilotage?
3. C'est une ceinture de sécurité ou un masque à oxygène?
4. C'est un oreiller ou une couverture?
5. C'est la sortie ou l'aile?
6. C'est un steward ou une hôtesse de l'air?
7. C'est une boisson ou un repas?

B **Qu'est-ce qui arrivera?** Répondez par «Absolument!» ou «J'espère que non».

1. On débarquera par une issue de secours.
2. On passera un film pendant le vol.
3. On mettra son gilet de sauvetage pendant le vol.
4. L'avion fera un amerrissage.
5. Les masques à oxygène tomberont.
6. On distribuera des écouteurs.
7. On servira une collation et des boissons.
8. Le pilote choisira une place dans la cabine de classe économique.
9. Les hôtesses de l'air piloteront l'avion.

166   CHAPITRE 7

ADDITIONAL PRACTICE

Student Tape Manual, Teacher's Edition, *Activité D*, page 70

C **À bord de l'avion.** Choisissez.

1. Le personnel de bord comprend ___.
   a. les stewards et les hôtesses de l'air
   b. le commandant de bord
   c. les passagers

2. ___ comprend le commandant de bord, les stewards et les hôtesses de l'air.
   a. Le personnel de bord
   b. L'équipage
   c. La liste des passagers

3. En cas d'un changement dans la pression de l'air de la cabine de l'avion, ___ tomberont automatiquement.
   a. les gilets de sauvetage
   b. les couvertures
   c. les masques à oxygène

4. En cas d'un atterrissage dans la mer ou dans l'océan (c'est-à-dire un amerrissage), les passagers mettront ___.
   a. un gilet de sauvetage
   b. une couverture
   c. une tablette rabattable

5. Pendant le décollage et l'atterrissage les passagers attacheront leur ___.
   a. couverture
   b. gilet de sauvetage
   c. ceinture de sécurité

6. ___ de chaque passager doit être en position verticale pendant le décollage et l'atterrissage.
   a. Le masque à oxygène
   b. Le coffre à bagages
   c. Le dossier du siège

7. Pendant le vol on passera ___.
   a. un repas
   b. un film
   c. plusieurs chaînes de musique

8. Une collation, c'est ___.
   a. un petit repas
   b. le départ de l'avion
   c. un plateau

9. Pendant le vol, il est interdit d'___.
   a. attacher sa ceinture de sécurité
   b. entrer dans le poste de pilotage
   c. entrer dans la cabine de classe affaires

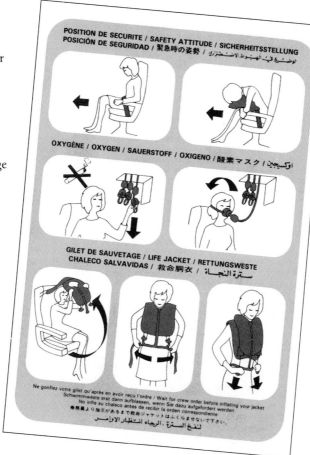

POSITION DE SECURITE / SAFETY ATTITUDE / SICHERHEITSSTELLUNG
POSICIÓN DE SEGURIDAD / 緊急時の姿勢 /

OXYGÈNE / OXYGEN / SAUERSTOFF / OXIGENO / 酸素マスク /

GILET DE SAUVETAGE / LIFE JACKET / RETTUNGSWESTE
CHALECO SALVAVIDAS / 救命胴衣 /

Ne gonflez votre gilet qu'après en avoir reçu l'ordre / Wait for crew order before inflating your jacket
Schwimmweste erst dann aufblasen, wenn Sie dazu aufgefordert werden
No infle su chaleco antes de recibir la orden correspondiente
乗務員より指示があるまで救命ジャケットはふくらませないで下さい。

CHAPITRE 7   **167**

Extension of *Exercice C*
   After completing the exercise, have students create sentences using each unused multiple-choice answer.

ANSWERS
Exercice C

1. a	6. c
2. b	7. b
3. c	8. a
4. a	9. b
5. c	

LEARNING FROM REALIA

   Have students designate the pictogram that represents each of the following sentences: *Il faut attacher sa ceinture de sécurité pendant le décollage et l'atterrissage. En cas d'amerrissage, vous trouverez un gilet de sauvetage au-dessous de votre siège. Mettez la tête sur les genoux. Les masques à oxygène tomberont automatiquement. Mettez le masque à oxygène sur le nez et la bouche.*

INDEPENDENT PRACTICE

   Assign any of the following:
1. Exercises, pages 166–167
2. Workbook, *Mots 1: A–D*, pages 69–70
3. Communication Activities Masters, *Mots 1: A–B*, pages 43–45
4. CD-ROM, Disc 2, pages 164–167

MOTS 2

Vocabulary Teaching Resources

1. Vocabulary Transparencies 7.2 (A & B)
2. Audio Cassette 5A/CD-4
3. Student Tape Manual, Teacher's Edition, *Mots 2: E–G*, pages 70–72
4. Workbook, *Mots 2: E–J*, pages 71–73
5. Communication Activities Masters, *Mots 2: C–D*, page 46
6. Computer Software, *Vocabulaire*
7. Chapter Quizzes, *Mots 2: Quiz 2*, page 35
8. CD-ROM, Disc 2, *Mots 2:* pages 168–171

Bell Ringer Review

Write the following on the board or use BRR Blackline Master 7-2: Answer the following questions:

1. **Quels cours suis-tu cette année?**
2. **Quels cours as-tu suivis l'année dernière?**
3. **Tu vivais avec tes grands-parents quand tu étais petit(e)?**

PRESENTATION *(pages 168–169)*

A. Have students close their books. Show Vocabulary Transparencies 7.2 (A & B) and have students repeat the words, phrases, and sentences after you or Cassette 5A/CD-4.

embarquer

débarquer

récupérer les bagages

un tapis roulant

un chariot à bagages

prendre l'autocar (m.)

prendre un taxi

arriver à l'aérogare (f.) = arriver au terminal

PANTOMIME

Have students act out the following:

Cherchez votre place. Mettez vos bagages sur le siège.
Ouvrez le coffre à bagages.
Mettez vos bagages dans le coffre à bagages.
Fermez le coffre à bagages.
Asseyez-vous. Attachez votre ceinture de sécurité.
Remettez votre siège en position verticale.

Le steward arrive. Il vous donne des écouteurs. Prenez-les.
Mettez les écouteurs.
Choisissez votre chaîne de musique.
Vérifiez s'il y a un gilet de sauvetage sous votre siège.
(après le vol)
Cherchez un chariot à bagages.
Récupérez vos bagages.
Mettez les bagages sur le chariot.

(continued on next page)

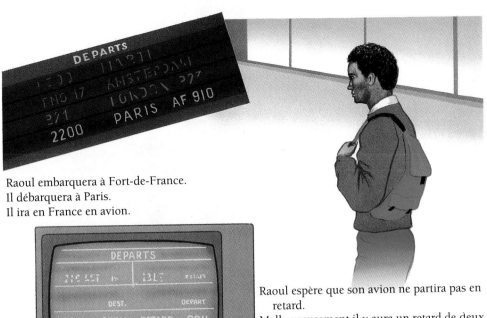

Raoul embarquera à Fort-de-France.
Il débarquera à Paris.
Il ira en France en avion.

Raoul espère que son avion ne partira pas en
  retard.
Malheureusement il y aura un retard de deux
  heures.
Mais le vol n'a pas été annulé.
Après ce long vol Raoul sera bien fatigué.

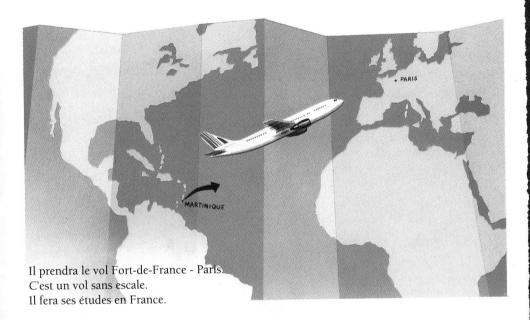

Il prendra le vol Fort-de-France - Paris.
C'est un vol sans escale.
Il fera ses études en France.

B. During the presentation ask questions such as the following about the vocabulary on page 168: *Est-ce que les passagers débarquent après le vol? Est-ce que les passagers débarquent après l'atterrissage? Où est-ce que leurs bagages arrivent? Sur quoi mettent-ils leurs bagages? Les passagers récupèrent leurs bagages? Comment peut-on aller en ville de l'aéroport? Ça coûte plus cher de prendre l'autocar ou de prendre un taxi?*

C. As you introduce the sentences on page 169, intersperse your presentation with questions such as the following: *Où ira Raoul? Où est-ce qu'il embarquera? Où est-ce qu'il débarquera? À quelle heure est son vol pour Paris? Il y aura un retard de combien d'heures? Comment sera-t-il après ce long voyage? Que fera-t-il à Paris?*

D. Have students open their books and read the new material.

GEOGRAPHY CONNECTION

You may wish to have students find Martinique on the Map Transparency of *Le Monde francophone* or on the map on page 437.

(*continued from page 168*)
Poussez le chariot.
Cherchez un taxi.
Mettez vos bagages dans le taxi.

ADDITIONAL PRACTICE

1. Have students scan the words on page 168 to find a verb that is related to each of the following nouns: *l'arrivée, le débarquement, l'embarquement.*

2. Have students scan the sentences on page 169 to find a noun related to the verbs: *voler, étudier.*

3. Student Tape Manual, Teacher's Edition, *Activité F,* page 71

PRESENTATION (*page 170*)

It is recommended that you go over the exercises orally in class before assigning them for homework. You may do them during your vocabulary presentation.

Note The verbs in these exercises are in the third person so that students need not manipulate forms.

Exercice A

Exercise A can be done with books either open or closed.

Exercices B and C

These exercises can be done with books either open or closed.

ANSWERS

Exercice A

1. Oui, Raoul ira en France.
2. Oui, il ira en France l'année prochaine.
3. Oui, il ira en France en avion.
4. Oui, il prendra le vol Fort-de-France–Paris.
5. Oui, c'est un vol sans escale.
6. Oui, Raoul embarquera à Fort-de-France.
7. Oui, il débarquera à Paris.
8. Oui, il récupérera ses bagages à l'aéroport.
9. Oui, ses bagages arriveront sur le tapis roulant numéro dix.
10. Oui, Raoul ira chercher un chariot à bagages.
11. Oui, il mettra ses bagages sur le chariot.
12. Oui, il prendra le car pour aller en ville.
13. Oui, il arrivera à l'aérogare des Invalides.
14. Oui, il y cherchera un taxi.

Exercice B

1. Raoul ira en France en avion.
2. Il embarquera à Fort-de-France.
3. Il débarquera à Paris.
4. Il sera fatigué après le vol.
5. Il prendra un car (un taxi) pour aller en ville.
6. Il fera ses études en France.

Exercice C

1. Oui, il espère que son avion partira à l'heure.
2. Non, il ne sera pas content s'il y a un retard.

170

Exercices

A Raoul ira en France l'année prochaine.   Répondez par «oui».

1. Raoul ira en France?
2. Il ira en France l'année prochaine?
3. Il ira en France en avion?
4. Il prendra le vol Fort-de-France - Paris?
5. C'est un vol sans escale?
6. Raoul embarquera à Fort-de-France?
7. Il débarquera à Paris?
8. Il récupérera ses bagages à l'aéroport?
9. Ses bagages arriveront sur le tapis roulant numéro dix?
10. Les bagages pèsent très lourd. Ils pèsent beaucoup. Raoul ira chercher un chariot à bagages?
11. Il mettra ses bagages sur le chariot?
12. Il prendra le car pour aller en ville?
13. Il arrivera à l'aérogare des Invalides?
14. Il y cherchera un taxi?

Voici une file de taxis devant l'aérogare des Invalides.

B Il le fera comment?   Répondez.

1. Raoul ira en France en avion ou en bateau?
2. Il embarquera à Fort-de-France ou à Paris?
3. Il débarquera à Fort-de-France ou à Paris?
4. Il sera fatigué après le vol ou avant le vol?
5. Il prendra un taxi ou un car pour aller en ville?
6. Il fera ses études à la Martinique ou en France?

C Le voyage de Raoul.   Répondez par «oui» ou «non».

1. Raoul espère que son avion partira à l'heure?
2. Il sera content s'il y a un retard?
3. Malheureusement il y aura un retard?
4. Le vol sera annulé?
5. Si le vol est annulé, l'avion ne partira pas?

Le marché de la rue Isambert à Fort-de-France

170   CHAPITRE 7

Activités de communication orale
Mots 1 et 2

A **Dans l'avion.** Travaillez avec un(e) camarade. Posez-lui des questions sur ces photos. Votre camarade vous répondra. Changez ensuite de rôles.

B **Pendant le vol.** Vous allez en avion de Miami à Pointe-à-Pitre. Pendant le vol vous avez besoin de plusieurs choses. Dites ce que vous voulez à l'hôtesse de l'air ou au steward (votre camarade). Il/Elle essaiera de vous aider.

avoir froid	vouloir écouter de la musique	vouloir dormir
avoir soif	vouloir manger quelque chose	
avoir très faim	vouloir regarder le film	

Élève 1: Je voudrais dormir.
Élève 2: Vous voulez une couverture?
Élève 1: Oui, s'il vous plaît.

C **Qui est-ce?** Décrivez à un(e) camarade ce qu'une hôtesse de l'air, un steward, un pilote ou un passager fait pendant un vol. Votre camarade identifiera la personne dont vous parlez.

Élève 1: Il pilote l'avion.
Élève 2: C'est le commandant de bord.

D **Qu'est-ce que c'est?** Travaillez avec un(e) camarade. Décrivez-lui quelque chose qu'on peut trouver à bord d'un avion. Votre camarade devinera (vous dira) ce que vous décrivez.

Élève 1: On met le repas sur cette chose.
Élève 2: C'est un plateau.

---

3. Oui, malheureusement il y aura un retard.
4. Non, le vol ne sera pas annulé.
5. Oui, si le vol est annulé, l'avion ne partira pas.

Bell Ringer Review

Write the following on the board or use BRR Blackline Master 7-3: Answer the following questions about students in your school:

1. Qui est le meilleur joueur de football américain?
2. Qui reçoit les meilleures notes?
3. Qui chante le mieux?
4. Qui est le (la) meilleur(e) en sciences?
5. Qui parle français le mieux?

Activités de communication orale
Mots 1 et 2

PRESENTATION *(page 171)*

It is not necessary to have students complete all the activities. Select those which you consider most appropriate. You may wish to have groups complete different activities.

ANSWERS

Activités A, B, C, and D
Answers will vary.

Structure Teaching Resources

1. Workbook, *Structure: A–F,* pages 74–76
2. Student Tape Manual, Teacher's Edition, *Structure: A–C,* pages 72–73
3. Audio Cassette 5A/CD-4
4. Communication Activities Masters, *Structure: A–C,* pages 47–49
5. Computer Software, *Structure*
6. Chapter Quizzes, *Structure:* Quizzes 3–5, pages 36–38
7. CD-ROM, Disc 2, pages 172–175

Le futur des verbes réguliers

PRESENTATION *(page 172)*

A. Elicit more examples of the *futur proche.*

B. In step 2, stress that the *-e* is dropped from *-re* verbs.

C. Have the students repeat the verb forms after you.

D. Ask students what the future endings remind them of. Write the forms of *avoir* on the board and point out the similarity.

Note In the CD-ROM version, this structure point is presented via an interactive electronic comic strip.

Exercices

PRESENTATION *(pages 172–173)*

Exercises A, B, C, D, E, and F

Exercises A and C can be done with books either open or closed. Exercises B, D, E, and F are to be done with books open.

ANSWERS

Exercice A

1. Oui, il étudiera en France.
2. Oui, il prendra l'avion...
3. Oui, il prendra un vol...
4. Oui, il choisira...

172

STRUCTURE

Le futur des verbes réguliers

Telling What You and Other People Will Do

1. You have already learned that actions that will take place in the near future can be expressed in French by using the verb *aller* and the infinitive.

   Il va aller en France la semaine prochaine.
   Il va faire ses études à Toulouse.

2. There is also a future tense that corresponds to the English "will." It is very easy to form the future. You add the future endings to the infinitive of *-er* and *-ir* verbs. With *-re* verbs, you drop the *-e* before adding the endings. Study the following forms.

INFINITIVE	PARLER	FINIR	ATTENDRE	ENDINGS
STEM	parler-	finir-	attendr-	
FUTURE	je parlerai tu parleras il/elle/on parlera nous parlerons vous parlerez ils/elles parleront	je finirai tu finiras il/elle/on finira nous finirons vous finirez ils/elles finiront	j'attendrai tu attendras il/elle/on attendra nous attendrons vous attendrez ils/elles attendront	-ai -as -a -ons -ez -ont

Exercices

A **Raoul étudiera en France.**
Répondez par «oui».

1. Raoul étudiera en France?
2. Il prendra l'avion pour aller en France?
3. Il prendra un vol sans escale?
4. Il choisira une place non-fumeurs?
5. Il arrivera fatigué?
6. Il dînera pendant le vol?
7. Il regardera un film?
8. Il dormira un peu?
9. Il arrivera à Paris à l'heure?
10. Il prendra le car pour aller en ville?

172   CHAPITRE 7

Le Sacré-Cœur de Balata à la Martinique

DID YOU KNOW?

Le Sacré-Cœur de Balata (l'église de Balata) se trouve près de Fort-de-France, la capitale de la Martinique. L'église est une réplique miniature de la basilique du Sacré-Cœur à Paris. (Voir la photo du Sacré-Cœur à Paris, page 198.)

B **On embarquera.** Faites des phrases d'après le modèle.

> embarquer à l'heure
> *On embarquera à l'heure.*

1. décoller à l'heure
2. atterrir en retard
3. s'amuser pendant le vol
4. dîner à bord
5. écouter de la musique
6. mettre des écouteurs
7. dormir un peu
8. attacher sa ceinture de sécurité
9. mettre son gilet de sauvetage
10. respirer à l'aide du masque à oxygène

C **Demain.** Donnez des réponses personnelles.

1. Demain tu arriveras à l'école à quelle heure?
2. Tu y resteras jusqu'à quelle heure?
3. Tu rentreras chez toi à quelle heure?
4. Comment rentreras-tu chez toi?
5. Tu regarderas la télé?
6. À quelle heure est-ce que tu dîneras?
7. Avant le dîner tu mettras le couvert?
8. Qui débarrassera la table?

D **Tu donneras une fête?** Posez des questions à Laurent Legrand.

> donner une fête
> *Laurent, tu donneras une fête?*

1. donner une fête
2. inviter des amis
3. préparer des hors-d'œuvre
4. jouer de la guitare
5. mettre des disques
6. danser

E **À l'hôtel.** Répondez d'après les indications.

1. À quelle heure est-ce qu'Agnès arrivera à l'hôtel? (à trois heures)
2. Tu y arriveras à la même heure? (oui)
3. Agnès et toi, à qui parlerez-vous? (au réceptionniste)
4. Qu'est-ce que vous remplirez? (une fiche d'enregistrement)
5. Tu choisiras quelle chambre? (une chambre qui donne sur la cour)
6. Qu'est-ce qu'Agnès demandera? (le prix de la chambre)
7. Qui montera les valises? (le porteur)
8. Qu'est-ce qu'il vous donnera? (la clé)

F **Au futur.** Complétez les mini-conversations en utilisant le futur.

1. danser

    JULIE: Vous ___ pendant la fête?
    ALAIN: Bien sûr que nous ___. Tous nos copains ___.

2. prendre

    MARIE-FRANCE: Vous ___ le train pour aller au Canada?
    BERNARD: Non, je ne crois pas. Nous ___ l'avion.
    MARIE-FRANCE: Vos copains aussi ___ l'avion?

CHAPITRE 7 **173**

5. Oui, il arrivera fatigué.
6. Oui, il dînera pendant le vol.
7. Oui, il regardera un film.
8. Oui, il dormira un peu.
9. Oui, il arrivera à l'heure.
10. Oui, il prendra le car...

Exercice B

1. On décollera à l'heure.
2. On atterrira en retard.
3. On s'amusera pendant le vol.
4. On dînera à bord.
5. On écoutera de la musique.
6. On mettra des écouteurs.
7. On dormira un peu.
8. On attachera sa ceinture de sécurité.
9. On mettra son gilet de sauvetage.
10. On respirera à l'aide du masque à oxygène.

Exercice C
    Answers will vary.

Exercice D

1. Laurent, tu donneras une fête?
2. ... tu inviteras des amis?
3. ... tu prépareras des hors-d'œuvre?
4. ... tu joueras de la guitare?
5. ... tu mettras des disques?
6. ... tu danseras?

Exercice E

1. Agnès arrivera à l'hôtel à trois heures.
2. Oui, j'y arriverai à la même heure.
3. Agnès et moi, nous parlerons au réceptionniste.
4. Nous remplirons une fiche d'enregistrement.
5. Je choisirai une chambre qui donne sur la cour.
6. Agnès demandera le prix de la chambre.
7. Le porteur montera les valises.
8. Il nous donnera la clé.

Exercice F

1. danserez, danserons, danseront
2. prendrez, prendrons, prendront

INTERDISCIPLINARY CONNECTIONS

Ask the music teacher to give a brief talk on Caribbean music in your class. Have him or her bring examples of Caribbean music with French lyrics to play for the students.

If your school has a chorus, have your students teach the music students one or more of the songs to perform for the annual concert.

INDEPENDENT PRACTICE

Assign any of the following:
1. Exercises, pages 172–173
2. Workbook, *Structure: A–B*, pages 74–75
3. Communication Activities Masters, *Structure: A*, page 47
4. CD-ROM, Disc 2, pages 172–173

Les verbes être, faire et aller *au futur*

PRESENTATION (page 174)

Guide students through the topic and have them repeat the verb forms after you.

Exercices

PRESENTATION (page 174)

Exercice A

Exercise A can be done with books either open or closed.

Note The beach vocabulary in this exercise was originally presented in *Bienvenue*, Chapter 9.

Extension of Exercice A: Speaking

After completing Exercise A, have students invent original sentences telling what they will do at the beach. For example: *J'irai à la plage où je prendrai un bain de soleil.*

Exercice B

Exercise B is to be done with books open. You may wish to have students do Exercise B in pairs. After some practice, have them present the mini-conversations to the class.

ANSWERS

Exercice A

1. Oui, l'hiver prochain Émilie fera un voyage.
2. Oui, elle ira à la Martinique.
3. Oui, elle fera le voyage en avion.
4. Oui, elle sera fatiguée après le vol.
5. Oui, je ferai le voyage avec Émilie.
6. Oui, nous irons ensemble à la Martinique.
7. Oui, nous y ferons des excursions ensemble.
8. Oui, nous irons à la plage.
9. Oui, nous prendrons des bains de soleil.
10. Oui, nous serons bronzé(e)s.

Exercice B

1. irez, irons, iront
2. ferez, ferons, feront
3. serez, serons, seront

Les verbes *être*, *faire* et *aller* au futur

Expressing the Future of Some Important Irregular Verbs

The verbs *être*, *faire*, and *aller* have an irregular stem in the future. Study the following.

INFINITIVE	ÊTRE	FAIRE	ALLER
STEM	ser-	fer-	ir-
FUTURE	je serai tu seras il/elle/on sera nous serons vous serez ils/elles seront	je ferai tu feras il/elle/on fera nous ferons vous ferez ils/elles feront	j'irai tu iras il/elle/on ira nous irons vous irez ils/elles iront

Exercices

A **Un voyage à la Martinique.** Répondez par «oui».

1. L'hiver prochain Émilie fera un voyage?
2. Elle ira à la Martinique?
3. Elle fera le voyage en avion?
4. Elle sera fatiguée après le vol?
5. Tu feras le voyage avec Émilie?
6. Vous irez ensemble à la Martinique?
7. Vous y ferez des excursions ensemble?
8. Vous irez à la plage?
9. Vous prendrez des bains de soleil?
10. Vous serez bronzé(e)s?

B **Qu'est-ce que vous ferez?** Complétez les mini-conversations en utilisant le futur.

1. aller

   JEANNE: Vous ___ à la fête si Éric vous invite?
   MICHEL: Bien sûr que nous ___ à la fête. Tous nos copains ___ à la fête si Éric les invite.

2. faire

   CARINE: Vous ___ un voyage cet été?
   PHILIPPE: Oui, nous ___ un voyage au Canada. Marc et Suzanne ___ le voyage avec nous.

3. être

   LAURE: Vous êtes en retard aujourd'hui mais vous ___ à l'heure demain, n'est-ce pas?
   OLIVIER: Oui, nous ___ à l'heure. Les autres élèves aussi ___ à l'heure.

St.-Pierre et la Montagne Pelée

174   CHAPITRE 7

LEARNING FROM PHOTOS

(Explain that *une nuée ardente* is a tremendous cloud of burning ash and hot gases.)

You may wish to give students the following information about the photo: *La montagne Pelée est une montagne volcanique. Elle se trouve dans la partie nord de la Martinique. L'éruption de Pelée en 1902 a totalement détruit la ville de Saint-Pierre et a causé la mort de 40 000 personnes. Ça a été une véritable tragédie. Une nuée ardente a accompagné l'éruption.*

Deux pronoms dans la même phrase

Referring to People and Things Already Mentioned

1. It is possible to use both a direct and an indirect object pronoun in the same sentence. Look at the following sentences in which both pronouns are used.

   Le steward nous servira le dîner. Il *nous le* servira.
   Le steward me donnera les écouteurs. Il *me les* donnera.

2. The pronouns *me, te, nous,* and *vous* always precede the pronouns *le, la, l',* or *les.* In the negative *ne* comes before the pronouns. Study the following.

(ne)	before	me te nous vous	before	le la les	before	verbe	before	(pas)

   Le commandant ne *nous le* servira pas.
   Le commandant ne *me les* donnera pas.

3. Remember that in the *passé composé,* the past participle must agree with the direct object pronoun that precedes it.

   Il t'a donné la couverture?   **Oui, il me *l'*a donnée.**
   Il t'a donné les écouteurs?   **Oui, il me *les* a donnés.**

Exercices

A À bord de l'avion. Répondez en utilisant des pronoms.

1. L'hôtesse de l'air te dit le titre du film?
2. Elle te donne les écouteurs?
3. Elle t'explique la route du vol?
4. Elle te montre le gilet de sauvetage?
5. Pendant le vol, le steward te sert le dîner?
6. Il te sert le dîner sur un plateau?

B Pendant le vol. Refaites l'Exercice A d'après le modèle.

    L'hôtesse de l'air vous dit le titre du film?
    Oui, elle nous le dit.

C Qui te l'a acheté(e)? Répondez d'après le modèle.

    J'ai une nouvelle cassette.
    Sans blague! Qui te l'a achetée?

1. J'ai un nouveau téléphone sans fil.
2. J'ai une nouvelle moto.
3. J'ai de nouveaux disques.
4. J'ai un nouveau zappeur.
5. J'ai un nouveau magnétoscope.
6. J'ai de nouvelles cassettes.

CHAPITRE 7   **175**

Deux pronoms dans la même phrase

PRESENTATION *(page 175)*

Go over steps 1–3 with the class and have students repeat the model sentences.

Note The use of *lui* and *leur* in sentences with two pronouns will be taught in the next chapter.

Exercices

PRESENTATION *(page 175)*

Exercices A, B, and C

Exercises A, B, and C can be done with books either open or closed.

ANSWERS

Exercice A

Students may answer with *oui* or *non.*

1. Oui, elle me le dit.
2. Oui, elle me les donne.
3. Oui, elle me l'explique.
4. Oui, elle me le montre.
5. Oui, il me le sert.
6. Oui, il me le sert sur un plateau.

Exercice B

1. Oui, elle nous le dit. (Non, elle ne nous le dit pas.)
2. Oui, elle nous les donne. (Non, elle ne nous les donne pas.)
3. Oui, elle nous l'explique. (Non, elle ne nous l'explique pas.)
4. Oui, elle nous le montre. (Non, elle ne nous le montre pas.)
5. Oui, il nous le sert. (Non, il ne nous le sert pas.)
6. Oui, il nous le sert sur un plateau. (Non, il ne nous le sert pas...)

Exercice C

1. Sans blague! Qui te l'a acheté?
2. ... Qui te l'a achetée?
3. ... Qui te les a achetés?
4. ... Qui te l'a acheté?
5. ... Qui te l'a acheté?
6. ... Qui te les a achetées?

ADDITIONAL PRACTICE

Student Tape Manual, Teacher's Edition, *Activités A–C,* pages 72–73

INDEPENDENT PRACTICE

Assign any of the following:
1. Exercises, pages 174–175
2. Workbook, *Structure: C–F,* pages 75–76
3. Communication Activities Masters, *Structure: B–C,* pages 48–49
4. Computer Software, *Structure*
5. CD-ROM, Disc 2, pages 174–175

CONVERSATION

CONVERSATION

Scènes de la vie *Tu partiras à quelle heure?*

MONIQUE: Ton avion partira à quelle heure?

RAOUL: À vingt heures dix.

MONIQUE: Et tu arriveras à Paris à quelle heure?

RAOUL: Avec le décalage horaire on arrivera à six heures et demie du matin.

MONIQUE: C'est long. Tu seras fatigué. Tu vas dîner avant d'aller à l'aéroport?

RAOUL: Non, je ne crois pas. On nous servira le dîner à bord.

MONIQUE: On passera un film?

RAOUL: Je crois, mais je ne voyage pas souvent, tu sais. C'est la première fois que je vais en France.

MONIQUE: Et tu seras hyper-intelligent quand tu retourneras à la Martinique!

RAOUL: Eh oui! Je serai diplômé de l'Université de Paris!

MONIQUE: C'est vraiment chouette! C'est super! Je te souhaite beaucoup de succès.

A **Un vol à Paris.** Répondez d'après la conversation.

1. L'avion partira de Fort-de-France à quelle heure?
2. Et il arrivera à Paris à quelle heure?
3. C'est long, le vol Fort-de-France–Paris?
4. Raoul sera fatigué quand il arrivera à Paris?
5. Il dînera avant d'aller à l'aéroport?
6. Pourquoi pas?
7. On passera un film à bord?
8. Monique dit que quand Raoul rentrera de Paris, il sera très intelligent. Pourquoi?

176 CHAPITRE 7

Bell Ringer Review

Write the following on the board or use BRR Blackline Master 7-4: Fill in the blanks with *ce qui* or *ce que.*

1. Je ne sais pas ___ Martine veut faire.
2. Dis-moi ___ tu vois.
3. Les enfants demandent ___ est dans la voiture.
4. Le médecin veut savoir ___ s'est passé.
5. ___ je dois envoyer, c'est ce colis.

PRESENTATION *(page 176)*

A. Have students close their books. Play the Conversation Video or have them listen as you read the conversation or play Cassette 5A/CD-4. (Use *Activité E* in the Student Tape Manual to check oral comprehension.)

B. Call on pairs to read the conversation with as much expression as possible. In the second half, Raoul should sound a bit nervous and Monique very excited.

Note In the CD-ROM version, students can play the role of either one of the characters and record the conversation.

Note Remind students that the 24-hour clock is used when referring to flights. Also point out that the prefix *hyper-* is very popular these days, as are the words *chouette* and *super*.

ANSWERS

Exercice A

1. L'avion partira de Fort-de-France à 20h10.
2. Il arrivera à Paris à 6h30 du matin.
3. Oui, c'est long.

LEARNING FROM PHOTOS

1. Tell students that Raoul and Monique are leaving the Bibliothèque Schœlcher in Fort-de-France. See DID YOU KNOW? on page 178 for information about Victor Schœlcher.
2. Point out to students that the French flag is flown on public buildings in Martinique since it is a department of France.
3. Have students say as much about the photo as they can.

Activités de communication orale

A Que ferez-vous? Vous allez à Paris en avion. Pendant le vol, vous parlez avec Martine Duclos, qui est assise à côté de vous. Elle vous pose des questions sur votre voyage. Répondez-lui.

1. Qu'est-ce que tu feras quand tu seras à Paris?
2. Combien de temps est-ce que tu resteras?
3. Qu'est-ce que tu feras quand tu retourneras aux États-Unis?

Martine Duclos

B Un voyage en avion. Regardez l'horaire et choisissez une destination. Posez des questions au sujet de votre vol à l'agent de la ligne aérienne (votre camarade). Il/Elle vous répondra d'après l'horaire. Vous voulez savoir:

1. l'heure du départ du vol
2. la durée du vol
3. l'heure de l'arrivée du vol

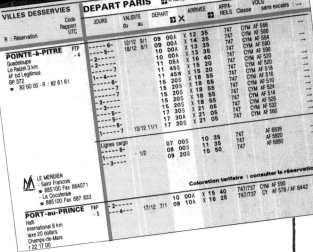

4. Oui, il sera fatigué quand il arrivera à Paris.
5. Non, il ne dînera pas avant d'aller à l'aéroport.
6. Parce qu'on leur servira le dîner à bord.
7. Il croit que oui.
8. Parce qu'il sera diplômé de l'Université de Paris.

Activités de communication orale

PRESENTATION (*page 177*)

Activité A

In the CD-ROM version of this activity, students can interact with an on-screen native speaker.

ANSWERS

Activités A and B
    Answers will vary.

READING STRATEGIES
(pages 178–179)

Pre-reading

Tell students they are going to learn more about Raoul Castellar, the young man in the *Conversation,* and about the island where he lives.

Reading

A. You may wish to break the reading into several parts. Present one paragraph thoroughly, reading it to the students as they follow along in their books, and interspersing your reading with your own comprehension questions. Then have students read the next paragraph silently.

B. When reading aloud, you may wish to intersperse the reading with the *Compréhension* questions on page 179.

Post-reading

Call on volunteers to tell in their own words what they have learned about Raoul and about Martinique.

Note Students may listen to a recorded version of the *Lecture* on the CD-ROM.

IL SERA DIPLÔMÉ DE L'UNIVERSITÉ DE PARIS

*R*aoul Castellar habite à Schœlcher, un village tout près de Fort-de-France. Fort-de-France est la capitale de la Martinique. Cette année Raoul est en terminale au Lycée Bellevue à Fort-de-France. Mais en mai il passera le bachot (le bac). Il sera reçu[1] sans aucun doute. Raoul a toujours eu de très bonnes notes.

Au mois d'août il partira pour la France. Il veut être médecin et il étudiera à la Faculté de Médecine de l'Université de Paris. Les cours commenceront en octobre mais Raoul veut être à Paris à la fin d'août. Il veut avoir le temps de s'installer et de se familiariser un peu avec la vie parisienne. Et Raoul veut voyager avant la rentrée universitaire[2]. Il a très envie de[3] connaître la France.

Raoul est de la Martinique et il fera ses études en France. Pourquoi? La Martinique est un département d'outre-mer depuis 1946. Les Martiniquais sont des citoyens[4] français et leur système d'enseignement (d'éducation) est le même que celui de la France métropolitaine. Quand un(e) élève

martiniquais(e) est reçu(e) au bachot il ou elle peut s'inscrire à l'université en France. C'est pour cette raison que Raoul ira à l'université en France.

Vous connaissez la Martinique? Non? Vous savez quelque chose de la Martinique? Non? Un peu peut-être? La Martinique n'est pas du tout loin des États-Unis. C'est une île tropicale dans la mer des Caraïbes. Beaucoup de Martiniquais vivent de la culture du sucre[5] et des fruits tropicaux. D'autres vivent du tourisme. Pas mal de Français, de Canadiens (surtout des Québécois) et d'Américains passent leurs vacances d'hiver à la Martinique. Ils fuient[6] le froid du nord et vont s'amuser sur de jolies plages tropicales. Ce n'est pas mal, n'est-ce pas?

[1] Il sera reçu   *he'll pass*
[2] avant la rentrée universitaire   *before classes start*
[3] il a très envie de   *he's very eager to*
[4] des citoyens   *citizens*
[5] la culture du sucre   *the growing of sugar cane*
[6] fuient   *flee, escape from*

DID YOU KNOW?

Raoul habite à Schœlcher. Cette petite ville tout près de Fort-de-France porte le nom d'un homme politique français, Victor Schœlcher. Il est né à Paris en 1804. Il a servi comme député de la Martinique et de la Guadeloupe. C'est lui qui a préparé le décret qui a aboli l'esclavage dans les colonies.

Les Martiniquais parlent français et créole. Le créole est un dialecte franco-africain. La plupart des[7] Martiniquais sont d'origine africaine. Raoul a très envie de faire la connaissance d'autres jeunes des pays francophones d'Afrique.

En France il connaîtra bien sûr des jeunes du Zaïre, du Sénégal, du Mali, de la Côte d'Ivoire, etc. Ce sont tous des pays africains francophones.

[7] la plupart des *most*

Étude de mots

A Quelle est la définition?

1. s'inscrire
2. la rentrée universitaire
3. la terminale
4. faire des études
5. universitaire
6. l'enseignement
7. francophone

a. étudier
b. l'éducation
c. qui parle français
d. de l'université
e. la dernière année de lycée
f. quand les cours recommencent
g. immatriculer, entrer dans

Compréhension

B Vous avez compris? Répondez.

1. À quel lycée va Raoul?
2. Il est en quelle année?
3. Raoul ira où en août?
4. Qu'est-ce qu'il fera en France?
5. Les cours commenceront quand?
6. Pourquoi arrivera-t-il à Paris à la fin d'août?
7. Qu'est-ce que la Martinique?

C Des données sur la Martinique.
Répondez par «oui» ou «non».

1. La Martinique est une péninsule.
2. La Martinique est un pays indépendant.
3. La Martinique est dans la mer Méditerranée.
4. Schœlcher est la capitale de la Martinique.
5. Beaucoup de Martiniquais vivent de la culture des légumes.
6. Il y a beaucoup de stations de sports d'hiver à la Martinique.
7. Il fait toujours chaud à la Martinique.
8. La Martinique a le même système d'enseignement que la France.

Un champ de canne à sucre

DID YOU KNOW?

Depuis le 17e siècle, la plus importante industrie des Antilles est la production du sucre.

Aux 17e et 18e siècles, les colons américains ont importé de la mélasse (*molasses*) des Antilles. Ils l'utilisaient pour faire du rhum, une industrie qui rapportait gros. Pour forcer les colons à acheter leur mélasse uniquement aux agriculteurs anglais, le Parlement a voté le «Molasses Act» en 1733 et le «Sugar Act» en 1764. Les impôts qui ont resulté de ces lois ont été une des causes indirectes de la Guerre d'Indépendance.

Étude de mots

ANSWERS

Exercice A

1. g   4. a   7. c
2. f   5. d
3. e   6. b

Compréhension

PRESENTATION (*pages 179–180*)

Exercices B and C

Exercices B and C require factual recall. However, Exercise C has students look back at the selection and scan for some information as well.

Extension of *Exercice C*

After completing Exercise C, you may wish to have students correct the false statements.

ANSWERS

Exercice B

1. Il va au Lycée Bellevue à Fort-de-France.
2. Il est en terminale.
3. Il ira en France.
4. Il fera ses études en France.
5. Ils commenceront en octobre.
6. Il arrivera à Paris à la fin d'août parce qu'il veut avoir le temps de s'installer et de se familiariser un peu avec la vie parisienne. Et il veut voyager.
7. La Martinique est une île dans la mer des Caraïbes.

Exercice C

1. Non. (La Martinique est une île.)
2. Non. (La Martinique est un département d'outre-mer de la France.)
3. Non. (La Martinique est dans la mer des Caraïbes.)
4. Non. (Fort-de-France est la capitale de la Martinique.)
5. Non. (Beaucoup de Martiniquais vivent de la culture du sucre et des fruits tropicaux.)
6. Non. (Il n'y a pas de stations de sports d'hiver à la Martinique.)
7. Oui.
8. Oui.

Exercices D and E

In Exercise D, students are expected to scan for the necessary information. Exercise E challenges students' critical thinking skills.

ANSWERS

Exercice D

1. Raoul Castellar
2. Schœlcher
3. la Martinique
4. Fort-de-France
5. le sucre, des fruits tropicaux
6. le tourisme
7. la mer des Caraïbes
8. le créole
9. 1946
10. le Zaïre, le Sénégal, le Mali, la Côte d'Ivoire...

Exercice E

1. Les Martiniquais sont des citoyens français parce que la Martinique est un département d'outre-mer de la France.
2. Ils vont à la Martinique pour passer leurs vacances d'hiver parce qu'ils fuient le froid du nord et vont s'amuser sur de jolies plages tropicales.
3. C'est un dialecte franco-africain.
4. Ils parlent le créole parce que la plupart des Martiniquais sont d'origine africaine.

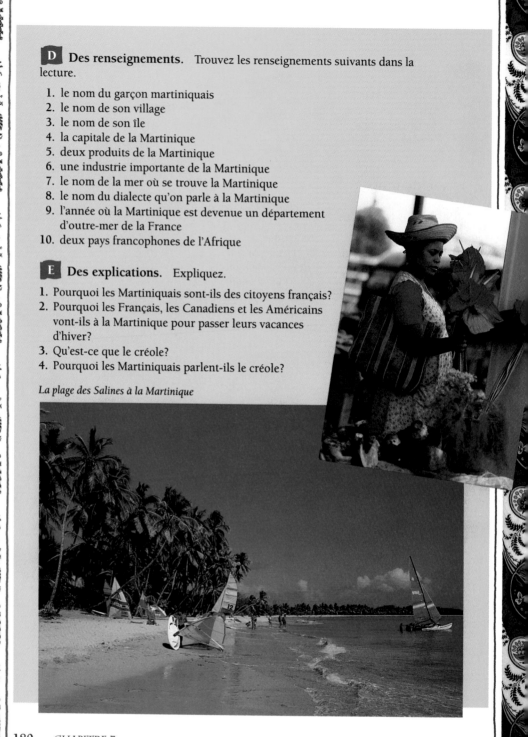

D **Des renseignements.** Trouvez les renseignements suivants dans la lecture.

1. le nom du garçon martiniquais
2. le nom de son village
3. le nom de son île
4. la capitale de la Martinique
5. deux produits de la Martinique
6. une industrie importante de la Martinique
7. le nom de la mer où se trouve la Martinique
8. le nom du dialecte qu'on parle à la Martinique
9. l'année où la Martinique est devenue un département d'outre-mer de la France
10. deux pays francophones de l'Afrique

E **Des explications.** Expliquez.

1. Pourquoi les Martiniquais sont-ils des citoyens français?
2. Pourquoi les Français, les Canadiens et les Américains vont-ils à la Martinique pour passer leurs vacances d'hiver?
3. Qu'est-ce que le créole?
4. Pourquoi les Martiniquais parlent-ils le créole?

La plage des Salines à la Martinique

180 CHAPITRE 7

180

DÉCOUVERTE CULTURELLE

Comme la Martinique est un département d'outre-mer (D.O.M.) de la France, les Martiniquais sont des citoyens français. Par conséquent, les Martiniquais voyagent avec un passeport de l'Union Européenne. Quand ils arrivent en France, les Martiniquais ne passent ni par l'immigration ni à la douane.

La Guadeloupe, une autre île dans la mer des Caraïbes, est aussi un département d'outre-mer. La capitale de la Guadeloupe est Pointe-à-Pitre. Les Guadeloupéens, comme les Martiniquais, vivent de la culture du sucre, de la culture des fruits tropicaux et du tourisme.

Une très petite, très jolie île française dans la mer des Caraïbes est Saint-Barthélemy.

St.-Barthélemy: une vue de la côte

Le carnaval à la Guadeloupe: des enfants déguisés

Haïti est un autre pays francophone dans la mer des Caraïbes. Mais Haïti n'est pas un département de la France. Haïti est un pays indépendant. C'est le seul pays noir de notre hémisphère et la première république indépendante noire du monde. Sa capitale est Port-au-Prince. En Haïti on parle français et créole. Mais le créole qu'on parle en Haïti n'est pas le même créole qu'on parle à la Martinique ou à la Guadeloupe.

Haïti a connu toute une série de crises politiques et économiques. C'est le pays le plus pauvre de notre hémisphère. Mais il faut espérer que la situation changera radicalement dans un proche avenir[1].

[1] dans un proche avenir *in the near future*

CHAPITRE 7   **181**

OPTIONAL MATERIAL

Découverte culturelle

PRESENTATION *(page 181)*

Before doing the reading selection with the class, prepare some *vrai/faux* statements about it and write them on the board. After reading, have students correct the false statements. For example: *Haïti est un pays très riche. (Faux. Haïti est un pays très pauvre.)*

Note Students may listen to a recorded version of the *Découverte culturelle* on the CD-ROM.

Note You may wish to have students follow events in Haiti in the newspaper. Ask them to clip out news articles and make a bulletin board display of the latest developments in the sad situation of this wonderful country.

HISTORY CONNECTION

Christophe Colomb a découvert les îles de la Martinique et de la Guadeloupe. Il a découvert la Guadeloupe en 1493 et la Martinique en 1502. Les Français ont colonisé les îles à partir de 1635.

GEOGRAPHY CONNECTION

La Martinique et la Guadeloupe sont des îles des Petites Antilles. La Guadeloupe est formée de deux îles: Basse-Terre et Grande-Terre, séparées par un bras de mer, la rivière Salée.

Haïti est une des Grandes Antilles. Cette île est divisée en deux états indépendants: la République Dominicaine et Haïti.

DID YOU KNOW?

Saint-Barthélemy is an 8-square-mile island of hills and sheltered inlets in the Caribbean. It was named for Christopher Columbus' brother Bartholomeo when Columbus discovered the island in 1493. The tiny island has only one real town, Gustavia, but is noted for its gourmet French cuisine. Once a retreat for the wealthy, the island has expanded its tourist trade in recent times.

INDEPENDENT PRACTICE

Assign any of the following:
1. Workbook, *Un Peu Plus*, pages 77–82
2. *Étude de mots* and *Compréhension* exercises, pages 179–180
3. CD-ROM, Disc 2, pages 178–181

OPTIONAL MATERIAL

PRESENTATION

(pages 182–183)

Have students read the captions silently and enjoy the photographs. Encourage them to ask questions and express opinions.

Note In the CD-ROM version, students can listen to the recorded captions and discover a hidden video behind one of the photos.

CROSS-CULTURAL COMPARISON

Ask students what other countries have *Carnaval* or Mardi Gras celebrations. (Answer: Italy, France, Guadeloupe, Brazil, Canada, and the United States.)

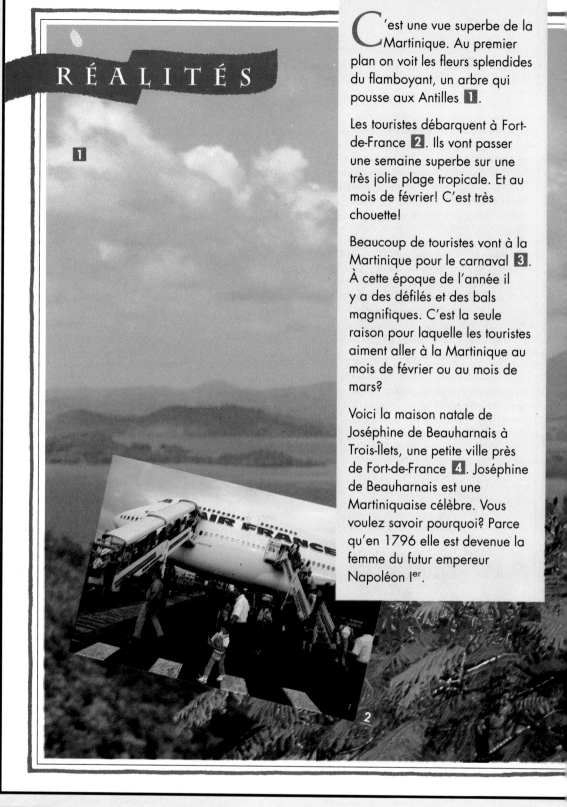

RÉALITÉS

C'est une vue superbe de la Martinique. Au premier plan on voit les fleurs splendides du flamboyant, un arbre qui pousse aux Antilles **1**.

Les touristes débarquent à Fort-de-France **2**. Ils vont passer une semaine superbe sur une très jolie plage tropicale. Et au mois de février! C'est très chouette!

Beaucoup de touristes vont à la Martinique pour le carnaval **3**. À cette époque de l'année il y a des défilés et des bals magnifiques. C'est la seule raison pour laquelle les touristes aiment aller à la Martinique au mois de février ou au mois de mars?

Voici la maison natale de Joséphine de Beauharnais à Trois-Îlets, une petite ville près de Fort-de-France **4**. Joséphine de Beauharnais est une Martiniquaise célèbre. Vous voulez savoir pourquoi? Parce qu'en 1796 elle est devenue la femme du futur empereur Napoléon Ier.

COMMUNITIES

Have students work in groups. Assign each group a different French-speaking country or city that has a Mardi Gras (*Carnaval*) celebration. Ask them to write to the tourist office of that place for information on the celebration. Once students have received the information, have the groups give an oral presentation to the class. Students can then compare and contrast the Mardi Gras customs in different francophone countries.

You may also wish to plan your own Mardi Gras celebration for National Foreign Language Week, which is the first week of March.

183

HISTORY CONNECTION

Marie-Joséphine Rose Tascher de La Pagerie (1763–1814), first wife of Napoleon Bonaparte, was born in Martinique, West Indies. In 1779, at age 16, she married the French army officer Alexandre, vicomte de Beauharnais, who was guillotined in 1794 during the Reign of Terror. Two years later she married Napoleon and in 1804 became empress of France. Napoleon divorced her in 1809.

In the little village of Les Trois-Îlets is the Musée de La Pagerie dedicated to the memory of Joséphine Bonaparte. La Pagerie was Joséphine's birthplace. The main house on the estate blew down in a hurricane when Joséphine was three. The stone building that served as the kitchen houses the museum. Memorabilia includes family portraits, antique furnishings like her childhood bed, documents such as her marriage certificate, and a love letter written to her by Napoleon in 1796.

(For more information on Joséphine de Beauharnais and Napoleon, refer to *Lettres et sciences,* page 220.)

ADDITIONAL PRACTICE

Assign any of the following:
1. Student Tape Manual, Teacher's Edition, *Deuxième Partie,* pages 75–77
2. Situation Cards, Chapter 7

CULMINATION

CULMINATION

RECYCLING

These activities encourage students to use all the language they have learned in the chapter and recombine it with material from previous chapters. It is not necessary to do all the activities with all students. You may select the ones you consider most appropriate or allow students to choose the ones they wish to do.

INFORMAL ASSESSMENT

The *Activités de communication orale* lend themselves to assessing speaking and listening abilities. Use the evaluation criteria given on page 22 of this Teacher's Wraparound Edition.

Activités de communication orale
ANSWERS
Activités A and B
Answers will vary.

Activités de communication écrite
ANSWERS
Activités A and B
Answers will vary.

OPTIONAL MATERIAL

Réintroduction et recombinaison
PRESENTATION (page 185)
Exercices A and B

Exercise A recycles airline vocabulary presented in *Bienvenue*, Chapter 7. Exercise B recycles the use of third-person direct and indirect object pronouns occurring alone in a sentence. It serves as a lead-in to the next chapter, where students will learn to use two third-person object pronouns in the same sentence.

Activités de communication orale

A **C'est son premier vol.** Travaillez en petits groupes. Imaginez qu'un(e) élève va faire son premier voyage en avion. Expliquez-lui tout ce qu'il/elle fera à partir du moment où il/elle arrivera à l'aéroport de départ jusqu'au moment où il/elle quittera l'aéroport d'arrivée.

> Élève 1: D'abord tu feras enregistrer tes bagages au comptoir de la compagnie aérienne.
> Élève 2: Puis tu iras à la porte d'embarquement de ton avion.

B **La Martinique.** Your French class has decided to go to Martinique over spring break. You and a classmate are in charge of planning the flight. Working together, decide what airline your group will use, where you'll fly to in Martinique, how long the flight will last, what class you'll fly, what food will be served, what film will be shown, where you'll stay, and what you'll do when you get there. Then report to the class for their reaction. The class decides which group has planned the best trip.

Activités de communication écrite

A **Le service à bord.** Imaginez que vous avez pris un vol New York—Paris. Écrivez une lettre à la compagnie aérienne. Dans votre lettre, indiquez que le service à bord a été mauvais. Expliquez pourquoi vous n'avez pas été satisfait(e) de votre vol.

B **Un beau voyage.** Écrivez deux paragraphes sur la Martinique. Dites si vous voulez y aller un jour et pourquoi.

184 CHAPITRE 7

Have students look at the map of Martinique as you ask the following questions: *D'après la carte quels sports peut-on faire à la Martinique? (de la plongée sous-marine, de la voile, de la planche à voile, de la natation) Est-ce qu'il y a beaucoup de plages? Il y a des poissons tropicaux à la Martinique? Quelle sorte de végétation est-ce qu'il y a? Il y a des palmiers? Des fleurs exotiques?*

Display Communication Transparency C-7. Have students work in groups and make up as many questions as they can about the illustration. Then have the groups take turns asking and answering the questions.

184

Réintroduction et recombinaison

A **Un voyage en avion.** Répondez par «oui» ou «non».

1. Toutes les lignes aériennes qui desservent un aéroport ont un comptoir dans cet aéroport pour servir leurs passagers.
2. Avant d'embarquer il faut faire enregistrer tous les bagages, même les petits bagages à main.
3. Au comptoir de la ligne aérienne un agent de la ligne vérifiera vos billets.
4. Si vous faites un voyage international, il faut avoir un passeport.
5. Si vous n'avez pas de passeport, l'agent de la ligne aérienne vous en donnera un.
6. Au comptoir, l'agent vous donnera une carte d'embarquement.
7. Beaucoup de passagers qui voyagent fréquemment préfèrent une place côté couloir parce qu'il y a un peu plus de place pour les jambes.
8. Après un voyage international il faut passer par l'immigration et à la douane.
9. Après un vol intérieur il faut passer par le contrôle de sécurité.

B **À l'aéroport.** Récrivez les phrases en utilisant un pronom.

1. J'ai *les billets*.
2. Tu as *les passeports*?
3. Tu vois *l'agent de la ligne aérienne*?
4. Tu parles *à l'agent*?
5. Oui, je parle *à l'agent*.
6. Tu donnes ton billet *à l'agent*?
7. Il regarde *ton billet*?
8. Tu donnes ta valise *à l'agent*.
9. Il pèse *ta valise*.
10. À bord, tu parleras *aux hôtesses de l'air*?
11. Tu parleras *aux stewards*?
12. Le personnel de bord dira «bonjour» *aux passagers*?
13. Tu montreras ta carte d'embarquement *au steward*?
14. Il regardera *ta carte d'embarquement*?

Vocabulaire

NOMS
l'avion (m.)
l'appareil (m.)
l'aile (f.)
la cabine
  première classe
  classe affaires
  classe économique
le passager
la passagère
l'équipage (m.)
le pilote
le commandant de bord
le poste de pilotage
le personnel de bord
le steward

l'hôtesse (f.) de l'air
la ceinture de sécurité
le masque à oxygène
le gilet de sauvetage
l'issue (f.) de secours
la sortie de secours
le coffre à bagages
le siège réglable
le dossier du siège
la tablette rabattable
les écouteurs (m.)
la chaîne
la couverture
l'oreiller (m.)
le repas
la collation
le plateau

la boisson
le vol
le décollage
l'atterrissage (m.)
le retard
les bagages (m.)
  à main
le tapis roulant
le chariot à bagages
l'aérogare (f.)
le terminal
l'autocar (m.),
  le car
le taxi

ADJECTIF
fatigué(e)

VERBES
embarquer
débarquer
piloter
annuler
distribuer
passer un film
récupérer les bagages

AUTRES MOTS
ET EXPRESSIONS

il est interdit de
plusieurs
malheureusement
sans escale

ANSWERS

Exercice A

1. Oui.
2. Non. (On ne doit pas faire enregistrer les petits bagages à main.)
3. Oui.
4. Oui.
5. Non. (Il faut obtenir un passeport avant d'aller à l'aéroport.)
6. Oui.
7. Oui.
8. Oui.
9. Non. (Avant un vol intérieur il faut passer par le contrôle de sécurité.)

Exercice B

1. Je les ai.
2. Tu les as?
3. Tu le vois?
4. Tu lui parles?
5. Oui, je lui parle.
6. Tu lui donnes ton billet?
7. Il le regarde?
8. Tu lui donnes ta valise?
9. Il la pèse.
10. À bord, tu leur parleras?
11. Tu leur parleras?
12. ... leur dira «bonjour»?
13. Tu lui montreras...
14. Il la regardera?

ASSESSMENT RESOURCES

1. Chapter Quizzes
2. Testing Program
3. Situation Cards
4. Communication Transparency C-7
5. Computer Software: Practice/Test Generator

VIDEO PROGRAM

INTRODUCTION   (27:58)

PHILIPPE ARRIVE DE   (28:31)
FORT-DE-FRANCE

STUDENT PORTFOLIO

Written assignments which may be included in students' portfolios are the *Activités de communication écrite* on page 184 and any writing activities from the *Un Peu Plus* section in the Workbook.

 Note Students may create and save both oral and written work using the Electronic Portfolio feature on the CD-ROM.

INDEPENDENT PRACTICE

Assign any of the following:
1. Activities and exercises, pages 184–185
2. Communication Activities Masters, pages 43–49
3. CD-ROM, Disc 2, pages 184–185

CHAPITRE 8

CHAPTER OVERVIEW

In this chapter students will learn to give directions to pedestrians and drivers. They will also learn vocabulary related to driving both on the open road and in the city. They will learn to use the future tense with *quand,* to form sentences with direct object pronouns and *lui* or *leur,* and to form adverbs.

The cultural focus of the chapters is on driving in France.

CHAPTER OBJECTIVES

By the end of this chapter, students will know:

1. vocabulary associated with road travel, various traffic situations, and pedestrian traffic
2. how to give and ask for directions and express location
3. the future tense of irregular verbs
4. the use of the future tense in complex sentences with *quand*
5. the use of *lui* and *leur* in sentences with direct object pronouns, in the present as well as in the *passé composé*
6. the formation of regular adverbs

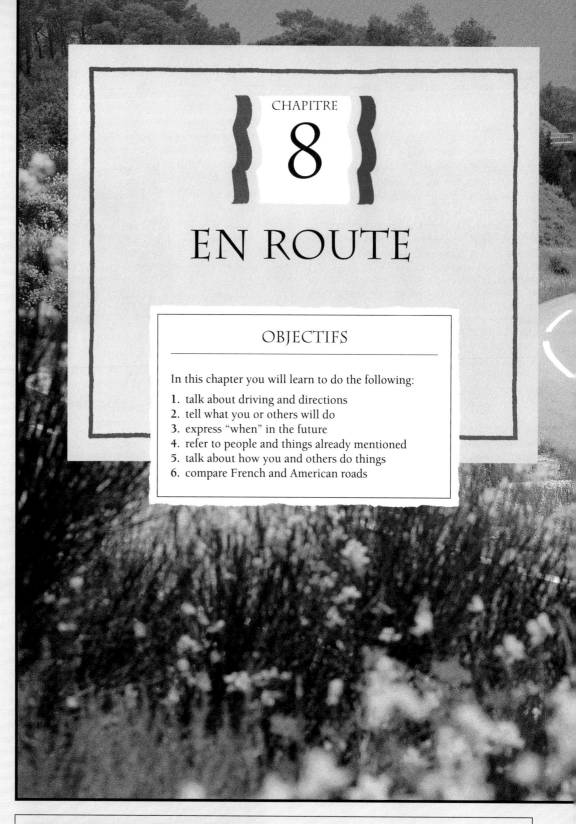

CHAPITRE
8

EN ROUTE

OBJECTIFS

In this chapter you will learn to do the following:

1. talk about driving and directions
2. tell what you or others will do
3. express "when" in the future
4. refer to people and things already mentioned
5. talk about how you and others do things
6. compare French and American roads

CHAPTER PROJECTS

(optional)

1. Have students do research on Brittany and give an oral report to the class. In their report, have them include some of the special characteristics of this region and its people.
2. Have students prepare a report on Breton *pardons.*
3. Have students prepare a report on the monuments of Carnac.
4. Have students do research on the Montmartre section of Paris and give an oral report to the class.

CHAPTER 8 RESOURCES

1. Workbook
2. Student Tape Manual
3. Audio Cassette 5B/CD-4
4. Bell Ringer Review Blackline Masters
5. Vocabulary Transparencies
6. Communication Transparency C-8
7. Communication Activities Masters
8. Situation Cards
9. Conversation Video
10. Videocassette/Videodisc, Unit 2
11. Video Activities Booklet, Unit 2
12. Lesson Plans
13. Computer Software: Practice/Test Generator
14. Chapter Quizzes
15. Testing Program
16. Internet Activities Booklet
17. CD-ROM Interactive Textbook
18. Map Transparencies
19. Performance Assessment

Pacing

This chapter will require eight to ten class sessions. Pacing will depend on the length of the class, and the age and aptitude of your students.

For more information on planning your class, see the Lesson Plans, which offer guidelines for 45- and 55-minute classes and **Block Scheduling**.

Exercices vs. *Activités*

The exercises and activities are color-coded. Exercises, which provide guided practice to prepare students for independent communication, are coded in blue. Communicative activities, which give students opportunities for creative, open-ended expression, are coded in red.

INTERDISCIPLINARY CONNECTIONS

Have students ask the Driver's Ed instructor at your school for a copy of the American and international pictograms for highways. Explain in French what the different international symbols mean. Have students find the equivalent American pictograms.

INTERNET ACTIVITIES

(optional)

These activities, student worksheets, and related teacher information are in the *À bord* Internet Activities Booklet and on the Glencoe Foreign Language Home Page at: **http://www.glencoe.com/secondary/fl**

MOTS 1

Bell Ringer Review

Write the following on the board or use BRR Blackline Master 8-1: Write the following words under the appropriate heading: *Le train* or *L'avion.*

le compartiment
la cabine
le contrôleur
le commandant de bord
le steward
la voiture gril-express
la ceinture de sécurité
le gilet de sauvetage
le poste de pilotage
l'aile
le quai
le coffre à bagages
la correspondance

PRESENTATION (pages 188–189)

A. Have students close their books. Show Vocabulary Transparencies 8.1 (A & B) and ask students to repeat the words, phrases, and sentences after you or Cassette 5B/CD-4.

B. You may wish to use toy cars to demonstrate *doubler, changer de voie, ralentir, accélérer, rouler vite.*

VOCABULAIRE

MOTS 1

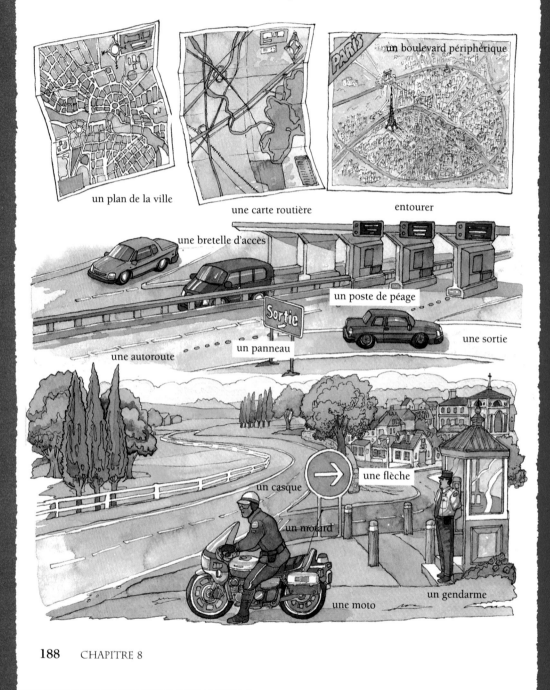

un boulevard périphérique
un plan de la ville
une carte routière
entourer
une bretelle d'accès
un poste de péage
une autoroute
un panneau
une sortie
un casque
une flèche
un motard
un gendarme
une moto

ADDITIONAL PRACTICE

After practicing the *Mots 1* vocabulary, write the following on the board or on a transparency and have students match each verb on the left with the corresponding noun on the right.

1. circuler	a. la sortie
2. limiter	b. le ralentissement
3. conduire	c. la conduite
4. sortir	d. la limite, la limitation
5. ralentir	e. la circulation

la circulation
un bouchon
une caravane
une file de voitures
un camion
une jeep
doubler
changer de voie
ralentir
accélérer
rouler vite

Les points noirs sont les endroits où il y a souvent de gros bouchons.

Les heures de pointe sont les heures où il y a beaucoup de circulation.

Quand il y a beaucoup de circulation il est impossible de rouler vite. Il y a des ralentissements.

Si un automobiliste roule trop vite, il aura une contravention (un P.V.).

S'il ne respecte pas la limitation de vitesse, le gendarme l'arrêtera.

Il lui demandera son permis de conduire et sa carte grise.

L'automobiliste paiera une amende.

Il ne pourra pas se tirer facilement de cette mauvaise situation.

CHAPITRE 8   **189**

C. After presenting the sentences on page 189, ask questions to elicit the vocabulary. For example: *Cette voiture double? Est-ce qu'elle accélère ou ralentit? Une caravane est plus grande qu'une voiture? Qu'est-ce que le motard porte sur la tête?*, etc.

D. After some practice, you may wish to vary the presentation by having students chant the following to a rap beat:
C'est le motard, le motard
C'est le motard qui a, qui a
C'est le motard qui a une moto, une moto
Ah oui, c'est le motard qui a une moto
Le motard, le motard
Repeat the stanza, changing *une moto* to *un casque*. Then:
C'est le panneau, le panneau
C'est le panneau qui a une flèche, une flèche
Ah oui, c'est le panneau qui a une flèche
Le panneau, le panneau

Vocabulary Expansion

You may wish to give students the following additional words:

un poids lourds	tractor-trailer, big rig
une camionnette	a van
un toit ouvrant	a sun roof
une berline	a sedan

CROSS-CULTURAL COMPARISON

La carte grise is a motor vehicle registration card. In France motor vehicle registration is renewed once a year as it is in the U.S. In France, however, you can buy your new registration sticker, *la vignette*, at a *bureau de tabac*.

Exercices

PRESENTATION (*pages 190–191*)

Exercice A

Exercise A is to be done with books open.

Extension of Exercice B

Exercise B requires only a *oui* or *non* answer. However, you may wish to have students correct the false statements in order for them to practice the new vocabulary as much as possible.

Exercice C

Exercise C can be done with books open or closed.

Exercice D

Have students scan the *Mots 1* vocabulary as they do Exercise D.

ANSWERS

Exercice A

1. C'est une route à quatre voies.
2. C'est une caravane.
3. Le gendarme est à pied.
4. C'est une carte routière.
5. Le panneau indique l'accès.
6. C'est un camion.
7. C'est un poste de péage.

Exercice B

1. Non. (Il y a une bretelle de sortie à la sortie de l'autoroute.)
2. Non. (Il faut changer de voie quand on va doubler.)
3. Oui.
4. Non. (Il y a des ralentissements quand il y a beaucoup de circulation.)
5. Non. (Il faut accélérer pour doubler une autre voiture.)
6. Oui.
7. Non. (Il faut ralentir ou s'arrêter quand on arrive à un croisement dangereux.)
8. Oui.
9. Oui.
10. Oui.

Exercices

A **Qu'est-ce que c'est?** Identifiez.

1. C'est une route à deux voies ou à quatre voies?
2. C'est un camion ou une caravane?

3. Le gendarme est à moto ou à pied?

4. C'est un plan de la ville ou une carte routière?

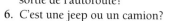

5. Le panneau indique l'accès ou la sortie de l'autoroute?
6. C'est une jeep ou un camion?

7. C'est un poste de péage ou une bretelle d'accès?

B **Sur la route.** Répondez par «oui» ou «non».

1. Il y a une bretelle d'accès à la sortie de l'autoroute?
2. Il est interdit de changer de voie quand on va doubler?
3. Quand il y a un bouchon, il y a beaucoup de circulation?
4. Il y a des ralentissements quand il y a très peu de circulation?
5. Il faut ralentir pour doubler une autre voiture?
6. Le motard surveille la circulation sur l'autoroute?
7. Il faut rouler vite et accélérer quand on arrive à un croisement dangereux?
8. Sur de nombreux panneaux il y a des flèches qui indiquent la direction (le sens) qu'on doit prendre?
9. Les boulevards périphériques entourent les grandes villes?
10. Quand il y a un gros bouchon, il y a une longue file de voitures?

C Sur l'autoroute. Répondez.

1. Il y a une autoroute près de chez toi?
2. C'est une autoroute à péage?
3. On paie le péage à la sortie de l'autoroute ou est-ce qu'il y a plusieurs postes de péage sur l'autoroute?
4. Sur l'autoroute y a-t-il des points noirs?
5. Quelles sont les heures de pointe dans ta ville?
6. Faut-il respecter la limitation de vitesse?
7. Si un automobiliste roule trop vite, est-ce que le gendarme l'arrêtera?
8. Qu'est-ce qu'il lui demandera?
9. Qu'est-ce qu'il lui donnera?
10. Qu'est-ce que l'automobiliste paiera?
11. Il pourra se tirer facilement de cette mauvaise situation?
12. Dans l'état où tu habites, est-ce que les motocyclistes sont obligés de porter un casque? Et les cyclistes?

D Des définitions. Donnez le mot ou l'expression convenable.

1. rouler moins vite
2. rouler plus vite
3. les heures où il y a beaucoup de circulation
4. les endroits où il y a beaucoup de circulation
5. ce qu'il y a à l'entrée de l'autoroute
6. passer d'une voie à une autre sur l'autoroute
7. dépasser une voiture qui roule dans le même sens
8. la personne qui surveille la circulation sur l'autoroute
9. le contraire de «permis», «autorisé»
10. celui qui conduit une voiture

CHAPITRE 8   **191**

Exercice C

1. Oui, il y a une autoroute près de chez moi. (Non, il n'y a pas d'autoroute...)
2. Oui, c'est une autoroute à péage. (Non, ce n'est pas une autoroute à péage.)
3. On paie le péage à la sortie de l'autoroute. (Il y a plusieurs postes de péage sur l'autoroute.)
4. Oui, sur l'autoroute il y a des points noirs. (Non, ... il n'y a pas de points noirs.)
5. Les heures de pointe dans ma ville sont (de sept heures à neuf heures du matin et de quatre heures et demie à sept heures du soir).
6. Oui, il faut respecter la limitation de vitesse.
7. Oui, si un automobiliste roule trop vite, le gendarme l'arrêtera.
8. Il lui demandera son permis de conduire et sa carte grise.
9. Il lui donnera une contravention.
10. L'automobiliste paiera une amende.
11. Non, il ne pourra pas se tirer facilement de cette mauvaise situation.
12. Oui, dans l'état où j'habite, les motocyclistes (les cyclistes) sont obligés de porter un casque. (Non, ... ne sont pas obligés de porter de casque.)

Exercice D

1. ralentir
2. accélérer
3. les heures de pointe
4. les points noirs
5. une bretelle d'accès
6. changer de voie
7. doubler
8. le motard, le gendarme
9. interdit
10. l'automobiliste

VOCABULAIRE

MOTS 2

Bell Ringer Review

Write the following on the board or use BRR Blackline Master 8-2: Write as many words and expressions as you can think of which have to do with giving directions.

PRESENTATION *(pages 192–193)*

A. Pointing to Vocabulary Transparencies 8.2 (A & B), have students repeat the words, phrases, and sentences after you or Cassette 5B/CD-4.

B. Use gestures and dramatizations to convey the meaning of *à droite, à gauche, devant, derrière, à côté de, tout droit, en face de, tourner,* and *faire demi-tour.*

COOPERATIVE LEARNING

Have students work in teams to practice giving directions in French to commonly known local places. Each team should choose one or two sets of directions to present to the class. The others guess where they are being directed.

ADDITIONAL PRACTICE

Student Tape Manual, Teacher's Edition, *Activité E,* page 81

Le feu va changer.
Quand le feu changera, les piétons pourront
    traverser la rue.

Elle ne sait pas y aller.
L'agent, lui, saura.
Si elle demande son chemin à l'agent,
    il pourra le lui indiquer.

un embouteillage

Les rues du centre-ville sont encombrées.

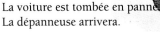

une dépanneuse

La voiture est tombée en panne.
La dépanneuse arrivera.

Note Ask students to say what other French word they see in the word *un embouteillage*. Tell students that the French use "bottle" imagery to describe traffic jams just as we do in English when we use the word "bottleneck." A traffic jam is also called *un bouchon*.

Teaching Tip You may wish to lead into the object pronoun grammar point of this chapter by calling students' attention to this sentence on page 193: *Si elle demande son chemin à l'agent, il pourra le lui indiquer.* Ask students which word is replaced by *le* and which by *lui*.

CRITICAL THINKING ACTIVITY

(*Thinking skills: evaluating consequences; problem-solving*)

Read the following to the class or write it on the board or on a transparency:

1. Expliquez en français pourquoi il est important de regarder à droite et à gauche avant de traverser la rue.
2. Qu'est-ce qu'on peut faire pour essayer d'éviter les embouteillages?

Exercices

PRESENTATION (pages 194–195)

Exercices A and B

Exercises A and B can be done with books either open or closed. After completing them, call on one student to retell the story of each exercise in his/her own words.

ANSWERS

Exercice A

1. Oui, les piétons attendent sur le trottoir.
2. Oui, ils attendent au coin de la rue.
3. Non, le feu est rouge.
4. Non, les piétons ne peuvent pas traverser la rue.
5. Oui, le feu changera.
6. Oui, les piétons pourront traverser la rue.
7. Oui, ils pourront traverser quand le feu changera.
8. Oui, ils devront traverser dans le passage pour piétons.
9. Oui, l'agent de police règle la circulation. Oui, il porte une casquette.
10. Oui, les rues du centre-ville sont encombrées.
11. Oui, une voiture est tombée en panne.
12. Oui, la dépanneuse arrivera.

Exercice B

1. Il va dans le mauvais sens.
2. Il doit faire demi-tour.
3. Il doit aller tout droit.
4. Il doit aller tout droit jusqu'au troisième croisement.
5. Il y a un stop là.
6. Au stop il doit tourner à gauche.
7. Oui, s'il demande son chemin à l'agent, l'agent saura le lui indiquer.

Exercices

A À pied en ville. Répondez.

1. Les piétons attendent sur le trottoir?
2. Ils attendent au coin de la rue?
3. Le feu est vert?
4. Les piétons peuvent traverser la rue?
5. Le feu changera?
6. Les piétons pourront traverser la rue?
7. Ils pourront traverser quand le feu changera?
8. Ils devront traverser dans le passage pour piétons?
9. L'agent de police règle la circulation? Il porte une casquette?
10. Les rues du centre-ville sont encombrées?
11. Une voiture est tombée en panne?
12. La dépanneuse arrivera?

B C'est le mauvais sens. Répondez d'après les indications.

1. Il va dans le bon sens ou dans le mauvais sens? (le mauvais sens)
2. Il doit doubler ou faire demi-tour? (faire demi-tour)
3. Et alors il doit aller tout droit ou tourner à droite? (aller tout droit)
4. Il doit aller tout droit jusqu'où? (jusqu'au troisième croisement)
5. Qu'est-ce qu'il y a là? (un stop)
6. Au stop il doit tourner dans quel sens? (à gauche)
7. S'il demande son chemin à l'agent, l'agent saura le lui indiquer?

L'Opéra de Paris: le palais Garnier

C **Où est le café?** Repondez d'après le dessin.

1. Le café est à droite ou à gauche du théâtre?
2. Le cinéma est à côté du restaurant ou derrière le restaurant?
3. Le parc est à côté du restaurant ou en face du café?
4. La voiture est garée devant l'école ou derrière l'école?
5. Le cinéma est derrière le théâtre ou en face du théâtre?

Activités de communication orale
Mots 1 et 2

A **Qu'est-ce que c'est?** Décrivez à un(e) camarade un objet ou une personne qu'on trouve d'habitude dans la rue ou sur la route. Il/Elle l'identifiera.

> Élève 1: Cette personne surveille la circulation.
> Élève 2: C'est un gendarme.

B **Une soirée.** Vous organisez une fête chez vous pour votre anniversaire. Téléphonez à un(e) camarade pour l'inviter à la fête. Indiquez-lui le chemin. Votre camarade prendra des notes et vous les relira pour être sûr(e) qu'il/elle ne s'est pas trompé(e).

C **Votre ville…** Michel Passavant, un ami français, veut savoir si vous savez conduire et comment est la circulation dans votre ville. Répondez à ses questions.

Michel Passavant

1. Tu as ton permis de conduire?
2. Tu as une voiture?
3. Où sont les points noirs dans ta ville?
4. Quelles sont les heures de pointe?
5. Il est difficile de circuler dans ta ville?

CHAPITRE 8 **195**

STRUCTURE

Structure Teaching Resources

1. Workbook, *Structure: A–F*, pages 87–89
2. Student Tape Manual, Teacher's Edition, *Structure: A–B*, pages 83–84
3. Audio Cassette 5B/CD-4
4. Communication Activities Masters, *Structure: A–D*, pages 52–54
5. Computer Software, *Structure*
6. Chapter Quizzes, *Structure:* Quizzes 3–6, pages 41–44
7. CD-ROM, Disc 2, pages 196–201

Le futur des verbes irréguliers

PRESENTATION *(page 196)*

Guide students through the explanation and have them repeat the verb forms after you.

Exercices

ANSWERS

Exercice A

1. Oui (Non), on (n')ira (pas)...
2. Oui (Non), on (ne) pourra (pas) prendre le train.
3. Oui (Non), on (n')ira (pas) à Notre-Dame.
4. Oui (Non), on (n')y verra (pas) des (de) gargouilles...
5. Oui (Non), on (ne) voudra (pas) dîner en ville.
6. Oui (Non), ils (ne) pourront (pas) aller sans veste...
7. Oui (Non), on (ne) devra (pas) téléphoner...
8. Oui (Non), on (ne) saura (pas) comment aller...
9. Oui (Non), on (n')aura (pas) un (de) dessert super...
10. Oui (Non), on (ne) pourra (pas) payer l'addition...

STRUCTURE

Le futur des verbes irréguliers — *Telling What You or Others Will Do*

Some verbs have an irregular stem for the formation of the future tense. Study the following.

INFINITIVE	STEM	FUTURE
avoir	aur-	j' aurai
savoir	saur-	je saurai
voir	verr-	je verrai
envoyer	enverr-	j' enverrai
pouvoir	pourr-	je pourrai
devoir	devr-	je devrai
recevoir	recevr-	je recevrai
vouloir	voudr-	je voudrai
venir	viendr-	je viendrai

Exercices

A **On ira en ville.** Répondez.

1. On ira en ville la semaine prochaine?
2. On pourra prendre le train?
3. On ira à Notre-Dame?
4. On y verra des gargouilles fantastiques?
5. On voudra dîner en ville?
6. Les garçons pourront aller sans veste au restaurant?
7. On devra téléphoner à l'avance pour réserver?
8. On saura comment aller au restaurant?
9. On aura un dessert super dans ce restaurant?
10. On pourra payer l'addition par chèque?

B **Pauline ne sera pas très contente.** Répondez.

1. L'année prochaine, Pauline recevra de mauvaises notes?
2. Elle voudra les voir?
3. Elle sera contente quand elle verra ses mauvaises notes?
4. Elle voudra les montrer à ses parents?
5. Ses parents seront fâchés quand ils les verront?
6. Elle leur montrera ses notes?
7. Pauline pourra sortir avec ses copains?

LEARNING FROM PHOTOS

Ask students what this is. Some may not realize it is one of the *gargouilles* (Ex. A, item 4) found on the roof of Notre-Dame. You may wish to tell the class that gargoyles serve as rainspouts on Gothic cathedrals and are often in the form of fantastical or grotesque creatures.

C **Tu voudras lui organiser une surprise-partie?** Répondez.

1. Tu voudras organiser une surprise-partie pour l'anniversaire d'Émilie?
2. Tu enverras des invitations à tous ses amis?
3. Tu leur enverras les invitations demain?
4. Tous ses amis pourront aller à la fête?
5. Ils viendront tous avec des cadeaux?
6. Émilie recevra beaucoup de cadeaux?
7. Elle sera surprise quand elle verra ses amis?

D **Tu sais ce que tu vas faire?** Répétez la petite conversation.

GUY: Qu'est-ce que tu vas faire demain?
LUC: Je crois que je vais aller à la piscine.
GUY: Tu vas y aller tout seul ou avec ta petite amie?
LUC: Je vais le savoir plus tard. Je vais te donner un coup de fil.

Maintenant répétez la conversation en mettant les verbes au futur.

E **Vous irez à Nantes l'année prochaine?** Mettez au futur les verbes indiqués.

Vous allez à Nantes? Je vous ___ (dire) ce que vous ___ (pouvoir) faire pour
y arriver vite. Vous ___ (prendre) l'A11. Pour quitter la ville vous ___
(prendre) le Boulevard Raspail jusqu'à la Place Denfert-Rochereau. Vous ___
(traverser) la place et vous ___ (continuer) tout droit. Il y a quelques feux
avant d'arriver au Boulevard Périphérique. Vous ne ___ (prendre) pas le
Boulevard Périphérique. Vous ___ (continuer) tout droit et vous ___ (voir) un
panneau qui indique Chartres.
C'est l'A11. Vous ___ (passer) par
Chartres et vous ___ (continuer)
sur l'A11 jusqu'au Mans. Vous ___
(sortir) au Mans et là vous ___
(voir) un panneau qui indique la
N23. Vous ___ (prendre) la N23
jusqu'à Nantes. Je ne sais pas si vous
___ (avoir) le temps, mais vous
devez vous arrêter quelques minutes
pour voir Angers. La N23 passe par
Angers.

Exercice B
1. Oui, elle recevra...
2. Non, elle ne voudra pas...
3. Non, elle ne sera pas contente...
4. Non, elle ne voudra pas...
5. Oui, ils seront fâchés quand ils les verront.
6. Oui, elle leur montrera...
7. Non, elle ne pourra pas sortir avec ses copains.

Exercice C
1. Oui, je voudrai organiser une surprise-partie pour l'anniversaire d'Émilie. (Non, je ne voudrai pas organiser...)
2. Oui, j'enverrai des invitations à tous ses amis. (Non, je n'enverrai pas d'...)
3. Oui, je leur enverrai les invitations demain. (Non, je ne leur enverrai pas les...)
4. Oui, tous ses amis pourront aller à la fête. (Non, tous ses amis ne pourront pas aller...)
5. Oui, ils viendront tous avec des cadeaux. (Non, ils ne viendront pas tous...)
6. Oui, Émilie recevra beaucoup de cadeaux. (Non, Émilie ne recevra pas...)
7. Oui, elle sera surprise quand elle verra ses amis. (Non, elle ne sera pas surprise...)

Exercice D
Guy: Qu'est-ce que tu feras demain?
Luc: Je crois que j'irai à la piscine.
Guy: Tu y iras tout seul ou avec ta petite amie?
Luc: Je le saurai plus tard. Je te donnerai un coup de fil.

Exercice E
1. dirai
2. pourrez
3. prendrez
4. prendrez
5. traverserez
6. continuerez
7. prendrez
8. continuerez
9. verrez
10. passerez
11. continuerez
12. sortirez
13. verrez
14. prendrez
15. aurez

INDEPENDENT PRACTICE

Assign any of the following:
1. Exercises, pages 196–197
2. Workbook, *Structure: A–C,* pages 87–88
3. Communication Activities Masters, *Structure: A,* page 52
4. CD-ROM, Disc 2, pages 196–197

Le futur après quand

PRESENTATION   *(page 198)*
    Guide students through the explanation and provide and elicit additional examples.

Exercices

PRESENTATION   *(pages 198–199)*
Exercices A, B, and C
    Exercises A and C are to be done with books open. Exercise B can be done with books either open or closed.
Exercices B and C
    Point out that *acheter* is slightly irregular in the future with its *accent grave* in the second syllable.

ANSWERS
Exercice A
1. ... le feu changera.
2. ... le feu sera rouge.
3. ... les voitures s'arrêteront.
4. ... l'agent de police leur indiquera qu'ils pourront traverser.

Exercice B
1. Oui, je serai content(e) quand j'aurai mon permis de conduire. (Non, je ne serai pas content[e] quand j'aurai...)
2. J'aurai mon permis de conduire quand j'aurai (16) ans.
3. Oui, je saurai conduire quand je recevrai mon permis.
4. Oui, j'achèterai une voiture quand j'aurai assez d'argent. (Non, je n'achèterai pas de...)
5. Oui, je ferai de longs voyages quand j'aurai ma nouvelle voiture. (Non, je ne ferai pas de longs voyages...)

Montmartre: la basilique du Sacré-Cœur et la Place du Tertre

Le futur après *quand*   *Expressing "When" in the Future*

When the verb in the main clause is in the future, the verb in the clause introduced by *quand* must also be in the future. In English you use the present tense, but in French you always use the future.

> **Nous partirons quand ils arriveront.**
> **Quand elle ira à Paris elle visitera le Sacré-Cœur.**

Exercices

A **Les piétons traverseront la rue quand?**   Complétez la phrase.

   Les piétons traverseront la rue quand...

1. Le feu change.   3. Les voitures s'arrêtent.
2. Le feu est rouge.   4. L'agent de police leur indique qu'ils peuvent traverser.

B **Un jour j'aurai mon permis de conduire.**   Donnez des réponses personnelles.

1. Tu seras content(e) quand tu auras ton permis de conduire?
2. Tu auras ton permis de conduire quand tu auras quel âge?
3. Tu sauras conduire quand tu recevras ton permis?
4. Tu achèteras une voiture quand tu auras assez d'argent?
5. Tu feras de longs voyages quand tu auras ta nouvelle voiture?

198   CHAPITRE 8

ADDITIONAL PRACTICE

1. After completing Exercises A, B, and C, have students write five sentences beginning with: *Quand je serai adulte...*
2. Student Tape Manual, Teacher's Edition, *Activité A,* page 83

DID YOU KNOW?

    You may wish to tell students that throughout the nineteenth century, Montmartre was a favorite gathering place for many writers, artists, and musicians including Berlioz, Toulouse-Lautrec, and Nerval. Today, artists still gather in the Place du Tertre adjacent to the Sacré-Cœur to paint portraits and sell their works.

C Quand j'aurai de l'argent. Faites des phrases d'après le modèle.

> avoir de l'argent / acheter quelque chose
> *Quand j'aurai de l'argent, j'achèterai quelque chose.*

1. avoir assez d'argent / acheter une voiture
2. avoir mon permis de conduire / faire des voyages en voiture
3. être sur l'autoroute / faire attention aux panneaux routiers
4. savoir conduire / conduire prudemment
5. voir un motard / ralentir

Deux pronoms dans la même phrase: *le, la, les* avec *lui, leur*

Referring to People and Things Already Mentioned

1. You have already seen that *me, te, nous,* and *vous* can be used with the direct object pronouns *le, la,* and *les.* You can also use *lui* and *leur* with *le, la,* and *les.* Note, however, that the order is different. Study the following.

Je donne *le* plan à Jean.	Je *le lui* donne.
Je donne *la* carte routière à Marie.	Je *la lui* donne.
Je donne *les* clés à Marie.	Je *les lui* donne.
J'ai donné *le* plan aux copains.	Je *le leur* ai donné.
J'ai donné *la* carte routière aux copains.	Je *la leur* ai donnée.
J'ai donné *les* clés aux copains.	Je *les leur* ai données.

2. Note that *le, la,* and *les* come before *lui* and *leur.*

(ne)	*before*	le la les	*before*	lui leur	*before*	verbe	(pas)

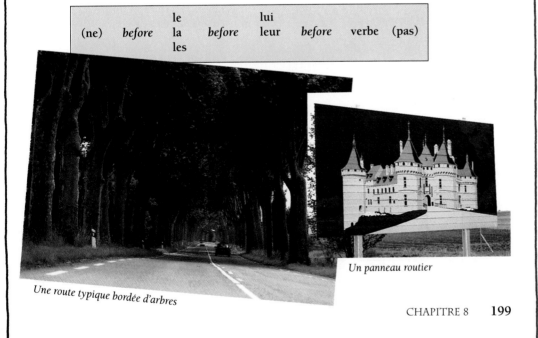

Un panneau routier

Une route typique bordée d'arbres

CHAPITRE 8   **199**

Exercices

ANSWERS

Exercice A

1. Oui, Martin la lui donnera.
2. Oui, il la lui écrira.
3. Oui, il la leur donnera.
4. Oui, il la leur lira.
5. Oui, il la leur lira en anglais (en français).

Exercice B

1. Oui, je le lui ai donné.
2. Oui, je le lui ai donné.
3. Oui, je les lui ai donnés.
4. Oui, je la lui ai donnée.
5. Oui, je les leur ai données.
6. Oui, je les leur ai donnés.
7. Oui, je les leur ai donnés.
8. Oui, je le leur ai donné.

Exercice C

1. Non, je ne le lui ai pas lu.
2. Non, je ne le lui ai pas vendu.
3. Non, je ne la lui ai pas expliquée.
4. Non, je ne la leur ai pas écrite.
5. Non, je ne les lui ai pas montrées.
6. Non, je ne les lui ai pas envoyés.

La formation des adverbes

Exercices

A Martin la lui donnera, j'en suis certain.
Répondez en utilisant des pronoms.

1. Martin lui donnera l'adresse?
2. Il lui écrira l'adresse?
3. Et il donnera l'adresse à ses amis?
4. Il leur lira l'adresse?
5. Il leur lira l'adresse en anglais ou en français?

B Que tu es généreux! Répondez d'après le modèle en utilisant des pronoms.

> Les billets d'avion? Tu les as donnés à Michèle?
> *Oui, je les lui ai donnés.*

1. Le téléphone sans fil? Tu l'as donné à Lucien?
2. Le téléviseur? Tu l'as donné à Monique?
3. Les disques? Tu les as donnés à Dominique?
4. La guitare? Tu l'as donnée à Philippe?
5. Les cassettes? Tu les as données à tes amis?
6. Les livres? Tu les as donnés à tes cousins?
7. Les timbres? Tu les as donnés à tes cousines?
8. L'ordinateur? Tu l'as donné à tes frères?

C Non! Répondez d'après le modèle en utilisant des pronoms.

> Tu as donné les cassettes à Jean-Paul?
> *Non, je ne les lui ai pas données.*

1. Tu as lu le livre au petit enfant?
2. Tu as vendu le magnétophone à Annette?
3. Tu as expliqué la pièce à Paul?
4. Tu as écrit la lettre à tes parents?
5. Tu as montré les cartes routières à Claudine?
6. Tu as envoyé les livres à Luc?

La formation des adverbes

Talking About How You and Others Do Things

---

1. You form most adverbs in French by adding *-ment* to the feminine form of the adjective. Study the following.

MASCULIN	FÉMININ	ADVERBE
certain	certaine	certainement
complet	complète	complètement
annuel	annuelle	annuellement
sérieux	sérieuse	sérieusement

2. However, if the masculine form of the adjective ends in a vowel, you add -ment to the masculine form.

MASCULIN	ADVERBE
poli	poliment
vrai	vraiment
absolu	absolument

3. Note the spelling of the adverbial form of adjectives that end in -ent or -ant.

évident	évidemment
prudent	prudemment
courant	couramment

Exercices

A **Un cours de conduite.** Répondez d'après les indications.

1. Il a suivi un cours de conduite? (certainement)
2. Quand l'a-t-il suivi? (récemment)
3. Il a beaucoup appris? (évidemment)
4. Avant de suivre le cours, comment conduisait-il? (dangereusement)
5. Comment conduit-il maintenant? (prudemment)

B **Quel est l'adverbe?** Pour chaque adjectif, donnez l'adverbe et faites une phrase avec cet adverbe.

1. heureux
2. certain
3. poli
4. direct
5. constant
6. fréquent
7. sérieux
8. correct
9. parfait
10. vrai

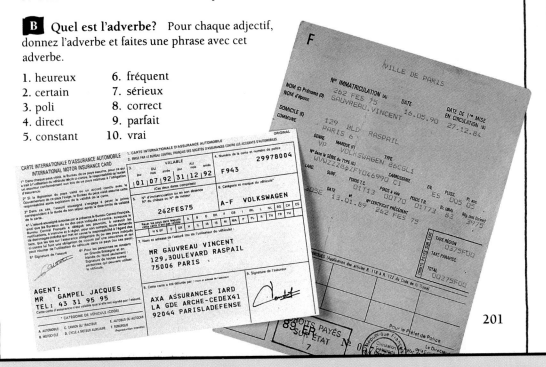

201

PRESENTATION *(page 201)*

Exercices A and B

Exercises A and B can be done with books either open or closed.

ANSWERS

Exercice A

1. Oui, il a certainement suivi un cours de conduite.
2. Il l'a suivi récemment.
3. Oui, évidemment il a beaucoup appris.
4. Avant de suivre le cours, il conduisait dangereusement.
5. Il conduit prudemment maintenant.

Exercice B

Sentences will vary. Adverb formation is as follows:

1. heureusement
2. certainement
3. poliment
4. directement
5. constamment
6. fréquemment
7. sérieusement
8. correctement
9. parfaitement
10. vraiment

LEARNING FROM REALIA	INDEPENDENT PRACTICE

LEARNING FROM REALIA

1. Ask students what these documents are. Who should have them? Where should they be kept? (*dans la voiture, dans la boîte à gants*)
2. Ask the following questions about the realia: *Où habite Vincent Gauvreau? Il a quelle marque de voiture? Quel est le numéro de sa plaque d'immatriculation? Sa voiture est assurée? Comment s'appelle son agent?*

INDEPENDENT PRACTICE

Assign any of the following:

1. Exercises, pages 200–201
2. Workbook, *Structure: F,* page 89
3. Communication Activities Masters, *Structure: D,* page 54
4. Computer Software, *Structure*
5. CD-ROM, Disc 2, pages 200–201

CONVERSATION

Bell Ringer Review

Write the following on the board or use BRR Blackline Master 8-6: Fill in the blanks with *qui* or *que.*

1. Je connais le garçon _____ travaille au supermarché.
2. Il a une voiture _____ j'aime beaucoup.
3. C'est la voiture _____ est devant sa maison.
4. Voilà le garçon _____ je connais.
5. C'est le garçon _____ a les cheveux roux.

PRESENTATION *(page 202)*

A. Tell students they will hear a conversation in which a person asks directions.
B. Have students close their books. Play the Conversation Video or have them listen as you read the conversation or play Cassette 5B/CD-4.
C. Have students practice reading the conversation in pairs with as much expression as possible. (Use *Activité D* in the Student Tape Manual to check oral comprehension.)
D. As pairs present the conversation to the class, have a third student act out the directions given.

Note In the CD-ROM version, students can play the role of either one of the characters and record the conversation.

ANSWERS

Exercice A

1. Michel cherche l'Hôtel François 1er.
2. Il va dans le mauvais sens.
3. Il faut faire demi-tour.
4. L'Hôtel François 1er est sur la place François 1er.
5. Non, Michel ne le sait pas.

Scènes de la vie   *Je vais dans le bon sens?*

MICHEL: Pardon, Mademoiselle. L'Hôtel François 1er, c'est bien par là?
UNE FILLE: L'Hôtel François 1er? C'est sur la place François 1er.
MICHEL: Je m'excuse, Mademoiselle, mais je ne suis pas d'ici. Où est la place François 1er, s'il vous plaît?
LA FILLE: Vous allez dans le mauvais sens. Il faut faire demi-tour. Allez tout droit, et à la quatrième rue tournez à gauche. Continuez tout droit jusqu'au premier feu. Au feu tournez à droite. C'est la place François 1er et à cent mètres à gauche vous verrez l'hôtel.

A **Il demande son chemin.**   Répondez d'après la conversation.

1. Michel cherche quel hôtel?
2. Il va dans le bons sens ou dans le mauvais sens?
3. Qu'est-ce qu'il faut faire?
4. L'Hôtel François 1er est dans quelle rue?
5. Michel sait où est la place François 1er?
6. Il demande son chemin à une fille?
7. Elle le lui indique?
8. Il doit aller tout droit jusqu'à quelle rue?
9. Alors il doit tourner à droite ou à gauche?
10. Il doit continuer jusqu'où?
11. Au feu il doit tourner à gauche ou à droite?
12. L'hôtel sera à gauche ou à droite?

COGNAC

HÔTEL *** NN

FRANÇOIS 1er

EL FRANÇOIS 1er

3 place François 1er
16100 COGNAC
Tél. 45 32 07 18

DID YOU KNOW?

François 1er, King of France from 1515 to 1547, was born in Cognac in 1494 in the Château des Valois, which can still be visited today.

Activités de communication orale

A **Le plan de Paris.** Vous êtes Place de la Concorde à Paris. Regardez le plan à la page 436 et choisissez un monument (un musée, un parc, etc.) que vous voulez visiter. Dites à votre camarade le chemin que vous allez prendre et il/elle devinera où vous voulez aller.

> Élève 1: Je quitte la Place de la Concorde et je traverse le pont. Je tourne à gauche sur le quai d'Orsay et je continue tout droit.
> Élève 2: Tu vas au Musée d'Orsay, n'est-ce pas?

B **Vendeur de voitures.** Vous êtes vendeur/vendeuse de voitures. Un des clients suivants (votre camarade) veut acheter un véhicule et ne sait pas quel type de véhicule choisir—une jeep, un camion, une caravane, une moto, une décapotable, une voiture de sport ou un break. Posez des questions à votre client(e) pour l'aider à faire son choix. Changez ensuite de rôles.

CLIENTS
un(e) étudiant(e)
un homme de 40 ans avec six enfants
un jeune couple
un(e) lycéen(ne)
une vieille dame

une vieille dame

> Élève 1: Vous voulez une petite voiture ou une grande voiture?
> Élève 2: Une petite voiture qui roule vite.
> Élève 1: Ah bon? Alors, je vous propose de choisir une jeep.

Paris: Place de la Concorde

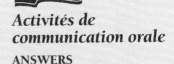

6. Oui, il demande son chemin à une fille.
7. Oui, elle le lui indique.
8. Il doit aller tout droit jusqu'à la quatrième rue.
9. Il doit tourner à gauche.
10. Il doit continuer jusqu'au premier feu.
11. Au feu il doit tourner à droite.
12. L'hôtel sera à gauche.

Bell Ringer Review

Write the following on the board or use BRR Blackline Master 8-7: Complete the sentences with the future tense of the indicated verbs.

1. L'année prochaine, ma famille ____ un voyage à Montréal. (faire)
2. Nous ____ en avion. (aller)
3. Mes parents ____ à tous les musées. (aller)
4. Moi, je ____ des achats. (faire)
5. Le voyage ____ fantastique. (être)

Activités de communication orale

ANSWERS

Activités A and B
Answers will vary.

INDEPENDENT PRACTICE

Assign any of the following:
1. Exercise and activities, pages 202–203
2. CD-ROM, Disc 2, pages 202–203

LECTURE ET CULTURE

LECTURE ET CULTURE

Bell Ringer Review

Write the following on the board or use BRR Blackline Master 8-8: You are working for Air France and have been assigned to train new flight attendants. Write five things you would tell them. Example: **Montrez les sorties de secours aux passagers.**

READING STRATEGIES
(*pages 204–205*)

Pre-reading

Ask students to tell what they already know about *le Mont-Saint-Michel* and *la Bretagne*.

Reading

Select some paragraphs of the reading and go over them thoroughly by reading aloud and asking your own comprehension questions. Allow students to read other paragraphs silently and come up with their own questions.

Post-reading

Have students pretend they have just visited Rennes and Mont-Saint-Michel, and have them write a postcard in French describing their experience.

Note Students may listen to a recorded version of the *Lecture* on the CD-ROM.

VOYAGE AU MONT-SAINT-MICHEL

*J'*aime bien la France. Quand je te dirai ce que j'y fais, tu sauras pourquoi je l'aime tellement. J'en suis sûr.

L'autre jour j'avais un peu faim et je suis allé dans un petit café pour manger quelque chose. À la table d'à côté il y avait un jeune couple français. Ils ont remarqué (vu) que j'avais un petit drapeau[1] américain sur mon sac à dos. Ils m'ont demandé si j'étais américain.

Quand je leur ai dit que oui, ils ont commencé à me parler parce qu'ils voulaient parler anglais. Ils m'ont demandé ce que je faisais en France. Je leur ai répondu que j'avais envie de voir tout le pays et que le lendemain[2] je partais pour Rennes, en Bretagne. Quelle coïncidence! Eux aussi, ils allaient à Rennes pour rendre visite à leurs parents. Ils y allaient en voiture et ils m'ont invité à les accompagner. C'était vraiment sympa de leur part. Pendant tout le voyage nous avons beaucoup parlé—en anglais et en français. Eux, ils voulaient améliorer[3] leur anglais et moi, je voulais améliorer mon français.

Après deux heures de route, ils se sont arrêtés pour faire le plein. Ils m'ont invité à prendre quelque chose au restoroute. J'ai proposé de payer mais ils

---
[1] drapeau   *flag*
[2] le lendemain   *the next day*
[3] améliorer   *to improve*

Un restoroute près de Beaune, en Bourgogne

Rennes: la Place de la Mairie

DID YOU KNOW?

A week-long fire in 1720 destroyed half of Rennes. Hence, the older sections with cobblestoned streets and 15th-century houses like the ones pictured here differ from the more modern architecture of the rebuilt sections of the city. Rennes was also badly damaged by bombings in World War II.

Une vue aérienne du Mont-Saint-Michel

magnifiques. De l'abbaye et du haut des remparts, il y a une vue incroyable.

Demain Raoul et moi irons à La Baule. La Baule est une grande station balnéaire sur la côte sud de la Bretagne. Là nous ferons du camping. Moi, j'ai un sac de couchage[6] et Raoul va s'en acheter un. À La Baule on pourra se baigner[7] s'il ne pleut pas. Mais je sais qu'en Bretagne il pleut souvent. Zut! Qu'est-ce que je ferai s'il pleut, moi qui vais dormir à la belle étoile (en plein air) dans mon sac de couchage? Ça m'est égal. De toute façon je m'amuserai, même si je suis un peu mouillé.

Oui, je m'amuserai. Voilà pourquoi j'aime tellement la France. Je rencontre des tas de gens qui viennent de pays différents avec des cultures différentes: des Tunisiens, des Marocains, des Ivoiriens (de la Côte d'Ivoire), des Sénégalais. Je parle une autre langue, je visite des villes superbes, de charmants villages et des sites historiques et pittoresques.

Tu iras un jour en France? Quand tu viendras ici, tu verras. Tu sauras pourquoi j'aime tellement ce pays. Tu l'aimeras aussi, je t'assure.

n'ont pas voulu. Je sais que je me suis fait de très bons amis et je suis certain qu'on se reverra, en France ou en Amérique.

De Rennes j'ai pris le car pour le Mont-Saint-Michel. J'ai passé la nuit dans une auberge de jeunesse[4] où j'ai rencontré Raoul Castellar, un étudiant martiniquais. Aujourd'hui Raoul et moi visitons le Mont-Saint-Michel. C'est très impressionnant! Je ne sais pas comment te le décrire. C'est un îlot, une petite île, mais pas vraiment. Ça dépend de la marée[5]. Quand la marée est haute, le Mont-Saint-Michel est entouré d'eau. Mais quand la marée est basse, la baie est presque à sec et on peut arriver au Mont-Saint-Michel à pied ou en voiture. En haut du mont il y a une abbaye superbe. Et les vieux remparts sont

La Baule en Bretagne

---

[4] une auberge de jeunesse *a youth hostel*
[5] la marée *the tide*
[6] un sac de couchage *a sleeping bag*
[7] se baigner *to swim*

CHAPITRE 8 **205**

Étude de mots

ANSWERS

Exercice A

1. d   5. a
2. f   6. c
3. b   7. e
4. g

Compréhension

PRESENTATION *(page 206)*

Exercice B

You may wish to ask these questions as students read the *Lecture*.

Exercice C

Students can either scan the *Lecture* for the answers to these questions or you may challenge them to answer from memory in their own words.

ANSWERS

Exercice B

1. Le jeune homme est allé au café parce qu'il avait un peu faim.
2. Un jeune couple français était à la table d'à côté.
3. Ils ont commencé à parler anglais au jeune homme parce qu'ils ont remarqué qu'il avait un petit drapeau américain sur son sac à dos (parce qu'ils voulaient parler anglais).
4. Le jeune homme allait à Rennes (en Bretagne) le lendemain.
5. Le jeune couple allait à Rennes aussi.
6. Ils y allaient pour rendre visite à leurs parents.
7. Le jeune homme est descendu à Rennes.
8. Il est allé au Mont-Saint-Michel.
9. Il y est arrivé en car.
10. Le jeune homme a passé la nuit dans une auberge de jeunesse.
11. Il a rencontré Raoul Castellar, un étudiant martiniquais.
12. Ils ont visité le Mont-Saint-Michel.
13. Ils iront à La Baule.
14. Oui, ils feront du camping.
15. Oui, ils se baigneront à La Baule s'il ne pleut pas.

206

Étude de mots

A **Quelle est la définition?** Trouvez le mot ou l'expression qui correspond.

1. un couple	a. un monastère
2. faire le plein	b. un petit hôtel
3. une auberge	c. un restaurant sur l'autoroute
4. un îlot	d. un homme et une femme
5. une abbaye	e. j'avais envie
6. un restoroute	f. mettre de l'essence dans le réservoir
7. je voulais	g. une petite île

Compréhension

B **Vous avez compris?** Répondez d'après la lecture.

1. Pourquoi le jeune homme est-il allé au café?
2. Qui était à la table d'à côté?
3. Pourquoi ont-ils commencé à parler anglais au jeune homme?
4. Où allait le jeune homme le lendemain?
5. Où allait le jeune couple?
6. Pour quoi faire?
7. Où est descendu le jeune homme?
8. Où est-il allé après Rennes?
9. Comment y est-il arrivé?
10. Où le jeune homme a-t-il passé la nuit?
11. Qui a-t-il rencontré?
12. Qu'est-ce qu'ils ont visité?
13. Où iront-ils demain?
14. Ils feront du camping?
15. Ils se baigneront à La Baule?

C **Des renseignements.** Répondez d'après la lecture.

1. Qu'est-ce que le Mont-Saint-Michel?
2. Qu'est-ce qu'il y a au Mont-Saint-Michel?
3. Où est le Mont-Saint-Michel?
4. Qu'est-ce que La Baule?
5. Où est La Baule?
6. Quel temps fait-il souvent en Bretagne?

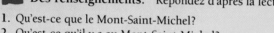

INDEPENDENT PRACTICE

Assign any of the following:
1. *Étude de mots* and *Compréhension* exercises, page 206
2. Workbook, *Un Peu Plus*, pages 90–93
3. CD-ROM, Disc 2, pages 204–206

DID YOU KNOW?

1. You may wish to tell students the following about the photo on page 207: *Le Périgord est connu pour son art préhistorique. La célèbre grotte de Lascaux se trouve dans cette région.*
2. Ask students why they think the hotel in the top photo is called *Hôtel Cro-Magnon*.

DÉCOUVERTE CULTURELLE

En France le réseau (système) routier est excellent. Il y a de grandes autoroutes à péage. Si vous regardez une carte routière de la France vous verrez:

A   Autoroute, presque toujours à péage

N   Route Nationale, c'est une route à grande circulation

D   Route départementale

V   Chemin vicinal (rural), ce sont de petits chemins qui relient des villages. Ils sont souvent très pittoresques.

Vous parlez à quelqu'un en France et vous voulez dire «thruway» ou «freeway». Vous allez choisir quel mot en français? Exprimez les idées suivantes en français—*interstate, county road, country road.*

Le camping est assez populaire en France. En France il y a beaucoup de terrains de camping. Si le camping vous intéresse, vous pourrez vous adresser au Touring Club de France. On vous enverra la brochure «Indicateur du camping-caravaning».

© MICHELIN, Map No 63 Vannes/La Baule/Angers, édition 1992. Permission No. 9611564

Un camping dans le Périgord

---

1. Le Mont-Saint-Michel est un îlot.
2. Il y a une abbaye superbe en haut du mont.
3. Le Mont-Saint-Michel se trouve en Bretagne.
4. La Baule est une grande station balnéaire.
5. La Baule se trouve sur la côte sud de la Bretagne.
6. Il pleut souvent en Bretagne.

Bell Ringer Review

Write the following on the board or use BRR Blackline Master 8-9: Write three facts about Martinique.

OPTIONAL MATERIAL

Découverte culturelle

PRESENTATION (*page 207*)

A. Focus on the topic by discussing road trips you or students have taken.

B. Have students look at the French road map on page 212 and point out the N and D routes to them.

C. Have the students read the selection silently.

Note Students may listen to a recorded version of the *Découverte culturelle* on the CD-ROM.

LEARNING FROM PHOTOS

Have students look at the road sign. Ask: *La route 134 est quel genre de route? Qu'est-ce qui indique ça?*

RÉALITÉS

OPTIONAL MATERIAL

PRESENTATION
(pages 208–209)

A. Have students read the captions and enjoy the photos together.
B. Have volunteer poets write poems about Mont-Saint-Michel as seen in the photo.

Note In the CD-ROM version, students can listen to the recorded captions and discover a hidden video behind one of the photos.

RÉALITÉS

C'est une vue superbe du Mont-Saint-Michel **1**.

C'est une borne kilométrique le long de la route à la campagne **2**. C'est une route départementale ou une route nationale? Il y a combien de kilomètres d'ici à Captieux?

Voici un alignement de menhirs en Bretagne **3**.

Voici des femmes et des hommes en costume breton traditionnel **4**.

DID YOU KNOW?

According to legend, Saint Michael the Archangel appeared to Aubert, the bishop of Avranches, and inspired him to build a church on a small island off the coast of Normandy. The original church was completed in 1144, but was added to in the 13th century to accommodate the monks and the increasing number of pilgrims. During the 15th and 16th centuries, interior buildings were rebuilt in Gothic style. The 17th century, however, witnessed the decline of the abbey as the monks began to rebel against the strict discipline of their order. The abbey was converted to a prison before the French Revolution. Only in this century have monks regained the right to live and work there.

209

ADDITIONAL PRACTICE

Assign any of the following:
1. Student Tape Manual, Teacher's Edition, *Deuxième Partie*, pages 86–88
2. Situation Cards, Chapter 8

COOPERATIVE LEARNING

Display Communication Transparency C-8. Have students work in groups and make up as many questions as they can about the illustration. Have groups take turns asking and answering the questions.

RECYCLING

These activities encourage students to use all the language they have learned in the chapter and recombine it with material from previous chapters. It is not necessary to do all the activities with all students. You may select the ones you consider most appropriate or permit students to choose the ones they wish to do.

INFORMAL ASSESSMENT

Use the oral and written activities in this section as a review at the end of the chapter or to evaluate speaking and writing skills. To evaluate oral skills, use the evaluation criteria that appear on page 22 of this Teacher's Wraparound Edition.

Activités de communication orale

ANSWERS

Activités A and B
Answers will vary.

Activités de communication écrite

ANSWERS

Activités A and B
Answers will vary.

OPTIONAL MATERIAL

Réintroduction et recombinaison

PRESENTATION *(pages 210–211)*

Exercices A, B, and C

Exercise A recycles the use of infinitives after auxiliaries and also practices the future after *quand*. Exercise B reintroduces the differences between the use of the *passé composé* and the imperfect. Exercise C reviews structures and vocabulary for giving directions, learned in this chapter.

210

Activités de communication orale

A **Que ferez-vous?** Demandez à un(e) camarade ce qu'il/elle fera quand:

il/elle aura des vacances   il/elle sera diplômé(e)
il/elle aura son permis de conduire   il/elle sera adulte

Élève 1: Quand tu auras des vacances, que feras-tu?
Élève 2: Quand j'aurai des vacances, j'irai à San Francisco avec ma famille.

B **Flash circulation.** Vous et votre camarade travaillez pour la station de radio de votre ville. L'un(e) de vous est dans le studio et pose des questions à l'autre, qui se trouve dans une voiture dans la ville.

Élève 1: Comment est la circulation, là où vous êtes?
Élève 2: Eh bien, je suis dans la rue (Main), et il y a un énorme embouteillage. Je conseille aux automobilistes de prendre la rue (High)...

Activités de communication écrite

A **Une visite.** Vos amis français viennent aux USA pour vous rendre visite. Dans une lettre, écrivez-leur comment venir chez vous de l'aéroport.

B **Quelle chance!** Vous avez enfin votre permis de conduire. Vos parents vous ont prêté leur voiture pour la première fois hier. Écrivez tout ce que vous avez fait, où vous êtes allé(e), etc.

Réintroduction et recombinaison

A **Je veux et je vais si je peux.** Répondez.

1. Dites plusieurs choses que vous voulez faire.
2. Dites plusieurs choses que vous allez faire.
3. Dites plusieurs choses que vous pouvez faire.
4. Dites plusieurs choses que vous devez faire.
5. Dites plusieurs choses que vous voulez faire mais que vous ne pouvez pas faire parce que vous devez faire quelque chose d'autre.
6. Dites plusieurs choses que vous ferez quand vous serez adulte.

210 CHAPITRE 8

B **Un petit accident.** Répondez d'après les indications.

1. Est-ce que l'automobiliste conduisait prudemment? (oui)
2. Il roulait trop vite? (non)
3. Il est arrivé à un croisement? (oui)
4. Il y avait un feu au croisement? (oui)
5. Le feu changeait quand il y est arrivé? (oui)
6. Il a ralenti? (oui)
7. Il s'est arrêté? (oui)
8. Il a brûlé le feu (grillé le feu rouge)? (non, il s'est arrêté)
9. Mais il a eu un accident? (oui)
10. Le conducteur qui le suivait a vu le feu? (non)
11. Il s'est arrêté? (non)
12. Et il est rentré dans l'autre voiture? (oui)
13. L'accident était sérieux? (non)
14. Pourquoi pas? (Les deux voitures ne roulaient pas vite.)

C **Comment y aller.** Expliquez à quelqu'un qui vous demande son chemin comment aller de chez vous au centre commercial ou au centre-ville.

Vocabulaire

NOMS

le boulevard périphérique
l'autoroute (f.)
la bretelle d'accès
la sortie
le poste de péage
le panneau
la flèche
la circulation
le sens
le ralentissement
le bouchon
l'embouteillage (m.)
la file (de voitures)
le point noir
l'heure (f.) de pointe
l'automobiliste (m. et f.)
le permis de conduire
la carte grise
la carte routière
le plan de la ville
l'agent (m.) de police
la casquette
le gendarme

le motard
le casque
la limitation de
    vitesse
l'amende (f.)
la contravention
le centre-ville
le trottoir
le coin
le feu
les piétons (m.)
le passage pour
    piétons
l'endroit (m.)
la voiture
le camion
la caravane
la jeep
la moto(cyclette)
la dépanneuse

ADJECTIFS

gros(se)
encombré(e)

VERBES

accélérer
rouler
ralentir
changer de voie
doubler
tourner
traverser
respecter
arrêter
entourer

AUTRES MOTS ET EXPRESSIONS

faire demi-tour
se tirer d'une mauvaise
    situation
tomber en panne
demander son chemin
à droite
à gauche
tout droit
à côté de
en face de
devant
derrière

CHAPITRE 8   **211**

211

INDEPENDENT PRACTICE

Assign any of the following:
1. Activities and exercises, pages 210–211
2. Communication Activities Masters,
   pages 50–54
3. CD-ROM, Disc 2, pages 210–211

ANSWERS

Exercice A
  Answers will vary.

Exercice B

1. Oui, l'automobiliste conduisait prudemment.
2. Non, il ne roulait pas trop vite.
3. Oui, il est arrivé à un croisement.
4. Oui, il y avait un feu au croisement.
5. Oui, le feu changeait quand il y est arrivé.
6. Oui, il a ralenti.
7. Oui, il s'est arrêté.
8. Non, il s'est arrêté.
9. Oui, il a eu un accident.
10. Non, le conducteur qui le suivait n'a pas vu le feu.
11. Non, il ne s'est pas arrêté.
12. Oui, il est rentré dans l'autre voiture.
13. Non, l'accident n'était pas sérieux.
14. Parce que les deux voitures ne roulaient pas vite.

Exercice C
  Answers will vary.

ASSESSMENT RESOURCES

1. Chapter Quizzes
2. Testing Program
3. Situation Cards
4. Communication Transparency C-8
5. Computer Software: Practice/Test Generator
6. Performance Assessment

VIDEO PROGRAM

INTRODUCTION   (30:49)

ANNE ET PATRICE   (31:13)
PERDENT LEUR CHEMIN

RÉVISION

CHAPITRES 5-8

OVERVIEW

This section reviews key grammatical structures and vocabulary from Chapters 5–8. The topics were first presented on the following pages: two object pronouns in the same sentence, pages 175, 199; the future tense, pages 172, 174, 196, 198.

REVIEW RESOURCES

1. Bell Ringer Review Blackline Masters R8-1 & R8-2, page 23
2. Workbook, Self-Test 2, pages 94–99
3. Videocassette/Videodisc, Unit 2
4. Video Activities Booklet, Unit 2: Chapters 5–8, pages 17–37
5. Computer Software, Chapters 5–8
6. Testing Program, Unit Test: Chapters 5–8, pages 60–64
7. Performance Assessment
8. CD-ROM, Disc 2, *Révision:* pages 212–215
9. CD-ROM, Disc 2, Self-Tests 5–8
10. CD-ROM, Disc 2, Game: *Le Tour de France*
11. Lesson Plans

Conversation

PRESENTATION *(page 212)*

A. Have students close their books and listen as you read the conversation to the class.
B. Call on pairs of volunteers to read the conversation aloud.
C. Have one student summarize the conversation.

Note Point out that in everyday conversation, a native speaker would say *C'est pas la peine.*

212

Conversation   *Sur la route*

GILLES: Mais qu'est-ce qui se passe? Ce n'est pas possible. Une heure et on n'a même pas fait un kilomètre. Pourquoi payer pour prendre l'autoroute? Ce n'est pas la peine.

MÉLANIE: Ça doit être un accident! Sors à la prochaine sortie. On prendra la Nationale 6. Ça sera plus long mais on a le temps. Et à la vitesse où on va maintenant on arrivera à la même heure.

GILLES: D'accord. Tu as la carte?

MÉLANIE: Elle est dans le sac à l'arrière.

GILLES: Tu me la passes, s'il te plaît... Merci... Alors, la prochaine sortie, c'est Auxerre-Nord. Là, comme tu as dit, on prendra la Nationale 6 jusqu'à Saulieu... Quand on arrivera à Saulieu, on restera sur la droite et on rejoindra la Départementale 980 jusqu'à Autun. Voilà, c'est simple.

MÉLANIE: Oui, mais maintenant on va voir combien de temps on met pour sortir de l'autoroute!

A Quelle circulation!
Répondez d'après la conversation.

1. Gilles et Mélanie sont sur l'autoroute ou sur une route secondaire?
2. Est-ce que ça roule bien?
3. Pourquoi, d'après Mélanie?
4. Faut-il payer pour prendre l'autoroute en France?
5. Que vont faire Gilles et Mélanie?
6. Où sortiront-ils de l'autoroute?
7. Quelle route prendront-ils?
8. D'après Mélanie, est-ce qu'ils sortiront bientôt de l'autoroute?

© MICHELIN, Map No 238 *Centre Berry-Nivernais*, édition 1992. Permission No. 9611564

COOPERATIVE LEARNING

Have students work in teams. Ask them to write directions from one place to another using a map. They should write the starting point but not the ending point. Teams exchange maps and directions. The second team must follow the directions and see if they arrive at the destination the first team intended.

Structure

Deux pronoms dans la même phrase

1. When two object pronouns are used, the order is as follows.

		me te nous vous		le la les		lui leur				
(ne)	*before*		*before*		*before*		*before*	verbe	*before*	(pas)

Tu te laves les cheveux? Non, je me les suis lavés hier!

2. Pronouns usually come before the verb or the helping verbs *avoir* and *être* in the *passé composé*. They cannot be separated from the verb or the helping verb; therefore, negations go around the verb or the helping verb.

> **Ses conseils? Je *ne* les suis *jamais*.**
> **Ses conseils? Je *ne* les ai *jamais* suivis.**

Remember that when a verb is conjugated with *avoir* in the *passé composé*, its past participle agrees with a preceding direct object.

3. In affirmative commands, the pronoun follows the verb. It is linked to the verb by a hyphen. In negative commands, pronouns come before the verb.

> **Écoutez-moi.   Ne m'écoutez pas.**
> **Regardez-la.   Ne la regardez pas.**

A **C'est une bonne infirmière.** Remplacez les mots en italique par des pronoms.

> **Elle a donné les pansements aux médecins.**
> *Elle les leur a donnés.*

1. Elle a pris *la tension aux malades*.
2. Elle a fait *sa piqûre à Mélanie*.
3. Elle a pris *le pouls à Mme Delors*.
4. Elle a donné *ses médicaments à M. Vernier*.

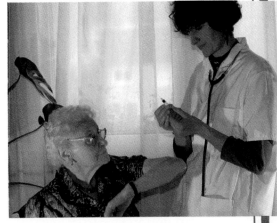

B **D'accord.** Répondez d'après le modèle.

> **Passe-moi le sac, s'il te plaît.**
> *D'accord! Je te le passe.*

1. Donne-moi les billets!
2. Prête-nous ta carte!
3. Envoie-nous les renseignements.
4. Écris-moi son adresse.

CHAPITRES 5-8 RÉVISION   **213**

Write the following on the board or use BRR Blackline Master R8-2: Complete the sentences with the present tense of the indicated verbs.

1. Ce week-end nous ____ en ville. (aller)
2. Mes sœurs ____ aller dans le magasin de disques. (vouloir)
3. Ma mère ____ un colis à ma tante. (envoyer)
4. Je ____ tous mes amis. (voir)
5. Tu ____ avec nous? (venir)

Le futur

PRESENTATION (*pages 214–215*)

Guide students through steps 1–5. Have individuals read the verb forms aloud.

Le futur

1. For regular verbs, the future tense is formed by adding the following endings to the infinitive, which is the future stem. However, *-re* verbs drop the final *-e* before adding the endings.

INFINITIVE		FUTURE	
		STEM	ENDING
parler finir attendre	je tu il/elle/on nous vous ils/elles	*parler* *finir* *attendr*	-ai -as -a -ons -ez -ont

2. Most irregular verbs that end in *-re* have a regular future stem.

dire	je *dirai*	lire	je *lirai*	conduire	je *conduirai*
écrire	j' *écrirai*	ouvrir	j' *ouvrirai*	prendre	je *prendrai*
vivre	je *vivrai*	suivre	je *suivrai*	connaître	je *connaîtrai*

3. Verbs with spelling changes keep the spelling change in the future stem. Note that *préférer* is an exception. It has a regular future stem: *je préférerai*.

INFINITIVE	PRESENT	FUTURE
acheter	j'achète	j'*achèterai*
appeler	j'appelle	j'*appellerai*
essayer	j'essaie	j'*essaierai*

4. Study the future stems of common irregular verbs.

INFINITIVE	STEM	INFINITIVE	STEM
aller	*ir-*	pleuvoir	*pleuvr-*
avoir	*aur-*	pouvoir	*pourr-*
courir	*courr-*	recevoir	*recevr-*
devoir	*devr-*	savoir	*saur-*
envoyer	*enverr-*	tenir	*tiendr-*
être	*ser-*	venir	*viendr-*
faire	*fer-*	voir	*verr-*
falloir	*faudr-*	vouloir	*voudr-*

ADDITIONAL PRACTICE

After completing Exercises D–F on page 215, have students redo Bell Ringer Review R8-2 using the future tense.

5. When the verb in the main clause is in the future, the verb following *quand* must be in the future too.

Quand j'aurai le temps, j'irai chez le coiffeur.

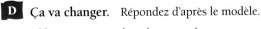 **C** **L'avenir.** Répondez d'après le modèle.

avoir beaucoup d'enfants
Tu auras beaucoup d'enfants.

1. être riche
2. faire de longs voyages
3. aller dans des pays exotiques
4. avoir beaucoup d'amis
5. vouloir beaucoup de choses
6. pouvoir les acheter

Une belle plage à la Martinique

D **Ça va changer.** Répondez d'après le modèle.

Nous ne voyons jamais nos amis.
Vous verrez bientôt vos amis.

1. Nous ne sortons jamais.
2. Nous ne voyons jamais les derniers films.
3. Nous n'allons jamais au cinéma.
4. Nous ne savons pas parler français.
5. Nous ne recevons jamais nos amis.
6. Nous ne sommes jamais heureux.

E **Quand?** Complétez avec les verbes entre parenthèses. Utilisez le temps qui convient.

1. Je vous téléphonerai quand je ___ à Paris. (être)
2. Quand je suis arrivé, il ___ déjà là. (être)
3. Quand il est arrivé, il m'___ immédiatement. (téléphoner)
4. Quand on est en retard, on ___. (s'excuser)
5. Quand vous ___ à la Martinique, nous visiterons l'île ensemble. (aller)

Activités de communication orale

 **A** **Un accident.** Racontez (ou inventez) un accident de la route. Vous pouvez inclure les éléments suivants: le type de voitures, le genre de route, la gravité de l'accident (blessés), l'intervention des services de secours, etc.

L'année dernière ma cousine a eu un accident de la route. Elle roulait vite sur l'autoroute quand…

B **À l'avenir.** Vous êtes très sûr(e) de ce que vous voulez faire plus tard, donc vous utilisez le futur quand vous en parlez à votre camarade.

Élève 1: Qu'est-ce que tu feras plus tard?
Élève 2: Je serai médecin. Je suivrai des cours de biologie…

Exercices

PRESENTATION *(page 215)*

Exercices C and D

Exercises C and D can be done with books either open or closed.

Exercice E

Exercise E is to be done with books open. Advise students that Exercise E requires careful attention to choice of verb tense.

ANSWERS

Exercice C

1. Tu seras riche.
2. Tu feras de longs voyages.
3. Tu iras dans des pays exotiques.
4. Tu auras beaucoup d'amis.
5. Tu voudras beaucoup de choses.
6. Tu pourras les acheter.

Exercice D

1. Vous sortirez bientôt.
2. Vous verrez bientôt les derniers films.
3. Vous irez bientôt au cinéma.
4. Vous saurez bientôt parler français.
5. Vous recevrez bientôt vos amis.
6. Vous serez bientôt heureux.

Exercice E

1. serai
2. était
3. a téléphoné
4. s'excuse
5. irez

Activités de communication orale

ANSWERS

Activités A and B

Answers will vary.

INDEPENDENT PRACTICE

Assign any of the following:

1. Exercises and activities, page 215
2. Workbook, Self-Test 2, pages 94–99
3. CD-ROM, Disc 2, page 215
4. CD-ROM, Disc 2, Self-Tests 5–8
5. CD-ROM, Disc 2, Game: *Le Tour de France*

MÉDECINE: SECOURISME

Médecine: Secourisme

OVERVIEW

It is recommended that you allow students to choose the readings that interest them. If a student has no particular interest in a topic, it is not necessary for him or her to read about it in a foreign language. All the readings in this section are optional. They can be given to individual groups to read, they can be assigned as outside reading for extra credit, or they can be done in class as an additional reading.

See page 106 in this Teacher's Wraparound Edition for information on presenting the readings at different levels of intensity.

Avant la lecture

PRESENTATION *(page 216)*

A. Have the students do the activities in the *Avant la lecture* section.
B. Explain to students that the information they are going to read originally appeared in a magazine. The article explains what to do if you are the first to arrive at the scene of an accident.
C. Have the students scan the reading for cognates. There are approximately 20.

Lecture

PRESENTATION *(pages 216–217)*

Most students are already familiar with much of the information in the reading selection from their health courses. For this reason, it is suggested that you let the students read the selection silently.

Avant la lecture

1. Imagine there is a car accident and you are the first one on the scene. Make a list of all the things you would do, *in order of priority*.
2. Compare your list with your classmates' and make a final list you all agree upon.

Lecture

Les accidents de voiture sont de plus en plus nombreux. Vous vous dites peut-être que vous ne pouvez rien faire parce que vous n'êtes pas médecin. Il n'en est rien. Voici ce que vous pouvez faire:

- Tout d'abord, allumez les feux de détresse[1] de la voiture pour alerter les autres voitures.
- Coupez ensuite le contact et mettez le frein à main.
- Faites signe de ralentir aux voitures qui arrivent.
- Téléphonez ou faites téléphoner à la police et donnez avec précision le lieu de l'accident, le nombre de blessés[2], etc.
- Parlez au blessé, même s'il n'a pas l'air[3] d'être conscient: cela le rassurera et diminuera les effets de l'état de choc.
- Ne déplacez[4] pas le blessé, mais donnez-lui la main.

- Si la victime est inconsciente et ne respire pas, faites-lui du bouche à bouche: mettez-lui doucement la tête en arrière. Pincez-lui fortement le nez et ouvrez-lui la bouche. Mettez votre bouche sur la sienne et soufflez de l'air dedans. Inspirez et ressoufflez dans la bouche du blessé.

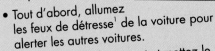

LEARNING FROM ILLUSTRATIONS

After completing the reading selection, you may wish to have students describe the illustrations in their own words.

SCIENCES

Recommencez jusqu'à ce que le blessé respire seul, sans votre aide. Dans le cas d'un bébé, mettez votre bouche sur sa bouche et son nez.

• Si la victime est inconsciente mais qu'elle respire encore, allongez-la sur le côté. Si vous la mettez sur le dos, elle risque de s'étouffer[5]. Pour qu'elle reste dans cette position, pliez[6] son genou et son coude[7] supérieurs. Couvrez la victime avec un vêtement pour la protéger du froid.

• Si le blessé saigne[8] abondamment, rassurez-le d'abord, car la vue du sang[9] fait souvent peur[10]. Installez le blessé confortablement, si vous le pouvez, et appuyez fortement sur la blessure. Enlevez de temps en temps votre main pour voir si le sang coule toujours. Il vous faudra peut-être une bonne dizaine de minutes avant de pouvoir arrêter l'hémorragie.

• Dans tous les cas, gardez votre sang-froid et ne paniquez pas. Votre aide peut être très précieuse.

[1] feux de détresse *hazard lights*
[2] blessés *injured*
[3] même s'il n'a pas l'air *even if he doesn't seem*
[4] déplacez *move*
[5] s'étouffer *to choke*
[6] pliez *bend*
[7] coude *elbow*
[8] saigne *bleeds*
[9] sang *blood*
[10] fait peur *scares people*

Après la lecture

A Un accident de la route.
Choisissez.

1. La première chose à faire est ___.
   a. de faire signe aux autres voitures
   b. d'allumer les feux de détresse
   c. de couper le contact

2. Parlez au blessé ___.
   a. même s'il est inconscient
   b. s'il a chaud
   c. s'il a froid

3. Si la victime est consciente, allongez-la ___.
   a. sur le dos
   b. sur le ventre
   c. sur le côté

4. Le bouche à bouche sert à ___.
   a. rassurer la victime
   b. étouffer la victime
   c. faire respirer la victime

5. Si la victime saigne abondamment, il faut ___.
   a. appuyer sur la blessure
   b. voir si le sang coule
   c. voir s'il y a une hémorragie

B Contre les accidents de la route.
Dans de nombreux pays, les accidents de la route sont causés par des conducteurs en état d'ivresse (*intoxicated*). D'après vous, quelles mesures peuvent être adoptées pour réduire le nombre de ce genre d'accidents?

C Une lettre. Écrivez une lettre au maire (*mayor*) de votre ville pour lui faire part de vos conclusions.

Après la lecture
PRESENTATION (*page 217*)
A. Go over Exercise A in the *Après la lecture* section.
B. In addition to Exercises B and C, you may wish to do the following activities:
   1. Have students explain in their own words in French how to administer mouth-to-mouth resuscitation.
   2. Have students name three things they can do to help an injured person remain calm.

Exercices
ANSWERS
Exercice A
1. b
2. a
3. c
4. c
5. a

Exercices B and C
   Answers will vary.

Littérature: Jules Verne (1828–1905)

Note This reading selection will interest students who like science-fiction. Students will read an excerpt from *Sans dessus dessous* by Jules Verne in Glencoe French 3, *En voyage*, page 420.

Avant la lecture

PRESENTATION *(page 218)*

A. Tell the students to look at the dates of Jules Verne's birth and death. The fact that he lived and wrote so many years ago makes his work truly remarkable. Tell students: *Jules Verne a écrit ses romans avant l'exploration aérienne, spatiale et sous-marine.*

B. Have the students look at the photos to familiarize themselves with the type of information they will encounter in the reading selection.

Lecture

PRESENTATION *(pages 218–219)*

You can have the students read the selection silently or aloud.

LITTÉRATURE: JULES VERNE (1828–1905)

Avant la lecture

1. What science fiction films did you see recently? Did you enjoy them or not? Why or why not? Do you think science fiction is art?
2. According to you, which science fiction phenomena will become reality during your lifetime?

Lecture

Jules Verne a introduit en France le roman[1] d'anticipation scientifique ou de science-fiction, comme on l'appelle aujourd'hui. Son père était avocat[2], mais lui préférait être écrivain[3]. Il a commencé par écrire des pièces de théâtre. L'une d'elles a été mise en scène[4] par Alexandre Dumas, l'auteur des *Trois Mousquetaires*. Puis, il a écrit des nouvelles[5] qui parlent déjà de voyages, le thème principal de son œuvre. Jules Verne s'intéressait beaucoup aux travaux scientifiques de son époque qu'il voulait faire connaître au grand public. Des années plus tard, les explorations que Jules Verne avait décrites dans ses romans sont devenues réalité: exploration aérienne dans *Cinq Semaines en ballon*, exploration spatiale dans *De la Terre*[6] à la *Lune*[7], exploration sous-marine dans *Vingt Mille Lieues sous les mers*.

«Vingt Mille Lieues sous les mers» (1870)

La plongée sous-marine de nos jours

218

SCIENCES

Astronautes marchant dans l'espace

«De la Terre à la Lune» (1865)

Le cinéma s'est emparé[8] des romans de Jules Verne et en a fait des spectacles impressionnants. L'acteur anglais David Niven a immortalisé le héros du *Tour du monde en quatre-vingts jours*, Philéas Fogg. Et le grand acteur James Mason a incarné le capitaine Nemo (nemo = «personne», en latin) dans *Vingt Mille Lieues sous les mers*.

La plupart des découvertes de Jules Verne ont été réalisées et même dépassées[9], mais ses livres continuent à fasciner. Il est intéressant de savoir que le premier sous-marin atomique s'est appelé le *Nautilus*, nom du sous-marin du capitaine Nemo, et que l'un des cratères sur la face cachée[10] de la Lune s'appelle *Jules Verne*.

[1] roman *novel*
[2] avocat *lawyer*
[3] écrivain *writer*
[4] mise en scène *directed*
[5] nouvelles *short stories*
[6] Terre *Earth*
[7] Lune *Moon*
[8] s'est emparé *took*
[9] dépassées *surpassed*
[10] cachée *dark*

Après la lecture

A **Jules Verne.** Vrai ou faux?

1. Jules Verne venait d'une famille de mathématiciens.
2. Une de ses pièces a été mise en scène par Alexandre Dumas.
3. Les romans de Jules Verne parlent surtout de voyages.
4. Le premier sous-marin atomique s'est appelé *Jules Verne*.
5. On a fait des films de certains romans de Jules Verne.
6. Nemo veut dire «invisible».

B **Ses romans.** Citez les titres des romans où Jules Verne parle:

— d'un voyage autour du monde
— d'une aventure sous-marine
— d'une aventure spatiale

C **Ses descendants.** Écrivez.

1. Le commandant Cousteau a fait de nombreuses explorations sous-marines. Faites un rapport sur l'une d'elles.
2. Faites un rapport sur la dernière en date des explorations spatiales américaines.

Après la lecture

PRESENTATION (page 219)

You may wish to ask students the following questions: *Avez-vous vu un ou plusieurs des films mentionnés dans cette lecture? Lequel ou lesquels? Si vous êtes fana de cinéma, vous connaissez David Niven? James Mason? Dites ce que vous savez au sujet de ces acteurs de cinéma.*

Exercices

ANSWERS

Exercice A

1. faux
2. vrai
3. vrai
4. faux
5. vrai
6. faux

Exercice B

Le Tour du monde en quatre-vingts jours
Vingt Mille Lieues sous les mers
De la Terre à la Lune

Exercice C

Answers will vary.

Histoire: Joséphine et Napoléon

Note This reading selection will interest students who enjoy history and biography. For more information on Napoleon and a poem by Victor Hugo on Napoleon's disastrous Russian campaign—*La Retraite de Russie*—see Glencoe French 4, *Trésors du temps*, pages 289–293 and 296–297.

Avant la lecture

PRESENTATION *(page 220)*

A. Have students tell anything they know from their history courses about Napoleon.

B. You may wish to have students look for the following information as they read the selection.
   1. le nom du premier mari de Joséphine
   2. le nombre d'enfants qu'ils ont eus
   3. le nom du deuxième mari de Joséphine
   4. les pays que Napoléon a conquis
   5. la raison de la séparation de Joséphine et Napoléon
   6. la date de la mort de Joséphine
   7. le pays envahi par Napoléon en 1812
   8. la bataille où Napoléon a été battu

Lecture

PRESENTATION *(pages 220–221)*

You may have the students read the selection aloud or silently.

HISTOIRE: JOSÉPHINE ET NAPOLÉON

Avant la lecture

1. Martinique is one of the French West Indies. Read about Martinique at the time of the French Revolution and Napoleon.
2. Read about the prestigious career of Napoleon.

Lecture

Joséphine (Marie-Josèphe) Tascher de la Pagerie est née en 1763 à Trois-Îlets, à la Martinique, aux Antilles. En 1779, elle épouse[1] Alexandre de Beauharnais. Ils vivront en France et auront deux enfants, Eugène et Hortense. Mais en 1789, c'est la Révolution, et les Beauharnais sont des aristocrates. En 1794, Alexandre de Beauharnais est guillotiné. Joséphine et ses

Prud'hon: «L'Impératrice Joséphine»

enfants échappent à la mort[2].

En 1795, Joséphine rencontre Napoléon Bonaparte et elle l'épouse l'année suivante. Napoléon n'est que général, mais il a d'autres ambitions... Par le coup d'État du 18 brumaire An VII (9 novembre 1799), il prend le pouvoir[3]. En 1804, il se fait sacrer[4] empereur des Français sous le nom de Napoléon Ier, et il sacre lui-même Joséphine, impératrice.

Pendant quelque temps, Joséphine est la femme de l'homme le plus puissant[5] du monde. En effet, Napoléon a conquis l'Italie, l'Espagne, l'Égypte, les Pays-Bas et une grande partie de l'Europe centrale.

Jacques-Louis David: «Le Sacre»

SCIENCES

David: «Bonaparte au Grand-Saint-Bernard»

Mais pour survivre, cet empire a besoin d'un héritier[6], et malheureusement Joséphine ne peut plus avoir d'enfant. Alors, en 1809, malgré[7] l'amour qu'il a encore pour sa femme, Napoléon la répudie pour se marier avec la fille de l'empereur d'Autriche. Joséphine se retire au château de La Malmaison que Napoléon avait acheté pour elle. Elle gardera toujours beaucoup d'influence sur Napoléon, avec qui elle correspondra jusqu'à sa mort, en 1814.

Quant à[8] Napoléon, sa chance tourne[9] en 1812, quand il envahit la Russie et doit battre en retraite. En 1814, battu par les coalitions européennes, il abdique. Il essaie de revenir en 1815, mais il est battu à Waterloo et envoyé en exil dans l'île de Sainte-Hélène, où il mourra en 1821.

[1] épouse *marries*
[2] échappent à la mort *escape death*
[3] le pouvoir *power*
[4] se fait sacrer *has himself crowned*
[5] puissant *powerful*
[6] un héritier *heir*
[7] malgré *in spite of*
[8] quant à *as for*
[9] sa chance tourne *his luck changes*

Après la lecture

A **Napoléon et Joséphine.** Répondez aux questions.

1. Où est la Martinique?
2. Pourquoi Alexandre de Beauharnais a-t-il été guillotiné?
3. Qu'était Napoléon quand il a rencontré Joséphine?
4. En quelle année Napoléon devient-il empereur?
5. Combien d'années a-t-il été empereur?
6. Pourquoi Joséphine et Napoléon ont-ils divorcé?

B **Napoléon après Joséphine.**
Napoléon s'est remarié. Faites des recherches, et écrivez la suite de l'histoire.

C **Couples célèbres.** Napoléon et Joséphine font partie des couples célèbres de l'Histoire. Pouvez-vous réunir les personnages suivants?

> Roméo
> Cléopâtre
> Robin
> Ferdinand
> Marion
> Iseult
> Juliette
> Tristan
> Isabelle
> Marc Antoine

D **Où est la vérité** (*truth*)? L'Histoire de chaque pays interprète les événements et les personnages historiques de façons différentes. L'image que se font les Américains de Napoléon vient des Anglais qui étaient ses ennemis. Racontez l'histoire de Napoléon «à l'anglaise», puis «à la française».

LETTRES ET SCIENCES **221**

Après la lecture
Exercices

PRESENTATION *(page 221)*
Exercises C and D are rather difficult and should be assigned only to very able students.

ANSWERS

Exercice A

1. La Martinique est aux Antilles.
2. Il a été guillotiné parce qu'il était aristocrate.
3. Il était général.
4. Il devient empereur en 1804.
5. Il a été empereur pendant dix ans.
6. Ils ont divorcé parce que Joséphine ne pouvait plus avoir d'enfant.

Exercice B
Answers will vary.

Exercice C
Roméo et Juliette
Cléopâtre et Marc Antoine
Robin et Marion
Ferdinand et Isabelle
Tristan et Iseult

Exercice D
Answers will vary.

ART CONNECTION

For student art activities related to the paintings on pages 220–221 and for more information on David, Prud'hon and the Napoleonic era, please refer to Fine Art Transparencies F-2, F-3, and F-4.

INTERDISCIPLINARY CONNECTIONS

Have your students share the information from this reading with the World History class. Have both classes work together to create a bilingual timeline with all significant dates. This timeline may be posted in the history or French classroom.

CHAPITRE 9

CHAPTER OVERVIEW

In this chapter students will learn vocabulary and structures associated with caring for clothing and requesting services at a laundromat or dry cleaning establishment. They will also learn to use the conditional mood and the causative *faire*.

The cultural focus of Chapter 9 is on garment cleaning services available in France. The chapter also deals with some areas of France which are of interest to campers and backpackers.

CHAPTER OBJECTIVES

By the end of this chapter, students will know:

1. vocabulary associated with dry cleaners, laundromats and doing laundry
2. vocabulary associated with clothing, including features of garments and types of materials
3. the conditional of regular and irregular verbs
4. *si* clauses: complex sentences containing present-future and imperfect-conditional tense combinations
5. causative constructions with *faire* + infinitive

{ CHAPITRE
9 }

LA TEINTURERIE ET LA LAVERIE AUTOMATIQUE

OBJECTIFS

In this chapter you will learn to do the following:

1. talk about taking care of your clothes
2. take your clothes to a laundry or dry cleaner when in a French-speaking country
3. express conditions
4. express more conditions
5. say what you or others have someone else do
6. compare dry cleaners and laundromats in France and the U.S.
7. learn about some spots for nature lovers in France

CHAPTER PROJECTS

(optional)
1. Have students prepare a simple manual in French on how to use a washing machine.
2. Have students conduct a debate on bullfighting, with one team for and the other against.

Pacing

This chapter will require eight to ten class sessions. Pacing will depend on the length of the class, the age of the students, and student aptitude.

For more information on planning your class, see the Lesson Plans, which offer guidelines for 45- and 55-minute classes and **Block Scheduling.**

Exercices vs. *Activités*

The exercises and activities are color-coded. Exercises, which provide guided practice to prepare students for independent communication, are coded in blue. Communicative activities, which give students opportunities for creative, open-ended expression, are coded in red.

INTERNET ACTIVITIES

(optional)

These activities, student worksheets, and related teacher information are in the *À bord* Internet Activities Booklet and on the Glencoe Foreign Language Home Page at: **http://www.glencoe.com/secondary/fl**

LEARNING FROM PHOTOS

After practicing the *Mots 1* and 2 vocabulary, come back to this photo and have students describe it in as much detail as possible.

VOCABULAIRE

MOTS 1

Bell Ringer Review

Write the following on the board or use BRR Blackline Master 9-1: Make a list of all the words you can remember having to do with clothing.

PRESENTATION (*pages 224–225*)

A. Introduce the new words and sentences using Vocabulary Transparencies 9.1 (A & B). Have students repeat each word after you or Cassette 6A/CD-5. Ask questions about each illustration during your presentation.

B. Have students open their books and read the new words and sentences.

C. After presenting and practicing all the vocabulary, have pairs make up a conversation between the woman and the customer at the dry cleaner's.

À LA TEINTURERIE

le nettoyage à sec

le repassage
repasser

le pressing

chiffonné(e)

de l'amidon (m.)

AMIDON

faire nettoyer à sec

Julie porte son pull à la teinturerie.

Teinturerie / Pressing

14 vendredi
15 samedi

Elle revient le lendemain.

À LA LAVERIE AUTOMATIQUE

faire la lessive

LAVERIE

de la lessive

le linge sale

le linge propre

la machine à laver

sécher

un sèche-linge

rétrécir

plier

laver

Georges lave sa chemise.

Daniel ne lave pas sa chemise.
Il fait laver sa chemise.
Il la fait laver.

CHAPITRE 9   **225**

Note Point out to students that a word can sometimes have more than one meaning. *Porter* might mean "wear" or "take." *Il porte une chemise blanche. Il porte sa chemise à la laverie.* The word *lessive* might mean "soap powder" or "laundry to be washed." *Il faut faire la lessive. D'abord il faut mettre de la lessive dans la machine à laver.*

Exercices

PRESENTATION (*page 226*)

Exercice A

Exercise A is to be done with books open.

Exercice B

Exercise B can be done with books either open or closed.

Extension of *Exercice B*: Writing

After completing Exercise B, have students write sentences using the alternate multiple choice items.

ANSWERS

Exercice A

1. Monsieur Celle lave le linge sale.
2. Il met le linge sale dans la machine à laver.
3. Il lave la chemise.
4. Il met de la lessive dans la machine à laver.
5. Madame Celle repasse la chemise.
6. Elle repasse le linge chiffonné.
7. Olivier le fait nettoyer à sec.
8. Pour le nettoyage à sec il doit porter ses vêtements à la teinturerie.

Exercice B

1. a	5. b
2. b	6. c
3. c	7. c
4. c	8. b

Exercices

A Laver ou faire nettoyer à sec? Répondez d'après les dessins.

1. Monsieur Celle lave le linge sale ou le linge propre?
2. Il met le linge sale dans la machine à laver ou dans le lave-vaisselle?
3. Il lave la chemise ou repasse la chemise?
4. Il met de la lessive ou de l'amidon dans la machine à laver?

5. Madame Celle lave la chemise ou repasse la chemise?
6. Elle repasse le linge sale ou le linge chiffonné?
7. Olivier lave le pull ou le fait nettoyer à sec?
8. Pour le nettoyage à sec il doit porter ses vêtements à la laverie automatique ou à la teinturerie?

B Le linge. Complétez.

1. Il y a du linge sale. Il faut faire ___.
   a. la lessive
   b. les courses
   c. la cuisine

2. La chemise est sale. Il faut la ___.
   a. plier
   b. laver
   c. repasser

3. On ne peut pas la laver. Il faut ___.
   a. l'amidonner
   b. la mettre dans le lave-vaisselle
   c. la faire nettoyer à sec

4. Le pantalon est chiffonné. Il faut le ___.
   a. plier
   b. laver
   c. repasser

5. Je ne veux pas le repasser moi-même. Je vais le ___.
   a. mettre
   b. faire repasser
   c. laver

6. Pour le nettoyage à sec on porte ses vêtements à ___.
   a. la laverie automatique
   b. la machine à laver
   c. la teinturerie

7. Ce chemisier est délicat. Si je le lave il va ___.
   a. chiffonner
   b. être sale
   c. rétrécir

8. Julie porte son pull à la teinturerie. Le teinturier lui dit qu'il l'aura pour ___.
   a. hier
   b. le lendemain
   c. l'année prochaine

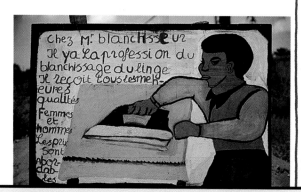

226 CHAPITRE 9

INDEPENDENT PRACTICE

Assign any of the following:
1. Exercises, page 226
2. Workbook, *Mots 1: A*, page 100
3. Communication Activities Masters, *Mots 1: A–B*, pages 55–56
4. CD-ROM, Disc 3, pages 224–226

VOCABULAIRE

MOTS 2

D'AUTRES VÊTEMENTS

un pantalon

une veste

un collant

un imper(méable)

un complet

un tailleur

un short

un tee-shirt

une matière

une chemise en coton

une cravate

un chemisier en soie

un tissu

des chaussures (f.) en cuir

une robe en laine

un blouson en jean

Le coton, la soie et la laine sont des matières.
Le tricot et le jersey sont des tissus.

un pull en tricot

une jupe en jersey

Vocabulary Teaching Resources

1. Vocabulary Transparencies 9.2 (A & B)
2. Audio Cassette 6A/CD-5
3. Student Tape Manual, Teacher's Edition, *Mots 2: D–F*, pages 92–93
4. Workbook, *Mots 2: B–E*, pages 100–101
5. Communication Activities Masters, *Mots 2: C–D*, pages 57–58
6. Computer Software, *Vocabulaire*
7. Chapter Quizzes, *Mots 2: Quiz 2*, page 46
8. CD-ROM, Disc 3, *Mots 2:* 227–230

Bell Ringer Review

Write the following on the board or use BRR Blackline Master 9-2: Make a list of words and expressions you might need when shopping for clothes.

PRESENTATION (*pages 227–228*)

A. Present the new words using Vocabulary Transparencies 9.2 (A & B). Have students repeat each expression and sentence after you or Cassette 6A/CD-5.

B. Personalize the presentation with descriptions of what you or students are wearing. For example: *Regardez Marie. Elle porte une jupe rouge et un pull blanc. Et Joseph? Qu'est-ce qu'il porte? (Un blouson en jean, une chemise en coton, et un jean.)*, etc.

C. Have students repeat the mini-conversations after you using as much expression as possible.

D. You may wish to ask the following questions during your presentation: *Où est-ce que le jeune homme a fait une tache? Et la jeune fille, qu'est-ce qu'elle a perdu? Qu'est-ce que le jeune homme a cassé? Il a cassé la fermeture éclair de son blouson? Qu'est-ce que le garçon a déchiré? La jeune fille peut laver son pull? Le pull est en laine? La laine rétrécit?*

228   CHAPITRE 9

ADDITIONAL PRACTICE

1. You may wish to ask students the following additional questions about the illustrations: *Que porte l'homme qui a fait une tache? Et la fille qui a perdu un bouton? Comment est le garçon qui a cassé sa fermeture éclair? Que porte le garçon qui a déchiré sa manche?*, etc.

2. Student Tape Manual, Teacher's Edition, *Activités E–F,* page 93

Exercices

A **Qu'est-ce qu'il porte?** Choisissez un camarade de classe et décrivez ce qu'il porte.

B **Qu'est-ce qu'elle porte?** Choisissez une camarade de classe et décrivez ce qu'elle porte.

C **Des vêtements pour homme.** Voici des mannequins. Décrivez ce qu'ils portent. Donnez tous les détails possibles.

D **Des vêtements pour femme.** Voici un autre mannequin. Décrivez tout ce qu'elle porte. Donnez tous les détails possibles.

YVESSAINTLAURENT

variation

INFORMATIONS : (1) 45 08 91 00.

CHAPITRE 9 **229**

Exercices

PRESENTATION (*pages 229–230*)

Exercices A, B, C, and D

Exercises A and B are to be done with books closed. Exercises C and D are to be done with books open.

Note Students have already learned that the words *la vedette* and *la star* are always feminine, even when they refer to males. The word *mannequin,* on the other hand, is always masculine, even when it refers to female models.

ANSWERS

Exercice A

Answers will vary.

Exercice B

Answers will vary.

Exercice C

Answers will vary but may include the following:

L'homme à droite porte un complet bleu marine (en flanelle), une chemise blanche (en coton), une cravate bleu marine et rouge (en soie) et des chaussures noires (en cuir). Il a des lunettes de soleil à la main. L'homme à gauche porte un complet gris (en flanelle), une chemise blanche (en coton), une cravate noire et rouge (en soie), des chaussures (qu'on ne voit pas sur la photo). Il a un imperméable à la main.

Exercice D

Answers will vary but may include the following:

Elle porte un tailleur gris, un chemisier blanc (en coton ou en soie), des gants noirs et un collant noir.

229

Exercice E

1. b
2. c
3. c
4. c

Bell Ringer Review

Write the following on the board or use BRR Blackline Master 9-3: Complete the following sentences using the future tense.

1. Quand j'aurai vingt-cinq ans...
2. Quand je passerai le prochain examen de français...
3. Quand mes amis viendront chez moi...
4. Quand le professeur quittera cette classe...

Activités de communication orale
Mots 1 et 2

PRESENTATION *(page 230)*

It is not necessary to have students do all the activities. Select those which you consider most appropriate. You may wish to have groups do different activities.

Activité B

 In the CD-ROM version of this activity, students can interact with an on-screen native speaker.

ANSWERS
Activités A, B, and C
Answers will vary.

RECYCLING

You may wish to quickly review the vocabulary from *Bienvenue*, Chapter 10, which deals with shopping for clothing, as it fits in well with the lexicon of this chapter.

230

E De petits problèmes. Complétez.

1. Ah, zut! Il manque ___ à ma chemise. Je ne peux pas la porter.
   a. une manche
   b. un bouton
   c. un bâton
2. Il a laissé tomber de la pizza. Il y a ___ sur sa veste.
   a. une fermeture
   b. une manche
   c. une tache
3. Cette veste n'a pas de boutons. Elle a ___.
   a. une manche
   b. un repassage
   c. une fermeture éclair
4. Il ne faut pas la laver car elle est ___.
   a. en coton
   b. en jean
   c. en soie

Activités de communication orale
Mots 1 et 2

A La lessive. Travaillez avec un(e) camarade. Faites une liste de vos vêtements et dites en quelle matière ils sont. Votre camarade vous dira s'il/si elle laverait ou ferait nettoyer à sec ces vêtements. Changez ensuite de rôles.

> Élève 1: J'ai deux pulls en laine.
> Élève 2: À ta place je les ferais nettoyer.

B Qui fait la lessive chez vous? Vous êtes dans une laverie automatique en France avec votre amie française Sylvie. Elle veut savoir qui fait la lessive chez vous en Amérique. Répondez-lui.

1. Qui fait la lessive chez toi?
2. Qui repasse?
3. Qui plie le linge propre?
4. Tu fais nettoyer tes pulls ou tu les laves?

Sylvie

C À la laverie automatique. Imaginez que vous êtes dans une laverie automatique à Paris. Vous ne savez pas comment procéder. Vous demandez de l'aide à un(e) étudiant(e) français(e) qui fait sa lessive. Employez les expressions suivantes.

attendre une demi-heure	mettre la lessive
choisir la température	mettre le linge
fermer la machine	mettre les pièces
mettre l'eau de Javel *(bleach)*	sortir le linge

> Élève 1: Je mets les vêtements?
> Élève 2: Non, tu mets d'abord la lessive.
> Élève 1: Et après, je mets... ?

230   CHAPITRE 9

INDEPENDENT PRACTICE

Assign any of the following:
1. Exercises and activities, pages 229–230
2. Workbook, *Mots 2: B–E*, pages 100–101
3. Communication Activities Masters, *Mots 2: C–D*, pages 57–58
4. Computer Software, *Vocabulaire*
5. CD-ROM, Disc 3, pages 227–230

STRUCTURE

Le conditionnel — *Expressing Conditions*

1. You use the conditional in French, as you do in English, to express what would happen under certain circumstances. You form the conditional by adding the endings for the imperfect to the stem used for the future. Study the following forms of the conditional of regular verbs.

INFINITIVE	PARLER	FINIR	VENDRE	ENDINGS
STEM	parler-	finir-	vendr-	
CONDITIONAL	je parlerais	je finirais	je vendrais	-ais
	tu parlerais	tu finirais	tu vendrais	-ais
	il/elle/on parlerait	il/elle/on finirait	il/elle/on vendrait	-ait
	nous parlerions	nous finirions	nous vendrions	-ions
	vous parleriez	vous finiriez	vous vendriez	-iez
	ils/elles parleraient	ils/elles finiraient	ils/elles vendraient	-aient

2. The conditional is usually expressed in English by "would."

À ta place, je prendrais le train. — *If I were you, I would take the train.*

Il me donnerait de l'argent, mais il n'en a pas. — *He would give me some money but he doesn't have any.*

Je le ferais mais je n'ai pas le temps. — *I would do it but I don't have the time.*

3. Study the following irregular verbs.

INFINITIVE	CONDITIONAL
être	je serais
faire	je ferais
aller	j'irais
avoir	j'aurais
savoir	je saurais
pouvoir	je pourrais
devoir	je devrais
recevoir	je recevrais
voir	je verrais
envoyer	j'enverrais
vouloir	je voudrais
venir	je viendrais

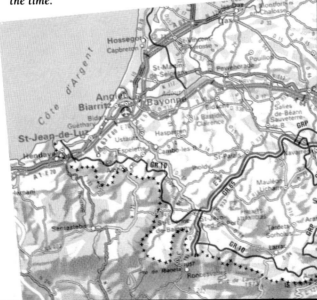

DID YOU KNOW?

Have students locate St.-Jean-de-Luz and Biarritz on the map on this page. Tell them that these cities are resort towns on the Atlantic coast close to the Spanish border.

Biarritz became fashionable when Emperor Napoleon III started spending his holidays there during the 19th century to enjoy the fine sand beaches.

Just south of Biarritz is the smaller town of St.-Jean-de-Luz. Its old streets, colorful harbor, elegant beach, and casinos make it a popular tourist destination. Louis XIV and Marie-Thérèse were married there on June 9, 1660.

PRESENTATION *(page 232)*

Exercices A and B

Exercises A and B can be done with books either open or closed.

ANSWERS

Exercice A

1. Oui, à ta place, je laverais mon linge sale moi-même. (Non,... je ne laverais pas...)
2. Oui, je le porterais à la laverie automatique. (Non, je ne le porterais pas à...)
3. Oui, je le mettrais dans la machine à laver. (Non, je ne le mettrais pas...)
4. Je le sécherais à la laverie automatique (à l'hôtel).
5. Oui, je le plierais. (Non, je ne le plierais pas.)
6. Oui, je laverais mon pull en laine. (Non, je ne laverais pas...)
7. Oui, je le porterais à la teinturerie. (Non, je ne le porterais pas...)
8. Oui, je le ferais nettoyer à sec. (Non, je ne le ferais pas nettoyer à sec.)

Exercice B

1. Oui, je travaillerais. (Non, je ne travaillerais pas.)
2. Oui, je voyagerais souvent. (Non, je ne voyagerais pas...)
3. J'irais...
4. Oui, je visiterais toutes les grandes villes du monde. (Non, je ne visiterais pas...)
5. Oui, je dînerais tous les soirs au restaurant. (Non, je ne dînerais pas...)
6. Oui, j'achèterais beaucoup de vêtements. (Non, je n'achèterais pas...)
7. Oui, je serais très chic. (Non, je ne serais pas...)
8. Oui, j'aurais une grande voiture de sport. (Non, je n'aurais pas...)
9. J'habiterais dans une grande maison à la campagne (dans un grand appartement en ville).
10. Oui, je donnerais de l'argent aux pauvres. (Non, je ne donnerais pas d'argent...)

---

4. You can also use the conditional to make a polite request. You are already familiar with the expression *je voudrais*.

> **Je voudrais du pain, s'il vous plaît.**

5. Note that *pouvoir* in the conditional means "could." *Devoir* in the conditional means "should."

> **Tu pourrais parler au prof.**
> **Tu devrais étudier plus. Je crois que ça serait une bonne idée.**

Exercices

A Le linge sale? Moi, je le laverais. *Répondez.*

1. À ma place, tu laverais ton linge sale toi-même?
2. Tu le porterais à la laverie automatique?
3. Tu le mettrais dans la machine à laver?
4. Tu le sécherais à la laverie automatique ou à l'hôtel?
5. Tu le plierais?
6. Tu laverais ton pull en laine?
7. Tu le porterais à la teinturerie?
8. Tu le ferais nettoyer à sec?

B Tout ce que je ferais si j'étais riche. *Répondez.*

1. Tu travaillerais?
2. Tu voyagerais souvent?
3. Où irais-tu?
4. Tu visiterais toutes les grandes villes du monde?
5. Tu dînerais tous les soirs au restaurant?
6. Tu achèterais beaucoup de vêtements?
7. Tu serais très chic?
8. Tu aurais une grande voiture de sport?
9. Tu habiterais dans un grand appartement en ville ou dans une grande maison à la campagne?
10. Tu donnerais de l'argent aux pauvres?

Une belle maison près de Cognac

LEARNING FROM PHOTOS

1. Ask students the following questions about the top photo: *Qu'est-ce qu'un lavomatique? À quelle heure est-il ouvert le matin? Ça coûte combien pour laver 20kg de lessive? 13kg? Ça coûte combien pour sécher la lessive pendant 30 minutes? À ton avis, ça coûte cher?*
2. Ask students to describe what the people in the bottom photo are wearing.

C **Je le connais très bien. Je sais ce qu'il ferait.** Complétez au conditionnel.

1. Jean ___. (voyager)
2. Il ___ beaucoup ça. (aimer)
3. Il ___ beaucoup de voyages. (faire)
4. Ses amis et lui ___ beaucoup de villes intéressantes. (visiter)
5. Ils ___ le français. (apprendre)
6. Ils ___ un cours à Paris. (suivre)
7. Ils s'y ___ beaucoup d'amis. (faire)
8. Moi aussi, je ___ voyager. (vouloir)
9. Je ___ avec mes copains. (voyager)
10. Nous ___ dans une île de la mer des Caraïbes peut-être. (aller)
11. Je ___ des bains de soleil. (prendre)
12. Je ___. (bronzer)
13. Et toi, qu'est-ce que tu ___? (faire)
14. Tu ___ mieux aller à la Martinique ou en France? (aimer)

D **On ferait du camping.** Répondez d'après les indications.

1. Tes copains aimeraient faire du camping? (oui)
2. Ils iraient où? (dans un camping à la montagne)
3. Tu les accompagnerais? (oui)
4. Vous dresseriez une tente? (oui)
5. Tu aiderais tes copains? (bien sûr)
6. Où dormirais-tu? (dans un sac de couchage)
7. Où est-ce que tu mettrais le sac de couchage? (dans la tente)
8. Qui préparerait le petit déjeuner le matin? (Romain)

Le Lac d'Orédon dans les Pyrénées

E **Après les cours.** Demandez poliment. Posez des questions au professeur d'après le modèle.

> **pouvoir m'aider**
> *Monsieur (Madame), est-ce que vous pourriez m'aider?*

1. être libre après les cours
2. avoir le temps de m'aider
3. vouloir bien m'expliquer le conditionnel
4. pouvoir me donner des devoirs supplémentaires
5. savoir quel livre explique le mieux la grammaire française

CHAPITRE 9 **233**

Les propositions avec si
PRESENTATION *(page 234)*

Write the sequence of tenses on the board and have students read the sample sentences aloud. Elicit and discuss other examples.

Exercices
ANSWERS

Exercice A

1. Oui (Non), si j'ai de l'argent, je (ne) ferai (pas) un grand voyage.
2. Oui (Non), si je fais un voyage, j'irai (je n'irai pas) en France.
3. Oui (Non), si je vais en France, je (ne) visiterai (pas) Paris.
4. Oui (Non), si je visite Paris, je (ne) monterai (pas) sur la tour Eiffel.
5. Oui (Non), si je monte sur la tour Eiffel, je (ne) prendrai (pas) des (de) photos.
6. Oui (Non), si je fais des photos, je (ne) les montrerai (pas) à mes amis.

Exercice B

1. Oui (Non), si j'avais de l'argent, je (ne) ferais (pas) un grand voyage.
2. Oui (Non), si je faisais un voyage, j'irais (je n'irais pas) en France.
3. Oui (Non), si j'allais en France, je (ne) visiterais (pas) Paris.
4. Oui (Non), si je visitais Paris, je (ne) monterais (pas) sur la tour Eiffel.
5. Oui (Non), si je montais sur la tour Eiffel, je (ne) prendrais (pas) des (de) photos.
6. Oui (Non), si je faisais des photos, je (ne) les montrerais (pas) à mes amis.

Exercice C

1. étais
2. passe
3. avons
4. irait

Les propositions avec *si*   *Expressing More Conditions*

The *si* clauses, "if" clauses in English, have the following sequence of tenses.

SI + PRÉSENT	FUTUR
Si j'ai de l'argent,	je ferai un grand voyage.

SI + IMPARFAIT	CONDITIONNEL
Si j'avais de l'argent,	je ferais un grand voyage.

Exercices

A Avec des *si*... Donnez des réponses personnelles.

1. Si tu as de l'argent, tu feras un grand voyage?
2. Si tu fais un voyage, tu iras en France?
3. Si tu vas en France, tu visiteras Paris?
4. Si tu visites Paris, tu monteras sur la tour Eiffel?
5. Si tu montes sur la tour Eiffel, tu prendras des photos?
6. Si tu fais des photos, tu les montreras à tes amis?

B Encore avec des *si*... Donnez des réponses personnelles.

1. Si tu avais de l'argent, tu ferais un grand voyage?
2. Si tu faisais un voyage, tu irais en France?
3. Si tu allais en France, tu visiterais Paris?
4. Si tu visitais Paris, tu monterais sur la tour Eiffel?
5. Si tu montais sur la tour Eiffel, tu prendrais des photos?
6. Si tu faisais des photos, tu les montrerais à tes amis?

C Si j'étais toi. Complétez.

1. Si j' ___ (être) toi je prendrais un imper.
2. Si elle ___ (passer) par Paris elle me téléphonera.
3. Nous viendrons vous voir si nous ___ (avoir) le temps.
4. Il n' ___ (aller) pas à la laverie automatique s'il avait une machine à laver.

La tour Eiffel la nuit

ADDITIONAL PRACTICE

1. After completing Exercises A–C, you may wish to have students complete these sentences.
   S'il y avait un accident, je...
   Si je ratais mon train, je...
   S'il y avait trop de circulation sur l'autoroute, je...
   S'il y avait trop de circulation au centre-ville, je...
   Si je ne savais pas le numéro de téléphone de mon ami, je...
   Si je n'avais pas le temps de lui écrire, je...
   Si mon père était malade, je...

2. Student Tape Manual, Teacher's Edition, *Activités A–B*, page 94

Faire et un autre verbe

Saying What You or Others Have Someone Else Do

1. You use the verb *faire* + an infinitive to express what you have someone else do for you. Study the following sentences.

> **Je lave ma chemise moi-même.**
> **Je ne lave pas ma chemise moi-même. Je fais laver ma chemise.**
>
> **Il construit sa maison.**
> **Il ne construit pas sa maison lui-même. Il fait construire sa maison.**

2. If an object pronoun is used, it precedes the *faire* construction.

> **Je ne lave pas la chemise moi-même.**
> **Je la fais laver.**

Exercices

A **Tu le fais toi-même ou tu le fais faire?** Répondez d'après les indications.

1. Tu laves le chemisier? (non)
2. Tu le fais laver? (oui)
3. Où est-ce que tu le fais laver? (à la laverie automatique)
4. Tu nettoies la veste? (non)
5. Tu la fais nettoyer à sec? (oui)
6. Où est-ce que tu la fais nettoyer à sec? (à la teinturerie)
7. Tu repasses le pantalon? (non)
8. Tu le fais repasser? (oui)
9. Où est-ce que tu le fais repasser? (à la teinturerie)

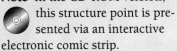

B **Le prof me fait étudier.** Donnez des réponses personnelles.

1. Le/La prof te fait beaucoup parler dans la classe de français?
2. Il/Elle te fait lire?
3. Il/Elle te fait chanter des chansons françaises?
4. Il/Elle te fait passer des examens?
5. Il/Elle te fait faire des devoirs?

Faire et un autre verbe

PRESENTATION *(page 235)*

A. Guide students through steps 1 and 2.
B. Tell students that when someone performs an action himself or herself, only one verb is used. If a person has someone else do the action, *faire* is used with the verb.

Note In the CD-ROM version, this structure point is presented via an interactive electronic comic strip.

Exercices

ANSWERS

Exercice A

1. Non, je ne lave pas le chemisier.
2. Oui, je le fais laver.
3. Je le fais laver à la laverie automatique.
4. Non, je ne nettoie pas la veste.
5. Oui, je la fais nettoyer à sec.
6. Je la fais nettoyer à sec à la teinturerie.
7. Non, je ne repasse pas le pantalon.
8. Oui, je le fais repasser.
9. Je le fais repasser à la teinturerie.

Exercice B

1. Oui, le/la prof me fait beaucoup parler... (Non, le/la prof ne me fait pas beaucoup parler...)
2. Oui, il/elle me fait lire. (Non, il/elle ne me fait pas lire.)
3. Oui, il/elle me fait chanter des chansons françaises. (Non, il/elle ne me fait pas chanter de chansons...)
4. Oui, il/elle me fait passer des examens. (Non, il/elle ne me fait pas passer d'examens.)
5. Oui, il/elle me fait faire des devoirs. (Non, il/elle ne me fait pas faire de devoirs.)

ADDITIONAL PRACTICE

After completing Exercises A and B, ask students if the subject is acting alone or having someone else perform the action:

1. Je lave ma chemise.
2. Je fais laver ma chemise.
3. Je repasse ma chemise.
4. Je fais repasser ma chemise.
5. Je lave ma voiture.
6. Je fais laver ma voiture.

INDEPENDENT PRACTICE

Assign any of the following:
1. Exercises, pages 234–235
2. Workbook, *Structure: C–E*, pages 103–104
3. Communication Activities Masters, *Structure: B–C*, page 60
4. Computer Software, *Structure*
5. CD-ROM, Disc 3, pages 234–235

CONVERSATION

CONVERSATION

Bell Ringer Review

Write the following on the board or use BRR Blackline Master 9-5: Answer the questions using pronouns. Example: Tu as donné ta photo à ton ami(e)? Non, je ne la lui ai pas donnée.

1. Tu as donné tes livres à tes copains?
2. Tu as expliqué ton devoir au (à la) prof?
3. Tu as vendu ton stylo à ton camarade?
4. Tu as montré ta composition au gendarme?
5. Tu as chanté la chanson à tous les élèves?

PRESENTATION *(page 236)*

A. Tell students they will hear a conversation between Didier and a woman at a laundry.
B. Have them close their books and watch the Conversation Video or listen as you read the conversation or play the recorded audio version.
C. Have students read along with you or Cassette 6A/CD-5. (Use *Activité E* in the Student Tape Manual to check oral comprehension.)
D. Have students practice reading the conversation in pairs, then call on two students to present it to the class.

Note In the CD-ROM version, students can play the role of either one of the characters and record the conversation.

Exercices

ANSWERS

Exercice A

1. chemises
2. laver, repasser
3. amidonnées
4. amidon

236

Scènes de la vie *À la laverie*

DIDIER: Je voudrais faire laver et repasser ces deux chemises, s'il vous plaît.
L'EMPLOYÉE: Pas de problème, Monsieur. Vous les voulez amidonnées?
DIDIER: Non, pas d'amidon.
L'EMPLOYÉE: D'accord, Monsieur.

A **Pas d'amidon.** Complétez d'après la conversation.

1. Didier a deux ___.
2. Il voudrait les faire ___ et ___.
3. Il ne les veut pas ___.
4. Il ne veut pas d'___.

B **Les chemises de Didier.** Répondez d'après la conversation.

1. Didier va laver ses chemises?
2. Il va les repasser?
3. Il voudrait les faire laver et repasser?
4. Il a combien de chemises?
5. Il voudrait de l'amidon?

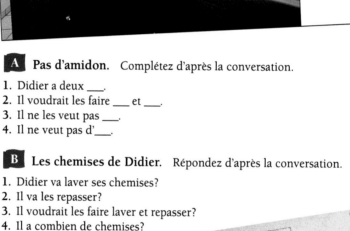

ADDITIONAL PRACTICE

Present the following conversation to the students. It takes place at a *teinturerie*. Then ask the questions that follow.

L'employé: Oui, Monsieur?
Olivier: J'aimerais faire nettoyer cette veste.
L'employé: Oui, Monsieur. Vous la voulez pour quand?
Olivier: Je pourrais l'avoir pour demain après-midi?
L'employé: Pas de problème, Monsieur. Vers quatre heures. Ça vous convient?
Olivier: Parfait.

1. Olivier est où?
2. Qu'est-ce qu'il veut?
3. Le teinturier peut nettoyer sa veste?
4. Olivier veut la faire nettoyer à sec?
5. Pour quand veut-il sa veste?

Activités de communication orale

A J'aimerais… Vous parlez à un(e) camarade. Dites-lui ce que vous aimeriez faire demain. Demandez-lui s'il/si elle aimerait faire les mêmes choses et pourquoi.

B Si j'étais… Demandez à un(e) camarade ce qu'il/elle ferait s'il/si elle était l'une des personnes suivantes. Ensuite changez de rôles.

> extraterrestre   professeur
> millionnaire   disc-jockey

> Élève 1: Qu'est-ce que tu ferais si tu étais millionnaire?
> Élève 2: Si j'étais millionnaire, j'achèterais un yacht et je vivrais en France, sur la Côte d'Azur.

C Mes parents me font faire… Travaillez avec un(e) camarade. Il/Elle vous dira ce qu'on lui fait faire chez lui/elle. Dites-lui si on vous fait faire la même chose chez vous. Ensuite posez-lui une autre question.

> Élève 1: Mes parents me font faire la vaisselle tous les soirs. Et toi?
> Élève 2: Moi, mes parents me font mettre le couvert et débarrasser la table. Est-ce que tes parents te font faire la lessive?

Exercice B
1. Non, il ne va pas laver ses chemises.
2. Non, il ne va pas les repasser.
3. Oui, il voudrait les faire laver et repasser.
4. Il a deux chemises.
5. Non, il ne voudrait pas d'amidon.

> **Bell Ringer Review**
>   *Write the following on the board or use BRR Blackline Master 9-6:* Form adverbs from the following adjectives:
>
> | | |
> |---|---|
> | évident | vrai |
> | heureux | récent |
> | complet | sérieux |
> | direct | annuel |

Activités de communication orale
ANSWERS
Activités A, B, and C
  Answers will vary.

LEARNING FROM PHOTOS

  Have students say as much as they can about the photo.

INDEPENDENT PRACTICE

  Assign any of the following:
1. Exercises and activities, pages 236–237
2. CD-ROM, Disc 3, pages 236–237

LECTURE ET CULTURE

READING STRATEGIES
(*pages 238–239*)

Pre-reading

Have students turn to the map on page 240. Point out the Pyrenees, Bayonne, and the Camargue to them.

Reading

Call on volunteers to read four to five sentences at a time aloud. After each person reads, ask the class your own comprehension questions or those on page 240.

Post-reading

Call on volunteers to describe Flore's experiences in their own words.

Note Students may listen to a recorded version of the *Lecture* on the CD-ROM.

OÙ EST LA LAVERIE?

«Bonjour! Je m'appelle Flore et je fais de la randonnée pédestre[1]. Je viens de terminer[2] une randonnée de deux semaines dans les Pyrénées. Et maintenant, me voici à Bayonne. Après quinze jours dans mon sac à dos tous mes vêtements sont bien sales et chiffonnés. Je vais les faire laver ici à Bayonne avant de partir pour la Camargue. Je voudrais bien les laver moi-même mais ce n'est pas possible car il n'y a pas de machine à laver à l'auberge de jeunesse[3]. Je vais chercher une laverie automatique dans les pages jaunes.

Ah, voilà une laverie tout près d'ici, rue Denis».

Flore a mis son linge sale dans un sac en plastique et elle est allée à la laverie. Elle l'a trouvée sans problème. Elle croyait que la laverie serait automatique et qu'elle pourrait laver son linge elle-même, mais comme dans beaucoup de laveries en France, il y avait un employé, un gentil jeune homme qui a expliqué à Flore qu'il prendrait son linge et le mettrait dans la machine à laver. Elle pourrait le récupérer dans les deux heures.

Deux heures plus tard, Flore est revenue à la laverie et son linge était prêt. Le gentil jeune homme lui a rendu son linge bien propre et soigneusement[4] plié, sauf son pull, qu'il n'a pas lavé

En randonnée dans le Parc national des Écrins

parce qu'il est en laine. Flore l'a payé et lui a donné un petit pourboire pour le remercier. Elle est rentrée à l'auberge de jeunesse où elle a remis les vêtements dans son sac à dos. Le lendemain elle est partie pour la Camargue faire une autre randonnée.

[1] je fais de la randonnée pédestre   *I'm backpacking*
[2] je viens de terminer   *I have just finished*
[3] l'auberge de jeunesse   *youth hostel*
[4] soigneusement   *carefully*

DID YOU KNOW?

Le Parc national des Écrins, qui se trouve dans la région Rhône-Alpes, est le plus grand et le plus élevé des parcs nationaux de France.

Étude de mots

A **Quel est le mot?** Trouvez dans la lecture le mot ou l'expression qui correspond.

1. deux semaines
2. pas propre
3. une section de l'annuaire qui donne les numéros de téléphone des magasins, etc.
4. un hôtel pour les jeunes gens
5. une somme d'argent qu'un client donne comme récompense pour un service

Randonnées
Le Haut Entre deux Mers à pied, à cheval, à vélo

Des campeurs dans les Pyrénées

Étude de mots

ANSWERS

Exercice A

1. quinze jours
2. sale
3. les pages jaunes
4. une auberge de jeunesse
5. un pourboire

LEARNING FROM PHOTOS

Challenge students to say as much as they can about the photos on pages 238–239. How do these outdoor scenes compare to similar ones in the U.S.?

INDEPENDENT PRACTICE

Assign any of the following:
1. *Étude de mots* exercises, page 239
2. CD-ROM, Disc 3, pages 238–239

Compréhension

ANSWERS

Exercice B

1. Flore fait de la randonnée pédestre depuis deux semaines.
2. Elle fait de la randonnée pédestre dans les Pyrénées.
3. Elle est maintenant à Bayonne.
4. Elle a beaucoup de linge sale parce que tous ses vêtements ont été dans son sac à dos pendant deux semaines.
5. Elle a trouvé l'adresse de la laverie dans les pages jaunes.
6. Non, elle n'a pas lavé son linge elle-même.
7. Un gentil jeune homme l'a mis dans la machine à laver.
8. Quand il l'a sorti de la machine à laver, il a soigneusement plié le linge.
9. Il n'a pas lavé le pull de Flore parce qu'il était (est) en laine.

Exercice C

Students find the places on the map.

Compréhension

B **Vous avez compris?** Répondez d'après la lecture.

1. Que fait Flore depuis deux semaines?
2. Où fait-elle de la randonnée pédestre?
3. Elle est maintenant dans quelle ville?
4. Pourquoi a-t-elle beaucoup de linge sale?
5. Où a-t-elle trouvé l'adresse de la laverie?
6. Elle a lavé son linge elle-même?
7. Qui l'a mis dans la machine à laver?
8. Quand il l'a sorti de la machine à laver, qu'est-ce qu'il a fait du linge?
9. Il n'a pas lavé le pull de Flore. Pourquoi?

C **Savez-vous où se trouve...?** Trouvez sur la carte.

1. Bayonne
2. Les Pyrénées
3. La Camargue

DID YOU KNOW?

The Camargue region has only about 10,000 inhabitants. The region has had a recent economic rebirth due to the cultivation of rice (*la culture du riz*).

CRITICAL THINKING ACTIVITY

(Thinking skills: making inferences)
Read the following to the class or write it on the board or on a transparency:
Pourquoi la Camargue intéresserait-elle une personne comme Flore qui aime la nature?

DÉCOUVERTE CULTURELLE

Flore a passé quinze jours dans les Pyrénées où elle a fait de la randonnée pédestre. Et maintenant elle va en Camargue. Flore est une vraie naturaliste. Pourquoi veut-elle aller en Camargue? La Camargue est une région très pittoresque dans le delta du Rhône. C'est aujourd'hui un parc naturel régional. En Camargue il y a beaucoup d'oiseaux[1] exotiques. Il y a aussi des troupeaux de taureaux[2] et de chevaux sauvages. Les gardians surveillent ces troupeaux ou «manades». Les gardians sont les «cowboys» français.

Encore un peu de géographie! Les Pyrénées sont les montagnes qui forment la frontière entre la France et l'Espagne. Quelles sont les montagnes qui forment la frontière entre la France et la Suisse? Le Rhône est un fleuve important qui prend sa source dans les Alpes suisses. Il est alimenté[3] par de très grands glaciers. Le Rhône est le plus abondant des fleuves français. Dans le sud, le Rhône forme un delta tout près d'Arles. La Camargue se trouve dans le delta du Rhône. Ce fleuve se jette dans la mer Méditerranée ou dans l'océan Atlantique? Quels sont les autres fleuves français? Quel est le fleuve qui traverse Paris? Vous avez dit la Seine? Vous avez raison!

[1] oiseaux *birds*
[2] troupeaux de taureaux *herds of bulls*
[3] alimenté *fed*

Des gardians en Camargue

Les Pyrénées

INDEPENDENT PRACTICE

Assign any of the following:
1. Workbook, *Un Peu Plus*, pages 105–106
2. *Compréhension* exercises, page 240
3. CD-ROM, Disc 3, pages 240–241

DID YOU KNOW?

The horses of the Camargue belong to a very old race. They are famous for their hardiness, endurance, sure-footedness, and handling.

Bell Ringer Review

Write the following on the board or use BRR Blackline Master 9-7: What did you do this morning before you left for school? Write five sentences. Example: *Je me suis réveillé(e) à sept heures.*

OPTIONAL MATERIAL

Découverte culturelle
PRESENTATION *(page 241)*

A. Have students refer to the map on page 240 or the one on page 435. (You may wish to use the France Map Transparency.)
B. Have students read the selection silently.

Note Students may listen to a recorded version of the *Découverte culturelle* on the CD-ROM.

GEOGRAPHY CONNECTION

1. Have students find the following rivers on the map of France on page 435 or on the France Map Transparency: *le Rhin, la Loire, la Garonne.*
2. The following is a slightly rewritten version of comments about the Camargue from the *Guide Michelin:*
La Camargue n'est pas une des plus belles régions de Provence. Mais elle est intéressante. Le touriste y ressentira une profonde impression de solitude. Les meilleures époques pour visiter sont mai et octobre. On évitera ainsi le soleil et les moustiques de l'été. La Camargue ne convient guère (très peu) aux touristes qui recherchent l'animation et les distractions élégantes. Mais elle plaira aux amateurs de calmes paysages d'eau, de solitude, de vastes horizons et d'air marin.

RÉALITÉS

Bell Ringer Review

Write the following on the board or use BRR Blackline Master 9-8: Complete the sentences with the correct forms and tense of the verbs in parentheses.

1. Vous avez acheté du pain et vous ____ à la caisse? (payer)
2. J'____ toujours un stylo pour écrire mes devoirs. (employer)
3. Quand nous étions petits, notre tante nous ____ souvent des cadeaux. (envoyer)
4. Au cours de maths, nous ____ une calculatrice. (employer)
5. Quand Paul et Marc seront riches, ils ____ de l'argent à leurs parents. (envoyer)

OPTIONAL MATERIAL

PRESENTATION
(pages 242–243)

Allow students time to enjoy the photos on their own. Answer any questions they may have.

Note In the CD-ROM version, students can listen to the recorded captions and discover a hidden video behind one of the photos.

1

2

oici de petits chevaux blancs typiques de la Camargue **1**. Ces chevaux sont élevés dans cette région. Tu les trouves beaux?

Voici des maisons en Camargue **2**. Tu aimerais vivre dans une de ces maisons? Pourquoi? La Camargue est un parc naturel très pittoresque qui se trouve dans le delta du Rhône.

Voilà une jeune fille dans une laverie **3**. Après avoir fait de la randonnée pédestre pendant quinze jours, elle a beaucoup de linge sale. C'est une laverie automatique ou est-ce qu'il y a des employés qui lavent le linge?

Chaque année il y a trois grands pèlerinages aux Saintes-Maries-de-la-Mer, un joli port de pêche en Camargue. Ces hommes font partie du pèlerinage d'octobre **4**.

DID YOU KNOW?

According to legend, a boat without oars landed on the southwest corner of the Camargue carrying, among others, Mary Magdalene, Mary Jacoby (sister of the Virgin), Mary Salome (mother of James and John), and Lazarus. The saints Mary Jacoby and Mary Salome remained in the area and the town Saintes-Maries-de-la-Mer was named in their honor.

Two pilgrimages are held each year, one in May and the other in October. After Mass, *gardians*, herdsmen of the longhorn bulls, lead the procession followed by figures of the saints, carried in a little blue boat. The Bishop and the local clergy follow the images to the shore where the Bishop blesses the sea. After the religious ceremony, the *gardians* participate in branding bulls, a bull-run, and bullfights.

3

4

243

ADDITIONAL PRACTICE

Assign any of the following:
1. Student Tape Manual, Teacher's Edition, *Deuxième Partie,* pages 96–98
2. Situation Cards, Chapter 9

RECYCLING

These activities encourage students to use all the language they have learned in the chapter and recombine it with material from previous chapters. It is not necessary to do all the activities with all students. You may select the ones you consider most appropriate or permit students to choose the ones they wish to do.

INFORMAL ASSESSMENT

You may wish to use the oral and written exercises in this section as a review at the end of the chapter or to evaluate speaking and writing skills. For suggestions on grading the oral activities, see the evaluation criteria on page 22 of this Teacher's Wraparound Edition.

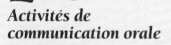

Activités de communication orale

ANSWERS

Activités A and B

Answers will vary.

Activités de communication écrite

ANSWERS

Activités A, B, and C

Answers will vary.

Activités de communication orale

A **Si j'avais…** Demandez à un(e) camarade ce qu'il/elle ferait s'il/si elle avait les choses suivantes. Ensuite changez de rôles.

> plus de temps   sa propre voiture
> plus d'argent   son propre avion

> Élève 1: Qu'est-ce que tu ferais si tu avais plus de temps?
> Élève 2: Si j'avais plus de temps, j'irais à la plage tous les jours.

B **Que vais-je bien mettre?** Vous êtes invité(e) dans différents endroits et vous ne savez pas quoi mettre. Vous demandez conseil à un(e) camarade.

> Élève 1: Je suis invitée à l'Opéra demain. Qu'est-ce que tu mettrais à ma place?
> Élève 2: Je ne sais pas, moi. Ta robe longue noire.
> Élève 1: Si tu faisais du ski, qu'est-ce que tu mettrais comme vêtements?
> Élève 2: Je mettrais des gants et un bonnet en laine, un anorak et un pantalon de ski.

Activités de communication écrite

A **Si je gagnais la loterie…** Décrivez toutes les choses que vous feriez si vous gagniez la loterie.

B **J'adore la nature!** Imaginez que vous avez fait une randonnée pédestre en Camargue ou dans un parc national américain pendant deux semaines. Dans une lettre à un(e) ami(e), décrivez tout ce que vous avez vu et fait.

C **Quelle horreur!** C'est la première fois que vous faites la lessive pour votre famille et tout se passe très mal. La machine ne marche pas bien, tous les vêtements rétrécissent, vous mettez de l'eau de Javel (*bleach*) sur le chemisier vert de votre mère, vous mettez ensemble le blanc et les couleurs, etc. Décrivez cette expérience horrible et les réactions de votre famille.

244 CHAPITRE 9

COOPERATIVE LEARNING

Have teams create original conversations between two or more people at the following places:
1. à la laverie
2. à la teinturerie
3. au grand magasin
4. au rayon de vêtements pour hommes
5. au rayon de vêtements pour femmes
6. au rayon de chaussures

PAIRED ACTIVITY

Display Communication Transparency C-9. Have pairs of students make up the conversation between the mother and daughter in the illustration. Have different pairs present their conversations to the class.

Réintroduction et recombinaison

A **Des vêtements.** Répondez d'après le dessin.

1. C'est la boutique d'un grand couturier ou un grand magasin?
2. C'est le rayon prêt-à-porter?
3. Ce sont des vêtements pour hommes?
4. Il y a des soldes ou pas?
5. Il y a des rabais (réductions)?
6. Quand il y a des rabais, les vêtements sont plus chers ou meilleur marché?

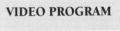

B **Le contraire.** Trouvez le contraire.

1. large   a. étroit
2. long   b. au-dessus
3. haut   c. bas
4. au-dessous   d. bon marché
5. cher   e. court

C **Une petite enquête.** Donnez des réponses personnelles.

1. Quelle est la taille de ton chemisier ou de ta chemise?
2. Quelle est la pointure de tes tennis?
3. Tu préfères les manches longues ou les manches courtes?
4. Tu préfères les talons bas ou les talons hauts?
5. Tu préfères faire tes achats dans une boutique ou dans un grand magasin?

Vocabulaire

NOMS
la laverie automatique
la machine à laver
le sèche-linge
le linge
la lessive
l'amidon (m.)
la teinturerie
le pressing
le nettoyage à sec

la veste
le blouson
la chemise
la cravate
le pantalon

le complet
l'imper(méable) (m.)
le tee-shirt
le short
le pull
la chaussure
le chemisier
la jupe
la robe
le tailleur
le collant

le tissu
la matière
le bouton
la fermeture éclair

la manche
la tache

ADJECTIFS
chiffonné(e)
sale
propre

VERBES
porter
laver
sécher
repasser
plier
nettoyer à sec
rétrécir

déchirer
casser

AUTRES MOTS ET EXPRESSIONS
en coton
en cuir
en jean
en laine
en soie
en tricot
en jersey
à ta (sa, votre, etc.) place
faire la lessive
il manque + nom

CHAPITRE 9   **245**

INDEPENDENT PRACTICE

Assign any of the following:
1. Activities and exercises, pages 244–245
2. Communication Activities Masters, pages 55–60
3. CD-ROM, Disc 3, pages 244–245

OPTIONAL MATERIAL

Réintroduction et recombinaison

PRESENTATION *(page 245)*

These review exercises recycle vocabulary and structures from *Bienvenue,* Chapter 10.

ANSWERS
Exercice A
1. C'est un grand magasin.
2. Oui, c'est le rayon prêt-à-porter.
3. Oui, ce sont des vêtements pour hommes.
4. Oui, il y a des soldes.
5. Oui, il y a des rabais.
6. Quand il y a des rabais, les vêtements sont meilleur marché.

Exercice B
1. a
2. e
3. c
4. b
5. d

Exercice C
Answers will vary.

ASSESSMENT RESOURCES

1. Chapter Quizzes
2. Testing Program
3. Situation Cards
4. Communication Transparency C-9
5. Computer Software: Practice/Test Generator

VIDEO PROGRAM

INTRODUCTION   (33:32)

QUELLE CATASTROPHE!   (34:01)

245

CHAPTER OVERVIEW

In this chapter students will learn vocabulary associated with the public transportation system in a French-speaking country. They will increase their ability to ask and understand directions. They will learn to use the pronoun *en* to refer to people and to use the pronouns *y* and *en* with other pronouns. They will once again be exposed to the various ways of asking questions and learn to express the idea "to have just done something."

The cultural focus of Chapter 10 is on public transportation in and around Paris.

CHAPTER OBJECTIVES

By the end of this chapter, students will know:

1. vocabulary associated with taking the subway
2. vocabulary associated with taking the bus
3. the pronoun *en* used to refer to people
4. the position of the pronouns *y* and *en* when used together or with other pronouns in the same sentence
5. the various ways to form questions
6. the use of the construction *venir de* + infinitive

CHAPITRE

10

LES TRANSPORTS EN COMMUN

OBJECTIFS

In this chapter you will learn to do the following:

1. use the Parisian public transportation system
2. refer to people and things already mentioned
3. request information formally and informally
4. tell what you and others have just done
5. discuss the Parisian public transportation system and life in the Paris suburbs

CHAPTER PROJECTS

(optional)

1. Have students study the Paris *métro* map on page 268. They should choose a starting point and destination and write out the directions necessary to get from one to the other.
2. Have groups prepare questions they feel would be most useful when making their way about an unfamiliar French city.
3. Have groups research and compare various aspects of French and American cities and suburbs. Possible topics might include: public transportation, populations of city centers vs. suburbs, number of commuters, etc.

247

CHAPTER 10 RESOURCES

1. Workbook
2. Student Tape Manual
3. Audio Cassette 6B/CD-5
4. Bell Ringer Review Blackline Masters
5. Vocabulary Transparencies
6. Communication Transparency C-10
7. Communication Activities Masters
8. Situation Cards
9. Conversation Video
10. Videocassette/Videodisc, Unit 3
11. Video Activities Booklet, Unit 3
12. Lesson Plans
13. Computer Software: Practice/Test Generator
14. Chapter Quizzes
15. Testing Program
16. Internet Activities Booklet
17. CD-ROM Interactive Textbook

Pacing

This chapter will require eight to ten class sessions. Pacing will depend on the length of the class, the age of the students, and student aptitude.

For more information on planning your class, see the Lesson Plans, which offer guidelines for 45- and 55-minute classes and **Block Scheduling.**

Exercices vs. *Activités*

The exercises and activities are color-coded. Exercises, which provide guided practice to prepare students for independent communication, are coded in blue. Communicative activities, which give students opportunities for creative, open-ended expression, are coded in red.

COMMUNITIES

If you live in an area with a public transportation system, have students prepare a brochure for French-speaking visitors on how to use it. Then send it to the local Chamber of Commerce or the nearest foreign student exchange organization.

INTERNET ACTIVITIES

(optional)

These activities, student worksheets, and related teacher information are in the *À bord* Internet Activities Booklet and on the Glencoe Foreign Language Home Page at: http://www.glencoe.com/secondary/fl

VOCABULAIRE

MOTS 1

Vocabulary Teaching Resources

1. Vocabulary Transparencies 10.1(A & B)
2. Audio Cassette 6B/CD-5
3. Student Tape Manual, Teacher's Edition, *Mots 1: A–C,* pages 99–101
4. Workbook, *Mots 1: A–C,* pages 108–109
5. Communication Activities Masters, *Mots 1: A–B,* pages 61–62
6. Chapter Quizzes, *Mots 1:* Quiz 1, page 50
7. CD-ROM, Disc 3, *Mots 1:* pages 248–250

Bell Ringer Review

Write the following on the board or use BRR Blackline Master 10-1: List all the words and expressions you can remember that have to do with train travel.

PRESENTATION (*pages 248–249*)

A. Have students close their books. Using Vocabulary Transparencies 10.1 (A & B), have students repeat the words, phrases, and sentences after you or Cassette 6B/CD-5.

B. Ask either/or and yes/no questions to elicit the vocabulary. Then point in random order to illustrations on the Vocabulary Transparencies and ask *Qu'est-ce que c'est?*

C. Have students open their books and read pages 248–249. Model the correct pronunciation as necessary.

LE MÉTRO

la station (de métro)

le métro

le quai

un distributeur automatique

un guichet

un carnet

un ticket

la direction Vincennes

un escalier mécanique = un escalator

la direction La Défense

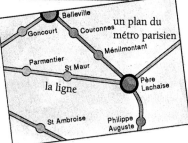

un plan du métro parisien

la ligne

Les deux lignes se croisent à cette station.

un trottoir roulant

248 CHAPITRE 10

ADDITIONAL PRACTICE

Have pairs or groups of students write and present short skits in which they must refer to a map, buy a ticket, ask for directions, etc.

la correspondance

Les voyageurs changent de ligne.
Ils prennent la correspondance.

Le métro vient de partir.

CHAPITRE 10   249

D. Have students repeat the mini-conversations with as much expression as possible.

E. You may wish to ask the following questions about the illustrations: *Est-ce que les voyageurs attendent le métro sur le quai? Est-ce qu'on peut acheter les tickets au guichet et au distributeur automatique? Est-ce que les voyageurs prennent la correspondance là où les deux lignes se croisent? Est-ce qu'on peut descendre sur le quai par l'escalier mécanique? Le métro vient de partir? Les voyageurs l'ont raté? Où est la station de métro la plus proche? Il faut prendre quelle direction pour aller Place de la Bastille?*

F. Have students repeat the mini-conversation on the right, substituting different place names. They can refer to the *métro* map on page 268.

CRITICAL THINKING ACTIVITY

(*Thinking skill: problem-solving*)
     Read the following to the class or write it on the board or on a transparency:
Vous êtes à Paris avec un ami qui ne parle pas français. Vous prenez le métro pour aller au Louvre. Il y a beaucoup de monde dans la station. Quand vous montez en voiture, vous ne voyez pas votre ami. Que faites-vous?

PRESENTATION *(page 250)*

Exercice A

🎧 Exercise A is to be done with books open.

Exercice B

Exercise B is to be done with books open.

Extension of *Exercice B*

After completing Exercise B, have one student read the entire exercise as a story.

ANSWERS

Exercice A

1. C'est l'entrée du métro.
2. C'est un distributeur automatique.
3. C'est un ticket.
4. C'est un escalier mécanique.
5. C'est le métro.

Exercice B

1. proche
2. quai
3. guichet, distributeur automatique
4. carnet
5. escalier mécanique
6. plan du métro
7. croisent
8. correspondance
9. trottoir roulant
10. métro

Exercices

A **Qu'est-ce que c'est?** Répondez d'après les photos.

1. C'est l'entrée du métro ou le quai?

2. C'est un guichet ou un distributeur automatique?

3. C'est un ticket ou un carnet?

4. C'est un trottoir roulant ou un escalier mécanique?

5. C'est le métro ou un autobus?

B **Dans la station de métro.** Complétez.

1. Quand je ne sais pas où se trouve la station de métro la plus ___, je demande à quelqu'un.
2. Je vais prendre le métro. Je descends sur le ___.
3. Je peux acheter ou prendre les billets au ___ ou au ___.
4. Je peux acheter les billets un par un ou je peux acheter un ___.
5. Je prends l'___ pour descendre sur le quai de la station de métro.
6. Je ne sais pas la direction que je dois prendre. Je vais regarder le ___.
7. Beaucoup de lignes se ___ à la station qui s'appelle Châtelet.
8. On peut prendre la ___ dans une station où deux lignes se croisent.
9. Quand je change de ligne, je prends le ___ quand la correspondance est longue.
10. Zut! Le ___ vient de partir. Je l'ai raté!

250 CHAPITRE 10

LEARNING FROM PHOTOS

Assign one photo from Exercise A to each team of students. Teams write composite descriptions of their photo, with as much detail as possible.

ADDITIONAL PRACTICE

Student Tape Manual, Teacher's Edition, *Activité C,* page 101

VOCABULAIRE

MOTS 2

L'AUTOBUS

le numéro

un arrêt

un autobus (m.)

un conducteur

un ticket

une machine = un appareil

oblitérer (valider) le ticket

une portière

un bouton

appuyer sur le bouton

Pour demander un arrêt, on appuie sur le bouton.
Il est interdit de s'appuyer contre la portière.

CHAPITRE 10   **251**

Vocabulary Teaching Resources

1. Vocabulary Transparencies 10.2 (A & B)
2. Audio Cassette 6B/CD-5
3. Student Tape Manual, Teacher's Edition, *Mots 2: D–F,* pages 101–103
4. Workbook, *Mots 2: D–G,* pages 109–110
5. Communication Activities Masters, *Mots 2: C–D,* pages 63–64
6. Computer Software, *Vocabulaire*
7. Chapter Quizzes, *Mots 2:* Quiz 2, page 51
8. CD-ROM, Disc 3, *Mots 2:* pages 251–254

Bell Ringer Review

Write the following on the board or use BRR Blackline Master 10-2: Complete the following sentences:

1. Si je reçois de bonnes notes cette année,...
2. Si je vois mon ami(e) après ce cours,...
3. Si je vais au cinéma ce week-end,...
4. Si je dois faire mes devoirs ce soir,...
5. Si je pose une question au professeur,...

PRESENTATION *(pages 251–252)*

A. Pointing to Vocabulary Transparencies 10.2 (A & B), have students repeat the new words, phrases and sentences after you or Cassette 6B/CD-5.

INDEPENDENT PRACTICE

Assign any of the following:

1. Exercises, page 250
2. Workbook, *Mots 1: A–C,* pages 108–109
3. Communication Activities Masters, *Mots 1: A–B,* pages 61–62
4. CD-ROM, Disc 3, pages 248–250

B. Ask students questions such as: *Où est-ce qu'on attend l'autobus? On attend le 38 à cet arrêt d'autobus? Qui conduit l'autobus? On met son ticket dans la machine ou le conducteur prend le ticket? On met le ticket dans l'appareil pour l'oblitérer? Pour demander un arrêt, on appuie sur le bouton ou contre la portière? Il est interdit de s'appuyer contre la portière?*

C. To elicit the new vocabulary on this page, ask questions such as: *Par où est-ce qu'on descend de l'autobus? On monte par le milieu ou l'avant? Est-ce que le jeune homme veut descendre de l'autobus? Il a poussé une femme? Elle est contente ou fâchée? Qu'est-ce qu'il dit pour s'excuser? Quels sont les deux terminus de la ligne 27?*

INFORMAL ASSESSMENT
(Mots 2)

Show Vocabulary Transparencies 10.2 (A & B). Call on students to point to and identify various items at random.

Vocabulary Expansion

You may wish to teach the expression *faire exprès*. Have students look at the center illustration on page 252. Ask: *Le garçon a poussé la femme? Il voulait le faire? Il savait qu'il l'avait poussée? Non. Alors il l'a poussée mais il ne l'a pas fait exprès.*

On descend de l'autobus par l'arrière ou par le milieu.
La descente est interdite par l'avant.
On monte par l'avant.

Le garçon veut descendre.

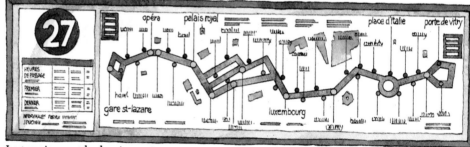

Le terminus est le dernier arrêt.
Le trajet est le voyage que fait un autobus d'un terminus à l'autre.

252   CHAPITRE 10

ADDITIONAL PRACTICE

1. After completing Exercises A, B, and C, have students listen to these definitions and supply a word or expression that means the same.
   le dernier arrêt
   le contraire de «monter»
   le voyage que fait un autobus d'un terminus à l'autre
   Pardonnez-moi.

la partie antérieure d'un véhicule
la partie postérieure d'un véhicule
celui qui conduit l'autobus
pas permis
se servir de quelque chose comme support

2. Student Tape Manual, Teacher's Edition, *Activités E–F,* pages 102–103

Exercices

A Un autobus parisien. Répondez d'après la photo.

1. De quelle couleur est l'autobus?
2. Quel est le numéro de l'autobus?
3. Quel est le terminus?

B L'arrêt de l'autobus. Répondez d'après le panneau.

1. Où êtes-vous?
2. Combien de lignes passent par ce point?
3. Le premier bus commence à circuler à quelle heure du lundi au samedi?
4. Le dernier bus est à quelle heure?
5. Quel est le terminus de cette ligne?

C Les autobus parisiens. Répondez par «oui» ou «non».

1. Les lignes des autobus parisiens sont numérotées?
2. À l'avant de la voiture (de l'autobus) il y a un tableau qui indique tous les arrêts de la ligne?
3. Les autobus parisiens n'ont qu'une seule portière?
4. On utilise les mêmes tickets pour prendre l'autobus et le métro?
5. Il faut valider son ticket avant de monter dans l'autobus?
6. Il faut crier au conducteur quand on veut descendre?
7. Il y a des machines à l'avant de l'autobus pour oblitérer ou valider son ticket?
8. Pour demander un arrêt, il faut appuyer sur un bouton?
9. Il est interdit de descendre de l'autobus par l'arrière?
10. La descente est interdite par le milieu?
11. Beaucoup de passagers s'appuient contre la portière pendant tout le trajet?
12. Le terminus est le dernier arrêt de l'autobus?
13. Il faut pousser tout le monde pour descendre de l'autobus?

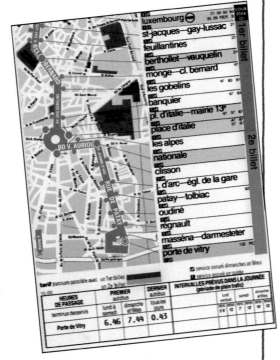

Exercices

PRESENTATION (page 253)

Exercice C

Exercise C can be done with books either open or closed. You may wish to have students correct the false statements.

ANSWERS

Exercice A

1. L'autobus est vert.
2. C'est le 38.
3. C'est Porte d'Orléans.

Exercice B

1. Nous sommes à Luxembourg.
2. Six lignes passent par ce point.
3. Le premier bus commence à circuler à 6h46 du lundi au samedi.
4. Le dernier bus est à 0h43.
5. Le terminus de cette ligne est Porte de Vitry.

Exercice C

1. Oui.
2. Oui.
3. Non. (Les autobus parisiens ont trois portières.)
4. Oui.
5. Non. (Il faut valider son ticket dans la machine qui se trouve à l'avant de l'autobus.)
6. Non. (Il faut appuyer sur le bouton quand on veut descendre.)
7. Oui.
8. Oui.
9. Non. (Il est interdit de descendre de l'autobus par l'avant.)
10. Non. (La descente est interdite par l'avant.)
11. Non. (Il est interdit de s'appuyer contre la portière pendant le trajet.)
12. Oui.
13. Non. (Il ne faut pas pousser tout le monde pour descendre de l'autobus.)

LEARNING FROM REALIA

Have students look at the bus schedule and route map as you ask: *Quels sont les terminus de cette ligne? L'autobus fait combien d'arrêts entre Luxembourg et Porte de Vitry? Il vous faut combien de billets pour aller de Luxembourg à la Place d'Italie? De Luxembourg à la Porte de Vitry?*

INDEPENDENT PRACTICE

Assign any of the following:

1. Exercises, page 253
2. Workbook, *Mots 2: D–G*, pages 109–110
3. Communication Activities Masters, *Mots 2: C–D*, pages 63–64
4. Computer Software, *Vocabulaire*
5. CD-ROM, Disc 3, pages 251–253

Bell Ringer Review

Write the following on the board or use BRR Blackline Master 10-3: Complete the sentences with the conditional of the verbs in parentheses.

1. À sa place, je ___ au professeur. (parler)
2. Nous ___ , mais nous devons aller à la gare. (attendre)
3. À ma place, lequel ___ -tu? (choisir)
4. Vous ___ à la fête si vous étiez invité(e)? (danser)
5. Il ___ finir ses devoirs, mais il doit faire la lessive. (vouloir)

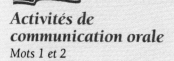

Activités de communication orale

Mots 1 et 2

PRESENTATION *(page 254)*

It is not necessary to have students complete all the activities. Select those you consider most appropriate. You may wish to have groups complete different activities.

Activité B

In the CD-ROM version of this activity, students can interact with an on-screen native speaker.

ANSWERS

Activités A, B, and C

Answers will vary.

Culture Note You may wish to tell students that the Paris *métro* runs every night until 1 a.m. If you miss the last *métro,* you must take the *Noctambus* home from Châtelet. These buses run every hour from 1 a.m. until around 5 a.m. These buses are indicated by a black owl in a yellow circle.

Activités de communication orale

Mots 1 et 2

A **Où est le métro?** Vous êtes à Paris et vous voulez prendre le métro. Demandez les renseignements suivants à votre ami(e) français(e) (votre camarade).

1. où se trouve la station de métro la plus proche
2. où on peut acheter des tickets
3. comment on descend sur le quai
4. où on vérifie la direction qu'on doit prendre

B **Les autobus dans votre ville.** Votre ami Étienne veut savoir comment se servir des transports en commun dans votre ville. Répondez à ses questions.

1. Il y a un métro ou seulement des autobus?
2. Où est-ce qu'on peut acheter des tickets?
3. Où est-ce qu'on peut trouver un horaire?
4. Dans l'autobus, comment est-ce qu'on indique qu'on veut descendre?

Étienne

C **Un sondage: Les transports en commun.** Travaillez en petits groupes. Choisissez un chef et un(e) secrétaire. Le chef demandera aux autres comment leurs parents vont au travail et comment les membres du groupe viennent à l'école. Le/La secrétaire présentera les résultats à la classe.

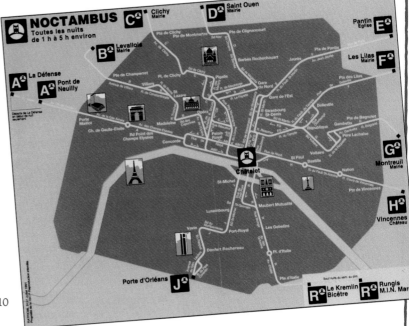

254 CHAPITRE 10

LEARNING FROM REALIA

Ask students to find the following places on the map as you say:

1. Vous avez peut-être lu quelque chose sur la Grande Arche dans *Lettres et sciences,* page 111. La Grande Arche est à La Défense. Trouvez La Défense sur le plan.
2. Vous savez que beaucoup de gens aiment acheter leurs vêtements au marché aux puces. Il y a un marché aux puces à Saint-Ouen. Trouvez Saint-Ouen sur le plan.
3. Le célèbre Arc de Triomphe est à Charles-de-Gaulle-Étoile. Trouvez l'Arc de Triomphe.
4. L'Opéra-Bastille se trouve Place de la Bastille. Trouvez cette place sur le plan.

Le pronom *en* avec des personnes

Talking About People Already Mentioned

1. You have already learned that *en* replaces *de* + a thing. You can also use *en* to replace a person when it is used with *un, une, des,* or an expression of quantity (*beaucoup de, assez de,* etc.).

Il a un cousin?	Oui, il *en* a un.
Tu as des frères?	Oui, j'*en* ai trois.
Elle a beaucoup d'amis?	Oui, elle *en* a beaucoup.

2. When a verb is followed by the preposition *de* + a noun referring to a specific person or persons, you use a stress pronoun (*lui, elle, eux, elles*) instead of *en* to replace the noun.

Il parle de son père.	Il parle de *lui.*
Il a besoin de sa mère.	Il a besoin d'*elle.*

Exercice

A **À toi.** Répondez en utilisant un pronom.

1. Tu parles souvent de tes cours?
2. Tu parles de tes parents?
3. Tu as des amis?
4. Tu as besoin de tes amis?
5. Tu as besoin d'argent?
6. Tu parles de ton professeur de français?

Le pronom en *avec des personnes*

PRESENTATION (*page 255*)

A. Guide students through steps 1–2. Read the sentences on the left and have students chorally read those on the right.

B. Elicit answers with either *en* or with *de* + a stress pronoun by asking questions such as: *Tu as un cousin? Tu parles de ton cousin? Tu as un frère? Tu parles de ton frère? Tu as une cousine? Tu parles de ta cousine? Tu as une tante? Tu parles de ta tante?*

ANSWERS

Exercice A

1. Oui, j'en parle souvent. (Non, je n'en parle pas souvent.)
2. Oui, je parle d'eux. (Non, je ne parle pas d'eux.)
3. Oui, j'en ai. (Non, je n'en ai pas.)
4. Oui, j'ai besoin d'eux. (Non, je n'ai pas besoin d'eux.)
5. Oui, j'en ai besoin. (Non, je n'en ai pas besoin.)
6. Oui, je parle de lui (d'elle). (Non, je ne parle pas de lui [d'elle].)

PRESENTATION *(page 256)*

Guide students through steps 1–3. Have students read the model sentences aloud. Provide additional examples.

Exercices

PRESENTATION *(page 256)*

Exercice A

You may wish to use the recorded version of this exercise.

Exercice B

Exercise B is to be done with books open. You may wish to have pairs practice the conversation and present it to the class.

Note Point out that the typical French expression *Bof!* in Exercise B is really not translatable. It may connote indifference, doubt, or irony, depending on the context.

ANSWERS

Exercice A

1. Paul m'en a donné trois.
2. Il m'en reste un maintenant.
3. Je lui en ai donné un.
4. Je lui en ai donné un.
5. En tout, je leur en ai donné deux.

Exercice B

lui, en
m'en
vous, en
m'en
lui, en
lui, en

Exercice C

1. Il y en a au moins quarante.
2. Il y en a très peu.
3. Il y en a beaucoup.
4. Il y en a deux.
5. Il y en a deux.
6. Il y en a plusieurs.

Un autre pronom avec y ou *en*   *Referring to People and Things Already Mentioned*

1. When you use *en* with any other pronoun, it always comes last.

   L'employé t'a donné combien de tickets?   **Il m'*en* a donné deux.**
   Il vend des tickets aux passagers?   **Oui, il leur *en* vend.**
   Il parle à Paul du métro?   **Oui, il lui *en* parle.**

2. You seldom use the pronoun *y* with any other pronoun except *en*. When you use *y* and *en* in the same sentence, *en* is always last.

   Il y *en* a deux sur la table.

3. When you use *y* with a pronoun other than *en*, *y* comes last.

   Il t'a rencontré à la station de métro?   **Oui, il m'*y* a rencontré.**

Exercices

A   **Il ne m'en reste qu'un.**   *Répondez.*

1. Paul t'a donné combien de tickets? (trois)
2. Il t'en reste combien maintenant? (un)
3. Tu as donné combien de tickets à René? (un)
4. Et tu as donné combien de tickets à Marie? (un)
5. En tout, tu leur en as donné combien?

B   **Je lui en ai parlé.**   *Complétez la conversation.*

—Vous avez parlé à votre père de vos problèmes financiers?
—Ah, oui. Je ___ ___ ai parlé.
—Il vous a donné de l'argent?
—Oui, il ___ ___ a donné.
—Il ___ ___ a donné beaucoup?
—Bof! Il ___ ___ a donné un peu.
—Et vous ___ ___ avez parlé combien de fois?
—Je ___ ___ ai parlé au moins trois fois.

C   **Il y en a beaucoup.**   *Répondez avec un pronom.*

1. Il y a combien de places? (au moins quarante)
2. Il y a combien de places libres? (très peu)
3. Il y a combien de passagers? (beaucoup)
4. Il y a combien de portières dans le bus? (deux)
5. Il y a combien d'appareils pour oblitérer les tickets? (deux)
6. Il y a combien de boutons pour demander un arrêt? (plusieurs)

256   CHAPITRE 10

Marseille: Un distributeur automatique dans le métro

INDEPENDENT PRACTICE

Assign any of the following:
1. Exercises, page 256
2. Workbook, *Structure: B–C*, pages 111–113
3. Communication Activities Masters, *Structure: B*, pages 66–67
4. CD-ROM, Disc 3, page 256

ADDITIONAL PRACTICE

Student Tape Manual, Teacher's Edition, *Activité A*, page 103

Les questions
Requesting Information

1. You have been asking questions since you began your study of French. The most common way to make a question in spoken French is simply to use a rising intonation at the end of a statement. If you use a question word such as *quand, comment, etc.*, you put it at the end of the sentence.

> **Jacques part?**
> **Il part quand?**
> **Il part avec qui?**

2. Another way to form a question in French is to place *est-ce que* before a statement. If a question word is used, *est-ce que* follows it.

> **Est-ce que Jacques part?**
> **Quand est-ce qu'il part?**
> **Avec qui est-ce qu'il part?**

3. A third way of asking a question is by using inversion, that is, reversing the order of the subject and verb.

> **Parlez-vous français?**
> **Où veux-tu aller?**
> **Combien coûte un ticket de métro?**

   a. When the pronouns *il(s), elle(s)* and *on* are inverted, there is a /t/ sound between the subject and verb. This /t/ sound is represented by the *t* or the *d* already present at the end of the verb. If the verb ends in a vowel, you add a *-t-* between the subject and verb.

> **Où prend-il le métro?**
> **Comment vont-elles au bureau?**
> **À quelle station monte-t-elle?**
> **Où va-t-on?**

   b. When the verb is in the *passé composé*, you invert the subject and the helping verb, *avoir* or *être*.

> **Combien as-tu payé?**

   The same rule applies to verbs followed by an infinitive.

> **Combien peux-tu payer?**

   c. With a noun subject, both the noun and the pronoun *il(s)* or *elle(s)* are used.

> **Marie parle-t-elle français?**

   This type of inversion is used mostly in written French.

Bell Ringer Review

Write the following on the board or use BRR Blackline Master 10-4: Write the following words under the appropriate heading: La teinturerie or La laverie automatique.
l'amidon
la machine à laver
la lessive
le nettoyage à sec
plier
le pressing
le repassage
le sèche-linge

Les questions

PRESENTATION (*pages 257–258*)

Students have had a good deal of practice hearing and, hopefully, producing questions in the ways described here. You may wish to have students read this material silently. Then have them read the model questions aloud. The more students hear and form questions on their own, the more comfortable they will be with them.

Note The exercises that follow the presentation have students practice the formation of questions with specific word orders. When students are speaking on their own, it is recommended that you let them use any word order they are comfortable with. When they are doing formal writing, you may require that they use inversion.

Note In the CD-ROM version, this structure point is presented via an interactive electronic comic strip.

Exercices

ANSWERS

Exercice A

Answers will vary. Students will form questions with rising intonation, *est-ce que,* inversion, or *n'est-ce pas.* For example:

1. **Vous êtes français? Est-ce que vous êtes français? Êtes-vous français? Vous êtes français, n'est-ce pas?**

Exercice B

1. **À quelle heure est-ce que son frère se réveille?**
2. **Quand est-ce que le petit garçon se brosse les dents?**
3. **Où est-ce que tes amis s'amusent?**
4. **À quelle heure est-ce que vous vous couchez?**
5. **Comment est-ce que les élèves s'habillent?**

Exercice C

1. **Où Marie habite-t-elle?**
2. **Comment Marie est-elle?**
3. **Où Marie étudie-t-elle l'anglais?**
4. **Avec qui Marie fait-elle de l'anglais?**
5. **D'où Madame Richards vient-elle?**
6. **Comment Marie va-t-elle à l'école?**
7. **À quelle heure Marie prend-elle le métro?**

Exercice D

1. **À quelle école allez-vous?**
2. **À quelle école Robert pense-t-il aller?**
3. **Combien de cours suivez-vous ce semestre?**
4. **Combien de cours Robert va-t-il suivre?**
5. **Quels cours préférez-vous?**
6. **Comment allez-vous à l'école?**
7. **Comment Robert va-t-il à l'école?**
8. **Avec qui suivez-vous le cours de français?**
9. **Avec qui Robert pense-t-il suivre le cours de français?**
10. **Depuis quand étudiez-vous le français?**

4. The expression *n'est-ce pas* can be placed after the statement to ask for confirmation. The answer may be "yes" or "no."

> **Jacques parle francais, n'est-ce pas?**
> **Tu le connais, n'est-ce pas?**

Exercices

A **J'ai des questions à vous poser.** Posez des questions de trois façons différentes.

1. Vous êtes français.
2. Vous parlez français.
3. Vous habitez à Paris.
4. Vous avez un appartement en ville.
5. Vous travaillez à Paris.
6. Vous êtes artiste.
7. Vous allez au travail en bus.

B **Tous les jours.** Refaites les phrases d'après le modèle.

> **À quelle heure Marie se lève-t-elle?**
> *À quelle heure est-ce que Marie se lève?*

1. À quelle heure son frère se réveille-t-il?
2. Quand le petit garçon se brosse-t-il les dents?
3. Où tes amis s'amusent-ils?
4. À quelle heure vous couchez-vous?
5. Comment les élèves s'habillent-ils?

C **Des questions.** Écrivez des questions d'après le modèle.

> **Marie habite *à Paris.***
> *Où Marie habite-t-elle?*

1. Marie habite *rue Saint-Dominique.*
2. Marie est *très sympathique.*
3. Marie étudie l'anglais *à l'école.*
4. Marie fait de l'anglais *avec Madame Richards.*
5. Madame Richards vient *d'Angleterre.*
6. Marie va à l'école *en métro.*
7. Marie prend le métro *à neuf heures.*

Attention !
Ne mets pas tes main...
sur la porte : tu risque...
de te faire pincer très fo...

D **De quelle école Robert pense-t-il être diplômé?** Récrivez les questions suivantes en utilisant l'inversion.

1. Vous allez à quelle école?
2. Robert pense aller à quelle école?
3. Vous suivez combien de cours ce semestre?
4. Robert va suivre combien de cours?
5. Vous préférez quels cours?
6. Vous allez à l'école comment?
7. Robert va à l'école comment?
8. Vous suivez le cours de français avec qui?
9. Robert pense suivre le cours de français avec qui?
10. Vous étudiez le français depuis quand?

LEARNING FROM REALIA

You may wish to ask the students what the message is in this announcement and where they think the announcement appears. (Answer: on the doors of the Paris *métro.*) What new cognates do you see? (*risquer, pincer.*)

E **Un voyage.** Faites une question en utilisant l'inversion.

1. François a fait un voyage en France l'année dernière. (quand)
2. Il est allé à l'aéroport avec ses copains. (où)
3. L'avion a fait deux escales. (combien)
4. Le vol était complet. (comment)
5. L'avion est arrivé à cinq heures du matin. (à quelle heure)
6. François était fatigué. (comment)
7. Il est allé récupérer ses bagages. (où)
8. Ses bagages sont arrivés sur le tapis roulant numéro huit. (où)

Venir de

Telling What You and Others Have Just Done

You use *venir* in the present tense with *de* + infinitive to indicate that an action has just taken place.

Les voyageurs viennent de descendre du métro.	*The passengers just got off the subway.*
Le métro vient de partir.	*The subway just left.*

Exercices

A **La journée d'Alexandre.** Répondez.

1. Il est sept heures et demie du matin. Alexandre vient de se lever ou de se coucher?
2. Il est midi. Il vient de déjeuner ou de dîner?
3. Il est quatre heures et demie de l'après-midi. Il vient d'entrer dans la classe ou de rentrer du lycée?
4. Il est sept heures du soir. Il vient de dîner ou de prendre le petit déjeuner?
5. Il est dix heures du soir. Il vient de regarder la télé ou de dîner?
6. Il est onze heures du soir. Il vient de se lever ou de se coucher?

B **Qu'est-ce que tout le monde vient de faire?**
Donnez des réponses personnelles.

1. Moi, je ___.
2. Mon père ___.
3. Mes copains ___.
4. Nous ___.
5. Vous ___.

Arrêt Bus Scolaire

Exercice E

1. Quand François a-t-il fait un voyage en France?
2. Où est-il allé avec ses copains?
3. Combien d'escales l'avion a-t-il fait?
4. Comment le vol était-il? (Comment était le vol?)
5. À quelle heure l'avion est-il arrivé?
6. Comment François était-il? (Comment était François?)
7. Où est-il allé?
8. Où ses bagages sont-ils arrivés?

Venir de
PRESENTATION *(page 259)*

A. Guide students through the explanation and have them read the model sentences aloud.

B. You may wish to have students repeat one sentence, such as *Je viens d'arriver*, in all forms. For example: *Je viens d'arriver. Tu viens d'arriver. Il/Elle/On vient d'arriver*, etc.

Exercices
PRESENTATION *(page 259)*

Exercises A and B can be done with books either open or closed.

ANSWERS
Exercice A

1. Alexandre vient de se lever.
2. Il vient de déjeuner.
3. Il vient de rentrer du lycée.
4. Il vient de dîner.
5. Il vient de regarder la télé.
6. Il vient de se coucher.

Exercice B
Answers will vary.

ADDITIONAL PRACTICE	INDEPENDENT PRACTICE
Student Tape Manual, Teacher's Edition, *Activité B*, page 104	Assign any of the following: 1. Exercises, pages 258–259 2. Workbook, *Structure: D*, page 113 3. Communication Activities Masters, *Structure: C–D*, pages 68–69 4. Computer Software, *Structure* 5. CD-ROM, Disc 3, pages 257–259

CONVERSATION

Bell Ringer Review

Write the following on the board or use BRR Blackline Master 10-5: Complete the following sentences:

1. Je ferais un voyage si...
2. J'achèterais une Mercedes si...
3. Mes pulls rétréciraient si...
4. Je parlerais très bien le français si...
5. Je serais très content(e) si...

PRESENTATION *(page 260)*

A. Have students close their books. Play the Conversation Video or have them listen as you read the conversation or play Cassette 6B/CD-5.
B. Have students open their books and read along with you or the cassette. (Use *Activité D* in the Student Tape Manual to check oral comprehension.)
C. Ask why François is confused. Have students tell where he shows his confusion.
D. Call on a pair of volunteers to read the conversation to the class. Tell the student who plays François to sound confused when appropriate.
E. You may wish to go over the comprehension exercise that follows.
F. Have one student tell the story in the conversation in his/her own words.

Note In the CD-ROM version, students can play the role of either one of the characters and record the conversation.

ANSWERS

Exercice A

1. d'ici
2. quelle ligne il doit prendre
3. à La Motte-Picquet-Grenelle
4. à Ternes

Scènes de la vie   *Le métro*

FRANÇOIS: Pardon, Mademoiselle. Je ne suis pas d'ici et je ne sais pas quelle ligne je dois prendre.
LA FEMME: Vous voulez aller où?
FRANÇOIS: À La Motte-Picquet-Grenelle.
LA FEMME: Voilà! Vous êtes ici à Ternes. Vous allez prendre cette ligne direction Porte Dauphine jusqu'à Charles de Gaulle-Étoile.
FRANÇOIS: Charles de Gaulle-Étoile?
LA FEMME: Oui, c'est la prochaine station. À Charles de Gaulle-Étoile vous prenez la correspondance.
FRANÇOIS: Correspondance?
LA FEMME: Oui, vous changez à Charles de Gaulle-Étoile. Vous prenez la direction Nation et vous descendez à La Motte-Picquet.
FRANÇOIS: Merci, Mademoiselle. Vous êtes très aimable.
LA FEMME: Je vous en prie.

A **François prend le métro.** Complétez d'après la conversation.

1. François n'est pas ___.
2. Il ne sait pas ___.
3. Il veut aller ___.
4. François est maintenant ___.
5. Il va prendre la correspondance à ___.
6. «Prendre la correspondance» veut dire ___.
7. À Charles de Gaulle-Étoile il va prendre le métro direction ___.
8. Il va ___ à La Motte-Picquet-Grenelle.

260 CHAPITRE 10

LEARNING FROM PHOTOS

Have students say as much as they can about the photos.

Activités de communication orale

A **Questions.** Travaillez en petits groupes. En cinq minutes, écrivez autant de questions que possible sur le métro et les autobus à Paris. Posez vos questions à un autre groupe. Le groupe qui répondra correctement au plus grand nombre de questions gagnera.

B **Une matinée typique.** Posez des questions à un(e) camarade sur ce qu'il/elle fait le matin. Prenez des notes et présentez-les ensuite à la classe. Puis, changez de rôles. Demandez à votre camarade:

1. à quelle heure il/elle quitte la maison et avec qui
2. comment il/elle va au lycée
3. à quelle heure il/elle y arrive
4. quel est son premier cours, dans quelle salle et quel est le nom du professeur

C **Il y en a...** Un(e) élève d'une autre école (votre camarade) vous pose des questions sur votre école. Il/Elle veut savoir:

1. combien d'élèves il y a dans votre école
2. combien d'élèves il y a dans la plupart des cours
3. combien de clubs il y a
4. combien de bons profs il y a

> Élève 1: Il y a combien de profs de français?
> Élève 2: Il y en a trois.

D **Où suis-je?** Dites à un(e) camarade plusieurs choses que vous venez de faire et il/elle vous dira où vous êtes allé(e). Ensuite changez de rôles.

> Élève 1: Je viens d'acheter des timbres.
> Élève 2: Tu es allé(e) à la poste. Et moi, je viens de…

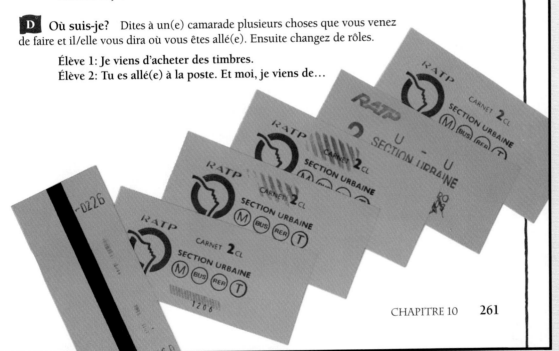

LECTURE ET CULTURE

Bell Ringer Review

Write the following on the board or use BRR Blackline Master 10-7: Write two articles of clothing that could be made from each of the following materials. Example: une chemise et une robe en coton

le coton
le cuir
la laine
la soie
le jean

READING STRATEGIES

(pages 262–263)

Pre-reading

A. You may wish to follow some of the procedures suggested in previous chapters for the presentation of the reading.

B. You may wish to review the family vocabulary from Chapter 2.

Note You may wish to tell students that *«métro-boulot-dodo»* is a popular expression in French meaning "the daily grind, the daily routine." It implies a dull, humdrum life and derives from the commuter's experience of taking the *métro* to work, putting in a day's work, then getting back on the *métro* to go home, often to the suburbs. Additional comments on life in the suburbs and in the city appear in the workbook. There the results of some recent polls are given.

Reading

Have students read the *Lecture* silently.

Post-reading

Ask students to compare their city or town and lifestyle to life in Paris and its suburbs.

Note Students may listen to a recorded version of the *Lecture* on the CD-ROM.

MÉTRO-BOULOT-DODO

«Métro-boulot-dodo» est une expression qu'on entend souvent en France dans la région parisienne. Mais qu'est-ce que cela veut dire? «Métro» veut dire «voyage», «boulot» est l'argot[1] pour «travail», et «dodo» est l'abbréviation de «dormir» utilisée quand on parle aux bébés.

Cette expression, «métro-boulot-dodo», a une signification sociale, car elle est utilisée pour décrire la vie des banlieusards—c'est-à-dire les gens qui habitent la banlieue de Paris. Comme vous l'avez déjà appris, pas mal de banlieusards en France sont des ouvriers ou des employés de bureau. Les moins aisés[2] habitent des H.L.M. (Habitations à Loyer Modéré). Les H.L.M. ne coûtent pas très cher car elles sont subventionnées[3] par le gouvernement. Les H.L.M. sont de très grands immeubles d'une vingtaine d'étages avec des appartements modestes mais

[1] l'argot *slang*
[2] aisés *well-off, rich*
[3] subventionnées *subsidized*

Les voyageurs attendent le train à Sèvres.

LEARNING FROM PHOTOS

You may wish to ask the students the following questions about the photo: *C'est une station de métro ou une gare? Sur le train on voit «SNCF»: c'est le métro ou le train? Il y a beaucoup de monde sur le quai? D'après vous, c'est l'heure de pointe? À votre avis, où vont ces gens?*

DID YOU KNOW?

Sèvres is a suburb of Paris between Paris and Versailles. The town lends its name to the fine neo-classical porcelain that has been made there at the French Royal Porcelain Factory since 1756. Pieces of Sèvres porcelain, coveted by distinguished collectors since the 18th century, can be found in the world's major museums.

Des H.L.M. dans la banlieue parisienne

propres et confortables. À proximité des H.L.M. il y a souvent un supermarché, des terrains de jeux et de sport, et des garderies d'enfants[4].

Beaucoup de gens, surtout ceux qui habitent une ville comme Paris où il y a beaucoup d'activités culturelles, etc., considèrent que la vie dans les H.L.M. de banlieue est ennuyeuse[5] et monotone. L'expression «métro-boulot-dodo» reflète cette monotonie: on se lève le matin, on prend le métro pour aller au *boulot*—au bureau ou à l'usine— et on rentre le soir pour dormir, ou comme disent les parents à leurs bébés, pour *faire dodo*.

[4] des garderies d'enfant   *day-care centers*
[5] ennuyeuse   *boring*

Étude de mots

A **Les définitions?** Trouvez le mot ou l'expression qui correspond.

1. un bébé
2. utilisé
3. un banlieusard
4. la banlieue
5. un ouvrier
6. aisé
7. un immeuble
8. confortable
9. une garderie d'enfants
10. faire dodo

a. un bâtiment qui a des appartements
b. la région autour d'une grande ville
c. dormir
d. un travailleur manuel
e. où tout est fait pour rendre la vie facile
f. celui qui habite la banlieue
g. une crèche municipale
h. assez riche, avec assez de ressources financières
i. employé
j. un très petit enfant

Étude de mots

ANSWERS

Exercice A

1. j   6. h
2. i   7. a
3. f   8. e
4. b   9. g
5. d   10. c

Compréhension

PRESENTATION (page 264)

You may wish to complete these exercises as students read the *Lecture*. Exercises B and C have students reading and scanning for information. Exercise D challenges their critical thinking skills.

ANSWERS

Exercice B

1. métro: voyage
2. boulot: travail
3. dodo: dormir

Exercice C

1. Un banlieusard est une personne qui habite la banlieue (de Paris).
2. Beaucoup de banlieusards sont des ouvriers ou des employés de bureau.
3. Une H.L.M. est un très grand immeuble d'une vingtaine d'étages avec des appartements (modestes mais propres et confortables).
4. Le gouvernement subventionne les H.L.M.
5. Il y a souvent un supermarché, des terrains de jeux et de sport, et des garderies d'enfants à proximité des H.L.M.
6. Les appartements sont modestes mais propres et confortables.
7. Les gens qui habitent la ville considèrent la vie dans les H.L.M. ennuyeuse et monotone.

Exercice D

Answers will vary.

264

Compréhension

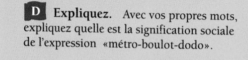 **Qu'est-ce que cela veut dire?**   Expliquez la signification des mots suivants.

1. métro
2. boulot
3. dodo

C **Les H.L.M.**   Répondez.

1. Qu'est-ce qu'un banlieusard?
2. Que font beaucoup de banlieusards? Ce sont des médecins, ce sont des ouvriers...?
3. Qu'est-ce qu'une H.L.M.?
4. Qui subventionne les H.L.M.?
5. Qu'est-ce qu'il y a à proximité des H.L.M.?
6. Comment sont les appartements dans les H.L.M.?
7. Comment les gens qui habitent la ville considèrent-ils la vie dans les H.L.M.?

D **Expliquez.**   Avec vos propres mots, expliquez quelle est la signification sociale de l'expression «métro-boulot-dodo».

LEARNING FROM PHOTOS

Have students say as much as they can about the photos. Talking about them will recycle much of the vocabulary from *Bienvenue*, Chapter 6. (You may wish to give them the word for umbrella, *un parapluie*, since there is an umbrella in both of these photos.)

INDEPENDENT PRACTICE

Assign any of the following:
1. *Étude de mots* and *Compréhension* exercises, pages 263–264
2. Workbook, *Un Peu Plus*, pages 114–117
3. CD-ROM, Disc 3, pages 262–264

DÉCOUVERTE CULTURELLE

Les métros en France sont composés de plusieurs voitures ou rames de deuxième classe. Les métros n'ont plus de voitures de première classe.

On peut acheter les tickets à l'entrée de la station au guichet ou au distributeur automatique. On peut les acheter un par un ou on peut acheter un carnet. Un carnet a dix tickets. Et n'oubliez pas que vous pouvez utiliser ces tickets dans l'autobus aussi bien que dans le métro. Dans l'autobus, il faut valider le ticket dans la machine qui se trouve à l'avant de la voiture. Si vous n'avez pas de ticket, vous pouvez en acheter un au conducteur, mais c'est plus cher.

Aux heures de pointe (d'affluence), le métro et les autobus sont bien sûr bondés[1]. Il y a un monde fou[2] mais heureusement à ces heures-là, ils passent fréquemment.

Les métros aujourd'hui roulent sur pneus. Ils sont confortables et ne font pas de bruit. Ils sont même presque silencieux.

Pour les autobus, les arrêts sont facultatifs. Ils ne sont pas obligatoires. Il faut indiquer au conducteur que vous voulez descendre. Pour cela, il faut appuyer sur un des boutons pour demander l'arrêt. Un signal «arrêt demandé» s'allume alors à l'avant de la voiture de l'autobus devant le conducteur.

[1] bondés   *packed*
[2] un monde fou   *crowds of people*

Bell Ringer Review
Write the following on the board or use BRR Blackline Master 10-8: Write three facts you have learned about the French region of the Camargue.

OPTIONAL MATERIAL

Découverte culturelle
PRESENTATION (*page 265*)

Although the *Découverte* is optional, you may wish to have all students read it since it contains some important information about public transportation. Have students read the selection silently.

Note Students may listen to a recorded version of the *Découverte culturelle* on the CD-ROM.

ADDITIONAL PRACTICE

After reading and discussing the *Découverte culturelle*, you may wish to ask the following questions: *Les métros en France ont combien de voitures? Combien de classes de voiture y a-t-il? Où est-ce qu'on peut acheter les tickets? Comment peut-on acheter les tickets? Est-ce que les tickets de métro sont valables dans les autobus? Pourquoi les trains du métro sont-ils presque silencieux? Comment les arrêts d'autobus sont-ils? Qu'est-ce qu'il faut faire pour demander un arrêt?*

RÉALITÉS

RÉALITÉS

Bell Ringer Review

Write the following on the board or use BRR Blackline Master 10-9: Write five sentences telling what you have people do for you. Example: Je fais préparer mon déjeuner.

OPTIONAL MATERIAL

PRESENTATION
(pages 266–267)

Allow students to read the captions and look at the photos for enjoyment. Solicit questions and comments.

Note In the CD-ROM version, students can listen to the recorded captions and discover a hidden video behind one of the photos.

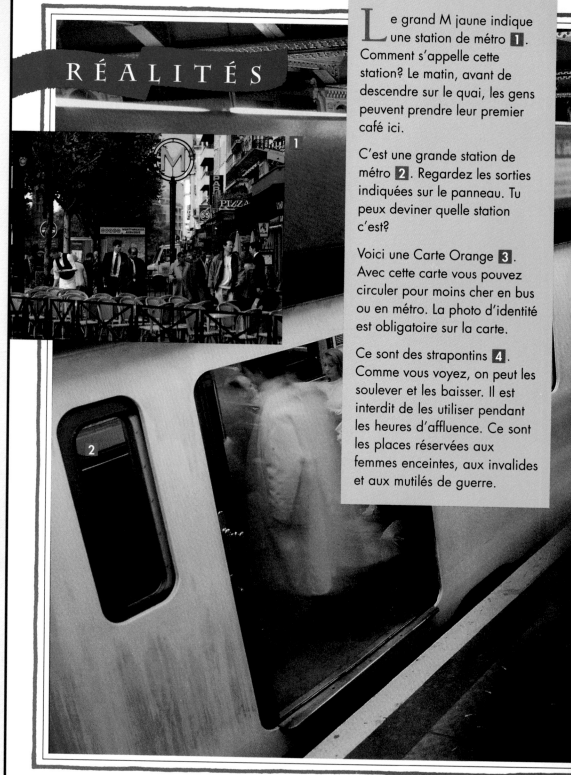

Le grand M jaune indique une station de métro **1**. Comment s'appelle cette station? Le matin, avant de descendre sur le quai, les gens peuvent prendre leur premier café ici.

C'est une grande station de métro **2**. Regardez les sorties indiquées sur le panneau. Tu peux deviner quelle station c'est?

Voici une Carte Orange **3**. Avec cette carte vous pouvez circuler pour moins cher en bus ou en métro. La photo d'identité est obligatoire sur la carte.

Ce sont des strapontins **4**. Comme vous voyez, on peut les soulever et les baisser. Il est interdit de les utiliser pendant les heures d'affluence. Ce sont les places réservées aux femmes enceintes, aux invalides et aux mutilés de guerre.

DID YOU KNOW?

The tickets used for the *métro* and the buses are the same. Buying one ticket at a time is more expensive than buying special value packages. *Un carnet,* a booklet of ten tickets, costs almost half the price of buying ten single tickets. The tickets are not dated and can be used at any time. Two dated passes allow unlimited access for short durations: the *Formule 1* for one day and the *Le Paris Visite* for several days. The *Coupon Jaune,* a weekly pass, and the *Carte Orange,* a monthly pass, are also dated. The cost of these passes varies, of course, depending on the length of time the pass is valid.

les 4 places ci-dessous sont réservées par priorité
- aux mutilés de guerre
- aux aveugles civils, aux invalides du travail
- aux infirmes civils
- aux femmes enceintes et aux personnes
  accompagnées d'enfants âgés de moins de 4 ans
- aux personnes âgées de 75 ans et plus

places réservées

267

HISTORY CONNECTION

The first *métro (chemin de fer métropolitain)* line from Porte Maillot to Porte de Vincennes on the Right Bank opened on July 19, 1900. Hector Guimard designed many of the early stations in the exotic Art Nouveau style. The best remaining examples of his work are at the Porte Dauphine and Abbesses stations. Now 15 lines, and nearly 125 miles of rail, crisscross Paris, connecting about 367 stations and providing inexpensive transportation to millions of Parisians and visitors.

ADDITIONAL PRACTICE

Assign any of the following:
1. Student Tape Manual, Teacher's Edition, *Deuxième Partie*, pages 105–109
2. Situation Cards, Chapter 10
3. Communication Transparency C-10

RECYCLING

These activities encourage students to use the vocabulary and grammar from this chapter in open-ended situations. They also provide an opportunity to recycle vocabulary and structures from earlier chapters and from *Bienvenue*. It is not necessary to do all the activities with all students. You may select the ones you consider most appropriate or permit students to choose the ones they would like to do.

INFORMAL ASSESSMENT

Use the oral and written exercises in this section as a review at the end of the chapter or to evaluate speaking and writing skills. For suggestions on assigning an oral grade, see the evaluation criteria on page 22 of this Teacher's Wraparound Edition.

Activités de communication orale

ANSWERS

Activités A and B
Answers will vary.

Activité de communication écrite

ANSWERS

Activité A
Answers will vary.

Réintroduction et recombinaison

PRESENTATION *(page 269)*

Exercise A recycles various types of adjectives. Exercise B recycles the third-person plural verb forms in the present indicative. This is in preparation for the next chapter, in which students

Activités de communication orale

A **Les transports en commun.** Travaillez avec un(e) camarade pour comparer les transports en commun de votre ville et ceux de Paris. Décidez quelle ville a les meilleurs transports en commun et justifiez votre opinion.

> Élève 1: Il y a un métro à Paris.
> Élève 2: Il n'y a pas de métro dans ma ville.

B **Dans le métro.** Un(e) de vos camarades qui ne connaît pas bien le métro parisien veut aller à plusieurs endroits. Il/Elle choisit ces endroits et vous lui expliquez comment y aller. Changez ensuite de rôles.

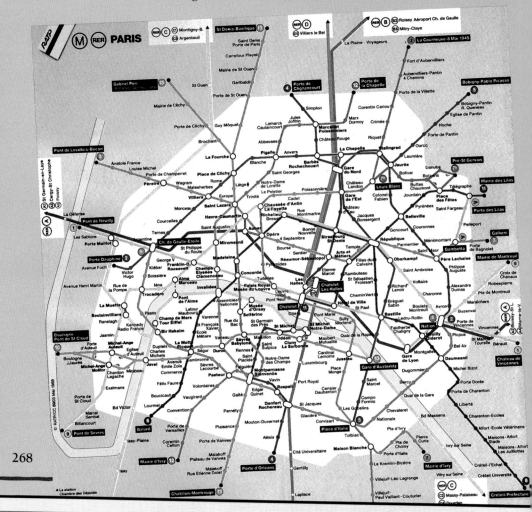

268

Have students work in teams. Using the *métro* map, one team gives the name of the terminus of a *métro* line (Porte d'Orléans, for example) and the other teams have to find the other terminus of that line (Porte de Clignancourt) in the shortest amount of time. The winner is the team which comes up with the correct answer first the most often.

The *métro* station Solférino on page 269 commemorates the town in Italy where the French and Sardinians fought a bloody battle against the Austrians in 1859. Shocked by the huge losses, Napoleon III arranged a preliminary peace soon afterward with Francis Joseph, the Austrian emperor. Several Paris *métro* and train stations are named after battles: Austerlitz, Wagram, Stalingrad, etc.

Activité de communication écrite

A **Prenez le bus ou le métro!** Le club d'écologie de votre école fait une campagne pour encourager les gens à prendre le bus ou le métro. Avec un(e) camarade, dessinez une affiche. N'oubliez pas de donner plusieurs raisons pour lesquelles on devrait prendre le bus ou le métro.

Réintroduction et recombinaison

A **Les Dejarnac.** Complétez.

Les Dejarnac ont un ___ (beau) appartement dans un ___ (vieux) immeuble dans un très ___ (beau) quartier de Paris. Ils habitent dans le septième. ___ (Quel) ligne ou ___ (quel) lignes de métro desservent le septième? La ligne numéro douze. Les deux terminus de ___ (ce) ligne sont Mairie d'Issy et Porte de la Chapelle. Les Dejarnac habitent près de la ___ (joli) station de métro Solférino.

La station de métro Solférino dans le 7ème arrondissement

B **La vie de Dominique.** Récrivez les phrases en remplaçant «Dominique» par «les amis de Dominique».

1. Dominique habite à Lyon.
2. Dominique part pour l'école à sept heures.
3. Dominique prend l'autobus.
4. Elle attend l'autobus au coin de la rue.
5. Elle descend de l'autobus devant le lycée.
6. Elle ouvre son sac à dos.
7. Elle écrit des poèmes.
8. Elle dit toujours bonjour à ses amis.

Vocabulaire

NOMS

les transports (m.) en commun

le métro
la station (de métro)
le guichet
le distributeur automatique
le ticket
le carnet
le plan du métro
la ligne
la direction

le quai
l'escalier mécanique (m.)
l'escalator (m.)
le trottoir roulant

l'autobus (m.)
l'arrêt (m.)
le numéro
le conducteur
la machine
l'appareil (m.)
la portière
le bouton
la descente

l'avant (m.)
le milieu
l'arrière (m.)
le terminus
le trajet

ADJECTIFS
interdit(e)
proche

VERBES
monter
descendre
valider

oblitérer
s'appuyer
appuyer sur
pousser
se croiser

AUTRES MOTS ET EXPRESSIONS
là-bas
au coin de
changer de ligne
prendre la correspondance
venir de + infinitif
il est interdit de

CHAPITRE 10   **269**

---

will learn the forms of the present subjunctive, which are based on the third-person plural of the present indicative.

Exercice A

1. bel
2. vieil
3. beau
4. Quelle
5. quelles
6. cette
7. jolie

Exercice B

1. Les amis de Dominique habitent à Lyon.
2. Les amis de Dominique partent pour l'école à sept heures.
3. Les amis de Dominique prennent l'autobus.
4. Les amis de Dominique attendent l'autobus au coin de la rue.
5. Les amis de Dominique descendent de l'autobus devant le lycée.
6. Les amis de Dominique ouvrent leur sac à dos.
7. Les amis de Dominique écrivent des poèmes.
8. Les amis de Dominique disent toujours bonjour à leurs amis.

CHAPTER OVERVIEW

In this chapter students will learn to describe and discuss several important holidays and family celebrations as well as to extend holiday greetings. Students will also be introduced to the subjunctive and its use in expressions of necessity and possibility.

The cultural focus of the chapter is on important holiday celebrations in France, both religious and national.

CHAPTER OBJECTIVES

By the end of this chapter, students will know:

1. vocabulary dealing with holidays and celebrations
2. vocabulary dealing with weddings
3. the subjunctive mood
4. forms of regular and irregular verbs in the present subjunctive
5. the use of the subjunctive with impersonal expressions
6. dates and numbers above 1,000

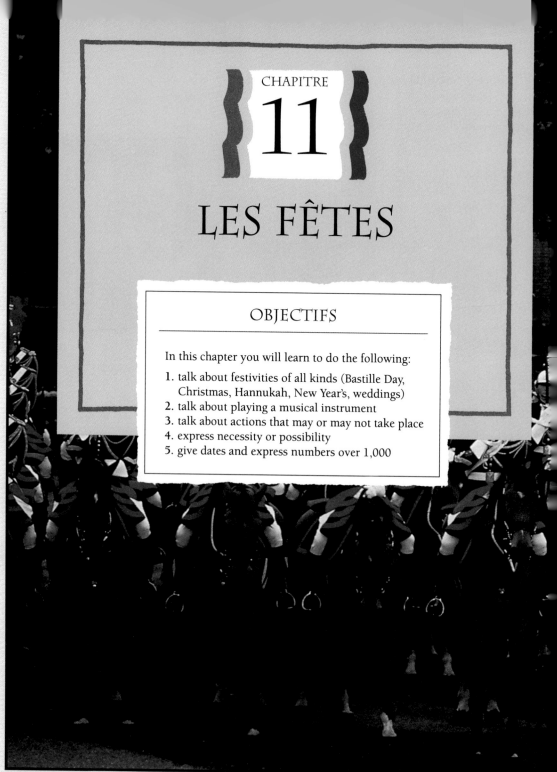

CHAPITRE

{ 11 }

LES FÊTES

OBJECTIFS

In this chapter you will learn to do the following:

1. talk about festivities of all kinds (Bastille Day, Christmas, Hannukah, New Year's, weddings)
2. talk about playing a musical instrument
3. talk about actions that may or may not take place
4. express necessity or possibility
5. give dates and express numbers over 1,000

CHAPTER PROJECTS

(optional)

1. Have students prepare original greeting cards for various holidays and occasions. They should write the greeting in French. You may wish to use the cards for a bulletin board display.
2. Have students select a holiday that interests them and prepare a report about it.
3. Have students select a holiday that is celebrated in both France and the United States and prepare a report comparing the ways in which the holiday is celebrated in each country.
4. Have the students prepare a report on *le 14 juillet.*

271

Pacing

This chapter will require eight to ten class sessions. Pacing will depend on the length of the class, the age of the students, and student aptitude.

For more information on planning your class, see the Lesson Plans, which offer guidelines for 45- and 55-minute classes and **Block Scheduling**.

Exercices vs. *Activités*

The exercises and activities are color-coded. Exercises, which provide guided practice to prepare students for independent communication, are coded in blue. Communicative activities, which give students opportunities for creative, open-ended expression, are coded in red.

INTERNET ACTIVITIES

(optional)

These activities, student worksheets, and related teacher information are in the *À bord* Internet Activities Booklet and on the Glencoe Foreign Language Home Page at: **http://www.glencoe.com/secondary/fl**

DID YOU KNOW?

The *Garde républicaine de Paris* is an arm of the national police force under the Department of Defense. Their appearance, with gleaming sabers, shining helmets with plumes, varnished boots, and flashing breastplates, is unequaled for state functions like the Bastille Day parade. The *Garde* provides color and pagentry, but they are also honored for their service as a riot squad and in battle.

Bell Ringer Review

Write the following on the board or use BRR Blackline Master 11-1: Write three facts about public transportation in Paris.

PRESENTATION (pages 272–273)

A. Have students close their books. Introduce the new words by pointing to the items on Vocabulary Transparencies 11.1 (A & B) and having students repeat after you or Cassette 7A/CD-6.

B. As you are presenting the vocabulary, you may wish to ask the following questions: *La fête nationale française est le 4 juillet ou le 14? Le 14 juillet il y a un grand défilé? Les soldats défilent au pas? Il y a beaucoup de monde dans les tribunes? Le maire et les notables regardent le défilé? Quels instruments y a-t-il dans la fanfare? Comment s'appelle l'hymne national français? Où faut-il que les enfants se mettent? Quand est-ce qu'il y a des feux d'artifice? Où est-ce que les orchestres jouent? Où est-ce que les gens dansent?*

La fête nationale française est le 14 juillet.
Les soldats défilent au pas.
Ils passent devant les tribunes.

PANTOMIME GAME

Write the following expressions on cards and distribute them to students to mime. The rest of the class tries to guess what instrument is being played.

jouer de la guitare	jouer du tambour
jouer du piano	jouer des cymbales
jouer de l'accordéon	jouer du violon
jouer du trombone	

La fanfare joue l'hymne national, «La Marseillaise».
Il faut que les enfants se mettent au premier rang.
Après, il faut que tout le monde applaudisse.

un feu d'artifice

la batterie

Le soir du 14 juillet, on tire des feux d'artifice.
Des orchestres jouent dans les rues.
Les gens dansent dans les rues.

C. Have students open their books and read the new words and expressions.

Vocabulary Expansion

You may wish to give students the names of these musical instruments:

un violon	une clarinette
un piano	un saxophone
une harpe	un cornet
un orgue	un tuba
une flûte	un gong
un hautbois	un triangle
un piccolo	une grosse caisse

ADDITIONAL PRACTICE

1. You may wish to ask students the following additional questions about the *Mots 1* vocabulary: *Il faut que tout le monde applaudisse après «La Marseillaise»? Qui joue l'hymne national, la fanfare ou l'orchestre? La batterie est dans la fanfare? On tire des feux d'artifice le 14 ou le 4 juillet en France? Et aux États-Unis?*

2. Student Tape Manual, Teacher's Edition, *Activité B,* page 111

Exercices

PRESENTATION *(page 274)*

Exercice A

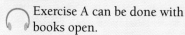

Exercise A can be done with books open.

Exercices B and C

Exercises B and C can be done with books open or closed.

Extension of *Exercice B*

After completing Exercise B, have students correct each false statement.

ANSWERS

Exercice A

1. a
2. a
3. c
4. c
5. c
6. c
7. a

Exercice B

1. Oui.
2. Non.
3. Oui.
4. Non.
5. Oui.
6. Oui.
7. Oui.
8. Oui.
9. Non.

Exercice C

Answers will vary.

Exercices

A Fêtes nationales. Choisissez.

1. Aux États-Unis, le 4 juillet est ___.
   a. la fête nationale
   b. l'hymne national
   c. le drapeau américain

2. Dans une fanfare, il y a ___.
   a. des trompettes
   b. des guitares
   c. des accordéons

3. On tire des feux d'artifice ___.
   a. le matin
   b. pendant le défilé
   c. le soir

4. Le 14 juillet en France, les soldats ___.
   a. se mettent au premier rang
   b. applaudissent
   c. défilent au pas

5. Le maire et les notables sont ___.
   a. dans la fanfare
   b. dans les tribunes
   c. devant la mairie

6. Après que la fanfare joue l'hymne national, on ___.
   a. danse
   b. se lève
   c. applaudit

7. Les notables sont ___.
   a. des gens importants
   b. des soldats
   c. des musiciens

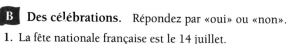

B Des célébrations. Répondez par «oui» ou «non».

1. La fête nationale française est le 14 juillet.
2. La fête nationale française est le même jour que la fête nationale américaine.
3. L'hymne national français s'appelle «La Marseillaise», et l'hymne national des États-Unis s'appelle «The Star-Spangled Banner».
4. On applaudit quand on n'aime pas quelque chose.
5. Aux États-Unis, le 4 juillet, on tire des feux d'artifice.
6. En France le 14 juillet, il y a un grand défilé militaire.
7. Dans une fanfare, les musiciens jouent de la trompette, du trombone, du tambour et des cymbales.
8. Les soldats passent devant le maire et les notables.
9. Le 4 juillet aux États-Unis, les orchestres jouent «La Marseillaise».

C Un peu de musique. Donnez des réponses personnelles.

1. Tu joues dans la fanfare ou dans l'orchestre de ton école?
2. Tu as des amis qui y jouent?
3. Est-ce que tu joues d'un instrument?
4. De quel instrument est-ce que tu joues? De la guitare? Du piano? Du violon?
5. De quel instrument est-ce que tu aimerais jouer? De la flûte? Du saxophone? De la batterie?
6. Est-ce qu'il y a des défilés là où tu habites?
7. À quelles dates y a-t-il des défilés?
8. Quand y a-t-il des feux d'artifice?

LEARNING FROM PHOTOS

Have students say anything they can about the photos. What day do they think it is? *(C'est le quatorze juillet.)*

INDEPENDENT PRACTICE

Assign any of the following:
1. Exercises, page 274
2. Workbook, *Mots 1: A–E*, pages 119–120
3. Communication Activities Masters, *Mots 1: A–B*, pages 70–72
4. CD-ROM, Disc 3, pages 272–274

VOCABULAIRE

MOTS 2

LES FÊTES DE FIN D'ANNÉE
NOËL

Joyeux Noël!

un arbre de Noël = un sapin

le Père Noël

une cheminée

des souliers (m.)

un cadeau de Noël

Il faut que les enfants soient sages s'ils veulent recevoir des cadeaux de Noël.

un chant de Noël

la messe de minuit

HANOUKA

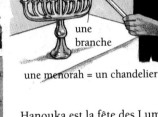

une bougie

une branche

une menorah = un chandelier

Hanouka est la fête des Lumières.
C'est une fête juive.
La fête dure huit jours.
Pendant la fête, les enfants allument les
   bougies de la menorah.

CHAPITRE 11   275

VOCABULAIRE

MOTS 2

Vocabulary Teaching Resources

1. Vocabulary Transparencies 11.2 (A & B)
2. Audio Cassette 7A/CD-6
3. Student Tape Manual, Teacher's Edition, *Mots 2: D–F*, pages 113–115
4. Workbook, *Mots 2: F–I*, pages 121–122
5. Communication Activities Masters, *Mots 2: C–D*, pages 73–74
6. Computer Software, *Vocabulaire*
7. Chapter Quizzes, *Mots 2: Quiz 2*, page 57
8. CD-ROM, Disc 3, *Mots 2:* pages 275–278

Bell Ringer Review

Write the following on the board or use BRR Blackline Master 11-2: Write the following words under the appropriate head: *Le métro* or *L'autobus*. l'arrêt, le bouton, le conducteur, la direction, le distributeur automatique, l'escalier mécanique, le guichet, le numéro, la portière, le quai, la station, le terminus, le trottoir roulant

PRESENTATION (pages 275–276)

A. Have the students repeat each word after you or Cassette 7A/CD-6 as they look at the illustrations on Vocabulary Transparencies 11.2 (A & B).

B. You may wish to ask the following questions during your presentation: *Qui apporte les cadeaux de Noël? Qui reçoit les cadeaux de Noël? Il faut qu'ils soient sages? Où sont les souliers? Les cadeaux de Noël sont dans les souliers et sous*

l'arbre de Noël? Quel est votre chant de Noël préféré? Quel est un autre nom pour la fête des Lumières? C'est une fête juive ou chrétienne? Qui allume les bougies de la menorah?

C. You may wish to ask the following questions about the New Year's Eve vocabulary: *Les gens célèbrent quelle fête? Le repas s'appelle le réveillon? Et les festivités font aussi partie du réveillon? Les gens se souhaitent «Bonne Année» et «Bonne Santé»? Il y a des décorations? Quelles sortes de décorations? Vous envoyez des cartes de vœux?*

D. When presenting the wedding vocabulary on page 276, you may wish to have the students stage a mock wedding ceremony.

Vocabulary Expansion

You may wish to give students the names of a few Christmas carols in French: *Mon beau sapin* ("O Christmas Tree"), *Minuit, chrétiens* ("O Holy Night"), *Douce nuit, sainte nuit* ("Silent Night"), *Les anges dans nos campagnes* ("Angels We Have Heard on High").

LE JOUR DE L'AN

Bonne Année!

Bonne Santé!

des guirlandes (f.)

un serpentin

des décorations (f.)

des confettis (m.)

Bonne Année

une carte de vœux

Le réveillon est le repas fait pendant la nuit de Noël et la nuit précédant le jour de l'An.
Les festivités qui accompagnent le repas font aussi partie du réveillon.
Tout le monde se souhaite une Bonne Année.

LE MARIAGE

le garçon d'honneur

les mariés

la demoiselle d'honneur

une alliance

le marié

la mariée

La cérémonie religieuse a lieu à l'église.
On se marie à l'église.

276   CHAPITRE 11

PANTOMIME

Have students mime the following actions:
Ouvrez votre cadeau de Noël.
Chantez un chant de Noël.
Allumez une bougie.
Signez la carte de vœux.
Souhaitez à quelqu'un une Bonne Année.

ADDITIONAL PRACTICE

Student Tape Manual, Teacher's Edition, *Activité E,* page 114

Exercices

A Noël et Hanouka. Répondez d'après les indications.

1. On célèbre Noël en quel mois? (décembre)
2. C'est quel jour Noël? (le vingt-cinq)
3. La messe de minuit est quel jour? (le vingt-quatre)
4. Qui apporte les cadeaux de Noël? (le Père Noël)
5. Qui reçoit les cadeaux? (les enfants sages)
6. Où est-ce que les enfants laissent leurs souliers? (devant la cheminée)
7. Qui remplit les souliers de cadeaux? (le Père Noël)
8. Quel est l'arbre de Noël traditionnel? (le sapin)
9. Où vont les catholiques le soir du vingt-quatre décembre? (à la messe de minuit)
10. Qu'est-ce qu'ils chantent pendant la messe de minuit? (des chants de Noël)
11. La menorah, ou le chandelier qu'on utilise pendant la fête des Lumières, a combien de branches? (neuf)
12. Qui célèbre la fête des Lumières? (les Juifs)
13. La fête des Lumières, ou Hanouka, est en quel mois? (décembre)
14. Elle dure combien de jours? (huit)
15. Qu'est-ce que les enfants allument? (les bougies de la menorah)

B C'est quelle fête? Décidez.

1. Il y a des défilés.
2. C'est le premier janvier.
3. On va à la messe de minuit.
4. On allume une à une les bougies d'un chandelier à neuf branches.
5. Il y a une fanfare.
6. Cette fête juive dure huit jours.
7. On reçoit des cadeaux dans ses souliers.
8. Il y a des confettis, des guirlandes et des serpentins.
9. Les festivités qui accompagnent le repas font aussi partie du réveillon.

C Les fêtes de fin d'année. Donnez des réponses personnelles.

1. Qu'est-ce que tu célèbres comme fête de fin d'année?
2. Comment est-ce que tu la célèbres?
3. Est-ce que tu as un grand repas de famille?
4. Qu'est-ce que tu fais la nuit précédant le jour de l'An? Tu invites des gens? Tu mets des décorations?
5. Tu envoies des cartes de vœux? À quelle date? À qui?
6. Qu'est-ce que tu souhaites à ta famille et à tes amis à Noël?
7. Et qu'est-ce que tu leur souhaites au jour de l'An?

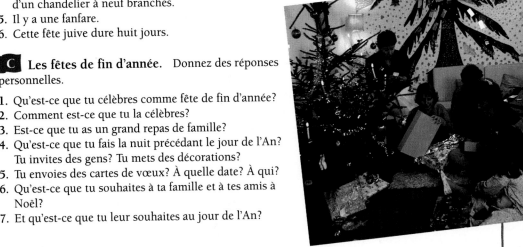

Exercices

PRESENTATION *(page 277)*

Extension of *Exercice A*

After completing the exercise, have one student supply the answers for 1–10, and another for 11–15. Then have a student give a description of Christmas in his/her own words and another give a description of Hanukkah.

Exercice B

You may wish to use the recorded version of this exercise.

ANSWERS

Exercice A

1. On célèbre Noël en décembre.
2. C'est le vingt-cinq (décembre).
3. C'est le vingt-quatre (décembre).
4. Le Père Noël apporte les cadeaux de Noël.
5. Les enfants sages reçoivent les cadeaux.
6. Les enfants laissent leurs souliers devant la cheminée.
7. Le Père Noël remplit les souliers de cadeaux.
8. Le sapin est l'arbre de Noël traditionnel.
9. Les catholiques vont à la messe de minuit le soir du vingt-quatre décembre.
10. Ils chantent des chants de Noël pendant la messe de minuit.
11. La menorah a neuf branches.
12. Les Juifs célèbrent la fête des Lumières.
13. La fête des Lumières (Hanouka) est en décembre.
14. Elle dure huit jours.
15. Les enfants allument les bougies de la menorah.

Exercice B

1. la fête nationale
2. le jour de l'An
3. Noël
4. Hanouka
5. la fête nationale
6. Hanouka
7. Noël
8. le jour de l'An
9. Noël, le jour de l'An

Exercice C

Answers will vary.

PAIRED ACTIVITY

You may wish to have students do Exercise C in pairs. They can compare what their families do.

LEARNING FROM PHOTOS

Call on a student to describe the photograph in as much detail as possible.

Exercices

PRESENTATION *(page 278)*

Extension of *Exercice D*

    After completing the exercise, have students correct each false statement.

ANSWERS

Exercice D

1. Non.
2. Oui.
3. Non.
4. Oui.
5. Non.

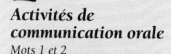

Activités de communication orale
Mots 1 et 2

PRESENTATION

Extension of *Activité A*

    After completing the activity, have each student give a description of one of his/her family holiday celebrations.

ANSWERS

Activités A, B, and C

    Answers will vary.

D   **Le jour du mariage.**   Répondez par «oui» ou «non».

1. Monsieur le maire célèbre la cérémonie religieuse.
2. Il faut que les mariés aient des alliances.
3. Il faut que le Père Noël soit présent au mariage.
4. La cérémonie religeuse a lieu à l'église.
5. Les demoiselles d'honneur se marient avec les garçons d'honneur.

Activités de communication orale
Mots 1 et 2

A   **Les fêtes familiales.**   Travaillez avec un(e) camarade. Demandez-lui comment il/elle célèbre une fête familiale. Ensuite dites-lui ce que vous faites pendant une fête familiale et comparez vos coutumes.

> Élève 1: Chez nous, on décore notre arbre de Noël une semaine avant Noël.
> Élève 2: Chez nous, on ne célèbre pas Noël, on célèbre Hanouka.

B   **Moments musicaux.**   Travaillez en petits groupes. Choisissez un chef et un(e) secrétaire. Le chef demandera les renseignements suivants aux membres du groupe. Le/La secrétaire prendra des notes et présentera les résultats à la classe.

1. qui joue d'un instrument
2. qui joue dans la fanfare du lycée
3. qui joue dans l'orchestre du lycée
4. qui joue dans un groupe

C   **C'est quelle fête?**   Décrivez une fête à un(e) camarade. Il/Elle essaiera de deviner quelle fête vous décrivez.

> Élève 1: On tire des feux d'artifice le soir.
> Élève 2: C'est la fête nationale française.

INDEPENDENT PRACTICE

    Assign any of the following:
1. Exercises and activities, pages 277–278
2. Workbook, *Mots 2: F–I,* pages 121–122
3. Communication Activities Masters, *Mots 2: C–D,* pages 73–74
4. Computer Software, *Vocabulaire*
5. CD-ROM, Disc 3, pages 275–278

STRUCTURE

Le subjonctif

Talking about Actions that May or May Not Take Place

1. The verbs studied thus far have been in the indicative mood. The indicative refers to an action that does, did, or will definitely take place. The subjunctive mood, which we are about to learn, is used to express an action that may, but not necessarily, take place.

2. Compare the following sentences.

   Grégoire fait ses devoirs.
   Il *faut que* Grégoire *fasse* ses devoirs.

   The first statement above is an independent statement of fact: "Greg does his homework." The second sentence contains a dependent clause: "that Greg do his homework." The sentence is introduced by: "It is necessary." Even though it is necessary for Greg to do his homework, it does not mean that he will in fact do it. Since the action may or may not occur, the verb is in the subjunctive, not the indicative.

3. You form the present subjunctive of regular verbs by dropping the *-ent* ending from the *ils/elles* form of the present indicative and adding the subjunctive endings to this stem. Study the following.

INFINITIVE	PARLER	FINIR	VENDRE	ENDINGS
STEM	ils *parl*ent	ils *finiss*ent	ils *vend*ent	
SUBJUNCTIVE	que je parle	que je finisse	que je vende	-e
	que tu parles	que tu finisses	que tu vendes	-es
	qu'il } parle qu'elle	qu'il } finisse qu'elle	qu'il } vende qu'elle	-e
	que nous parlions	que nous finissions	que nous vendions	-ions
	que vous parliez	que vous finissiez	que vous vendiez	-iez
	qu'ils } parlent qu'elles	qu'ils } finissent qu'elles	qu'ils } vendent qu'elles	-ent

CHAPITRE 11 **279**

STRUCTURE

Structure Teaching Resources

1. Workbook, *Structure: A–I*, pages 123–125
2. Student Tape Manual, Teacher's Edition, *Structure: A–E*, pages 115–117
3. Audio Cassette 7A/CD-6
4. Communication Activities Masters, *Structure: A–C*, pages 75–76
5. Computer Software, *Structure*
6. Chapter Quizzes, *Structure: Quizzes 3–5*, pages 58–60
7. CD-ROM, Disc 3, pages 279–283

Le subjonctif

Note The basic concept we wish to have students understand is that the subjunctive is used when we do not know if the action will take place. If we know that it is or will be a reality, we use the indicative. When we do not know if it is or will be a reality, we use the subjunctive. When students understand this concept, they will not have to memorize a long list of phrases that are followed by the subjunctive.

You may also wish to give students the following simple outline: *Indicative:* indicates or points something out; factual, objective; stands alone, independent *Subjunctive:* subjective, not objective, not factual; cannot stand alone, depends upon something else, dependent

PRESENTATION (*pages 279–280*)

A. Thoroughly and carefully go over steps 1 and 2. It is important that students understand this concept.

B. Write the verb forms on the board.

C. Have the students repeat the verb forms aloud.

D. Have students repeat each verb in the chart in step 4 in the *je* and *nous* forms.
E. Have students repeat all forms of the verbs in the chart in step 5.
F. Have students read the model sentences in step 6 aloud.

Note In the CD-ROM version, this structure point is presented via an interactive electronic comic strip.

Exercices

PRESENTATION *(page 280)*

All the exercises on pages 280–281 can be done with books open or closed. It is recommended that you go over each exercise the first time with books closed. Then have the students open their books and read the exercises for additional reinforcement.

Note The purpose of these exercises is to give students initial practice with the verb forms of the subjunctive. For this reason, the introductory clause *il faut que* is constant.

Exercice A

Exercise A uses only verbs in which the difference between the indicative and subjunctive forms can be heard.

ANSWERS

Exercice A

1. Oui, il faut qu'on écrive au Père Noël.
2. Oui, il faut qu'on lise mes cartes de vœux.
3. Oui, il faut qu'on aille au défilé.
4. Oui, il faut qu'on se dise «Bonne Année!».
5. Oui, il faut que je parte pour aller au feu d'artifice.
6. Oui, il faut que vous mettiez des guirlandes.

---

4. Most verbs, regular as well as irregular, form the subjunctive this way.

INFINITIVE	STEM	SUBJUNCTIVE	
ouvrir	*ouvrent*	que j'ouvre	que nous ouvrions
partir	*partent*	que je parte	que nous partions
dormir	*dorment*	que je dorme	que nous dormions
servir	*servent*	que je serve	que nous servions
mettre	*mettent*	que je mette	que nous mettions
lire	*lisent*	que je lise	que nous lisions
écrire	*écrivent*	que j'écrive	que nous écrivions
vivre	*vivent*	que je vive	que nous vivions
suivre	*suivent*	que je suive	que nous suivions
dire	*disent*	que je dise	que nous disions
conduire	*conduisent*	que je conduise	que nous conduisions
connaître	*connaissent*	que je connaisse	que nous connaissions

5. Few verbs are irregular in the subjunctive. Those that are, are very important. Study the following irregular verbs in the present subjunctive.

FAIRE	ÊTRE	AVOIR	ALLER
que je fasse	que je sois	que j'aie	que j'aille
que tu fasses	que tu sois	que tu aies	que tu ailles
qu'il / qu'elle } fasse	qu'il / qu'elle } soit	qu'il / qu'elle } ait	qu'il / qu'elle } aille
que nous fassions	que nous soyons	que nous ayons	que nous allions
que vous fassiez	que vous soyez	que vous ayez	que vous alliez
qu'ils / qu'elles } fassent	qu'ils / qu'elles } soient	qu'ils / qu'elles } aient	qu'ils / qu'elles } aillent

6. Remember that *il faut que* is always followed by the subjunctive.

Il faut que les enfants *soient* sages.
Il faut que tu *ailles* au magasin acheter des cadeaux de Noël.
Il faut qu'on *fasse* le réveillon chez moi cette année.

Exercices

A Il faut qu'on le fasse. Répondez par «oui».

1. Il faut qu'on écrive au Père Noël?
2. Il faut qu'on lise tes cartes de vœux?
3. Il faut qu'on aille au défilé?
4. Il faut qu'on se dise «Bonne Année!»?
5. Il faut que tu partes pour aller au feu d'artifice?
6. Il faut que nous mettions des guirlandes?

INDEPENDENT PRACTICE

Assign any of the following:
1. Exercises, pages 280–281
2. Workbook, *Structure: A–B,* page 123
3. Communication Activities Masters, *Structure: A,* page 75
4. CD-ROM, Disc 3, pages 279–281

B **Pour recevoir des cadeaux du Père Noël.** Répondez par «oui».

1. Il faut que les enfants soient sages toute l'année?
2. Il faut qu'ils aient de bonnes notes à l'école?
3. Il faut qu'ils décorent l'arbre de Noël?
4. Il faut qu'ils mettent leurs souliers devant la cheminée?
5. Il faut qu'ils aillent à la messe de minuit?
6. Il faut qu'ils fassent réveillon avec leurs parents?
7. Il faut qu'ils chantent des chants de Noël?
8. Il faut qu'ils souhaitent «Joyeux Noël» à tout le monde?

C **Le mariage en France.** Répondez par «oui».

1. Il faut que les fiancés annoncent leur mariage?
2. Il faut qu'ils choisissent des alliances?
3. Il faut qu'ils aient une demoiselle et un garçon d'honneur?
4. Il faut qu'ils disent «oui» devant Monsieur le maire?
5. Il faut qu'ils aillent à l'église pour la cérémonie religieuse?

D **Il faut que je fasse tellement de choses.** Donnez des réponses personnelles.

1. Il faut que tu te lèves de bonne heure?
2. Il faut que tu ailles à l'école?
3. Il faut que tu sois toujours à l'heure?
4. Il faut que tu dises «bonjour» au prof?
5. Il faut que tu fasses tes devoirs?
6. Il faut que tu passes un examen?
7. Il faut que tu réussisses à ton examen?

E **Vous êtes occupé(e)s?**
Dites à des camarades ce qu'il faut qu'ils fassent. Suivez le modèle.

> faire vos devoirs
> *Il faut que vous fassiez vos devoirs.*

1. étudier pour demain
2. préparer la fête
3. choisir des cadeaux
4. aller au magasin
5. faire des achats
6. aller au marché
7. faire les courses
8. rentrer chez vous
9. préparer le dîner
10. mettre le couvert
11. servir le dîner

Noël à Paris: une rue illuminée

Exercice B

1. Oui, il faut que les enfants soient sages toute l'année.
2. Oui, il faut qu'ils aient...
3. Oui, il faut qu'ils décorent...
4. Oui, il faut qu'ils mettent...
5. Oui, il faut qu'ils aillent...
6. Oui, il faut qu'ils fassent...
7. Oui, il faut qu'ils chantent...
8. Oui, il faut qu'ils souhaitent...

Exercice C

1. Oui, il faut que les fiancés annoncent leur mariage.
2. Oui, il faut qu'ils choisissent...
3. Oui, il faut qu'ils aient...
4. Oui, il faut qu'ils disent...
5. Oui, il faut qu'ils aillent...

Exercice D

Answers will vary but all should contain *il faut que* + the subjunctive of the verb.

Exercice E

1. Il faut que vous étudiiez pour demain.
2. ... que vous prépariez la fête.
3. ... que vous choisissiez des cadeaux.
4. ... que vous alliez au magasin.
5. ... que vous fassiez des achats.
6. ... que vous alliez au marché.
7. ... que vous fassiez les courses.
8. ... que vous rentriez chez vous.
9. ... que vous prépariez le dîner.
10. ... que vous mettiez le couvert.
11. ... que vous serviez le dîner.

LEARNING FROM PHOTOS

You may wish to ask the following questions about the photo: *La rue est illuminée? Il y a beaucoup de lumières? Pourquoi? C'est quelle saison de l'année? Où est la rue? Les lumières sont jolies? Est-ce que vous aimeriez être à Paris à Noël?*

ADDITIONAL PRACTICE

Student Tape Manual, Teacher's Edition, *Activités A–C*, pages 115–116

Le subjonctif avec les expressions impersonnelles

Note Once again, the concept we would like to emphasize is that even though an action is necessary (or important or good), it is not certain that it will take place. Since we do not know if it will take place, the subjunctive is used.

PRESENTATION (*page 282*)

Have the students read the expressions and the model sentences aloud.

Exercices

PRESENTATION (*page 282*)

Exercice B

You may wish to use the recorded version of this exercise.

ANSWERS

Exercice A

1. Il (n')est (pas) important que nous parlions bien.
2. ... que nous écrivions bien.
3. ... que nous lisions bien.
4. ... que nous suivions des cours.
5. ... que nous disions toujours...
6. ... que nous suivions...
7. ... que nous conduisions.
8. ... que nous conduisions prudemment.

Exercice B

1. ... que j'aille...
2. ... que je réussisse...
3. ... que je trouve...
4. ... que je me marie.
5. ... que je choisisse...
6. ... que j'aie...
7. ... que j'aie...

Exercice C

Answers will vary but all will include a form of the subjunctive.

1. Il faut que je suive...
2. Il est nécessaire que j'arrive à...
3. ... que je sois à l'heure.
4. ... que je sois poli(e)...
5. ... que j'aie...
6. ... que je lise...

Le subjonctif avec les expressions impersonnelles

Expressing Necessity or Possibility

1. Here are some other expressions that are always followed by the subjunctive in French.

il est nécessaire que	**il est possible que**
il est important que	**il est impossible que**
il est bon que	**il est juste que**
il est temps que	**il vaut mieux que (il est préférable que)**

2. These expressions of necessity or possibility require the subjunctive because the information in the clause introduced by *que* is not necessarily a fact. The action referred to may or may not take place.

   Il est nécessaire que vous fassiez vos devoirs.
   Il est possible que tu aies trop de choses à faire.
   Il est impossible que Jean finisse demain.

Exercices

A **Qu'est-ce que vous en pensez?** Faites des phrases avec «il est important que» ou «il n'est pas important que».

1. Nous parlons bien.
2. Nous écrivons bien.
3. Nous lisons beaucoup.
4. Nous suivons des cours.
5. Nous disons toujours la vérité.
6. Nous suivons un cours de conduite.
7. Nous conduisons.
8. Nous conduisons prudemment.

B **C'est possible ou pas?** Faites des phrases d'après le modèle.

   Je vais à l'université.
   Il est possible que j'aille à l'université.

1. Je vais à l'université.
2. Je réussis aux examens.
3. Je trouve un bon travail.
4. Je me marie.
5. Je choisis un mari (une femme) très riche.
6. J'ai des enfants.
7. J'ai beaucoup de succès.

C **À l'école.** Donnez des réponses personnelles.

1. Il faut que tu suives combien de cours?
2. Il est nécessaire que tu arrives à l'école à quelle heure?
3. Il est important que tu sois à l'heure?
4. Il est important que tu sois poli(e) avec les profs?
5. Il est possible que tu aies un examen aujourd'hui?
6. Il est bon que tu lises beaucoup de livres?

INDEPENDENT PRACTICE

Assign any of the following:
1. Exercises, pages 282–283
2. Workbook, *Structure: C–I*, pages 124–125
3. Communication Activities Masters, *Structure: B–C*, pages 75–76
4. CD-ROM, Disc 3, pages 282–283

Les nombres au-dessus de 1.000

Giving Dates and Expressing Numbers Over 1,000

1. Note the way the numbers 1,000 and above are expressed in French.

   > **1.000 mille**
   > **1.001 mille un**
   > **1.100 mille cent** ou **onze cents**
   > **1.492 mille quatre cent quatre-vingt-douze** ou **quatorze cent quatre-vingt-douze**

   It is also possible to leave a space instead of using a period: 1 000, 1 492. Dates, however, have no periods or spaces: 1789, 1492, etc.

2. Note that *mille* never takes an *-s*.

   > **2.000 deux mille**
   > **5.000 cinq mille**
   > **3.500 trois mille cinq cents**

3. You use *un* with *million*, and *million* is followed by *de*.

   > **1.000.000 un million (de personnes)**
   > **2.000.000 deux millions (d'habitants)**

Exercices

A **Un peu d'histoire de France.** Lisez à haute voix.

1. La Révolution a commencé en 1789.
2. Jeanne d'Arc est née en 1412.
3. Marie-Antoinette est morte en 1793.
4. Charles de Gaulle a été président de la République de 1958 à 1968.
5. Napoléon a régné de 1804 à 1814.
6. La Tunisie a reçu son indépendance en 1956.

B **Moi!** Donnez des réponses personnelles.

1. En quelle année es-tu né(e)?
2. En quelle année as-tu commencé tes études à l'école primaire?
3. En quelle année termineras-tu tes études secondaires?

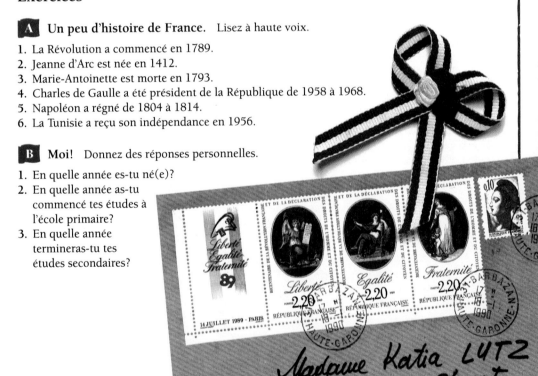

CONVERSATION

Bell Ringer Review

Write the following on the board or use BRR Blackline Master 11-3: Rewrite the following sentences, replacing the italicized words with pronouns.

1. Je vois trois *guichets* dans la gare.
2. Marc va rencontrer *ses amis devant le guichet.*
3. L'homme a vendu deux *carnets aux élèves.*
4. J'ai parlé *à Colette* hier soir.
5. Il y a beaucoup *de gâteaux* à la pâtisserie.

PRESENTATION *(page 284)*

A. Have students close their books. Play the Conversation Video or have them listen to the conversation on Cassette 7A/CD-6.
B. Have the students repeat each line of the conversation after you. (Use *Activité G* in the Student Tape Manual to check oral comprehension.)
C. Have two students read the conversation with as much expression as possible. The student reading the part of Érica should try to project a certain amount of disbelief.

Note In the CD-ROM version, students can play the role of either one of the characters and record the conversation.

ANSWERS

Exercice A

1. Les deux copains parlent du défilé du quatorze juillet.
2. Oui, il faut que Serge y aille.
3. Il faut qu'il y aille parce qu'il joue dans la fanfare, et la fanfare va défiler.
4. Il joue du trombone.
5. Non, elle ne sait pas qu'il joue du trombone.

284

Scènes de la vie *C'est bientôt le 14 juillet*

ÉRICA: Tu vas aller au défilé du quatorze juillet?
SERGE: Bien sûr... Il *faut* que j'y aille!
ÉRICA: Pourquoi? Tu y vas avec tes parents?
SERGE: Non, mais la fanfare va défiler.
ÉRICA: Oui, et alors?
SERGE: Tu veux rigoler ou quoi? Tu sais bien que je joue dans la fanfare!
ÉRICA: Ah oui? Je ne savais pas! Tu joues de quel instrument?
SERGE: Du trombone.
ÉRICA: Vraiment? Il faut que j'aille voir ça!
SERGE: Et il faudra que tu applaudisses quand je passerai!

A **Ils vont au défilé?** Répondez d'après la conversation.

1. De quoi les deux copains parlent-ils?
2. Serge va au défilé?
3. Pourquoi faut-il qu'il y aille?
4. Il joue de quel instrument?
5. Érica sait que son ami joue du trombone?
6. Érica va aller au défilé? Pourquoi?
7. Quand faudra-t-il qu'elle applaudisse?

284   CHAPITRE 11

ADDITIONAL PRACTICE

You may wish to ask your students the following questions: *Qui joue d'un instrument? Vous jouez de quel instrument? Y a-t-il une fanfare à votre école? Quand défile-t-elle? Est-ce que la fanfare joue l'hymne national américain? Quand? Est-ce que tout le monde applaudit?*

Activités de communication orale

A **À faire absolument.** Vous discutez avec un(e) camarade. Dites au moins trois choses qu'il faut que vous fassiez ce soir. Demandez à votre camarade s'il faut qu'il/elle fasse les mêmes choses ou pas.

> Élève 1: Il faut que j'aille au supermarché. Et toi? Il faut que tu y ailles aussi?
> Élève 2: Non, moi, il faut que j'aille au stade.

B **De bonnes résolutions.** Travaillez avec un(e) camarade. Imaginez que c'est le jour de l'An et que vous et votre camarade prenez trois bonnes résolutions pour la nouvelle année.

> Élève 1: Il faut que je sois plus gentil(le) avec mon petit frère et ma petite sœur.
> Élève 2: Moi, il faut que je sois plus aimable avec mes parents.

C **Le réveillon.** Travaillez en petits groupes. Imaginez que vous organisez une fête pour le Nouvel An. Dites tout ce qu'il faut que vous ayez, que vous fassiez, etc.

> Élève 1: Il faut que nous ayons des guirlandes roses et blanches.
> Élève 2: Il faut que nous achetions des confettis.
> Élève 3: Il faut que tout le monde arrive à 10 heures…

D **Deux avis valent mieux qu'un.** Faites une liste des choses que vous voudriez faire. Lisez votre liste à un(e) camarade. Votre camarade vous dira ce qu'il faut faire pour réaliser votre objectif. Ensuite changez de rôles.

> Élève 1: Je voudrais perdre cinq kilos.
> Élève 2: Il est important que tu fasses de l'exercice. Il faut que tu manges moins.

E **Chantons en français!** Travaillez avec les élèves de la chorale (*chorus*) de l'école. Apprenez-leur des chansons françaises (des chants de Noël, l'hymne national français, etc.). Demandez-leur de chanter une de ces chansons au concert annuel.

---

6. Oui, elle va aller au défilé parce qu'elle veut voir Serge dans la fanfare.
7. Il faudra qu'elle applaudisse quand Serge passera.

Activités de communication orale
PRESENTATION *(page 285)*

These activities encourage students to reincorporate previously learned vocabulary and structures and use them on their own. You may wish to select those activities that you consider most appropriate. You may also wish to allow students to select the activities they would like to do.

Activité E
The music and lyrics to *La Marseillaise* are on the French 3 Audio Program: Cassette 8B/CD-8 and in the Student Tape Manual, Teacher's Edition, *Chapitre 4,* page 112.

Extension of *Activité E*
See COMMUNITIES below.

ANSWERS
Activités A, B, C, and D
Answers will vary.

COMMUNITIES

If you are studying this chapter during the Christmas season, have the students learn some French Christmas carols and go caroling in the community.

INDEPENDENT PRACTICE

Assign any of the following:
1. Exercise and activities, pages 284–285
2. CD-ROM, Disc 3, pages 284–285

LECTURE ET CULTURE

Bell Ringer Review

Write the following on the board or use BRR Blackline Master 11-4: Complete the sentences with the correct form and tense of the verb in parentheses.

1. Ce matin j'___ l'autobus pour aller au lycée. (prendre)
2. On ___ sur le bouton pour demander un arrêt. (appuyer)
3. Quand j'étais jeune, je ___ prendre le métro. (préférer)
4. Si j'avais une voiture, je la ___ prudemment. (conduire)
5. Demain je ___ encore à l'arrêt d'autobus. (être)

READING STRATEGIES
(pages 286–287)

Note It is recommended that you present the reading selection as thoroughly as you feel is necessary, based on the interests of your students.

Pre-reading

Tell students they are going to read about two important celebrations in the lives of many French people: marriage and Christmas.

Reading

A. Have students read the selection once silently.

B. Call on an individual to read about half a paragraph aloud. Call on other students to answer comprehension questions about what was read.

Post-reading

Call on volunteers to summarize the *Lecture* in their own words.

Note Students may listen to a recorded version of the *Lecture* on the CD-ROM.

LES FÊTES FAMILIALES

*D*eux grandes fêtes familiales en France et aux États-Unis sont le mariage et Noël.

Ce jeune couple se marie à la mairie.

LE MARIAGE

En France, un garçon peut se marier à dix-huit ans, une fille à quinze ans. Pour se marier plus jeune, il faut que le couple demande et obtienne une autorisation spéciale. Le mariage civil est obligatoire et il est célébré avant le mariage religieux. Seuls les mariés, leurs pères et mères, les proches parents[1] et les témoins[2] assistent[3] à la cérémonie qui est célébrée par le maire, dans la salle des mariages de la mairie.

---
[1] les proches parents   *the close relatives*
[2] les témoins   *the witnesses*
[3] assistent   *attend*

La cérémonie religieuse a lieu à l'église. À la campagne, il n'est pas rare que le cortège aille à l'église à pied. En ville, on y arrive en voiture.

Après la cérémonie, il y a une réception chez les parents de la mariée, dans une salle louée pour l'occasion ou dans un restaurant. Après un déjeuner ou un buffet superbe, la mariée coupe le gâteau de mariage. Au dessert ou au moment où l'on sert le champagne, on porte des toasts aux mariés.

NOËL

Noël est toujours une fête joyeuse. Toute la famille se réunit pour un grand souper. Les enfants mettent leurs souliers devant la cheminée. Il est important que le Père Noël les voie quand il arrive pendant la nuit, parce

On se souhaite «Joyeux Noël».

286   CHAPITRE 11

LEARNING FROM PHOTOS

After going over the reading selection, have students describe the photos of the wedding and Christmas celebration.

que c'est lui qui les remplit de cadeaux. Pas mal d'enfants y mettent des bottes qui peuvent contenir plus de cadeaux que des chaussures. De toute façon[4], les enfants savent qu'il est indispensable qu'ils soient sages pendant toute l'année pour recevoir des cadeaux du Père Noël.

Le soir du 24 décembre, beaucoup de gens assistent à la messe de minuit. Après la messe, on rentre à la maison pour le réveillon. Le repas traditionnel commence avec des huîtres ou du boudin blanc[5], il continue avec une dinde farcie aux marrons[6], et il finit avec une bûche de Noël. On mange, on boit[7], on parle et on s'amuse beaucoup. Tout le monde est content d'être réuni et d'attendre le Père Noël!

[4] De toute façon   *anyway, in any case*
[5] des huîtres ou du boudin blanc   *oysters or white sausage*
[6] farcie aux marrons   *stuffed with chestnuts*
[7] boit   *drinks*

Étude de mots

A   **Quelle est la définition?**   Choisissez.

1. demander
2. obtenir
3. la bûche de Noël
4. civil
5. religieux
6 le souper
7. indispensable
8. sage

a. recevoir
b. le repas du soir
c. avoir besoin, solliciter
d. qui concerne l'Église
e. absolument nécessaire
f. le gâteau de Noël
g. gentil(le), obéissant(e)
h. qui concerne l'État

B   **Des définitions.**   Trouvez dans la lecture les mots qui correspondent à ces définitions.

1. de la famille
2. un homme et une femme
3. de rigueur, absolument nécessaire
4. ceux qui se marient
5. le défilé des mariés et de leurs parents et amis
6. pleine de joie
7. un rite de l'Église catholique

Grand-père découpe la dinde et le petit Romain regarde la bûche de Noël.

PRESENTATION   *(page 287)*

Exercice B

If necessary, have students scan the reading as they do Exercise B.

ANSWERS

Exercice A

1. c
2. a
3. f
4. h
5. d
6. b
7. e
8. g

Exercice B

1. familial(e)
2. un couple
3. indispensable
4. les mariés
5. le cortège
6. joyeuse
7. la messe (de minuit)

Compréhension

PRESENTATION *(page 288)*

Exercise C has students look for information. Exercise D deals with factual recall. Exercise E has students make comparisons.

ANSWERS

Exercice C

1. le mariage et Noël
2. dix-huit ans
3. quinze ans
4. le maire
5. les mariés, leurs pères et mères, les proches parents, les témoins et le maire

Exercice D

1. Non, le mariage civil est obligatoire.
2. Le mariage civil a lieu dans la salle des mariages de la mairie.
3. Le mariage religieux a lieu à l'église.
4. La réception a lieu chez les parents de la mariée, dans une salle louée pour l'occasion ou dans un restaurant.
5. On porte les toasts au dessert ou au moment où l'on sert le champagne.
6. À la campagne, le cortège va souvent à l'église à pied.
7. En ville, le cortège va à l'église en voiture.
8. Toute la famille se réunit pour un grand souper.
9. Les enfants mettent leurs souliers devant la cheminée.
10. Le Père Noël les remplit.
11. Il les remplit de cadeaux.
12. Beaucoup de gens vont à la messe de minuit le soir du 24 décembre.

Exercice E

Answers will vary.

Compréhension

C **Des renseignements.** Trouvez les renseignements suivants dans la lecture.

1. deux fêtes importantes en France
2. l'âge auquel un garçon peut se marier en France
3. l'âge auquel une fille peut se marier en France
4. celui qui célèbre le mariage civil
5. ceux qui doivent assister au mariage civil

D **Vous avez compris?** Répondez d'après la lecture.

1. Est-ce que le mariage religieux est suffisant en France?
2. Où le mariage civil a-t-il lieu?
3. Où le mariage religieux a-t-il lieu?
4. Où la réception a-t-elle lieu?
5. Quand porte-t-on les toasts?
6. À la campagne, comment est-ce que le cortège va à l'église?
7. En ville, comment le cortège va-t-il à l'église?
8. Que fait la famille pour Noël?
9. Où est-ce que les enfants mettent leurs souliers?
10. Qui les remplit?
11. Avec quoi les remplit-il?
12. Où beaucoup de gens vont-ils le soir du 24 décembre?

E **Des comparaisons.** Comparez les festivités de Noël en France et les festivités de Noël aux États-Unis.

LEARNING FROM PHOTOS

Have students describe the wedding photo in as much detail as possible.

DÉCOUVERTE CULTURELLE

*L*a fête nationale française est le 14 juillet, date qui marque le commencement de la Révolution de 1789. Ce jour-là, le peuple de Paris prit possession de la forteresse de la Bastille. La Bastille était une prison pour les ennemis du roi[1], et donc symbolisait la tyrannie de la monarchie. Traditionnellement le 14 juillet, il y a dans toute la France des cérémonies officielles le matin, et des réjouissances[2] populaires le soir. À la nuit tombante[3], les gens sortent pour aller voir les feux d'artifice, et pour aller danser dans des bals en plein air.

Aux États-Unis, un garçon peut se marier dans la plupart des états à l'âge de dix-huit ans et une fille à l'âge de seize ans. Remarquez que l'âge légal varie d'un état à l'autre. En France, c'est le même âge dans tout le pays. On peut se marier à quel âge, en France?

De nos jours, il n'est pas rare que les fiancés dressent une «liste» des cadeaux qu'ils voudraient recevoir. Ils la déposent dans un magasin. Les amis et les parents vont au magasin et consultent la liste.

En France, comme aux États-Unis, il y a une communauté juive. Comme les autres Français, les Juifs doivent se marier civilement avant de se marier religieusement. Après le mariage civil, les Juifs ont un mariage religieux célébré par un rabbin. La cérémonie religieuse a lieu dans une synagogue ou dans une salle louée pour la circonstance. Pendant la cérémonie, le marié brise[4] un verre pour assurer le succès du couple.

Le défilé du 14 juillet à Paris

Hanouka, la fête des Lumières, est une fête juive. Elle commémore la reconsécration du temple de Jérusalem par les Maccabées après la révolte contre Antiochos IV, roi de Syrie, en 167 avant Jésus-Christ. À l'époque biblique, une menorah à sept branches restait allumée toute l'année, de jour et de nuit, dans le temple de Jérusalem. La menorah de la fête des Lumières a neuf branches. Ce sont les enfants qui allument les bougies—une bougie chaque soir que dure la fête. La bougie au centre du chandelier est allumée le premier soir, et elle sert à allumer les autres bougies. La fête dure huit jours. Hanouka est une fête joyeuse, surtout pour les enfants qui reçoivent un cadeau chaque jour. Mais il y a aussi des bonbons et des gâteaux pour les adultes.

[1] roi   *king*
[2] réjouissances   *festivities*
[3] à la nuit tombante   *at nightfall*
[4] brise   *breaks*

Découverte culturelle

Note The first section deals with *le 14 juillet,* the second with *le mariage,* and the third with *Hanouka.*

PRESENTATION *(page 289)*

You may want to choose sections of this *Découverte* that you think will be of particular interest to your students. Different students may read different sections.

Note Students may listen to a recorded version of the *Découverte culturelle* on the CD-ROM.

INDEPENDENT PRACTICE

Assign any of the following:
1. *Compréhension* exercises, page 288
2. Workbook, *Un Peu Plus,* pages 126–129
3. CD-ROM, Disc 3, pages 288–289

RÉALITÉS

Bell Ringer Review

Write the following on the board or use BRR Blackline Master 11-5: Put the following conversation in logical order.

1. C'est de la part de qui?
2. Je peux lui laisser un message?
3. Pourrais-je parler à Chantal Vernier, s'il vous plaît?
4. Allô!
5. D'accord. Allez-y.
6. De Robert Bonnard.
7. Je suis désolée, mais elle n'est pas là.
8. Un moment. Ne quittez pas.

OPTIONAL MATERIAL

PRESENTATION
(*pages 290–291*)

Have the students look at the photographs for enjoyment.

Note In the CD-ROM version, students can listen to the recorded captions and discover a hidden video behind one of the photos.

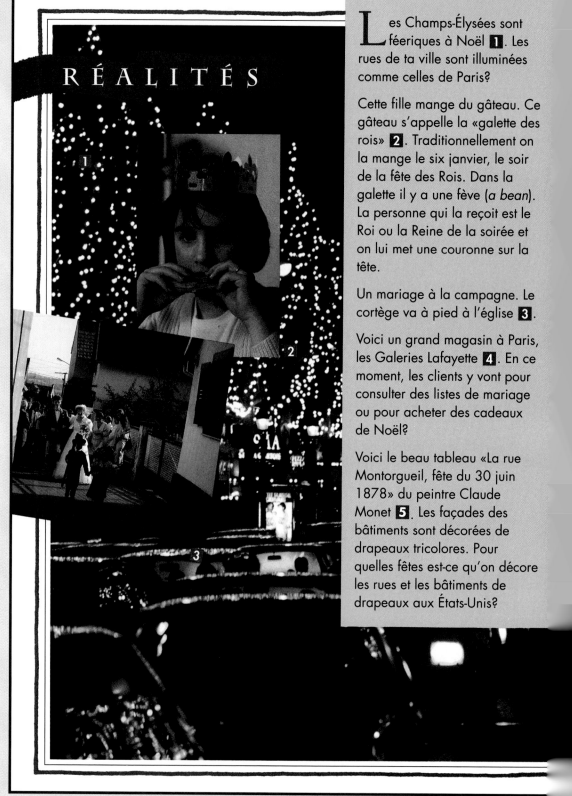

Les Champs-Élysées sont féeriques à Noël **1**. Les rues de ta ville sont illuminées comme celles de Paris?

Cette fille mange du gâteau. Ce gâteau s'appelle la «galette des rois» **2**. Traditionnellement on la mange le six janvier, le soir de la fête des Rois. Dans la galette il y a une fève (*a bean*). La personne qui la reçoit est le Roi ou la Reine de la soirée et on lui met une couronne sur la tête.

Un mariage à la campagne. Le cortège va à pied à l'église **3**.

Voici un grand magasin à Paris, les Galeries Lafayette **4**. En ce moment, les clients y vont pour consulter des listes de mariage ou pour acheter des cadeaux de Noël?

Voici le beau tableau «La rue Montorgueil, fête du 30 juin 1878» du peintre Claude Monet **5**. Les façades des bâtiments sont décorées de drapeaux tricolores. Pour quelles fêtes est-ce qu'on décore les rues et les bâtiments de drapeaux aux États-Unis?

COMMUNITIES

If there is a French bakery in your area, you may wish to buy a *galette des rois* for the 6th of January; or, if your school has a Home Economics department, you may wish to ask for its assistance in making one.

5

4

291

ART CONNECTION

Ask your students if they know any other paintings by Monet or if they know the names of any other Impressionist painters. (Another painting by Monet, *La Gare Saint-Lazare,* is pictured on page 98.) Ask them to tell you as much as they can about these artists and the Impressionist movement.

Note For art activities related to Claude Monet and *La rue Montorgueil, fête du 30 juin 1878,* please refer to Fine Art Transparency F-5.

ADDITIONAL PRACTICE

Assign any of the following:
1. Student Tape Manual, Teacher's Edition, *Deuxième Partie,* pages 119–120
2. Situation Cards, Chapter 11

RECYCLING

These activities encourage students to use all the language they have learned in the chapter and recombine it with material from previous chapters. It is not necessary to do all the activities with all students. You may select the ones you consider most appropriate or allow students to choose the ones they wish to do.

INFORMAL ASSESSMENT

The *Activités de communication orale* lend themselves to assessing speaking and listening abilities. For guidelines on assigning an oral grade, use the evaluation criteria given on page 22 of this Teacher's Wraparound Edition.

Activités de communication orale

PRESENTATION (page 292)

Activité A

This activity encourages students to do some realistic critical thinking.

Activité B

In the CD-ROM version of this activity, students can interact with an on-screen native speaker.

ANSWERS

Activités A, B, and C

Answers will vary.

Activités de communication écrite

ANSWERS

Activités A and B

Answers will vary.

Activités de communication orale

A **Un bon mariage.** Travaillez avec un(e) camarade. Discutez des qualités essentielles que vous aimeriez trouver chez un mari ou une femme idéale. Décidez si vous êtes d'accord ou pas.

> Élève 1: À mon avis, il est important que le mari aide sa femme avec les enfants. Tu es d'accord?
> Élève 2: Oui, je suis d'accord. Il est important aussi que le mari fasse la cuisine…

B **Un peu d'imagination!** Imaginez que vous allez vous marier avec un(e) Français(e). Votre camarade Véronique, très surprise, vous pose des questions. Répondez-lui.

1. Quand est-ce que vous allez vous marier?
2. Où aura lieu la cérémonie?
3. Ce sera à quelle heure?
4. Vous aurez un déjeuner assis ou un buffet?
5. Combien de personnes est-ce que vous inviterez?

Véronique

C **Ma fête préférée?** Demandez à votre camarade quelle fête il/elle préfère et pourquoi: le 4 juillet, Noël ou le jour de l'An. Ensuite changez de rôles.

Activités de communication écrite

A **Noël.** Vous êtes français(e). Écrivez une lettre à une amie américaine. Dites-lui ce que vous avez fait à Noël l'année dernière ou ce que vous ferez à Noël l'année prochaine.

B **Faire-part de mariage.** Regardez le faire-part de mariage à droite. Écrivez le faire-part de votre mariage tel que vous l'avez décrit dans l'Activité orale B. N'oubliez pas les renseignements suivants:

1. votre nom et celui de votre fiancé(e)
2. la date du mariage
3. le nom de vos parents
4. le lieu et l'heure du mariage

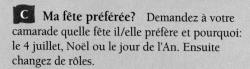

Madame Maurice Fischer,
Monsieur Oscar Lenotte,
Monsieur et Madame Ivan Lenotte,
sont heureux de vous faire part du mariage de
Monsieur Jean-Hubert Lenotte, leur petit-fils
et fils, avec Mademoiselle Laurence de Brye.

Et vous prient d'assister ou de vous unir
d'intention à la Messe de Mariage qui sera
célébrée le Samedi 5 Octobre 1991, à 14 heures 30,
en l'Église Notre-Dame d'Auteuil.
Le consentement des époux sera reçu par le
Père Jean-Luc Rayonneau (s.j.).

COOPERATIVE LEARNING

Display Communication Transparency C-11. Have groups make up as many questions as they can about the wedding reception. Then have groups take turns asking and answering the questions.

Réintroduction et recombinaison

A **Mes petits frères.** Complétez au présent avec le verbe indiqué.

1. Ils ___ des chants de Noël. (apprendre)
2. Ils ___ des leçons de chant. (prendre)
3. Ils ___ leurs cartes de vœux. (envoyer)
4. Ils ___ avec nous à la messe de minuit. (venir)
5. Ils ___ encore au Père Noël. (croire)
6. Ils ___ beaucoup de cadeaux. (recevoir)

B **Le voyage de noces** (*Honeymoon*). Complétez au passé composé avec le verbe indiqué.

1. Paul et Marie ___ hier. (se marier)
2. Leur mariage ___ à Notre-Dame. (avoir lieu)
3. Ils ___ beaucoup de cadeaux. (recevoir)
4. Tout le monde ___ à la réception. (s'amuser)
5. Leurs amis et leurs parents leur ___ beaucoup de succès. (souhaiter)
6. Paul et Marie ___ à la Martinique. (aller)
7. Ils ___ ce matin. (arriver)

Vocabulaire

NOMS

Le 14 juillet
la fête nationale
le défilé
l'hymne (m.) national
le drapeau
le maire
le notable
la tribune
le soldat
le feu d'artifice

la fanfare
le tambour
les cymbales (f.)
la trompette
le trombone
l'orchestre (m.)
le musicien
l'accordéon (m.)
la guitare
le piano
le violon
la flûte
le saxophone
la batterie

Noël
le Père Noël
l'arbre (m.) de Noël
le sapin
la cheminée
les souliers (m.)
le cadeau de Noël
le chant de Noël
la messe de minuit

Le jour de l'An
la carte de vœux
le réveillon
les confettis (m.)
le serpentin
les décorations (f.)
la guirlande
les festivités (f.)

Hanouka
la fête des Lumières
la menorah
le chandelier
la branche
la bougie

Le Mariage
la cérémonie
le marié
la mariée
les mariés (m.)
la demoiselle d'honneur
le garçon d'honneur
l'alliance (f.)
la mairie
l'église (f.)

VERBES
allumer
applaudir
célébrer
défiler
durer
se marier
se souhaiter

ADJECTIFS
militaire
national(e)
religieux, religieuse
juif, juive
sage

AUTRES MOTS ET EXPRESSIONS
Joyeux Noël!
Bonne Année!

avoir lieu
défiler au pas
jouer d'un instrument
  de musique
se mettre au premier
  rang
tirer un feu d'artifice
faire partie de

il est important que
il est impossible que
il est juste que
il est nécessaire que
il est possible que
il est temps que
il est préférable que
il faut que
il vaut mieux que

Réintroduction et recombinaison

PRESENTATION (*page 293*)

Exercise A reviews the *ils/elles* form of the types of verbs students will use to form the subjunctive in the next chapter. Exercise B once again reviews the *passé composé* with *avoir* and *être*.

ANSWERS

Exercice A

1. apprennent
2. prennent
3. envoient
4. viennent
5. croient
6. reçoivent

Exercice B

1. se sont mariés
2. a eu lieu
3. ont reçu
4. s'est amusé
5. ont souhaité
6. sont allés
7. sont arrivés

ASSESSMENT RESOURCES

1. Chapter Quizzes
2. Testing Program
3. Situation Cards
4. Communication Transparency C-11
5. Computer Software: Practice/Test Generator

VIDEO PROGRAM

INTRODUCTION   (38:26)

IL FAUT QUE TU VIENNES!   (38:58)

STUDENT PORTFOLIO

Written assignments which may be included in students' portfolios are the *Activités de communication écrite* on page 292 and any writing activities from the *Un Peu Plus* section in the Workbook.

Note Students may create and save both oral and written work using the Electronic Portfolio feature on the CD-ROM.

INDEPENDENT PRACTICE

Assign any of the following:
1. Activities and exercises, pages 292–293
2. Communication Activities Masters, pages 70–76
3. CD-ROM, Disc 3, pages 292–293

CHAPTER OVERVIEW

In this chapter students will learn to discuss many aspects of their school life. They will learn some additional uses of the subjunctive and the verbs *rire* and *sourire*.

The cultural focus of the chapter is on secondary school education in France. Students will be able to compare and contrast their school life with that of their French-speaking counterparts.

CHAPTER OBJECTIVES

By the end of this chapter, students will know:

1. vocabulary associated with school life
2. the forms of additional irregular verbs in the subjunctive
3. the use of the subjunctive to express wishes, preferences, and demands
4. the use of the subjunctive vs. the use of the infinitive
5. the irregular verbs *rire* and *sourire*

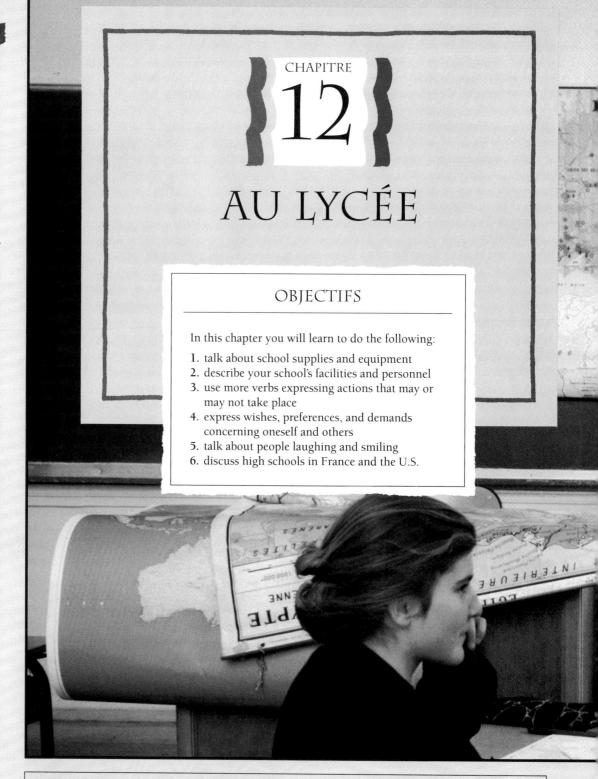

CHAPITRE 12

AU LYCÉE

OBJECTIFS

In this chapter you will learn to do the following:

1. talk about school supplies and equipment
2. describe your school's facilities and personnel
3. use more verbs expressing actions that may or may not take place
4. express wishes, preferences, and demands concerning oneself and others
5. talk about people laughing and smiling
6. discuss high schools in France and the U.S.

CHAPTER PROJECTS

(optional)

1. Have students prepare a magazine article for French students concerning school life in a typical American high school. You may suggest that they use the *Lecture* on page 310 as a model.
2. Have the students prepare a report on the educational system of the United States.
3. Have students prepare a report on the educational system in France.
4. Have students write an essay on the importance of a good education.

295

Pacing

This chapter will require eight to ten class sessions. Pacing will depend on the length of the class, the age of the students, and student aptitude.

For more information on planning your class, see the Lesson Plans, which offer guidelines for 45- and 55-minute classes and **Block Scheduling.**

Exercices vs. *Activités*

The exercises and activities are color-coded. Exercises, which provide guided practice to prepare students for independent communication, are coded in blue. Communicative activities, which give students opportunities for creative, open-ended expression, are coded in red.

INTERNET ACTIVITIES

(*optional*)

These activities, student worksheets, and related teacher information are in the *À bord* Internet Activities Booklet and on the Glencoe Foreign Language Home Page at: **http://www.glencoe.com/secondary/fl**

LEARNING FROM PHOTOS

After presenting the vocabulary in this chapter, have the students describe the people in the photo. Then have them describe what is going on in the photo.

VOCABULAIRE

MOTS 1

Vocabulary Teaching Resources

1. Vocabulary Transparencies 12.1 (A & B)
2. Audio Cassette 7B/CD-6
3. Student Tape Manual, Teacher's Edition, *Mots 1: A–C*, pages 121–123
4. Workbook, *Mots 1: A–D*, pages 130–131
5. Communication Activities Masters, *Mots 1: A–B*, pages 77–78
6. Chapter Quizzes, *Mots 1:* Quiz 1, page 61
7. CD-ROM, Disc 3, *Mots 1:* pages 296–299

Bell Ringer Review

Write the following on the board or use BRR Blackline Master 12-1: Make a list of all the words and expressions you know in French that are related to school.

PRESENTATION (pages 296–297)

A. Have students repeat each word after you or Cassette 7B/CD-6 as they look at Vocabulary Transparencies 12.1 (A & B).

B. Call a student to the front of the room and have him/her point to items on the transparency and ask, *Qu'est-ce que c'est?*

LE MATÉRIEL SCOLAIRE

un journal

un cartable

un livre scolaire

un sac à dos

une gomme

un dictionnaire

effacer

un emploi du temps

une encyclopédie

un feutre

un magazine

une calculatrice

un stylo(-bille)

une diapo(sitive)

une machine à traitement de texte

un ordinateur

un projecteur

un écran

une machine à écrire

le panneau d'affichage

la sonnerie

COOPERATIVE LEARNING

Have students work in groups to write definitions of the vocabulary words on page 296. Then have group members take turns giving a definition and see if the other groups can guess what word is being defined.

faire une rédaction
faire ses devoirs

taper à la machine

faire un exposé

Le prof veut que vous fassiez vos devoirs.
Il veut que vous appreniez vos leçons.
La prof veut que tous ses élèves fassent leurs
     devoirs.
Elle veut qu'ils apprennent leurs leçons.
Les profs exigent que vous finissiez vos
     devoirs.
Ils exigent que vous veniez en classe
     préparés.

échouer à
un examen

recevoir de bonnes notes
être reçu(e) à un examen

Votre professeur veut que vous soyez reçu(e)
     aux examens.
La prof veut que tous ses élèves soient reçus
     aux examens.

Tous les profs insistent pour que vous
     arriviez en classe à l'heure.

Les profs sont sympa. Ils rient avec leurs élèves.
Les élèves aiment que les profs rient avec eux.

CHAPITRE 12   297

C. Have students open their books
   and read the sentences on page
   297 after you.
D. You may wish to ask the following questions about the sentences: *Le professeur veut que
   ses élèves fassent leurs devoirs?
   Il veut qu'ils apprennent leurs
   leçons? Le professeur exige que
   les élèves finissent leurs devoirs?
   Il exige que les élèves viennent en
   classe préparés? Le professeur
   veut que les élèves soient reçus
   aux examens?*, etc.

Note The word *un exposé* refers to
an oral report more often than to a
written one.

Exercices

PRESENTATION (page 298)

Exercice A

Exercise A can be done with books open or closed.

Exercice B

Exercise B must be done with books open so that students may refer to the illustrations.

ANSWERS

Exercice A

Answers will vary.

Exercice B

1. C'est un écran.
2. Ce sont des encyclopédies.
3. C'est un sac à dos.
4. C'est un projecteur.
5. C'est un stylo-bille.
6. C'est une diapo.
7. C'est une calculatrice.
8. C'est un magazine.

Exercices

A Tu as le matériel scolaire nécessaire? Donnez des réponses personnelles.

1. Tu portes tes livres dans un cartable ou dans un sac à dos?
2. Tu as à peu près combien de livres scolaires cette année?
3. Tu préfères écrire avec un crayon, un feutre ou un stylo-bille?
4. Tu fais tes devoirs de maths au crayon?
5. Si tu fais une erreur, tu l'effaces avec une gomme?
6. Tu utilises une calculatrice pour faire tes devoirs de maths?
7. Tu suis un cours d'informatique pour apprendre à utiliser un ordinateur?
8. Tu consultes souvent ton emploi du temps ou tu le connais par cœur?
9. Quand tu prépares une rédaction, tu la tapes à la machine?
10. Tu as une machine à écrire, une machine à traitement de texte ou un ordinateur?
11. Dans ton école, est-ce qu'une sonnerie annonce la fin de chaque classe?
12. Tu cherches une définition dans une encyclopédie ou dans un dictionnaire?

B Qu'est-ce que c'est? Identifiez.

1. C'est un écran ou un emploi du temps?
2. Ce sont des livres scolaires ou des encyclopédies?
3. C'est un cartable ou un sac à dos?
4. C'est un projecteur ou un panneau d'affichage?
5. C'est un feutre ou un stylo-bille?
6. C'est un film ou une diapo?
7. C'est un ordinateur ou une calculatrice?
8. C'est un magazine ou un journal?

ADDITIONAL PRACTICE

Student Tape Manual, Teacher's Edition, *Activité C,* page 123

C Questions d'enseignement. Répondez par «oui» ou «non».

1. Les profs veulent que tes camarades et toi appreniez vos leçons?
2. Les profs exigent que vous soyez à l'heure?
3. Les profs aiment que vous arriviez en classe en retard?
4. Vos parents exigent que vous ayez de bonnes notes?
5. Vos parents veulent que vous soyez reçu(e) aux examens?
6. Vos camarades de classe veulent que vous échouiez aux examens?
7. Le prof d'anglais exige que vous écriviez vos rédactions à la main?
8. La prof de français insiste pour que vous lui donniez des devoirs tapés à la machine?

D Ce que je fais. Donnez des réponses personnelles.

1. Tu lis quels magazines?
2. Tu lis quels journaux?
3. Tu suis combien de cours ce semestre?
4. Tu fais à peu près combien d'exposés par semaine?
5. Tu consultes quelles encyclopédies ou quels dictionnaires?
6. Tu connais des profs qui rient avec leurs élèves?

299

PRESENTATION (*continued*)
Exercice C
  When doing Exercise C, students need only answer *oui* or *non*. The purpose of the exercise is to provide receptive practice with the subjunctive.

ANSWERS
Exercice C
1. Oui.
2. Oui.
3. Non.
4. Oui.
5. Oui.
6. Non.
7. Oui. (Non.)
8. Oui. (Non.)

Exercice D
  Answers will vary.

Vocabulary Teaching Resources

1. Vocabulary Transparencies 12.2 (A & B)
2. Audio Cassette 7B/CD-6
3. Student Tape Manual, Teacher's Edition, *Mots 2: D–G*, pages 123–125
4. Workbook, *Mots 2: E–G*, pages 132–133
5. Communication Activities Masters, *Mots 2: C–D*, pages 78–79
6. Computer Software, *Vocabulaire*
7. Chapter Quizzes, *Mots 2: Quiz 2*, page 62
8. CD-ROM, Disc 3, *Mots 2:* pages 300–303

Bell Ringer Review

Write the following on the board or use BRR Blackline Master 12-2: Write the following words under the appropriate heading: *Le 14 juillet* or *Noël*. le cadeau, le chant, la cheminée, le défilé, le drapeau, la fanfare, les feux d'artifice, la messe de minuit, le sapin, le soldat, les souliers, les tribunes

PRESENTATION (pages 300–301)

A. Present the vocabulary by showing Vocabulary Transparencies 12.2 (A & B) and having the students repeat the new words and expressions after you or Cassette 7B/CD-6.
B. Tell students: *Les grandes vacances sont les vacances d'été, et le premier jour des cours après ces vacances s'appelle «la rentrée (des classes)».*

VOCABULAIRE

MOTS 2

LE LYCÉE

le professeur principal

les lycéens

une lycéenne   un lycéen

la cour du lycée

le proviseur [1]
M. le Proviseur

[1] A female principal is called *la directrice.*

M. le Censeur

le censeur [2]

[2] A female vice-principal is also called *le censeur.*

La rentrée des classes est le jour où les cours recommencent après les grandes vacances.

le bureau de vie scolaire

Activités de la semaine

la conseillère d'éducation
(le conseiller d'éducation)

la conseillère d'orientation
(le conseiller d'orientation)

300 CHAPITRE 12

CRITICAL THINKING ACTIVITY

(Thinking skill: making inferences)
Read the following to the class or write it on the board or on a transparency:
Tous les élèves sont contents d'avoir des vacances. Mais il y a aussi des élèves qui attendent la rentrée des classes avec plaisir. Pourquoi?

la cantine

le surveillant   (la surveillante)

la salle de permanence

le terrain de basket

le gymnase

le terrain de hand

la piste de course

la documentaliste
(le documentaliste)

une carte

une brosse

le CDI (le Centre de Documentation et d'Information)

La prof enseigne la géographie.
Un élève efface le tableau.

La plupart des cours au lycée sont
  obligatoires.
Quelques cours ne sont pas obligatoires.
  Ils sont facultatifs.

Le baccalauréat (le bac, le bachot) est
  l'examen que l'on passe en dernière année
  de lycée. Si l'on est reçu, on obtient le
  diplôme du baccalauréat.

Note The *conseiller d'éducation*
has several administrative functions (student school attendance,
passes and authorizations, cafeteria supervision) as well as being in
charge of discipline and acting as
liaison between students, faculty,
and administration. The *conseillers d'orientation* are guidance
counselors. Their job is to inform
students and parents about the
educational system, careers, and
training requirements, and to
guide students in their choice of
courses and programs.

CROSS-CULTURAL COMPARISON

1. The word *bibliothèque* is
   still used when speaking
   of a library, but the term
   *CDI (Centre de Documen-
   tation et d'Information)* is
   increasingly common. It is
   used in the same way as
   "resource center" or
   "media center" in English.
2. *Une salle de permanence*
   can be translated as "study
   hall," but as students will
   learn later in the chapter,
   the two are somewhat
   different. Students go to
   the *salle de permanence*
   if a teacher is absent, for
   example. The expression
   often used is *Je vais en
   perm.*

302

Exercices

A **Un lycée.** *Complétez.*

1. Le directeur d'un lycée s'appelle le ___ si c'est un homme ou la ___ si c'est une femme.
2. La personne qui l'aide est le ___.
3. Les ___ sont les élèves d'un lycée.
4. Le conseiller ou la conseillère d'___ aide les élèves à choisir leurs cours.
5. Le prof de chimie ___ la chimie.
6. Le prof efface le tableau avec une ___.

7. Le / La documentaliste travaille au ___.
8. À la récréation, les élèves vont dans la ___.
9. On utilise souvent une ___ dans la classe de géographie.
10. On déjeune à la ___.
11. Le dessin est facultatif, mais les maths sont ___.
12. En été il y a les ___. Il n'y a pas de cours.
13. La ___ a lieu au mois de septembre.

B **Lycée ou *high school*?** *Choisissez le mot ou l'expression qui correspond.*

1. *vice-principal*
2. *homeroom teacher*
3. *dean of discipline*
4. *guidance counselor*
5. *study hall*
6. *resource center, media center*

a. le conseiller (la conseillère) d'éducation
b. le conseiller (la conseillère) d'orientation
c. le censeur
d. le Centre de Documentation et d'Information
e. la salle de permanence
f. le professeur principal

C **Mon école.** *Donnez des réponses personnelles.*

1. Quel est le nom de ton école?
2. Il y a à peu près combien d'élèves dans ton école?
3. Tu es en quelle classe?
4. Qui est le proviseur ou la directrice de ton école?
5. Il y a aussi un censeur? Comment s'appelle-t-il / elle?
6. Qui est ton conseiller ou ta conseillère d'orientation?
7. Qui est ton conseiller ou ta conseillère d'éducation?
8. Est-ce que tu vas à la salle de permanence? Est-ce qu'il y a toujours un(e) surveillant(e) quand tu y es?
9. L'année scolaire est divisée en semestres ou en trimestres?
10. Cette année, quels cours sont obligatoires? Et quels cours sont facultatifs?
11. En quelle année est-ce que tu vas obtenir ton diplôme?

D **Où à l'école?** *Complétez.*

1. On déjeune à ___.
2. On consulte des encyclopédies, des diapos, etc. au ___.
3. On fait de la gymnastique dans ___.
4. On joue au basket sur ___.

5. On parle au conseiller d'orientation au ___.
6. On fait ses devoirs dans ___.
7. On joue au hand-ball sur ___.
8. On court sur ___.

302   CHAPITRE 12

Activités de communication orale
Mots 1 et 2

A **Qu'est-ce que c'est?** Décrivez à un(e) camarade un objet qu'on trouve dans la salle de classe. Votre camarade vous dira ce que c'est.

> Élève 1: On l'utilise pour effacer le tableau.
> Élève 2: C'est une brosse.

B **C'est comment, ton école?** Vous parlez à Jean-Luc Giraudon, un jeune Français qui va passer l'année dans votre école. Il vous pose des questions sur votre vie scolaire. Répondez-lui.

1. Quels sont les cours obligatoires?
2. Quels sont les cours facultatifs?
3. Tu avais combien de cours l'année dernière?
4. Quel était ton prof favori l'année dernière?

Jean-Luc Giraudon

C **Les habitudes de travail.** Travaillez en petits groupes. Choisissez un chef et un(e) secrétaire. Le chef demandera les renseignements suivants aux membres du groupe. Le/La secrétaire prendra des notes et présentera les résultats à la classe.

1. Tu écris tes devoirs à la main ou tu les tapes?
2. Où fais-tu tes devoirs? Au CDI, à la salle de permanence ou à la maison?
3. Tu utilises un dictionnaire ou une encyclopédie quand tu fais tes devoirs?
4. Tu écoutes de la musique quand tu fais tes devoirs?
5. Tu fais tes devoirs seul(e) ou avec un(e) ami(e)?

D **Dans ton sac à dos.** Travaillez avec un(e) camarade. Vous allez deviner ce que votre camarade a dans son sac à dos. Suggérez une chose et votre camarade vous dira si c'est exact. Changez ensuite de rôles.

> Élève 1: Tu as trois livres scolaires dans ton sac à dos.
> Élève 2: Non, j'en ai quatre. Et toi, tu as deux stylos et un feutre dans ton sac à dos.

E **C'est super!** Travaillez en petits groupes. Dites ce que vous aimez bien à votre lycée et ce que vous aimez moins. Chaque personne mentionnera au moins deux choses.

> Élève 1: Je trouve que nous avons un bon terrain de basket. Et les profs sont fantastiques!
> Élève 2: Moi, je n'aime pas la cantine, mais le CDI est excellent.

CHAPITRE 12　303

Activités de communication orale
Mots 1 et 2

PRESENTATION *(page 303)*
You may wish to select the activities you consider most appropriate. As an alternative, you might allow students to select the activities they would like to participate in. Different groups of students can work on different activities.

Activité B
In the CD-ROM version of this activity, students can interact with an on-screen native speaker.

ANSWERS
Activités A, B, C, D, and *E*
Answers will vary.

INDEPENDENT PRACTICE

Assign any of the following:
1. Exercises and activities, pages 302–303
2. Workbook, *Mots 2: E–G,* pages 132–133
3. Communication Activities Masters, *Mots 2: C–D,* pages 78–79
4. Computer Software, *Vocabulaire*
5. CD-ROM, Disc 3, pages 300–303

STRUCTURE

Structure Teaching Resources

1. Workbook, *Structure: A–H*, pages 134–136
2. Student Tape Manual, Teacher's Edition, *Structure: A–C*, pages 126–127
3. Audio Cassette 7B/CD-6
4. Communication Activities Masters, *Structure: A–D*, pages 80–82
5. Computer Software, *Structure*
6. Chapter Quizzes, *Structure: Quizzes 3–6*, pages 63–66
7. CD-ROM, Disc 3, pages 304–307

D'autres verbes au présent du subjonctif

PRESENTATION *(page 304)*

A. Have students redo Exercise A on page 293 in order to review the third-person plural of the present indicative of these verbs.

B. Have them repeat the verb forms in steps 1 and 2 after you.

Exercices

PRESENTATION *(page 304)*

Exercice A

This exercise uses only introductory expressions that students already know. The focus is on the forms of the new verbs.

ANSWERS

Exercice A

1. Il faut qu'elle voie...
2. Il est nécessaire qu'elle appelle le conseiller d'éducation.
3. Il est temps qu'elle vienne...
4. Il est bon qu'elle apprenne...
5. Il vaut mieux qu'elle achète...
6. Il est impossible qu'elle comprenne tout.
7. Il est juste qu'elle reçoive...

STRUCTURE

D'autres verbes au présent du subjonctif

More Verbs Expressing Actions That May or May not Take Place

1. Some verbs have two stems in the present subjunctive. All forms except *nous* and *vous* have one stem. The *nous* and *vous* forms have another.

INFINITIF	SUBJONCTIF	
prendre	que je *prenne*	que nous *prenions*
apprendre	que j' *apprenne*	que nous *apprenions*
comprendre	que je *comprenne*	que nous *comprenions*
venir	que je *vienne*	que nous venions
recevoir	que je *reçoive*	que nous recevions
devoir	que je *doive*	que nous *devions*

2. Verbs that have a spelling change in the present indicative keep the same spelling change in the present subjunctive.

INFINITIF	SUBJONCTIF	
voir	que je *voie*	que nous *voyions*
croire	que je *croie*	que nous *croyions*
appeler	que j' *appelle*	que nous *appelions*
acheter	que j' *achète*	que nous *achetions*
répéter	que je *répète*	que nous *répétions*

Exercices

A **Alice suit un cours de français.** Faites des phrases avec l'expression indiquée.

1. Elle voit le conseiller d'orientation. (il faut que)
2. Elle appelle le conseiller d'éducation. (il est nécessaire que)
3. Elle vient avec nous au cours de français. (il est temps que)
4. Elle apprend le français. (il est bon que)
5. Elle achète un dictionnaire français. (il vaut mieux que)
6. Elle comprend tout. (il est impossible que)
7. Elle reçoit de bonnes notes. (il est juste que)

304 CHAPITRE 12

LEARNING FROM PHOTOS

Ask the students to describe what is going on in the photo.

B Vous aussi. Récrivez les phrases de l'Exercice A en remplaçant «elle» par «vous». Suivez le modèle.

> Vous comprenez le professeur de français. (il est possible que)
> *Il est possible que vous compreniez le professeur de français.*

Le subjonctif avec des expressions de volonté

Expressing Wishes, Preferences and Demands Concerning Others

1. You use the subjunctive with the following verbs which express a wish, a preference, or a demand.

vouloir que	*to want*
souhaiter que	*to wish*
aimer (mieux) que	*to like (better)*
préférer que	*to prefer*
désirer que	*to desire*
exiger que	*to demand, require*
insister pour que	*to insist*

2. These verbs require the subjunctive because they describe wishes or desires concerning people's actions. Regardless of whether one wishes, prefers, demands, or insists that another person do something, one can never be sure that he or she will actually do it. The action may or may not take place. For this reason the subjunctive is used.

> Les parents de Philippe *veulent qu'il fasse* de la gymnastique.
> Ils *exigent qu'il aille* au gymnase tous les jours.

Exercices

A Je veux que tu... Commencez par «je veux».

1. Tu viens avec moi au lycée.
2. Tu es à l'heure.
3. Tu parles au prof principal.
4. Tu écris une rédaction.
5. Tu vas au Centre de Documentation et d'Information.
6. Tu fais des recherches sur la Révolution de 1789.
7. Tu lis des magazines et des journaux.
8. Tu reçois une bonne note.

B Notre prof de français. Dites ce que votre prof de français exige que vous fassiez, vos camarades et vous.

> étudier la leçon
> *Notre prof de français exige que nous étudiions la leçon.*

1. parler à haute voix
2. lire un journal français
3. écrire de petits paragraphes
4. apprendre les mots nouveaux

ANSWERS

Exercice B

1. ... vous voyiez...
2. ... que vous appeliez...
3. ... que vous veniez...
4. ... que vous appreniez...
5. ... que vous achetiez...
6. ... que vous compreniez...
7. ... que vous receviez...

Le subjonctif avec des expressions de volonté

PRESENTATION (*page 305*)

A. Have students repeat the verbs aloud.
B. When explaining step 2, emphasize once again that the subjunctive is used because we don't know if the action of the verb will take place.
C. Have students read the model sentences from step 2 aloud.

Note In the CD-ROM version, this structure point is presented via an interactive electronic comic strip.

Exercices

PRESENTATION (*page 305*)

Extension of *Exercice B*

Have students add their own statements.

ANSWERS

Exercice A

1. Je veux que tu viennes...
2. ... que tu sois...
3. ... que tu parles...
4. ... que tu écrives...
5. ... que tu ailles...
6. ... que tu fasses...
7. ... que tu lises...
8. ... que tu reçoives...

Exercice B

1. Notre prof de français exige que nous parlions à haute voix.
2. ... que nous lisions un journal français.
3. ... que nous écrivions de petits paragraphes.
4. ... que nous apprenions les mots nouveaux.

Exercice C

1. Oui, je préfère que tu l'appelles.
2. Oui, je veux que tu lui dises de venir.
3. Oui, j'aimerais qu'il aille au café.
4. Oui, je veux qu'il soit là à six heures.
5. Oui, je voudrais que Michel vienne avec lui.

Exercice D

1. ... que nous finissions...
2. ... que nous sortions...
3. ... que nous dînions...
4. ... que nous allions...
5. ... que nous voyions...
6. ... que nous prenions...

L'infinitif ou le subjonctif

PRESENTATION *(page 306)*

Go over the explanation with the students. Have them read the model sentences aloud.

Exercices

PRESENTATION *(page 306)*

Exercice A

Exercise A contrasts the use of the subjunctive with the use of the infinitive.

Exercice B

You may wish to use the recorded version of this exercise.

Exercice A

1. Oui, Maman veut dormir un peu.
2. Elle veut que je dorme.
3. Oui, mon frère préfère sortir.
4. Mon frère veut que je sorte.
5. Oui (Non), Thomas (ne) veut (pas) faire ses devoirs.
6. Il veut que je lui fasse ses devoirs.
7. Florence voudrait acheter un dictionnaire. (Elle voudrait que je l'achète.)
8. Je veux venir avec vous. (Je veux que Suzanne vienne.)

C Je téléphone pour toi. Répondez par «oui».

1. Tu préfères que je l'appelle?
2. Tu veux que je lui dise de venir?
3. Tu aimerais qu'il aille au café?
4. Tu veux qu'il soit là à six heures?
5. Tu voudrais que Michel vienne avec lui?

D Il aimerait que nous fassions quelque chose. Commencez par «il aimerait que».

1. Nous finissons notre travail à l'heure.
2. Nous sortons ce soir.
3. Nous dînons dans son restaurant favori.
4. Nous allons ensuite au cinéma.
5. Nous voyons un film en version originale.
6. Nous prenons un café après le film.

L'infinitif ou le subjonctif

Expressing Wishes, Preferences and Demands Concerning Oneself and Others

You use the subjunctive when the subject of the dependent clause and the subject of the main clause are not the same. You use the infinitive when there is only one subject. Compare the following.

DIFFERENT SUBJECTS	SAME SUBJECT
Tu veux que *je* sois reçu à l'examen. *Il* aimerait que *nous* fassions du sport.	*Tu* veux être reçue à l'examen. *Il* aimerait faire du sport.

Exercices

A La même personne ou quelqu'un d'autre? Répondez.

1. Maman veut dormir un peu?
2. Elle veut que tu dormes?
3. Ton frère préfère sortir?
4. Ton frère veut que tu sortes?
5. Thomas veut faire ses devoirs?
6. Il veut que tu lui fasses ses devoirs?
7. Florence voudrait acheter un dictionnaire ou elle voudrait que tu l'achètes?
8. Tu veux venir avec nous ou tu veux que Suzanne vienne?

B Qu'est-ce qu'ils veulent? Répondez d'après le modèle.

> Ils veulent que tu y ailles.
> *Oui, je sais. Et je <u>veux</u> y aller.*

1. Ils veulent que tu fasses le voyage.
2. Ils veulent que tu viennes avec eux.
3. Ils veulent que tu conduises.
4. Ils veulent que tu prennes ta voiture.
5. Ils veulent que tu achètes une carte.
6. Ils veulent que tu partes immédiatement.

ADDITIONAL PRACTICE

1. After completing Exercises A–D, you may wish to have students complete the following paragraph:
   Mes parents veulent que je... , mais moi, je ne veux pas... . Je préfère... parce que... , mais eux, ils insistent pour que je...
2. Student Tape Manual, Teacher's Edition, *Activités A–B*, page 126

C Votre préférence. Dites ce que vous préférez.

1. aller à la salle de permanence ou au Centre de Documentation et d'Information
2. parler au conseiller d'éducation ou au conseiller d'orientation
3. lire des journaux ou des magazines
4. mettre vos livres dans un sac à dos ou dans un cartable
5. écrire avec un feutre ou un stylo-bille

D Que veux-tu que tes amis fassent? Commencez par «je veux qu'ils».

1. sortir
2. prendre le métro
3. venir me voir
4. aller au café avec moi
5. voir le nouveau film de Whoopi Goldberg
6. le voir en version originale

Les verbes *rire* et *sourire*

Talking about People Laughing and Smiling

1. Study the following forms of the present indicative of the verbs *rire*, "to laugh," and *sourire*, "to smile."

RIRE
je ris
tu ris
il/elle/on rit
nous rions
vous riez
ils/elles rient

SOURIRE
je souris
tu souris
il/elle/on sourit
nous sourions
vous souriez
ils/elles sourient

2. Note the past participles of these verbs:

Quand il a vu ses notes, il a *ri*.
La prof a *souri* parce que tout le monde a eu «A» à l'examen.

Exercice

A Ha, ha! Répondez.

1. Tu ris quand tu es avec tes copains?
2. Vous riez en classe?
3. Les professeurs sont contents quand les élèves rient trop?
4. Le professeur de français sourit?
5. Tu souris quand tu es content(e)?

Exercice B

1. Oui, je sais. Et je <u>veux</u> faire le voyage.
2. ... Et je <u>veux</u> venir avec eux.
3. ... Et je <u>veux</u> conduire.
4. ... Et je <u>veux</u> prendre ma voiture.
5. ... Et je <u>veux</u> acheter une carte.
6. ... Et je <u>veux</u> partir...

Exercice C

Answers will vary but all begin with Je préfère + infinitif.

Exercice D

1. Je veux qu'ils sortent.
2. ... qu'ils prennent le métro.
3. ... qu'ils viennent me voir.
4. ... qu'ils aillent au café avec moi.
5. ... qu'ils voient le nouveau film de Whoopi Goldberg.
6. ... qu'ils le voient en version originale.

Les verbes *rire et sourire*

PRESENTATION *(page 307)*

Have the students repeat the verb forms and model sentences after you.

ANSWERS

Exercice A

1. Oui, je ris quand je suis avec mes copains.
2. Oui (Non), nous (ne) rions (pas) en classe.
3. Non, les professeurs ne sont pas contents quand les élèves rient trop.
4. Oui (Non), le professeur de français (ne) sourit (pas).
5. Oui, je souris quand je suis content(e).

LEARNING FROM PHOTOS

Have students look at the sign in the top photo and say when they would go to the various places listed. Example: *Quand j'ai besoin d'un livre, je vais au CDI.*

INDEPENDENT PRACTICE

Assign any of the following:
1. Exercises, pages 306–307
2. Workbook, *Structure: E–H*, pages 135–136
3. Communication Activities Masters, *Structure: C–D*, pages 81–82
4. CD-ROM, Disc 3, pages 306–307

CONVERSATION

Bell Ringer Review

Write the following on the board or use BRR Blackline Master 12-3: Think about a wedding you attended, or imagine one. Write five sentences about it.

PRESENTATION *(page 308)*

A. Have students close their books. Play the Conversation Video or have them repeat the conversation once after you or Cassette 7B/CD-6. (Use *Activité E* in the Student Tape Manual to check oral comprehension.)

B. Call on pairs to read the conversation.

C. Have pairs act out the conversation for the class. Allow them to make any logical changes.

Note In the CD-ROM version, students can play the role of either one of the characters and record the conversation.

Exercice

PRESENTATION *(page 308)*

Extension of *Exercice A*

Have students retell the story of the conversation in their own words, basing their summary on their answers to the exercise.

ANSWERS

Exercice A

1. Sylvie a cinq cours cette année.
2. Trois cours sont obligatoires et deux cours sont facultatifs.
3. Madame Lafarge est son professeur principal.
4. Madame Lafarge est sympa.
5. Elle exige que les élèves arrivent en classe à l'heure.
6. Quand ses élèves sont en retard, elle les envoie chez le censeur.
7. Sylvie se dépêche parce qu'elle doit aller en classe.

308

CONVERSATION

Scènes de la vie *Sympa, mais stricte*

JEANNE: Tu as combien de cours cette année?
SYLVIE: J'en ai cinq. C'est dur, tu sais!
JEANNE: Ils sont tous obligatoires?
SYLVIE: Non, j'en ai deux qui sont facultatifs.
JEANNE: Qui est ton prof principal?
SYLVIE: Madame Lafarge.
JEANNE: Ah, oui. Je la connais. Elle est sympa, non?
SYLVIE: Oui, on rit bien avec elle, mais elle a une manie…
JEANNE: Elle exige que vous soyez toujours à l'heure. C'est ça?
SYLVIE: C'est ça! Une minute de retard, et elle nous envoie chez le censeur!
JEANNE: Ah, oui! Je me souviens…
SYLVIE: Zut! Ça sonne! Il faut que j'y aille, sinon…

A **Sylvie et son professeur.** Corrigez les phrases.

1. Sylvie a quatre cours cette année.
2. Tous ses cours sont obligatoires.
3. Monsieur Laforgue est son professeur principal.
4. Madame Lafarge n'est pas du tout sympa.
5. Elle permet toujours aux élèves d'arriver en classe en retard.
6. Quand ses élèves sont en retard, elle les envoie chez le proviseur.
7. Sylvie se dépêche parce qu'elle doit aller chez le censeur.

	Lundi	Mardi	Mercredi	Jeudi
8h - 8h30				
8h30 - 9h30				
9h30 - 10h30	anglais	anglais	sport	
10h30 - 11h30	espagnol			
11h30 - 12h30		français	français	histoire et géographie
12h30 - 13h				
13h30 - 14h	français	histoire et géographie	maths	
14h - 15h			histoire et	espagnol
15h - 16h		espagnol	géographie	maths
16h - 17h	biologie			
17h - 18h				

308 CHAPITRE 12

PAIRED ACTIVITY

Have students work in pairs to make up a conversation similar to this one, substituting information about their own school and teachers.

COOPERATIVE LEARNING

Have students work in groups to compare their own class schedules with the French student's schedule. Ask them to make a list of similarities and differences between American and French schedules. As groups read their lists to the class, have the others classify the statements under the appropriate heading: *En France* or *Aux États-Unis*.

Activités de communication orale

A **Ce que veulent mes parents.** Travaillez avec un(e) camarade. Dites-lui au moins trois choses que vos parents veulent toujours que vous fassiez. Demandez-lui si ses parents veulent qu'il/elle fasse les mêmes choses.

> Élève 1: Mes parents veulent toujours que j'aie de bonnes notes. Et toi? Est-ce que tes parents veulent toujours que tu aies de bonnes notes?
>
> Élève 2: Bien sûr! Ils veulent que je sois le premier (la première) de la classe!

B **Le lycée idéal.** Qu'est-ce que vous voudriez changer dans votre lycée? Travaillez en petits groupes. Chaque membre du groupe va proposer un changement. Comparez vos résultats et ceux des autres groupes.

> Élève 1: Je voudrais qu'il y ait plus de cours facultatifs.
>
> Élève 2: Je voudrais que les profs donnent moins de devoirs.

C **Tes préférences.** Un(e) camarade vous dira ce qu'il/elle voudrait que vous fassiez avec lui/elle ce week-end. Dites-lui ce que vous préférez faire. Vous pouvez employer la liste suivante. Changez ensuite de rôles.

> acheter de nouvelles cassettes
> écouter de la musique
> étudier
> faire tes devoirs
> prendre le petit déjeuner au restaurant
> venir chez moi
> voir un film

> Élève 1: Je voudrais bien que tu ailles au cinéma avec moi.
>
> Élève 2: Mais moi j'ai envie d'aller à la fête de Sandra.

309

Activités de communication orale

ANSWERS

Activités A, B, and C

Answers will vary.

LECTURE ET CULTURE

COLLÈGE ET LYCÉE

*E*n France, l'enseignement secondaire est divisé en deux cycles. Le premier cycle, de quatre ans (sixième, cinquième, quatrième, troisième), est enseigné dans un collège. Le deuxième cycle, de trois ans (seconde, première, terminale), est enseigné dans un lycée. C'est-à-dire que de 11 ans à 15 ans, les élèves français font leurs études dans un collège, et que de 15 ans à 18 ans, ils étudient dans un lycée.

En France, comme aux États-Unis, il y a pas mal de magazines destinés aux jeunes comme vous. En général, ces magazines consacrent[1] leur numéro[2] de la fin août à la rentrée des classes. Voyons ce que dit l'un de ces magazines de la rentrée dans un lycée.

Avant de partir pour l'école, il faut prendre le temps de manger un vrai petit déjeuner—des tartines beurrées, des céréales, un yaourt. Le jour de la rentrée, vous ferez connaissance avec votre professeur principal qui vous emmènera[3] dans votre première salle de classe. Ce prof vous donnera votre emploi du temps. Vous aurez au moins six ou sept autres profs, chacun avec sa propre personnalité et sa propre spécialité. Tous voudront que vous ayez de bonnes notes et que vous soyez reçus aux examens.

Le proviseur est le capitaine du lycée. Dans un très grand lycée, le proviseur n'a pas beaucoup de contacts avec les élèves. Le censeur a souvent plus de contacts. Si vous arrivez en retard à l'école ou si vous avez un problème avec un prof, il faudra que vous alliez au bureau de vie scolaire, voir le conseiller d'éducation. C'est lui (ou elle) qui s'occupe de l'ordre et de la discipline. Si vous voulez des renseignements sur les cours que vous devez suivre, etc., vous pouvez aller parler au conseiller d'orientation.

[1] consacrent *devote*
[2] numéro *issue*
[3] emmènera *will take*

Au lycée, rien de changé: comme au collège, vous allez toujours en perm, c'est-à-dire à la salle de permanence, quand vous avez une heure de libre entre deux classes, ou quand un prof est absent. En perm, il y a toujours des surveillants (les pions), qui vous surveillent bien sûr. Comme au collège, les surveillants exigent que vous fassiez vos devoirs et que vous appreniez vos leçons en silence. Si vous ne voulez pas être envoyé(e) chez le conseiller d'éducation, ne riez pas en perm!

Quand vous voulez savoir si un de vos profs est absent, il y a toujours le panneau d'affichage à l'entrée du lycée qui indique les absences des profs, les dates des vacances, les rendez-vous des clubs, etc.

Si vous avez un exposé à préparer, vous pouvez toujours aller au Centre de Documentation et d'Information pour y faire des recherches. S'il y a une encyclopédie ou une diapo que vous n'arrivez pas à trouver, la documentaliste vous aidera. Il faudra que vous suiviez ses conseils[4].

Le déjeuner! Vous le prendrez à la cantine du lycée. Il sera sans doute libre-service[5]: vous choisirez ce que vous voulez manger et vous le mettrez sur un plateau.

Après les cours, vous vous amuserez un peu avec vos copains dans la cour du lycée ou sur le terrain de sport. Mais n'oubliez pas que vous aurez beaucoup de devoirs à faire pour le lendemain!

[4] conseils   *advice*
[5] libre-service   *self-service*

LEARNING FROM PHOTOS

Have the students say as much as they can about the photos on pages 310–311.

Étude de mots

ANSWERS
Exercice A
1. a
2. e
3. f
4. b
5. d
6. c

Compréhension

ANSWERS
Exercice B
1. Un lycée est une école du deuxième cycle de l'enseignement secondaire en France.
2. Les élèves passent trois ans au lycée.
3. Le professeur principal donne aux élèves leur emploi du temps.
4. Les lycéens ont à peu près sept ou huit profs.
5. Ils vont à la salle de permanence si un de leurs profs est absent.
6. Les surveillants (les pions) surveillent les élèves en salle de permanence.
7. Ils exigent que les élèves fassent leurs devoirs et qu'ils apprennent leurs leçons en silence.
8. Si un élève rit en perm, il va être envoyé chez le conseiller d'éducation.

Exercice C
1. le Centre de Documentation et d'Information
2. la salle de classe
3. la salle de permanence
4. la cantine
5. la cour du lycée ou le terrain de sport
6. l'entrée du lycée

Étude de mots

A Quelle est la définition? Choisissez.

1. terminer	a. finir, le contraire de «commencer»
2. les lycéens	b. le travail qu'il faut faire pour l'école
3. les pions	c. le directeur d'un lycée
4. les devoirs	d. le début (le commencement) des cours
5. la rentrée	e. les élèves d'un lycée
6. le proviseur	f. les surveillants

Compréhension

B Vous avez compris? Répondez d'après la lecture.

1. Qu'est-ce qu'un lycée en France?
2. Les élèves passent combien d'années au lycée?
3. Le premier jour de classe, qui donne aux élèves leur emploi du temps?
4. Les lycéens ont à peu près combien de profs?
5. Où vont-ils si un de leurs profs est absent?
6. Qui surveille les élèves en salle de permanence?
7. Qu'est-ce qu'ils exigent des élèves?
8. Qu'est-ce qui se passe si un élève rit en perm?

C Dans quel endroit? Indiquez où d'après la lecture.

1. On trouve des magazines, des journaux, des diapos, etc.
2. On suit un cours.
3. On a une heure de libre et des devoirs à faire.
4. On déjeune.
5. On s'amuse avec les copains.
6. On trouve le panneau d'affichage.

Un terrain de sport au Lycée Pasteur à Neuilly

LEARNING FROM PHOTOS

Have students note the name of the school in the photo. Ask: *Qui était Pasteur?*

DÉCOUVERTE CULTURELLE

Le système scolaire en France est assez compliqué et il change fréquemment. Mais voici une description générale:

ÉCOLE	ÂGE DE L'ÉLÈVE	DURÉE
École maternelle	de 2 à 6 ans	quatre ans
École primaire	de 6 à 11 ans	cinq ans
Collège (Secondaire-Premier cycle)	de 11 à 15 ans	quatre ans
Collège d'enseignement technique (Secondaire-Deuxième cycle-cycle court)	de 15 à 17 ans	deux ans
Lycée (Secondaire-Deuxième cycle-cycle long)	de 15 à 18 ans	trois ans

La plupart des élèves en France sont externes. C'est-à-dire qu'ils ne viennent à l'école que pour les cours. Ils habitent chez eux mais déjeunent souvent à la cantine de l'école.

La plupart des écoles sont mixtes, c'est-à-dire que les filles et les garçons étudient ensemble. Et la majorité (à peu près 80%) sont publiques, et non pas privées. L'enseignement public s'appelle aussi l'enseignement laïque, c'est-à-dire non-religieux.

Les écoliers passent à peu près 30 heures par semaine à l'école pendant une période de 32 semaines. Le mercredi est leur jour de congé. Généralement, il n'y a pas cours le samedi après-midi.

Dès la sixième—la première année de collège—tous les élèves étudient une langue étrangère. En quatrième, ils peuvent commencer à étudier le latin. Et en quatrième aussi, ils peuvent commencer à étudier une deuxième langue étrangère! À votre avis, est-ce que les langues ont de l'importance pour les Français?

OPTIONAL MATERIAL

Découverte culturelle

Culture Note In recent years the French educational system has undergone many changes, and changes are continuing to take place. The system is no longer as rigid as it once was.

Note Students may listen to a recorded version of the *Découverte culturelle* on the CD-ROM.

COOPERATIVE LEARNING

Have teams make up as many questions as they can about the photos on pages 310–313. Then have them call on members of other teams to answer.

INDEPENDENT PRACTICE

Assign any of the following:
1. *Étude de mots* and *Compréhension* exercises, page 312
2. Workbook, *Un Peu Plus*, pages 137–139
3. CD-ROM, Disc 3, pages 310–313

RÉALITÉS

Bell Ringer Review

Write the following on the board or use BRR Blackline Master 12-6: Complete each sentence with the present subjunctive of the verb in parentheses.

1. C'est le jour de l'An. Il faut que tout le monde ____ ici. (être)
2. Il faut que nous ____ chez Tante Anne avec les décorations. (aller)
3. Il faut que mes cousins ____ le réveillon avec nous. (faire)
4. Il faut qu'ils ____ des confettis et des guirlandes. (avoir)
5. Il faut que tout le monde ____ heureux. (être)

OPTIONAL MATERIAL

PRESENTATION
(pages 314–315)

Have students look at the photographs for enjoyment. Have them read the information that accompanies each photo. They may wish to answer the questions embedded in the captions but it is not necessary that they do so.

Note In the CD-ROM version, students can listen to the recorded captions and discover a hidden video behind one of the photos.

Ces trois copines viennent de sortir du lycée **1**. À ton avis, où vont-elles après les cours? Et toi, où vas-tu après tes cours?

En France, de nombreux lycéens se servent d'une mobylette pour aller au lycée **2**. Ces garçons quittent le Lycée Beaulieu tous les jours à 4 heures et demie. Et toi, comment vas-tu à l'école? À quelle heure finissent tes cours?

C'est bientôt la rentrée des classes **3**. Dans ce magasin on vend des sacs à dos pour la rentrée. Qu'est-ce que tu mets dans ton sac à dos?

Dans la cour du lycée, des élèves discutent de leurs devoirs **4**. À ton avis, c'est pendant la récréation ou le matin avant les cours?

315

ADDITIONAL PRACTICE

1. Student Tape Manual, Teacher's Edition, *Deuxième Partie,* pages 128–130
2. Situation Cards, Chapter 12

COOPERATIVE LEARNING

Display Communication Transparency C-12. Have groups make up as many questions as they can about the illustrations. Have the groups take turns asking and answering the questions.

CULMINATION

RECYCLING

These activities encourage students to use all the language they have learned in the chapter and recombine it with material from previous chapters. It is not necessary to do all the activities with all students. You may select the ones you consider most appropriate or allow students to choose the ones they wish to do.

INFORMAL ASSESSMENT

The *Activités de communication orale* lend themselves to assessing speaking and listening abilities. For grading suggestions, see the evaluation criteria given on page 22 of this Teacher's Wraparound Edition.

Activités de communication orale

ANSWERS

Activités A and B
Answers will vary.

Activités de communication écrite

ANSWERS

Activités A and B
Answers will vary.

Activités de communication orale

A Non, non! Travaillez avec un(e) camarade. Votre camarade va jouer le rôle d'un parent exigeant. Il/Elle va exiger ou insister pour que vous fassiez quelque chose. Et vous, vous allez protester. Changez ensuite de rôles.

> Élève 1: Je veux que tu rentres avant minuit.
> Élève 2: Ah, non! C'est le week-end. Je peux rentrer plus tard.

B Chez le conseiller d'éducation. Vous avez fait quelque chose en classe que votre prof n'a pas aimé. Il faut que vous alliez voir le conseiller (la conseillère) d'éducation (votre camarade). Il/Elle vous demandera ce que vous avez fait. Répondez-lui et il/elle utilisera les verbes suivants pour vous dire ce qu'il faut faire. Changez ensuite de rôles.

insister pour que	préférer que
exiger que	souhaiter que
vouloir que	aimer mieux que

> Élève 1: Qu'est-ce que tu as fait?
> Élève 2: Je rigolais avec un copain pendant que le prof enseignait.
> Élève 1: Alors j'exige que tu écoutes ton professeur et que tu ne rigoles plus en classe.

Activités de communication écrite

A Mon école. Votre ami(e) français(e) vous a demandé de lui décrire votre école. Il/Elle veut savoir si votre école est petite ou grande, publique ou privée, combien d'élèves il y a, etc. Écrivez-lui et donnez-lui une description de votre école.

B Mon cours favori. Écrivez un paragraphe dans lequel vous décrivez votre cours favori. Expliquez pourquoi c'est votre cours favori.

LEARNING FROM REALIA

Review the days of the week. Ask students which day is missing on the Scrabble "board."

COOPERATIVE LEARNING

For a change of pace, bring three or four French **Scrabble** games to class and have students play in teams. Allow them to look up words in the vocabulary at the back of the book. (If the French version of **Scrabble** is not available, you may use the English version, but the letter distribution is somewhat different.)

Réintroduction et recombinaison

A **Les cours.** Faites une liste des cours que vous suivez ce semestre. Ensuite écrivez au moins deux phrases pour décrire ce que vous faites dans chaque cours.

B **À l'école, demain.** Complétez au futur.

1. Je ___ de bonne heure demain. (se lever)
2. Je ___ un vrai petit déjeuner. (prendre)
3. Je ___ des fruits et des céréales. (manger)
4. Je ___ pour l'école. (partir)
5. Je ___ le métro. (prendre)
6. Je ___ à l'école à huit heures. (être)
7. Je ___ «bonjour» à mon prof principal. (dire)
8. De neuf heures et demie à dix heures et demie, j'___ en perm car j'___ une heure de libre. (aller, avoir)
9. Je ___ mes devoirs dans la salle de permanence. (faire)
10. Je ___ à la cantine et je ___ tout ce que je ___ manger sur un plateau. (déjeuner, mettre, vouloir)

C **À l'école, hier.** Refaites l'Exercice B. Changez le mot «demain» de la première phrase en «hier», et faites tous les changements nécessaires.

Vocabulaire

NOMS
le matériel scolaire
le cartable
le sac à dos
le feutre
le stylo(-bille)
la gomme
la brosse
le livre scolaire
le dictionnaire
l'encyclopédie (f.)
la carte
le magazine
le journal
la diapo(sitive)
le projecteur
l'écran (m.)
l'ordinateur (m.)
la machine à traitement de texte

la machine à écrire
la calculatrice
le lycée
la cour du lycée
le panneau d'affichage
la sonnerie
le bureau de vie scolaire
la salle de permanence
le Centre de Documentation et d'Information (CDI)
le gymnase
le terrain de basket
le terrain de hand
la piste de course
la cantine
le lycéen
la lycéenne
le professeur principal
le (la) surveillant(e)

le conseiller (la conseillère) d'éducation
le conseiller (la conseillère) d'orientation
le (la) documentaliste
le proviseur
la directrice
le censeur
la rentrée des classes
l'emploi (m.) du temps
la rédaction
l'exposé (m.)
la note
le baccalauréat (bac, bachot)
le diplôme

ADJECTIFS
facultatif, facultative
obligatoire
principal(e)

scolaire
préparé(e)

VERBES
enseigner   obtenir
exiger   effacer
insister   rire
souhaiter   sourire

AUTRES MOTS ET EXPRESSIONS
apprendre ses leçons
faire ses devoirs
faire une rédaction
faire un exposé
taper à la machine
recevoir de bonnes notes
être reçu(e) à un examen
échouer à un examen

Réintroduction et recombinaison

PRESENTATION *(page 317)*

Exercise A reviews school vocabulary from Chapters 2 and 3 of *Bienvenue* and recombines it with the new vocabulary of this chapter. Exercise B reviews the future tense and Exercise C, the *passé composé*.

ANSWERS

Exercice A
Answers will vary.

Exercice B
1. me lèverai   7. dirai
2. prendrai   8. irai, aurai
3. mangerai   9. ferai
4. partirai   10. déjeunerai,
5. prendrai   mettrai,
6. serai   voudrai

Exercice C
1. me suis levé(e)
2. ai pris
3. ai mangé
4. suis parti(e)
5. ai pris
6. ai été
7. ai dit
8. suis allé(e), ai eu
9. ai fait
10. ai déjeuné, ai mis, ai voulu

ASSESSMENT RESOURCES

1. Chapter Quizzes
2. Testing Program
3. Situation Cards
4. Communication Transparency C-12
5. Performance Assessment
6. Computer Software: Practice/Test Generator

VIDEO PROGRAM

INTRODUCTION   (41:09)

ON PRÉPARE LE BAC   (42:00)

STUDENT PORTFOLIO

Written assignments which may be included in students' portfolios are the *Activités de communication écrite* on page 316 and any writing activities from the *Un Peu Plus* section in the Workbook.

Note Students may create and save both oral and written work using the Electronic Portfolio feature on the CD-ROM.

INDEPENDENT PRACTICE

Assign any of the following:
1. Activities and exercises, pages 316–317
2. Communication Activities Masters, pages 77–82
3. CD-ROM, Disc 3, pages 316–317

RÉVISION

CHAPITRES 9-12

OVERVIEW

This section reviews key grammatical structures and vocabulary from Chapters 9–12. The topics were first presented on the following pages: *en* or *y* used with other object pronouns, page 256; the present subjunctive, pages 279–280, 282, 304, 305, and 306; *si* clauses, page 234.

Conversation

PRESENTATION (*page 318*)

Note Students can guess from the context that *se cotiser* means "to chip in."

A. Read the conversation as they follow along in their books.
B. Break it into three parts and call on three pairs to read it aloud.
C. Intersperse the reading with the questions from Exercise A.

Conversation   *Le mariage de Christine*

LOUISE: Tu vas au mariage de Christine?

ÉMILIE: Oui, bien sûr. Il faut que je lui achète quelque chose. Qu'est-ce que tu lui donnes, toi?

LOUISE: Je ne sais pas, je n'ai pas encore décidé. Mais de toute façon Christine sait bien qu'on est tous fauchés. Je suis sûre qu'elle ne veut pas qu'on dépense trop pour elle. Ce qui compte, c'est qu'on soit là.

ÉMILIE: On pourrait peut-être se cotiser et lui acheter quelque chose tous ensemble.

LOUISE: Ce n'est pas une mauvaise idée. Mais il vaut mieux d'abord qu'on décide ce qu'on va lui acheter.

ÉMILIE: Je ne sais pas, moi. Des verres? Des assiettes?

LOUISE: Je crois que sa mère va lui en donner.

ÉMILIE: Des vidéocassettes?

LOUISE: Il vaut mieux qu'on attende qu'elle ait un magnétoscope!

ÉMILIE: Ouais...évidemment! Ça y est, j'ai une idée! Si tu voulais vraiment rester en contact avec les copains, qu'est-ce que tu ferais?

LOUISE: Ben, je ne sais pas, moi,...je leur téléphonerais souvent.

ÉMILIE: Voilà, c'est ça. On va lui acheter un répondeur automatique!

A **Cadeau de mariage.**   Répondez d'après la conversation.

1. Qu'est-ce qu'il faut qu'Émilie achète?
2. Est-ce que Christine croit que ses amis vont lui acheter un cadeau cher? Pourquoi?
3. Pourquoi ne vont-ils pas acheter de verres ou d'assiettes?
4. Pourquoi ne vont-ils pas lui acheter de vidéocassettes?
5. Comment reste-t-on en contact avec ses amis?
6. Quel cadeau suggère Émilie?

DID YOU KNOW?

Tell students that *ouais* is colloquial for *oui*, and *ben* is colloquial for *bien*.

Structure

Deux pronoms dans la même phrase

You have seen that two object pronouns can be used in the same sentence. *En* and *y* can be used along with the other object pronouns. Note the order.

me												
te		le		lui								
se	*before*	la	*before*		*before*	y	*before*	en	*before*	verbe		
nous		les		leur								
vous												

Il y a du lait?   Oui, je *t'en* donne.
Tu connais la rue Dufour?   Oui, je vais *t'y* conduire.
Il y a des pommes?   Oui, il y *en* a.

A   **C'est l'anniversaire de Marie.**   Remplacez les mots en italique par des pronoms.

1. Marc va apporter *des cadeaux à Marie.*
2. Catherine va nous faire *des sandwichs.*
3. Serge te prête *des cassettes.*
4. Corinne nous fait *des décorations.*
5. Je vais donner *des fleurs aux parents de Marie.*

Le subjonctif

1. The present subjunctive is formed by adding the subjunctive endings to the stem of the *ils* form of the present indicative. Most verbs, regular and irregular, form the subjunctive this way.

PRESENT INDICATIVE	PRESENT SUBJUNCTIVE		
	il faut que je		-e
	il faut que tu		-es
ils *choisiss* -ent	il faut qu'il/elle	*choisiss*	-e
ils *mett* -ent	il faut que nous	*mett*	-ions
	il faut que vous		-iez
	il faut qu'ils/elles		-ent

2. Some very common verbs have irregular subjunctives.

aller: il faut que j'aille, que nous allions, qu'ils aillent
avoir: il faut que j'aie, que nous ayons, qu'ils aient
faire: il faut que je fasse, que nous fassions, qu'ils fassent
être: il faut que je sois, que nous soyons, qu'ils soient

INDEPENDENT PRACTICE

Assign any of the following:
1. Exercises, pages 318–319
2. CD-ROM, Disc 3, pages 318–319

ANSWERS

Exercice A

1. Un cadeau pour Christine.
2. Non, parce qu'elle sait que ses amis sont fauchés.
3. Parce que sa mère va lui en donner.
4. Parce qu'elle n'a pas de magnétoscope.
5. On leur téléphone souvent.
6. Un répondeur automatique.

Bell Ringer Review

Write the following on the board or use BRR Blackline Master R12-1: You are going to buy school supplies. List ten items you might need.

Structure
Deux pronoms dans la même phrase

PRESENTATION *(page 319)*

Note This section reviews pronouns and their order in a sentence.

Read the questions in the left-hand column and have students respond with the sentences in the right-hand column.

ANSWERS

Exercice A

1. Marc va lui en apporter.
2. Catherine va nous en faire.
3. Serge t'en prête.
4. Corinne nous en fait.
5. Je vais leur en donner.

Bell Ringer Review

Write the following on the board or use BRR Blackline Master R12-2: Complete the sentences with the correct form of the indicated verb.

1. Quand j'ai vu ce film, j'_____. (rire)
2. S'ils réussissent à l'examen, ils _____. (sourire)
3. Si nous allons à la fête, nous _____. (rire)
4. Philippe _____ toujours quand il parle à Catherine. (sourire)
5. Quand tu étais petit(e), tu _____ beaucoup? (rire)

PRESENTATION (pages 319–320)

A. Go over steps 1–2 with the students and have them repeat the verb forms aloud.

B. When presenting steps 3–4, emphasize once again that these expressions are followed by the subjunctive because it is not certain that the action expressed by the subjunctive verb will take place.

Exercices

PRESENTATION (page 320)

Exercices B and C

These exercises can be done with books open or closed.

ANSWERS

Exercice B

1. Il faut que tu fasses ta lessive plus souvent.
2. Il vaut mieux que tu ailles voir tes parents pour Noël.
3. Il est juste que tu lui rendes l'argent que tu lui dois.
4. Il est possible qu'il prenne le métro.
5. Il est impossible qu'elle soit déjà sortie.
6. Il est préférable qu'ils prennent un taxi.
7. Il est temps que j'arrête de fumer.
8. Il est important que je vienne avec vous.

Exercice C

1. Je préfère que vous partiez tout de suite.
2. J'exige que vous n'arriviez pas en retard.
3. Je souhaite que tu viennes avec ta mère.
4. J'insiste pour que vous passiez une semaine avec nous.
5. Je veux que nous ne dépensions pas trop d'argent.
6. J'aimerais que nous allions au cinéma.
7. Je préférerais que tu restes avec moi.

---

3. The subjunctive is used in subordinate clauses introduced by *que* after the following impersonal expressions.

il faut que	il est bon que
il vaut mieux que	il est temps que
il est préférable que	il est possible que
il est important que	il est impossible que
il est nécessaire que	il est juste que

Il est possible qu'il ne vienne pas seul.
Il est préférable que vous soyez à l'heure.

4. The subjunctive is also used after verbs expressing a wish, a preference, or a demand.

vouloir que	préférer que
souhaiter que	désirer que
aimer que	exiger que
aimer mieux que	insister pour que

Ses parents insistent pour qu'il vienne à Noël.
J'aimerais que vous soyez là.

B Quelques conseils. Utilisez les expressions entre parenthèses.

1. Fais ta lessive plus souvent. (Il faut que)
2. Va voir tes parents pour Noël. (Il vaut mieux que)
3. Rends-lui l'argent que tu lui dois. (Il est juste que)
4. Il prendra le métro. (Il est possible que)
5. Elle est déjà sortie. (Il est impossible que)
6. Ils prendront un taxi. (Il est préférable que)
7. J'arrête de fumer. (Il est temps que)
8. Je viens avec vous. (Il est important que)

C Prenons des décisions. Faites des phrases d'après le modèle.

> Partons tout de suite. Je préfère ça.
> *Je préfère que nous partions tout de suite.*

1. Partez tout de suite. Je préfère ça.
2. N'arrivez pas en retard. Je l'exige.
3. Viens avec ta mère. Je le souhaite.
4. Passez une semaine avec nous. J'insiste.
5. Ne dépensons pas trop d'argent. Je le veux.
6. Allons au cinéma. J'aimerais ça.
7. Reste avec moi. Je préférerais ça.

Une jolie station de métro à Montréal, au Canada

ADDITIONAL PRACTICE

You may wish to have the students write sentences telling what they do in each of the following places.

la cour du lycée
la salle de permanence
le gymnase
la cantine
le CDI
le bureau de vie scolaire

DID YOU KNOW?

The Montreal metro system, which uses the French innovation of rubber tires, is considered to be one of the world's quietest metros. The system has the capacity to carry 60,000 riders per hour and can transport passengers between the downtown area and the outskirts of the city in less that 20 minutes.

Les propositions avec *si*

Si clauses express possibilities or impossibilities. The following sequence of tenses is used.

POSSIBILITÉ	*SI* + PRÉSENT	FUTUR
	Si elle a le temps,	**elle ira au cinéma.**
IMPOSSIBILITÉ	*SI* + IMPARFAIT	CONDITIONNEL
	Si elle avait le temps,	**elle irait au cinéma.**

D **Le possible et l'impossible.** Complétez avec les verbes entre parenthèses.

1. S'il fait beau, j'___ faire du ski à Noël. (aller)
2. J'inviterai mes amis, si j'___ de l'argent. (avoir)
3. Si mes amis ne partent pas, ils ___ les fêtes chez eux. (passer)
4. Tout le monde ___ content si le réveillon est réussi. (être)
5. S'il n'y ___ pas Noël ou le jour de l'An, il n'y aurait pas de réveillon! (avoir)
6. Si on ___, on ferait un réveillon tous les soirs. (pouvoir)

Activités de communication orale

A **Des conseils.** Un(e) de vos ami(e)s (votre camarade) est malheureux/malheureuse (pas heureux/pas heureuse). Il/Elle vous dit ce qu'il/elle a, et vous lui donnez des conseils pour lui faire oublier ses ennuis (*troubles*).

> Élève 1: Personne ne m'aime.
> Élève 2: Écoute, si tu étais plus gentil(le) avec les autres, ils t'aimeraient mieux.

B **Un voyage imaginaire.** Racontez à vos camarades le voyage que vous feriez si vous aviez beaucoup d'argent. Dites où vous iriez, avec qui, par quel moyen de transport, etc.

Noël à Paris: «La Forêt enchantée»

Les propositions avec si

PRESENTATION *(page 321)*

A. Write the sequence of tenses on the board.
B. Have the students read the model sentences aloud.

ANSWERS

Exercice D

1. irai
2. ai
3. passeront
4. sera
5. avait
6. pouvait

Activités de communication orale

ANSWERS

Activités A and B
  Answers will vary.

LETTRES ET SCIENCES

OPTIONAL MATERIAL

Éducation: Charlemagne, Napoléon, Jules Ferry

OVERVIEW

You may wish to allow students to choose which of the three selections in this *Lettres et sciences* section they want to read, or you may wish to have the entire group read a particular selection.

See page 106 in this Teacher's Wraparound Edition for suggestions on presenting the readings at different levels of intensity.

Avant la lecture

PRESENTATION *(page 322)*

A. Give students a few moments to call to mind the school vocabulary they know in French.

B. Tell students they are going to read about three important phases in the history of French education. The system evolved from an elitist program to one made accessible to all people. Three individuals had a great deal to do with this evolution. Tell students to pay particular attention, as they read, to the changes taking place in the educational system.

C. Have students scan the reading selection for cognates.

Lecture

PRESENTATION *(pages 322–323)*

A. Have students read the selection silently.

B. You may wish to have them look for the answers to the *Après la lecture* Exercise A as they read.

LETTRES ET

ÉDUCATION: CHARLEMAGNE, NAPOLÉON, JULES FERRY

Avant la lecture

Pretend you have to explain the American system of education to a foreigner. Prepare an outline.

Lecture

Pendant très longtemps, le système éducatif français a été religieux et privé et, la plupart du temps réservé à une élite.

Les principes de l'enseignement[1] public ont été déterminés par la Révolution de 1789, mais il faudra attendre cent ans avant qu'ils ne soient établis dans la réalité. Ces principes sont les suivants:

- l'enseignement est public, c'est-à-dire commun à tous, et non réservé à une élite comme avant la Révolution;

- l'enseignement est divisé en trois degrés: primaire, secondaire et supérieur.
  Dans l'esprit[2] des Français, trois hommes ont été responsables de la création de l'enseignement en France: Charlemagne, Napoléon et Jules Ferry.

CHARLEMAGNE (742-814)

Charlemagne a commencé par être Charles Ier, roi[3] des Francs, en 768. Un peu plus de vingt ans après, il est devenu Charlemagne, empereur d'un immense empire qui comprenait ce qui est maintenant la France et une grande partie de l'Allemagne et de l'Italie. C'est pourquoi il fait partie de l'histoire de ces trois pays modernes.

En France, on dit souvent que c'est lui qui a «inventé» l'école. Ce n'est pas tout à fait vrai. Il existait déjà des écoles dans les monastères, en général pour les enfants des nobles qui voulaient devenir moines[4]. Mais on peut dire que Charlemagne a encouragé le développement de l'éducation par l'exemple qu'il a donné.

Comme la plupart des nobles de son époque, qui passaient leur temps à faire la guerre[5], Charlemagne n'était pas très instruit[6]. Mais il s'intéressait à la culture. Une fois empereur, il a commencé à faire des études: latin, mathématiques, astronomie… Et il s'est entouré[7] d'hommes de lettres et d'artistes qui venaient de toute l'Europe. L'empereur «à la barbe fleurie[8]» a donc ainsi contribué au développement de l'éducation en France.

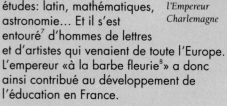

Dürer: portrait de l'Empereur Charlemagne

[1] l'enseignement *education*
[2] l'esprit *mind*
[3] roi *king*
[4] moines *monks*
[5] la guerre *war*
[6] instruit *educated*
[7] s'est entouré *surrounded himself with*
[8] à la barbe fleurie *with a flowing white beard*

322 LETTRES ET SCIENCES

322

SCIENCES

Napoléon Ier à La Malmaison, par François Gérard

NAPOLÉON Ier (1769-1821)

C'est à Napoléon que l'on doit la création des lycées, mais pour les garçons seulement. C'est aussi lui qui organise les structures de l'enseignement supérieur. L'enseignement devient très centralisé et entièrement dirigé par l'État. Mais il est encore réservé à une élite.

JULES FERRY (1832-1893)

Il faut attendre 1879 et Jules Ferry pour vraiment avoir l'enseignement public que la Révolution de 1789 avait promis à tous les Français.

Jules Ferry

Jules Ferry était avocat[1] et homme d'État. C'est lui qui, comme ministre de l'Éducation, a fait adopter les réformes qui sont à la base de l'enseignement public en France:

- l'enseignement est laïque (la plupart des écoles depuis le Moyen-Âge étaient des écoles religieuses);
- l'enseignement est gratuit[2] (puisque personne n'est obligé de payer, l'enseignement devient accessible à tous, riches ou pauvres);
- l'enseignement primaire est obligatoire;
- l'enseignement secondaire, jusque là réservé aux garçons, est étendu aux filles.

[1] avocat *lawyer*   [2] gratuit *free*

Après la lecture

A **L'école en France.** Vrai ou faux?

1. C'est Charlemagne qui a «inventé» l'école.
2. Charlemagne était très instruit.
3. Il était déjà empereur quand il a appris le latin.
4. Napoléon a développé l'enseignement pour les filles.
5. Il a établi un enseignement très centralisé.
6. Jules Ferry est vraiment le père de l'école en France.
7. Avant Jules Ferry, la plupart des écoles étaient des écoles publiques.
8. Jules Ferry a établi la gratuité de l'enseignement.

B **Qui a fait quoi?** Quelles ont été leurs contributions en matière d'enseignement?

> Charlemagne
> Napoléon
> Jules Ferry

C **Carrières.** Choisissez quelqu'un dans la classe et décidez si cette personne fera carrière dans:

> la politique
> l'enseignement
> la diplomatie
> les arts

Justifiez votre choix.

D **L'enseignement supérieur.** Les études supérieures en France sont pratiquement gratuites. Mais les conditions sont difficiles: il y a trop d'étudiants pour le nombre de places disponibles. Discutez des avantages et inconvénients des systèmes français et américains.

LETTRES ET SCIENCES   **323**

Après la lecture

PRESENTATION *(page 323)*

You may wish to have the students do the following vocabulary exercise. Write it on the board or on a transparency. Students match each expression with its opposite.

1. privé   a. commun à
2. religieux   tous
3. la réalité   b. petit
4. réservé à   c. public
   une élite   d. primaire
5. secondaire   e. l'imagination
6. immense   f. laïque
7. moderne   g. décourager
8. vrai   h. partiellement
9. encourager   i. ancien
10. entièrement j. faux
11. obligatoire k. pauvre
12. riche   l. facultatif

Exercices

ANSWERS

Exercice A

1. faux   5. vrai
2. faux   6. vrai
3. vrai   7. faux
4. faux   8. vrai

Exercice B

Answers will vary but may include:

Charlemagne a fait des études quand il était empereur. Il a donc encouragé l'éducation.

Napoléon a créé les lycées et a organisé les structures de l'enseignement supérieur.

Jules Ferry a fait adopter plusieurs réformes: l'enseignement laïque, l'enseignement gratuit, l'enseignement primaire obligatoire, l'enseignement secondaire pour les filles.

Exercices C and D

Answers will vary.

ART CONNECTION

For student art activities related to the paintings on pages 322–323, please refer to Fine Art Transparencies F-6 and F-7.

ADDITIONAL PRACTICE

Have students work in pairs to compare the French and American educational systems. One student mentions an aspect of the French system as outlined in the paragraph about Jules Ferry (*L'enseignement est laïque,* for example), and the other says whether the American system is the same.

Littérature: La Chanson de Roland

Note Since this selection deals with a famous literary piece, you may wish to have all students read it, at least quickly.

Students will read an excerpt from *La Chanson de Roland* in Glencoe French 4, *Trésors du temps*, pages 60–62.

Avant la lecture

PRESENTATION *(page 324)*

A. Have the students read the information in the *Avant la lecture* section.

B. Have the students scan the reading for cognates. There are approximately 18.

C. Give the students the following information: *La Westphalie est une ancienne province de l'Allemagne. Pampelune et Saragosse sont deux villes dans le nord de l'Espagne. Les Saxons qui ont colonisé la Bretagne sont un peuple germanique.*

Lecture

PRESENTATION *(pages 324–325)*

A. Have the students read the selection silently.

B. Have them look for the following information as they read: *Pourquoi Roland n'était-il pas avec Charlemagne quand celui-ci (Charlemagne) revenait en Westphalie?*
Note Ask the students for the English equivalent of *Richard Cœur de Lion.*

C. You may wish to do some additional word study with the students:

1. *en hâte:* The circumflex accent indicates that a letter was deleted. What letter do you think it is? If the letter were there, the word would be the same in English and French. What is the word?

2. The noun form of the verb *piller* is *le pillage.* Does this help you understand the meaning of *piller?*

LITTÉRATURE: LA CHANSON DE ROLAND

Avant la lecture

La Chanson de Roland is an epic poem which marks the beginning of French literature. It is based on a historical event that took place in 778 in the Pyrenees: a skirmish between the rear guard of Charlemagne's army and Basque highlanders, which claimed the life of Charlemagne's nephew, Roland.

The poem was written two centuries after the event, and its patriotic and religious fervor against the "infidels" reflects feelings prevalent at the end of the 10th century in Christian Europe, feelings which would lead to the Crusades of the 12th and 13th centuries.

From 1096 to 1265, there were eight Crusades. The third one involved the French king Philippe Auguste and the English king Richard Cœur de Lion, a Norman whose language was French. Make a report on that Crusade.

Lecture

La Chanson de Roland est la plus ancienne chanson de geste française. «Geste» veut dire «exploit». Les chansons de geste racontent les aventures de héros, en particulier de chevaliers[1] chrétiens qui luttent[2] contre les «infidèles». Les chansons de geste deviennent très populaires au début du XIIe siècle, au moment où les chrétiens d'Europe partent en croisade à Jérusalem pour la délivrer des Turcs. Les chansons de geste marquent le début de la littérature française.

La Chanson de Roland est un long poème épique qui raconte la mort de Roland, le neveu de Charlemagne, roi des Francs. L'histoire place l'événement en 778. Charlemagne est l'allié de certains chefs arabes d'Espagne qui ont besoin de son aide pour lutter contre d'autres chefs arabes. Charlemagne se bat[3] à leurs côtés

Mort de Roland à Ronceveaux, d'après A. le Neuville

SCIENCES

Le cor de Roland

à Pampelune et Saragosse. Mais il doit bientôt revenir en hâte vers la Westphalie où les Saxons se sont soulevés[4] contre lui. Il traverse les Pyrénées à l'ouest, passant par le col de Roncevaux[5].

Roland, lui, est resté en arrière pour surveiller les chariots qui transportent les bagages. Dans l'étroite gorge qu'est le col de Roncevaux, il est facile d'attaquer un petit nombre d'hommes coupés d'une armée, même si c'est la toute puissante[6] armée de Charlemagne. La nuit, des montagnards basques attaquent Roland et ses hommes pour piller les chariots. La légende dit que Roland sonne du cor[7] pour avertir[8] Charlemagne qui revient sur ses pas, mais trop tard: Roland est déjà mort. Il a près de lui sa belle épée[9], Durendal, qu'il a vainement essayé de briser[10] sur un rocher pour qu'elle ne tombe pas entre les mains de ses ennemis: c'est le rocher qui s'est brisé à sa place.

[1] chevaliers *knights*
[2] luttent *fight*
[3] il se bat *he fights*
[4] se sont soulevés *rose up*
[5] le col de Roncevaux *Roncesvalles Pass*
[6] puissante *powerful*
[7] sonne du cor *sounds his horn*
[8] avertir *warn*
[9] épée *sword*
[10] briser *break*

Baudoin rapportant à Charlemagne l'épée et le cor de Roland

Après la lecture

A **Charlemagne et Roland.** Répondez aux questions.

1. Que veut dire «geste» dans «chanson de geste»?
2. Qui était Charlemagne?
3. Pourquoi traverse-t-il les Pyrénées?
4. Pourquoi Roland est-il resté en arrière?
5. Qui attaque Roland?
6. Comment s'appelle son épée?
7. Pourquoi Roland essaie-t-il de briser son épée?
8. Comment Roland avertit-il Charlemagne?
9. Est-ce que Charlemagne arrive à temps pour sauver Roland?

B **Robin des Bois** (*Robin Hood*). Racontez l'histoire de Robin des Bois en français.

LETTRES ET SCIENCES **325**

Architecture: L'Art gothique: La cathédrale de Chartres

Avant la lecture

PRESENTATION *(page 326)*

A. Have the students look at the drawings to familiarize themselves with the architectural terms. (You may wish to display Fine Art Transparencies F-8 through F-11 as you read this selection.)

B. Explain to students that since France has so many architectural gems from so many different periods, the type of information in this selection is part of the general knowledge of all French students.

C. Have students scan the selection for cognates.

Note For more photos of Romanesque and Gothic architecture, see Glencoe French 4, *Trésors du temps*, pages 87 and 116–117.

Lecture

PRESENTATION *(pages 326–327)*

Have the students read the selection silently.

ARCHITECTURE: L'ART GOTHIQUE LA CATHÉDRALE DE CHARTRES

Avant la lecture

1. What kind of architecture do you find in American churches?
2. These drawings show the main features of Romanesque and Gothic architectures. Study their differences.

Lecture

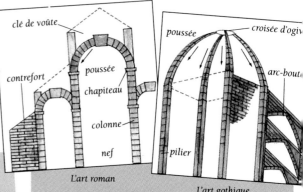

L'art roman

L'art gothique

L'art gothique est né en France au XIIe siècle. Il a été adopté ensuite dans tout l'Europe. Avant l'art gothique, il y avait l'art roman. Les églises romanes sont souvent massives et très sombres: leurs

Une basilique romane: La Madeleine de Vézelay

Une cathédrale gothique: la cathédrale de Chartres

murs sont épais[1] et ont de toutes petites ouvertures. Leurs voûtes[2] sont en demi-cercle, ou en «berceau». Les églises gothiques, elles, sont plus hautes et plus claires. Leurs voûtes sont sur des ogives qui se croisent. Ces voûtes sont plus légères et plus hautes parce qu'elles sont supportées par des piliers, eux-mêmes soutenus par des arcs-boutants.

Pour beaucoup, la cathédrale de Chartres est la plus belle des cathédrales gothiques. La cathédrale que l'on voit aujourd'hui n'est pas l'originale. En effet, en 1194, la cathédrale brûle[3]. Il ne reste que les tours, la façade, les fondations et la crypte. L'évêque[4] de Chartres et ses associés décident de faire reconstruire la cathédrale. Ils choisissent un architecte qui propose de construire une cathédrale encore plus belle que celle qui a brûlé. On ne connaît pas le nom de cet architecte, mais on l'appelle «le maître de Chartres».

Il faut plus de quarante ans pour reconstruire la cathédrale. Elle est alors plus haute et plus claire qu'avant. Sa voûte en berceau a été remplacée par une superbe voûte en ogive qui repose sur des piliers, ce qui permet aux murs d'être minces[5] et d'avoir de nombreux vitraux[6].

SCIENCES

La cathédrale de Chartres: le vitrail «Notre-Dame de la Belle Verrière»

Ces vitraux sont célèbres pour leur beauté, mais aussi pour leur bleu, «le bleu de Chartres», qui n'a jamais été reproduit. Quand la cathédrale de Chartres a été terminée, elle était si belle qu'elle est devenue un modèle pour tous les bâtisseurs[7] de cathédrales.

C'étaient les «compagnons» qui bâtissaient les cathédrales. Ils étaient organisés par métiers[8]: les tailleurs de pierre[9], les charpentiers, les couvreurs qui faisaient les toits[10], les verriers qui faisaient les vitraux. Les jeunes étaient d'abord apprentis pendant plusieurs années. Puis, ils devenaient «aspirants» et travaillaient sous la direction d'un maître. Ils voyageaient à pied de chantier[11] en chantier pour apprendre leur métier. Ensuite, ils devaient faire un travail qui était soumis au jugement des maîtres du métier. Si les maîtres jugeaient le travail parfait, l'aspirant était reçu compagnon. Il faisait serment[12] d'aider ses compagnons et de garder les secrets de fabrication du compagnonnage.

[1] épais *thick*
[2] voûtes *vaults*
[3] brûle *burns*
[4] évêque *bishop*
[5] minces *thin*
[6] vitraux *stained glass windows*
[7] bâtisseurs *builders*
[8] métiers *crafts*
[9] tailleurs de pierre *stone cutters*
[10] toits *roofs*
[11] chantier *construction site*
[12] faisait serment *pledged*

Une voûte en ogive

Après la lecture

A **L'art roman et l'art gothique.** Complétez.

1. L'art roman est né au Xe _____.
2. Saint-Patrick à New York est une _____ gothique.
3. Quand la cathédrale de Chartres a brûlé, l'évêque a décidé de la _____.
4. Les vitraux de Chartres sont admirés pour leur _____.
5. On ne connaît pas le _____ de l'architecte.
6. On n'a jamais pu _____ le «bleu de Chartres».
7. Au Moyen-Âge, les compagnons étaient groupés par _____.
8. Pour apprendre le métier, les apprentis travaillaient sur de nombreux _____.

B **Enquête.** Les cathédrales étaient construites à la gloire du dieu chrétien. Le catholicisme est la religion la plus importante en France. Ensuite viennent l'Islam, le protestantisme et le judaïsme. Faites une enquête sur les religions aux États-Unis.

LETTRES ET SCIENCES **327**

CHAPTER OVERVIEW

In this chapter students will learn vocabulary associated with good manners and some French social customs. They will learn the subjunctive forms of some irregular verbs and the use of the subjunctive with expressions of emotion.

The cultural focus of the chapter is on good manners, courtesy, and etiquette in France.

CHAPTER OBJECTIVES

By the end of this chapter students will know:

1. vocabulary associated with good and bad social and table manners
2. vocabulary for the parts of the body
3. vocabulary associated with emotions
4. vocabulary associated with introductions
5. irregular forms of *savoir, pouvoir,* and *vouloir* in the present subjunctive
6. the use of the subjunctive after expressions of emotion
7. the irregular verb *boire*

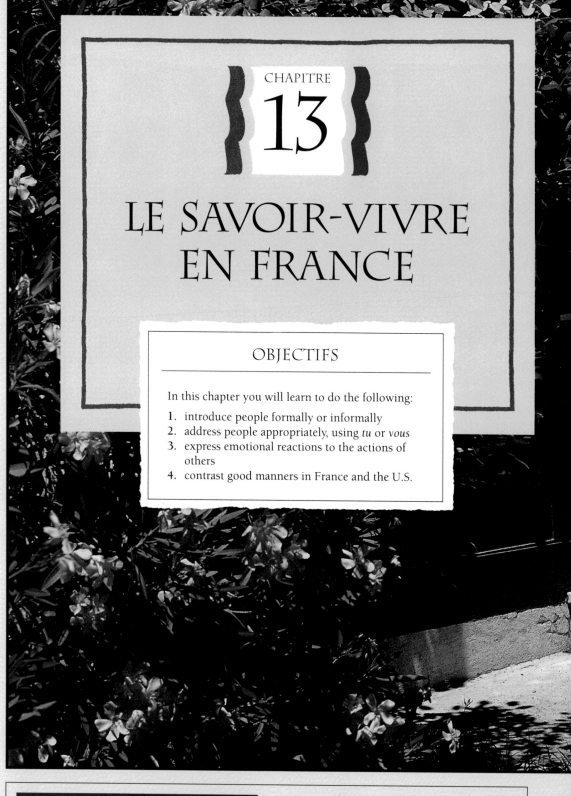

CHAPITRE

13

LE SAVOIR-VIVRE EN FRANCE

OBJECTIFS

In this chapter you will learn to do the following:

1. introduce people formally or informally
2. address people appropriately, using *tu* or *vous*
3. express emotional reactions to the actions of others
4. contrast good manners in France and the U.S.

CHAPTER PROJECTS

(optional)

1. Have students prepare in French a list of do's and don'ts concerning table manners in the United States.
2. Have students prepare a report that contrasts French and U.S. table manners.
3. Have students prepare a list of formal and informal greetings and farewells in French.
4. Have students make some simple drawings that depict good and bad manners. Have them write captions for their drawings. You may wish to use them for a bulletin board display.
5. Have the students write an article for a book entitled *Savoir-vivre.*

329

CHAPTER 13 RESOURCES

1. Workbook
2. Student Tape Manual
3. Audio Cassette 8A/CD-7
4. Bell Ringer Review Blackline Masters
5. Vocabulary Transparencies
6. Communication Transparency C-13
7. Communication Activities Masters
8. Situation Cards
9. Conversation Video
10. Videocassette/Videodisc, Unit 4
11. Video Activities Booklet, Unit 4
12. Lesson Plans
13. Computer Software: Practice/Test Generator
14. Chapter Quizzes
15. Testing Program
16. Internet Activities Booklet
17. CD-ROM Interactive Textbook
18. Map Transparencies
19. Fine Art Transparencies F-12 to F-15

Pacing

This chapter will require eight to ten class sessions. Pacing will depend on the length of the class, the age of the students, and student aptitude.

For more information on planning your class, see the Lesson Plans, which offer guidelines for 45- and 55-minute classes and **Block Scheduling**.

Exercices vs. *Activités*

The exercises and activities are color-coded. Exercises, which provide guided practice to prepare students for independent communication, are coded in blue. Communicative activities, which give students opportunities for creative, open-ended expression, are coded in red.

INTERNET ACTIVITIES

(optional)

These activities, student worksheets, and related teacher information are in the *À bord* Internet Activities Booklet and on the Glencoe Foreign Language Home Page at **http://www.glencoe.com/secondary/fl**

LEARNING FROM PHOTOS

Have the students describe the photo in their own words.

Vocabulary Teaching Resources

1. Vocabulary Transparencies 13.1 (A & B)
2. Audio Cassette 8A/CD-7
3. Student Tape Manual, Teacher's Edition, *Mots 1: A–D*, pages 131–133
4. Workbook, *Mots 1: A–B*, page 148
5. Communication Activities Masters, *Mots 1: A–B*, pages 83–84
6. Chapter Quizzes, *Mots 1: Quiz 1*, page 67
7. CD-ROM, Disc 4, *Mots 1:* pages 330–333

Bell Ringer Review

Write the following on the board or use BRR Blackline Master 13-1: List all the parts of the body that you remember in French.

PRESENTATION (*pages 330–331*)

A. Have students repeat the new words, phrases, and sentences after you or Cassette 8A/CD-7.
B. Point to the parts of the body (*un doigt, la main, le poignet, l'avant-bras, le coude, le pouce, la joue, la bouche, la lèvre*).
C. Dramatize the meaning of *bousculer, resquiller, se serrer la main, s'embrasser, manger la bouche fermée, manger la bouche ouverte, rompre un morceau de pain, couper le pain avec un couteau, s'essuyer les lèvres.*
D. Have students open their books and read pages 330–331.

bruyant

le bruit

mal élevé   impoli

bien élevé   poli

un doigt

la main

la joue

la bouche

le poignet

la lèvre

le pouce

l'avant-bras (m.)

le coude

bousculer

resquiller

330   CHAPITRE 13

ADDITIONAL PRACTICE

1. Have students describe the illustrations on pages 330–331 in as much detail as possible.
2. Student Tape Manual, Teacher's Edition, *Activité B*, page 132

Les amis ont rendez-vous dans un café.
Ils se retrouvent dans un café.
Les garçons se serrent la main.
Les filles s'embrassent.

Et toi, qu'est-ce que tu vas faire?

Les jeunes aiment se tutoyer.
Ils se tutoient facilement.
Le tutoiement est devenu très courant,
surtout entre adolescents.

Les garçons et les filles partagent
les frais quand ils sortent.
Chacun paie pour soi.

COMMENT SE TENIR À TABLE

la bouche
fermée

rompre

une serviette

la bouche
ouverte

Il faut rompre son morceau de pain avec les
doigts.
On ne coupe jamais le pain avec un couteau.

La serviette ne sert qu'à s'essuyer les lèvres.
Il est interdit de parler la bouche pleine.
Il faut manger la bouche fermée.

CHAPITRE 13   **331**

E. You may wish to ask the following questions about the illustrations: *Où est-ce que les amis ont rendez-vous? Ils s'y retrouvent? Que font les garçons? Que font les filles? Est-ce que les adolescents en France se tutoient facilement? Quand les jeunes gens sortent, qui paie? Est-ce que les garçons et les filles partagent les frais? En France, comment faut-il rompre son morceau de pain? On coupe le pain avec un couteau? Qu'est-ce qu'on fait avec une serviette?*, etc.

PANTOMIME GAME

Write the following words or phrases on index cards. Have students draw a card and mime the action. The class will guess what the person is doing.

bousculer
resquiller
se serrer la main
s'embrasser
manger la bouche fermée
manger la bouche ouverte
rompre un morceau de pain avec les doigts
couper le pain avec un couteau
s'essuyer les lèvres

ANSWERS

Exercice A

1. la joue
2. la bouche (la lèvre)
3. le coude
4. l'avant-bras
5. le poignet
6. le doigt
7. le pouce
8. la main

Exercice B

1. bien élevée
2. mal élevée
3. bien élevée
4. mal élevée
5. mal élevée
6. bien élevée
7. mal élevée
8. mal élevée

Exercices

A **Le corps.** Identifiez.

1.
2.
3.
4.
5.
6.
7.
8.

B **À vous de décider.** Gaby est bien élevée ou mal élevée? Prenez votre cahier et faites un tableau comme celui-ci.

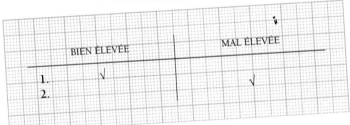

	BIEN ÉLEVÉE	MAL ÉLEVÉE
1.	√	√
2.		

1. Gaby se lève quand une personne âgée entre.
2. Elle ne regarde jamais la personne à qui elle parle, à qui elle s'adresse.
3. Quand elle rencontre une personne âgée dans l'autobus, par exemple, elle lui offre sa place. Elle ne veut pas que la personne âgée reste debout.
4. Elle fait beaucoup de bruit quand elle mange. Elle mange d'une façon bruyante.
5. Elle ne parle pas avec des mots. Elle fait des bruits. Elle grogne.
6. Elle dit toujours « merci » quand quelqu'un lui donne quelque chose ou fait quelque chose pour elle.
7. Elle aime parler la bouche pleine.
8. Elle se tient mal à table.

COOPERATIVE LEARNING

Have teams of students prepare a debate, each team taking one of the following sides:
1. **Les garçons et les filles doivent partager les frais quand ils sortent.**
2. **Les garçons et les filles ne doivent pas partager les frais. Ce sont les garçons (les filles) qui doivent payer.**

C C'est poli ou impoli? Décidez.

1. Quand on mange d'une façon bruyante, on montre qu'on apprécie ce qu'on mange.
2. Cette personne fait toujours beaucoup de bruit.
3. Quand on a rendez-vous avec des amis, on peut arriver avec une heure de retard.
4. Quand il y a un monde fou, c'est-à-dire beaucoup de monde, on bouscule les gens, on les pousse du coude.
5. Quand un garçon rencontre un ami, il lui serre la main.
6. Un jeune homme tutoie une vieille dame qu'il ne connaît pas bien.
7. Quand deux amies se retrouvent, elles s'embrassent sur les joues.
8. À table, on rompt son pain avec les doigts.
9. Et on s'essuie le nez avec sa serviette.
10. Il est absolument indispensable de resquiller quand les gens font la queue et que la queue est longue.

D Des définitions. Quel est le mot?

1. caractéristique d'une chose ou personne qui fait du bruit
2. s'adresser à quelqu'un en utilisant «tu»
3. le contraire de «la bouche ouverte»
4. chaque main en a cinq
5. avoir rendez-vous
6. diviser les frais
7. ce qu'on utilise pour couper quelque chose
8. ce qu'on utilise pour s'essuyer les lèvres
9. donner la main

PRESENTATION (*page 333*)

Exercice C

If there is disagreement, let the students argue their viewpoints.

Extension of *Exercice D*

After completing the exercise, you may wish to have students use each word in an original sentence.

ANSWERS

Exercice C

1. C'est impoli.
2. C'est impoli.
3. C'est impoli.
4. C'est impoli.
5. C'est poli.
6. C'est impoli.
7. C'est poli.
8. C'est poli.
9. C'est impoli.
10. C'est impoli.

Exercice D

1. bruyante
2. tutoyer
3. la bouche fermée
4. doigts
5. se retrouver
6. partager les frais (payer pour soi)
7. un couteau
8. une serviette
9. se serrer la main

LEARNING FROM PHOTOS

You may wish to ask: *D'après vous, de quoi parlent les deux hommes?*

INDEPENDENT PRACTICE

Assign any of the following:
1. Exercises, pages 332–333
2. Workbook, *Mots 1: A–B*, page 148
3. Communication Activities Masters, *Mots 1: A–B*, pages 83–84
4. CD-ROM, Disc 4, pages 330–333

VOCABULAIRE

MOTS 2

Vocabulary Teaching Resources

1. Vocabulary Transparencies 13.2 (A & B)
2. Audio Cassette 8A/CD-7
3. Student Tape Manual, Teacher's Edition, *Mots 2: E–G*, pages 134–136
4. Workbook, *Mots 2: C–D*, page 149
5. Communication Activities Masters, *Mots 2: C–D*, pages 85–86
6. Computer Software, *Vocabulaire*
7. Chapter Quizzes, *Mots 2: Quiz 2*, page 68
8. CD-ROM, Disc 4, *Mots 2:* pages 334–338

Bell Ringer Review

Write the following on the board or use BRR Blackline Master 13-2: Write five sentences telling what your French teacher wants you to do in class today. Begin each sentence with Le professeur veut que nous...

PRESENTATION (*pages 334–335*)

A. Using Vocabulary Transparencies 13.2 (A & B), have students repeat the new words, phrases, and sentences after you or Cassette 8A/CD-7.

B. Use facial expressions to convey the meaning of *avoir peur, être triste, être désolé, être surpris, être étonné, être content, être heureux, être fâché, être furieux.*

Note Explain to students that *être furieux* is stronger than *être fâché.*

334

VOCABULAIRE

MOTS 2

LES ÉMOTIONS

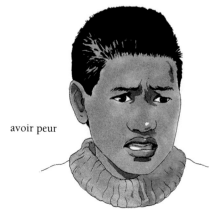

avoir peur

être triste

être désolée

regretter

Il a peur que tu ne viennes pas.

Elle a l'air désolée.
Elle est désolée que tu ne puisses pas venir.
Elle regrette que tu ne puisses pas venir.

être surpris

être étonné

être contente

être heureuse

être furieux

être fâché

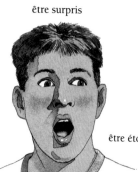

Pierre a l'air surpris (étonné).
Il est étonné que tu ne saches pas son numéro de téléphone.

Marie a l'air contente (heureuse).
Elle est contente que tu veuilles faire sa connaissance.

Il a l'air furieux.
Il est fâché que tu ne sois pas là.

334 CHAPITRE 13

PANTOMIME

You may wish to have a student or several students mime the following.

Vous êtes content(e).
Vous êtes fâché(e).
Vous êtes heureux (-se).
Vous êtes triste.
Vous êtes furieux (-se).
Vous êtes désolé(e).
Vous avez peur.
Vous êtes surpris(e).
Vous avez l'air étonné(e).

LES PRÉSENTATIONS

Je suis enchantée de faire votre connaissance, Monsieur.

Madame de la Rochefoucauld, je vous présente Monsieur Gauquelin.

Moi de même, Madame.

Christian, tu connais Olivier?

Non.

Olivier, Christian.

Bonjour.

Si vous venez de faire la connaissance de quelqu'un, vous pouvez dire:
— Je suis heureux (-se) de vous connaître.
— Je suis content(e) de vous connaître.
— Je suis enchanté(e) de faire votre connaissance.

Ou vous pouvez dire tout simplement:
— Enchanté(e).
— Bonjour.
— Salut.

CHAPITRE 13   **335**

ADDITIONAL PRACTICE

Ask students how they would react to the following situations using *Je suis...* :
1. Il n'y a pas de cours demain.
2. Vous avez «A» à l'examen de français.
3. Vous avez raté tous vos examens.
4. Vous avez eu un petit accident de voiture.
5. Vous vous êtes cassé la jambe.
6. Vous entendez quelqu'un à la porte à trois heures du matin.

Exercices

Exercices A and B

You may wish to have students do these exercises in pairs.

Exercice C

You may wish to have students do this exercise in pairs.

Extension of Exercice C

After completing the exercise, have students imagine a reason why the person is feeling the emotion. If the emotion is a negative one, have students say what the person can or should do.

ANSWERS

Exercice A

Answers will vary but may include:
Non.
Bonjour.

Exercice B

Answers will vary but may include:
Bonjour, Monsieur.
Moi de même.

Exercice C

1. Il a l'air content.
2. Elle a l'air désolée.
3. Elle a l'air surprise.
4. Elle a l'air fâchée.
5. Il a l'air triste.
6. Il a peur.

A **Un ami vous présente à un de ses copains.** Complétez le dialogue. Donnez des réponses simples.

> — Paul, tu connais Henri?
> — ___.
> — Henri, Paul.
> — ___.
> — Enchanté.

B **Votre mère vous présente au président.** Complétez le dialogue. Soyez extrêmement poli(e).

> — Monsieur Bolduc, je vous présente mon fils Cyrille (ma fille Nathalie).
> — Bonjour, Cyrille (Nathalie).
> — ___.
> — Je suis heureux de faire votre connaissance.
> — ___.

C **Comment sont-ils?** Répondez d'après les photos.

1. Il a l'air content ou triste?

2. Elle a l'air heureuse ou désolée?

3. Elle a l'air surprise ou fâchée?

4. Elle a l'air fâchée ou contente?

5. Il a l'air étonné ou triste?

6. Il a peur ou pas?

336   CHAPITRE 13

ADDITIONAL PRACTICE

Student Tape Manual, Teacher's Edition, *Activité G,* page 136

D Comment réagissez-vous? Choisissez et faites une phrase d'après le modèle.

> Vous avez gagné un million de dollars.
> *Je suis vraiment très surpris(e).*

1. Le Père Noël vous a apporté beaucoup de cadeaux.
2. Un ami vous présente la fille/le garçon de vos rêves.
3. Vous rencontrez dans la rue une amie que vous n'avez pas vue depuis longtemps.
4. Elle vous dit qu'elle a été très malade.
5. Votre ami(e) vous dit qu'il/elle ne vous aime plus.
6. Vous faites la queue à la poste et quelqu'un cherche à resquiller.
7. Votre meilleure amie vous annonce qu'elle va se marier demain.
8. Quelqu'un vous bouscule et vous fait tomber.

a. furieux (-se)
b. triste
c. étonné(e)
d. heureux (-se)
e. désolé(e)
f. content(e)
g. fâché
h. surpris(e)

E Laure est très émotive. Complétez chaque phrase avec le verbe qui convient.

1. Elle est contente que tu ___ faire sa connaissance.
2. Elle est surprise que tu ne ___ pas son adresse.
3. Elle est désolée que tu ne ___ pas là.
4. Elle a peur que tu ne ___ pas venir.
5. Elle regrette que tu ne ___ pas sa sœur.

a. connaisses
b. sois
c. puisses
d. saches
e. veuilles

Activités de communication orale
Mots 1 et 2

A Une personne bien élevée. Avec un(e) camarade, faites une liste de ce qu'une personne bien élevée doit faire. Vous devez trouver au moins six bonnes manières.

> Élève 1: Je trouve qu'une personne bien élevée doit toujours arriver à l'heure aux rendez-vous.
> Élève 2: Moi, je pense qu'une personne bien élevée doit répondre aimablement au téléphone.

B Une personne mal élevée. Maintenant, pensez un peu aux manières que vous n'aimez pas. Avec votre camarade, faites une liste de ce qui, selon vous, est mal élevé.

> Élève 1: Je déteste les personnes qui parlent la bouche pleine.
> Élève 2: Et moi, je n'aime pas les personnes qui vous bousculent dans la rue.

CHAPITRE 13   337

Exercices D and E
These exercises can be done with books open.

Extension of *Exercice D*
Have students write lists of additional situations. Have them choose a partner and find out how he/she would react to each situation on the list.

ANSWERS
Exercice D
Answers will vary, but may include:
1. Je suis vraiment très content(e).
2. Je suis vraiment très heureux (-se).
3. Je suis vraiment très surpris(e).
4. Je suis vraiment très désolé(e).
5. Je suis vraiment très triste.
6. Je suis vraiment très fâché(e).
7. Je suis vraiment très étonné(e).
8. Je suis vraiment très furieux (-se).

Exercice E
1. e
2. d
3. b
4. c
5. a

Activités de communication orale
Mots 1 et 2

PRESENTATION (*pages 337–338*)

Activités A, B, C, and D
It is suggested that you allow students to select the activities they would like to do.

ANSWERS
Activités A and B
Answers will vary.

338

PRESENTATION (continued)

Activité D

These paintings are reproduced on Fine Art Transparencies F-12 to F-15. The transparencies also provide notes on the painter and the period as well as student art appreciation activities.

Extension of Activité D

You may wish to have students work in groups. Have them bring in pictures of famous people from magazines. Each student describes one of the pictures while group members guess who is being described.

ANSWERS

Activité C

Answers will vary but may include:

1. Papa, je te présente mon amie Liliane.
2. Sylvie, je te présente mon amie Liliane.
3. Madame Hébert, je vous présente mon amie Liliane.
4. Liliane, tu connais ma petite sœur Julie?
5. Liliane, je te présente mon petit frère Gérard.

Activité D

Answers will vary.

C **Quelques présentations.** Votre cousine se marie. Vous êtes invité(e) ainsi que votre ami(e). Préparez-vous à faire quelques présentations. Travaillez avec deux camarades: l'un(e) joue votre ami(e), l'autre joue tous les autres rôles.

1. Vous présentez votre ami(e) à votre père.
2. Vous présentez votre ami(e) à votre cousine.
3. Vous présentez votre ami(e) à Madame Hébert, la mère du marié.
4. Vous présentez votre petite sœur à votre ami(e).
5. Vous présentez votre petit frère à votre ami(e).

D **Qui est-ce?** Regardez les portraits suivants. Décrivez un de ces personnages à votre camarade. Il/Elle doit deviner qui c'est.

> Élève 1: Cette dame a l'air heureuse et mystérieuse.
> Élève 2: C'est la Joconde!

Quentin de La Tour: «Autoportrait»

Édouard Manet: «Lola de Valence»

Léonard de Vinci: «La Joconde»

Jean-Baptiste Chardin: «Autoportrait»

STRUCTURE

Les verbes irréguliers *savoir, pouvoir, vouloir* au présent du subjonctif

Expressing the Subjunctive of Some Irregular Verbs

1. The verbs *savoir, pouvoir,* and *vouloir* are irregular in the present subjunctive. Study the following forms.

SAVOIR	POUVOIR	VOULOIR
que je sache	que je puisse	que je veuille
que tu saches	que tu puisses	que tu veuilles
qu'il sache	qu'il puisse	qu'il veuille
qu'elle sache	qu'elle puisse	qu'elle veuille
qu'on sache	qu'on puisse	qu'on veuille
que nous sachions	que nous puissions	que nous voulions
que vous sachiez	que vous puissiez	que vous vouliez
qu'ils sachent	qu'ils puissent	qu'ils veuillent
qu'elles sachent	qu'elles puissent	qu'elles veuillent

2. Now study the following examples.

Il faut *que vous sachiez* faire des présentations.
Je souhaite *qu'elle puisse* venir.
Il est possible *qu'elle veuille* faire ta connaissance.

Exercice

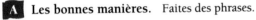

A **Les bonnes manières.** Faites des phrases.

Ils savent se tenir à table. (il faut)
Il faut qu'ils sachent se tenir à table.

1. Tu sais faire des présentations. (il est important)
2. Nous pouvons faire sa connaissance. (il est possible)
3. Ils peuvent faire ça. (il est impossible)
4. Il veut bien vous serrer la main. (je souhaite)
5. Elle sait parler français. (ils aimeraient)
6. Elle veut bien te présenter son frère. (il faut)
7. Vous voulez faire sa connaissance aussi. (il est possible)
8. Je peux venir le voir. (il est impossible)

CHAPITRE 13   **339**

Les verbes irréguliers savoir, pouvoir, vouloir au présent du subjonctif

PRESENTATION *(page 339)*

A. Have students repeat the verb forms after you.
B. Have students read the model sentences aloud.

Exercice

PRESENTATION *(page 339)*

It is recommended that you go over Exercise A in class before assigning it for homework.

ANSWERS
Exercice A

1. Il est important que tu saches faire des présentations.
2. Il est possible que nous puissions faire sa connaissance.
3. Il est impossible qu'ils puissent faire ça.
4. Je souhaite qu'il veuille bien vous serrer la main.
5. Ils aimeraient qu'elle sache parler français.
6. Il faut qu'elle veuille bien te présenter son frère.
7. Il est possible que vous vouliez faire sa connaissance aussi.
8. Il est impossible que je puisse venir le voir.

Le subjonctif après les expressions d'émotion

PRESENTATION (page 340)

Note The use of the subjunctive after these expressions does not conform to the notion that the subjunctive is used when it is not certain that the action of the verb will take place. In these cases, the subjunctive is used because of the subjective nature of the statement. What makes one person happy could make another one sad, etc.

A. Go over steps 1–2 with students.

B. Have students read the model sentences aloud.

Note In the CD-ROM version, this structure point is presented via an interactive electronic comic strip.

Exercices

PRESENTATION (pages 340–341)

Exercices A and B

These exercises can be done with books open or closed.

Exercice C

Have two students read the conversation to the class.

ANSWERS

Exercice A

Answers will vary. Each answer will begin *Je suis content(e)* or *Je suis désolé(e)* and end with the clause indicated.

Exercice B

1. Oui, je suis triste que Françoise ne soit pas encore là.
2. Oui, j'ai peur qu'elle ne vienne pas.
3. Oui, je suis surpris(e) qu'elle puisse faire le voyage.
4. Oui, je suis content(e) qu'elle le fasse.
5. Oui, je suis étonné(e) qu'elle sache conduire.
6. Oui, je suis désolé(e) que sa sœur ne veuille pas l'accompagner.

Exercice C

1. Oui, Anne est heureuse que Laurent vienne pour Noël.
2. Oui, elle est désolée que Richard ne puisse pas venir.

340

Le subjonctif après les expressions d'émotion

Expressing Emotional Reactions to the Actions of Others

1. Verbs and expressions of emotion such as joy, surprise, anger, and fear require the subjunctive because they are subjective. The following are some of the most commonly used expressions that deal with emotions.

avoir peur	être furieux (-se)	être désolé(e)
être content(e)	être étonné(e)	regretter
être heureux (-se)	être surpris(e)	
être fâché(e)	être triste	

2. Study the following examples.

Ils *ont peur* que leur chien ne *sache* pas bien se tenir.
Nous *sommes heureux* que vous *puissiez* venir.
Je *suis désolé* que tu ne *veuilles* pas faire sa connaissance.

Exercices

A **Content(e) ou désolé(e)?** Dites si vous êtes content(e) ou désolé(e).

1. que Paul ne vienne pas
2. qu'il connaisse votre sœur
3. qu'il ait l'air triste
4. qu'il ne sache pas votre numéro de téléphone
5. qu'il veuille faire la connaissance de vos parents
6. qu'il ne puisse pas vous fixer un rendez-vous

B **Françoise vient ou pas?** Répondez par «oui».

1. Tu es triste que Françoise ne soit pas encore là?
2. Tu as peur qu'elle ne vienne pas?
3. Tu es surpris(e) qu'elle puisse faire le voyage?
4. Tu es content(e) qu'elle le fasse?
5. Tu es étonné(e) qu'elle sache conduire?
6. Tu es désolé(e) que sa sœur ne veuille pas l'accompagner?

C **Je suis contente qu'il vienne.** Répétez la conversation.

VIRGINIE: Laurent vient pour Noël?
ANNE: Oui. Je suis contente que Laurent puisse faire le voyage. Mais je suis désolée que Richard ne vienne pas avec lui.
VIRGINIE: Je suis un peu étonnée que Richard ne veuille pas venir avec son frère.

Répondez d'après la conversation.

1. Anne est heureuse que Laurent vienne pour Noël?
2. Elle est désolée que Richard ne puisse pas venir?
3. Virginie est surprise que Richard ne vienne pas avec Laurent?

D Opinions et émotions. Complétez.

1. Je regrette que vous...
2. Je suis vraiment étonné(e) que vous...
3. Je suis désolé(e) que vous...
4. J'ai peur que vous...
5. Je suis fâché(e) que vous...
6. Je ne suis pas du tout content(e) que vous...
7. Je suis vraiment furieux (-se) que vous...

Le verbe *boire* — *Talking About What People Drink*

1. Study the following forms of the present indicative of the verb *boire*, "to drink."

BOIRE	
je bois	nous buvons
tu bois	vous buvez
il/elle/on boit	ils/elles boivent

2. Note that the past participle of *boire* is *bu*.

> Comme il avait très soif, il a bu toute une bouteille d'eau.

Exercices

A Ce que je bois. Dites si vous en buvez ou pas.

1. Du lait
2. De l'eau minérale
3. Du thé
4. Du café
5. Du coca
6. Du vin
7. Du champagne
8. Du jus d'orange

B Question de goût. Complétez avec *boire*.

1. Tu ___ de l'eau avec tes repas?
2. Je ne sais pas si c'est vrai, mais quelqu'un m'a dit qu'on ne doit pas ___ d'eau pendant les repas.
3. Nous les Américains, nous ___ du café pendant les repas, mais les Français jamais, sauf au petit-déjeuner.
4. Les Français ___ du vin pendant le déjeuner ou le dîner. Et ils ___ du café après.
5. Vous ___ votre café avec du lait ou sans lait?
6. Moi, je ___ du coca avec les repas.
7. Qu'est-ce que tu as ___ ce matin au petit déjeuner?

---

3. Oui, Virginie est un peu surprise que Richard ne vienne pas avec Laurent.

Exercice D
Answers will vary.

Le verbe boire

PRESENTATION (*page 341*)

Have students read the verb forms and the model sentence aloud.

Exercices

ANSWERS

Exercice A

1. Je (ne) bois (pas) du (de) lait.
2. Je (ne) bois (pas) de l'eau (d'eau) minérale.
3. Je (ne) bois (pas) du (de) thé.
4. Je (ne) bois (pas) du (de) café.
5. Je (ne) bois (pas) du (de) coca.
6. Je (ne) bois (pas) du (de) vin.
7. Je (ne) bois (pas) du (de) champagne.
8. Je (ne) bois (pas) du (de) jus d'orange.

Exercice B

1. bois
2. boire
3. buvons
4. boivent, boivent
5. buvez
6. bois
7. bu

CRITICAL THINKING ACTIVITY

(*Thinking skill: identifying consequences*)
Read the following to the class or write it on the board or on a transparency:
On ne doit pas boire de boissons alcoolisées parce que...

INDEPENDENT PRACTICE

Assign any of the following:
1. Exercises, pages 339–341
2. Workbook, *Structure: A–G*, pages 150–151
3. Communication Activities Masters, *Structure: A–C*, pages 87–89
4. Computer Software, *Structure*
5. CD-ROM, Disc 4, pages 339–341

CONVERSATION

PRESENTATION *(page 342)*

A. Have students close their books. Play the Conversation Video or have them listen as you read the conversation or play the recorded version on Cassette 8A/CD-7. (Use *Activité F* in the Student Tape Manual to check oral comprehension.)

B. Have two students read the conversation aloud with as much expression as possible. Have them use intonation to indicate their opinion of Fabienne.

Note In the CD-ROM version, students can play the role of either one of the characters and record the conversation.

ANSWERS

Exercice A

1. Elles pratiquent le basket.
2. Non, il n'y a pas assez de joueuses dans leur équipe.
3. Elle s'appelle Fabienne Daumale.
4. Non, mais elle la voit à la cantine.
5. Non, elle la trouve très mal élevée.

Scènes de la vie   *Mal élevée, mais championne*

ANNE-SOPHIE: Tu as trouvé quelqu'un pour l'équipe de basket?

CAMILLE: Oui. Fabienne Daumale. Tu la connais?

ANNE-SOPHIE: Je la vois à la cantine. C'est une horreur, cette fille! Elle bouscule tout le monde, elle parle la bouche pleine, mange avec ses doigts, boit à la bouteille. Et en plus, elle a toujours l'air furieuse!…

CAMILLE: Écoute, elle ne se tient peut-être pas très bien à table, mais sur un terrain de basket, elle est extra.

ANNE-SOPHIE: Si tu le dis, je veux bien… Mais, je regrette qu'on ne puisse pas trouver quelqu'un de plus sympa.

CAMILLE: Tiens, la voilà. Je vais vous présenter. Je sais que tu vas changer d'avis. Salut, Fabienne! Tu connais Anne-Sophie?

FABIENNE: De vue seulement. Salut!

ANNE-SOPHIE: Salut!

A **L'esprit d'équipe.**   Répondez d'après la conversation.

1. Anne-Sophie et Camille pratiquent quel sport?
2. Est-ce qu'il y a assez de joueuses dans leur équipe?
3. Comment s'appelle celle que Camille a trouvée?
4. Est-ce qu'Anne-Sophie connaît Fabienne?
5. Elle la trouve bien élevée?
6. Pourquoi? Qu'est-ce que Fabienne fait, d'après Anne-Sophie?
7. Pour Camille, est-ce qu'il est important que Fabienne se tienne mal à table?
8. Qu'est-ce qu'Anne-Sophie regrette?
9. Quand Camille présente Anne-Sophie à Fabienne, est-ce qu'Anne-Sophie montre qu'elle est fâchée?
10. Qu'est-ce qu'elle dit à Fabienne?

342   CHAPITRE 13

ADDITIONAL PRACTICE

Have students debate the following question: *Anne-Sophie va changer d'avis vis-à-vis de Fabienne? Pourquoi ou pourquoi pas? Justifiez votre réponse.*

LEARNING FROM PHOTOS

Have students describe the game in the photo. (Sports vocabulary was presented in Chapter 9 of *Bienvenue*.)

6. Elle bouscule tout le monde, parle la bouche pleine, mange avec ses doigts, boit à la bouteille et elle a toujours l'air furieuse.
7. Non, pour Camille il n'est pas important que Fabienne se tienne mal à table.
8. Elle regrette qu'on ne puisse pas trouver quelqu'un de plus sympa.
9. Non, Anne-Sophie ne montre pas qu'elle est fâchée.
10. Elle dit «Salut!»

Activités de communication orale

A **Pas content(e).** Un(e) de vos camarades n'est pas content(e) pour une raison quelconque. Vous êtes d'accord (ou pas d'accord).

> Élève 1: Je ne suis pas content qu'il fasse mauvais.
> Élève 2: Moi non plus, je ne suis pas contente qu'il fasse mauvais. (Moi si, parce que j'aimerais aller au cinéma.)

B **Le Rose et le Noir.** Votre camarade Pierre est toujours pessimiste: il voit tout en noir. Vous êtes toujours optimiste: vous voyez tout en rose. Avec Pierre vous préparez un pique-nique pour dimanche. Pierre exprime ses inquiétudes mais vous restez optimiste. Par exemple, Pierre dit: «J'ai peur qu'il fasse mauvais dimanche.» Vous lui répondez: «Mais non, il va faire très beau!»

1. J'ai peur qu'il fasse trop froid pour un pique-nique.
2. J'ai peur que la nourriture ne soit pas bonne.
3. J'ai peur que personne ne vienne.

Pierre

CHAPITRE 13   343

Activités de communication orale

PRESENTATION *(page 343)*

Activités A and B
Allow students to choose the activity they would like to do.

Activité B
In the CD-ROM version of this activity, students can interact with an on-screen native speaker.

ANSWERS
Activités A and B
Answers will vary.

LECTURE ET CULTURE

Bell Ringer Review

Write the following on the board or use BRR Blackline Master 13-6: Complete each sentence with the correct form of the indicated verb.

1. Je crois que tu ____ trop de coca. (boire)
2. Je ne pense pas que tu ____ être fâché. (devoir)
3. Je suis sûr(e) que Maman ____ contente de te voir. (être)
4. Je doute qu'elle ____ te chercher à l'aéroport. (venir)

READING STRATEGIES
(pages 344–345)

Pre-reading

Ask students to summarize what they have learned so far about the use of *tu* and *vous*.

Reading

A. Have students read the selection once silently.
B. Now go over the *Lecture* again, having individuals read four or five sentences aloud. Ask your own comprehension questions as they read or use the questions in Exercise D on page 346.
C. Have students role-play greetings and leave-takings using the French handshake and the kiss on the cheeks.

Post-reading

Call on volunteers to summarize in their own words what they have learned about good manners in France.

Note Students may listen to a recorded version of the *Lecture* on the CD-ROM.

LE SAVOIR-VIVRE EN FRANCE

Dans toutes les sociétés du monde, il existe des règles de politesse que l'on doit respecter pour avoir de bonnes manières. Ce qui peut être très poli dans une société n'est pas du tout poli dans une autre. Quelles sont les règles de politesse qu'on doit suivre en France pour ne pas avoir l'air mal élevé?

En général, il faut savoir que les Français attachent plus d'importance aux convenances[1] que nous, les Américains. Autrement dit, nous sommes un peu plus décontractés[2] qu'eux. Par exemple, quand un Français rencontre un ami, ils se serrent la main, même s'ils sont bons amis. Les jeunes le font également quand ils se rencontrent.

Les Français s'embrassent aussi. Une femme embrassera une autre femme ou un homme. On embrasse sur les joues,

jamais sur les lèvres. Les embrassades marquent un certain signe d'intimité ou de parenté. Dans le nord du pays les hommes ne s'embrassent presque jamais, mais dans le sud ils s'embrassent très volontiers comme en Espagne, en Italie ou en Grèce.

Quand on dit «bonjour», «au revoir» ou «merci» à quelqu'un, il est presque toujours de rigueur d'ajouter «Madame», «Mademoiselle» ou «Monsieur».

L'emploi des noms est différent aussi. Aux États-Unis on a l'habitude d'appeler par son prénom une personne dont on vient de faire la connaissance. En France, on ne fait pas ça. On peut appeler quelqu'un par son prénom seulement (uniquement) si on est intime avec cette personne, si cette personne est très jeune ou si elle vous a demandé expressément de l'appeler par son prénom.

Quand on les présente, les Français utilisent «Monsieur», «Madame» ou «Mademoiselle», sans le nom de famille. Puis quand ils connaissent quelqu'un, mais ne sont pas intimes—comme avec un voisin, par exemple—ils utilisent «Monsieur», «Madame» ou «Mademoiselle» suivi du nom de famille.

[1] convenances *social customs, conventions*
[2] décontractés *informal*

LEARNING FROM PHOTOS

You may wish to ask students: *Qu'est-ce que ces personnes disent?*

Ce qui est très important en France, c'est l'emploi du «tu» et du «vous»— le tutoiement et le vouvoiement. En général, on ne tutoie pas: un professeur, un patron ou une patronne[3], une personne plus âgée, un(e) commerçant(e) ou une personne qu'on ne connaît pas très bien. Actuellement les gens tutoient plus facilement. Les jeunes se tutoient toujours quand ils se parlent. Comme c'est vous l'étranger ou l'étrangère, il vaut mieux attendre qu'on vous tutoie avant de tutoyer aussi. Il faut que vous sachiez que les Français ne sont pas contents qu'on prenne l'initiative de les tutoyer, s'ils ne sont pas prêts à le faire.

En France comme partout, il existe des règles concernant l'exactitude. Persuadés que «L'exactitude est la politesse des rois», les Français essaient toujours d'arriver à l'heure exacte à un rendez-vous d'affaires[4]. Mais s'ils sont invités chez des parents ou chez des amis, ils se permettent souvent d'arriver avec un peu de retard.

[3] un patron ou une patronne   *boss*
[4] un rendez-vous d'affaires   *business meeting*

ORDRE DE LA COURTOISIE FRANCAISE
Fondé en 1952 et régi par la loi de 1901
56, avenue Simon-Bolivar, 75019 Paris
Pour maintenir en France une tradition et une Chevalerie

1997

Madame Yvonne Menard
Croix de Chevalier

Membre de l'Ordre, se fait un honneur de perpétuer une tradition française, et apprécie à sa valeur la Courtoisie et l'obligeance de tous.

Le Grand Chancelier,   Le Titulaire,

Étude de mots

A **Quelle est la définition?** Choisissez le mot ou l'expression qui correspond.

1. l'habitude
2. les voisins
3. tutoyer
4. vouvoyer
5. le commerçant

a. dire «vous» à quelqu'un
b. la coutume
c. celui qui vend des marchandises
d. ceux qui habitent à côté
e. dire «tu» à quelqu'un

B **Des mots semblables.** Il y a des mots qui ressemblent à ceux-ci en anglais? Quels sont ces mots?

1. la société
2. la politesse
3. la formalité
4. l'adulte

5. embrasser
6. intime
7. l'exactitude
8. respecter

«L'exactitude est la politesse des rois.»

CHAPITRE 13   345

COMMUNITIES

Have students look at the award certificate on this page. Have them write to the *Ordre de la Courtoisie française* to find out more about this award and the organization itself.

CRITICAL THINKING ACTIVITY

(Thinking skill: making inferences)

You may wish to have students explain the meaning of the proverb *L'exactitude est la politesse des rois* in their own words. (Tell them that *l'exactitude* means *la ponctualité* in this context.)

C **Le nom et le verbe.** Choisissez le nom qui correspond au verbe.

1. rencontrer
2. employer
3. habituer
4. connaître
5. tutoyer
6. embrasser

a. l'emploi
b. le tutoiement
c. la connaissance
d. l'embrassade
e. la rencontre
f. l'habitude

Compréhension

D **Des coutumes.** Corrigez les phrases d'après la lecture.

1. En général, les Américains attachent plus d'importance aux convenances que les Français.
2. Les Français sont plus décontractés que les Américains.
3. Les Français ne se serrent presque jamais la main.
4. Il n'y a que les adultes qui se serrent la main.
5. Les femmes n'embrassent que les autres femmes.
6. On s'embrasse sur les lèvres.
7. Les hommes dans le nord du pays s'embrassent très volontiers.
8. Il est poli de dire «bonjour» ou «merci» sans rien ajouter.

E **Les noms.** Donnez des réponses personnelles.

1. Quel est ton prénom?
2. Quel est ton nom de famille?
3. Qui appelles-tu par son prénom?
4. Qui appelles-tu par son nom de famille?
5. Compare l'emploi des prénoms en France et aux États-Unis.

F **Les bonnes manières en France.**
Répondez d'après la lecture.

1. Qu'est-ce que le savoir-vivre?
2. Qu'est-ce qu'il faut savoir pour ne pas avoir l'air mal élevé en France?
3. En France qui peut-on tutoyer?
4. Et qui doit-on vouvoyer?

M. et Mme Boursicot

vous redisent le plaisir qu'ils ont eu de passer auprès de vous la journée de Noël, dont ils gardent le meilleur souvenir, et vous adressent tous leurs vœux pour la nouvelle année.

Tél. (1) 45 60 03 86   *8, Rue Jourdan, 75016 Paris*

DÉCOUVERTE CULTURELLE

«S'il vous plaît» et «merci» sont des mots ou expressions qu'on doit utiliser souvent en France et en Amérique. Mais il y a une petite différence intéressante. En Amérique, si quelqu'un vous demande si vous voulez quelque chose, vous répondrez, «Yes, please». Mais en France, on dit tout simplement «S'il vous plaît». Aux États-Unis, si quelqu'un vous demande si vous voulez quelque chose et que vous ne le voulez pas, vous direz, «No, thank you». En France on dit tout simplement «Merci». Autrement dit, dans certaines circonstances—à table, par exemple—«s'il vous plaît» veut dire «oui» et «merci» veut dire «non».

Il est très important de ne pas paraître mal élevé(e) à table. En France, il est poli d'appuyer légèrement les poignets sur la table (mais jamais les avant-bras ni les coudes) et de garder les mains sur la table pendant le repas.

En France, on ne coupe jamais le pain avec un couteau. Il faut rompre son morceau de pain avec ses doigts.

On boit le café après le repas, pas avec. Avec le repas, on boit du vin et de l'eau minérale.

347

LEARNING FROM PHOTOS

Have students look at the second photo from the top. Demonstrate the French way of using a knife and fork. Then ask a student to explain, in French, the American way of using these utensils.

DID YOU KNOW?

During World War II some American spies were spotted and captured by the Nazis because their table manners gave them away. In spite of their excellent command of the language, some of them failed to use eating utensils in the European fashion and thus aroused suspicion.

Bell Ringer Review

Write the following on the board or use BRR Blackline Master 13-7: Complete each sentence with the correct form of the verb.

1. Nous ____ beaucoup ____ pendant ce film. (rire)
2. Elle est très réservée. Elle ne ____ pas souvent. (sourire)
3. Nous sommes bien élevés. Nous ne ____ pas en permanence. (rire)
4. J'ai essayé d'amuser l'enfant, mais il n'____ pas ____. (sourire)
5. Quand j'étais jeune, je ____ beaucoup. (rire)

OPTIONAL MATERIAL

PRESENTATION
(*pages 348–349*)

Have students look at the photographs for enjoyment. Answer any questions they may have and solicit comments.

Note In the CD-ROM version, students can listen to the recorded captions and discover a hidden video behind one of the photos.

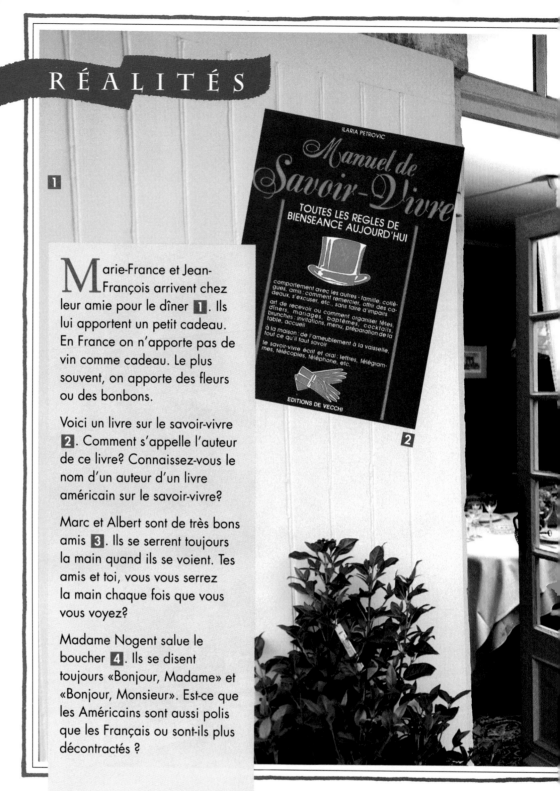

Marie-France et Jean-François arrivent chez leur amie pour le dîner **1**. Ils lui apportent un petit cadeau. En France on n'apporte pas de vin comme cadeau. Le plus souvent, on apporte des fleurs ou des bonbons.

Voici un livre sur le savoir-vivre **2**. Comment s'appelle l'auteur de ce livre? Connaissez-vous le nom d'un auteur d'un livre américain sur le savoir-vivre?

Marc et Albert sont de très bons amis **3**. Ils se serrent toujours la main quand ils se voient. Tes amis et toi, vous vous serrez la main chaque fois que vous vous voyez?

Madame Nogent salue le boucher **4**. Ils se disent toujours «Bonjour, Madame» et «Bonjour, Monsieur». Est-ce que les Américains sont aussi polis que les Français ou sont-ils plus décontractés ?

ADDITIONAL PRACTICE

1. Student Tape Manual, Teacher's Edition,
   Deuxième Partie, pages 138–140
2. Situation Cards, Chapter 13

CULMINATION

Bell Ringer Review

Write the following on the board or use BRR Blackline Master 13-8: Complete each sentence with the present subjunctive of the verb in parentheses.

1. Le proviseur veut que nous ___ beaucoup. (apprendre)
2. Le censeur veut que Frédéric ___ tout ce qu'elle dit. (comprendre)
3. La conseillère d'orientation veut que je ___ à son bureau. (venir)
4. Le conseiller d'éducation veut que vous ___ de bonnes notes. (recevoir)
5. Les profs veulent que tu ___ le censeur. (voir)

RECYCLING

These activities encourage students to use all the language they have learned in the chapter and recombine it with material from previous chapters.

INFORMAL ASSESSMENT

Use the oral and written exercises in this section as a review at the end of the chapter or to evaluate speaking and writing skills. For guidelines on assigning oral grades, see the evaluation criteria on page 22 of this Teacher's Wraparound Edition.

Activités de communication orale

ANSWERS

Activités A and B
Answers will vary.

Activités de communication écrite

ANSWERS

Activités A, B, and C
Answers will vary.

350

Activités de communication orale

A **Comparaisons.** Travaillez avec un(e) camarade. Comparez les règles de politesse française et les règles de politesse américaines.

B **Le savoir-vivre aux États-Unis.** Vous parlez à Laure et à Romain, deux amis français. Laure et Romain pensent bientôt faire un voyage aux États-Unis. Ils vous demandent de leur dire les choses qu'ils doivent savoir pour ne pas avoir l'air impolis ou mal élevés quand ils seront aux États-Unis. Parlez à Laure et Romain et dites-leur comment ils doivent traiter les Américains.

Activités de communication écrite

A **Le savoir-vivre en France.** Imaginez que vous écrivez un petit livre sur le savoir-vivre. Faites une liste de cinq choses qu'on doit faire en France pour être poli. Et faites une liste de cinq choses qu'on ne doit pas faire en France parce qu'elles seraient considérées comme impolies ou mal élevées.

B **Les bonnes manières.** Faites une liste de ce que vous considérez comme étant de bonnes manières. Faites-en une autre pour les mauvaises manières. Décrivez ce que vos parents ou vos profs insistent pour que vous fassiez ou pour que vous ne fassiez pas.

C **Vous avez soif?** Composez une publicité pour une nouvelle boisson que vous voulez lancer sur le marché. Dites qui boit cette boisson, quand, pourquoi, avec qui, etc.

Le jus d'orange Tropiques: la nouvelle boisson fraîche des îles!

Je le bois matin, midi et soir!

350 CHAPITRE 13

COOPERATIVE LEARNING

Have students work in groups to prepare as many questions as they can about the café scene on Communication Transparency C-13. (The illustration reviews the chapter vocabulary, food vocabulary, and hairstyles.) Then have the groups take turns asking and answering the questions.

INDEPENDENT PRACTICE

Assign any of the following:
1. Activities and exercises, pages 350–351
2. Communication Activities Masters, pages 83–89
3. CD-ROM, Disc 4, pages 350–351

Réintroduction et recombinaison

A **Les goûts.** Répondez d'après le modèle.

> le dessert
> *Moi, j'aime beaucoup le dessert. Mais je ne mange pas de dessert.*
> *Si je mange du dessert, je grossirai.*

1. les tartes
2. le chocolat
3. les glaces
4. les bonbons
5. les gâteaux

B **On va prendre le train.** Répondez en utilisant *le, la, les* ou *en*.

1. Thérèse prend le train?
2. Elle prend son billet au guichet?
3. Elle achète deux billets?
4. Elle attend le train sur le quai?
5. Dans le train, elle trouve sa place sans difficulté?
6. Le contrôleur vérifie les billets?
7. Il ramasse les billets?
8. Thérèse lit le journal pendant le voyage?

C **Yves est français.** Répondez par «oui».

1. Yves est allé au café hier soir?
2. Il a vu ses copains et copines?
3. Ils se sont parlé?
4. Ils ont pris quelque chose?
5. Ils ont partagé les frais?
6. Quand les parents d'Yves étaient jeunes, ils allaient aussi au café?
7. Ils se vouvoyaient?
8. Est-ce que les coutumes ont changé?

Vocabulaire

NOMS	ADJECTIFS	VERBES	AUTRES MOTS ET EXPRESSIONS
la main	bien élevé(e)	présenter	avoir l'air
le doigt	mal élevé(e)	s'embrasser	avoir peur
le pouce	bruyant(e)	se tutoyer	faire la connaissance de
le poignet	enchanté(e)	se retrouver	moi de même
l'avant-bras (m.)	content(e)	regretter	se serrer la main
le coude	heureux, heureuse	s'essuyer	se tenir bien/mal
la lèvre	fâché(e)	couper	partager les frais
la bouche	furieux, furieuse	servir à	
la joue	poli(e)	bousculer	
la serviette	impoli(e)	resquiller	
le bruit	surpris(e)	rompre	
le savoir-vivre	étonné(e)		
les présentations (f.)	triste		
le tutoiement	désolé(e)		
	courant(e)		

Réintroduction et recombinaison

PRESENTATION *(page 351)*

Exercise A reviews partitive vs. definite articles; Exercise B, object pronouns and train vocabulary; and Exercise C, the imperfect vs. the *passé composé.*

ANSWERS

Exercice A

1. ... les tartes. ... de tartes. ... des tartes...
2. ... le chocolat. ... de chocolat. ... du chocolat
3. ... les glaces. ... de glaces. ... des glaces
4. ... les bonbons. ... de bonbons. ... des bonbons
5. ... les gâteaux. ... de gâteaux. ... des gâteaux

Exercice B

1. Oui, elle le prend.
2. Oui, elle le prend...
3. Oui, elle en achète deux.
4. Oui, elle l'attend...
5. Oui, elle la trouve...
6. Oui, il les vérifie.
7. Oui, il les ramasse.
8. Oui, elle le lit pendant le voyage.

Exercice C

Answers begin with *Oui* and repeat the wording of the question.

ASSESSMENT RESOURCES

1. Chapter Quizzes
2. Testing Program
3. Situation Cards
4. Communication Transparency C-13
5. Computer Software: Practice/Test Generator

STUDENT PORTFOLIO

Written assignments which may be included in students' portfolios are the *Activités de communication écrite* on page 350 and any writing activities from the *Un Peu Plus* section in the Workbook.

Note Students may create and save both oral and written work using the Electronic Portfolio feature on the CD-ROM.

VIDEO PROGRAM

INTRODUCTION   (44:03)

À TABLE   (44:26)

CHAPITRE 14

CHAPTER OVERVIEW

In this chapter students will learn about the life-styles of the people of the Maghreb—Tunisia, Algeria, and Morocco—and the French influence in those countries. Students will also learn to use the subjunctive after expressions of doubt and the infinitive after a preposition.

CHAPTER OBJECTIVES

By the end of this chapter students will know:

1. vocabulary associated with life in North Africa
2. the use of the subjunctive with expressions of doubt
3. the use of the indicative with *il me semble que* and *il paraît que*
4. the use of the infinitive after prepositions

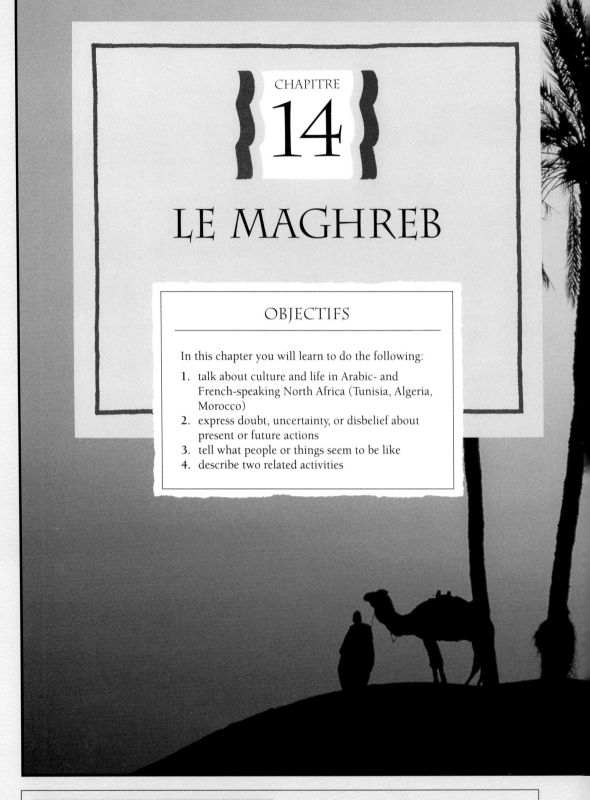

CHAPITRE 14

LE MAGHREB

OBJECTIFS

In this chapter you will learn to do the following:

1. talk about culture and life in Arabic- and French-speaking North Africa (Tunisia, Algeria, Morocco)
2. express doubt, uncertainty, or disbelief about present or future actions
3. tell what people or things seem to be like
4. describe two related activities

CHAPTER PROJECTS

(optional)

1. Have students prepare a report on one of the three countries of the Maghreb: Tunisia, Algeria, or Morocco.
2. If students are interested in religion, have them prepare a report on the role of Islam in the daily life of its adherents.
3. Have the students prepare a report on the Roman ruins in Tunisia.
4. If students are interested in cooking, have them prepare a report on the cuisine of the Maghreb. There are many interesting dishes besides the famous couscous. Students might prepare some dishes to share with the class. (See *Activité B,* page 374.)

352

353

CHAPTER 14 RESOURCES

1. Workbook
2. Student Tape Manual
3. Audio Cassette 8B/CD-7
4. Bell Ringer Review Blackline Masters
5. Vocabulary Transparencies
6. Communication Transparency C-14
7. Communication Activities Masters
8. Situation Cards
9. Conversation Video
10. Videocassette/Videodisc, Unit 4
11. Video Activities Booklet, Unit 4
12. Lesson Plans
13. Computer Software: Practice/Test Generator
14. Chapter Quizzes
15. Testing Program
16. Internet Activities Booklet
17. CD-ROM Interactive Textbook

Pacing

This chapter will require eight to ten class sessions. Pacing will depend on the length of the class, the age of the students, and student aptitude.

For more information on planning your class, see the Lesson Plans, which offer guidelines for 45- and 55-minute classes and **Block Scheduling**.

Exercices vs. *Activités*

The exercises and activities are color-coded. Exercises, which provide guided practice to prepare students for independent communication, are coded in blue. Communicative activities, which give students opportunities for creative, open-ended expression, are coded in red.

INTERNET ACTIVITIES

(optional)

These activities, student worksheets, and related teacher information are in the *À bord* Internet Activities Booklet and on the Glencoe Foreign Language Home Page at: **http://www.glencoe.com/secondary/fl**

VOCABULAIRE

MOTS 1

Vocabulary Teaching Resources

1. Vocabulary Transparencies 14.1 (A & B)
2. Audio Cassette 8B/CD-7
3. Student Tape Manual, Teacher's Edition, *Mots 1: A–C*, pages 141–143
4. Workbook, *Mots 1: A–C*, pages 155–156
5. Communication Activities Masters, *Mots 1: A–B*, pages 90–92
6. Chapter Quizzes, *Mots 1:* Quiz 1, page 72
7. CD-ROM, Disc 4, *Mots 1:* pages 354–357

Bell Ringer Review

Put the following on the board or use BRR Blackline Master 14-1: Divide your paper into two columns headed *Poli* and *Impoli*. Write the following words and phrases in the appropriate columns:
arriver à un rendez-vous à l'heure
bousculer
se servir d'une serviette pour s'essuyer les lèvres
faire du bruit quand quelqu'un veut dormir
manger la bouche fermée
manger la bouche ouverte
parler la bouche pleine
partager les frais
resquiller
se serrer la main
tutoyer une marchande

PRESENTATION (pages 354-355)

A. Have the students close their books. Using Vocabulary Transparencies 14.1 (A & B), present the new words. Point to each item and have the students repeat the word after you or Cassette 8B/CD-7.

Il paraît qu'il faut marchander dans un souk.

354   CHAPITRE 14

PAIRED ACTIVITY

Have students work in pairs to make up a conversation at a market. One student takes the part of a customer and the other that of a merchant. The pair bargain for an item that the merchant is selling. You may wish to call on volunteers to present their conversations to the class.

un minaret

un muezzin

une mosquée

Les musulmans prient en direction de la Mecque.

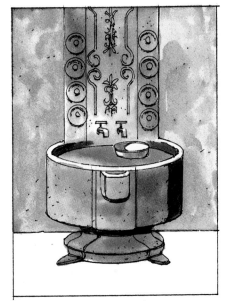

un hammam = un bain turc

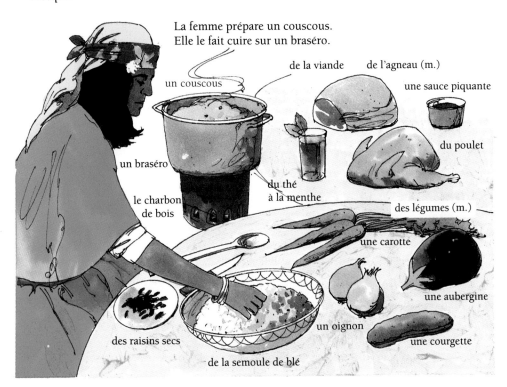

La femme prépare un couscous.
Elle le fait cuire sur un braséro.

de la viande   de l'agneau (m.)

un couscous

une sauce piquante

du poulet

un braséro

du thé à la menthe

le charbon de bois

des légumes (m.)

une carotte

une aubergine

des raisins secs

un oignon

une courgette

de la semoule de blé

CHAPITRE 14   **355**

B. Have the students open their books and read the new words.
C. Call on two students to read the mini-conversation on page 354 with as much expression as possible.
D. As you present the new vocabulary on page 355, you may wish to ask the students the following questions: *Le muezzin est dans le minaret? Les musulmans prient dans la mosquée? Ils prient en direction de quelle ville? Où est-ce que la femme prépare son couscous? Elle le prépare avec quels ingrédients? Le thé à la menthe est dans une tasse ou dans un verre?*, etc.

Bell Ringer Review

Put the following on the board or use BRR Blackline Master 14-2: Prepare a list of foods you know in French.

Culture Note The woman's dress on this page is typical of that worn by Berber women. The Berbers are a Muslim people of North Africa and the Sahara. They have their own language, Berber, although most also speak Arabic. They number around 20 million, and millions of other North Africans are of mixed Berber and Arabic ancestry.

Note There is a photo of a dish of couscous on page 366.

THE FRANCOPHONE WORLD

For additional information on and photos of North Africa, see *Bienvenue, Le Monde francophone*, pages 111, 222, 327, and 436.

Exercices

PRESENTATION (page 356)

Exercice A

For this exercise, books must be open so that students may refer to the illustrations.

Exercice B

Exercise B can be done with books open or closed.

Extension of Exercice B

After completing Exercise B, you may wish to call on a student to retell the story in the exercise in his/her own words.

ANSWERS

Exercice A

1. C'est un voile.
2. C'est une ruelle.
3. C'est un atelier.
4. C'est un souk.
5. C'est une mosquée.
6. C'est un minaret.
7. C'est un muezzin.
8. C'est un hammam.
9. C'est en cuir.

Exercice B

1. Oui, Madame Bouraoui porte un voile.
2. Oui, elle s'enveloppe dans un châle.
3. Oui, elle habite dans la médina.
4. Oui, elle prépare le thé à la menthe sur un braséro.
5. Oui, elle y met du charbon de bois.

Exercices

A Qu'est-ce que c'est? Répondez d'après les dessins.

1. C'est un voile ou un châle?

2. C'est un grand boulevard ou une ruelle?

3. C'est une boutique ou un atelier?

4. C'est un centre commercial ou un souk?

5. C'est une mosquée ou une église?

6. C'est une tour ou un minaret?

7. C'est un muezzin ou un maroquinier?

8. C'est un hammam ou une piscine?

9. C'est en laine ou en cuir?

B Madame Bouraoui. Répondez par «oui».

1. Madame Bouraoui porte un voile?
2. Elle s'enveloppe dans un châle?
3. Elle habite dans la médina?
4. Elle prépare le thé à la menthe sur un braséro?
5. Elle y met du charbon de bois?

356 CHAPITRE 14

ADDITIONAL PRACTICE

Student Tape Manual, Teacher's Edition, *Activité C*, page 143

C **Le couscous.** Faites une liste des ingrédients nécessaires pour préparer un bon couscous.

D **Des définitions.** Quel est le mot?

1. une pièce de tissu destinée à protéger quelqu'un du froid
2. une petite rue étroite
3. ce qu'on peut utiliser pour faire un feu quand on n'a pas le gaz ou l'électricité
4. un édifice religieux musulman
5. parler à Dieu
6. un plat très populaire en Algérie, en Tunisie et au Maroc
7. une boisson chaude qu'on boit beaucoup au Maghreb
8. des personnes qui prient en direction de la Mecque
9. discuter avec un marchand pour acheter quelque chose à meilleur prix
10. la monnaie tunisienne
11. un autre nom pour le Maroc, l'Algérie et la Tunisie

Une Tunisienne voilée

Un musulman en prière

CHAPITRE 14   **357**

Exercice C

Il faut avoir de la semoule de blé, des légumes (des carottes, des aubergines, des oignons, des courgettes), des raisins secs, de la viande (de l'agneau, du poulet) et une sauce piquante pour préparer un bon couscous.

Note There is a recipe for couscous on page 148 of the Student Tape Manual, Teacher's Edition (page 264, Student Edition).

Exercice D

1. un châle
2. une ruelle
3. du charbon de bois
4. une mosquée
5. prier
6. le couscous
7. le thé à la menthe
8. des musulmans
9. marchander
10. le dinar
11. le Maghreb

LEARNING FROM PHOTOS

1. Students will learn in this chapter that although some Tunisian women wear a veil, the majority do not. The veil is becoming more commonplace, however, in all the countries of the Maghreb due to the influence of Islamic fundamentalism.
2. Ask the following about the photo on the left: *L'homme est jeune ou vieux? De quelle religion est-il? Il lit la Bible ou le Coran?*

INDEPENDENT PRACTICE

Assign any of the following:
1. Exercises, pages 356–357
2. Workbook, *Mots 1: A–C,* pages 155–156
3. Communication Activities Masters, *Mots 1: A–B,* pages 90–92
4. CD-ROM, Disc 4, pages 354–357

VOCABULAIRE

MOTS 2

Vocabulary Teaching Resources

1. Vocabulary Transparencies 14.2 (A & B)
2. Audio Cassette 8B/CD-7
3. Student Tape Manual, Teacher's Edition, *Mots 2: D–F,* pages 143–145
4. Workbook, *Mots 2: D–E,* pages 156–157
5. Communication Activities Masters, *Mots 2: C–D,* pages 92–93
6. Computer Software, *Vocabulaire*
7. Chapter Quizzes, *Mots 2: Quiz 2,* page 73
8. CD-ROM, Disc 4, *Mots 2:* pages 358–361

Bell Ringer Review

Put the following on the board or use BRR Blackline Master 14-3: Put the following conversation in logical order.

Mlle Chénier, je vous présente M. Ledoux.

Moi de même, Mademoiselle.

M. Ledoux, vous connaissez Mlle Chénier?

Je suis heureuse de vous connaître, Monsieur.

Non, mais je voudrais bien faire sa connaissance.

PRESENTATION (*pages 358–359*)

A. Present the new words using Vocabulary Transparencies 14.2 (A & B). Then point to items on the transparencies at random and have students identify them. Have students repeat each word after you or Cassette 8B/CD-7.

une palmeraie = une plantation de palmiers

358   CHAPITRE 14

le soleil

la croûte de sel

un chott = un lac salé

Djamila est tunisienne et maghrébine.
Elle est étudiante. Elle fait ses études à
Monastir.

—Je doute que tu connaisses le désert du
Sahara.
—Où est le Sahara?
—Je crois que c'est en Afrique.
—Je ne crois pas que ce soit en Afrique.
—Je suis sûr que c'est en Afrique.

CHAPITRE 14   **359**

B. Call on a pair of students to
read the conversation. This
conversation introduces the
grammatical concept being
taught in this chapter.
C. Ask students if they think the
two students on this page are
from North Africa. Why or
why not?

Culture Note In the illustration,
Djamila is wearing clothing typi-
cal of that worn by middle-class
Tunisian women.

Vocabulary Expansion

You may wish to give stu-
dents some other words denot-
ing plantations or groves that,
like *palmeraie*, are formed from
the name of a fruit tree.
la pommeraie
l'orangeraie
la bananeraie

ADDITIONAL PRACTICE

1. You may wish to ask students the following additional questions about the
illustrations: *Il fait très chaud dans le
désert? Les chameaux ont besoin de
beaucoup d'eau? Ils boivent beaucoup? Il
y a des palmiers dans l'oasis? Les palmiers
donnent des dattes? La figue est un fruit ou
un légume? Un chott est une oasis ou un lac
salé? Où se trouvent les chotts? Comment est*
*Djamila? Elle a les cheveux comment? Elle a
l'air sympathique? De quoi parlent le garçon
et la fille? Ils connaissent le Sahara?*
2. Student Tape Manual, Teacher's Edition,
Activités E–F, pages 144–145

Exercices

PRESENTATION (page 360)

Exercice A

You may wish to have students use the words in Exercise A in original sentences.

Exercices B and C

After completing each exercise, you may wish to have a student describe the Sahara in his/her own words.

ANSWERS

Exercice A

1. i	6. a
2. e	7. j
3. f	8. b
4. h	9. d
5. g	10. c

Exercice B

1. Oui, le Sahara est un désert.
2. Le Sahara est en Afrique.
3. Oui, les déserts ont des oasis.
4. Oui, dans les oasis il y a souvent des palmiers.
5. Oui, il y a des palmiers qui donnent des dattes.
6. Oui, le soleil brille très fort dans le Sahara.

Exercice C

1. désert
2. Afrique
3. oasis
4. croûte (de sel)
5. palmier
6. figues, dattes
7. palmeraies
8. chameau
9. caravanes
10. sable

Exercices

A Quelle est la définition? Choisissez.

1. un désert
2. le Sahara
3. un Maghrébin
4. un Tunisien
5. une oasis
6. un palmier
7. une palmeraie
8. une dune
9. un chameau
10. un chott

a. un arbre qui donne des dattes
b. une montagne de sable
c. un lac salé dans le désert tunisien
d. un animal qui peut rester sans boire pendant très longtemps
e. un désert d'Afrique
f. un habitant du Maghreb
g. un endroit dans le désert où il y a de l'eau et des palmiers
h. un homme qui vit en Tunisie
i. une région presque sans eau et sans végétation
j. une plantation de palmiers

B Un désert. Répondez.

1. Est-ce que le Sahara est un désert?
2. Où est le Sahara?
3. Les déserts ont des oasis?
4. Dans les oasis il y a souvent des palmiers?
5. Y a-t-il des palmiers qui donnent des dattes?
6. Le soleil brille très fort dans le Sahara?

Les jardins de Ghardaïa: une oasis du Sahara

C Le Sahara. Complétez.

1. Le Sahara est un grand ___.
2. Le Sahara est en ___.
3. Dans le Sahara il y a quelques ___, c'est-à-dire, des endroits fertiles où il y a de l'eau.
4. En été quand il fait très chaud et que le soleil brille très fort, le sel des chotts forme une ___.
5. Le ___ du Maghreb est un arbre qui donne des dattes.
6. Les ___ et les ___ sont des fruits délicieux.
7. Dans certaines oasis, il y a des ___ immenses avec des milliers de palmiers.
8. Dans le Sahara on peut voyager à dos de ___.
9. Quand on voyage dans le Sahara, on voit souvent des ___ de chameaux qui vont d'une oasis à une autre.
10. Dans certaines régions du Sahara, le ___ forme de grandes dunes.

DID YOU KNOW?

Ghardaïa is one of five towns in the Mzab, a group of oases in the Sahara in northern Algeria. Many of the Berber inhabitants are merchants. Men wear the traditional flowing Arab clothes, and women dress according to religious custom, that is, they are veiled in public.

You may wish to have students say as much as they can about the photo.

ADDITIONAL PRACTICE

You may wish to ask students the following questions about U.S. geography:

Est-ce qu'il y a des déserts aux États-Unis? Où? Comment sont-ils? Est-ce qu'on y trouve des chameaux, des dunes, des palmeraies, des chotts et des oasis? Est-ce que les oasis des déserts américains ressemblent à Ghardaïa?

Dans la médina de Marrakech, un marchand de tapis

Activités de
communication orale
Mots 1 et 2

PRESENTATION *(page 361)*

These activities encourage students to use the new vocabulary of the chapter on their own.

ANSWERS

Activités A, B, and C
Answers will vary.

Activités de communication orale

Mots 1 et 2

A **Les souks.** Vous êtes dans les souks de la médina de Casablanca. On y vend de très beaux objets en cuir. Vous aimeriez bien acheter un sac. Vous parlez au maroquinier (votre camarade).

1. Il vous demande ce que vous voulez.
2. Il vous montre un grand sac. Vous en voulez un petit.
3. Il vous montre un sac rouge, mais vous préférez un sac vert.
4. Il vous donne le sac vert. Vous voulez savoir le prix.
5. Vous croyez que le prix est trop élevé. Vous marchandez.

B **J'ai marchandé.** Décrivez ce qui vient de se passer avec le maroquinier (votre camarade). Dites si vous avez acheté le grand sac ou le petit sac vert. Expliquez pourquoi. Le maroquinier donnera son point de vue sur ce qui s'est passé.

C **Le Sahara.** Comment imaginez-vous le Sahara? Travaillez en petits groupes. Décrivez-le en quelques phrases. Vous pouvez même faire un dessin.

      Élève 1: J'imagine qu'il fait très, très chaud au Sahara.
      Élève 2: J'imagine qu'il y a des palmiers.

CHAPITRE 14   **361**

LEARNING FROM PHOTOS

You may wish to explain to students that the medina of Marrakech is one of the most famous of the entire Maghreb. Ask the following questions about the photo: *C'est la boutique d'un marchand de tapis? D'après vous, le marchand vend un tapis à l'homme assis à côté de lui? Les deux hommes marchandent? Ou est-ce qu'ils parlent d'autres choses?*

INDEPENDENT PRACTICE

Assign any of the following:
1. Exercises and activities, pages 360–361
2. Workbook, *Mots 2: D–E,* pages 156–157
3. Communication Activities Masters, *Mots 2: C–D,* pages 92–93
4. Computer Software, *Vocabulaire*
5. CD-ROM, Disc 4, pages 358–361

STRUCTURE

Structure Teaching Resources

1. Workbook, *Structure: A–F,* pages 158–159
2. Student Tape Manual, Teacher's Edition, *Structure: A–E,* pages 146–148
3. Audio Cassette 8B/CD-7
4. Communication Activities Masters, *Structure: A–C,* pages 94–95
5. Computer Software, *Structure*
6. Chapter Quizzes, *Structure:* Quizzes 3–5, pages 74–76
7. CD-ROM, Disc 4, pages 362–365

Bell Ringer Review

Write the following on the board or use BRR Blackline Master 14-4: Complete the following sentences:

1. J'ai peur que...
2. Luc est désolé que...
3. Anne est surprise que...
4. Je suis content(e) que...
5. Je suis fâché(e) que...

Le subjonctif avec les expressions de doute

PRESENTATION *(page 362)*

Have the students read the model sentences aloud.

Note In the CD-ROM version, this structure point is presented via an interactive electronic comic strip.

Exercices

PRESENTATION *(pages 362-363)*

Exercice A

Exercise A can be done with books open or closed.

Extension of *Exercice B*

After completing Exercise B, have a student describe the Sahara in his/her own words.

362

Le subjonctif avec les expressions de doute

Expressing Doubt or Uncertainty

1. In French, any verb or expression that implies doubt, uncertainty, or disbelief about present and future actions is followed by the present subjunctive.

> Je doute
> Je ne pense pas
> Je ne crois pas
> Je ne suis pas sûr(e)
> Je ne suis pas certain(e) ⎬ qu'ils soient là.
> Ça m'étonnerait
> Il n'est pas évident
> Il n'est pas sûr
> Il n'est pas certain

2. Note that many verbs or expressions of uncertainty or disbelief are actually expressions of certainty or belief in the negative. Expressions of certainty or belief are followed by the indicative. Compare the following pairs of sentences:

CERTAINTY → INDICATIVE

Je suis sûr qu'ils partiront.
Je crois qu'elle est musulmane.
Il est certain qu'il fera beau.
Il est probable que j'irai au Maroc.

UNCERTAINTY → SUBJUNCTIVE

Je ne suis pas sûr qu'ils partent.
Je ne crois pas qu'elle soit musulmane.
Il n'est pas certain qu'il fasse beau.
Il est peu probable que j'aille au Maroc.

Exercices

A **Tu en doutes?** Répondez.

1. Tu doutes que je connaisse le Maghreb?
2. Tu doutes que je fasse un voyage au Maghreb l'année prochaine?
3. Tu doutes que j'aille en Tunisie?
4. Tu doutes que je sache faire le thé à la menthe?
5. Tu doutes que j'aie une amie tunisienne.

La baie de Hammamet, en Tunisie

362   CHAPITRE 14

B Le désert du Sahara. Répondez.

1. Tu crois que le Sahara est le plus grand désert du monde?
2. Tu crois que le Sahara est en Afrique?
3. Tu crois qu'il fait toujours chaud au Sahara?
4. Tu crois qu'il y fait du vent?
5. Tu crois qu'il y a des oasis?
6. Tu crois que la vie au Sahara est difficile?

C La géographie, ça n'est pas mon fort! Complétez.

1. Je doute que le Sahara ___ en Amérique. (être)
2. Je crois que le Sahara ___ en Afrique. (être)
3. Je ne suis pas sûr(e) que le Sahara ___ le plus vaste désert du monde. (être)
4. Moi, je crois que oui. Je suis certain(e) que c'___ le plus vaste désert du monde. (être)
5. Je crois que le Sahara ___ de l'océan Atlantique à la mer Rouge. (s'étendre)
6. Je ne pense pas qu'il y ___ beaucoup d'oasis. (avoir)
7. Ça m'étonnerait qu'on ___ encore rencontrer beaucoup de chameaux au Sahara. (pouvoir)
8. Il est certain qu'il y ___ beaucoup de palmiers dans les oasis. (avoir)

Une vieille carte postale: vue du Sahara

D Certain ou pas? Commencez par les expressions indiquées.

1. La capitale de la Tunisie est Tunis. (Je crois)
2. Tunis est une grande ville cosmopolite. (Il est probable)
3. Tunis a une médina. (Il est certain)
4. La médina de Tunis a de très grands souks. (Je ne doute pas)
5. Les marchés arabes s'appellent des souks. (Je crois)
6. Tunis a de jolies banlieues. (Je doute)
7. Vous n'avez pas raison. (Je suis certain[e])
8. Carthage et Sidi-Bou-Saïd sont de très jolis villages de la banlieue de Tunis. (Je suis sûr[e])
9. Nous allons faire un voyage en Tunisie. (Je crois)
10. J'y vais. (Moi, ça m'étonnerait)
11. Il y va. (Il est peu probable)

CHAPITRE 14   **363**

ANSWERS

Exercice A

1. Oui, je doute que tu connaisses le Maghreb.
2. Oui, je doute que tu fasses un voyage au Maghreb l'année prochaine.
3. Oui, je doute que tu ailles en Tunisie.
4. Oui, je doute que tu saches faire le thé à la menthe.
5. Oui, je doute que tu aies une amie tunisienne.

Exercice B

1. Oui, je crois que le Sahara est le plus grand désert du monde.
2. Oui, je crois que le Sahara est en Afrique.
3. Oui, je crois qu'il fait toujours chaud au Sahara.
4. Oui, je crois qu'il y fait du vent.
5. Oui, je crois qu'il y a des oasis.
6. Oui, je crois que la vie au Sahara est difficile.

Exercice C

1. soit	5. s'étend
2. est	6. ait
3. soit	7. puisse
4. est	8. a

Exercice D

1. Je crois que la capitale de la Tunisie est Tunis.
2. Il est probable que Tunis est une grande ville cosmopolite.
3. Il est certain que Tunis a une médina.
4. Je ne doute pas que la médina de Tunis a de très grands souks.
5. Je crois que les marchés arabes s'appellent des souks.
6. Je doute que Tunis ait de jolies banlieues.
7. Je suis certain(e) que vous n'avez pas raison.
8. Je suis sûr(e) que Carthage et Sidi-Bou-Saïd sont de très jolis villages de la banlieue de Tunis.
9. Je crois que nous allons faire un voyage en Tunisie.
10. Moi, ça m'étonnerait que j'y aille.
11. Il est peu probable qu'il y aille.

Les expressions il me semble que *et* il paraît que

PRESENTATION *(page 364)*

Go over the explanation with the students. Then have them read the model sentences aloud.

Exercice

PRESENTATION *(page 364)*

Exercise A can be done with books open or closed.

ANSWERS

Exercice A

1. Je crois que tu as raison. Il me semble qu'elle est malade.
2. Je crois que tu as raison. Il me semble qu'elle perd des kilos.
3. Je crois que tu as raison. Il me semble qu'elle maigrit.
4. Je crois que tu as raison. Il me semble qu'elle a toujours l'air triste.
5. Je crois que tu as raison. Il me semble qu'elle n'a pas envie de travailler.
6. Je crois que tu as raison. Il me semble qu'elle n'a aucune énergie.

L'infinitif après les prépositions

PRESENTATION *(page 364)*

Have students read the model sentences aloud.

Les expressions *il me semble que et il paraît que* — Telling What People or Things Seem to Be Like

Note that *il paraît que* and *il me semble que* (or *il lui semble que, il vous semble que,* etc.) are followed by the indicative. Study the following.

> **Il paraît qu'elle va passer ses vacances au Maroc.**
> *Apparently, she's going to spend her vacation in Morocco.*
>
> **Il me semble qu'elle va souvent au Maroc.**
> *It seems to me that she goes to Morocco often.*

Exercice

A **Elle est malade.** Répondez d'après le modèle.

> **Il paraît qu'elle est malade.**
> *Je crois que tu as raison. Il me semble qu'elle est malade.*

1. Il paraît qu'elle est malade.
2. Il paraît qu'elle perd des kilos.
3. Il paraît qu'elle maigrit.
4. Il paraît qu'elle a toujours l'air triste.
5. Il paraît qu'elle n'a pas envie de travailler.
6. Il paraît qu'elle n'a aucune énergie.

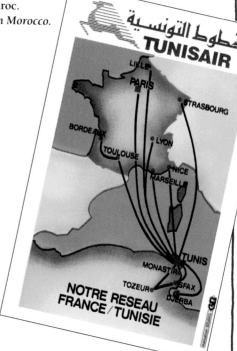

L'infinitif après les prépositions — Describing Two Related Activities

1. You have already used the infinitive form of the verb in several constructions. Review the following.

> Jacqueline va *faire* une petite excursion à Carthage.
> Elle aime *visiter* les sites archéologiques.
> Elle pense y *aller* demain.

2. You also use the infinitive form of the verb after a preposition in French. Study the following.

> Elle est allée au souk *pour faire* des achats.
> *Avant d'aller* au souk elle est allée à la banque.
> Elle y est allée *pour changer* de l'argent.
> Elle ne peut rien acheter *sans payer.*

364 CHAPITRE 14

Exercices

A En Tunisie! Répondez.

1. Elle est allée à l'agence de voyage pour prendre ses billets?
2. Elle y est allée avant de partir pour l'aéroport?
3. Elle est partie sans dire «au revoir»?
4. Elle a voyagé en Tunisie sans parler arabe?
5. Elle a visité Tunis et ses environs avant d'aller à Tozeur?
6. Elle est allée à Tozeur pour voir les chotts?

B Une étudiante sérieuse. Répondez d'après le modèle.

> Elle fait ses devoirs. Ensuite elle regarde la télé.
> *Elle fait ses devoirs avant de regarder la télé.*

1. Elle fait ses devoirs. Ensuite elle téléphone à ses copains.
2. Elle fait ses devoirs. Ensuite elle écoute des cassettes.
3. Elle fait ses devoirs. Ensuite elle regarde une vidéo.
4. Elle fait ses devoirs. Ensuite elle sort.
5. Elle fait ses devoirs. Ensuite elle lit un magazine.

C Pourquoi faire des études? Répondez d'après le modèle.

> Nous étudions parce que nous voulons apprendre.
> *Nous étudions pour apprendre.*

1. Nous étudions parce que nous voulons réussir.
2. Nous étudions parce que nous voulons avoir de bonnes notes.
3. Nous étudions parce que nous voulons trouver un bon travail.
4. Nous étudions parce que nous voulons apprendre.
5. Nous étudions parce que nous voulons obtenir notre diplôme.

Le chott El Fedjadj en Tunisie

CHAPITRE 14 **365**

Bell Ringer Review

Write the following on the board or use BRR Blackline Master 14-6: Complete each sentence with the correct form of the verb in parentheses.

1. Il n'est pas évident que tu ____ venir. (pouvoir)
2. Il faut que vous ____ conduire. (savoir)
3. Ça m'étonnerait que tu ____ Tom Cruise! (connaître)
4. Mes parents veulent que je ____ nager. (savoir)
5. Il est important que vous ____ réussir. (vouloir)

PRESENTATION (page 366)

A. Have students close their books. Play the Conversation Video or have them repeat the conversation once after you or Cassette 8B/CD-7. (Use *Activité E* in the Student Tape Manual to check oral comprehension.)
B. Call on two students to read the conversation with as much expression as possible.

Note Explain to students that *avoir une faim de loup* is a colloquial expression meaning *avoir très faim.*

Note In the CD-ROM version, students can play the role of either one of the characters and record the conversation.

Exercices

ANSWERS

Exercice A

1. Je pense qu'elle est française.
2. Marc est américain.
3. Oui, ils ont faim.
4. Lisette connaît la cuisine tunisienne.
5. Marc ne la connaît pas.
6. Oui, ils vont aller à un restaurant tunisien.

Scènes de la vie *Allons dîner à la tunisienne!*

LISETTE: J'ai faim.
MARC: Moi aussi, j'ai une faim de loup.
LISETTE: Tu veux manger tunisien? Ah, zut! J'ai oublié. Toi, l'Américain, ça m'étonnerait que tu connaisses la cuisine tunisienne.
MARC: Ça t'étonnerait que je la connaisse? Tout juste! Je ne la connais pas.
LISETTE: Mais je suis sûre que tu aimeras ça. On va commander un bon couscous.
MARC: Qu'est-ce que tu as dit? Un «cou» quoi?
LISETTE: Un couscous. Répète, *couscous.*
MARC: Couscous. Mais c'est quoi, un couscous?
LISETTE: C'est de la semoule de blé servie avec de la viande, des légumes et une sauce un peu piquante. C'est délicieux!

A **Où vont-ils dîner?** Répondez d'après la conversation.

1. Lisette est française ou américaine? Qu'est-ce que vous en pensez?
2. Et Marc, il est américain ou français?
3. Ils ont faim?
4. Qui connaît la cuisine tunisienne?
5. Qui ne la connaît pas?
6. Ils vont aller à un restaurant tunisien?
7. Vous pensez qu'ils vont en Tunisie pour dîner?
8. Qu'est-ce qu'ils vont commander?
9. Qu'est-ce qu'un couscous?
10. Vous connaissez la cuisine tunisienne?

B **Langage familier.** Dites d'une façon plus familière.

1. J'ai très faim.
2. Je vais aller à un restaurant tunisien.

LEARNING FROM PHOTOS

You may wish to explain to students that both Tunisian and Moroccan restaurants are very popular in France. Have students say as much as they can about the photos.

Activités de communication orale

Sophie

A **En Tunisie.** Vous venez de rentrer d'un voyage en Tunisie. Votre amie Sophie, qui va bientôt y aller aussi, voudrait des renseignements. Répondez à ses questions.

1. On utilise quelle monnaie en Tunisie?
2. Où est-ce que je devrais aller pour acheter des objets en cuir?
3. Qu'est-ce que je devrais manger?
4. Qu'est-ce qu'il y a dans un couscous?

B **Connaissez-vous le Maghreb?** Parmi les affirmations suivantes, certaines sont exactes et certaines sont fausses. Discutez-en avec un(e) camarade.

1. Le Sahara est le plus grand désert du monde.
2. Casablanca est en Algérie.
3. L'Algérie a 22.600.000 habitants.
4. La Mecque est en Arabie Saoudite.
5. Les chotts se trouvent dans les grandes villes maghrébines.
6. La baie de Hammamet est au Maroc.

> Élève 1: Je crois que c'est vrai que le Sahara est le plus grand désert du monde.
> Élève 2: Moi, je ne suis pas sûr(e) que ce soit vrai, mais je ne sais pas la bonne réponse.

C **À votre avis.** Voici une liste de sujets. Avec votre camarade, discutez de ces sujets en utilisant «je pense» ou «je crois» et «je ne pense pas» ou «je ne crois pas».

1. Les cheveux longs sont plus jolis que les cheveux courts.
2. Les cours facultatifs sont plus intéressants que les cours obligatoires.
3. La technologie cause la pollution.
4. Les médias ont une bonne influence sur les jeunes.
5. Les jeunes d'aujourd'hui sont mal élevés.
6. La musique rock est meilleure que la musique classique.

B. 1. Vrai.
2. Faux. (Casablanca est au Maroc.)
3. Vrai.
4. Vrai.
5. Faux. (Les chotts se trouvent dans le désert.)
6. Faux. (Voir la photo à la page 362.)

---

7. Non, je ne pense pas qu'ils aillent en Tunisie pour dîner.
8. Ils vont commander un couscous.
9. C'est de la semoule de blé servie avec de la viande, des légumes et une sauce un peu piquante.
10. Oui (Non), je (ne) connais (pas) la cuisine tunisienne.

Exercice B
1. J'ai une faim de loup.
2. Je vais manger tunisien.

Activités de communication orale

PRESENTATION *(page 367)*

You may wish to allow students to select the activities they would like to do.

Activité A

In the CD-ROM version of this activity, students can interact with an on-screen native speaker.

ANSWERS

Activités A and C
Answers will vary.

Activité B
Note The correct answers to the false statements appear at the bottom of the student page.

INDEPENDENT PRACTICE

Assign any of the following:
1. Exercises and activities, pages 366–367
2. CD-ROM, Disc 4, pages 366–367

LECTURE ET CULTURE

READING STRATEGIES
(pages 368–369)

Pre-reading

Give students a brief oral review of the reading in French.

Reading

A. Read a paragraph to students as they follow along in their books.

B. Call on an individual to read three or four sentences.

C. Ask your own questions concerning the sentences just read by the student or use the questions in Exercise B on page 370. Call on other students to respond. Continue in this way until the selection has been completed.

D. Have the students read the selection for homework.

Post-reading

Assign the *Étude de mots* and *Compréhension* exercises to be written for homework.

Note Students may listen to a recorded version of the *Lecture* on the CD-ROM.

UNE MAGHRÉBINE VOUS PARLE

*B*onjour, mes amis! Je m'appelle Farida Ashour. Je suis Maghrébine. C'est-à-dire que je suis du Maghreb. Je doute que vous connaissiez le Maghreb. Il est possible que vous ne sachiez même pas où ça se trouve. En arabe, le Maghreb veut dire «là où le soleil se couche». C'est le nom qu'on donne aux trois pays d'Afrique du Nord: Maroc, Algérie et Tunisie. Moi, je suis tunisienne et comme les Marocains et les Algériens, je parle arabe et français.

Pourquoi le français? Parce que la Tunisie, l'Algérie et le Maroc étaient, il n'y a pas encore si longtemps, des colonies françaises. Elles sont devenues indépendantes entre 1955 et 1962, et l'influence française est encore très forte. Par exemple, tous les enfants du Maghreb apprennent le français comme deuxième langue dès l'école primaire.

Comme je vous l'ai dit, je suis tunisienne. Je suis de Tunis, notre capitale. Je fais des études universitaires à Tunis. Ma sœur est agent de police. Et vous savez que je vous parle d'un pays islamique. Dans certains pays islamiques, les femmes ne peuvent pas sortir dans la rue sans être voilées. Vous verrez de temps en temps des femmes voilées en Tunisie mais la plupart des Tunisiennes ne portent pas le voile. Notre ancien président, M. Bourguiba, a insisté sur l'émancipation des femmes.

Presque toutes les écoles en Tunisie sont mixtes, et beaucoup de femmes vont à l'université et participent à la vie active. Bourguiba a aboli la polygamie en 1960. Mais encore aujourd'hui, il n'est pas rare qu'un jeune couple ne se connaisse pas avant de se marier. Ce sont les familles des mariés qui organisent et décident le mariage. Ça commence à changer un peu, mais le «dating» tel que[1] vous le connaissez n'existe pas chez nous.

La plupart des Tunisiens sont musulmans; par conséquent, nous ne mangeons pas de porc et nous ne buvons pas d'alcool. Les hommes prient cinq fois par jour vers la Mecque, la

---

[1] tel que *as*

Marrakech: la place Djemaa-el-Fna

Des artisans dans un atelier au Maroc

ville sainte[2] des musulmans. Nous n'avons pas de clergé, mais nous avons des imams ou guides religieux qui interprètent le Coran. Si vous nous rendez visite en Tunisie, vous entendrez le muezzin appeler à la prière du haut du minaret de nos mosquées.

Je vous ai dit que les Tunisiennes ne portent pas le voile. Mais si vous allez dans les souks de Tunis vous verrez beaucoup de femmes en sifsari. Le sifsari est une sorte de voile ou très grand châle en tissu blanc. Il est très ample et la femme s'enveloppe dedans. La plupart du temps, le sifsari couvre la tête et le corps, mais laisse le visage à découvert[3].

Toutefois[4], certaines femmes utilisent le sifsari pour se couvrir une partie du visage.

Vous me demandez ce que c'est qu'un souk? Un souk est un marché arabe couvert. Il y a beaucoup de ruelles dans un souk. De chaque côté de ces ruelles il y a de petites boutiques et ateliers qui offrent tous les mêmes produits. Ainsi[5] il y a le souk des maroquiniers, qui vendent toutes sortes d'objets en cuir. Quand on se promène dans les souks, il faut faire attention, car il est très facile de se perdre dans ces ruelles. Mais je vous assure qu'il n'est pas dangereux de se promener dans les souks et que c'est vraiment fascinant. Et puis si vous savez marchander, vous vous amuserez bien.

Pour trouver les souks, il faut aller dans la médina. La médina est la partie ancienne de nos villes et on l'appelle souvent le quartier arabe pour le différencier des quartiers récents d'origine européenne.

[2] sainte   *holy*
[3] à découvert   *exposed, uncovered*
[4] toutefois   *still, nevertheless*
[5] ainsi   *thus*

Étude de mots

A **Qu'est-ce qui va ensemble?** Choisissez le contraire.

1. le soleil se couche
2. le nord
3. une colonie
4. l'école primaire
5. boire
6. une ruelle

a. l'école secondaire
b. un boulevard
c. le soleil se lève
d. manger
e. le sud
f. un pays indépendant

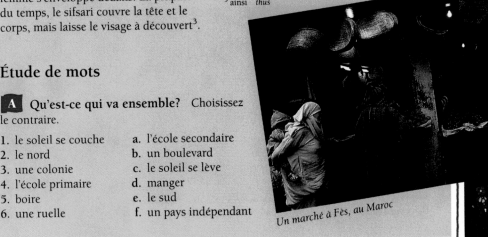

Un marché à Fès, au Maroc

ANSWERS

Exercice A

1. c
2. e
3. f
4. a
5. d
6. b

THE FRANCOPHONE WORLD

Fès, or Fez, is a commerical and religious center on the trade routes linking the Atlantic Ocean and the Mediterranean Sea. A Moroccan ruler, Idris II, founded the city as his capital in 808 and built its famous Mosque of Mulai Idris. The city is also home to one of the oldest universities in the world, Karaouiyine University, founded in 859.

The fez, a brimless, cylindrical red hat that is worn by eastern Mediterranean men, takes its name from this city.

Compréhension

PRESENTATION (page 370)

Exercice B

You may ask the questions in this exercise as you are going over the reading selection.

Exercice C

You may wish to allow the students to look up the information for Exercise C in the *Lecture*, or you may expect them to produce it from memory.

ANSWERS

Exercice B

1. Elle s'appelle Farida Ashour.
2. Elle est du Maghreb (de Tunisie).
3. Le Maghreb est en Afrique du Nord.
4. Elle est tunisienne.
5. Elle est musulmane.
6. Sa première langue est l'arabe.
7. Sa deuxième langue est le français.
8. Elle fait ses études à Tunis.

Exercice C

1. le Maroc, l'Algérie, la Tunisie
2. Tunis
3. l'arabe
4. le français
5. l'Islam
6. M. Bourguiba
7. un souk
8. la médina
9. une mosquée
10. le muezzin

Exercice D

1. La plupart des Tunisiennes ne sont pas voilées.
2. Oui.
3. Oui.
4. Le grand livre religieux des musulmans est le Coran.
5. La médina est la partie ancienne d'une ville du Maghreb.
6. La médina est toujours d'origine arabe.

Compréhension

B **Farida.** Répondez d'après la lecture.

1. Comment s'appelle la jeune fille qui nous parle?
2. Elle est d'où?
3. Où est le Maghreb?
4. Quelle est sa nationalité?
5. Quelle est sa religion?
6. Quelle est sa première langue?
7. Quelle est sa deuxième langue?
8. Où fait-elle ses études?

C **Des renseignements.** Trouvez les renseignements suivants dans la lecture.

1. les trois pays du Maghreb
2. la capitale de la Tunisie
3. la langue officielle des pays du Maghreb
4. la deuxième langue étudiée à l'école
5. la religion officielle des pays du Maghreb
6. le nom du président de la Tunisie de 1957 à 1987
7. un marché arabe couvert
8. le quartier ancien d'une ville du Maghreb
9. un édifice religieux islamique
10. l'homme qui appelle à la prière du haut du minaret

D **Oui ou non?** Corrigez les phrases fausses.

1. La plupart des Tunisiennes sont voilées.
2. Les mosquées ont des minarets.
3. L'Islam n'a pas de clergé.
4. Le grand livre religieux des musulmans est la Bible.
5. La médina est la partie moderne d'une ville du Maghreb.
6. La médina est toujours d'origine européenne.

Deux vues du Sahara: un mirage et un couple à dos de chameau

DÉCOUVERTE CULTURELLE

Un hammam est un bain turc. Pour obéir à leur religion, les musulmans doivent aller une fois par semaine au hammam.

Les femmes maghrébines qui n'habitent pas dans des maisons modernes font la cuisine sur des «canouns». Ce sont de petits braséros en terre cuite qui contiennent du charbon de bois.

Les pays du Maghreb ne sont pas industrialisés. Ce sont tous des pays en voie de développement. Comme dans tous les pays en voie de développement, le chômage[1] est un problème sérieux. Il y a des gens qui cherchent du travail sans pouvoir en trouver. À cause du chômage, beaucoup de Maghrébins émigrent en France pour y chercher du travail. Les Maghrébins constituent le plus grand groupe de travailleurs immigrés en France.

Le Sahara tunisien commence par les chotts. Les chotts sont des lacs salés en hiver qui se recouvrent d'une croûte de sel en été. Les chotts sont spectaculaires car l'été, ils scintillent[2] et créent des mirages. Il est très facile de se perdre dans les chotts car on croit qu'on voit un

Ruines romaines à Carthage, en Tunisie

village quand en fait il n'y a rien. Ce n'est qu'un mirage. Et entre les chotts et les dunes de sable, il y a des oasis qui sont comme de petites îles fertiles dans le désert. On y trouve de l'eau et des palmiers, et des hommes qui cultivent les palmeraies avec l'aide de leurs chameaux.

Au 9e siècle avant Jésus-Christ, la reine[3] phénicienne Didon fonde Carthage. Carthage devient la capitale d'une grande république maritime. Au 3e siècle avant Jésus-Christ, les guerres puniques opposent Rome et Carthage. Aujourd'hui Carthage est une très jolie banlieue de Tunis. Beaucoup de gens aisés qui travaillent à Tunis y habitent. La partie de Carthage où se trouvent les ruines les plus importantes a été déclarée parc archéologique national.

[1] chômage   *unemployment*
[2] scintillent   *glitter*
[3] reine   *queen*

Le marché de Ghardaïa en Algérie

OPTIONAL MATERIAL

Découverte culturelle

PRESENTATION *(page 371)*

You may wish to have students look once again at the photographs in this chapter that depict aspects of the Maghreb that are described in this section.

Note Students may listen to a recorded version of the *Découverte culturelle* on the CD-ROM.

THE FRANCOPHONE WORLD

Roman Carthage was the third largest city in the empire after Rome and Alexandria. The city was enclosed by ramparts; a second protective wall enclosed the citadel and its temple. Multi-story houses stood in the center of town, and villas on the outskirts. Water for large public baths was supplied by aqueduct. The theater held 10,000 people, and the amphitheater 35,000. Today one can visit the museum and admire a beautiful collection of ceramics, masks, statuettes, amulets, and ivory objects.

The Carthage Festival, an international art festival, is held annually at the ancient ruins.

INDEPENDENT PRACTICE

Assign any of the following:
1. *Étude de mots* and *Compréhension* exercises, pages 369–370
2. Workbook, *Un Peu Plus*, pages 160–163
3. CD-ROM, Disc 4, pages 368–371

RÉALITÉS

Regardez ces belles montagnes enneigées au Maroc, près de Marrakech **1**. Ce sont les montagnes du Haut-Atlas. La plus haute montagne de l'Afrique du Nord se trouve dans le Haut-Atlas: il s'agit du djebel Toubkal (4165 m).

Voici le port d'Alger sur la Méditerranée **2**. Alger est le premier port du Maghreb.

Les ruines romaines à Tipasa en Algérie **3**. Cette ville est située sur la Méditerranée.

C'est une palmeraie à Ghardaïa, une oasis en Algérie **4**.

Voici la Mosquée de Paris dans le 5ème arrondissement **5**. Cette mosquée est fréquentée par les Maghrébins de Paris.

HISTORY CONNECTION

For more information about the French involvement in Algeria and the Algerian War for Independence, you may wish to refer students to the reading about De Gaulle in *Lettres et sciences*, pages 426–427.

373

DID YOU KNOW?

Near the Jardin des Plantes in Paris is the Paris Mosque, a beautiful white mosque complete with minaret. Some sections are open to the public: the sunken gardens and tiled patios, the *hammams,* or Turkish baths (men and women visit on different days), and the restaurant serving couscous and mint tea. The prayer rooms are closed to the public.

ADDITIONAL PRACTICE

Assign any of the following:
1. Student Tape Manual, Teacher's Edition, *Deuxième Partie*, pages 148–150
2. Situation Cards, Chapter 14

RECYCLING

These activities encourage students to use all the language they have learned in the chapter and recombine it with material from previous chapters. It is not necessary to do all the activities with all students. You may select the ones you consider most appropriate or permit students to choose the ones they wish to do.

INFORMAL ASSESSMENT

The *Activités de communication orale* lend themselves to assessing speaking and listening abilities. For guidelines on assigning an oral grade, see the evaluation criteria given on page 22 of this Teacher's Wraparound Edition.

Activités de communication orale

PRESENTATION *(page 374)*

Activité A

Before assigning *Activité A,* you may wish to do the **Communities** activity suggested below.

Extension of *Activité B*

Have students write invitations to the North African dinner in French and send them to the other classes.

ANSWERS

Activité A

Answers will vary.

Activités de communication écrite

PRESENTATION *(page 374)*

Before assigning the written activities, you may wish to do the **Communities** activity suggested below.

ANSWERS

Activités A and B

Answers will vary.

374

Activités de communication orale

A **Un voyage en Tunisie.** Travaillez avec un(e) camarade. Vous êtes agent de voyage. Votre client(e) (votre camarade) veut faire un voyage en Tunisie. Dites ce qu'il faut absolument qu'il/elle fasse pendant son voyage. Votre camarade peut être d'accord avec vous ou non. Faites plusieurs recommandations.

> Élève 1: Il faut absolument que vous visitiez un marché couvert.
> Élève 2: Oui, je voudrais bien voir un marché couvert.
> Élève 1: Il faut absolument que vous mangiez un couscous.
> Élève 2: Merci, mais je n'aime pas le couscous.

B **Un dîner maghrébin.** Avec vos camarades, préparez un couscous et d'autres plats maghrébins à la maison. (Voir la recette «Couscous marocain aux sept légumes» à la page 148 du Student Tape Manual Teacher's Edition.) Apportez ces plats à l'école. Invitez d'autres classes de français à les manger avec vous. Si possible, essayez de trouver de la musique nord-africaine à jouer pendant le dîner. N'oubliez pas de parler français.

Activités de communication écrite

A **Mon journal.** Vous revenez d'un voyage au Maghreb. Décrivez ce que vous avez vu, mangé et observé.

B **Des comparaisons.** Écrivez une lettre à un(e) ami(e) en comparant le climat, le paysage, la vie, la nourriture, les vêtements et les villes du Maghreb et ceux de votre pays. Quelles en sont les différences?

Une porte dans les remparts de Fès, au Maroc

374 CHAPITRE 14

COMMUNITIES

Invite a French-speaking person from North Africa to your class to talk about life in his/her country, or ask a local travel agent to show slides, films, or brochures about North Africa to the class.

STUDENT PORTFOLIO

Written assignments which may be included in students' portfolios are the *Activités de communication écrite* on page 374 and any writing activities from the *Un Peu Plus* section in the Workbook.

Note Students may create and save both oral and written work using the Electronic Portfolio feature on the CD-ROM.

Réintroduction et recombinaison

A **Le dernier film que tu as vu.** Répondez en utilisant un pronom.

1. Tu as aimé le film?
2. Tu as vu le film hier soir?
3. Tu es allé(e) au cinéma avec qui?
4. Tu as lu les sous-titres?
5. Tu as compris le dialogue?
6. Tu as vu la vedette?
7. Tu as admiré les costumes?

B **Un peu de géographie.** Complétez avec une préposition.

1. Je veux aller ___ Tunisie.
2. La Tunisie est ___ Afrique.
3. On peut aller ___ France ___ Tunisie en avion ou en bateau.
4. Je voudrais bien aller aussi ___ Maroc.
5. Tu vas aller ___ Rabat, la capitale ___ Maroc?
6. Tunis est la capitale ___ Tunisie.

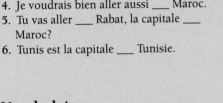

Vocabulaire

NOMS
l'Afrique (f.)
le Maghreb
le Maroc
l'Algérie (f.)
la Tunisie
la Mecque
le Sahara

le désert
le soleil
le sable
la dune
le chott
le lac salé
la croûte de sel

l'oasis (f.)
la palmeraie
la plantation
le palmier

la datte
la figue
le chameau
la caravane

les musulmans (m.)
la mosquée
le minaret
le muezzin
le hammam
le bain turc
le voile
le châle

la médina
le souk
le marché arabe couvert
la ruelle
l'atelier (m.)
le maroquinier
l'objet (m.) en cuir

le dinar
le thé à la menthe
le braséro
le charbon de bois

le couscous
la semoule de blé
l'agneau (m.)
l'aubergine (f.)
la courgette
les raisins secs
la sauce piquante

ADJECTIFS
maghrébin(e)
tunisien(ne)
salé(e)

VERBES
marchander
s'envelopper

prier
douter

AUTRES MOTS ET EXPRESSIONS
il paraît
il me (te, lui, etc.) semble
il est certain
il est sûr
il est évident
ça m'étonnerait
être sûr(e)
être certain(e)
faire cuire

CHAPITRE 14   **375**

INDEPENDENT PRACTICE

Assign any of the following:
1. Activities and exercises, pages 374–375
2. Communication Activities Masters, pages 90–95
3. CD-ROM, Disc 4, pages 374–375

Réintroduction et recombinaison

PRESENTATION *(page 375)*

Exercise A reviews the *passé composé* of verbs with *être* and *avoir*. This review prepares students for the past subjunctive in the next chapter. Exercise B reviews prepositions with countries and cities.

Exercices

ANSWERS

Exercice A

1. Oui (Non), je (ne) l'ai (pas) aimé.
2. Oui (Non), je (ne) l'ai (pas) vu hier soir.
3. J'y suis allé(e) avec (mes amis).
4. Oui (Non), je (ne) les ai (pas) lus.
5. Oui (Non), je (ne) l'ai (pas) compris.
6. Oui (Non), je (ne) l'ai (pas) vue.
7. Oui (Non), je (ne) les ai (pas) admirés.

Exercice B

1. en   4. au
2. en   5. à, du
3. de, en   6. de la

ASSESSMENT RESOURCES

1. Chapter Quizzes
2. Testing Program
3. Situation Cards
4. Communication Transparency C-14
5. Computer Software: Practice/Test Generator

VIDEO PROGRAM

INTRODUCTION   (48:35)

VIVE LA DIFFÉRENCE!   (49:09)

CHAPTER OVERVIEW

In this chapter students will learn to talk about life on a farm. Students will also learn the past subjunctive and the use of the subjunctive after certain conjunctions.

The cultural focus of the chapter is on agriculture in France and some of the problems confronting the French farmer today.

CHAPTER OBJECTIVES

By the end of this chapter students will know:

1. vocabulary associated with farming and country life
2. vocabulary associated with farm animals and the sounds they make
3. the forms and uses of the past subjunctive
4. the use of the subjunctive after certain conjunctions

CHAPTER 15 RESOURCES

1. Workbook
2. Student Tape Manual
3. Audio Cassette 9A/CD-8
4. Bell Ringer Review Blackline Masters
5. Vocabulary Transparencies
6. Communication Transparency C-15
7. Communication Activities Masters
8. Situation Cards
9. Conversation Video
10. Videocassette/Videodisc, Unit 4
11. Video Activities Booklet, Unit 4
12. Lesson Plans
13. Computer Software: Practice/Test Generator
14. Chapter Quizzes
15. Testing Program
16. Internet Activities Booklet
17. CD-ROM Interactive Textbook
18. Map Transparencies

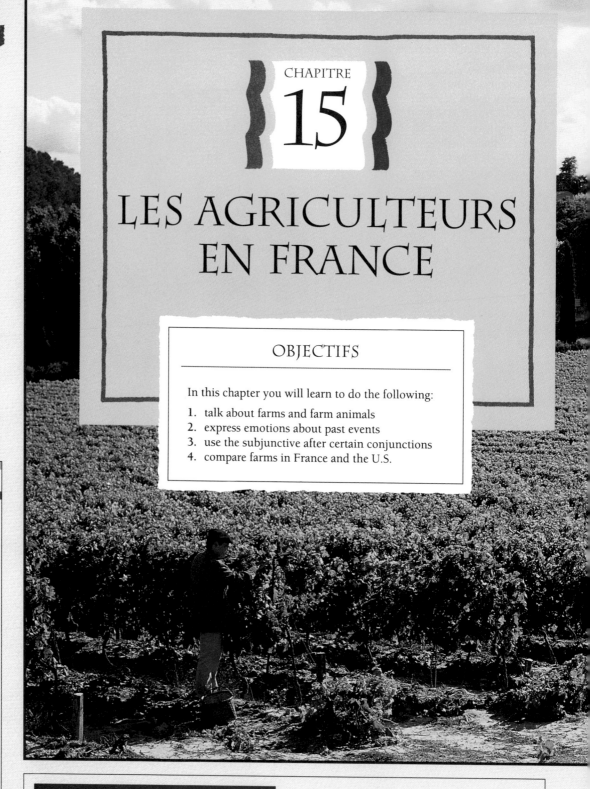

CHAPITRE

15

LES AGRICULTEURS EN FRANCE

OBJECTIFS

In this chapter you will learn to do the following:

1. talk about farms and farm animals
2. express emotions about past events
3. use the subjunctive after certain conjunctions
4. compare farms in France and the U.S.

CHAPTER PROJECTS

(optional)

Have students make a large map of France. Ask students to bring in pictures of French food products from magazines and have them glue them in the appropriate region on the map.

Pacing
This chapter will require eight to ten class sessions. Pacing will depend on the length of the class, the age of the students, and student aptitude.

For more information on planning your class, see the Lesson Plans, which offer guidelines for 45- and 55-minute classes and **Block Scheduling**.

Note It is recommended that the degree of thoroughness with which you present this chapter be determined by how interested your students are in farming, agriculture, and animals.

Exercices vs. *Activités*

The exercises and activities are color-coded. Exercises, which provide guided practice to prepare students for independent communication, are coded in blue. Communicative activities, which give students opportunities for creative, open-ended expression, are coded in red.

INTERNET ACTIVITIES

(optional)

These activities, student worksheets, and related teacher information are in the *À bord* Internet Activities Booklet and on the Glencoe Foreign Language Home Page at: http://www.glencoe.com/secondary/fl

LEARNING FROM PHOTOS

After presenting the vocabulary in this chapter, have students come back to this page and describe the photo in as much detail as possible.
(The village pictured in the photo is Ansouis, a medieval village in Provence.)

VOCABULAIRE

MOTS 1

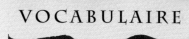

Vocabulary Teaching Resources

1. Vocabulary Transparencies 15.1 (A & B)
2. Audio Cassette 9A/CD-8
3. Student Tape Manual, Teacher's Edition, *Mots 1: A–D*, pages 151–153
4. Workbook, *Mots 1: A–E*, pages 164–166
5. Communication Activities Masters, *Mots 1: A–B*, pages 96–98
6. Chapter Quizzes, *Mots 1:* Quiz 1, page 77
7. CD-ROM, Disc 4, *Mots 1:* pages 378–381

Bell Ringer Review

Write the following on the board or use BRR Blackline Master 15-1: Make a list of the animals you know in French.

PRESENTATION (pages 378–379)

A. You may wish to have students listen to Cassette 9A/CD-8 as you point to each item on Vocabulary Transparencies 15.1 (A & B).

B. Have the students repeat each new word after you at least twice as you point to the illustration on the transparency.

C. Call on students to point to items on the transparencies and identify them with the proper word or expression.

À LA CAMPAGNE

une ferme · un hangar · les bâtiments (m.) · une étable · une grange · du foin · une vache

un champ · un pré · de l'herbe (f.) · un vignoble

le bétail

un troupeau

un mouton

un cheval

un bœuf

un veau

un agneau

une poule

un lapin

un cochon

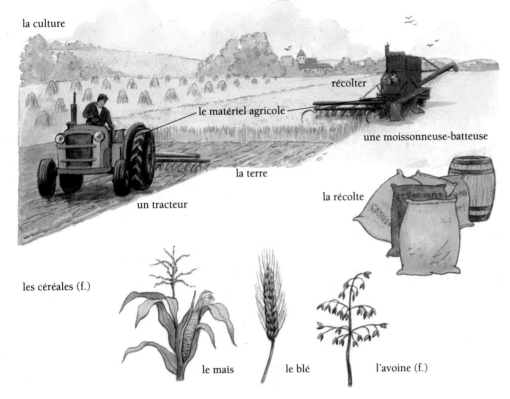

la culture

récolter

le matériel agricole

une moissonneuse-batteuse

la terre

la récolte

un tracteur

les céréales (f.)

le maïs

le blé

l'avoine (f.)

L'élevage est la production et l'entretien des
animaux domestiques, surtout du bétail.
La culture est l'action de cultiver (travailler)
la terre.

CHAPITRE 15   **379**

D. You may wish to ask the following questions about the animals on page 379: *Testez vos connaissances: De tous les animaux que vous voyez sur cette page, lesquels donnent du lait?*

Note Additional animal vocabulary is introduced on page 383 along with the animal sounds.

INFORMAL ASSESSMENT
(Mots 1)

Show the Vocabulary Transparencies, point to items at random, and call on students to identify them.

DID YOU KNOW?

The average French person consumes 72 kilos of bread a year.

Exercices

PRESENTATION (*page 380*)

Exercice A

🎧 You may wish to use the recorded version of this exercise.

ANSWERS

Exercice A

1. un bâtiment
2. un animal
3. un bâtiment
4. un animal
5. un animal
6. un animal
7. un bâtiment
8. un animal
9. un animal
10. un animal

Exercice B

Answers will vary; accept any of the following:

1. Le cheval mange de l'avoine, du maïs, du foin, de l'herbe et des carottes.
2. La poule mange du maïs, du blé et de l'avoine.
3. Le lapin mange des carottes, de la laitue, du maïs et de l'avoine.
4. Le cochon mange du maïs, de l'avoine et du blé.
5. Le mouton mange de l'herbe, du blé, du maïs, de l'avoine et du foin.
6. La vache mange de l'herbe, de l'avoine, du maïs et du foin.

Exercices

Une ferme en Normandie

A Un bâtiment ou un animal? Choisissez.

1. une grange
2. une poule
3. une étable
4. une vache
5. un cochon
6. un lapin
7. un hangar
8. un cheval
9. un veau
10. un agneau

B Ils ont faim! Que mangent les animaux suivants? Choisissez.

Que mange le lapin?
Le lapin mange des carottes.

Point out Normandy on the France Map Transparency or on the map of France on page 435. Tell students that half-timbered buildings with thatched roofs (*un toit de chaume*) are common in this region. As students look at the photos of French farms throughout the chapter, have them pay particular attention to the architecture of the farmhouses.

Student Tape Manual, Teacher's Edition, *Activité D*, page 153

C L'élevage ou la culture? Choisissez.

1. les champs
2. les prés
3. une étable
4. le bétail
5. les céréales
6. les animaux domestiques
7. un troupeau
8. la récolte

D L'agriculture. Répondez.

1. Les fermes se trouvent à la campagne ou à la ville?
2. L'agriculture moderne emploie des chevaux et bœufs ou des tracteurs et des moissonneuses-batteuses?
3. Les animaux qui sont gardés ensemble forment une étable ou un troupeau?
4. On met le matériel agricole dans un hangar ou une grange?
5. On met la récolte dans la grange ou l'étable?
6. Les vignobles produisent des céréales ou du raisin pour le vin?
7. La culture est l'action de cultiver la terre ou la production et l'entretien des animaux domestiques?
8. On récolte le blé avec des moissonneuses-batteuses ou avec des tracteurs?

Des vignobles dans le Midi

Exercices
PRESENTATION *(continued)*
Exercice C

🎧 You may wish to use the recorded version of this exercise.

Exercice D

Have the students answer the questions with complete sentences.

ANSWERS
Exercice C

1. la culture
2. l'élevage
3. l'élevage
4. l'élevage
5. la culture
6. l'élevage
7. l'élevage
8. la culture

Exercice D

1. Les fermes se trouvent à la campagne.
2. L'agriculture moderne emploie des tracteurs et des moissonneuses-batteuses.
3. Les animaux qui sont gardés ensemble forment un troupeau.
4. On met le matériel agricole dans un hangar.
5. On met la récolte dans la grange.
6. Les vignobles produisent du raisin pour le vin.
7. La culture est l'action de cultiver la terre.
8. On récolte le blé avec des moissonneuses-batteuses.

LEARNING FROM PHOTOS

Explain to students: *Le Midi, c'est le sud de la France.* Have them say as much as they can about the photos.

INDEPENDENT PRACTICE

Assign any of the following:

1. Exercises, pages 380–381
2. Workbook, *Mots 1: A–E*, pages 164–166
3. Communication Activities Masters, *Mots 1: A–B*, pages 96–98
4. CD-ROM, Disc 4, pages 378–381

VOCABULAIRE

MOTS 2

Vocabulary Teaching Resources

1. Vocabulary Transparencies 15.2 (A & B)
2. Audio Cassette 9A/CD-8
3. Student Tape Manual, Teacher's Edition, *Mots 2: E–G*, pages 154–155
4. Workbook, *Mots 2: F–G*, page 167
5. Communication Activities Masters, *Mots 2: C–D*, pages 98–99
6. Computer Software, *Vocabulaire*
7. Chapter Quizzes, *Mots 2: Quiz 2*, page 78
8. CD-ROM, Disc 4, *Mots 2*, pages 382–385

Bell Ringer Review

Write the following on the board or use BRR Blackline Master 15-2: Write the following words under the appropriate heading: Le souk or Le désert.

l'atelier, la caravane, le chameau, le chott, le dinar, la dune, marchander, le marché, le maroquinier, la médina, l'oasis, l'objet en cuir, le palmier, la ruelle, le sable

PRESENTATION (*pages 382–383*)

A. Have students close their books. Present the new words by pointing to items on Vocabulary Transparencies 15.2 (A & B). Have students repeat the words and expressions after you or Cassette 9A/CD-8.

LA VIE DU FERMIER

le lever du soleil

le coucher du soleil

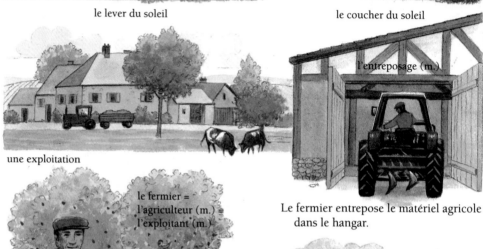

l'entreposage (m.)

une exploitation

le fermier = l'agriculteur (m.) = l'exploitant (m.)

Le fermier entrepose le matériel agricole dans le hangar.

Le fermier gagne de l'argent pourvu qu'il ait une bonne récolte.

Il travaille jusqu'à ce que le soleil se couche. Il travaille jusqu'au coucher du soleil.

382 CHAPITRE 15

ADDITIONAL PRACTICE

Student Tape Manual, Teacher's Edition, *Activité F*, page 154

meuh — la vache

hi-han — l'âne (m.)

miaou — le chat

wa wa — le chien

groin groin — le cochon

bê — le mouton

coin-coin — le canard

glouglou — le dindon

cuicui — l'oiseau (m.)

cocorico — le coq

B. After presenting the animal vocabulary, ask the students the following questions and have them produce the sound the animal makes: *Que fait le chien? Que fait le chat? Que fait le cochon? Que fait l'oiseau? Que fait le canard? Que fait la vache? Que fait le dindon? Que fait le coq? Que fait le mouton? Que fait l'âne?*

DID YOU KNOW?

The *coq gaulois* has been the French national symbol since the French Revolution. The rooster's cry, *cocorico,* is an expression of victory, "Three cheers for France!"

Exercices

PRESENTATION *(page 384)*

All the exercises on this page can be done with books open.

Exercice A

You may wish to use the recorded version of this exercise.

ANSWERS

Exercice A

1. i
2. e
3. a
4. g
5. f
6. h
7. d
8. b
9. c

Exercice B

1. lever du soleil
2. fermier
3. coucher du soleil
4. exploitation
5. entrepose
6. entreposage

Exercice C

1. meuh
2. hi-han
3. glouglou
4. groin groin
5. cuicui
6. miaou
7. wa wa
8. coin-coin
9. bê
10. cocorico

Exercice D

1. c
2. e
3. a
4. b
5. d

Exercices

A **La terminologie agricole.** Choisissez le mot ou l'expression qui correspond.

1. les céréales
2. la culture
3. entreposer
4. une ferme
5. le matériel agricole
6. récolter
7. le troupeau
8. le bétail
9. l'élevage

a. mettre dans un entrepôt
b. les bœufs, les chevaux, etc.
c. la production et l'entretien des animaux
d. un groupe d'animaux de la même espèce
e. l'action de cultiver la terre
f. les tracteurs et les moissonneuses-batteuses
g. une exploitation
h. amasser
i. le blé et autres grains

B **Une ferme.** Complétez.

1. Le jour commence avec le ___.
2. Le ___ se lève au lever du soleil.
3. Le jour finit avec le ___.
4. Une ferme s'appelle une ___.
5. Le fermier ___ son matériel agricole dans le hangar.
6. Il est important qu'il ait un lieu pour l'___ de son matériel.

C **Les cris des animaux.** Répondez.

1. Que fait la vache?
2. Et l'âne?
3. Et le dindon?
4. Et le cochon?
5. Et l'oiseau?
6. Et le chat?
7. Et le chien?
8. Et le canard?
9. Et le mouton?
10. Et le coq?

D **Encore un peu de terminologie agricole.** Choisissez le nom qui correspond au verbe.

1. récolter
2. élever
3. cultiver
4. entreposer
5. entretenir

a. la culture
b. l'entreposage
c. la récolte
d. l'entretien
e. l'élevage

Un troupeau de moutons et un champ de choux-fleurs

384 CHAPITRE 15

LEARNING FROM PHOTOS

Have students say as much about each photo as they can.

Activités de communication orale
Mots 1 et 2

A **À la ferme.** Vous parlez à un(e) ami(e) français(e) (votre camarade). Quand votre ami(e) était petit(e), il/elle habitait dans une ferme. Vous voulez savoir:

1. où se trouvait cette ferme
2. s'il y avait des prés autour de la ferme
3. quels étaient les bâtiments
4. quels animaux il y avait

B **Qui suis-je?** Un(e) élève imitera en français le cri d'un animal. Les autres élèves devineront quel animal c'est.

> Élève 1: Meuh!
> Les autres élèves: C'est la vache.

C **Les produits agricoles.** Travaillez avec un(e) camarade. Faites une liste de la nourriture que vous avez chez vous. Votre camarade vous dira avec quoi chaque produit est fait ou d'où il vient. Ensuite changez de rôles.

> Élève 1: Il y a du pain.
> Élève 2: On fait le pain avec du blé.

D **À la ferme.** Travaillez avec un(e) camarade. Sans le nommer, décrivez un animal, un bâtiment ou quelque chose d'autre qu'on trouve dans une ferme. Votre camarade devinera ce que c'est. Ensuite changez de rôles.

> Élève 1: Le fermier entrepose ça dans le hangar.
> Élève 2: C'est le matériel agricole.

Activités de communication orale
Mots 1 et 2

PRESENTATION *(page 385)*

It is recommended that you allow students to select the activities they would like to do.

ANSWERS

Activités A, B, C, and D
Answers will vary.

INTERDISCIPLINARY CONNECTIONS

Ask the art teacher to have his/her students make cards like this one showing different animals. (The artists in your class can do the same.) Have any students studying other languages (or of different nationalities), make cards showing the animal sounds in "their" language.

INDEPENDENT PRACTICE

Assign any of the following:
1. Exercises and activities, pages 384–385
2. Workbook, *Mots 2: F–G*, page 167
3. Communication Activities Masters, *Mots 2: C–D*, pages 98–99
4. Computer Software, *Vocabulaire*
5. CD-ROM, Disc 4, pages 382–385

Structure Teaching Resources

1. Workbook, *Structure: A–D,* pages 168–169
2. Student Tape Manual, Teacher's Edition, *Structure: A–B,* page 156
3. Audio Cassette 9A/CD-8
4. Communication Activities Masters, *Structure: A–B,* page 100
5. Computer Software, *Structure*
6. Chapter Quizzes, *Structure:* Quizzes 3–4, pages 79–80
7. CD-ROM, Disc 4, pages 386–389

Bell Ringer Review

Write the following on the board or use BRR Blackline Master 15-3: Complete the sentences:

1. Je doute que...
2. Ça m'étonnerait que...
3. Il n'est pas certain que...
4. Le professeur de français n'est pas sûr que...
5. Mes copains ne croient pas que...

Le passé du subjonctif

PRESENTATION *(page 386)*

A. Have students repeat the verb forms aloud.
B. Have students read the model sentences aloud.

Le passé du subjonctif

Expressing Emotions About Past Events

1. You form the past subjunctive by using the present subjunctive of the verb *avoir* or *être* and the past participle.

PARLER	ALLER	SE LEVER
que j' **aie parlé**	que je **sois allé(e)**	que je me **sois levé(e)**
que tu **aies parlé**	que tu **sois allé(e)**	que tu te **sois levé(e)**
qu'il **ait parlé**	qu'il **soit allé**	qu'il se **soit levé**
qu'elle **ait parlé**	qu'elle **soit allée**	qu'elle se **soit levée**
qu'on **ait parlé**	qu'on **soit allé**	qu'on se **soit levé**
que nous **ayons parlé**	que nous **soyons allé(e)s**	que nous nous **soyons levé(e)s**
que vous **ayez parlé**	que vous **soyez allé(e)(s)**	que vous vous **soyez levé(e)(s)**
qu'ils **aient parlé**	qu'ils **soient allés**	qu'ils se **soient levés**
qu'elles **aient parlé**	qu'elles **soient allées**	qu'elles se **soient levées**

2. The past subjunctive is used after the same expressions or verbs as the present subjunctive. It indicates that an action or event was completed in the past.

> Je regrette que vous soyez arrivés en retard.
> Mais je suis content que vous soyez venus chez nous.

Des oliviers devant une maison près d'Arles

LEARNING FROM PHOTOS		

Have students find Avignon on the France Map Transparency or on the map of France on page 435. Tell them that Arles is just south of Avignon on the Rhône and that stone houses with tile roofs are common in the South of France. Have students describe the photo. You can give them the following expressions:

une maison en pierre	a stone house
un toit en tuiles	a tile roof
des volets	shutters

Des vignobles en Provence

Exercices

A **L'accident de Jacques.** Répondez d'après le modèle.

> **Jacques s'est blessé hier.**
> *Je regrette que Jacques se soit blessé hier.*

1. Jacques a eu un accident.
2. Il est tombé.
3. Il est allé à l'hôpital.
4. Il s'est cassé la jambe.
5. Le médecin lui a mis la jambe dans le plâtre.

B **Le mauvais temps.** Répondez d'après le modèle.

> **Il a fait très chaud ici.**
> *Je suis désolé(e) qu'il ait fait très chaud.*

1. Il a fait très sec tout l'été.
2. Toutes les plantes sont mortes.
3. Les fermiers ont eu une très mauvaise récolte.
4. Les agriculteurs ont perdu beaucoup d'argent.
5. Ils ont gagné très peu d'argent.

C **Un mariage.** Commencez chaque phrase par «Robert est content que».

1. Nous avons décidé de nous marier.
2. Nous lui avons envoyé un faire-part.
3. Nous l'avons invité à la réception.
4. Marie a été invitée aussi.
5. Marie a accepté l'invitation.

Le subjonctif après des conjonctions

Note Bearing in mind the concept that the subjunctive is used when the action of the verb may or may not take place, one would expect some of these conjunctions to be followed by the indicative rather than the subjunctive. This, however, is not the case. You may wish to point this out to the students. For example: *Il va sortir bien qu'il pleuve.* The subjunctive is used in this sentence even though the action expressed by the verb is definitely taking place. Note that this sentence can convey the meaning "He is going to go out even though it is raining" or "He is going to go out even though it may rain."

Note In the CD-ROM version, this structure point is presented via an interactive electronic comic strip.

Exercices

Exercice A
Exercise A can be done with books open or closed.

ANSWERS

Exercice A

1. Oui, le fermier se lève de bonne heure.
2. Oui, de temps en temps, il se lève avant que le soleil ne se lève.
3. Oui, il travaille bien qu'il pleuve.
4. Oui, il travaille bien qu'il fasse mauvais temps.
5. Oui, il travaille dur pour avoir une bonne récolte.
6. Oui, tout le monde est content que les fermiers aient une bonne récolte.
7. Oui, les fermiers gagnent assez d'argent pourvu que la récolte soit bonne.
8. Oui, il est possible que les fermiers perdent de l'argent à moins que la récolte ne soit bonne.

Le subjonctif après des conjonctions / *Using the Subjunctive After Certain Conjunctions*

1. You use the subjunctive after the following conjunctions.

bien que	*although*
pourvu que	*provided that*
à moins que	*unless*
sans que	*without*
pour que	*in order that, so that*
avant que	*before*
jusqu'à ce que	*until*

Robert fera le voyage *bien qu*'il n'*ait* pas assez d'argent.
Il ira *pourvu que* tu y *ailles* aussi.
Et je sais que tu ne feras pas le voyage *à moins que* ton frère (ne) le *fasse.*

2. When the subjects of the main and subordinate clauses are the same, *pour que, sans que, avant que,* and *à moins que* + subjunctive become *pour, sans, avant de* and *à moins de* + infinitive.

Ils travaillent pour gagner de l'argent.

3. In careful speech, the conjunctions *à moins que* and *avant que* are often used with *ne.* The *ne* does not, however, make the sentence negative.

Il faut que je parte *avant qu*'il *n'*arrive.
Il est impossible qu'elle le sache *à moins que* vous *ne* lui ayez dit.

Exercices

A **La vie du fermier.** Répondez par «oui» ou «non».

1. Le fermier se lève de bonne heure?
2. De temps en temps, il se lève avant que le soleil ne se lève?
3. Il travaille bien qu'il pleuve?
4. Il travaille bien qu'il fasse mauvais temps?
5. Il travaille dur pour avoir une bonne récolte?
6. Tout le monde est content que les fermiers aient une bonne récolte?
7. Les fermiers gagnent assez d'argent pourvu que la récolte soit bonne?
8. Il est possible que les fermiers perdent de l'argent à moins que la récolte ne soit bonne?

La Touraine: un fermier trait ses chèvres

LEARNING FROM PHOTOS

You may wish to ask students what goat's milk is used for. Explain to them that *le fromage de chèvre* is one of the three hundred different kinds of cheeses produced in France. Remind them that a typical French meal always ends with cheese before dessert and coffee. If your class has never tasted French cheeses, you may want to bring some to class.

PAIRED ACTIVITY

Have students work in pairs to complete the following statements:
Je ferai le voyage bien que...
J'irai en France pourvu que...
Mais je ne partirai pas jusqu'à ce que...
Je ne ferai pas le voyage sans que...

B De toute façon j'irai. Répondez par «oui».

1. Vous irez à la campagne bien qu'il fasse mauvais temps?
2. Vous irez en voiture bien qu'il y ait beaucoup de circulation?
3. Vous attendrez jusqu'à ce qu'il y ait moins d'embouteillages?
4. Vous attendrez jusqu'à ce que les heures de pointe soient passées?
5. Vous conduirez pendant la nuit à moins que vous ne soyez trop fatigué(e)?
6. Vous arriverez chez eux sans qu'ils le sachent?

C Les fermiers. Complétez.

1. Les fermiers travaillent bien qu'il ___. (faire mauvais)
2. Ils travaillent bien qu'il ___ très mauvais temps. (faire)
3. Malheureusement les récoltes ne poussent pas à moins qu'il n'y ___ du soleil ou de la pluie en quantité suffisante. (avoir)
4. À moins qu'il ___ demain, les légumes vont mourir. (pleuvoir)
5. Les agriculteurs n'auront pas assez de revenu à moins que la récolte ne ___ bonne. (être)
6. Ils ne pourront pas continuer sans que le gouvernement (l'État) ___. (intervenir)
7. L'État leur donnera de l'argent pour qu'ils ___ continuer à exploiter leurs fermes. (pouvoir)

Des champs cultivés près d'Albi

D Pourquoi la prof enseigne-t-elle? Complétez.

La prof enseigne pour que ses élèves...

1. apprendre
2. être mieux informés
3. pouvoir discuter avec intelligence
4. parler bien le français
5. savoir beaucoup de choses
6. être bien élevés
7. réussir dans la vie
8. être bien préparés pour faire des études universitaires

Exercice B

1. Oui, j'irai à la campagne bien qu'il fasse mauvais temps.
2. Oui, j'irai en voiture bien qu'il y ait beaucoup de circulation.
3. Oui, j'attendrai jusqu'à ce qu'il y ait moins d'embouteillages.
4. Oui, j'attendrai jusqu'à ce que les heures de pointe soient passées.
5. Oui, je conduirai pendant la nuit à moins que je ne sois trop fatigué(e).
6. Oui, j'arriverai chez eux sans qu'ils le sachent.

Exercice C

1. fasse mauvais
2. fasse
3. ait
4. pleuve
5. soit
6. intervienne
7. puissent

Exercice D

1. La prof enseigne pour que ses élèves apprennent.
2. ... pour que ses élèves soient mieux informés.
3. ... pour que ses élèves puissent discuter avec intelligence.
4. ... pour que ses élèves parlent bien le français.
5. ... pour que ses élèves sachent beaucoup de choses.
6. ... pour que ses élèves soient bien élevés.
7. ... pour que ses élèves réussissent dans la vie.
8. ... pour que ses élèves soient bien préparés pour faire des études universitaires.

CONVERSATION

Bell Ringer Review

Write the following on the board or use BRR Blackline Master 15-4: Complete the sentences with the indicative or subjunctive of the verbs in parentheses.

1. Je ne crois pas que nous ___ au Maghreb cette année. (aller)
2. Il est certain que vous y ___ l'année prochaine. (voyager)
3. Je suis sûr(e) que cette région ___ très belle. (être)
4. Ça m'étonnerait que mes parents ne ___ pas la visiter. (vouloir)
5. Mais il n'est pas certain qu'ils ___ assez d'argent. (avoir)

PRESENTATION *(page 390)*

A. Have students close their books. Play the Conversation Video or have them listen to the recorded version on Cassette 9A/CD-8. (Use *Activité D* in the Student Tape Manual to check oral comprehension.)

B. Have two students read the conversation with as much expression as possible.

Note In the CD-ROM version, students can play the role of either one of the characters and record the conversation.

ANSWERS

Exercice A
1. Caroline est de la ville.
2. Chantal est de la campagne.
3. Chantal préfère la ville.
4. Caroline préfère la campagne.
5. Chantal en a assez de vivre à la campagne parce qu'elle ne veut plus conduire les vaches au pré, garder les moutons et donner à manger aux cochons...

390

CONVERSATION

Scènes de la vie *L'herbe est toujours plus verte chez le voisin.*

CHANTAL: Comme tu as de la chance de vivre en ville!

CAROLINE: Pourquoi? Tu n'aimes pas vivre à la campagne?

CHANTAL: Ça non, alors! J'en ai assez de conduire les vaches au pré, de garder les moutons et de donner à manger aux cochons...

CAROLINE: C'est vrai? Je devrais changer de place avec toi! Moi j'adorerais ça, être fermière: donner de l'herbe aux lapins, de l'avoine aux chevaux, du maïs aux poules...

CHANTAL: Mais dis donc, tu en sais des choses! Tu as vu ça au cinéma?

CAROLINE: Tu rigoles, mais quand j'avais dix ans j'ai passé l'été dans une ferme. À la fin je voulais rester là-bas. Mes parents ont dû me kidnapper pour que je revienne à la maison!

A **Rat des villes et rat des champs.** Répondez d'après la conversation.

1. Qui est de la ville?
2. Qui est de la campagne?
3. Qui préfère la ville?
4. Qui préfère la campagne?
5. Pourquoi est-ce que Chantal en a assez de vivre à la campagne?
6. Qu'est-ce que Caroline ferait si elle était fermière?
7. Qu'est-ce qui s'est passé quand elle avait dix ans?
8. Est-ce qu'elle a aimé ces vacances à la ferme?

Des vaches dans un pâturage en Dordogne

390 CHAPITRE 15

CRITICAL THINKING ACTIVITY

(Thinking skills: seeing relationships; supporting statements with reasons)

1. Ask students to explain in French the meaning of the saying: *L'herbe est toujours plus verte chez le voisin.*
2. Ask them if they think the saying rings true and why.

COOPERATIVE LEARNING

Have students work together in small groups to prepare a debate on life in the country vs. life in the city.

Activités de communication orale

A   Une jolie ferme.   Travaillez en petits groupes. Chaque groupe écrira autant de questions que possible au sujet des deux photos et posera ces questions aux autres groupes. Le groupe qui répondra correctement au plus grand nombre de questions gagnera.

B   Des expressions avec des animaux.   Travaillez avec un(e) camarade. Choisissez une des expressions suivantes sans la nommer. Expliquez-la en d'autres mots à votre camarade. Il/Elle vous dira quelle expression c'est.

avoir une faim de loup
avoir une fièvre de cheval
avoir un rire de cheval
compter les moutons
être malade comme un chien
être mère poule
être fier (*proud*) comme un coq
Il fait un temps de chien (de cochon).
jouer au chat et à la souris
manger comme un cochon
Quand le chat n'est pas là, les souris
   dansent.
suer comme un bœuf

Élève 1: J'ai très, très faim.
Élève 2: Tu as une faim de loup.

Il sue comme un bœuf!

6. Si Caroline était fermière, elle donnerait de l'herbe aux lapins, de l'avoine aux chevaux, du maïs aux poules...
7. Quand elle avait dix ans, elle a passé l'été dans une ferme.
8. Oui, elle a beaucoup aimé ces vacances à la ferme.

Activités de communication orale
PRESENTATION (*page 391*)

Activités A and B
   Allow students to choose the activities they would like to do.

Extension of *Activité B*
   If you have any artists in your class, have them illustrate other animal expressions from the list and label them in French.

ANSWERS
Activités A and B
   Answers will vary.

You may wish to ask students if they can figure out the meaning and/or English equivalents of other French proverbs and sayings:
Vouloir, c'est pouvoir.
L'appétit vient en mangeant.
Dis-moi qui tu hantes, je te dirai qui tu es.
Qui ne risque rien, n'a rien.
Un «tiens» vaut mieux que deux «tu
   l'auras».

INDEPENDENT PRACTICE

Assign any of the following:
1. Exercise and activities, pages 390–391
2. CD-ROM, Disc 4, pages 390–391

LECTURE ET CULTURE

Bell Ringer Review

Write the following on the board or use BRR Blackline Master 15-5: Complete each sentence with an infinitive and any other necessary words.

1. Pour ____ un couscous, il faut avoir de l'agneau, des légumes et de la semoule de blé.
2. Avant de ____ la petite Mimi doit faire ses devoirs.
3. Anne travaille pour ____.
4. Dans le souk, avant de (d') ____ il faut toujours marchander.

READING STRATEGIES
(page 392)

The extent to which your students are interested in agriculture and life in a rural area should determine the thoroughness with which you present this reading selection.

Pre-reading

You may wish to read parts of the selection to students before calling on individuals to read.

Reading

A. Call on a student to read a few sentences.
B. Ask comprehension questions about the sentences just read. Call on other students to answer.

Post-reading

After going over the reading selection in class, you can assign it for homework and have students write the *Étude de mots* and *Compréhension* exercises that follow.

Note Students may listen to a recorded version of the *Lecture* on the CD-ROM.

LES AGRICULTEURS

*L*a plupart des agriculteurs français sont des propriétaires-exploitants. C'est-à-dire que ce sont des agriculteurs qui sont propriétaires de la terre qu'ils cultivent. Il y a aussi des fermiers qui louent la terre qu'ils cultivent. Les propriétaires de cette terre sont des avocats[1] ou des industriels qui habitent la ville. Ils n'ont rien à voir avec[2] l'exploitation de la ferme. Le fermier qui loue la terre est propriétaire de la récolte.

En Touraine on fabrique du fromage de chèvre

Une grande exploitation en Provence

On va faire connaissance avec la famille Fauvet. La famille Fauvet est une famille d'agriculteurs. Ils ont une ferme à quelques kilomètres de Soual dans le Sud-Ouest de la France. Monsieur

Fauvet est un propriétaire-exploitant. Sa ferme n'est pas très grande. Il a quinze hectares[3], mais pas d'un seul tenant[4]. Il possède ici tout près de la maison un petit champ et à trois kilomètres au nord, un autre champ. Ces petits champs isolés s'appellent des îlots.

La vie de Monsieur Fauvet et de sa femme, comme la vie des agriculteurs du monde entier, est réglée sur le lever et le coucher du soleil. M. Fauvet se lève tôt et se couche tôt pour profiter des heures de jour et travailler la terre.

Les Fauvet habitent une petite maison en pierre[5]. La maison est entourée d'une

---

[1] avocats   *lawyers*
[2] rien à voir avec   *nothing to do with*
[3] hectares   *hectares (1 hectare = 2.47 acres)*
[4] d'un seul tenant   *in one piece*
[5] en pierre   *stone, made of stone*

LEARNING FROM PHOTOS

Have students look at the photos of French farms on these two pages and elsewhere in the chapter. Ask them what differences they notice between French and American farms.

étable, d'une grange et d'un hangar où M. Fauvet entrepose le matériel. Il travaille du matin au soir. Après le dîner, comme la plupart des familles rurales, les Fauvet regardent la télé. En semaine, seule Solange, la fille cadette[6], reste à la maison. Gilbert, âgé de 17 ans et Madeleine, âgée de 15 ans, font leurs études dans un lycée à Albi. Ils sont internes et ne rentrent chez eux que pour les week-ends. Gilbert et Madeleine, comme beaucoup d'enfants d'agriculteurs, disent que la vie de fermier ne les intéresse pas. Quand ils termineront leurs études, ils veulent aller travailler en ville.

Les agriculteurs d'une petite exploitation ont beaucoup de problèmes économiques. Il faut souvent qu'ils s'endettent pour acheter du matériel agricole moderne. Bien que ces machines coûtent très cher, elles sont nécessaires à la bonne exploitation de la terre. Il faut que l'exploitant les achète. Le revenu que lui rapporte sa petite propriété, surtout les années où la récolte n'est pas bonne, n'est pas suffisant pour couvrir ses frais. Il faut de temps en temps que les agriculteurs demandent au gouvernement de les aider, de les subventionner. C'est vraiment pour ces raisons économiques que les jeunes ne sont pas très tentés par la vie à la campagne.

[6] la fille cadette   *youngest daughter*

Une ferme à Trémolat, en Dordogne

Étude de mots

A Qui est-ce?

1. celui qui se dédie à l'agriculture
2. celui qui a une propriété
3. celui qui a une petite propriété agricole, et qui la travaille, la cultive, l'exploite

B Quel est le contraire? Choisissez.

1. louer
2. d'un seul tenant
3. le matin
4. le lever
5. tôt
6. interne
7. beaucoup de
8. cher
9. le revenu

a. bon marché
b. externe
c. acheter
d. peu de
e. en îlots
f. le coucher
g. le soir
h. les frais
i. tard

CHAPITRE 15   393

Compréhension

PRESENTATION (*page 394*)

Exercice C

Exercice C requires factual recall. You can ask these questions as you are presenting the reading.

Exercice D

This exercise asks students to find correct information.

Exercices E and F

These exercises make students use their critical thinking skills.

ANSWERS

Exercice C

1. La ferme des Fauvet est à quelques kilomètres de Soual.
2. Soual est dans le Sud-Ouest de la France.
3. M. Fauvet est un propriétaire-exploitant.
4. Non, sa propriété n'est pas d'un seul tenant.
5. Non, les Fauvet ont une maison en pierre.
6. La maison est entourée d'une étable, d'une grange et d'un hangar.
7. M. Fauvet entrepose son matériel agricole dans le hangar.
8. Les Fauvet regardent la télé après le dîner.
9. Les Fauvet ont trois enfants.
10. Deux enfants font leurs études en ville.

Exercice D

1. b
2. b
3. a
4. b
5. a

Exercices E and F

Answers will vary.

Compréhension

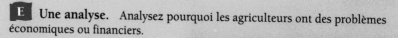

C **Les Fauvet.** Répondez d'après la lecture.

1. Où est la ferme des Fauvet?
2. Où est Soual?
3. M. Fauvet est quel type d'agriculteur?
4. Sa propriété est d'un seul tenant?
5. Les Fauvet ont une maison en bois?
6. De quoi la maison est-elle entourée?
7. Où M. Fauvet entrepose-t-il son matériel agricole?
8. Que font les Fauvet après le dîner?
9. Les Fauvet ont combien d'enfants?
10. Combien d'enfants font leurs études en ville?

D **Les fermiers.** Choisissez.

1. La plupart des agriculteurs en France sont des ___.
   a. industriels
   b. propriétaires-exploitants

2. ___ est le propriétaire de la récolte.
   a. Le propriétaire de la terre
   b. Le fermier qui loue la terre

3. La vie des agriculteurs est réglée sur ___.
   a. le lever et le coucher du soleil
   b. le matériel agricole

4. Les enfants des familles d'agriculteurs veulent ___.
   a. rester à la campagne
   b. aller travailler en ville

5. ___ fait partie du matériel agricole moderne.
   a. Le tracteur
   b. Le cheval

E **Une analyse.** Analysez pourquoi les agriculteurs ont des problèmes économiques ou financiers.

F **Savez-vous pourquoi?**
Expliquez pourquoi la plupart des enfants d'agriculteurs veulent quitter la campagne et aller chercher du travail en ville.

Un champ de blé près des Eyzies, en Dordogne

INDEPENDENT PRACTICE

Assign any of the following:
1. *Étude de mots* and *Compréhension* exercises, pages 393–394
2. Workbook, *Un Peu Plus,* pages 170–174
3. CD-ROM, Disc 4, pages 392–395

DÉCOUVERTE CULTURELLE

Vous avez lu que Monsieur Fauvet a une ferme de quinze hectares, mais pas d'un seul tenant. Il a plusieurs petits champs appelés «îlots». Pourquoi ces îlots existent-ils en France? Le responsable de cette division est le code civil de Napoléon. Si un paysan[1] avait trois fils et trois champs, chacun de valeur égale, il ne pouvait pas léguer[2] un champ entier à chacun de ses trois fils. Il était obligé de donner un tiers (1/3) de chaque champ à chaque fils. C'est à cause de ce régime que la campagne française est devenue une mosaïque

La Vallée d'Ossau dans les Pyrénées

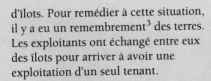

d'îlots. Pour remédier à cette situation, il y a eu un remembrement[3] des terres. Les exploitants ont échangé entre eux des îlots pour arriver à avoir une exploitation d'un seul tenant.

On peut distinguer en France deux types d'exploitation. Il y a de grandes exploitations extrêmement modernisées et de petites exploitations qui suivent des méthodes d'agriculture plus traditionnelles. Les grandes exploitations se trouvent surtout dans les plaines du nord et dans le Bassin Parisien. Les petites exploitations se trouvent surtout dans le Sud-Ouest.

En 1960, en France, 25 pour cent de la population active était dans l'agriculture. Aujourd'hui, c'est 6 pour cent. Mais il y a des paysans qui adorent la campagne. Ils ne changent pas leur mode de vie, et ils ne le changeraient pour rien au monde.

[1] un paysan   *peasant*
[2] léguer   *bequeath, leave*
[3] remembrement   *regrouping*

Vue aérienne de la campagne provençale

395

CROSS-CULTURAL COMPARISON

You may wish to give students the following information:

Le blé est présent dans toutes les régions de la France, mais en particulier dans le Nord et les régions du Bassin parisien.

Now ask students: **Le blé est présent dans quelles régions des États-Unis? Ces régions ressemblent à la photo de la Dordogne à la page 394?**

OPTIONAL MATERIAL

Découverte culturelle

PRESENTATION *(page 395)*

A. Before reading the selection, focus on the topic by having students look at the photo at the bottom of the page. Ask: *Comment s'appellent ces petits champs isolés?*

B. Have the students read the selection silently.

Note Students may listen to a recorded version of the *Découverte culturelle* on the CD-ROM.

LEARNING FROM PHOTOS

Have the students look at the bottom photo. Ask: *Vous pouvez voir les petits îlots? Identifiez-les. Ces îlots sont dans une vallée? Les montagnes sont hautes? Qu'est-ce qu'il y a au-dessus des montagnes?*

395

RÉALITÉS

Bell Ringer Review

Write the following on the board or use BRR Blackline Master 15-6: Put the conversation in logical order.

—J'adore ce sac rouge. C'est combien?

—Ah, je regrette. C'est trop cher. 35 dinars.

—40 dinars. Et c'est mon dernier prix.

—C'est 50 dinars, Mademoiselle.

—Vous désirez, Mademoiselle?

—D'accord, Mademoiselle. 40 dinars.

—35 dinars! C'est impossible! 45 dinars.

OPTIONAL MATERIAL

PRESENTATION
(pages 396–397)

A. Have the students look at the photos for enjoyment.

B. If a student has a flair for poetry, some of these photos may inspire him or her to write a poem.

Note In the CD-ROM version, students can listen to the recorded captions and discover a hidden video behind one of the photos.

Voici de petits arbres fruitiers près de Trémolat en Dordogne **1**. Tu vois les jolies fleurs? Ce sont des coquelicots.

C'est une maison typique en Normandie **2**. Tu vois les pommiers et les vaches? La Normandie est connue pour ses pommes et ses produits laitiers.

Voici un village à la campagne **3**. Aimeriez-vous mieux habiter dans un petit village comme celui-ci ou dans une grande ville comme Paris? Voyez-vous des tracteurs dans les rues de votre ville ou village?

Cet homme travaille dans un vignoble en Bourgogne **4**. Il cueille les grappes de raisin au mois de septembre. La récolte du raisin s'appelle les vendanges.

L'homme sur le tracteur verse le raisin dans une cuve **5**.

Voici un champ de tournesols en Provence **6**. Ce champ ressemble à un tableau, n'est-ce pas? Quel artiste a peint un tableau magnifique représentant des tournesols dans le Midi de la France?

4

5

6

397

ADDITIONAL PRACTICE

1. Student Tape Manual, Teacher's Edition,
   Deuxième Partie, pages 158–159
2. Situation Cards, Chapter 15

RECYCLING

These activities encourage students to use all the language they have learned in the chapter and recombine it with material from previous chapters. It is not necessary to do all the activities with all students. You may select the ones you consider most appropriate or permit students to choose the ones they wish to do.

INFORMAL ASSESSMENT

Use the oral and written exercises in this section as a review at the end of the chapter or to evaluate speaking and writing skills. For guidelines on assigning oral grades, see the evaluation criteria on page 22 of this Teacher's Wraparound Edition.

Activités de communication orale

PRESENTATION (page 398)

Activité B

In the CD-ROM version of this activity, students can interact with an on-screen native speaker.

ANSWERS

Activités A and B

Answers will vary.

Activités de communication écrite

ANSWERS

Activités A, B, and C

Answers will vary.

Activités de communication orale

A À la campagne. Avec un(e) camarade, comparez la vie d'un agriculteur en France et celle d'un agriculteur aux États-Unis. Comparez leurs problèmes.

> Élève 1: **En France les agriculteurs se lèvent à 5 heures du matin.**
> Élève 2: **Aux États-Unis aussi.**

B À la ville ou à la campagne? Vous aimez la campagne et votre camarade française, Anne, aime la ville. Discutez avec elle des avantages et des inconvénients de la vie à la ville et à la campagne.

1. J'adore la ville parce qu'il y a beaucoup de choses à faire. Pas toi?
2. J'aime m'asseoir à la terrasse d'un café et regarder les gens qui passent. Pas toi?
3. J'aime sortir le soir. Pas toi?

Anne

Activités de communication écrite

A J'adore la campagne. Faites une description d'une des photos qui vous plaît dans le chapitre. Écrivez au moins un paragraphe.

B Moi je préfère… Faites deux listes: une des avantages et des inconvénients de la vie à la campagne, et une autre pour la vie à la ville. Expliquez où vous préféreriez habiter et pourquoi.

C Dans une ferme. Vous allez passer l'été dans une ferme en France. Dans une lettre à vos hôtes *(hosts)*, demandez-leur où se trouve leur ferme, comment elle est, quels animaux ils ont, ce qu'ils cultivent, et de vous décrire une journée typique. Échangez vos lettres avec vos camarades qui y répondront.

STUDENT PORTFOLIO

Written assignments which may be included in students' portfolios are the *Activités de communication écrite* on page 398 and any writing activities from the *Un Peu Plus* section in the Workbook.

Note Students may create and save both oral and written work using the Electronic Portfolio feature on the CD-ROM.

Réintroduction et recombinaison

A **Les animaux.** Donnez le pluriel.

1. L'agneau devient un mouton.
2. L'oiseau chante.
3. Le cheval mange de l'avoine.
4. Voilà un troupeau de moutons.
5. La vache est un animal domestique.

B **Toujours le meilleur.** Complétez avec «meilleur» ou «mieux».

1. Robert est le ___ élève de la classe.
2. Paul est un très bon élève, il n'y a pas de doute. Mais Roger est ___.
3. La vedette chante ___ que les autres.
4. Je crois qu'elle a une ___ voix, plus jolie.

Une vieille étable en pierre près de Tours

C **Une visite à la ferme.** Complétez au passé.

1. Quand j'___ dans le Sud-Ouest de la France, j'___ la ferme des Charpentier. (être, visiter)
2. Les Charpentier ___ dans une jolie petite maison en pierre. (habiter)
3. Mme Charpentier m'___ à prendre un café. (inviter)
4. J'___ le hangar où M. Charpentier ___ tout son matériel agricole. (voir, entreposer)
5. Il n'y a pas de doute, M. Charpentier ___ dur. (travailler)

Vocabulaire

NOMS

le fermier
l'agriculteur (m.)
l'exploitant (m.)

la ferme
l'exploitation (f.)
le bâtiment
la grange
l'étable (f.)
le hangar

le matériel agricole
le tracteur
la moissonneuse-batteuse

la production
l'entreposage (m.)
l'entretien (m.)

le lever du soleil
le coucher du soleil

la campagne
la terre
l'herbe (f.)
le foin
le pré
le champ
le vignoble

la culture
la récolte
les céréales (f.)
le blé
le maïs
l'avoine (f.)
l'élevage (m.)

le bétail
le troupeau
l'animal (m.) domestique
la vache
le bœuf
le veau
le cheval
l'âne (m.)
le mouton
l'agneau (m.)
le cochon
le lapin
le coq
la poule
le dindon
le canard
le chien

le chat
l'oiseau (m.)
le cri

VERBES

cultiver
récolter
entreposer

CONJONCTIONS

avant que
à moins que
bien que
jusqu'à ce que
pour que
pourvu que
sans que

CHAPITRE 15 **399**

Réintroduction et recombinaison

PRESENTATION *(page 399)*

Exercise A reviews plurals ending in *-x*. Exercise B practices the difference between the use of the adjective *meilleur* and the adverb *mieux*. Exercise C reviews once again the difference between the imperfect and the *passé composé*.

ANSWERS

Exercice A

1. Les agneaux deviennent des moutons.
2. Les oiseaux chantent.
3. Les chevaux mangent de l'avoine.
4. Voilà des troupeaux de moutons.
5. Les vaches sont des animaux domestiques.

Exercice B

1. meilleur
2. meilleur
3. mieux
4. meilleure

Exercice C

1. étais, ai visité
2. habitaient
3. a invité(e)
4. ai vu, entreposait
5. travaillait

ASSESSMENT RESOURCES

1. Chapter Quizzes
2. Testing Program
3. Situation Cards
4. Communication Transparency C-15
5. Computer Software: Practice/Test Generator

VIDEO PROGRAM

INTRODUCTION (53:05)

UNE FERME EN NORMANDIE (53:37)

ADDITIONAL PRACTICE

Use the Communication Transparency C-15 to review city and country vocabulary. Then ask students which scene they prefer and why.

INDEPENDENT PRACTICE

Assign any of the following:
1. Activities and exercises, pages 398–399
2. Communication Activities Masters, pages 96–100
3. CD-ROM, Disc 4, pages 398–399

CHAPTER OVERVIEW

In this chapter students will learn to identify and discuss professions. They will also learn how their knowledge of French can help them in their future careers. They will learn vocabulary needed at a job interview and how to prepare a curriculum vitae. They will also learn to use the subjunctive in relative clauses and as a command.

The cultural focus of the chapter is on jobs and the importance of the French language in the business world.

CHAPTER OBJECTIVES

By the end of this chapter students will know:

1. vocabulary dealing with professions and trades
2. vocabulary dealing with job seeking and working
3. the use of the subjunctive in relative clauses
4. the use of the subjunctive after a superlative
5. the use of the subjunctive as an imperative

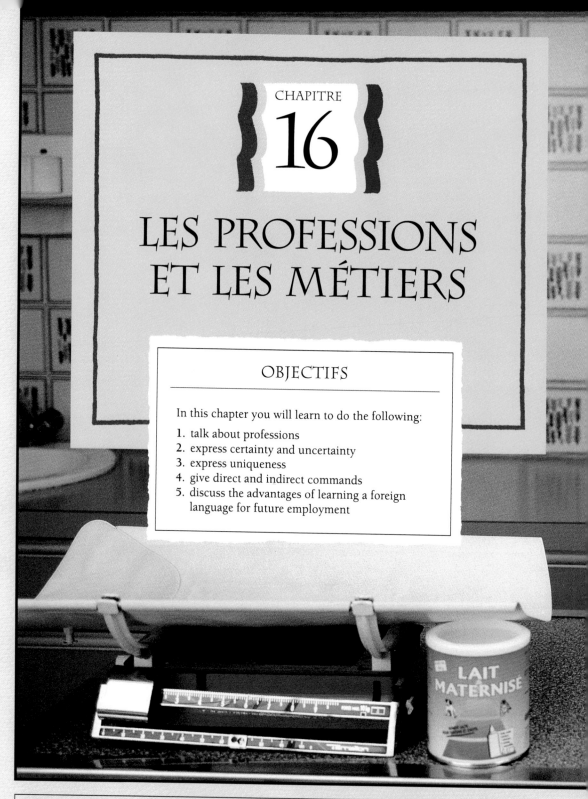

CHAPITRE

16

LES PROFESSIONS ET LES MÉTIERS

OBJECTIFS

In this chapter you will learn to do the following:

1. talk about professions
2. express certainty and uncertainty
3. express uniqueness
4. give direct and indirect commands
5. discuss the advantages of learning a foreign language for future employment

CHAPTER PROJECTS

(optional)

Have students prepare a report on what they think they would like to do when they complete their education and how French will possibly help them in their career.

COMMUNITIES

Have students prepare their curriculum vitae in French to pursue summer or future employment at an American company that does business in the French-speaking world. They might like to use the French CV on page 414 as a model.

401

CHAPTER 16 RESOURCES

1. Workbook
2. Student Tape Manual
3. Audio Cassette 9B/CD-8
4. Bell Ringer Review Blackline Masters
5. Vocabulary Transparencies
6. Communication Transparency C-16
7. Communication Activities Masters
8. Situation Cards
9. Conversation Video
10. Videocassette/Videodisc, Unit 4
11. Video Activities Booklet, Unit 4
12. Lesson Plans
13. Computer Software: Practice/Test Generator
14. Chapter Quizzes
15. Testing Program
16. Internet Activities Booklet
17. CD-ROM Interactive Textbook
18. Map Transparencies
19. Performance Assessment

Pacing

This chapter will require eight to ten class sessions. Pacing will depend on the length of the class, the age of the students, and student aptitude.

Note The Lesson Plans offer guidelines for 45- and 55-minute classes and **Block Scheduling.**

Exercices vs. *Activités*

The exercises and activities are color-coded. Exercises, which provide guided practice to prepare students for independent communication, are coded in blue. Communicative activities, which give students opportunities for creative, open-ended expression, are coded in red.

INTERNET ACTIVITIES

(optional)

These activities, student worksheets, and related teacher information are in the *À bord* Internet Activities Booklet and on the Glencoe Foreign Language Home Page at: http://www.glencoe.com/secondary/fl

LEARNING FROM PHOTOS

After presenting the vocabulary in this chapter, have students say as much as they can about the photo. Then ask them: *Aimeriez-vous être vétérinaire? Pourquoi?*

Vocabulary Teaching Resources

1. Vocabulary Transparencies 16.1 (A & B)
2. Audio Cassette 9B/CD-8
3. Student Tape Manual, Teacher's Edition, *Mots 1: A–C*, pages 160–162
4. Workbook, *Mots 1: A–C*, pages 175–176
5. Communication Activities Masters, *Mots 1: A–B*, pages 101–102
6. Chapter Quizzes, *Mots 1: Quiz 1*, page 81
7. CD-ROM, Disc 4, *Mots 1:* pages 402–405

Bell Ringer Review

Write the following on the board or use BRR Blackline Master 16-1: Make a list of the trades and professions you know in French.

PRESENTATION (pages 402–403)

A. Using Vocabulary Transparencies 16.1 (A & B), have the students repeat the new words and expressions after you or Cassette 9B/CD-8.
B. Have the students open their books and read pages 402–403.
C. Call on students to point to items on the transparencies and name the professions.

Note To clarify the meaning of *cadre,* explain that it is a salaried employee at the managerial level—from lower management to upper management: *un cadre inférieur, un cadre moyen, un cadre supérieur.* A feminine form for the word does not exist: one would say *une femme cadre.*

le lieu de travail
un bureau
une secrétaire
un directeur
un informaticien
la profession
un ingénieur
une comptable
un cadre
une femme cadre
un magasin
un commerçant

402 CHAPITRE 16

COOPERATIVE LEARNING

Have students work in groups. Each person chooses a profession from *Mots 1.* The group works together to draw up a list of courses that students would need to take to pursue the profession they chose. Groups can compare lists for the same professions and see if they agree.

une mairie

une assistante
sociale

un fonctionnaire

un tribunal

une avocate

un juge

un théâtre

un comédien =
un acteur

une comédienne =
une actrice

un chanteur

une danseuse

un technicien

le métier

PRESENTATION (*page 403*)

D. You may wish to ask the following questions about the vocabulary on this page: *Où est-ce que l'assistante sociale travaille? Et le fonctionnaire? Le juge a l'air sévère? L'avocate et le juge travaillent au tribunal? Qui est sur la scène? Le rideau se lève quand la pièce commence? Il tombe à la fin de la pièce? Que fait le chanteur? Et la danseuse? Qui porte des écouteurs? Tous ces gens aiment leur métier?*

Vocabulary Expansion

It is possible that a student will want to know the name of a profession or trade not presented in this chapter. Since it would be impossible to list every profession in this Teacher's Wraparound Edition, have the student look up the word in a bilingual dictionary.

PANTOMIME GAME

Write the following on several index cards and distribute them to students to mime. The rest of the class guesses what profession each student is miming.

Vous êtes danseur (danseuse).

Vous êtes chanteur (chanteuse).

Vous êtes commerçant(e).

Vous êtes comédien(ne).

Vous êtes juge.

Vous êtes informaticien(ne).

Vous êtes secrétaire.

Exercices

Exercice A

🎧 Exercise A must be done with books open.

Exercices B and C

Exercises B and C review vocabulary related to work and professions that was taught in earlier chapters of *À bord* and *Bienvenue*.

Exercice C

🎧 You may wish to use the recorded version of this exercise.

ANSWERS

Exercice A

1. C'est un bureau.
2. C'est une usine.
3. C'est une mairie.
4. C'est une boutique (un grand magasin).
5. C'est une pharmacie.
6. C'est un atelier.
7. C'est un cinéma (un théâtre).
8. C'est un tribunal.

Exercice B

Answers will vary but may include:

1. Des ouvriers et des contre-maîtres...
2. Des fonctionnaires et des assistantes sociales...
3. Des médecins, des chirurgiens et des infirmiers...
4. Des directeurs, des secrétaires, des comptables et des informaticiens...
5. Des pilotes, des hôtesses de l'air et des stewards...
6. Des professeurs, des censeurs, des proviseurs, des documentalistes, des conseillers d'orientation et d'éducation...
7. Des banquiers...
8. Des pharmaciens...
9. Des contrôleurs...
10. Des réceptionnistes...
11. Des acteurs (des comédiens) et des techniciens...
12. Des vendeurs et des commerçants...
13. Des pompistes...
14. Des teinturiers...

Exercices

A **Les lieux de travail.** Répondez d'après les dessins.

1. C'est une école ou un bureau?

2. C'est un bureau ou une usine?

3. C'est une mairie ou une église?

4. C'est une boutique ou un grand magasin?

5. C'est un hôpital ou une pharmacie?

6. C'est un atelier ou une boutique?

7. C'est un théâtre ou un cinéma?

8. C'est un tribunal ou une ferme?

B **Qui travaille où?** Répondez. Utilisez toutes les professions et métiers que vous connaissez.

1. Qui travaille dans une usine?
2. Qui travaille dans une mairie?
3. Qui travaille dans un hôpital?
4. Qui travaille dans un bureau?
5. Qui travaille à bord d'un avion?
6. Qui travaille dans une école?
7. Qui travaille dans une banque?
8. Qui travaille dans une pharmacie?
9. Qui travaille dans un train?
10. Qui travaille dans un hôtel?
11. Qui travaille dans un théâtre?
12. Qui travaille dans un magasin?
13. Qui travaille dans une station-service?
14. Qui travaille dans une teinturerie?

PAIRED ACTIVITY

Have students work in pairs. Students take turns describing one of the illustrations in Exercise A without saying which one it is and guessing which place of employment is being described.

C Qui fait ce travail? Répondez.

1. Il/Elle aide le chirurgien.
2. Il/Elle fait des ordonnances.
3. Il/Elle opère ou fait des interventions chirurgicales.
4. Il/Elle aide les criminels à se défendre devant le juge.
5. Il/Elle vend des marchandises.
6. Il/Elle chante.
7. Il/Elle danse.
8. Il/Elle tient les livres de compte.
9. Il/Elle coupe les cheveux.
10. Il/Elle aide les élèves à prendre des décisions.
11. Il/Elle travaille dans une usine.
12. Il/Elle travaille au CDI.
13. Il/Elle crée des routes, des bâtiments, etc.

Cet homme travaille dans une usine à Cognac.

D Une profession que j'aimerais. Répondez d'après le modèle.

agent de police
Oui, j'aimerais être agent de police. (Non, je n'aimerais pas être agent de police).

1. médecin
2. directeur/directrice d'une usine
3. avocat(e)
4. dentiste
5. pharmacien/pharmacienne
6. acteur/actrice
7. pilote
8. comptable
9. assistant(e) social(e)
10. informaticien/informaticienne
11. fonctionnaire

Ce scientifique fait de la recherche au CNRS à Paris.

405

Exercice C

1. l'infirmier (-ière)
2. le/la pharmacien(ne)
3. le/la chirurgien(ne)
4. l'avocat(e)
5. le vendeur (la vendeuse)
6. le chanteur (la chanteuse)
7. le danseur (la danseuse)
8. le/la comptable
9. le coiffeur (la coiffeuse)
10. le/la conseiller (-ère) d'orientation
11. l'ouvrier (-ière)
12. le/la documentaliste
13. l'ingénieur (la femme ingénieur)

Exercice D

1. Oui (Non), j'aimerais (je n'aimerais pas) être médecin.
2. Oui (Non), j'aimerais (je n'aimerais pas) être directeur (-trice) d'une usine.
3. Oui (Non), j'aimerais (je n'aimerais pas) être avocat(e).
4. Oui (Non), j'aimerais (je n'aimerais pas) être dentiste.
5. Oui (Non), j'aimerais (je n'aimerais pas) être pharmacien(ne).
6. Oui (Non), j'aimerais (je n'aimerais pas) être acteur (actrice).
7. Oui (Non), j'aimerais (je n'aimerais pas) être pilote.
8. Oui (Non), j'aimerais (je n'aimerais pas) être comptable.
9. Oui (Non), j'aimerais (je n'aimerais pas) être assistant(e) social(e).
10. Oui (Non), j'aimerais (je n'aimerais pas) être informaticien(ne).
11. Oui (Non), j'aimerais (je n'aimerais pas) être fonctionnaire.

VOCABULAIRE

MOTS 2

Vocabulary Teaching Resources

1. Vocabulary Transparencies 16.2 (A & B)
2. Audio Cassette 9B/CD-8
3. Student Tape Manual, Teacher's Edition, *Mots 2: D–F,* pages 163–164
4. Workbook, *Mots 2: D–E,* pages 176–177
5. Communication Activities Masters, *Mots 2: C–D,* page 103
6. Computer Software, *Vocabulaire*
7. Chapter Quizzes, *Mots 2: Quiz 2,* page 82
8. CD-ROM, Disc 4, *Mots 2:* pages 406–409

Bell Ringer Review

Write the following on the board or use BRR Blackline Master 16-2: Write the following words under the appropriate heading: L'élevage or La culture.

le bétail
le blé
le canard
les céréales
le cochon
le dindon
la moissonneuse-batteuse
le mouton
la récolte
le tracteur

PRESENTATION (*pages 406–407*)

A. Have the students close their books. Introduce the new words by pointing to the items on Vocabulary Transparencies 16.2 (A & B) and having the students repeat after you or Cassette 9B/CD-8.

VOCABULAIRE

MOTS 2

un bureau de placement

chercher du travail

le service du personnel

un curriculum vitae (CV)

un entretien

une carrière

poser sa candidature

être candidat à un poste

une (petite) annonce

une demande d'emploi

Paris, le 3 octobre

Éditions Gaillard
Service du Personnel
7, rue Magellan
75008 Paris

Messieurs,

Suite à votre annonce dans LE MONDE du 15 septembre dernier, je me permets de poser ma candidature au poste d'information.
Comme le montrera mon curriculum vitae que je joins à cette lettre, je viens de terminer mes études en informatique et j'ai effectué

Il est libre immédiatement. Il peut commencer à travailler demain.

LEARNING FROM ILLUSTRATIONS

After completing the chapter, you may wish to have students write a job application letter like the one above in response to one of the job ads on pages 408, 416, or 420. For other examples of this type of business correspondence, consult the appendices of a French/English dictionary.

COMMUNITIES

Have students write to international organizations which offer student jobs in French-speaking countries and request information about summer job possibilities.

une entreprise

un salaire
une employée   un employeur

travailler pour une
grosse société

être à son compte

Elle travaille à plein temps (40 heures
par semaine).

Elle travaille à mi-temps (à peu près 20
heures par semaine).

Il est au chômage.
Il y a chômage quand il n'y a pas d'emplois.

CHAPITRE 16   **407**

B. Ask questions such as: *La femme cherche du travail? Elle a donné son curriculum vitae à ce monsieur du bureau de placement? Quand va-t-on au bureau de placement? Elle a vu une petite annonce dans le journal? C'était pour quel poste?*, etc.

C. You may wish to ask the following questions about the illustrations on page 407: *IBM est une grosse société ou une petite entreprise? C'est l'employé qui reçoit ou qui paie un salaire? Qui paie les salaires? Monsieur Milhaud travaille chez lui. Il travaille pour une grosse société ou il est à son compte? Monsieur Cortot est au chômage. Pourquoi? Madame Legendre travaille à plein temps. Elle travaille combien d'heures par semaine?*, etc.

D. Have the students open their books and read the new words and expressions.

ADDITIONAL PRACTICE

Student Tape Manual, Teacher's Edition,
Activités E–F, pages 163–164

Exercices

PRESENTATION (pages 408–409)

Extension of Exercice A

After completing the exercise, you may wish to have a student retell the story in his/her own words.

Exercice B

Exercise B is to be done with books open.

Extension of Exercice B

After completing the exercise, you may wish to have the students use the words in the first column in original sentences.

ANSWERS

Exercice A

1. Oui, elle cherche du travail.
2. Elle lit une annonce dans le journal.
3. Isère, S.A. cherche des candidats.
4. Elle pose sa candidature.
5. Elle va au service du personnel de la compagnie.
6. Elle remplit une demande d'emploi.
7. Elle donne son curriculum vitae à la réceptionniste au service du personnel.
8. Bien sûr qu'elle a des références.
9. Elle est diplômée en informatique.
10. Elle va avoir un entretien.
11. Elle peut commencer à travailler immédiatement.

Exercice B

1. d
2. b
3. h
4. g
5. j
6. c
7. a
8. f
9. e
10. i

Exercice C

Answers will vary.

Exercices

A Elle cherche du travail. Répondez d'après les indications.

1. Régine cherche du travail? (oui)
2. Qu'est-ce qu'elle lit? (une annonce dans le journal)
3. Quelle compagnie ou société cherche des candidats? (Isère, S.A. [Société Anonyme])
4. Que fait Régine? (poser sa candidature)
5. Où va Régine? (au service du personnel de la compagnie)
6. Qu'est-ce qu'elle remplit? (une demande d'emploi)
7. Qu'est-ce qu'elle donne à la réceptionniste au service du personnel? (son curriculum vitae)
8. Elle a des références? (bien sûr)
9. Régine est diplômée en quoi? (informatique)
10. Qu'est-ce qu'elle va avoir? (un entretien)
11. Quand est-ce qu'elle peut commencer à travailler? (immédiatement)

B Des définitions. Trouvez les mots qui correspondent.

1. les petites annonces
2. un poste
3. être à son compte
4. être libre immédiatement
5. travailler à plein temps
6. être au chômage
7. travailler à mi-temps
8. un bureau de placement
9. une entreprise
10. un(e) employé(e)

a. travailler à peu près 20 heures par semaine
b. un emploi
c. être sans travail
d. ce qu'on lit dans le journal quand on cherche du travail
e. une société
f. l'endroit où on va quand on cherche du travail
g. pouvoir commencer à travailler tout de suite
h. travailler pour soi
i. quelqu'un qui travaille pour un employeur
j. travailler 40 heures par semaine

C Mon travail. Donnez des réponses personnelles.

1. Tu travailles ou tu aimerais travailler?
2. Où?
3. Tu travailles ou tu aimerais travailler à plein temps ou à mi-temps?
4. Tu as un salaire? C'est un bon salaire ou pas?

Nantes: Une jeune femme cherche du travail à l'ANPE.

LEARNING FROM PHOTOS AND REALIA

1. In the caption under the top photo, the acronym *ANPE* stands for *Agence nationale pour l'emploi.* You may wish to ask the following questions about the photo: *Que fait la jeune femme? Pourquoi? Qu'est-ce qu'il y a sur le panneau d'affichage?*

2. You may wish to ask students the following questions about the ad: *Qui a écrit cette annonce? Quelle est sa profession? Qu'est-ce qu'elle offre? Est-ce qu'elle veut enseigner les débutants seulement? Elle offre des cours le soir? Elle préfère enseigner à des particuliers? Quel est son numéro de téléphone?*

D Ce domaine vous intéresse? Répondez d'après le modèle.

l'architecture
Oui, l'architecture m'intéresse. (Non, l'architecture ne m'intéresse pas.)

1. les sciences naturelles
2. les sciences politiques
3. la médecine
4. l'enseignement
5. la criminologie
6. les finances et la comptabilité
7. la chirurgie
8. l'informatique
9. le commerce
10. la publicité
11. le marketing
12. le tourisme
13. la danse
14. l'art

Activités de communication orale
Mots 1 et 2

A Qu'est-ce qu'ils font, tes parents? Vous parlez à un(e) ami(e) français(e) (votre camarade). Demandez-lui ce que ses parents font.

> Élève 1: Que fait ton père?
> Élève 2: Il est comptable.
> Élève 1: Et ta mère, qu'est-ce qu'elle fait?

B Tu travailles après les cours? Travaillez en petits groupes. Choisissez un chef et un(e) secrétaire. Le chef demandera aux autres:

1. qui travaille
2. ce qu'il/elle fait
3. où il/elle travaille
4. combien d'heures par semaine il/elle travaille
5. combien il/elle gagne de l'heure

Le/La secrétaire prendra des notes et présentera les résultats à la classe.

C Ce que je veux faire plus tard. Demandez à un(e) camarade ce qu'il/elle veut faire plus tard et pourquoi. Ensuite changez de rôles.

> Élève 1: Qu'est-ce que tu veux faire plus tard?
> Élève 2: Je voudrais être prof parce que j'aime enseigner.

D Quelle est sa profession ou son métier? Travaillez en petits groupes. Sur une feuille de papier, décrivez plusieurs professions ou métiers sans les nommer. Pour chaque profession ou métier, indiquez ce qu'on fait et où on travaille. Ensuite lisez vos descriptions à la classe. Les autres groupes devineront quelles professions ou métiers vous décrivez.

> Groupe 1: Cette personne travaille dans un bureau et tape à la machine.
> Groupe 2: C'est un/une secrétaire.

CHAPITRE 16   409

Exercice D
1. Oui (Non), les sciences naturelles (ne) m'intéressent (pas).
2. Oui (Non), les sciences politiques (ne) m'intéressent (pas).
3. Oui (Non), la médecine (ne) m'intéresse (pas).
4. Oui (Non), l'enseignement (ne) m'intéresse (pas).
5. Oui (Non), la criminologie (ne) m'intéresse (pas).
6. Oui (Non), les finances et la comptabilité (ne) m'intéressent (pas).
7. Oui (Non), la chirurgie (ne) m'intéresse (pas).
8. Oui (Non), l'informatique (ne) m'intéresse (pas).
9. Oui (Non), le commerce (ne) m'intéresse (pas).
10. Oui (Non), la publicité (ne) m'intéresse (pas).
11. Oui (Non), le marketing (ne) m'intéresse (pas).
12. Oui (Non), le tourisme (ne) m'intéresse (pas).
13. Oui (Non), la danse (ne) m'intéresse (pas).
14. Oui (Non), l'art (ne) m'intéresse (pas).

Activités de communication orale
Mots 1 et 2

PRESENTATION *(page 409)*

You may wish to have students choose the activities they would like to do.

ANSWERS
Activités A, B, C, and D
Answers will vary.

INDEPENDENT PRACTICE

Assign any of the following:
1. Exercises and activities, pages 408–409
2. Workbook, *Mots 2: D–E*, pages 176–177
3. Communication Activities Masters, *Mots 2: C–D*, page 103
4. Computer Software, *Vocabulaire*
5. CD-ROM, Disc 4, pages 406–409

STRUCTURE

Structure Teaching Resources

1. Workbook, *Structure: A–C*, pages 178–179
2. Student Tape Manual, Teacher's Edition, *Structure: A–D*, pages 164–165
3. Audio Cassette 9B/CD-8
4. Communication Activities Masters, *Structure: A–C*, pages 104–106
5. Computer Software, *Structure*
6. Chapter Quizzes, *Structure: Quizzes 3–5*, pages 83–85
7. CD-ROM, Disc 4, pages 410–413

Le subjonctif dans les propositions relatives

PRESENTATION (*page 410*)

Have the students read the model sentences aloud.

Exercices

PRESENTATION (*page 410*)

When you are going over these exercises, you may wish to ask students why they did or did not use the subjunctive.

Exercice A

You may wish to use the recorded version of this exercise.

ANSWERS

Exercice A

Answers begin with *Oui* and repeat the wording of the question.

Exercice B

1. **ait, connaisse, puisse**
2. **soit**
3. **a, veut, peut**
4. **sache, connaisse**

Le subjonctif dans les propositions relatives

Expressing Certainty and Uncertainty

1. You know that clauses introduced by the relative pronouns *qui* and *que* describe people or things.

> **Nous avons un secrétaire qui parle très bien le français.**

2. It is possible to use the subjunctive in a relative clause. It indicates uncertainty as to whether the person or thing in question exists or not. Compare the following.

CERTAINTY	UNCERTAINTY
J'ai un ami qui *sait* conduire. Il a un métier qui *est* intéressant.	Je cherche quelqu'un qui *sache* conduire. Il cherche un métier qui *soit* intéressant.

Exercices

A On cherche un représentant. Répondez par «oui».

1. La Société Isère cherche un représentant?
2. Ils ont un poste qui paie bien?
3. Ils cherchent quelqu'un qui ait de l'expérience dans la vente?
4. Ils veulent quelqu'un qui ait voyagé?
5. Ils ont besoin d'une personne qui connaisse des langues?
6. Ils cherchent un candidat qui soit libre immédiatement?

B On a besoin de certaines qualifications. Complétez.

1. La Société Isère cherche quelqu'un qui ___ de l'expérience, qui ___ bien le français et l'anglais et qui ___ voyager. (avoir, connaître, pouvoir)
2. Le directeur du personnel m'a dit qu'ils ont besoin de quelqu'un qui ___ libre immédiatement. (être)
3. Ils ont eu des candidats. Il y a une candidate qui ___ de l'expérience, qui ___ et qui ___ commencer à travailler immédiatement. (avoir, vouloir, pouvoir)
4. Malheureusement elle ne parle que le français et la société continue à chercher quelqu'un qui ___ parler anglais et qui ___ le marché américain. (savoir, connaître)

Le subjonctif après un superlatif

Expressing Uniqueness

1. You use the subjunctive in a relative clause that modifies a superlative or an expression such as *le seul, le premier, le dernier*, or *personne* and *rien*. These expressions all indicate uniqueness and therefore express the speaker's opinion, not facts.

> **C'est le meilleur livre que j'aie jamais lu.**
> **Martine est la seule personne qui sache le faire.**
> **Il n'y a personne qui puisse le faire.**
> **C'est le dernier emploi qu'il ait eu.**

2. The subjunctive is not used if there is no idea of uniqueness.

> **Le dernier livre que j'ai lu, c'était *Eugénie Grandet*.**

Exercices

A **Tu exagères!** Complétez.

1. C'est le meilleur livre que j'___ jamais ___. (lire)
2. C'est la meilleure photo que j'___ jamais ___. (prendre)
3. C'est la plus belle ville où je ___ jamais ___. (aller)
4. C'est le plus bel homme que j'___ jamais ___. (connaître)
5. C'est la plus belle femme que j'___ jamais ___. (voir)
6. C'est la voiture la plus luxueuse que j'___ jamais ___. (conduire)
7. C'est le seul homme qui ___ conduire cette voiture. (savoir)
8. C'est la seule personne qui ___ le faire. (pouvoir)

B **Il est déprimé.** Répondez par «non».

1. Il n'y a rien qui le fasse rire?
2. Il n'y a rien qui l'intéresse?
3. Il n'y a rien qu'il veuille faire?
4. Il n'y a rien qu'il fasse avec plaisir?

C **Qui? Personne?** Répondez d'après le modèle.

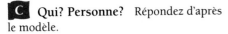

> **Qui le sait?**
> *Il n'y a personne ici qui le sache.*

1. Qui le sait?
2. Qui connaît ces trois langues?
3. Qui a de l'expérience?
4. Qui peut faire ce travail?
5. Qui veut remplir une demande d'emploi?

I.S.F.A.T.
TEL. 47.74.58.00
FORMATION—CONSEIL
LANGUES—INFORMATIQUE
35ème ETAGE

INDEPENDENT PRACTICE

Assign any of the following:
1. Exercises, pages 410–411
2. Workbook, *Structure: A–B*, pages 178–179
3. Communication Activities Masters, *Structure: A–B*, pages 104–105
4. CD-ROM, Disc 4, pages 410–411

Le subjonctif après un superlatif

PRESENTATION *(page 411)*

Go over the explanation with the students. Have them read the model sentences aloud.

Exercices

PRESENTATION *(page 411)*

Exercices B and C

You may wish to use the recorded version of these exercises.

ANSWERS

Exercice A

1. aie... lu
2. aie... prise
3. sois... allé(e)
4. aie... connu
5. aie... vue
6. aie... conduite
7. sache
8. puisse

Exercice B

1. Non, il n'y a rien qui le fasse rire.
2. Non, il n'y a rien qui l'intéresse.
3. Non, il n'y a rien qu'il veuille faire.
4. Non, il n'y a rien qu'il fasse avec plaisir.

Exercice C

1. Il n'y a personne ici qui le sache.
2. Il n'y a personne ici qui connaisse ces trois langues.
3. Il n'y a personne ici qui ait de l'expérience.
4. Il n'y a personne ici qui puisse faire ce travail.
5. Il n'y a personne ici qui veuille remplir une demande d'emploi.

Write the following on the board or use BRR Blackline Master 16-4: Complete the sentences.

1. **J'aime le cours de français bien que...**
2. **Je voudrais faire un voyage pourvu que...**
3. **Je ne regarde pas la télé à moins que...**
4. **Je ne sortirai pas ce week-end sans que...**
5. **Je veux rentrer chez moi avant que...**

Le subjonctif comme impératif

PRESENTATION *(page 412)*

Have the students read the verb forms and the model sentences aloud.

Note In the CD-ROM version, this structure point is presented via an interactive electronic comic strip.

Exercices

PRESENTATION *(pages 412–413)*

Exercice C

You may wish to use the recorded version of this exercise.

ANSWERS

Exercice A

1. sois
2. Sois
3. Sois
4. Sois
5. Aie
6. Aie
7. Aie
8. Aie
9. aie

Le subjonctif comme impératif   *Giving Direct and Indirect Commands*

1. Note that the command forms of the verbs *être*, *avoir*, and *savoir* resemble the subjunctive forms.

ÊTRE	AVOIR	SAVOIR
Sois!	Aie!	Sache!
Soyons!	Ayons!	Sachons!
Soyez!	Ayez!	Sachez!

2. You can use a subjunctive clause alone to express a command directed at a third party. These clauses start with *que*.

Qu'il parte tout de suite!	*Let him leave right away!*
Qu'ils viennent demain!	*Let them come tomorrow!*

3. *Que* is not used in common expressions such as:

Vive(nt) les vacances!	*Hurray for vacation!*
Ainsi soit-il!	*So be it!*

Exercices

A **Eh, Marc!** Dites quelque chose à votre copain Marc. Complétez.

1. Marc, ___ sage!
2. ___ prudent!
3. ___ à l'heure!
4. ___ poli!
5. ___ de la patience!
6. ___ de la pitié!
7. ___ confiance!
8. ___ du courage!
9. N'___ pas peur!

LEARNING FROM REALIA

Ask students what the brochure is about. Ask what crime is punishable by fines or imprisonment.

B **Eh, les amis!** Maintenant dites la même chose à Marc et Caroline.

C **Qu'elle le fasse!** Répondez d'après le modèle.

> Elle veut parler au directeur.
> *Qu'elle parle au directeur!*

1. Elle veut chercher du travail.
2. Elle veut travailler à plein temps.
3. Elle veut aller en France.
4. Elle veut travailler pour une entreprise multinationale.
5. Elle veut faire le tour du monde.
6. Elle veut connaître tous les pays du monde.

D **Bon! Alors qu'il le fasse.** Répondez d'après le modèle.

> Il peut le voir.
> *Qu'il le voie!*

1. Il peut le faire.
2. Il peut l'apprendre.
3. Il peut la conduire.
4. Il peut prendre la leçon d'espagnol maintenant.
5. Il peut y aller.

mairie de paris
informations ☎ 42.76.47.47.

VOUS SORTEZ DU
COLLEGE OU DU LEP
VOUS AVEZ DU MAL
A TROUVER
UN EMPLOI
TEL: 42-03-99-10
9H-17H JUSQU'AU 10

Deux avocats devant le Palais de Justice de Marseille

Exercice B
1. soyez
2. Soyez
3. Soyez
4. Soyez
5. Ayez
6. Ayez
7. Ayez
8. Ayez
9. ayez

Exercice C
1. Qu'elle cherche du travail!
2. Qu'elle travaille à plein temps!
3. Qu'elle aille en France!
4. Qu'elle travaille pour une entreprise multinationale!
5. Qu'elle fasse le tour du monde!
6. Qu'elle connaisse tous les pays du monde!

Exercice D
1. Qu'il le fasse!
2. Qu'il l'apprenne!
3. Qu'il la conduise!
4. Qu'il prenne la leçon d'espagnol maintenant!
5. Qu'il y aille!

CONVERSATION

CONVERSATION

PRESENTATION *(page 414)*

A. Have students close their books. Play the Conversation Video or have them listen to the recorded version on Cassette 9B/CD-8. (Use *Activité F* in the Student Tape Manual to check oral comprehension.)

B. Have two students read the conversation with as much expression as possible.

C. Go over the comprehension exercise.

D. Call on a student to retell the story of the conversation in his/her own words.

Note In the CD-ROM version, students can play the role of either one of the characters and record the conversation.

ANSWERS

Exercice A

1. Elle cherche du travail.
2. Elle a apporté son CV avec elle.
3. Elle cherche un poste de secrétaire dans une grosse société.
4. Oui, elle a une possibilité.
5. Il a besoin de quelqu'un qui connaisse bien l'anglais et l'espagnol.
6. Oui, elle parle bien l'anglais et l'espagnol parce qu'elle a vécu dix ans à New York et quatre ans à Madrid.
7. Elle parle d'une multinationale américaine.

Scènes de la vie *Au bureau de placement*

CONSEILLÈRE: Votre CV est intéressant. Quel genre de travail cherchez-vous?
SOPHIE: Secrétaire dans une grosse société.
CONSEILLÈRE: J'ai une possiblité, mais l'employeur a besoin de quelqu'un qui connaisse bien l'anglais et l'espagnol.
SOPHIE: J'ai vécu dix ans à New York et quatre ans à Madrid.
CONSEILLÈRE: Alors ce poste est pour vous! Vous travaillerez pour une multinationale américaine, ici à Paris. Le salaire est excellent. Le seul problème c'est que vous devez pouvoir voyager.
SOPHIE: Ce n'est pas un problème.
CONSEILLÈRE: Alors, je leur envoie tout de suite votre dossier et demande pour vous un entretien. Et n'ayez pas peur! Vous êtes la candidate idéale!

A **À la recherche d'un emploi.** Répondez d'après la conversation.

1. Que fait Sophie dans ce bureau de placement?
2. Qu'est-ce qu'elle a apporté avec elle?
3. Qu'est-ce qu'elle cherche comme poste?
4. Est-ce que la conseillère a une possibilité?
5. De quoi a besoin l'employeur?
6. Est-ce que Sophie parle bien l'anglais et l'espagnol? Pourquoi?
7. La conseillère parle de quel genre d'entreprise?
8. Quel problème peut-il y avoir?
9. Est-ce que Sophie veut essayer d'obtenir ce poste?
10. Que va faire pour elle la conseillère?

Un curriculum vitae

Françoise Bernet
65, Rue Archereau
Paris 75019
47.61.59.35

FORMATION
1986-90: Double Maîtrise en Droits français et anglais Programme Erasmus.
1990: Université de Paris I Panthéon-Sorbonne.
1986-89: Université de King's College. Londres.
1985-86: Université de Paris IV-Assas. 1ère année de Droit.
1984-85: Hypokhâgne classique. Lycée Fénelon. Paris. (Préparation à l'Ecole Normale Superieure)
Juin 84: Baccalauréat A1: Lettres et Mathématiques Mention Assez Bien
Scolarité: Sainte-Marie de Neuilly

LANGUES
Anglais: bilingue
Russe: lu et parlé. Cours de perfectionnement au Centre de Langue et Culture Russe (Lycée Fénelon).

EXPERIENCE PROFESSIONNELLE
Août 89: Biddle & Co. Cabinet d'avocats. Londres. 20 associés. Stagiaire au "Droit immobilier".
Juil 89: Druces & Attlee. Cabinet d'avocats. Londres. 15 associés. Stagiaire au Contentieux.
Août 86: Johnston Stokes & Masters. Cabinet d'avocats. Hong-Kong. 200 juristes. Stagiaire auprès de plusieurs associés.

PAIRED ACTIVITY

Have students work in pairs to prepare a skit about a job interview. One student plays the job applicant and the other plays the personnel director. Call on volunteers to present their skits to the class.

Activités de communication orale

A **Les meilleures professions ou métiers.** Travaillez avec un(e) camarade. Faites une liste des meilleures professions ou métiers par ordre de préférence. Ensuite échangez vos listes. Demandez à votre camarade s'il/si elle voudrait faire ces professions ou métiers.

> Élève 1: Tu aimerais être comptable?
> Élève 2: Non, ça paie bien, mais je ne suis pas assez fort(e) en maths.

B **Les meilleures choses.** Votre camarade français, Marc, sait que vous avez très bon goût. Il vous demande votre avis sur plusieurs choses. Répondez-lui.

1. Quel est le meilleur film que tu aies jamais vu?
2. Quel est le meilleur livre que tu aies jamais lu?
3. Quel est le meilleur repas que tu aies jamais mangé?
4. Quel est le meilleur professeur que tu aies jamais eu?

C **Qu'est-ce qui vous intéresse?** Travaillez en petits groupes. Choisissez un chef. Le chef jouera le rôle de conseiller/conseillère d'orientation dans votre école. Les autres membres du groupe lui parleront de ce qui les intéresse et lui demanderont de leur recommander une profession ou un métier. Il/Elle répondra.

> Élève 1: Je m'intéresse à la biologie.
> Élève 2: Tu pourrais être médecin ou infirmier/infirmière.

Marc

D **Je cherche quelqu'un…** Vous êtes le directeur/la directrice du personnel d'une société multinationale et le président de l'entreprise veut engager quelques personnes pour les postes suivants. Demandez-lui quelles sont les qualifications nécessaires pour deux ou trois des postes. Changez ensuite de rôles.

avocat(e)   secrétaire
comptable   ingénieur
interprète

> Élève 1: Pour le poste d'informaticien, qu'est-ce que vous cherchez?
> Élève 2: Je cherche quelqu'un qui connaisse parfaitement les ordinateurs qu'on utilise ici.

8. C'est que Sophie doit pouvoir voyager.
9. Oui, elle veut essayer d'obtenir ce poste.
10. Elle va leur envoyer tout de suite le dossier de Sophie et demander un entretien pour elle.

Activités de communication orale

PRESENTATION *(page 415)*

Allow students to choose the activity they would like to participate in. Different groups may do different activities.

Activité B

In the CD-ROM version of this activity, students can interact with an on-screen native speaker.

ANSWERS

Activités A, B, C, and D

Answers will vary.

LECTURE ET CULTURE

LECTURE ET CULTURE

LE FRANÇAIS ET VOTRE CARRIÈRE

Vous ne savez pas si le français vous sera utile dans votre carrière parce que vous n'avez pas encore décidé ce que vous ferez ni où vous travaillerez quand vous aurez votre diplôme. Mais il n'y a pas de doute que la connaissance d'une langue étrangère telle que[1] le français sera un atout[2].

De nos jours le commerce international est d'importance majeure. Ainsi, de nombreuses grosses sociétés américaines sont devenues multinationales. C'est-à-dire qu'elles se sont implantées à l'étranger[3]. Pour cette raison, il est possible que vous soyez engagé(e) par une compagnie ou société américaine et que votre bureau se trouve dans un pays francophone.

Souvenez-vous bien que le français en soi[4] n'est pas forcément une carrière.

Mais le français avec une autre spécialisation est un outil[5] de valeur incalculable. Si vous connaissez la comptabilité, la médecine, le marketing, le commerce, etc. et qu'en plus vous connaissez le français, vous pourrez faire un travail intéressant, voyager à l'étranger et gagner beaucoup d'argent. Vive le français!

[1] telle que   *such as*
[2] un atout   *advantage*
[3] à l'étranger   *abroad*
[4] en soi   *in itself*
[5] outil   *tool*

Étude de mots

A **Quel est le mot?**   Cherchez le mot dans la lecture.

1. faire un voyage
2. beaucoup de
3. une compagnie
4. une profession
5. qui est d'un autre pays
6. un avantage
7. un objet qu'on utilise pour faire un travail

CRITICAL THINKING ACTIVITY

(Thinking skill: seeing relationships)
Read the following to the class or write it on the board or on a transparency:
1. Faites une liste des avantages qu'a une personne qui parle plusieurs langues.
2. Classez ces avantages en catégories telles que: avantages culturels, avantages économiques, avantages commerciaux.

Compréhension

B **Votre carrière.** Répondez.

1. Croyez-vous que le français vous sera utile dans votre carrière?
2. Vous avez choisi une carrière? Si vous répondez oui, quelle carrière avez-vous choisie?
3. De nos jours, qu'est-ce qui est très important?
4. Qu'est-ce qui est un outil de valeur incalculable?

C **Vous avez compris?** Répondez d'après la lecture.

1. Il est possible de travailler pour une société américaine et de travailler à l'étranger?
2. Beaucoup de grosses sociétés américaines sont implantées à l'étranger?
3. La connaissance d'une langue telle que le français pourra vous être utile dans beaucoup de carrières différentes?

L'American Express à Paris

DÉCOUVERTE CULTURELLE

*O*n parle depuis longtemps de la présence des sociétés américaines à l'étranger. Mais de nos jours de plus en plus de sociétés d'autres pays sont devenues multinationales. Par conséquent, on voit beaucoup de sociétés européennes, japonaises, sud-américaines, etc. aux États-Unis. Ces sociétés multinationales emploient bien sûr des ressortissants (*citizens*) des pays où elles sont installées. Par conséquent, il est possible qu'un jour vous travailliez pour une société française ici aux États-Unis. Voici des entreprises françaises qui ont des filiales importantes aux États-Unis: Air France, le Crédit Lyonnais, Fabergé, L'Oréal, Michelin.

Compréhension

ANSWERS

Exercice B

1. Oui (Non), je crois que le français (ne) me sera (pas) utile dans ma carrière.
2. Oui (Non), j'ai (je n'ai pas) choisi une (de) carrière. (J'ai choisi...)
3. De nos jours, le commerce international est très important.
4. Le français avec une autre spécialisation est un outil de valeur incalculable.

Exercice C

1. Oui, il est possible de travailler pour une société américaine et de travailler à l'étranger.
2. Oui, beaucoup de grosses sociétés américaines sont implantées à l'étranger.
3. Oui, la connaissance d'une langue telle que le français pourra m'être utile dans beaucoup de carrières différentes.

OPTIONAL MATERIAL

Découverte culturelle

PRESENTATION *(page 417)*

Have students read the selection silently. Ask them if they can think of any other French companies that do business in the United States.

Note Students may listen to a recorded version of the *Découverte culturelle* on the CD-ROM.

LEARNING FROM PHOTOS

You may wish to tell the students that the American Express office in Paris is a place where Americans traveling abroad can have their mail held for them as well as buy traveler's checks, change money, etc.

INDEPENDENT PRACTICE

Assign any of the following:
1. *Étude de mots* or *Compréhension* exercises, pages 416–417
2. Workbook, *Un Peu Plus*, pages 180–183
3. CD-ROM, Disc 4, pages 416–417

RÉALITÉS

Bell Ringer Review

Write the following on the board or use BRR Blackline Master 16-7: Complete the sentences about this past school year.

1. Je suis content(e) que...
2. Je regrette que...
3. Je suis fâché(e) que...
4. Je suis triste que...
5. Je suis surpris(e) que...

OPTIONAL MATERIAL

PRESENTATION *(page 418)*

Have students look at the photographs for enjoyment.

Note In the CD-ROM version, students can listen to the recorded captions and discover a hidden video behind one of the photos.

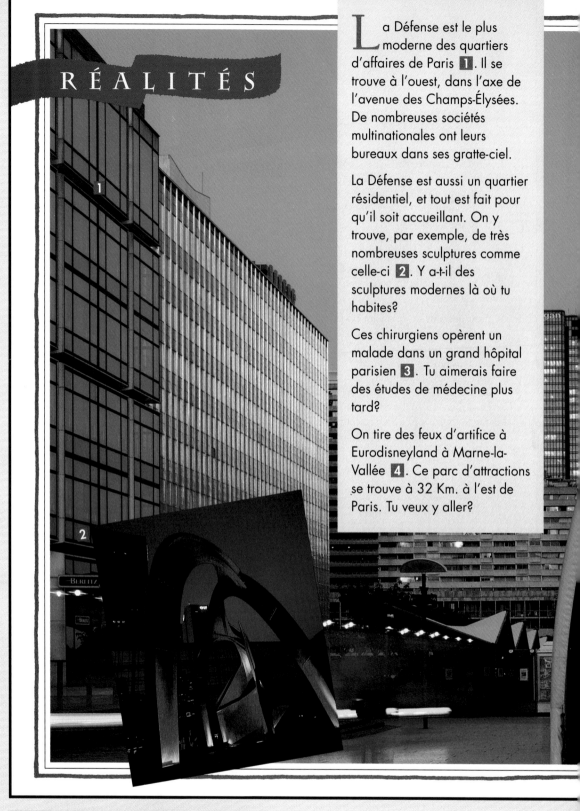

La Défense est le plus moderne des quartiers d'affaires de Paris **1**. Il se trouve à l'ouest, dans l'axe de l'avenue des Champs-Élysées. De nombreuses sociétés multinationales ont leurs bureaux dans ses gratte-ciel.

La Défense est aussi un quartier résidentiel, et tout est fait pour qu'il soit accueillant. On y trouve, par exemple, de très nombreuses sculptures comme celle-ci **2**. Y a-t-il des sculptures modernes là où tu habites?

Ces chirurgiens opèrent un malade dans un grand hôpital parisien **3**. Tu aimerais faire des études de médecine plus tard?

On tire des feux d'artifice à Eurodisneyland à Marne-la-Vallée **4**. Ce parc d'attractions se trouve à 32 Km. à l'est de Paris. Tu veux y aller?

DID YOU KNOW?

Eurodisneyland was initially decried by some Europeans as an unwelcome invasion of American pop culture. After several years of financial difficulty and a period of adaption to its new clientele, Eurodisneyland has established itself as a major European tourist destination. It was recently renamed Disneyland Paris in an attempt to give it a clearer sense of identity.

419

GEOGRAPHY CONNECTION

Have students find La Défense on the Paris Map Transparency or on the map on page 436. Tell them that the business district of La Défense with its skyscrapers and modern architecture looks more like an American city than a European one. The district takes its name from a monument commemorating the defense of Paris in 1871.

ADDITIONAL PRACTICE

Assign any of the following:
1. Student Tape Manual, Teacher's Edition, *Deuxième Partie,* pages 167–169
2. Situation Cards, Chapter 16

CULMINATION

Bell Ringer Review

Write the following on the board or use BRR Blackline Master 16-8: Complete the sentences with the past subjunctive of the verbs in parentheses.

1. Ses parents sont heureux que Charlotte ____ à la ferme. (aller)
2. Elle est surprise que les animaux ____ beaucoup de bruit. (faire)
3. Elle regrette qu'on ____ à cinq heures du matin. (se lever)
4. Elle est contente que les fermiers ____ une bonne récolte. (avoir)
5. Ils sont tristes qu'elle ____ partir. (devoir)

RECYCLING

These activities encourage students to use all the language they have learned in the chapter and recombine it with material from previous chapters. It is not necessary to do all the activities with all students. You may select the ones you consider most appropriate or permit students to choose the ones they wish to do.

INFORMAL ASSESSMENT

Use the oral and written exercises in this section as a review at the end of the chapter or to evaluate speaking and writing skills. For guidelines on assigning oral grades, see the evaluation criteria on page 22 of this Teacher's Wraparound Edition.

Activités de communication orale

ANSWERS

Activités A, B, and C
Answers will vary.

Activités de communication orale

A Un entretien. Travaillez avec un(e) camarade. Lisez les petites annonces du journal *Le Monde* et choisissez-en une qui vous intéresse. Votre camarade vous accordera un entretien pour ce poste. Préparez ensemble votre conversation et présentez-la à la classe.

B «Career Day». C'est *Career Day* dans votre école. Votre professeur vous a demandé de préparer un petit discours sur l'importance des langues étrangères. Dans votre discours dites pourquoi le français peut vous être utile plus tard. Donnez votre discours à une autre classe de français.

C Voulez-vous travailler à l'étranger? Travaillez avec un(e) camarade. Demandez-lui s'il/si elle aimerait travailler pour une société multinationale et pourquoi. Si votre camarade dit «oui», demandez-lui s'il/si elle préférerait travailler à l'étranger ou aux États-Unis et pourquoi.

> Élève 1: Tu aimerais travailler pour une société multinationale?
> Élève 2: Oui, parce que j'aimerais pouvoir utiliser mon français.
> Élève 1: Tu préférerais travailler ici ou à l'étranger?

Emplois de l'automobile

CONCESSION CITROEN
recherche
AGENT DE COMPTOIR
Location courte durée.
Une expérience Citer ou Grand Loir serait un plus.
Ecrire CV réf. A89145
à PREMIER CONTACT
34, rue de Rennes
92456 - Levallois cedex

JOB INTÉRESSANT
(Paris -12°)
Personnes Jeunes
Rémunération motivante.
Formation assurée.
Venez rejoindre une grande société d'études par téléphone.
Pour en savoir plus:
contactez
Sonia Dubon
32.45.81.39

Emplois divers

MAIRE DE BANLIEUE OUEST
recherche d'URGENCE
pour l'ouverture d'un JARDIN D'ENFANTS
PERSONNEL DIPLÔMÉ:
1 EDUCATRICE DE JEUNES ENFANTS (RESPONSABLE)
ou
1 PUERICULTRICE
et
1 AUXILIAIRE DE PUERICULTURE
Adr. lettre manuscrite à l'attention de M. le Maire avec photo et C.V.

URGENT!
SOCIÉTÉ HAUTE SÉCURITÉ
recrute Agents de Sécurité
Spécialistes en protection rapprochée. Réf. exigées.
Contacter le 21.67.64.34.

Activités de communication écrite

A Pour trouver du travail. Avec un(e) camarade faites une liste détaillée de tout ce qu'il faut faire pour trouver du travail. Que faut-il lire, comment doit-on procéder ensuite, comment faut-il s'habiller le jour de l'entretien, etc.? Comparez votre liste et celles de vos camarades.

B Vos aptitudes. Travaillez avec les élèves de commerce et de psychologie et votre professeur de français pour écrire un test d'orientation professionnelle. Faites passer ce test aux classes de français.

Réintroduction et recombinaison

A **Tous les temps.** Complétez.

1. chanter
   a. Il ___ aujourd'hui.
   b. Il ___ hier.
   c. Il ___ toujours quand il était enfant.
   d. Il ___ demain.
   e. Il ___ s'il n'avait pas mal à la gorge.
   f. Je veux qu'il ___.

2. aller
   a. Je ___ en France tous les ans.
   b. Je ___ en France l'année dernière.
   c. J'___ toujours en France quand mes cousins y habitaient.
   d. J'___ en France l'année prochaine.
   e. J'___ en France si j'avais plus d'argent.
   f. Il veut que j'___ en France.

3. prendre
   a. Ils ___ l'avion chaque fois qu'ils vont en Floride.
   b. Ils ___ l'avion hier.
   c. Ils ___ toujours l'avion parce qu'ils n'aimaient pas le train.
   d. Ils ___ l'avion quand ils iront en Floride.
   e. Ils ___ l'avion si les billets coûtaient moins cher.
   f. Tu préfères qu'ils ___ l'avion?

Vocabulaire

NOMS
le lieu de travail
la profession
le métier

la (grosse) société
l'entreprise (f.)
le bureau
le directeur, la directrice
le/la secrétaire
le/la comptable
l'informaticien(ne)
l'ingénieur, la femme ingénieur
le cadre, la femme cadre

la mairie
le/la fonctionnaire
l'assistant(e) social(e)

le tribunal

le juge
l'avocat(e)

le magasin
le commerçant, la commerçante

le théâtre
l'acteur (m.), l'actrice (f.)
le comédien, la comédienne
le chanteur, la chanteuse
le danseur, la danseuse
le technicien, la technicienne
le service du personnel
l'employeur, l'employeuse
l'employé(e)
l'emploi (m.)
le travail
le poste
la carrière
le salaire

le chômage
le bureau de placement
la (petite) annonce
la demande d'emploi
la candidature
le candidat, la candidate
le curriculum vitae (CV)
l'entretien (m.)

AUTRES MOTS ET EXPRESSIONS
à peu près
travailler à plein temps
travailler à mi-temps
être à son compte
être au chômage
chercher du travail
poser sa candidature
être candidat à un poste
être libre immédiatement

CHAPITRE 16   **421**

Activités de communication écrite

ANSWERS

Activités A and B
   Answers will vary.

OPTIONAL MATERIAL

Réintroduction et recombinaison

PRESENTATION   *(page 421)*

Exercice A
   This exercise reviews all verb tenses learned so far.

ANSWERS

1. a. chante   d. chantera
   b. a chanté   e. chanterait
   c. chantait   f. chante

2. a. vais   d. irai
   b. suis allé(e) e. irais
   c. allais   f. aille

3. a. prennent
   b. ont pris
   c. prenaient
   d. prendront
   e. prendraient
   f. prennent

ASSESSMENT RESOURCES

1. Chapter Quizzes
2. Testing Program
3. Situation Cards
4. Communication Transparency C-16
5. Performance Assessment
6. Computer Software: Practice/Test Generator

VIDEO PROGRAM

INTRODUCTION   (55:32)

LE FRANÇAIS ET   (56:15)
TA CARRIÈRE

STUDENT PORTFOLIO

   Written assignments which may be included in students' portfolios are the *Activités de communication écrite* on page 420 and any writing activities from the *Un Peu Plus* section in the Workbook.

Note Students may create and save both oral and written work using the Electronic Portfolio feature on the CD-ROM.

INDEPENDENT PRACTICE

Assign any of the following:
1. Activities and exercises, pages 420–421
2. Communication Activities Masters, pages 101–106
3. CD-ROM, Disc 4, pages 420–421

RÉVISION

CHAPITRES 13-16

OVERVIEW

This section reviews key vocabulary and the use of the subjunctive, which was taught in Chapters 11–16. Use of the subjunctive was presented on the following pages: 279–280, 282, 304, 305, 306, 339, 340, 362, 386, 388, 410, 411, 412.

REVIEW RESOURCES

1. Bell Ringer Review Blackline Masters, R16-1, page 44
2. Workbook, Self-Test 4, pages 184–190
3. Videocassette/Videodisc, Unit 4
4. Video Activities Booklet, Unit 4: Chapters 13–16, pages 55–73
5. Computer Software, Chapters 13–16
6. Testing Program, Unit Test: Chapters 13–16, pages 123–129
7. Performance Assessment
8. CD-ROM, Disc 4, *Révision*: pages 422–425
9. CD-ROM, Disc 4, Self-Tests 13–16
10. CD-ROM, Disc 4, Game: *Le Tour de France*
11. Lesson Plans

Conversation

PRESENTATION *(page 422)*

A. Call on two students to read the conversation aloud as the class listens with books closed.

B. Read the conversation again as students follow along in their books.

Note You may wish to have students find all the subordinate clauses in the conversation and explain why the subjunctive or the indicative is used in each one.

Conversation   *Une fête surprise*

ÉRIC: Mais où est-ce que Caroline et Rachid peuvent bien être? Ça m'étonne qu'ils ne soient pas encore là!

ANNE: Oui, c'est vrai. Pourvu qu'il ne leur soit pas arrivé quelque chose!

ÉRIC: Jean-Luc va être furieux qu'on ne soit pas là à temps.

ANNE: Oui, il veut vraiment que ce soit une surprise pour Véronique.

ÉRIC: Moi, je suis sûr qu'elle sait qu'on a organisé une fête pour elle.

ANNE: Oh, ça m'étonnerait qu'elle le sache.

ÉRIC: En tout cas, c'est formidable qu'elle ait été reçue à ses derniers examens de chirurgie.

ANNE: Oui, surtout qu'il paraît que ce n'était pas facile.

ÉRIC: Enfin, il faut l'appeler «Docteur Charpentier», maintenant!

ANNE: Je regrette, mais pour moi, ce sera toujours «Véro»!

A   Bravo, Véronique!   Répondez d'après la conversation.

1. Que font Éric et Anne?
2. De quelle origine est le nom Rachid?
3. Où vont les quatre amis?
4. Chez qui?
5. Pourquoi est-ce qu'il donne cette fête?
6. Quelle carrière Véronique a-t-elle choisie?
7. Est-ce qu'elle a fini ses études?
8. Comment doit-on l'appeler, maintenant?
9. Est-ce que ses amis vont l'appeler comme ça?

LEARNING FROM PHOTOS

You may wish to ask the following questions about the photo: *Quelle est la profession de cette femme? Qu'est-ce qu'elle va faire?*

Structure

L'emploi du subjonctif

The subjunctive (present or past) is used in subordinate clauses introduced by *que* to express actions that may or may not happen. However, the subjunctive is used only when the subject of the main clause is different from that of the subordinate clause. If the subjects are the same, the infinitive is used.

> *Je* veux qu'*il parte*. But *Je* veux *partir*.
> *Il* est content que *je parte*. But *Il* est content de *partir*.

The subjunctive (present or past) is used in the following cases.

1. After expressions of opinion, emotions, wishes, and demands

> *Il faut que j'aille* au Maroc.
> Je suis *contente* que tu *aies* pu venir.
> Elle *voudrait* que vous *soyez* là.

Such expressions include:

il faut que	il est bon que
il vaut mieux que	il est temps que
il est préférable que	il est possible que
il est important que	il est impossible que
il est nécessaire que	il est juste que
être content(e) que	être étonné(e) que
être heureux (-se) que	être surpris(e) que
être fâché(e) que	être triste que
être furieux (-se) que	être désolé(e) que
avoir peur que	préférer que
regretter que	désirer que
vouloir que	exiger que
souhaiter que	aimer mieux que
aimer que	insister pour que

Une mosquée à Marrakech

2. After expressions of doubt, uncertainty, or disbelief

> Je *doute* qu'il *vienne*.
> Il est *possible* que vous *veniez*.
> *Ça m'étonnerait* qu'ils *aient fini*.

Such expressions include:

il est possible que	il n'est pas évident que
il n'est pas certain que	ne pas penser que
il n'est pas sûr que	ne pas croire que
douter que	
ça (m') étonnerait que	

Bell Ringer Review

Write the following on the board or use BRR Blackline Master R16-1: You are going to a job interview. Write five questions you are going to ask the interviewer. Begin the questions with the following words.
Quand
Combien
Où
Quel
Qu'est-ce que

Structure
L'emploi du subjonctif

PRESENTATION (*pages 423–424*)

Note This section reviews all the uses of the subjunctive that students have learned. Once again, it is recommended that you emphasize that the subjunctive is used when it is uncertain that the action of the verb will take place.

Have students read the explanation silently.

LEARNING FROM PHOTOS

You may wish to ask the following questions about the photo: *Qu'est-ce qu'il y a devant la mosquée? Les musulmans prient dans la mosquée? Ils prient en direction de la Mecque? Du haut du minaret on a une belle vue sur la ville de Marrakech? Le muezzin est dans le minaret?*

PRESENTATION (*pages 424–425*)

You may wish to have students prepare these exercises before going over them in class.

ANSWERS

Exercice A

1. Pourvu qu'
2. avant que
3. bien qu'
4. jusqu'à ce que
5. à moins que
6. Bien qu'
7. pour qu'
8. sans que

Exercice B

1. Nous sommes désolés qu'il soit allé à la montagne sans nous.
2. Elle est fâchée que vous ne soyez pas venu(e)(s) la voir.
3. J'ai bien peur que vous n'ayez pas réussi.
4. Ils sont étonnés que tu aies fait ce travail.
5. Nathalie est heureuse que Pierre ait pu venir faire du ski avec elle.
6. Je regrette que vous ne m'en ayez pas parlé.
7. Il est furieux qu'ils aient pris des décisions sans lui.

---

3. After certain conjunctions expressing restriction or purpose

   > Je vais lui téléphoner *pour qu*'il *vienne*.

   Such conjunctions include:

bien que	pour que	sans que
pourvu que	avant que	
à moins que	jusqu'à ce que	

4. In relative clauses to express uncertainty or uniqueness

   > Je *cherche* un appartment qui *soit* près d'ici.
   > C'est *la seule* personne qui *ait compris*.

   Expressions of uniqueness include:

   > le seul, la seule, les seuls, les seules
   > le premier, la première, les premiers, les premières
   > le dernier, la dernière, les derniers, les dernières
   > personne
   > rien
   > all superlatives

A **Que de restrictions!** Utilisez les conjonctions suivantes:

bien que	pour que	avant que	sans que
pourvu que	à moins que	jusqu'à ce que	

1. ___ il ne soit pas encore parti!
2. Dépêche-toi de finir ___ ton père rentre.
3. Il a été reçu à son examen ___ il n'ait rien fait pendant l'année.
4. Tu resteras ici ___ tu aies fini tes devoirs.
5. Je peux venir avec vous ___ ma mère ait besoin de moi.
6. ___ il fasse froid, il est sorti sans anorak.
7. Je lui ai donné de l'argent ___ elle s'achète une robe.
8. Ils sont entrés ___ nous les voyions.

B **Que d'émotions!** Changez les phrases d'après le modèle.

> Je suis triste qu'il ne vienne pas avec nous.
> *Je suis triste qu'il ne soit pas venu avec nous.*

1. Nous sommes désolés qu'il aille à la montagne sans nous.
2. Elle est fâchée que vous ne veniez pas la voir.
3. J'ai bien peur que vous ne réussissiez pas.
4. Ils sont étonnés que tu fasses ce travail.
5. Nathalie est heureuse que Pierre puisse venir faire du ski avec elle.
6. Je regrette que vous ne m'en parliez pas.
7. Il est furieux qu'ils prennent des décisions sans lui.

En randonnée dans les Hautes-Alpes

C **Maintenant ou avant.** Mettez les verbes entre parenthèses au présent ou passé du subjonctif.

1. Nous sommes désolés qu'il ___ la cheville. (se tordre)
2. Je souhaite qu'ils ___ de bonnes études. (faire)
3. Vous n'êtes pas surpris qu'elle ne ___ pas là. (être)
4. Oh, là, là! Quelle chute! Pourvu qu'il ne ___ pas ___ la jambe! (se casser)
5. Nous aimerions que vous ___ dîner samedi. (venir)
6. Il n'est pas encore là. J'ai peur qu'il ___ notre rendez-vous. (oublier)

D **De deux phrases, une seule phrase.** Combinez les deux phrases suivantes d'après le modèle.

je pense / je pars demain
Je pense partir demain.

1. nous ne pensons pas / il a obtenu le poste
2. ils ne sont pas contents / on ne leur a pas téléphoné
3. elle a fait signe avant / elle a tourné à gauche
4. nous attendons / nous pouvons récupérer nos bagages
5. je ne suis pas sûr(e) / nous avons pris la bonne route
6. il regrette / je n'ai pas écouté ses conseils

E **Quel mode?** Utilisez le subjonctif, l'indicatif ou l'infinitif.

1. Il a déjà son billet! Je suis sûre qu'il ___. (resquiller)
2. Je regrette que tu ne me le ___ pas ___. (présenter)
3. Nous aimerions beaucoup les ___. (rencontrer)
4. Voulez-vous ___ avec moi demain? (déjeuner)
5. C'est le seul poste que nous ___. (avoir)
6. Ils sont entrés sans ___. (sonner)
7. Nous sommes absolument certains qu'ils ___ demain. (arriver)
8. Je crois qu'il faut que vous ___ une pièce d'abord. (introduire)

Une jolie vue du Loir près de Cloyes-sur-Loir

Activité de communication orale

A **Chez le conseiller d'orientation.** Vous parlez au conseiller/à la conseillère d'orientation de votre école (votre camarade) de ce que vous voulez faire plus tard. Il/Elle vous donne des conseils. Changez ensuite de rôles.

Élève 1: J'aimerais peut-être élever des chevaux.
Élève 2: Il faudrait que vous alliez vivre un peu à la campagne…

Exercice C

1. se soit tordu
2. fassent
3. soit
4. se soit... cassé
5. veniez
6. ait oublié

Exercice D

1. Nous ne pensons pas qu'il ait obtenu le poste.
2. Ils ne sont pas contents qu'on ne leur ait pas téléphoné.
3. Elle a fait signe avant de tourner à gauche.
4. Nous attendons de pouvoir récupérer nos bagages.
5. Je ne suis pas sûr(e) que nous ayons pris la bonne route.
6. Il regrette que je n'aie pas écouté ses conseils.

Exercice E

1. a resquillé
2. l'aies... présenté
3. rencontrer
4. déjeuner
5. ayons
6. sonner
7. arriveront
8. introduisiez

Activité de communication orale

ANSWERS

Activité A

Answers will vary.

LEARNING FROM PHOTOS

You may wish to ask students the following questions about the photo: *C'est en ville ou à la campagne? C'est une jolie vue du Loir. Le Loir est une montagne ou une rivière? Vous aimeriez vivre dans la maison qu'on voit sur la photo? Pourquoi?*

INDEPENDENT PRACTICE

Assign any of the following:

1. Exercises and activity, pages 424–425
2. Workbook, Self-Test 4, pages 184–190
3. Computer Software, Chapters 13–16
4. CD-ROM, Disc 4, pages 424–425
5. CD-ROM, Disc 4, Self-Tests 13–16
6. CD-ROM, Disc 4, Game: *Le Tour de France*

Politique: Charles de Gaulle (1890–1970)

OVERVIEW

It is recommended that you allow students to choose which of the three readings they would like to read. If a student has no interest in a particular topic, it is not necessary for him or her to read it.

See page 106 in this Teacher's Wraparound Edition for suggestions on presenting the readings at different levels of intensity.

Avant la lecture

Note This selection is quite easy, and students should have little difficulty understanding it.

PRESENTATION (page 426)

A. Go over the *Avant la lecture* questions with the students.
B. Have students scan the reading for cognates. There are approximately 45.

Lecture

PRESENTATION (pages 426–427)

Have the students read the selection silently.

POLITIQUE: CHARLES DE GAULLE (1890-1970)

Avant la lecture

1. What do you know about the Second World War? Who were the principal American and European statesmen of the time?
2. The major European countries had colonies in Africa. Which African countries are former French colonies?

Lecture

Le général Charles de Gaulle a été un des plus grands hommes d'État que la France ait connu. Il commence sa carrière militaire à l'École des officiers de Saint-Cyr. Pendant la Première Guerre mondiale, il est blessé[1] et fait prisonnier par les Allemands. Entre les deux guerres, il voit avec appréhension le danger que représente Hitler, mais personne en France ne veut l'écouter.

L'appel du général de Gaulle au peuple français, le 18 juin 1940

Au début de la Deuxième Guerre mondiale, lorsque la France capitule devant l'Allemagne, il part pour l'Angleterre, et le 18 juin 1940, il lance un appel à la BBC—la radio anglaise—où il encourage les Français à continuer la lutte[2]. De 1940 à 1944, il organise les Forces françaises libres qui combatteront avec les Alliés, et il coordonne la Résistance française de l'intérieur contre l'occupation allemande.

À la Libération, en juin 1944, le général

Le général de Gaulle sur les Champs-Élysées à la Libération de Paris

de Gaulle revient en France et devient président du Gouvernement provisoire de la République française. Il remet la France sur pied. Mais la Constitution ne permet pas à de Gaulle de gouverner comme il le veut, et il donne sa démission[3] en janvier 1946.

En 1958, la guerre d'Algérie divise les Français. Aucun gouvernement ne sait comment y mettre fin[4]. L'Algérie est alors un territoire français, avec une population de neuf millions de musulmans et un million de non-musulmans d'origine européenne. Les Algériens musulmans veulent leur indépendance, mais les non-musulmans, partisans de «l'Algérie française», s'y opposent.

En janvier 1959, le général de Gaulle devient président de la République. C'est

DID YOU KNOW?

Give students the following information about Charles de Gaulle: *Charles de Gaulle a eu une carrière militaire. Pendant la Première Guerre mondiale il est fait prisonnier par les Allemands. Il comprend le danger que représente Hitler. Pendant la Deuxième Guerre mondiale, il coordonne la Résistance française contre l'occupation allemande.*

SCIENCES

alors qu'il proclame le principe de l'autodétermination, ou droit des peuples à disposer d'eux-mêmes. Les Algériens voteront pour décider s'ils veulent rester français ou devenir indépendants. Les partisans de l'Algérie française organisent de violentes manifestations pour essayer de renverser[5] de Gaulle. Ils ne réussissent pas, et en 1962 l'Algérie devient indépendante.

Jusqu'en 1969, année où il se retire de la vie publique, de Gaulle travaille au rapprochement des pays d'Europe. Ainsi en 1963, il signe le traité de coopération franco-allemande qui marque la réconciliation de la France avec l'Allemagne.

Lorsqu'il meurt en 1970, le président Georges Pompidou annonce: «Le général de Gaulle est mort. La France est veuve[6]».

Le portrait officiel du Président Charles de Gaulle

[1] blessé *wounded*
[2] lutte *fight*
[3] donne sa démission *resigns*
[4] y mettre fin *to put an end to it*
[5] renverser *to overthrow*
[6] veuve *a widow*

Le discours du général de Gaulle à Alger, le 4 juin 1958

Après la lecture

A **Le général de Gaulle.** Répondez aux questions.

1. Qu'est-ce que le général de Gaulle a accompli en tant que militaire?
2. Qu'est-ce qu'il a accompli en tant qu'homme d'État?

B **Un grand homme d'État.** Choisissez un homme d'État que vous admirez et écrivez sa biographie en français.

C **Jeanne d'Arc.** Comme Jeanne d'Arc, de Gaulle pensait qu'il avait pour mission de sauver la France. Lisez la vie de Jeanne d'Arc et faites un parallèle entre Jeanne d'Arc et de Gaulle.

LETTRES ET SCIENCES **427**

Botanique: La Vie d'un arbre
Avant la lecture

Note Students who appreciate botany and ecology will enjoy this reading.

PRESENTATION *(page 428)*

A. Have the students give a brief definition of *photosynthesis* and *chlorophyll*, as suggested in the *Avant la lecture* section. Students will understand the selection more easily if they understand these terms. (See **Interdisciplinary Connections** below.)

B. Have the students look at the two illustrations to familiarize themselves with the technical vocabulary they will need.

C. Tell students to look for the following information as they read.
1. Comment est-ce qu'on peut déterminer l'âge d'un arbre?
2. Pourquoi les arbres sont-ils tellement importants pour les humains?

Lecture

PRESENTATION *(pages 428–429)*

Explain to students that they should try to get the general idea of the reading, but that it is not necessary that they understand every word. Have them read the selection silently.

BOTANIQUE: LA VIE D'UN ARBRE

Avant la lecture

Define the following: photosynthesis and chlorophyll.

Lecture

Un arbre est un être vivant. Comme les êtres humains, il a besoin de nourriture: protéines, lipides et sucres. Comment se nourrit-il? Grâce à l'eau et au soleil.

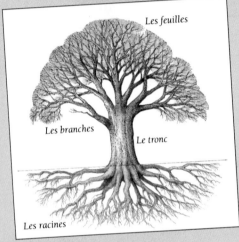

Dessin d'un arbre

Les racines de l'arbre absorbent l'eau qui forme la sève brute[1]. La sève brute monte dans l'arbre par des tubes appelés «vaisseaux conducteurs de sève». Elle monte jusqu'aux feuilles et là, il y a «photosynthèse».

La photosynthèse est une réaction chimique qui fabrique la sève élaborée, riche en protéines et en oxygène. Cette réaction se fait à partir de[2] l'eau de la sève brute et du gaz carbonique[3] de l'air. Mais il faut aussi du soleil. Cette énergie solaire, les feuilles la captent grâce à la chlorophylle. C'est la chlorophylle qui donne aux feuilles leur couleur verte.

La sève élaborée redescend ensuite dans l'arbre par d'autres vaisseaux conducteurs, situés dans un petit anneau[4], juste sous l'écorce de l'arbre. Cet anneau est la seule partie vivante de l'arbre — en effet, le cœur du tronc est du bois mort. Chaque année, un nouvel anneau se forme. On peut déterminer l'âge d'un arbre au nombre de ses anneaux.

Les arbres vivent à un rythme différent, selon les saisons. Au printemps, les bourgeons[5] éclatent, les fleurs apparaissent,

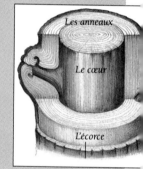

Coupe transversale du tronc d'un arbre

et bientôt les feuilles aussi. En automne, la sève ne circule pratiquement plus, les feuilles ne font plus de photosynthèse, donc leur couleur verte disparaît et d'autres pigments apparaissent. Puis les feuilles tombent et forment une couche[6] qui protège les racines du froid. Petit à petit, les feuilles se décomposent pour former de l'humus qui pénètre dans le sol et le nourrit de ses sels minéraux.

INTERDISCIPLINARY CONNECTIONS

Invite students from one of the science classes at your school to explain photosynthesis and chlorophyll to the class. Have them bring illustrations from their science books to compare with those in the reading.

DID YOU KNOW?

About one fourth of France is covered by forests, especially the northeastern plateaus, the central highlands, the southwestern coastal areas, and the slopes of the Alps, Jura, Pyrenees, and Vosges. Forests include both coniferous and deciduous trees. Along the Mediterranean and on Corsica, cork oaks, pine trees, and olive trees flourish. Because of the dryness, forest fires in these areas are common.

SCIENCES

Forêt Communale de Lacoste

La plupart des forêts du monde sont en danger, et pourtant les êtres humains ont absolument besoin des arbres pour survivre. La respiration des plantes est l'inverse de celle des hommes: les plantes absorbent du gaz carbonique et rejettent de l'oxygène. Les hommes absorbent de l'oxygène et rejettent du gaz carbonique. Nous nous complétons donc parfaitement. On dit souvent que la grande forêt d'Amazonie est le poumon[7] de la Terre.

Chaque minute qui passe voit disparaître trente hectares de forêt. Le déboisement[8] est critique parce que c'est toute la chaîne vivante qui est détruite. En effet, les arbres ne sont pas seulement indispensables pour les hommes, ils le sont aussi pour les insectes et autres animaux qui vivent dans la forêt. Un arbre nourrit une grande variété d'animaux: scarabées, écureuils[9], daims[10], etc. Dans certaines régions du monde, en France en particulier, il y a des programmes de reboisement, mais une forêt ne renaît pas en quelques années. Espérons qu'il n'est pas trop tard!

[1] sève brute *rising sap*
[2] à partir de *from*
[3] gaz carbonique *carbon dioxide*
[4] anneau *ring*
[5] bourgeons *buds*
[6] couche *cover*
[7] poumon *lung*
[8] déboisement *deforestation*
[9] écureuils *squirrels*
[10] daims *deer*

Après la lecture

A **Les arbres.** Vrai ou faux?

1. Un arbre n'a pas besoin de soleil.
2. La sève brute est riche en protéines et en oxygène.
3. Les couleurs des feuilles en automne sont dues à la chlorophylle.
4. Le cœur du tronc est la partie vivante de l'arbre.
5. Les feuilles protègent les racines de l'arbre pendant l'hiver.
6. L'humus est formé par des feuilles décomposées.
7. Les êtres humains et les plantes respirent de la même façon.
8. Les animaux ont besoin de la forêt.
9. Une forêt met longtemps à renaître.
10. Il y a très peu de forêts en danger dans le monde.

B **La vie d'un arbre.** Mettez en ordre les phrases suivantes:

— Il y a photosynthèse.
— Les racines absorbent l'eau.
— La sève brute monte jusqu'aux feuilles.
— Il fait du soleil.
— Il pleut.
— La sève élaborée redescend dans l'arbre.

C **Si les arbres parlaient.** Imaginez qu'un arbre près de chez vous puisse parler. Que dirait-il?

D **Contre le déboisement.** La plupart des forêts du monde sont en danger. Que devrait-on faire pour arrêter le déboisement de la planète?

LETTRES ET SCIENCES **429**

Littérature: La Littérature de langue française hors de France
Avant la lecture
PRESENTATION *(page 430)*

A. Go over the *Avant la lecture* activities with students. (You may wish to use *Le Monde francophone* Map Transparency or the map on page 437.)

B. Have students think about the following question: What comparisons could a writer make between a tree and an immigrant? Think in terms of an uprooted tree.

Lecture
PRESENTATION *(pages 430–431)*

Note Students will find it easier to understand the excerpt by Tahar Ben Jelloun if they have read the preceding *Lettres et sciences* selection about trees.

A. You may wish to have all students read the entire selection, or divide the class in half and have each group read about one author.

B. Have the students read the selection silently.

Note Students will read an excerpt from *La Réclusion solitaire* by Tahar Ben Jelloun in Glencoe French 3, *En voyage*, page 98.

LITTÉRATURE: LA LITTÉRATURE DE LANGUE FRANÇAISE HORS DE FRANCE

Avant la lecture

1. Faites une liste des pays francophones que vous connaissez.
2. Trouvez de quels pays viennent ces écrivains célèbres. Ils écrivent tous en français, mais ils ne sont pas français: Antonine Maillet, Birago Diop, Maurice Maeterlinck, Camara Laye, Jacques Roumain, Rachid Boudjedra, Charles Ramuz.

Lecture

Pendant longtemps, les écrivains de langue française ont pris la France comme modèle. Mais de nos jours, après deux guerres mondiales et les changements politiques et sociaux qui ont suivi, ces écrivains ont pris conscience de leur identité culturelle. Tout comme la création, la diffusion de la littérature de langue française n'est plus concentrée en France, Belgique et Suisse, mais existe au Maghreb (Algérie, Tunisie, Maroc), en Afrique noire, au Québec et aux Antilles.

TAHAR BEN JELLOUN
Tahar Ben Jelloun est né à Fès, au Maroc, en 1944. Romancier et poète, il reçoit le prix Goncourt en 1987, pour son roman *La Nuit sacrée*. Dans cet extrait de *La Réclusion solitaire* (1976), il compare les travailleurs

immigrés à des arbres.

«Nous sommes un pays déboisé de ses hommes. Des arbres arrachés[1] à la terre, comptabilisés et envoyés au froid. Quand nous arrivons en France, nos branches ne sont plus lourdes, les feuilles sont légères; elles sont mortes. Nos racines sont sèches et nous n'avons pas soif.

Si je nous compare à un arbre, c'est parce que tout tend à mourir en nous et la sève ne coule plus. Tout le monde trouve ‹normal› ce déboisement sélectif. Mais que peut un arbre arraché à l'aube[2] de sa vie? Que peut un corps étranger dans une terre fatiguée?»

(La Réclusion solitaire, Tahar Ben Jelloun, Éditions du Seuil, Paris, 1981, pp. 56-57)

[1] arrachés *torn*   [2] aube *dawn*

LÉOPOLD SÉDAR SENGHOR

Léopold Sédar Senghor est né à Djilor, au Sénégal, en 1906. Avec l'écrivain martiniquais Aimé Césaire, il fonde le mouvement de la «négritude[1]». Senghor se lance ensuite dans la politique. De 1963 à 1980, il sera

---

DID YOU KNOW?

Le terme «négritude» naît en 1934, dans un journal *L'Étudiant Noir*, lancé à Paris par trois écrivains de langue française: Léon-Gontran Damas, guyanais, Aimé Césaire, martiniquais et Léopold Sédar Senghor, sénégalais. Ce mouvement exaltait le retour à l'Afrique, le refus d'idéologies culturelles et littéraires européennes, tout comme l'a fait le mouvement «Black is beautiful» dans les années 60 aux États-Unis. La première expression de ce mouvement est littéraire, bien sûr, et poétique en particulier. En 1937 c'est *Pigments* de Damas. En 1939, c'est *Cahier d'un retour au pays natal* de Césaire. Après la Deuxième Guerre mondiale, Senghor publie *Chants d'Ombre*, poèmes auxquels il travaillait depuis longtemps. Mais après la guerre, les écrivains de la Négritude délaissent la littérature et deviennent hommes

(continued on next page)

président de la République du Sénégal.

Dans ses poèmes et ses écrits, Léopold Sédar Senghor célèbre la grandeur de la négritude et l'espoir de réconciliation des races. Le texte suivant est un extrait de *Négritude et humanisme* (1964).

"Un homme de l'Occident se représente difficilement la place qu'occupent les activités sociales, et parmi celles-ci, la littérature et l'art, dans le calendrier négro-africain. Elles n'occupent pas seulement «le dimanche» et les «soirées théâtrales», mais pour prendre l'exemple de la zone soudanienne, les huit mois de la saison sèche. On est alors tout occupé à ses relations avec les *Autres*: génies, Ancêtres, membres de la famille, de la tribu, du royaume[2], voire[3] étrangers. Ce ne sont que fêtes, et la Mort elle-même est une occasion de fête, de la *Fête* par excellence: fête des moissons[4] et fête des semailles[5]; naissances, initiations, mariages, funérailles; fêtes des corporations et fêtes des confréries. Et tous les soirs, ce sont les contes[6] des veillées[7] autour du foyer[8], les danses et les chants, les jeux gymniques, les drames et les comédies qu'éclairent[9] de hautes flammes. Et le travail qui célèbre les noces[10] de l'Homme et de la Terre, est encore relation et *poésie*. Ainsi les chants de travail: chants du paysan, du piroguier[11], du pâtre[12]. Car en Afrique noire, (...) toute littérature, tout art est poésie."

(*Liberté I: Négritude et humanisme*, Léopold Sédar Senghor, Éditions du Seuil, Paris, 1964)

[1] négritude *Black pride*
[2] royaume *kingdom*
[3] voire *nay, even*
[4] moissons *harvest*
[5] semailles *sowing*
[6] contes *stories*
[7] veillées *evening gatherings*
[8] foyer *fire*
[9] éclairent *lighted*
[10] noces *nuptials*
[11] piroguier *boatman*
[12] pâtre *shepherd*

La Fête des Vieux en Côte d'Ivoire

Après la lecture

A **Nord-africains en France.**
Répondez aux questions.

1. Quels sont les mots qui se rapportent à la vie d'un arbre?
2. Pourquoi ces hommes vont-ils travailler en France?
3. Y a-t-il des travailleurs immigrés aux États-Unis? De quel(s) pays viennent-ils? Que font-ils?

B **En Afrique noire.** Répondez aux questions.

1. À quelle époque de l'année ont lieu les activités sociales dans la zone soudanienne?
2. Qui sont les *Autres*?
3. Quelles sont les occasions de fête? Quelle est l'occasion de la *Fête* par excellence?
4. En quoi consistent les activités pendant les fêtes?
5. Que célèbre le travail?
6. Qu'est-ce que le travail, la littérature et l'art ont en commun en Afrique noire?
7. Y a-t-il aux États-Unis un mouvement semblable à celui de la «négritude» (en littérature ou dans les arts)? Faites des recherches.

Après la lecture

PRESENTATION *(page 431)*

Ask students to summarize in their own words the ideas expressed by Ben Jelloun and Senghor.

Exercices

ANSWERS

Exercice A

1. déboisé, arrachés, les branches, les feuilles, les racines, la sève, le déboisement
2. Ils vont y travailler parce qu'il y a beaucoup de chômage au Maghreb et ils ne peuvent pas y trouver de travail.
3. Answers will vary. Students might mention migrant farm workers from Mexico and Latin America and domestic and clothing industry workers from the Caribbean and Asia.

Exercice B

1. Elles ont lieu pendant les huit mois de la saison sèche.
2. Les *Autres* sont les génies, les Ancêtres, les membres de la famille, les membres de la tribu, les membres du royaume, les étrangers.
3. Les moissons, les semailles, les naissances, les initiations, les mariages, les funérailles, les corporations, les confréries sont tous des occasions de fête. La Mort est l'occasion de la Fête par excellence.
4. Il y a des contes, des danses, des chants, des jeux gymniques, des drames et des comédies.
5. Le travail célèbre les noces de l'Homme et de la Terre.
6. Ils sont tous poésie.
7. Answers will vary.

(continued)

politiques militant contre le colonialisme. En 1947 est publiée la revue *Présence Africaine* qui paraît à Paris et à Dakar et qui bénéficie immédiatement de l'appui de tous les intellectuels de l'époque, notamment Gide, Sartre et Camus. Le public commence alors à connaître la littérature africaine de langue française. L'âge d'or du roman africain commence. C'est Camara Laye avec *L'Enfant noir* (1953), *Ô pays mon beau peuple* de Sembene Ousmane. D'autres écrivains, tel que Birago Diop, reviennent aux sources et font connaître au monde la tradition orale africaine: ce sont *Les contes d'Amadou Koumba* (1947). De nos jours, la littérature africaine en langue française occupe une place de premier plan dans la littérature internationale.

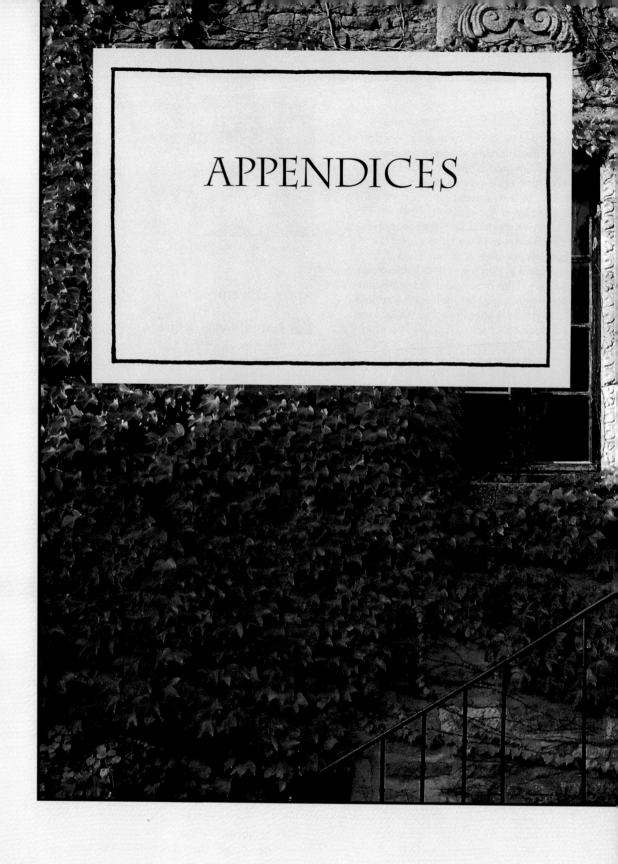

APPENDICES

433

CARTES

LA FRANCE

L'ANGLETERRE

Amsterdam

LES PAYS-BAS

La Mer
du Nord

52°

la Tamise

Londres

L'ALLEMAGNE

la Meuse

le Rhin

Bonn

Calais

Bruxelles

La Manche

Lille

LA BELGIQUE

le Mein

Amiens

LE LUXEMBOURG

Cherbourg

Luxembourg

Les Îles
Anglo-
Normandes

Le Havre

Rouen

Reims

Metz

le Rhin

Caen

la Seine

la Marne

Strasbourg

Nancy

LES VOSGES

la Moselle

le Danube

Paris

la Seine

Troyes

Rennes

Le Mans

Orléans

Chaumont

Ballon de Guebwiller
1424 m

LES VOSGES

Mulhouse

le Rhin

48°

Angers

Tours

la Loire

Dijon

la Saône

Besançon

L'AUTRICHE

Nantes

LE JURA

Berne

LA SUISSE

Poitiers

LA FRANCE

la Loire

Crêt de la Neige
1723 m

le Lac Léman

LES ALPES

La Rochelle

le Rhône

Genève

L'Océan
Atlantique

Vichy

Chamonix

Limoges

Clermont-
Ferrand

Lyon

Mont Blanc
4807 m

St-Étienne

LES ALPES

L'ITALIE

Le puy de Sancy
1886 m

la Dordogne

Grenoble

le Rhône

le Pô

Bordeaux

LE MASSIF
CENTRAL

Rodez

la Garonne

44°

Nîmes

Avignon

Nice

Bayonne

Toulouse

Montpellier

Aix-en-
Provence

Cannes

MONACO

Marseille

LES PYRÉNÉES

Toulon

l'Èbre

Vignemale
3298 m

Perpignan

L'ANDORRE

La Corse

La Mer
Méditerranée

Ajaccio

L'ESPAGNE

N

435

adrid

O — E

0   100   200

S

Kilomètres

La
Sardaigne

0°   4°   8°

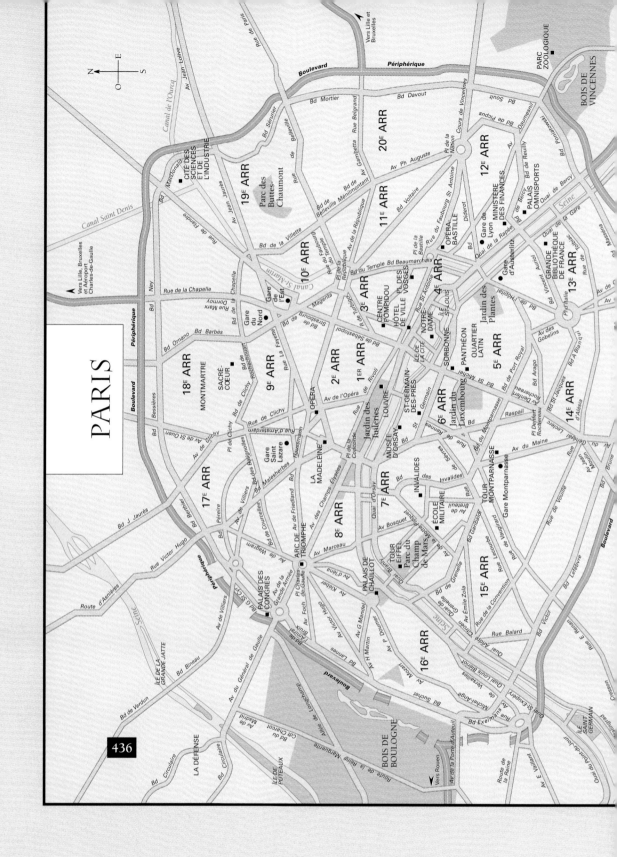

PARIS

436

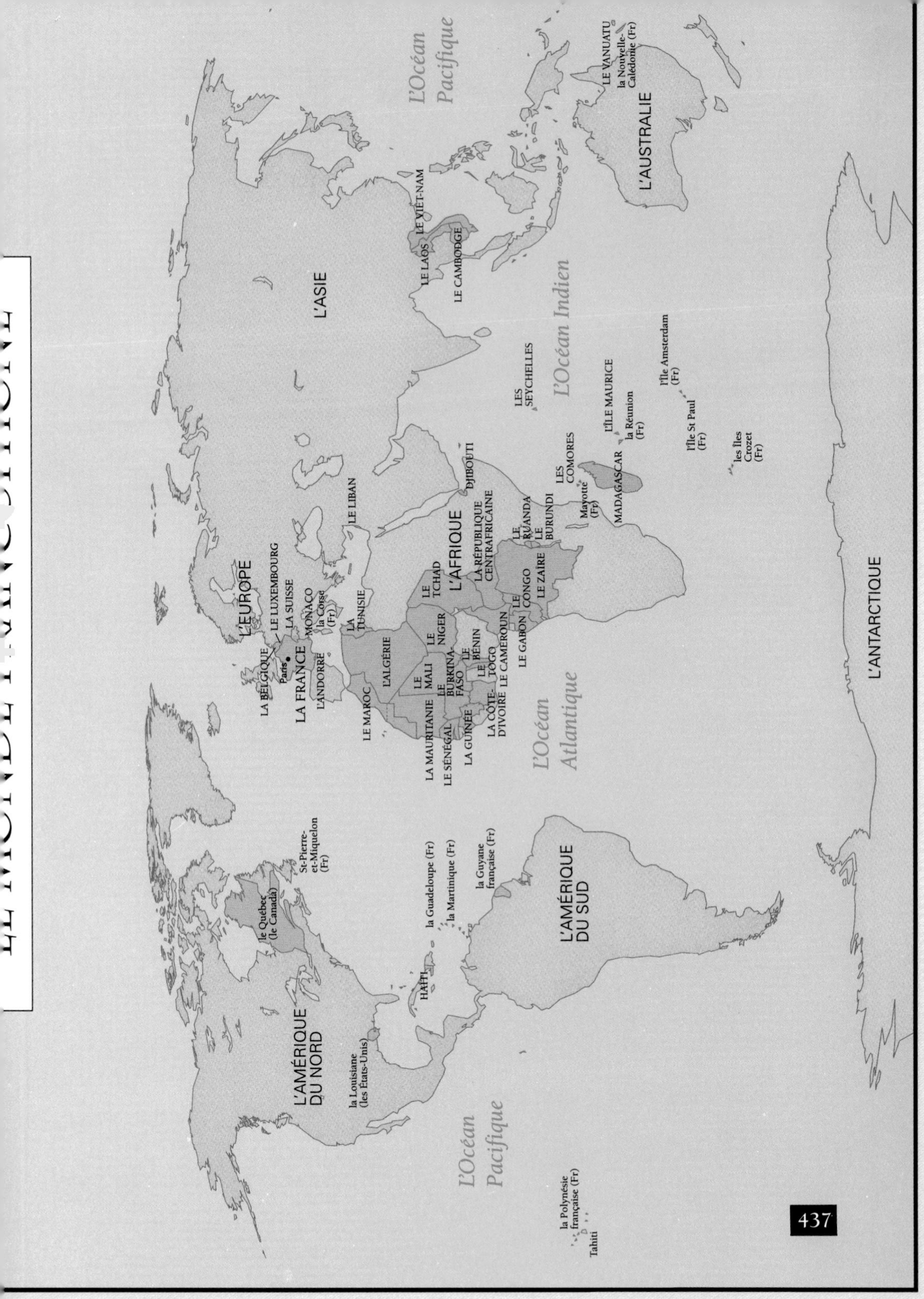

L'Océan
Pacifique

L'AUSTRALIE

LE VANUATU
la Nouvelle-
Calédonie (Fr)

L'ASIE

LE VIÊT-NAM
LE LAOS

LE CAMBODGE

L'Océan Indien

LES
SEYCHELLES

l'Île Amsterdam
(Fr)

l'ÎLE MAURICE
la Réunion
(Fr)

l'Île St Paul
(Fr)

les Îles
Crozet
(Fr)

LES
COMORES

Mayotte
(Fr)

MADAGASCAR

DJIBOUTI

LE LIBAN

L'AFRIQUE

LA RÉPUBLIQUE
CENTRAFRICAINE

LE
RWANDA
LE
BURUNDI

L'EUROPE

LE LUXEMBOURG
LA SUISSE
MONACO
la Corse
(Fr)
LA
TUNISIE

LE
TCHAD

LE GABON

LE
ZAÏRE

LE CONGO

LA BELGIQUE
Paris
LA FRANCE
L'ANDORRE

L'ALGÉRIE

LE
NIGER

LE CAMEROUN

LE MAROC

LE
MALI
LE
BURKINA
FASO
LE
BÉNIN
LE
TOGO

LA MAURITANIE
LE SÉNÉGAL
LA GUINÉE
LA CÔTE-
D'IVOIRE

L'Océan
Atlantique

St-Pierre-
et-Miquelon
(Fr)

la Guadeloupe (Fr)
la Martinique (Fr)

la Guyane
française (Fr)

L'AMÉRIQUE
DU SUD

le Québec
(le Canada)

HAÏTI

L'AMÉRIQUE
DU NORD

la Louisiane
(les États-Unis)

L'Océan
Pacifique

la Polynésie
française (Fr)
Tahiti

L'ANTARCTIQUE

437

PRONONCIATION
ET ORTHOGRAPHE

I. La transcription phonétique

[a]	la, là, avec	[ã]	dans, encore, temps
[é]	télé, chez, dîner, les	[õ]	non, regardons
[è]	elle, êtes, frère	[ẽ]	fin, demain
[i]	qui, il, lycée, dîne	[œ̃]	un
[ü]	tu, une		
[u]	vous, où, bonjour	[y]	fille, travailler
[ó]	au, beaucoup, allô		
[ò]	homme, alors	[sh]	chez, Michel
[œ̇]	deux, veut	[zh]	je, âge
[œ]	heure, sœur	[g]	garder, goûter, Guy

II. L'alphabet français

a b c d e f g h i j k l m n o p q r s t u v w x y z
Voyelles: a e i(y) o u
Consonnes: b c d f g h j k l m n p q r s t v w x z

III. Les accents

There are five written accent marks on French letters. These accents are part of the spelling of the word and cannot be omitted.

1. *L'accent aigu* (´) occurs over the letter *e*.

   le téléphone   élémentaire

2. *L'accent grave* (`) occurs over the letters *a, e,* and *u*.

   voilà   le frère   où

3. *L'accent circonflexe* (^) occurs over all vowels.

   le château   la fenêtre   le dîner   l'hôtel   août

4. *La cédille* (ç) appears only under the letter *c*. When the letter *c* is followed by an *a, o* or *u* it has a hard /k/ sound as in *ca*ve, *co*ca, *cu*lmination. The cedilla changes the hard /k/ sound to a soft /s/ sound.

   ça   garçon   commençons   reçu

5. *Le tréma* (¨) indicates that two vowels next to each other are pronounced separately.

   Noël   égoïste

VERBES

A. Verbes réguliers				B. Verbes réfléchis
INFINITIF	**parler** *to talk*	**finir** *to finish*	**répondre** *to answer*	**se laver** *to wash oneself*
PRÉSENT	je parle tu parles il parle nous parlons vous parlez ils parlent	je finis tu finis il finit nous finissons vous finissez ils finissent	je réponds tu réponds il répond nous répondons vous répondez ils répondent	je me lave tu te laves il se lave nous nous lavons vous vous lavez ils se lavent
IMPÉRATIF	parle parlons parlez	finis finissons finissez	réponds répondons répondez	lave-toi lavons-nous lavez-vous
PASSÉ COMPOSÉ	j'ai parlé tu as parlé il a parlé nous avons parlé vous avez parlé ils ont parlé	j'ai fini tu as fini il a fini nous avons fini vous avez fini ils ont fini	j'ai répondu tu as répondu il a répondu nous avons répondu vous avez répondu ils ont répondu	je me suis lavé(e) tu t'es lavé(e) il s'est lavé nous nous sommes lavé(e)s vous vous êtes lavé(e)(s) ils se sont lavés
IMPARFAIT	je parlais tu parlais il parlait nous parlions vous parliez ils parlaient	je finissais tu finissais il finissait nous finissions vous finissiez ils finissaient	je répondais tu répondais il répondait nous répondions vous répondiez ils répondaient	je me lavais tu te lavais il se lavait nous nous lavions vous vous laviez ils se lavaient
FUTUR	je parlerai tu parleras il parlera nous parlerons vous parlerez ils parleront	je finirai tu finiras il finira nous finirons vous finirez ils finiront	je répondrai tu répondras il répondra nous répondrons vous répondrez ils répondront	je me laverai tu te laveras il se lavera nous nous laverons vous vous laverez ils se laveront
CONDITIONNEL	je parlerais tu parlerais il parlerait nous parlerions vous parleriez ils parleraient	je finirais tu finirais il finirait nous finirions vous finiriez ils finiraient	je répondrais tu répondrais il répondrait nous répondrions vous répondriez ils répondraient	je me laverais tu te laverais il se laverait nous nous laverions vous vous laveriez ils se laveraient
SUBJONCTIF PRÉSENT	que je parle que tu parles qu'il parle que nous parlions que vous parliez qu'ils parlent	que je finisse que tu finisses qu'il finisse que nous finissions que vous finissiez qu'ils finissent	que je réponde que tu répondes qu'il réponde que nous répondions que vous répondiez qu'ils répondent	que je me lave que tu te laves qu'il se lave que nous nous lavions que vous vous laviez qu'ils se lavent
SUBJONCTIF PASSÉ	que j'aie parlé que tu aies parlé qu'il ait parlé que nous ayons parlé que vous ayez parlé qu'ils aient parlé	que j'aie fini que tu aies fini qu'il ait fini que nous ayons fini que vous ayez fini qu'ils aient fini	que j'aie répondu que tu aies répondu qu'il ait répondu que nous ayons répondu que vous ayez répondu qu'ils aient répondu	que je me sois lavé(e) que tu te sois lavé(e) qu'il se soit lavé que nous nous soyons lavé(e)s que vous vous soyez lavé(e)(s) qu'ils se soient lavés

VERBES **441**

C. Verbes avec changements d'orthographe

INFINITIF	**acheter**[1] *to buy*	**appeler** *to call*	**commencer**[2] *to begin*	**envoyer**[3] *to send*
PRÉSENT	j'achète tu achètes il achète nous achetons vous achetez ils achètent	j'appelle tu appelles il appelle nous appelons vous appelez ils appellent	je commence tu commences il commence nous commençons vous commencez ils commencent	j'envoie tu envoies il envoie nous envoyons vous envoyez ils envoient
IMPÉRATIF	achète achetons achetez	appelle appelons appelez	commence commençons commencez	envoie envoyons envoyez
PASSÉ COMPOSÉ	j'ai acheté tu as acheté il a acheté nous avons acheté vous avez acheté ils ont acheté	j'ai appelé tu as appelé il a appelé nous avons appelé vous avez appelé ils ont appelé	j'ai commencé tu as commencé il a commencé nous avons commencé vous avez commencé ils ont commencé	j'ai envoyé tu as envoyé il a envoyé nous avons envoyé vous avez envoyé ils ont envoyé
IMPARFAIT	j'achetais tu achetais il achetait nous achetions vous achetiez ils achetaient	j'appelais tu appelais il appelait nous appelions vous appeliez ils appelaient	je commençais tu commençais il commençait nous commencions vous commenciez ils commençaient	j'envoyais tu envoyais il envoyait nous envoyions vous envoyiez ils envoyaient
FUTUR	j'achèterai tu achèteras il achètera nous achèterons vous achèterez ils achèteront	j'appellerai tu appelleras il appellera nous appellerons vous appellerez ils appelleront	je commencerai tu commenceras il commencera nous commencerons vous commencerez ils commenceront	j'enverrai tu enverras il enverra nous enverrons vous enverrez ils enverront
CONDITIONNEL	j'achèterais tu achèterais il achèterait nous achèterions vous achèteriez ils achèteraient	j'appellerais tu appellerais il appellerait nous appellerions vous appelleriez ils appelleraient	je commencerais tu commencerais il commencerait nous commencerions vous commenceriez ils commenceraient	j'enverrais tu enverrais il enverrait nous enverrions vous enverriez ils enverraient
SUBJONCTIF PRÉSENT	que j'achète que tu achètes qu'il achète que nous achetions que vous achetiez qu'ils achètent	que j'appelle que tu appelles qu'il appelle que nous appelions que vous appeliez qu'ils appellent	que je commence que tu commences qu'il commence que nous commencions que vous commenciez qu'ils commencent	que j'envoie que tu envoies qu'il envoie que nous envoyions que vous envoyiez qu'ils envoient
SUBJONCTIF PASSÉ	que j'aie acheté que tu aies acheté qu'il ait acheté que nous ayons acheté que vous ayez acheté qu'ils aient acheté	que j'aie appelé que tu aies appelé qu'il ait appelé que nous ayons appelé que vous ayez appelé qu'ils aient appelé	que j'aie commencé que tu aies commencé qu'il ait commencé que nous ayons commencé que vous ayez commencé qu'ils aient commencé	que j'aie envoyé que tu aies envoyé qu'il ait envoyé que nous ayons envoyé que vous ayez envoyé qu'ils aient envoyé

[1] Verbes similaires: *emmener, se lever, peser, se promener, soulever*
[2] Verbe similaire: *effacer*
[3] Verbe similaire: *renvoyer*

Verbes avec changements d'orthographe				D. Verbes irréguliers
INFINITIF	manger[4] *to eat*	payer[5] *to pay*	préférer[6] *to prefer*	aller *to go*
PRÉSENT	je mange tu manges il mange nous mangeons vous mangez ils mangent	je paie tu paies il paie nous payons vous payez ils paient	je préfère tu préfères il préfère nous préférons vous préférez ils préfèrent	je vais tu vas il va nous allons vous allez ils vont
IMPÉRATIF	mange mangeons mangez	paie payons payez	préfère préférons préférez	va allons allez
PASSÉ COMPOSÉ	j'ai mangé tu as mangé il a mangé nous avons mangé vous avez mangé ils ont mangé	j'ai payé tu as payé il a payé nous avons payé vous avez payé ils ont payé	j'ai préféré tu as préféré il a préféré nous avons préféré vous avez préféré ils ont préféré	je suis allé(e) tu es allé(e) il est allé nous sommes allé(e)s vous êtes allé(e)(s) ils sont allés
IMPARFAIT	je mangeais tu mangeais il mangeait nous mangions vous mangiez ils mangeaient	je payais tu payais il payait nous payions vous payiez ils payaient	je préférais tu préférais il préférait nous préférions vous préfériez ils préféraient	j'allais tu allais il allait nous allions vous alliez ils allaient
FUTUR	je mangerai tu mangeras il mangera nous mangerons vous mangerez ils mangeront	je paierai tu paieras il paiera nous paierons vous paierez ils paieront	je préférerai tu préféreras il préférera nous préférerons vous préférerez ils préféreront	j'irai tu iras il ira nous irons vous irez ils iront
CONDITIONNEL	je mangerais tu mangerais il mangerait nous mangerions vous mangeriez ils mangeraient	je paierais tu paierais il paierait nous paierions vous paieriez ils paieraient	je préférerais tu préférerais il préférerait nous préférerions vous préféreriez ils préféreraient	j'irais tu irais il irait nous irions vous iriez ils iraient
SUBJONCTIF PRÉSENT	que je mange que tu manges qu'il mange que nous mangions que vous mangiez qu'ils mangent	que je paie que tu paies qu'il paie que nous payions que vous payiez qu'ils paient	que je préfère que tu préfères qu'il préfère que nous préférions que vous préfériez qu'ils préfèrent	que j'aille que tu ailles qu'il aille que nous allions que vous alliez qu'ils aillent
SUBJONCTIF PASSÉ	que j'aie mangé que tu aies mangé qu'il ait mangé que nous ayons mangé que vous ayez mangé qu'ils aient mangé	que j'aie payé que tu aies payé qu'il ait payé que nous ayons payé que vous ayez payé qu'ils aient payé	que j'aie préféré que tu aies préféré qu'il ait préféré que nous ayons préféré que vous ayez préféré qu'ils aient préféré	que je sois allé(e) que tu sois allé(e) qu'il soit allé que nous soyons allé(e)s que vous soyez allé(e)(s) qu'ils soient allés

[4] Verbes similaires: *changer, exiger, nager, voyager*
[5] Verbes similaires: *appuyer, employer, essayer, essuyer, nettoyer, tutoyer*
[6] Verbes similaires: *accélérer, célébrer, espérer, oblitérer, récupérer, sécher, suggérer*

Verbes irréguliers

INFINITIF	**s'asseoir** *to sit*	**boire** *to drink*	**conduire** *to drive*	**connaître** *to know*
PRÉSENT	je m'assieds tu t'assieds il s'assied nous nous asseyons vous vous asseyez ils s'asseyent	je bois tu bois il boit nous buvons vous buvez ils boivent	je conduis tu conduis il conduit nous conduisons vous conduisez ils conduisent	je connais tu connais il connaît nous connaissons vous connaissez ils connaissent
IMPÉRATIF	assieds-toi asseyons-nous asseyez-vous	bois buvons buvez	conduis conduisons conduisez	connais connaissons connaissez
PASSÉ COMPOSÉ	je me suis assis(e) tu t'es assis(e) il s'est assis nous nous sommes assis(es) vous vous êtes assis(e)(s) ils se sont assis	j'ai bu tu as bu il a bu nous avons bu vous avez bu ils ont bu	j'ai conduit tu as conduit il a conduit nous avons conduit vous avez conduit ils ont conduit	j'ai connu tu as connu il a connu nous avons connu vous avez connu ils ont connu
IMPARFAIT	je m'asseyais tu t'asseyais il s'asseyait nous nous asseyions vous vous asseyiez ils s'asseyaient	je buvais tu buvais il buvait nous buvions vous buviez ils buvaient	je conduisais tu conduisais il conduisait nous conduisions vous conduisiez ils conduisaient	je connaissais tu connaissais il connaissait nous connaissions vous connaissiez ils connaissaient
FUTUR	je m'assiérai tu t'assiéras il s'assiéra nous nous assiérons vous vous assiérez ils s'assiéront	je boirai tu boiras il boira nous boirons vous boirez ils boiront	je conduirai tu conduiras il conduira nous conduirons vous conduirez ils conduiront	je connaîtrai tu connaîtras il connaîtra nous connaîtrons vous connaîtrez ils connaîtront
CONDITIONNEL	je m'assiérais tu t'assiérais il s'assiérait nous nous assiérions vous vous assiériez ils s'assiéraient	je boirais tu boirais il boirait nous boirions vous boiriez ils boiraient	je conduirais tu conduirais il conduirait nous conduirions vous conduiriez ils conduiraient	je connaîtrais tu connaîtrais il connaîtrait nous connaîtrions vous connaîtriez ils connaîtraient
SUBJONCTIF PRÉSENT	que je m'asseye que tu t'asseyes qu'il s'asseye que nous nous asseyions que vous vous asseyiez qu'ils s'asseyent	que je boive que tu boives qu'il boive que nous buvions que vous buviez qu'ils boivent	que je conduise que tu conduises qu'il conduise que nous conduisions que vous conduisiez qu'ils conduisent	que je connaisse que tu connaisses qu'il connaisse que nous connaissions que vous connaissiez qu'ils connaissent
SUBJONCTIF PASSÉ	que je me sois assis(e) que tu te sois assis(e) qu'il se soit assis que nous nous soyons assis(es) que vous vous soyez assis(e)(s) qu'ils se soient assis	que j'aie bu que tu aies bu qu'il ait bu que nous ayons bu que vous ayez bu qu'ils aient bu	que j'aie conduit que tu aies conduit qu'il ait conduit que nous ayons conduit que vous ayez conduit qu'ils aient conduit	que j'aie connu que tu aies connu qu'il ait connu que nous ayons connu que vous ayez connu qu'ils aient connu

Verbes irréguliers

INFINITIF	**croire** *to believe*	**devoir** *to have to, to owe*	**dire** *to say*	**dormir** *to sleep*
PRÉSENT	je crois tu crois il croit nous croyons vous croyez ils croient	je dois tu dois il doit nous devons vous devez ils doivent	je dis tu dis il dit nous disons vous dites ils disent	je dors tu dors il dort nous dormons vous dormez ils dorment
IMPÉRATIF	crois croyons croyez	dois devons devez	dis disons dites	dors dormons dormez
PASSÉ COMPOSÉ	j'ai cru tu as cru il a cru nous avons cru vous avez cru ils ont cru	j'ai dû tu as dû il a dû nous avons dû vous avez dû ils ont dû	j'ai dit tu as dit il a dit nous avons dit vous avez dit ils ont dit	j'ai dormi tu as dormi il a dormi nous avons dormi vous avez dormi ils ont dormi
IMPARFAIT	je croyais tu croyais il croyait nous croyions vous croyiez ils croyaient	je devais tu devais il devait nous devions vous deviez ils devaient	je disais tu disais il disait nous disions vous disiez ils disaient	je dormais tu dormais il dormait nous dormions vous dormiez ils dormaient
FUTUR	je croirai tu croiras il croira nous croirons vous croirez ils croiront	je devrai tu devras il devra nous devrons vous devrez ils devront	je dirai tu diras il dira nous dirons vous direz ils diront	je dormirai tu dormiras il dormira nous dormirons vous dormirez ils dormiront
CONDITIONNEL	je croirais tu croirais il croirait nous croirions vous croiriez ils croiraient	je devrais tu devrais il devrait nous devrions vous devriez ils devraient	je dirais tu dirais il dirait nous dirions vous diriez ils diraient	je dormirais tu dormirais il dormirait nous dormirions vous dormiriez ils dormiraient
SUBJONCTIF PRÉSENT	que je croie que tu croies qu'il croie que nous croyions que vous croyiez qu'ils croient	que je doive que tu doives qu'il doive que nous devions que vous deviez qu'ils doivent	que je dise que tu dises qu'il dise que nous disions que vous disiez qu'ils disent	que je dorme que tu dormes qu'il dorme que nous dormions que vous dormiez qu'ils dorment
SUBJONCTIF PASSÉ	que j'aie cru que tu aies cru qu'il ait cru que nous ayons cru que vous ayez cru qu'ils aient cru	que j'aie dû que tu aies dû qu'il ait dû que nous ayons dû que vous ayez dû qu'ils aient dû	que j'aie dit que tu aies dit qu'il ait dit que nous ayons dit que vous ayez dit qu'ils aient dit	que j'aie dormi que tu aies dormi qu'il ait dormi que nous ayons dormi que vous ayez dormi qu'ils aient dormi

Verbes irréguliers

INFINITIF	écrire *to write*	être *to be*	faire *to do, to make*	lire *to read*
PRÉSENT	j'écris tu écris il écrit nous écrivons vous écrivez ils écrivent	je suis tu es il est nous sommes vous êtes ils sont	je fais tu fais il fait nous faisons vous faites ils font	je lis tu lis il lit nous lisons vous lisez ils lisent
IMPÉRATIF	écris écrivons écrivez	sois soyons soyez	fais faisons faites	lis lisons lisez
PASSÉ COMPOSÉ	j'ai écrit tu as écrit il a écrit nous avons écrit vous avez écrit ils ont écrit	j'ai été tu as été il a été nous avons été vous avez été ils ont été	j'ai fait tu as fait il a fait nous avons fait vous avez fait ils ont fait	j'ai lu tu as lu il a lu nous avons lu vous avez lu ils ont lu
IMPARFAIT	j'écrivais tu écrivais il écrivait nous écrivions vous écriviez ils écrivaient	j'étais tu étais il était nous étions vous étiez ils étaient	je faisais tu faisais il faisait nous faisions vous faisiez ils faisaient	je lisais tu lisais il lisait nous lisions vous lisiez ils lisaient
FUTUR	j'écrirai tu écriras il écrira nous écrirons vous écrirez ils écriront	je serai tu seras il sera nous serons vous serez ils seront	je ferai tu feras il fera nous ferons vous ferez ils feront	je lirai tu liras il lira nous lirons vous lirez ils liront
CONDITIONNEL	j'écrirais tu écrirais il écrirait nous écririons vous écririez ils écriraient	je serais tu serais il serait nous serions vous seriez ils seraient	je ferais tu ferais il ferait nous ferions vous feriez ils feraient	je lirais tu lirais il lirait nous lirions vous liriez ils liraient
SUBJONCTIF PRÉSENT	que j'écrive que tu écrives qu'il écrive que nous écrivions que vous écriviez qu'ils écrivent	que je sois que tu sois qu'il soit que nous soyons que vous soyez qu'ils soient	que je fasse que tu fasses qu'il fasse que nous fassions que vous fassiez qu'ils fassent	que je lise que tu lises qu'il lise que nous lisions que vous lisiez qu'ils lisent
SUBJONCTIF PASSÉ	que j'aie écrit que tu aies écrit qu'il ait écrit que nous ayons écrit que vous ayez écrit qu'ils aient écrit	que j'aie été que tu aies été qu'il ait été que nous ayons été que vous ayez été qu'ils aient été	que j'aie fait que tu aies fait qu'il ait fait que nous ayons fait que vous ayez fait qu'ils aient fait	que j'aie lu que tu aies lu qu'il ait lu que nous ayons lu que vous ayez lu qu'ils aient lu

Verbes irréguliers

INFINITIF	**mettre**[1] *to put*	**ouvrir**[2] *to open*	**partir**[3] *to leave*	**pouvoir** *to be able to*
PRÉSENT	je mets tu mets il met nous mettons vous mettez ils mettent	j'ouvre tu ouvres il ouvre nous ouvrons vous ouvrez ils ouvrent	je pars tu pars il part nous partons vous partez ils partent	je peux tu peux il peut nous pouvons vous pouvez ils peuvent
IMPÉRATIF	mets mettons mettez	ouvre ouvrons ouvrez	pars partons partez	(pas d'impératif)
PASSÉ COMPOSÉ	j'ai mis tu as mis il a mis nous avons mis vous avez mis ils ont mis	j'ai ouvert tu as ouvert il a ouvert nous avons ouvert vous avez ouvert ils ont ouvert	je suis parti(e) tu es parti(e) il est parti nous sommes parti(e)s vous êtes parti(e)(s) ils sont partis	j'ai pu tu as pu il a pu nous avons pu vous avez pu ils ont pu
IMPARFAIT	je mettais tu mettais il mettait nous mettions vous mettiez ils mettaient	j'ouvrais tu ouvrais il ouvrait nous ouvrions vous ouvriez ils ouvraient	je partais tu partais il partait nous partions vous partiez ils partaient	je pouvais tu pouvais il pouvait nous pouvions vous pouviez ils pouvaient
FUTUR	je mettrai tu mettras il mettra nous mettrons vous mettrez ils mettront	j'ouvrirai tu ouvriras il ouvrira nous ouvrirons vous ouvrirez ils ouvriront	je partirai tu partiras il partira nous partirons vous partirez ils partiront	je pourrai tu pourras il pourra nous pourrons vous pourrez ils pourront
CONDITIONNEL	je mettrais tu mettrais il mettrait nous mettrions vous mettriez ils mettraient	j'ouvrirais tu ouvrirais il ouvrirait nous ouvririons vous ouvririez ils ouvriraient	je partirais tu partirais il partirait nous partirions vous partiriez ils partiraient	je pourrais tu pourrais il pourrait nous pourrions vous pourriez ils pourraient
SUBJONCTIF PRÉSENT	que je mette que tu mettes qu'il mette que nous mettions que vous mettiez qu'ils mettent	que j'ouvre que tu ouvres qu'il ouvre que nous ouvrions que vous ouvriez qu'ils ouvrent	que je parte que tu partes qu'il parte que nous partions que vous partiez qu'ils partent	que je puisse que tu puisses qu'il puisse que nous puissions que vous puissiez qu'ils puissent
SUBJONCTIF PASSÉ	que j'aie mis que tu aies mis qu'il ait mis que nous ayons mis que vous ayez mis qu'ils aient mis	que j'aie ouvert que tu aies ouvert qu'il ait ouvert que nous ayons ouvert que vous ayez ouvert qu'ils aient ouvert	que je sois parti(e) que tu sois parti(e) qu'il soit parti que nous soyons parti(e)s que vous soyez parti(e)(s) qu'ils soient partis	que j'aie pu que tu aies pu qu'il ait pu que nous ayons pu que vous ayez pu qu'ils aient pu

[1] Verbe similaire: *remettre*
[2] Verbes similaires: *couvrir, découvrir, offrir, souffrir*
[3] Verbe similaire: *sortir*

Verbes irréguliers

INFINITIF	**prendre**[4] *to take*	**recevoir** *to receive*	**rire**[5] *to laugh*	**savoir** *to know*
PRÉSENT	je prends tu prends il prend nous prenons vous prenez ils prennent	je reçois tu reçois il reçoit nous recevons vous recevez ils reçoivent	je ris tu ris il rit nous rions vous riez ils rient	je sais tu sais il sait nous savons vous savez ils savent
IMPÉRATIF	prends prenons prenez	reçois recevons recevez	ris rions riez	sache sachons sachez
PASSÉ COMPOSÉ	j'ai pris tu as pris il a pris nous avons pris vous avez pris ils ont pris	j'ai reçu tu as reçu il a reçu nous avons reçu vous avez reçu ils ont reçu	j'ai ri tu as ri il a ri nous avons ri vous avez ri ils ont ri	j'ai su tu as su il a su nous avons su vous avez su ils ont su
IMPARFAIT	je prenais tu prenais il prenait nous prenions vous preniez ils prenaient	je recevais tu recevais il recevait nous recevions vous receviez ils recevaient	je riais tu riais il riait nous riions vous riiez ils riaient	je savais tu savais il savait nous savions vous saviez ils savaient
FUTUR	je prendrai tu prendras il prendra nous prendrons vous prendrez ils prendront	je recevrai tu recevras il recevra nous recevrons vous recevrez ils recevront	je rirai tu riras il rira nous rirons vous rirez ils riront	je saurai tu sauras il saura nous saurons vous saurez ils sauront
CONDITIONNEL	je prendrais tu prendrais il prendrait nous prendrions vous prendriez ils prendraient	je recevrais tu recevrais il recevrait nous recevrions vous recevriez ils recevraient	je rirais tu rirais il rirait nous ririons vous ririez ils riraient	je saurais tu saurais il saurait nous saurions vous sauriez ils sauraient
SUBJONCTIF PRÉSENT	que je prenne que tu prennes qu'il prenne que nous prenions que vous preniez qu'ils prennent	que je reçoive que tu reçoives qu'il reçoive que nous recevions que vous receviez qu'ils reçoivent	que je rie que tu ries qu'il rie que nous riions que vous riiez qu'ils rient	que je sache que tu saches qu'il sache que nous sachions que vous sachiez qu'ils sachent
SUBJONCTIF PASSÉ	que j'aie pris que tu aies pris qu'il ait pris que nous ayons pris que vous ayez pris qu'ils aient pris	que j'aie reçu que tu aies reçu qu'il ait reçu que nous ayons reçu que vous ayez reçu qu'ils aient reçu	que j'aie ri que tu aies ri qu'il ait ri que nous ayons ri que vous ayez ri qu'ils aient ri	que j'aie su que tu aies su qu'il ait su que nous ayons su que vous ayez su qu'ils aient su

[4] Verbes similaires: *apprendre, comprendre*
[5] Verbe similaire: *sourire*

Verbes irréguliers

INFINITIF	**servir**[6] *to serve*	**suivre** *to follow*	**venir**[7] *to come*	**vivre** *to live*
PRÉSENT	je sers tu sers il sert nous servons vous servez ils servent	je suis tu suis il suit nous suivons vous suivez ils suivent	je viens tu viens il vient nous venons vous venez ils viennent	je vis tu vis il vit nous vivons vous vivez ils vivent
IMPÉRATIF	sers servons servez	suis suivons suivez	viens venons venez	vis vivons vivez
PASSÉ COMPOSÉ	j'ai servi tu as servi il a servi nous avons servi vous avez servi ils ont servi	j'ai suivi tu as suivi il a suivi nous avons suivi vous avez suivi ils ont suivi	je suis venu(e) tu es venu(e) il est venu nous sommes venu(e)s vous êtes venu(e)(s) ils sont venus	j'ai vécu tu as vécu il a vécu nous avons vécu vous avez vécu ils ont vécu
IMPARFAIT	je servais tu servais il servait nous servions vous serviez ils servaient	je suivais tu suivais il suivait nous suivions vous suiviez ils suivaient	je venais tu venais il venait nous venions vous veniez ils venaient	je vivais tu vivais il vivait nous vivions vous viviez ils vivaient
FUTUR	je servirai tu serviras il servira nous servirons vous servirez ils serviront	je suivrai tu suivras il suivra nous suivrons vous suivrez ils suivront	je viendrai tu viendras il viendra nous viendrons vous viendrez ils viendront	je vivrai tu vivras il vivra nous vivrons vous vivrez ils vivront
CONDITIONNEL	je servirais tu servirais il servirait nous servirions vous serviriez ils serviraient	je suivrais tu suivrais il suivrait nous suivrions vous suivriez ils suivraient	je viendrais tu viendrais il viendrait nous viendrions vous viendriez ils viendraient	je vivrais tu vivrais il vivrait nous vivrions vous vivriez ils vivraient
SUBJONCTIF PRÉSENT	que je serve que tu serves qu'il serve que nous servions que vous serviez qu'ils servent	que je suive que tu suives qu'il suive que nous suivions que vous suiviez qu'ils suivent	que je vienne que tu viennes qu'il vienne que nous venions que vous veniez qu'ils viennent	que je vive que tu vives qu'il vive que nous vivions que vous viviez qu'ils vivent
SUBJONCTIF PASSÉ	que j'aie servi que tu aies servi qu'il ait servi que nous ayons servi que vous ayez servi qu'ils aient servi	que j'aie suivi que tu aies suivi qu'il ait suivi que nous ayons suivi que vous ayez suivi qu'ils aient suivi	que je sois venu(e) que tu sois venu(e) qu'il soit venu que nous soyons venu(e)s que vous soyez venu(e)(s) qu'ils soient venus	que j'aie vécu que tu aies vécu qu'il ait vécu que nous ayons vécu que vous ayez vécu qu'ils aient vécu

[6] Verbe similaire: *desservir*
[7] Verbes similaires: *devenir, revenir, se souvenir*

	Verbes irréguliers		E. Verbes impersonnels	
INFINITIF	**voir** *to see*	**vouloir** *to want*	**falloir** *to be necessary*	**pleuvoir** *to rain*
PRÉSENT	je vois tu vois il voit nous voyons vous voyez ils voient	je veux tu veux il veut nous voulons vous voulez ils veulent	il faut	il pleut
IMPÉRATIF	vois voyons voyez	veuille voulons veuillez		
PASSÉ COMPOSÉ	j'ai vu tu as vu il a vu nous avons vu vous avez vu ils ont vu	j'ai voulu tu as voulu il a voulu nous avons voulu vous avez voulu ils ont voulu	il a fallu	il a plu
IMPARFAIT	je voyais tu voyais il voyait nous voyions vous voyiez ils voyaient	je voulais tu voulais il voulait nous voulions vous vouliez ils voulaient	il fallait	il pleuvait
FUTUR	je verrai tu verras il verra nous verrons vous verrez ils verront	je voudrai tu voudras il voudra nous voudrons vous voudrez ils voudront	il faudra	il pleuvra
CONDITIONNEL	je verrais tu verrais il verrait nous verrions vous verriez ils verraient	je voudrais tu voudrais il voudrait nous voudrions vous voudriez ils voudraient	il faudrait	il pleuvrait
SUBJONCTIF PRÉSENT	que je voie que tu voies qu'il voie que nous voyions que vous voyiez qu'ils voient	que je veuille que tu veuilles qu'il veuille que nous voulions que vous vouliez qu'ils veuillent	qu'il faille	qu'il pleuve
SUBJONCTIF PASSÉ	que j'aie vu que tu aies vu qu'il ait vu que nous ayons vu que vous ayez vu qu'ils aient vu	que j'aie voulu que tu aies voulu qu'il ait voulu que nous ayons voulu que vous ayez voulu qu'ils aient voulu	qu'il ait fallu	qu'il ait plu

F. Verbes avec *être* au passé composé

aller (*to go*)	je suis allé(e)
arriver (*to arrive*)	je suis arrivé(e)
descendre (*to go down, to get off*)	je suis descendu(e)
entrer (*to enter*)	je suis entré(e)
monter (*to go up*)	je suis monté(e)
mourir (*to die*)	je suis mort(e)
naître (*to be born*)	je suis né(e)
partir (*to leave*)	je suis parti(e)
passer (*to go by*)	je suis passé(e)
rentrer (*to go home*)	je suis rentré(e)
rester (*to stay*)	je suis resté(e)
retourner (*to return*)	je suis retourné(e)
revenir (*to come back*)	je suis revenu(e)
sortir (*to go out*)	je suis sorti(e)
tomber (*to fall*)	je suis tombé(e)
venir (*to come*)	je suis venu(e)

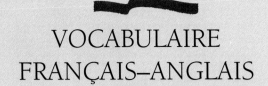

VOCABULAIRE
FRANÇAIS–ANGLAIS

The *Vocabulaire français–anglais* contains all productive and receptive vocabulary from Levels 1 and 2. The numbers following each entry indicate the chapter and vocabulary section in which the word is introduced. For example, **3.2** means that the word first appeared in Level 2, *Chapitre 3, Mots 2*. Numbers preceded by I indicate vocabulary introduced in Level 1; I-BV refers to the introductory *Bienvenue* chapter. Words without chapter references indicate receptive vocabulary (not taught in the *Mots* sections) in *À bord*.

The following abbreviations are used in this glossary.

adj.	adjective
adv.	adverb
conj.	conjunction
dem. adj.	demonstrative adjective
dem. pron.	demonstrative pronoun
dir. obj.	direct object
f.	feminine
fam.	familiar
form.	formal
ind. obj.	indirect object
inf.	infinitive
inform.	informal
interr.	interrogative
interr. adj.	interrogative adjective
interr. pron.	interrogative pronoun
inv.	invariable
m.	masculine
n.	noun
past part.	past participle
pl.	plural
poss. adj.	possessive adjective
prep.	preposition
pron.	pronoun
sing.	singular
subj.	subject
subjunc.	subjunctive

A

à at, in, to, I-3.1
   à la, à l' at the, in the, to the, I-5
   à l'avance in advance, 4.2
   à bord de on board, I-7.2
   à côté next door, I
   à côté de next to, I-5
   À demain. See you tomorrow., I-BV
   à demi-tarif half-price, I
   à destination de to (plane, train, etc.), I-7.1
   à domicile to the home, I
   à dos de chameau on camel(back), 14.2
   à droite de to, on the right of, I-5
   à l'étranger abroad, in a foreign country, I
   à gauche de to, on the left of, I-5
   à l'heure on time, I-8.1
   à l'intérieur inside, I
   à mi-temps part-time, I-3.2
   à la mode in style, "in", I
   à moins que (+ subjunc.) unless, 15
   à mon (ton, son, etc.) avis in my (your, his, etc.) opinion, I-10.2
   à partir de from . . . on; based on, I
   à peu près about, approximately, 16.2
   à pied on foot, I-5.2
   à plein temps full-time, I-3.2
   à point medium-rare (meat), I-5.2
   à propos de concerning, as regards, I
   à quelle heure? at what time?, I-2
   à ta (sa, votre, etc.) place if I were you (him, her, etc.), 9.2
   À tout à l'heure. See you later., I-BV
l' abbaye (f.) abbey
   abdiquer to abdicate
   abolir to abolish
   abondant(e) abundant
   abriter to house
   absolument absolutely, I
   absorber to absorb, I
   accélérer to speed up, go faster, I-12.1
   accepter to accept, I

l' accessoire (m.) accessory, I
l' accident (m.) accident, I-14.2
   accompagné(e) (de) accompanied (by), I
   accomplir to accomplish
l' accordéon (m.) accordion, 11.1
   accueillant(e) welcoming
   accueilli(e): bien accueilli(e) well-received, I
l' achat (m.) purchase, I
   faire des achats to shop, I-10.1
   acheter to buy, I-6.1
l' acidité (f.) acidity, I
l' acier (m.) steel
l' acte (m.) act, I-16.1
l' acteur (m.) actor (m.), I-16.1
   actif, active active, I-10
l' action (f.) action, I
l' activité (f.) activity, I
l' actrice (f.) actress, I-16.1
   actuel(le) current, present
   actuellement currently
l' addition (f.) check, bill (restaurant), I-5.2
   admirer to admire, I
l' adolescent(e) adolescent, teenager, I
   adopter to adopt, I
   adorable adorable, I
   adorer to love, I-3.2
l' adresse (f.) address, 1.2
l' adulte (m. et f.) adult, I
   adverse opposing, I-13.1
   aérien(ne) air, flight (adj.), I-9; aerial
   les tarifs aériens airfares, I
l' aérogare (f.) terminal with bus to airport, I-7.2
l' aérogramme (m.) airgram, 1.1
l' aéroport (m.) airport, I-7.1
   aérospatial(e) aerospace, I
les affaires (f. pl.) business; belongings, I
l' affiche (f.) poster
   affolé(e) panic-stricken, I
s' affronter to collide, I
   africain(e) African, I
l' Afrique (f.) Africa, 14.2
l' âge (m.) age, I-4.1
   Tu as quel âge? How old are you? (fam.), I-4.1
   âgé(e) old, I
l' agence (m.) de voyages travel agency
l' agenda (m.) appointment book, I-2.2
l' agent (m.) agent (m. and f.), I-7.1

   l'agent de police police officer (m. and f.), 8.2
l' agglomération (f.) populated area, I
s' agir de to be a matter of, be about
   agité(e) agitated, I
l' agneau (m.) lamb, 14.1
   agréable pleasant, I
l' agriculteur (m.) farmer (m. and f.), 15.2
l' aide (f.) help
   aider to help, I
l' aile (f.) wing, 7.1
   aimable nice (person), I-1.2
   aimer to like, love, I-3.2
   ainsi thus
l' air (m.) air, I
   en plein air outdoor(s), I
   aisé(e) well-off
   ajouter to add, I
l' alcoolisme (m.) alcoholism
   alerter to alert
l' algèbre (f.) algebra, I-2.2
l' Algérie (f.) Algeria, 14.1
l' aliment (m.) food, I
l' alimentation (f.) nutrition, diet, I
   alimenter to feed
l' Allemagne (f.) Germany, I-16
l' allemand (m.) German (language), I
   allemand(e) German, I
   aller to go, I-5.1
   aller à la pêche to go fishing, I-9.1
   aller pêcher to go fishing, I
l' allergie (f.) allergy, I-15.1
   allergique allergic, I-15.1
l' aller-retour (m.) round-trip ticket, I-8
l' aller simple (m.) one-way ticket, I-8.1
l' alliance (f.) wedding ring, 11.2
l' allié (m.) ally
   Allô. Hello. (when answering telephone), 3.2
   allonger to stretch out
   allumer to light, 11.2; to turn on (a TV, etc.), 2.1
l' allure (f.) allure, attractiveness
   alors so, then, well then, I
les Alpes (f. pl.) the Alps, I
l' alpinisme (m.) mountain climbing, I
l' altitude (f.) altitude, I
l' amateur (m.): l'amateur d'art art lover, I
l' ambulance (f.) ambulance, 6.1

améliorer   to improve
aménager   to renovate, transform, I
l' amende (f.)   fine, **8.1**
l' Américain(e)   American (person), I
américain(e)   American, I-1.1
l' Amérique (f.)   America, I-16
   l'Amérique du Nord   North America, I-16
   l'Amérique du Sud   South America, I-16
l' ami(e)   friend, I-1.2
l' amidon (m.)   starch, **9.1**
l' amitié (f.)   friendship, I
   Amitiés   Love (to close a letter)
l' amour (m.)   love
amusant(e)   funny, I-1.1
s' amuser   to have fun, I-11.2
l' an (m.): avoir... ans   to be . . . years old, I-4.1
   le jour de l'An   New Year's Day, **11.2**
l' ananas (m.)   pineapple
l' anatomie (f.)   anatomy, I
l' ancêtre (m.)   ancestor
ancien(ne)   old, I
l' âne (m.)   donkey, **15.2**
l' anesthésie (f.)   anesthesia, **6.2**
   faire une anesthésie   to give anesthesia, **6.2**
l' anesthésiste (m. et f.)   anesthesiologist, **6.2**
l' angine (f.)   throat infection, tonsillitis, I-15.1
l' anglais (m.)   English (language), I-2.2
l' Anglais(e)   Englishman (woman), I
l' Angleterre (f.)   England, I-16
l' animal (m.)   animal, I
   l'animal domestique   farm animal, **15.1**
animé(e)   lively, animated, I
l' anneau (m.)   ring
l' année (f.)   year, I-4.1
   l'année dernière   last year, I-13
   l'année scolaire   school year
   Bonne Année!   Happy New Year!, **11.2**
l' anniversaire (m.)   birthday, I-4.1
   Bon (Joyeux) anniversaire!   Happy birthday!, I
   C'est quand, ton anniversaire?   When is your birthday? (fam.), I-4.1

l' annonce (f.)   announcement, I-8.1
   la petite annonce   classified ad, **16.2**
annoncer   to announce, I-8.1
l' annuaire (m.)   telephone book, **3.1**
annuellement   yearly, annually, **8**
annuler   to cancel, **7.2**
l' anorak (m.)   ski jacket, I-14.1
antérieur(e)   previous, former, I
l' anthropologie (f.)   anthropology, I
l' antibiotique (m.)   antibiotic, I-15.1
l' anticyclone (m.)   high pressure area, I
antillais(e)   West Indian, I
les Antilles (f. pl.)   West Indies
antipathique   unpleasant (person), I-1.2
l' Antiquité (f.)   ancient times, I
anxieux, anxieuse   anxious, I
août (m.)   August, I-4.1
apparaître   to appear
l' appareil (m.)   machine, appliance
apparenté: le mot apparenté   cognate, I
l' appartement (m.)   apartment, I-4.2
appartenir   to belong
l' appel (m.)   call, **3.1**; appeal
   l'appel interurbain   long-distance call, **3.1**
appeler   to call, **3.1**
   s'appeler   to be called, be named, I-11.1
applaudir   to applaud, **11.1**
apporter   to bring, I
apprécier   to appreciate
l' appréhension (f.)   apprehension
apprendre (à)   to learn (to), I-9.1
   apprendre à quelqu'un à faire quelque chose   to teach someone to do something, I-14.1
   apprendre ses leçons   to learn one's lessons, **12.1**
l' apprenti(e)   apprentice
apprenti(e)   apprenticed
approprié(e)   appropriate
appuyer sur   to press, **10.2**
   s'appuyer contre   to lean (against), **10.2**
après   after, I-3.2
l' après-midi (m.)   afternoon, I-2

l' arbitre (m.)   referee, I-13.1
l' arbre (m.)   tree, I
   l'arbre de Noël   Christmas tree, **11.2**
l' arc-boutant (m.)   flying buttress
l' arche (f.)   arch, I
l' archipel (m.)   archipelago, I
l' architecte (m. et f.)   architect, I
l' architecture (f.)   architecture, I
l' argent (m.)   money, I-3.2
   l'argent liquide   cash, I-18.1
   l'argent de poche   allowance, I
l' Argentine (f.)   Argentina, I-16
l' argot (m.)   slang, I
l' aristocrate (m. et f.)   aristocrat, I
l' arme (f.)   weapon, I
l' armée (f.)   army, I
arraché(e)   torn
l' arrêt (m.)   stop, **10.2**
arrêter   to stop, **8.1**
   s'arrêter   to stop oneself, I-12.1
l' arrière (m.)   back (of an object), **10.2**
l' arrivée (f.)   arrival, I-7.2
   le tableau des départs et des arrivées   arrival and departure board, I
arriver   to arrive, I-3.1; to happen, I
l' arrondissement (m.)   district (in Paris), I
l' art (m.)   art, I-2.2
les articles (m. pl.) de sport   sporting goods, I
l' artisan(e)   craftsperson
artistique   artistic, I
l' ascenseur (m.)   elevator, I-4.2
l' asepsie (f.): pratiquer l'asepsie   to sterilize, disinfect, I
l' Asie (f.)   Asia, I-16
aspiré(e)   pulled in, I
l' aspirine (f.)   aspirin, I-15.1
s' asseoir   to sit (down), **2.1**
assez   fairly, quite; enough, I
   assez de (+ noun)   enough (+ noun), I-18
l' assiette (f.)   plate, I-5.2
   ne pas être dans son assiette   to be feeling out of sorts, I-15.1
assis(e)   seated, I-8.2
l' assistant(e)   assistant, I
   l'assistant(e) social(e)   social worker, **16.1**
assister (à)   to attend
l' association (f.)   association, I
associer   to associate, I

l' **assurance (f.)** insurance, I
assurer to insure, **1.2**; to assure
l' **astronome (m. et f.)**
astronomer, I
l' **atelier (m.)** workshop, **14.1**
l' **atmosphère (f.)** atmosphere, I
atomique atomic
l' **atout (m.)** advantage
attendre to wait (for), I-8.1
attendre la tonalité to wait
for the dial tone, **3.1**
l' **attente (f.): la salle d'attente**
waiting room, I-8.1
l' **attention (f.)** attention
Attention! Careful! Watch
out!, I
«Attention au départ!» "The
train is leaving!", **4.1**
**«Attention à la fermeture des
portes!»** "Watch the closing
doors!", **4.1**
faire attention to pay attention, I-6; be careful, I-9.1
atterrir to land, I-7.1
l' **atterrissage (m.)** landing
(plane), **7.1**
attirer to attract, I
attraper un coup de soleil to
get a sunburn, I-9.1
au at the, to the, in the, on
the (m. sing.), I-5
au bord de la mer by the
ocean; seaside, I-9.1
au contraire on the contrary, I
au début at the beginning
**au-dessous: la taille au-
dessous** the next smaller
size, I-10.2
au-dessus: la taille au-dessus
the next larger size, I-10.2
au-dessus de above, I
au fond de at the bottom of, I
au moins at least, I
au revoir goodbye, I-BV
au sujet de about, I
l' **aube (f.)** dawn
l' **auberge (f.) de jeunesse** youth
hostel, I
l' **aubergine (f.)** eggplant, **14.1**
aucun(e) any, none
audacieux, audacieuse auda-
cious, bold, I
augmenter to increase, I
aujourd'hui today, I-2.2
l' **aurore (f.)** dawn
ausculter to listen with a
stethoscope, I-15.2
aussi also, too, I-1.1; as
(comparisons), I-10
l' **Australie (f.)** Australia, I-16

autant de as many
l' **auteur (m.)** author (m. and
f.), I
l' **autobus (m.)** bus, **10.2**
l' **autocar (m.)** bus, coach, I-7.2
l' **autodétermination (f.)** self-
determination
l' **auto-école (f.)** driving school,
I-12.2
**automatique: le distributeur
automatique de billets**
automated teller machine
(ATM)
automatiquement
automatically
l' **automne (m.)** autumn, I-13.2
l' **automobiliste (m. et f.)**
motorist, **8.1**
l' **autoroute (f.)** highway, I
l'autoroute à péage toll
highway, I-12.2
autour de around, I
autre other, I-BV
Autre chose? Anything else?
(shopping), I-6.2
les autres others
autrefois in the past
l' **Autriche (f.)** Austria
aux at the, to the, in the, on the
(pl.), I-5
l' **avance (f.): à l'avance** in
advance, I
en avance early, ahead of
time, I-8.1
avancé(e) advanced, I
l' **avant (m.)** front, **10.2**
avant before (prep.), I-7.1
avant de (+ inf.) before
(+ verb), I
avant-hier the day before
yesterday, I-13
avant que (+ subjunc.)
before (conj.), **15**
l' **avantage (m.)** advantage
l' **avant-bras (m.)** forearm, **13.1**
avec with, I-5.1
Avec ça? What else?
(shopping), I-6.2
l' **avenir (m.)** future
dans un proche avenir in the
near future
l' **aventure (f.)** adventure, I
aventureux, aventureuse
adventurous
avertir to warn
l' **avion (m.)** airplane, I-7.1
en avion by plane, plane
(adj.), I-7.1
par avion (by) airmail, **1.2**
l' **avis (m.)** opinion, I

à mon avis in my opinion,
I-10.2
l' **avocat(e)** lawyer, **16.1**
l' **avoine (f.)** oats, **15.1**
avoir to have, I-4.1
avoir l'air to seem, **13.2**
avoir... ans to be . . . years
old, I-4.1
avoir besoin de to need,
I-11.1
avoir de la chance to be
lucky, I
avoir envie de to feel like
(doing something), **3.1**
avoir faim to be hungry, I-5.1
avoir une faim de loup to be
very hungry, I
avoir lieu to take place, **11.2**
avoir mal à to have a(n)
. . . -ache, to hurt, I-15.2
avoir l'occasion de (+ inf.)
to have the opportunity
(+ inf.), I
avoir peur (de) to be afraid
(of), **13.2**
avoir raison to be right, I
avoir soif to be thirsty, I-5.1
avoir tendance à (+ inf.) to
tend (+ inf.), I
avril (m.) April, I-4.1

B

le **baccalauréat (bac, bachot)**
French high school exam, **12.2**
le **bacon** bacon, I
bactérien(ne) bacterial, I-15.1
les **bagages (m. pl.)** luggage, I-7.1
les bagages à main carry-on
luggage, I-7.1
la **baguette** loaf of French bread,
I-6.1
la **baie** bay
se **baigner** to swim
le **bain** bath, I-11.2
prendre un bain to take a
bath, I-11.1
**le bain de soleil: prendre un
bain de soleil** to sunbathe,
I-9.1
le bain turc Turkish bath,
14.1
le **bal** ball, formal dance
la **balance** scale, **1.2**
le **balcon** balcony, I-4.2
la **balle** ball (tennis, etc.), I-9.2;
franc (slang), I-18.2
le **ballon** ball (soccer, etc.), I-13.1
la **banane** banana, I-6.2

la **bande dessinée** comic strip, I
la **banlieue** suburbs, I
le/la **banlieusard(e)** suburbanite
la **banque** bank, I-18.1
le **banquier**, la **banquière**
   banker, I
baptiser to christen, I
la **barbe** beard
   à la barbe fleurie with a
    flowing white beard
Barcelone Barcelona, I-16
bas(se) low, I-10
   à talons bas low-heeled
    (shoes), I-10
la **base: de base** basic, I
le **base-ball** baseball, I-13.2
la **basilique** basilica
le **basket(-ball)** basketball, I-13.2
le **bateau** boat, I
le **bâtiment** building, **15.1**
le **bâtisseur** builder
le **bâton** ski pole, I-14.1
la **batterie** drums, **11.1**
se **battre** to fight
   battre en retraite to retreat
    in battle
   battu(e) beaten
   bavarder to chat, I-4.2
   beau (bel) (m.) beautiful,
    handsome, I-4
   Il fait beau. It's nice weather.,
    I-9.2
   beaucoup a lot, I-3.1
   beaucoup de a lot of, many,
    I-10.1
   beaucoup de monde a lot of
    people, a crowd
la **beauté** beauty, I
les **Beaux-Arts (m. pl.)** fine arts, I
   beige (inv.) beige, I-10.2
le **beignet chinois** fortune cookie
le/la **Belge** Belgian (person), I
   belge Belgian, I
la **Belgique** Belgium, I
   belle (f.) beautiful, I-4
les **béquilles (f. pl.)** crutches,
   6.1
le **berceau** arbor; barrel vault
le **béribéri** beriberi, I
le **besoin** need, I
   avoir besoin de to need,
    I-11.1
le **bétail** livestock, **15.1**
la **bêtise** stupid thing, nonsense, I
le **beurre** butter, I-6.2
la **bibliothèque** library
le **bicentenaire** bicentennial, I
   bien fine, well, I-BV
   bien accueilli(e) well-
    received, I

   bien cuit(e) well-done
    (meat), I-5.2
   bien élevé(e) well-mannered,
    13.1
   bien que (+ subjunc.)
    although (conj.), **15**
   bien sûr of course, I
   bientôt soon, I
   Bienvenue! Welcome!, I
la **bière** beer, I
le **billet** bill (currency), I-18.1;
   ticket, I-7.1
   le billet aller-retour round-
    trip ticket, I-8.1
la **biologie** biology, I-2.2
le/la **biologiste** biologist, I
   bizarre strange, odd, I
la **blague: Sans blague!** No
   kidding!, I
   blanc, blanche white, I-10.2
la **blanchisserie** laundry
le **blé** wheat, **15.1**
le/la **blessé(e)** injured person
se **blesser** to hurt oneself, **6.1**
la **blessure** cut, wound, **6.1**
   bleu(e) blue, I-10.2
   bleu marine (inv.) navy blue,
    I-10.2
   blond(e) blond, I-1.1
   bloquer to block, I
le **blouson** jacket, I-10.1
le **bœuf** beef, I-6.1; ox, **15.1**
   boire to drink, **13**
le **bois** wood, the woods
la **boisson** beverage, I-5.1
la **boîte aux lettres** mailbox, **1.1**
la **boîte de conserve** can of food,
   I-6.2
   bon(ne) correct; good, I-9
   Bonne Année! Happy New
    Year!, **11.2**
   bon marché (inv.)
    inexpensive, I
   le bon numéro the right
    number, **3.1**
   Bonne Santé! Good health!
   bondé(e) packed
   Bonjour. Hello., I-BV
le **bonnet** ski cap, hat, I-14.1
le **bord: à bord de** aboard (plane,
   etc.), I-7.2
   au bord de la mer by the
    ocean, seaside, I-9.1
   bordé(e) (de) bordered, lined
    with, I
le **bordereau** receipt, I
la **borne** road marker
la **bosse** mogul (skiing), I-14.2
la **botanique** botany, I
la **botte** boot, I

la **bouche** mouth, I-15.1
la **boucherie** butcher shop, I-6.1
le **bouchon** traffic jam, **8.1**
   bouclé(e) wavy, **5.1**
le **boudin blanc** white sausage
   bouger to move, I
la **bougie** candle, **11.2**
le **bouillon de poulet** chicken
   soup, I
la **boulangerie-pâtisserie** bakery,
   I-6.1
la **boule** ball
   en boule curled up in a ball
   la boule de neige snowball,
    I-14.2
   les boules French bowling
le **boulevard périphérique**
   beltway, **8.1**
le **boulot** job (slang)
le **bourgeon** bud
   bousculer to shove, **13.1**
   bout (inf. bouillir) boils
    (verb), I
la **bouteille** bottle, I-6.2
la **boutique** shop, boutique, I
le **bouton** button **9.2**; bud, I
le **brancard** stretcher, **6.1**
la **branche** branch, **11.2**
le **bras** arm, **6.1**
le **braséro** charcoal grill, **14.1**
   Bravo! Good! Well done!, I
le **break** station wagon, I-12.1
le **Brésil** Brazil, I-16
la **Bretagne** Brittany, I
la **bretelle d'accès** on-ramp, **8.1**
le/la **Breton(ne)** person from
   Brittany, I
   breton(ne) from Brittany
la **brioche** sweet roll, I
   briser to break
   bronzé(e) tan, I
   bronzer to tan, I-9.1
la **brosse** brush, I; blackboard
   eraser, **12.2**
se **brosser (les dents, etc.)** to
   brush (one's teeth, etc.), I-11.1
le **bruit** noise, **13.1**
   brûler to burn
   brun(e) brunette, I-1.1; brown,
    I-10.2
le **brushing: faire un brushing** to
   blow-dry someone's hair, **5.2**
   brute: la sève brute rising,
    crude sap
   bruyant(e) noisy, **13.1**
la **bûche: la bûche de Noël**
   Christmas cake in shape of a log
le **bulletin de notes** report card, I
le **bulletin météorologique**
   weather report, I

le **bureau** desk, I-BV; office, **2.2**; bureau, I
   le bureau de change foreign exchange office (for foreign currency), I-18.1
   le bureau de location reservations office, **4.2**
   le bureau de placement employment agency, **16.2**
   le bureau de poste post office, **1.1**
   le bureau de tabac tobacco shop, **3.1**
   le bureau de vie scolaire school office, **12.2**
le **bus: en bus** by bus, I-5.
le **but** goal, I-13.1
   marquer un but to score a goal, I-13.1

C

ça that (dem. adj.), I-BV
   Ça coûte cher. It's (That's) expensive., I
   Ça fait combien? How much is it (that)?, I-6.2
   Ça fait... francs. That's . . . francs., I-6.2
   Ça fait mal. It (That) hurts., I-15.2
   ça m'étonnerait I would be very surprised, **14**
   Ça va. Fine., OK., I-BV
   Ça va? How's it going?, How are you? (inform.), I-BV
la **cabine** cabin (plane), I-7.1
   la cabine classe affaires business-class cabin, **7.1**
   la cabine classe économique coach-class cabin, **7.1**
   la cabine première classe first-class cabin, **7.1**
   la cabine téléphonique telephone booth, **3.1**
le **cabinet** office (doctor's), I
caché(e) dark, hidden
le **cadeau** gift, present, I-10.2
   le cadeau de Noël Christmas gift, **11.2**
cadet(te) younger, youngest
le **cadran** dial, **3.1**
   le téléphone à cadran dial phone, **3.1**
le **cadre, la femme cadre** executive, **16.1**
le **café** café; coffee, I-5.1
   le café au lait coffee with milk, I

la **cafétéria** cafeteria
le **cahier** notebook, I-BV
la **caisse** cash register, checkout counter, I-6.2
le **caissier, la caissière** cashier, I
le **calcium** calcium, I
le **calcul** calculation, I
la **calculatrice** calculator, I-BV
   calculer to calculate, I
le **calendrier** calendar
   calme quiet, calm, I
   calmer: Calmez-vous. Calm down., I
la **calorie** calorie, I
le/la **camarade** companion, friend, I
   le/la camarade de classe classmate
le **camion** truck, **8.1**
le **camp** side (in a sport or game), I-13.1
   le camp adverse opponents, other side, I-13.1
la **campagne** country(side), **15.1**
   la maison de campagne country house, I
le **campeur** camper
le **camping** campground
le **Canada** Canada, I-16
   canadien(ne) Canadian, I-9
le **canard** duck, **15.2**
le/la **candidat(e)** applicant, **16.2**
   être candidat(e) à un poste to be an applicant for a position, **16.2**
la **candidature** candidacy, **16.2**
   poser sa candidature to apply for a position, **16.2**
le **canne à sucre** sugar cane
le **canoë** canoe, I
la **cantine** school cafeteria, **12.2**
le **capitaine** captain
la **capitale** capital, I
   capituler to capitulate
   capter to collect, receive
le **car** bus (coach), I
   car because, for
le **caractère: à caractère familial** family-style, I
la **caractéristique** characteristic, I
la **caravane** caravan, **14.2**; trailer, **8.1**
le **carnet** book of ten subway tickets, **10.1**
   le carnet d'anniversaires birthday book, I
la **carotte** carrot, I-6.2
carré(e) square
le **carrefour** crossroads, I-12.2
la **carrière** career, **16.2**
le **cartable** bookbag, **12.1**

la **carte** card, **12.2**; menu, I-5.1; map, I
   la carte à mémoire speed-dial feature on a telephone
   la carte d'anniversaire birthday card, I
   la carte de crédit credit card, I-17.2
   la carte de débarquement landing card, I-7.2
   la carte d'embarquement boarding pass, I-7.1
   la carte grise automobile registration card, **8.1**
   la carte postale postcard, **1.1**
   la carte routière road map, **8.1**
   la carte verte insurance card, **8.1**
   la carte de vœux greeting card, **11.2**
le **cas** case
   en tout cas in any case, I
le **casier** cubbyhole
le **casque** helmet, **8.1**
la **casquette** cap, **8.2**
le **casse-cou** daredevil, I
   casser to break, **9.2**
   se casser to break (an arm, a leg, etc.), **6.1**
la **cassette** cassette, I-3.2
la **catégorie** category, I
la **cathédrale** cathedral, I
le **catholicisme** Catholicism
le/la **catholique** Catholic
le **cauchemar** nightmare, I
la **cause** cause, I
   causer to cause, I
   ce (cet) (m.) this, that (dem. adj.), I-8
   ce que c'est what it is, I
   Ce n'est rien. You're welcome., I-BV
la **ceinture de sécurité** seat belt, I-12.2
célèbre famous, I-1.2
célébrer to celebrate, **11.2**
célibataire single, unmarried, I
celle (f. sing.) this one, that one (dem. pron.), **5**
celles (f. pl.) these, those (dem. pron.), **5**
la **cellule** cell, I
   la cellule nerveuse nerve cell, I
celui (m. sing.) this one, that one (dem. pron.), **5**
celui-là that one (over there)
le **censeur** vice-principal, **12.2**
   cent hundred, I-5.2

les **centaines** (f. pl.) hundreds, I
centralisé(e) centralized
le **centre** center, middle, I
   au centre de in the heart of, I
   le centre commercial shopping center, I
   le Centre de Documentation et d'Information (CDI) school library, media center, **12.2**
le **centre-ville** downtown area, **8.2**
les **céréales** (f. pl.) cereal, grains, **15.1**
la **cérémonie** ceremony, **11.2**
certain(e) certain, I
   être certain(e) to be certain, **14**
   il est certain (que) it's certain (that), **14**
   pour certains for some people, I
certainement certainly, **8**
ces (pl.) these, those (dem. adj.), I-8
c'est it is, it's, I-BV
   c'est-à-dire that is, I
   C'est ça. That's right., I
   C'est combien? How much is it?, I-BV
   C'est une erreur. You have the wrong number., **3.2**
   C'est de la part de qui? Who's calling?, **3.2**
   C'est quand, ton anniversaire? When is your birthday? (fam.), I-4.1
   C'est quel jour? What day is it?, I-2.2
   C'est tout? Is that all?, I-6.2
cette (f.) this, that (dem. adj.), I-8
ceux (m. pl.) these, those (dem. pron.), **5**
chacun(e) each (one), I
la **chaîne** channel, **2.1**
   la chaîne hôtelière hotel chain, I
   la chaîne stéréo stereo, **2.1**
la **chaise** chair, I-BV
le **châle** shawl, **14.1**
le **chalet** chalet, I
la **chambre** room (in a hotel), I-17.1
   la chambre à coucher bedroom, I-4.2
   la chambre à deux lits double room, I-17.1
   la chambre à un lit single room, I-17.1

libérer la chambre to vacate the room, I-17.2
le **chameau** camel, **14.2**
   à dos de chameau on camel(back), **14.2**
le **champ** field, **15.1**
   le champ de manœuvres parade ground, I
le/la **champion(ne)** champion, I
le **championnat** championship, I
la **chance** luck, I
   avoir de la chance to be lucky, I
le **chandelier** candelabra, **11.2**
le **changement** change
changer (de) to change, I-8.2; to exchange, I-18.1
   changer de chaîne to change the channel, **2.1**
   changer de ligne to change (subway) lines, **10.1**
   changer de place to change places
   changer de train to change trains, **4.2**
   changer de voie to change lanes, **8.1**
le **chant** song
   le chant de Noël Christmas carol, **11.2**
chanter to sing, I-3.2
le **chanteur**, la **chanteuse** singer, **16.1**
le **chantier** construction site
chaque each, every, I-16.1
le **charbon de bois** charcoal, **14.1**
la **charcuterie** deli(catessen), I-6.1
charger to put in charge, I
le **chariot** shopping cart, I
   le chariot à bagages luggage cart, **7.2**
charmant(e) charming, I
le **charpentier** carpenter
le **chat** cat, I-4.1
   avoir un chat dans la gorge to have a frog in one's throat, I-15.2
châtain brown (hair), **5.2**
le **château** castle, mansion, **4.2**
chaud(e) warm, hot, I
   Il fait chaud. It's hot. (weather), I-9.2
chauffer to heat, I
les **chaussettes** (f. pl.) socks, I-10.1
les **chaussons** (m. pl.) slippers
les **chaussures** (f. pl.) shoes, I-10.1
   les chaussures de ski ski boots, I-14.1

les **chaussures de tennis** sneakers, tennis shoes, I-9.2
le **chef** head, boss, chief, I
la **cheminée** fireplace, **11.2**
la **chemise** shirt, I-10.1
le **chemisier** blouse, I-10.1
le **chèque (bancaire)** check, I-18.1
   le chèque de voyage traveler's check, I-17.2
cher, chère dear; expensive, I-10
   Ça coûte cher. It's (That's) expensive., I
chercher to look for, seek, I-5.1
   chercher du travail to look for work, **16.2**
le **cheval** (pl. les **chevaux**) horse, **15.1**
le **chevalier** knight
les **cheveux** (m. pl.) hair, I-11.1
   les cheveux en brosse brush cut, **5.1**
la **cheville** ankle, **6.1**
la **chèvre** goat
chez at the home (business) of, I-5
   chez soi home, I
chic (inv.) chic, stylish, I
le **chien** dog, I-4.1
chiffonné(e) wrinkled, **9.1**
le **chiffre** number, I
le **chignon** bun (of hair), **5.1**
le **Chili** Chile, I-16
la **chimie** chemistry, I-2.2
chimique chemical, I
le/la **chimiste** chemist, I
la **Chine** China, I-16
chinois(e) Chinese, I
la **chirurgie** surgery
le **chirurgien** surgeon (m. and f.), **6.2**
   le chirurgien-orthopédiste orthopedic surgeon, **6.2**
le **chocolat: au chocolat** chocolate (adj.), I-5.1
choisir to choose, I-7.1
le **choix** choice, I
le **choléra** cholera, I
le **cholestérol** cholesterol, I
le **chômage** unemployment, **16.2**
   être au chômage to be unemployed, **16.2**
la **chose** thing, I
le **chott** salt lake, **14.2**
Chouette! Great! (inform.), I-2.2
le **chou-fleur** cauliflower
chrétien(ne) Christian

Chroniques martiennes Martian
   Chronicles
la **chute: faire une chute** to fall,
   I-14.2
   ciao goodbye (inform.), I-BV
   ci-dessus above, I
le **ciel** sky, I-14.2
la **cigale** grasshopper, cicada, I
les **cils (m. pl.)** eyelashes, **5.2**
le **cinéma** movie theatre, movies,
   I-16.1
le/la **cinéphile** movie buff, I
   cinq five, I-BV
   cinquante fifty, I-BV
le **cintre** hanger, I-17.2
la **circonstance** circumstance
la **circulation** traffic, I-12.2;
   circulation, I
   la circulation à double sens
   two-way traffic, I
   circuler to circulate
les **ciseaux (m. pl.)** scissors, **5.2**
   citer to cite, mention, I
le/la **citoyen(ne)** citizen
le **citron pressé** lemonade, I-5.1
le/la **civilisé(e)** civilized person, I
   clair(e) light
la **classe** class (people), I-2.1
   en classe économique coach
   class (in plane), I
le **classement** classification, I
   classer to classify, I
le **clavier** keyboard
la **clé** key, I-12.1
le/la **client(e)** customer, I-10.1
le **climat** climate, I
la **clinique** private hospital
les **clous (m. pl.)** pedestrian
   crossing, I-12.2
le **club** club
   le club d'art dramatique
   drama club, I
   le club de forme health club,
   I-11.2
le **coca** Coca-Cola, I-5.1
le **cochon** pig, **15.1**
le **code postal** zip code, **1.2**
le **cœur** heart, I
le **coffre** trunk (of car), I
   le coffre à bagages luggage
   compartment, **7.1**
se **coiffer** to fix one's hair, **5.1**
le **coiffeur, la coiffeuse** hair
   stylist, **5.2**
la **coiffure** hairstyle, **5.1**
le **coin** corner, **8.2**
   au coin de at the corner of,
   10.1
   du coin neighborhood
   (adj.), I

le **col de Roncevaux** Roncesvalles
   Pass
le **colis** package, **1.2**
le **collaborateur, la collaboratrice**
   co-worker, associate, I
le **collant** pantyhose, I-10.1
la **collation** snack, **7.1**
le **collège** junior high, middle
   school, I
le/la **collègue** colleague
la **colline** hill
la **colonie de vacances** summer
   camp, I
   combattre to combat, fight, I
   combien (de) how much, how
   many, I-6.2
   Ça fait combien? How much
   is it (that)?, I-6.2
   C'est combien? How much is
   it (that)?, I-BV
le **combiné** telephone receiver
   comble packed (stadium),
   I-13.1
la **comédie** comedy, I-16.1
   la comédie musicale musical
   comedy, I-16.1
le/la **comédien(ne)** actor (actress),
   16.1
   comique funny, I-1.2
le **commandant de bord** captain
   (plane), **7.1**
   commander to order, I-5.1
   comme like, as; for, I
le **commencement** beginning, I
   commencer to begin, I
   comment how; what, I-1.2
   Comment est... ? What
   is . . . like? (description), I-1.1
   Comment t'appelles-tu?
   What's your name? (fam.),
   I-1.1
   Comment vas-tu? How are
   you? (fam.), I-BV
   Comment vous appelez-vous?
   What's your name? (form.),
   11.1
le/la **commerçant(e)** merchant, **16.1**
le **commerce** business
   commun(e) common, I
   en commun in common, I
la **communauté** community, I
le **compact disc** compact disc,
   I-3.2
la **compagnie aérienne** airline,
   I-7.1
le **compagnon** fellow-worker,
   journeyman
le **compagnonnage** guild
le **compartiment** compartment,
   I-7.2

le **complet** suit (man's), I-10.1
   complet, complète full,
   complete, **4.1**
   complètement completely
   compléter to complete, I
le **comportement** behavior, I
   composer to compose, I
   composer le numéro to dial a
   telephone number, **3.1**
   composter to stamp, validate
   (a ticket), I-8.1
   comprendre to understand,
   I-9.1; to include, **7**
le **comprimé** pill, tablet I-15.2
   compris(e) included (in the
   bill), I
   Le service est compris. The
   tip is included., I-5.2
   comptabilisé(e) accounted for
le/la **comptable** accountant, **16.1**
le **compte: le Compte-Chèques**
   Postal postal checking
   account
   le compte d'épargne savings
   account, I-18.1
   être à son compte to be self-
   employed, **16.2**
le **comptoir** counter, I-7.1
   concerner to concern
le/la **concierge** concierge, caretaker, I
le **concours** competition, contest, I
le **conducteur, la conductrice**
   driver, I-12.1
   conduire to drive, I-12.2
la **conduite: les leçons (f.) de con-**
   duite driving lessons, I-12.2
les **confettis (m. pl.)** confetti, **11.1**
   confiant(e) confident, I-1.1
le **confort** comfort, I
   confortable comfortable, I
la **confrérie** brotherhood
   congé: le jour de congé day off
la **connaissance: faire la connais-**
   sance de to meet, I
   connaître to know, I-16.2
   connu(e) known, I
la **conquête** conquest, I
   conquis(e) conquered
   consacrer to devote
   conscient(e) conscious
le **conseiller, la conseillère**
   d'éducation dean of
   discipline, **12.2**
le **conseiller, la conseillère**
   d'orientation guidance
   counselor, **12.2**
les **conseils (m. pl.)** advice
la **conséquence** consequence
   conséquent: par conséquent
   consequently

VOCABULAIRE FRANÇAIS-ANGLAIS   **461**

conservateur, conservatrice
conservative, I
conserve: la boîte de conserve
can of food, I-6.2
conserver to conserve, I
la consigne checkroom, I-8.1
la consigne automatique
locker, I-8.1
consommer to consume, I
construit(e) built, I
la consultation medical visit, I
le contact: mettre le contact
to start (a car), I-12.1
contaminer to contaminate, I
le conte story, tale, I
contenir to contain, I
content(e) happy, I-1.1
le contenu contents, 1.2
continu(e) continual,
ongoing, I
continuer to continue, I
la contractuelle meter maid,
I-12.2
le contraire opposite, I
au contraire on the
contrary, I
la contravention traffic ticket,
I-12.2
contre against, I-13.1
par contre on the other hand,
however, I
le contremaître, la contremaîtresse
foreman (woman), 2.2
le contrôle de sécurité security
(airport), I-7.1
passer par le contrôle de
sécurité to go through
security (airport), I
le contrôleur conductor (train),
I-8.2
convenable correct, I
les convenances (f. pl.) social
customs, conventions
convenir to fit, be suitable
la conversation conversation, I
la coopération cooperation, I
coordonner to coordinate
le copain friend, pal (m.), I-2.1
la copine friend, pal (f.), I-2.1
le coq rooster, 15.2
le coquelicot poppy
la coqueluche whooping cough, I
le cor horn
le Coran Koran
le corps body, I
correspondre to correspond, I
corriger to correct, I
le cortège procession, party
le costume costume, I-16.1
la côte coast, I

la Côte d'Azur French
Riviera, I
la Côte d'Ivoire Ivory Coast,
I-16
le côté side, 5.1
côté couloir aisle (seat), I-7.1
côté fenêtre window (seat),
I-7.1
se côtiser to chip in
le coton: en coton cotton (adj.),
9.2
la couche layer
coucher to put (someone) to
bed, I-11
se coucher to go to bed, I-11.1
le coucher du soleil sunset, 15.2
la couchette bunk (on a train),
I-8.2
le coude elbow, 13.1
couler to flow
la couleur color, I-10.2
De quelle couleur est... ?
What color is . . . ?, I-10.2
les coulisses (f. pl.): dans les
coulisses backstage, I
le couloir aisle, corridor, I-8.2
la voiture à couloir central
train car with central aisle,
4.1
la coupe haircut, 5.2; winner's cup
I-13.2
la coupe aux ciseaux haircut
with scissors, 5.2
la coupe au rasoir razor
haircut, 5.2
couper to cut, 5.2
se faire couper les cheveux
to get a haircut, 5
la cour courtyard, I-4.2; court, I
courageux, courageuse
courageous, brave, I
couramment fluently, 8
courant(e) common, 13.1;
current
le coureur runner, I-13.2
le coureur cycliste racing
cyclist, I-13.2
la courgette zucchini, 14.1
courir to run, 2.2
la couronne crown
couronné(e) crowned, I
le courrier mail, 1.1
le cours course, class, I-2.2
le cours facultatif elective,
12.2
le cours obligatoire required
course, 12.2
le cours du change exchange
rate, I-18.1
la course race, I-13.2

la course cycliste bicycle
race, I
les courses (f. pl.): faire les courses
to go grocery shopping, I-6.1
court(e) short, I-10.2
le court de tennis tennis court,
I-9.2
le couscous couscous (dish
made of semolina, meats, and
vegetables), 14.1
le/la cousin(e) cousin, I-4.1
le couteau knife, I-5.2
coûter to cost, I
Ça coûte cher. It's (That's)
expensive., I
la coutume custom, I
le couturier designer (of clothes),
I-10.1
le couvert table setting, I-5.2
mettre le couvert to set the
table, I-8
couvert(e): Le ciel est couvert.
The sky is overcast., I-14.2
la couverture blanket, I-17.2
le couvreur roofer
couvrir to cover, I-15
le crabe crab, I-6.1
la craie: le morceau de craie
piece of chalk, I-BV
le cratère crater
la cravate tie, I-10.1
le crayon pencil, I-BV
la crèche day-care center, I
créer to create, I
la crème cream, I-6.1
la crème pour le visage face
cream, 5.2
la crème solaire suntan
lotion, I-9.1
le crème coffee with cream (in a
café), I-5.1
la crémerie dairy store, I-6.1
le créole Creole (language), I
créole creole
la crêpe crepe, pancake, I-5.1
la crêperie crepe restaurant, I
crevé(e) exhausted, I
la crevette shrimp, I-6.1
le cri sound, 15.2
crier to shout, I
la crise crisis, I
la critique criticism, I
le/la critique critic, I
critique critical
critiquer to criticize, I
croire to believe, think, I-10.2
la croisade crusade
la croisée window
le croisement intersection, I-12.2
se croiser to cross (intersect), 10.1

la **croissance** growth, I
le **croissant** croissant, crescent roll, I-6.1
le **croque-monsieur** grilled ham and cheese sandwich, I-5.1
croustillant(e) crusty, I
la **croûte de sel** salt crust, **14.2**
la **croyance** belief, I
le **cube** cube, I
le **cubisme** Cubism, I
cueillir to pick, gather
la **cuillère** spoon, I-5.2
le **cuir: en cuir** leather (adj.), **9.2**
les objets (m. pl.) en cuir leather goods, **14.1**
la **cuisine** kitchen, I-4.2; cuisine (food), I
faire la cuisine to cook, I-6
cuit(e): bien cuit(e) well-done (meat), I-5.2
cultivé(e) cultivated
cultiver to cultivate, **15.1**
la **culture** culture, I; farming (raising crops), **15.1**
culturel(le) cultural, I
la **cure** cure, I
le **curriculum vitae (CV)** résumé, **16.2**
la **cuve** basin
le **cycle: le cycle de l'eau** water cycle, I
le **cyclisme** cycling, bicycle riding, I-13.2
le **cycliste** cyclist, I
les **cymbales (f. pl.)** cymbals, **11.1**

D

d'abord first, I-11.1
d'accord O.K., I-3
être d'accord to agree, I-2.1
le **daim** deer
la **dame** lady, I
le **danger: en danger** in danger, I
dangereux, dangereuse dangerous, I
dans in, I-BV
la **danse** dance, I
danser to dance, I-3.2
le **danseur**, la **danseuse** dancer, **16.1**
d'après according to, I
la **date: Quelle est la date aujourd'hui?** What is today's date?, I-4.1
la **datte** date (fruit), **14.2**
de from, I-1.1; of, belonging to, I-5
de bonne heure early, **2.2**

de côté aside, I-17.2
de loin by far, I
de nos jours today, nowadays, I
de plus en plus more and more, I
De quelle couleur est... ? What color is . . . ?, I-10.2
de rêve dream (adj.), I
De rien. You're welcome. (informal), I-BV
de temps en temps from time to time, occasionally, 4
le **débarquement** landing, deplaning, I
débarquer to get off (plane), I-7.2
débarrasser la table to clear the table, **2.1**
déboisé(e) stripped
le **déboisement** deforestation
déborder to overflow, I
debout standing, I-8.2
le **début** beginning, I
au début at the beginning
le/la **débutant(e)** beginner, I-14.1
le **décalage horaire** time difference, I
la **décapotable** convertible (car), I-12.1
décembre (m.) December, I-4.1
le **déchet** waste, I
déchirer to tear, **9.2**
décider (de) to decide (to), I
déclarer to declare, call, I
le **décollage** take-off (plane), **7.1**
décoller to take off (plane), I-7.1
se **décomposer** to decompose
décontracté(e) relaxed, informal
le **décor** set (for a play), I-16.1
le **décorateur (de porcelaine)** painter (of china), I
les **décorations (f. pl.)** decorations, **11.2**
découper to carve (meat)
découvert: à découvert exposed, uncovered
la **découverte** discovery, I
découvrir to discover, I-15
décrire to describe, I
décrocher to pick up a telephone receiver, **3.1**
dedans inside
dédié(e) dedicated, I
se **dédier** to dedicate (oneself)
défense de doubler no passing (traffic sign), I
le **défilé** parade, **11.1**

défiler to march, **11.1**
défiler au pas to march in step, **11.1**
définir to define, I
la **définition** definition, I
se **dégourdir (les jambes)** to stretch (one's legs)
le **degré** degree, I-14.2
Il fait... degrés. (Celsius) It's . . . degrees. (Celsius), I-14.2
dehors outside, I
en dehors de outside (of), I
déjà already, I-14
déjeuner to eat lunch, I-5.2
le **déjeuner** lunch, **2**
délicieux, délicieuse delicious, I-10
le **delta** delta, I
demain tomorrow, I-2.2
À demain. See you tomorrow., I-BV
la **demande d'emploi** job application, **16.2**
demander to ask (for), I
demander son chemin to ask the way, **8.2**
se **demander** to wonder, I
demi(e) half, I
et demie half past (time), I
le **demi-cercle** semi-circle; top of the key (on a basketball court), I-13.2
le **demi-kilo** half a kilo, 500 grams, I
la **démission: donner sa démission** to resign
le **demi-tarif: à demi-tarif** half-price, I
la **demoiselle d'honneur** maid of honor, **11.2**
la **dent** tooth, I-11.1
avoir mal aux dents to have a toothache, I-15
se brosser les dents to brush one's teeth, I-11.1
le **dentifrice** toothpaste, I-11.1
le **déodorant** deodorant, I-11.1
la **dépanneuse** tow-truck, **8.2**
le **départ** departure, I-7.1
le **département** one of 95 official regional divisions of France
le **département d'outre-mer** French overseas department, I
dépassé(e) surpassed
se **dépêcher** to hurry, **2.2**
dépendre (de) to depend (on), I
dépenser to spend (money), I-10.1
déplacer to move

la **dépression** low-pressure area (weather), I
depuis since, for, I-8.2
dériver to derive, I
dernier, dernière last, I-10
derrière behind, I-BV
des some, any, I-3; I-6; of the, from the, I-5
désagréable unpleasant, I-1.2
descendre to get off, I-8.2; to take down, I-8; to go down, I-14.1
la **descente** getting off (a bus), **10.2**
le **désert** desert, **14.2**
se **déshabiller** to get undressed, I
désirer to want, I
  Vous désirez? May I help you? (store); What would you like? (restaurant), I
désolé(e) sorry, **13.2**
  être désolé(e) to be sorry, **3.2**
le **dessert** dessert, I
desservir to serve, fly to, etc. (transportation), **4.2**
le **dessin** illustration, I
  le dessin animé cartoon, I-16.1
la **dessinatrice** illustrator, I
dessous: au-dessous smaller (size), I-10.2; below
dessus: au-dessus larger (size), I-10.2; above
le/la **destinataire** addressee, **1.2**
la **destruction** destruction, I
le **détergent** detergent, I
détester to hate, I-3.2
détruit(e) destroyed
deux two, I-BV
  les deux roues (f. pl.) two-wheeled vehicles, I
  tous (toutes) les deux both, I
deuxième second, I-4.2
  la Deuxième Guerre mondiale World War II, I
deuxièmement second of all, secondly, I
devant in front of, I-BV
le **développement** development, I
devenir to become, I-16
deviner to guess
la **devise** currency, I
le **devoir** homework (assignment), I-BV
  faire les devoirs to do homework, I-6
devoir to owe, I-18.2; must, to have to (+ verb), I-18
le **diagnostic: faire un diagnostic** to diagnose, I-15.2

le **diamant** diamond
la **diapo(sitive)** (photo) slide, **12.2**
dicter to dictate, I
le **dictionnaire** dictionary, **12.1**
le **dieu** god
la **différence** difference, I
différencier to distinguish, differentiate
différent(e) different, I
difficile difficult, I-2.1
la **difficulté: être en difficulté** to be in trouble, I
dimanche (m.) Sunday, I-2.2
diminuer to diminish
le **dinar** dinar (unit of currency in North Africa), **14.1**
la **dinde** turkey (food)
le **dindon** turkey (animal), **15.2**
le **dîner** dinner, I-4.2
dîner to eat dinner, I-4.2
dingue crazy
la **diphtérie** diphtheria, I
la **diplomatie** diplomacy
le **diplôme** diploma, **12.2**
diplômé(e): être diplômé(e) to get a degree from, I
dire to say, tell, I-12.2
directement directly, **3.1**
le **directeur, la directrice** manager, **16.1**
  la directrice high school principal (f.), **12.2**
la **direction: prendre la direction...** to take the . . . line (subway), **10.1**
diriger to direct, I
se **diriger** to head (towards)
discuter to discuss, I
le **diseur, la diseuse de bonne aventure** fortune-teller
disparaître to disappear, I
disponible available, **4.1**
le **disque** record, I-3.2
la **disquette** diskette (computer)
la **distance** distance, I
distingué(e) distinguished, I
distribuer to distribute, to deliver (mail), **1.1**
le **distributeur automatique** stamp machine, **1.1**; ticket machine, **10.1**
  le distributeur automatique de billets automated teller machine (ATM), I
divisé(e) divided, I
le **divorce** divorce, I
divorcer to divorce
dix ten, I-BV
dix-huit eighteen, I-BV

dix-neuf nineteen, I-BV
dix-sept seventeen, I-BV
la **dizaine** around ten
le **docteur** doctor (title), I
le **documentaire** documentary, I-16.1
le/la **documentaliste** school librarian, **12.2**
dodo sleep (slang)
le **doigt** finger, **6.1**
  le doigt de pied toe, **6.1**
le **dollar** dollar, I-3.2
le **dolmen** dolmen (prehistoric stone monument)
le **domaine** domain, field, I
le **domicile** home
  à domicile to the home, I
dominer to dominate
donc so, therefore
donner to give, I-3.2
  donner à manger à to feed, I
  donner un coup de fil to call on the telephone, **3.1**
  donner un coup de peigne to comb, **5.2**
  donner un coup de pied to kick, I-13.1
  donner sa démission to resign
  donner une fête to throw a party, I-3.2
  donner sur to face, overlook, I-17.1
dont of which, from which
doré(e) golden
dormir to sleep, I-7.2
  dormir à la belle étoile to sleep outdoors
le **dortoir** dormitory, I
le **dos** back (body), I
  à dos de chameau on camel(back), **14.2**
le **dossier** file
  le dossier du siège back of the seat, **7.1**
la **douane** customs, I-7.2
  passer à la douane to go through customs, I-7.2
doublé(e) dubbed (movies), I-16.1
doubler to pass (car), **8.1**
doucement gently
la **douche** shower, I
  prendre une douche to take a shower, I-11.1
la **douleur** pain
douloureux, douloureuse painful, I
le **doute: sans aucun doute** without a doubt, I

douter to doubt, **14.2**
doux, douce soft
la douzaine dozen, I-6.2
douze twelve, I-BV
le drame drama, I-16.1
le drap sheet, I-17.2
le drapeau flag, **11.1**
dresser to draw up (a list)
dribbler to dribble (basketball), I-13.2
le droit: le droit de vote right to vote
droite: à droite de to, on the right of, I-5
du of the, from the (m. sing.), I-5; some, any, I-6
du coin neighborhood (adj.), I
du tout: pas du tout not at all, I
la dune dune, **14.2**
la durée length (of time), I
durer to last, **11.2**

E

l' eau (f.) water, I
l'eau de Javel bleach
l'eau minérale mineral water, I-6.2
l'eau de toilette cologne, **5.2**
l' échange (m.) exchange, I
échapper (à) to escape
s' échapper to escape, I
l' écharpe (f.) scarf, I-14.1
échouer à un examen to fail an exam, **12.1**
éclairer to light
l' école (f.) school, I-1.2
l'école maternelle pre-school
l'école primaire elementary school, I
l'école secondaire junior high, high school, I
l' écolier, l'écolière pupil, schoolchild, I
l' écologiste (m. et f.) ecologist, I
l' économie (f.) economy, I
les économies (f. pl.): faire des économies to save money, I-18.2
économique economical, I
en classe économique in coach class (plane), I-7
l' écorce (f.) bark (of a tree)
écouter to listen (to), I-3.1
l' écouteur (m.) headphone, **7.1**
l' écran (m.) screen, I-7.1

l' écrevisse (f.) crawfish, I
écrire to write, I-12.2
l' écrit (m.) writing
l' écrivain (m.) writer (m. and f.), I
l' écureuil (m.) squirrel
éducatif, éducative educational, I
l' éducation (f.): l'éducation civique social studies, I-2.2
l'éducation (f.) physique physical education, I
effacer to erase, **12.1**
effectuer to perform
efficace efficient, I
égal: Ça m'est égal. I don't care.
également as well, also
égaliser to tie (score), I
l' église (f.) church, **11.2**
élaboré(e) worked on (adj.), refined
l' électricité (f.) electricity, I
électrique electric, I
électronique electronic
l' élément (m.) element, I
l' élevage (m.) farming (raising livestock), **15.1**
l' élève (m. et f.) student, I-1.2
élevé(e) high, I-15.
bien élevé(e) well brought-up, I
éliminer to eliminate, I
l' élite (f.) elite
elle she, it, I-1; her (stress pron.), I-9
elle-même herself
elles they (f.), I-2; them (stress pron.), I-9
l' embarquement (m.) boarding, leaving, I
embarquer to board (plane, etc.), I-7.2
embaumer to perfume
l' embouteillage (m.) traffic jam, **8.2**
l' embrassade (f.) embrace
s' embrasser to kiss (each other), **13.1**
Je t'embrasse Love (to close a letter)
émigrer to emigrate, I
l' émission (f.) TV show, **2.1**
emmener to bring, take (a person somewhere), **6.1**
émotif, émotive emotional
s' emparer to take
l' empereur (m.) emperor, I
l' empire (m.) empire
l' emploi (m.) job, **16.2**

la demande d'emploi job application, **16.2**
l'emploi du temps schedule, I
l' employé(e) employee, **16.2**
l'employé(e) des postes postal employee, **1.2**
employer to use, **1**
l' employeur, l'employeuse employer, **16.2**
emporter to bring (something), **4.2**
emprunter to borrow, I-18.2
en of it, of them, etc., I-18.2; in; as, I
en avance early, ahead of time, I-8.1
en avion plane (adj.), by plane, I-7.1
en baisse coming down (in value), I
en bas to, at the bottom, I
en boule in a ball, I
en ce moment right now, I
en classe in class, I
en commun in common, I
en dehors de outside (of); besides, I
en effet in fact, I
en exclusivité first-run (movie), I
en face de across from, opposite, **4.1**
en fait in fact, I
en fonction de in terms of, in accordance with, I
en général in general, I
en hausse going up (in value), I
en haut de on, to the top of, I
en plein(e) (+ noun) right in, on, etc. (+ noun), I
en plein air outdoor(s), I
en plus de besides, in addition, I
en première (seconde) in first (second) class, I-8.1
en provenance de arriving from (flight, train), I-7.1
en retard late, I-8.2
en solde on sale, I-10.2
en tout cas in any case, I
en version originale original language version, I-16.1
en ville in town, in the city, I
enceinte pregnant
enchanté(e) delighted, **13.2**
encombré(e) congested (road), **8.2**

encore still (adv.); another; again, I

encourager to encourage, I

l' encyclopédie (f.) encyclopedia, **12.1**

s' endetter to go into debt

s' endormir to fall asleep, I-11.1

l' endroit (m.) place, **8.1**

l' énergie (f.) energy, I

énergique energetic, I-1.2

l' enfant (m. et f.) child (m. and f.), I-4.1

enfin finally, I

engager to hire

l' engrais (m.) fertilizer, I

enlever to lift, remove

enneigé(e) covered with snow

l' ennemi (m.) enemy

l' ennui (m.) trouble, problem

ennuyeux, ennuyeuse boring

énormément enormously, I

l' enquête (f.) survey, opinion poll, I

enragé(e) rabid, enraged, I

enregistrer to record, **2.1**

enrhumé(e): être enrhumé(e) to have a cold, I-15.1

l' enseignement (m.) education; teaching, I

enseigner to teach, **12.2**

ensemble together, I-5.1

ensuite then, I-11.1

entendre to hear, I-8.1

l' enthousiasme (m.) enthusiasm, I

entier, entière entire, whole, I-10

entourer to surround, **8.1**

l' entracte (m.) intermission, I-16.1

entraîner to carry along, I

entre between, among, I-9.2

l' entrée (f.) entrance, I-4.2; admission, I

l' entreposage (m.) storage, **15.2**

entreposer to store, **15.2**

l' entreprise (f.) company, **16.2**

entrer to enter, I-3.1

l' entretien (m.) interview, **16.2**; upkeep, care, **15.1**

envahir to invade

l' enveloppe (f.) envelope, **1.1**

s' envelopper dans to wrap oneself up (in), **14.1**

l' environnement (m.) environment, I

envoler to fly away

envoyer to send, I-13.1

envoyé(e) en exil sent into exile

épais(se) thick

l' épée (f.) sword

l' épice (f.) spice

épicé(e) spicy, I

l' épicerie (f.) grocery store, I-6.1

l' époque (f.) period, times, era

épouser to marry

l' équilibre (m.) balance, I

équilibré(e) balanced, I

l' équipage (m.) flight crew, **7.1**

l' équipe (f.) team, I-13.1

équipé(e) equipped

l' équipement (m.) equipment, I

l' érable (m.) maple (tree)

le sirop d'érable maple syrup, I

erreur: C'est une erreur. You have the wrong number., **3.2**

l' escalator (m.) escalator, **10.1**

escale: sans escale nonstop (flight), **7.2**

l' escalier (m.) staircase, I-17.1

l'escalier mécanique (m.) escalator, **10.1**

l' espace (m.) space, I

l' Espagne (f.) Spain, I-16

l' espagnol (m.) Spanish (language), I-2.2

espagnol(e) Spanish, I

l' espèce (f.) species, group

les espèces (f. pl.): payer en espèces to pay cash, I-17.2

l' espionnage (m.) spying, I

l' esprit (m.) spirit

l' essence (f.) gas(oline), I-12.1

(l'essence) ordinaire regular gas, I-12.1

(l'essence) super sans plomb super unleaded gas, I-12.1

essentiel(le) essential, I

essentiellement essentially, I

s' essuyer to wipe (one's hands, etc.), **13.1**

l' est (m.) east, I

estimer to consider, I

l' estomac (m.) stomach, I

et and, I-1

et toi? and you? (fam.), I-BV

l' étable (f.) cowshed, **15.1**

établir to establish, I

l' établissement (m.) establishment

l'établissement de soins polyvalents multi-care center

l' étage (m.) floor (of a building), I-4.2

l' étal (m.) (market) stall, I

l' état (m.) state, I

en état d'ivresse intoxicated

l'homme (m.) d'état statesman, diplomat

les États-Unis (m. pl.) United States, I-13.2

l' été (m.) summer, I-9.1

en été in summer, I-9.1

éteindre to turn off (the T.V., etc.), **2.1**

étendu(e) extended

éternuer to sneeze, I-15.1

étonné(e) astonished, **13.2**

étonner: ça m'étonnerait I would be very surprised, **14**

s' étouffer to choke

étranger, étrangère foreign, I-16.1

à l'étranger abroad, in a foreign country

être to be, I-2.1

être à l'heure to be on time, I-8.1

être d'accord to agree, I-2.1

être de passage to be passing through

être désolé(e) to be sorry, **3.2**

être en avance to be early, I-8.1

être en bonne (mauvaise) santé to be in good (poor) health, I-15.1

être en retard to be late, I-8.2

être enrhumé(e) to have a cold, I-15.1

être reçu(e) à un examen to pass an exam, **12.1**

être vite sur pied to be back on one's feet in no time, I-15.2

ne pas être dans son assiette to be feeling out of sorts, I-15.2

l' être: l'être (m.) humain human being, I

l'être vivant living being

étroit(e) tight (shoes), narrow, I-10.2

l' étudiant(e) (university) student, I

étudier to study, I-3.1

européen(ne) European, I-9

eux them (m. pl. stress pron.), I-9

s' évaporer to evaporate, I

éveiller to wake (someone) up

l' événement (m.) event

éventuellement possibly, I

l' **évêque (m.)** bishop
évidemment obviously, **8**
évident: il est évident it's obvious, **14**
l' **évier (m.)** sink, **2.1**
évoquer to evoke, I
exact: C'est exact. That's correct.
l' **exactitude (f.)** exactness, promptness
exagérer to exaggerate
l' **examen (m.)** test, exam, I-3.1
passer un examen to take a test, I-3.1
réussir à un examen to pass a test, I-7
examiner to examine, I-15.2
excellent(e) excellent, I
exceptionnel(le) exceptional, I
Excusez-moi. Excuse me., I'm sorry., **4.1**
l' **exemple (m.)** example, I
par exemple for example, I
exercer to exert, to exercise
s' **exercer** to practice, I
exigeant(e) exacting, particular
exiger to require, **12.1**
l' **expansion (f.)** expansion, I
l' **expéditeur, l'expéditrice** sender, **1.2**
l' **expédition (f.)** expedition, I
expliquer to explain, I
l' **exploitant (m.)** farmer, **15.2**
l' **exploitation (f.)** farm, **15.2**
l' **explorateur (m.)** explorer, I
explorer to explore, I
l' **exposé (m.)** oral report, **12.1**
faire un exposé to give an oral report, **12.1**
exposer to exhibit, I
l' **exposition (f.)** exhibit, show, I-16.2
l' **express (m.)** espresso, black coffee, I-5.1
expressément expressly, purposely
s' **exprimer** to express oneself, I
exquis(e) exquisite, I
l' **extérieur (m.)** exterior, outside, I
externe day (student), non-resident
extra terrific (inform.), I-2.2
l' **extrait (m.)** extract
extraordinaire extraordinary, I
l' **extraterrestre (m.)** extraterrestrial
extrêmement extremely, I

F

la **fabrication** manufacture
la **fabrique** factory, **2.2**
fabriqué(e) made, I
fabriquer to make, **2.2**
fabuleux, fabuleuse fabulous, I
fâché(e) angry, I-12.2
facile easy, I-2.1
la **façon** way, manner, I
de toute façon anyway
d'une façon générale in a general way, I
le **facteur** mail carrier, **1.1**
la **facture** bill (hotel, etc.), I-17.2
facultatif, facultative elective, **12.2**
le **cours facultatif** elective (n.), **12.2**
faire to do, make, I-6.1
faire du (+ nombre) to take size (+ number), I-10.2
faire des achats to shop, make purchases, I-10.1
faire de l'aérobic to do aerobics, I-11.2
faire une anesthésie to give anesthesia, **6.2**
faire l'annonce to announce, I
faire attention to pay attention, I-6; to be careful, I-9.1
faire un brushing to blow-dry someone's hair, **5.2**
faire du camping to go camping
faire une chute to fall, take a fall, I-14.2
faire connaissance to meet, get acquainted
faire la connaissance de to meet (for the first time), **13.2**
faire une coupe (au rasoir, aux ciseaux) to give a haircut (with a razor, scissors), **5.2**
faire les courses to do the grocery shopping, I-6.1
faire cuire to cook, **14.1**
faire la cuisine to cook, I-6
faire demi-tour to make a U-turn, **8.2**
faire les devoirs to do homework, I
faire un diagnostic to diagnose, I-15.2
faire des économies to save money, I-18.2

faire enregistrer to check (luggage), I-7.1
faire des études to study, I-6
faire de l'exercice to exercise, I-1.2
faire un exposé to give an oral report, **12.1**
faire du français (etc.) to study French (etc.), I-6
faire de la gymnastique to do gymnastics, I-11.2
faire (+ inf.) to have something done for oneself
faire du jogging to jog, I-11.2
faire la lessive to do the laundry, **9.1**
faire le levé topographique to survey (land), I
faire de la monnaie to make change, I-18.1
faire de la natation to swim, go swimming, I
faire la navette to go back and forth, I
faire le numéro to dial a telephone number, **3.1**
faire une ordonnance to write a prescription, I-15.2
faire partie de to be a part of, I
faire du patin to skate, I-1.2
faire du patin à glace to ice-skate, I-14.2
faire du patin à roulettes to roller-skate, I
faire peur à to frighten, I
faire un pique-nique to have a picnic, I-6
faire une piqûre to give an injection, **6.2**
faire de la planche à voile to go windsurfing, I-9.1
faire le plein to fill up (a gas tank), I-12.1
faire de la plongée sous-marine to go deep-sea diving, I-9.1
faire des points de suture to give stitches, **6.2**
faire une promenade to take a walk, I-9.1
faire la queue to wait in line, I-8.1
faire une radiographie to do an X-ray, **6.2**
faire de la randonnée pédestre to go backpacking
faire une rédaction to write a composition or paper, **12.1**

faire un régime   to go on a diet, I
faire serment   to pledge
faire un shampooing   to shampoo, **5.2**
faire signe de (+ inf.)   to signal (someone) to do (something)
faire du ski   to ski, I-14.1
faire du ski nautique   to waterski, I-9.1
faire du sport   to play sports, I
faire du surf   to go surfing, I-9.1
faire du surf des neiges   to go snowboarding, I
faire sa toilette   to wash and groom oneself, I-11.1
faire la vaisselle   to do the dishes, **2.1**
faire les valises   to pack (suitcases), I-7.1
faire un voyage   to take a trip, I-7.1
se faire couper les cheveux   to get a haircut
le **faire-part**   invitation
le **fait**   fact, I
fait(e) à la main   handmade
familial(e)   family (adj.)
se **familiariser (avec)**   to familiar-ize oneself with
familier, familière   informal
la **famille**   family, I-4.1
la **famille à parent unique**   single-parent family, I
le/la **fana**   fan, I
la **fanfare**   marching band, **11.1**
fantaisiste   whimsical, I
fantastique   fantastic, I-1.2
farci(e)   stuffed
fasciner   to fascinate
fatigué(e)   tired, **7.2**
fauché(e)   broke (slang), I-18.2
faut: il faut (+ noun)   (noun) is (are) necessary, I
il faut (+ inf.)   one must, it is necessary to (+ verb), I-9.1
il faut que (+ subjunc.)   it is necessary that, **11**
le **fauteuil roulant**   wheelchair, **6.1**
faux, fausse   false, I
favori(te)   favorite, I-10
la **femme**   woman, I-2.1; wife, I-4.1
la **femme cadre**   (woman) executive
la **femme ingénieur**   (woman) engineer

la **femme médecin**   (woman) dcotor
la **fenêtre**   window, I
côté fenêtre   window (seat) (adj.), I-7.1
la **fente**   slot, **3.1**
la **ferme**   farm, **15.1**
fermé(e)   closed, I-16.2
la **fermeture éclair**   zipper, **9.2**
le **fermier**   farmer, **15.2**
la **fertilité**   fertility, I
les **festivités (f. pl.)**   festivities, **11.1**
la **fête**   holiday; party, I-3.2
la **fête des Lumières**   Festival of Lights, **11.2**
la **Fête des Mères (Pères)**   Mother's (Father's) Day, I
la **fête nationale**   national holiday, **11.1**
le **feu**   traffic light, I-12.2
les **feux (m. pl.) d'artifice**   fireworks, **11.1**
le **feu de détresse**   hazard light (on a car)
le **feu orange**   yellow traffic light, I-12.2
la **feuille**   leaf, I
la **feuille de papier**   sheet of paper, I-BV
le **feutre**   felt-tip pen, **12.1**
la **fève**   dried bean
février (m.)   February, I-4.1
la **fiche d'enregistrement**   registra-tion card (hotel), I-17.1
la **fièvre**   fever, I-15.1
la **fièvre jaune**   yellow fever, I
avoir une fièvre de cheval   to have a high fever, I-15.2
la **figue**   fig, **14.2**
la **figure**   face, I-11.1
la **file (de voitures)**   line (of cars), **8.1**
le **filet**   net shopping bag, I-6.1; net (tennis, etc.), I-9.2; rack (train), I
la **filiale**   branch office
la **fille**   girl, I-BV; daughter, I-4.1
le **film**   film, movie, I-16.1
le **film d'amour**   love story, I-16.1
le **film d'aventures**   adventure movie, I-16.1
le **film étranger**   foreign film, I-16.1
le **film d'horreur**   horror film, I-16.1
le **film policier**   detective movie, I-16.1
le **film de science-fiction**   science-fiction movie, I-16.1

le **fils**   son, I-4.1
fin(e)   fine, I
fines herbes: aux fines herbes   with herbs, I-5.1
finalement   finally, I
finir   to finish, I-7
fixe: à prix fixe   at a fixed price, I
le **flacon**   bottle
flamand(e)   Flemish
flambé(e)   flaming, I
le **flamboyant**   West Indian tree with bright red flowers
la **flamme**   flame
flâner   to stroll, I
le **fléau**   plague, evil
la **flèche**   arrow, **8.1**
le **fleuve**   river, I
flotter   to float, I
la **fluctuation**   fluctuation, I
la **flûte**   flute, **11.1**
le **foie**   liver, I
avoir mal au foie   to have indigestion, I-15
le **foin**   hay, **15.1**
la **fois**   time (in a series), I
le/la **fonctionnaire**   government worker, civil servant, **16.1**
le **fonctionnement**   functioning, I
fonctionner   to function, work, I
fond: au fond de   at the bottom of, I
le **fondateur, la fondatrice**   founder, I
fonder   to found, I
le **foot(ball)**   soccer, I-13.1
le **football américain**   football, I
la **force**   force, power, I
le **forcing: faire le forcing**   to put pressure on, I
la **forêt**   forest, I
le **forfait-journée**   lift ticket (skiing), I
la **forme**   form, shape, I
le **club de forme**   health club, I-11.2
être en forme   to be in shape, I-11.2
la **forme (physique)**   physical fitness, I
rester en forme   to stay in shape, I-11.2
se mettre en forme   to get in shape, I-11.2
former   to form; to train, I
le **formulaire**   form, data sheet, **6.2**
la **formule**   formula, I
le **fort**   fort, I
fort(e)   strong; good, I

fort (adv.) hard, I-9.2
fortement strong, hard
fou, folle crazy, I
le foulard scarf, I
la foule: venir en foule to crowd (into), I
se fouler to sprain, 6.1
la fourchette fork, I-5.2
le fourgon à bagages luggage car (train), 4.2
la fourmi ant, I
le foyer fire(side)
la fracture (compliquée) (multiple) fracture, 6.2
frais, fraîche fresh, cool
les frais (m. pl.) expenses, charges, I-17.2
    partager les frais to "go dutch," to share expenses, 13.1
la fraise strawberry, I
le franc franc, I-18.1
le français French (language), I-2.2
le/la Français(e) Frenchman (woman), I
français(e) French (adj.), I-1.1
la France France, I-16
franchement frankly, I
francophone French-speaking, I
la frange bangs, 5.1
frapper to hit, I-9.2
le frein à main emergency brake
freiner to brake, put on the brakes, I-12.1
fréquemment frequently, 4
fréquent(e) frequent, I
fréquenter to frequent, patronize
le frère brother, I-1.2
le fric money, dough (slang), I-18.2
    avoir plein de fric to have lots of money (slang), I-18.2
frisé(e) curly, 5.1
les frissons (m. pl.) chills, I-15.1
les frites (f. pl.) French fries, I-5.1
froid(e) cold, I-14.2
    avoir froid to be cold, I
    Il fait froid. It's cold. (weather), I-9.2
le fromage cheese, I-5.1
le front front (weather), I; forehead, 5.1
la frontière border, I
le fruit fruit, I-6.2
    les fruits de mer seafood, I
le fruitier fruit tree
    fuir to flee, escape from

fumer to smoke, I
fumeurs (adj. inv.) smoking (section), I-7.1
    non-fumeurs no smoking (section), I-7.1
les funérailles (f. pl.) funeral
furax furious (slang)
furieux, furieuse furious, 13.2
la fusée rocket, I
le futur future, I

G

le gadget gadget
le/la gagnant(e) winner, I-13.2
gagner to earn, I-3.2; to win, I-9.2
la galaxie galaxy, I
le galet pebble, I
le Gange Ganges River, I
le gant glove, I-14.1
    le gant de toilette washcloth, I-17.2
le garage garage, I-4.2
le garçon boy, I-BV
    le garçon d'honneur best man, 11.2
    garder to guard, I; to keep
la garderie d'enfants day-care center
le gardian French "cowboy"
le gardien de but goalie, I-13.1
la gare train station, I-8.1
    la gare d'arrivée station train arrives at, 4.2
    la gare de départ station train leaves from, 4.2
garer la voiture to park the car, I-12.2
gastronomique gastronomic, gourmet, I
le gâteau cake, I-6.1
gauche: à gauche de to, on the left of, I-5
le gaz gas, I
    le gaz carbonique carbon dioxide
le gel gel, 5.2
geler to freeze, I
    Il gèle. It's freezing. (weather), I-14.2
le gendarme police officer, 8.1
le général general, I-7
général: en général in general, I
généralement generally, I
généraliser to generalize, I
généraliste: le médecin généraliste general practitioner, I

généreux, généreuse generous, I-10, I
la générosité generosity, I
le génie genius
le genou knee, 6.1
le genre type, kind, I-16.1
les gens (m. pl.) people, I
gentil(le) nice (person), I-9
la géographie geography, I-2.2
la géométrie geometry, I-2.2
géométrique geometric, I
la geste exploit, heroic achievement
le gilet de sauvetage life vest, 7.1
la glace ice cream, I-5.1; mirror, I-11.1; ice, I-4.2
le glacier glacier
la glande gland, I
glisser to slip, slide, I
la gloire glory
le glucide carbohydrate, I
le golfe gulf, I
gominé(e) plastered down
la gomme eraser, 12.1
la gorge throat, I-15.1
    avoir un chat dans la gorge to have a frog in one's throat, I-15.2
    avoir la gorge qui gratte to have a scratchy throat, I-15.1
    avoir mal à la gorge to have a sore throat, I-15.1
gothique gothic
gourmand(e) fond of eating
goûter to taste
le gouvernement government, I
gouverner to govern
grâce à thanks to, I
le gradin bleacher (stadium), I-13.1
la graisse fat, I
    la graisse animale animal fat, I
la grammaire grammar
le gramme gram, I-6.2
grand(e) tall, big, I-1.1
    le grand couturier clothing designer, I-10.1
    le grand magasin department store, I-10.1
    de grand standing luxury (adj.), I
    la Grande-Bretagne Great Britain, I-16
    les Grands (m. pl.) Lacs the Great Lakes, I
    pas grand-chose not much, I
grandir to grow (up) (children), I

la **grand-mère** grandmother, I-4.1
le **grand-père** grandfather, I-4.1
les **grands-parents (m. pl.)** grandparents, I-4.1
la **grange** barn, **15.1**
la **grappe** bunch
le **gratte-ciel** skyscraper
gratuit(e) free
la **gratuité** costing no money
grave serious, I
  Ce n'est pas grave. Don't worry about it. (after an apology), **4.1**
la **gravité** seriousness
la **griffe** label, I
le **gril-express** snack bar (train), **4.1**
la **grippe** flu, I-15.1
gris(e) gray, I-10.2
grogner to grunt
gros(se) large, big
  Grosses bises Love and kisses (to close a letter)
grossir to gain weight, I-11.2
la **Guadeloupe** Guadeloupe, I
la **guerre** war
  la Deuxième Guerre mondiale World War II, I
  la Première Guerre mondiale World War I
le **guichet** ticket window, I-8.1; box office, I-16.1; counter window (in a post office), **1.2**
le **guide** guidebook, I-12.2
guillotiner to execute by guillotine
la **guirlande** garland, **11.2**
la **guitare** guitar
le **gymnase** gym(nasium), I-11.2
la **gymnastique** gymnastics, I-2.2
  faire de la gymnastique to do gymnastics, I-11.2

H

habillé(e) dressy, I-10.1
s' **habiller** to get dressed, I-11.1
l' **habitant(e)** resident, I
habiter to live (in a city, house, etc.), I-3.1
l' **habitude (f.): comme d'habitude** as usual
  d'habitude usually
le **hall** lobby, I-17.1
le **hammam** Turkish bath, **14.1**

handicapé(e) handicapped
le **hangar** shed, **15.1**
Hanouka Hanukkah, **11.2**
les **haricots (m. pl.) verts** green beans, I-6.2
la **hâte: en hâte** in haste, in a hurry
haut(e) high, I-10.2
  avoir... mètres de haut to be . . . meters high, I
  du haut de from the top of, I
  en haut de to, at the top of
  la **haute couture** high fashion, I
  à talons hauts high-heeled (shoes), I
le **haut** top, **5.1**
le **haut-parleur** loudspeaker, I-8.1
l' **hectare (m.)** hectare (= 2.47 acres)
l' **hémisphère (m.)** hemisphere
l' **hémorragie (f.)** hemorrhage
l' **herbe (f.)** grass, **15.1**
l' **héritier (m.)** heir
le **héros** hero, I
hésiter to hesitate
l' **heure (f.)** time (of day), I-2
  à quelle heure? at what time?, I-2
  À tout à l'heure. See you later., I-BV
  de bonne heure early, **2.2**
  être à l'heure to be on time, I-8.1
  les heures (f.) de pointe, les heures d'affluence rush hour, **8.1**
  Il est quelle heure? What time is it?, I-2
heureusement fortunately
heureux, heureuse happy, I-10.2
l' **hexagone (m.)** hexagon, I
hier yesterday, I-13.1
  avant-hier the day before yesterday, I-13
  hier matin yesterday morning, I-13
  hier soir last night, I-13
l' **histoire (f.)** history, I-2.2
l' **hiver (m.)** winter, I-14.1
  en hiver in winter, I-14.2
le **H.L.M.** low-income housing, I
le **hockey** hockey, I
  le hockey sur glace ice hockey, I
l' **homme (m.)** man, I-2.1
  l'homme d'affaires businessman

  l'homme d'état diplomat, statesman
les **honoraires (m. pl.)** fees (doctor), I
l' **hôpital (m.)** hospital, **6.1**
l' **horaire (m.)** schedule, timetable, I-8.1
l' **hormone (f.)** hormone, I
  hors des limites out of bounds, I-9.2
hospitalier, hospitalière hospital (adj.)
l' **hôte (m.)** host
l' **hôtel (m.)** hotel, I-17.1
l' **hôtesse (f.) de l'air** flight attendant (f.), I-7.2
huit eight, I-BV
l' **huître (f.)** oyster
humain(e) human, I
humanitaire humanitarian
humide wet, humid, I
humoristique humorous, I
l' **hydrate (m.) de carbone** carbohydrate, I
l' **hymne (m.) national** national anthem, **11.1**
hyper extremely
hystérique hysterical, I

I

l' **idéal(e)** ideal, I
l' **idée (f.)** idea, I
identifier to identify, I
il he, it, I-1
  Il est... heure(s). It's . . . o'clock, I-2
  Il est quelle heure? What time is it?, I-2
  il faut (+ noun) (noun) is (are) needed, I
  il faut (+ inf.) it is necessary to, one must (+ verb), I-9.1
  Il n'y a pas de quoi. You're welcome., I-BV
  il vaut mieux it is better, I
  il y a there is, there are, I-4.2; ago
l' **île (f.)** island, I
illuminé(e) illuminated, lighted
illustré(e) illustrated, I
l' **îlot (m.)** small island, plot of land
ils they (m.), I-2
l' **immeuble (m.)** apartment building, I-4.2
l' **immigration (f.)** immigration, I-7.2

passer à l'immigration to go through immigration (airport), I-7.2

immigré(e) immigrant

impatient(e) impatient, I-1.1

l' **impératrice (f.)** empress

l' **imper(méable) (m.)** raincoat, **9.2**

s' **implanter** to establish oneself (business)

impoli(e) impolite, **13.1**

important(e) important, I

  il est important que (+ subjunc.) it's important that, **11**

impossible: il est impossible que (+ subjunc.) it's impossible that, **11**

impressionnant(e) impressive

les **Impressionnistes (m. pl.)** Impressionists (painters), I

inauguré(e) inaugurated, I

incarner to play (role)

s' **incliner** to slope

inclure to include, I

inconnu(e) unknown, I

inconscient(e) unconscious

l' **inconvénient (m.)** disadvantage

incroyable incredible, I

l' **Inde (f.)** India, I

l' **indicatif (m.) de la ville** area code, **3.1**

l' **indicatif du pays** country code, **3.1**

l' **indication (f.)** cue, I

indiquer to indicate, I

industrialisé(e) industrialized, I

l' **industrie (f.)** industry, I

infectieux, infectieuse infectious, I

l' **infection (f.)** infection, I-15.1

infiltrer to seep (into), I

l' **infirmier, l'infirmière** nurse, **6.1**

influencer to influence, I

l' **informaticien(ne)** computer scientist, **16.1**

l' **informatique (f.)** computer science, I-2.2

l' **ingénieur, la femme ingénieur** engineer, **16.1**

l' **inondation (f.)** flood, I

inquiet, inquiète worried

l' **inquiétude (f.)** worry, concern

s' **inscrire** to register

insister to insist, **12.1**

inspirer to inhale

installer to settle (someone)

s' **installer** to get settled, move in

l' **institut (m.)** institute, I

l' **institution (f.)** institution, I

les **instructions (f. pl.)** instructions, I-9.1

instruit(e) educated

l' **instrument (m.)** instrument, I

intelligent(e) intelligent, I-1.1

interdit(e) forbidden, prohibited, I

  Il est interdit de stationner. No parking., I-12.2

intéressant(e) interesting, I-1.1

intéresser to interest, I

s' **intéresser à** to be interested in, I

l' **intérieur (m.)** interior, inside, I

intérieur(e) domestic (flight) (adj.), I-7.1

l' **interlocuteur, l'interlocutrice** person being spoken to

international(e) international, I-7.1

interne boarding (student), resident

interpréter to interpret

interrompre to interrupt

interurbain(e) long-distance (phone call), **3.1**

intitulé(e) titled

introduire to introduce

  introduire (une pièce) to put in (a coin), **3.1**

l' **inverse (m.)** opposite

l' **investissement (m.)** investment

inviter to invite, I-3.2

l' **islam (m.)** Islam

islamique Islamic

isoler to isolate, I

l' **issue (f.) de secours** emergency exit, **7.1**

l' **Italie (f.)** Italy, I-16

italien(ne) Italian, I-9

J

jamais ever, I

  ne... jamais never, I

la **jambe** leg, **6.1**

le **jambon** ham, I-5.1

janvier (m.) January, I-4.1

le **Japon** Japan, I-16

japonais(e) Japanese, I

le **jardin** garden, I-4.2

le **jasmin** jasmine

jaune yellow, I-10.2

je I, I-1.2

  Je t'en prie. You're welcome. (fam.), I-BV

  je voudrais I would like, I-5.1

  Je vous en prie. You're welcome. (form.), I-BV; Please, I beg of you., I

le **jean** jeans, I-10.1

  en jean denim (adj.), **9.2**

la **jeep** jeep, **8.1**

le **jersey: en jersey** jersey (adj.), **9.2**

jeter to throw, I

le **jeton** token, **3.2**

le **jeu** game

  les jeux de la lumière play of light, I

jeudi (m.) Thursday, I-2.2

la **jeune fille** girl, I

jeune young, I-4.1

les **jeunes (m. pl.)** young people, I

la **jeunesse** youth

le **jogging: faire du jogging** to jog, I-11.2

la **joie** joy

joindre to join

joli(e) pretty, I-4.2

la **joue** cheek, **13.1**

jouer to play, to perform, I-16.1

  jouer à (un sport) to play (a sport), I-9.2

  jouer d'un instrument de musique to play a musical instrument

le **jouet** toy, **2.2**

le **joueur, la joueuse** player, I-9.2

le **jour** day, I-2.2

  C'est quel jour? What day is it?, I-2.2

  le jour de l'An New Year's Day, **11.2**

  de nos jours today, nowadays, I

  par jour a (per) day, I-3

  tous les jours every day, I

le **journal** newspaper, I-8.1

  le journal intime diary, I

  le journal télévisé newscast, I

la **journée** day, I

Joyeux Noël! Merry Christmas!, **11.2**

le **judaïsme** Judaism

le **juge** judge (m. and f.), **16.1**

juif, juive Jewish, **11.2**

les **Juifs (m. pl.)** Jews

juillet (m.) July, I-4.1

  le 14 juillet July 14, French national holiday, **11.1**

juin (m.) June, I-4.1

la **jupe** skirt, I-10.1

la **jupette** tennis skirt, I-9.2

le **Jura** Jura Mountains, I

le **jury** selection committee, I

jusqu'à (up) to, until (prep.), I-13.2, I
    jusqu'à ce que (+ subjunc.) until (conj.), **15.2**
    jusqu'en bas de la piste to the bottom of the trail, I
juste: il est juste que (+ subjunc.) it's right that, **11**

K

le **kilo(gramme)** kilogram, I-6.2
le **kilomètre** kilometer, I
le **kiosque** newsstand, I-8.1
le **kleenex** tissue, Kleenex, I-15.1

L

la the (f.), I-1; her, it (dir. obj.), I-16
là there, I
là-bas over there, I-BV
le **laboratoire** laboratory, I
le **lac** lake, I
    les Grands Lacs (m. pl.) the Great Lakes, I
    le lac salé salt lake, **14.2**
laïc, laïque lay, non-religious
la **laine** wool, **9.2**
    en laine wool (adj.), **9.2**
laisser to leave (something behind), I
    laisser un message to leave a message, **3.2**
    laisser un pourboire to leave a tip, I-5.2
le **lait** milk, I-6.1
laitier: le produit laitier dairy product
la **laitue** lettuce, I-6.2
lancer to throw, I-13.2;
    lancer un appel to make an appeal
se **lancer** to get started
la **langue** language, I-2.2
le **lapin** rabbit, **15.1**
la **laque** hairspray, **5.2**
laquelle which one (f. sing. interr. pron.), **5**
large loose, wide, I-10.2
le **latin** Latin, I-2.2
la **lavande** lavender
laver to wash, I-11.1
    la machine à laver washing machine, **2.1**
se **laver** to wash oneself, I-11.1

se **laver les cheveux (la figure, etc.)** to wash one's hair (face, etc.), I-11
la **laverie automatique** laundromat, **9.1**
le **lave-vaisselle** dishwasher, **2.1**
le the (m.), I-1; him, it (dir. obj.), I-16.1
la **leçon** lesson, I-9.1
    la leçon de conduite driving lesson, I-12.2
la **lecture** reading, I
légendaire legendary, I
la **légende** legend, caption, I
léger, légère light
léguer to bequeath, leave
le **légume** vegetable, I-6.2
le **lendemain** the next day
lent(e) slow, I
lentement slowly, I
lequel which one (m. sing. interrog. pron.), **5**
les the (pl.), I-2; them (dir. obj.), I-16
lesquelles which ones (f. pl. interr. pron.), **5**
lesquels which ones (m. pl. interr. pron.), **5**
la **lessive** detergent, **9.1**
    faire la lessive to do the laundry, **9.1**
la **lettre** letter, **1.1**
leur their (sing. poss. adj.), I-5; (to) them (ind. obj.), I-17
leurs their (pl. poss. adj.), I-5
levant rising, I
le **levé: faire le levé topographique** to survey, I
se **lever** to get up, I-11.1
le **lever du soleil** sunrise, **15.2**
la **lèvre** lip, **5.2**
le **lexique** vocabulary, I
libérer la chambre to vacate the room, I-17.2
libre free, I-2.2
    être libre immédiatement to be available immediately, **16.2**
    libre-service self-service, I
le **lieu** place, I
    avoir lieu to take place, **11.2**
    le lieu de travail workplace, **16.1**
la **ligne** line, **3.1**
    les grandes lignes main lines (trains), I
    les lignes de banlieue commuter trains, **4.2**
la **limitation de vitesse** speed limit, I

les **limites (f. pl.)** boundaries (on tennis court), I-9.2
    hors des limites out of bounds I-9.2
la **limonade** lemon-lime drink, I
le **linge** laundry, **9.1**
la **lipide** fat, I
lire to read, I-12.2
le **lit** bed, I-8.2
le **litre** liter, I-6.2
littéraire literary, I
la **littérature** literature, I-2.2
la **livre** pound, I-6.2
le **livre** book, I-BV
    le livre scolaire textbook, **12.1**
la **location** rental, I
loin de far from, I-4.2
les **loisirs (m. pl.)** leisure activities, I-16
Londres London, I
le **long: le long de** along, I
    long(ue) long, I-10.2
    de longue portée long-range
    longtemps (for) a long time, I
la **longueur** length, I
lorsque when; while, I
louer to rent, I; to reserve (train seat), **4.2**
lourd(e) heavy, I
lui him (m. sing. stress pron.), I-9; (to) him, (to) her (ind. obj.), I-17.1
la **lumière** light, I
lundi (m.) Monday, I-2.2
la **lune** moon
les **lunettes (f. pl.)** (ski) goggles, I-14.1
    les lunettes de soleil sunglasses, I-9.1
la **lutte** fight
lutter to fight, I
le **luxe** luxury, I
luxueux, luxueuse luxurious, I
le **lycée** high school, I-1.2
le/la **lycéen(ne)** high school student, **12.2**

M

ma my (f. sing. poss. adj.), I-4
la **machine** machine, **10.2**
    la machine à écrire typewriter, **12.1**
    la machine à laver washing machine, **2.1**
    la machine à traitement de texte word processor, **12.1**

Madame (Mme) Mrs., Ms., I-BV
Mademoiselle (Mlle) Miss, Ms., I-BV
le **magasin** store, I-3.2
le **magazine** magazine, I-3.2
le **Maghreb** region of northwest Africa including Algeria, Morocco, and Tunisia, **14.1**
le/la **Maghrébin(e)** person from the Maghreb
maghrébin(e) from the Maghreb region of northwest Africa, **14.2**
le **magnétophone** tape recorder, **2.1**
le **magnétoscope** video recorder (VCR), **2.1**
magnifique magnificent, I
mai (m.) May, I-4.1
maigrir to lose weight, I-11.2
le **maillot de bain** bathing suit, I-9.1
la **main** hand, I-11.1
　fait(e) à la main handmade, I
　se serrer la main to shake hands, **13.1**
maintenant now, I-2
le **maire** mayor, **11.2**
la **mairie** town hall, **16.2**
mais but, I-1
　Mais oui (non)! Of course (not)!, I
le **maïs** corn, **15.1**
la **maison** house, I-3.1
le **maître** master, I
　le **maître d'hôtel** maitre d', I-5.2
mal badly, I
　avoir mal à to have a(n) . . . -ache, to hurt, I-15.1
　mal élevé(e) rude, **13.1**
　Où avez-vous mal? Where does it hurt?, I-15.2
　Pas mal. Not bad., I-BV
　pas mal de a lot, quite a few
　pas mal de fois rather often
le/la **malade** sick person, patient, I-15.1
malade sick, I-15.1
la **maladie** illness, I
　la **maladie sexuellement transmissible** sexually transmitted disease
malgré in spite of
malheureusement unfortunately, **7.2**
la **manade** herd of cattle (or horses)
la **Manche** English Channel, I
la **manche** sleeve, I-10.1

à manches longues (courtes) long- (short-)sleeved, I-10
manger to eat, I
la **mangue** mango, I
la **manie** mania
la **manière** manner, way, I
　avoir de bonnes manières to have good manners, I
la **manifestation** demonstration
manquer: il manque (+ noun) (noun) is (are) missing, **9.2**
le **maquillage** makeup, **5.2**
se **maquiller** to put on makeup, I-11.1
le **marathon** marathon, I
le **marbre** marble, I
le/la **marchand(e) (de fruits et légumes)** (produce) seller, I-6.2; merchant
marchander to bargain, **14.1**
la **marchandise** merchandise, I
le **marché** market, I-6.2
　le **marché arabe couvert** Arab covered market, **14.1**
marcher to walk, **6.1**
mardi (m.) Tuesday, I-2.2
la **marée** tide, I
le **mari** husband, I-4.1
le **mariage** marriage, **11.2**
le **marié** groom, **11.2**
marié(e) married, I
la **mariée** bride, **11.2**
se **marier** to get married, **11.2**
les **mariés (m.)** bride and groom, **11.2**
le **marin** sailor, I
le **Maroc** Morocco, I-16
le **maroquinier** leather worker, **14.1**
la **marque** make (of car), I-12.1
marquer un but to score a goal, I-13.1
le **marron** chestnut
marron (inv.) brown, I-10.2
mars (m.) March, I-4.1
martiniquais(e) from Martinique, I
la **Martinique** Martinique, **7.1**
le **mascara** mascara, **5.2**
le **masque à oxygène** oxygen mask, **7.1**
la **masse** mass, I
massif, massive massive
le **match** game, I-9.2
le **matériel agricole** farm equipment, **15.1**
le **matériel scolaire** school supplies, **12.1**
maternel(le): l'école maternelle pre-school

les **mathématiques (f. pl.)** mathematics, I
les **maths (f. pl.)** math, I-2.2
la **matière** subject (school), I-2.2; matter, I; material, **9.2**
le **matin** morning, in the morning, I-2
　du matin A.M. (time), I-2
la **matinée** morning, **2.2**
mauvais(e) bad; wrong, I
　Il fait mauvais. It's bad weather., I-9.2
　le **mauvais numéro** the wrong number, **3.1**
mauve mauve (color)
le **mazout** fuel oil, I
me (to) me (dir. and ind. obj.), I-15.2
la **mèche** lock of hair, **5.1**
la **Mecque** Mecca, **14.1**
le **médecin** doctor (m. and f.), I-15.2
　chez le médecin at, to the doctor's, I-15.2
　la **femme médecin** (woman) doctor
la **médecine** medicine (medical profession), I-15
médical(e) medical, I
le **médicament** medicine (remedy), I-15.2
la **médina** medina (old Arab section of northwest African towns), **14.1**
meilleur(e) better (adj.), I-10
　le **meilleur, la meilleure** the best, **6**
　Meilleurs souvenirs Yours (to close a letter)
le **membre** member, I
même same (adj.), I-2.1; even (adv.), I; itself
　la **lettre même** the letter itself
　lui-même (moi-même, etc.) himself (myself, etc.)
ménager, ménagère household
le **menhir** menhir (prehistoric stone monument)
la **menorah** menorah, **11.2**
mensuel(le) monthly
mental(e) mental, I
la **menthe: le thé à la menthe** mint tea, **14.2**
le **menu: le menu touristique** budget (fixed price) meal, I
la **mer** sea, I-9.1
　la **mer des Caraïbes** Caribbean Sea, I

la mer Méditerranée
Mediterranean Sea, I
merci thank you, I-BV
mercredi (m.) Wednesday, I-2.2
la **mère** mother, I-4.1
la mère poule mother hen
le **méridien** meridian, I
merveilleux, merveilleuse marvelous, I-10.2
mes my (pl. poss. adj.), I-4
le **message** message, **3.2**
laisser un message to leave a message, **3.2**
la **messe de minuit** midnight mass, **11.2**
la **mesure** measurement, I
sur mesure tailored (to one's measurements), tailor-made
mesurer to measure, I
le **métabolisme** metabolism, I
la **météo** weather forecast, I
la **météorologie** meteorology, the study of weather
météorologique meteorological, I
le **métier** profession, trade, **16.1**; craft
le **mètre** meter, I
métrique metric, I
le **métro** subway, I-4.2
en métro by subway, I-5.2
la station de métro subway station, I-4.2
métropolitain(e) metropolitan
mettre to put (on), to place, I-8.1; to put on (clothes), I-10; to turn on (appliance), I-10, I
mettre au point to come out with, develop, I
mettre de l'argent de côté to put money aside, save, I-18.2
mettre le contact to start the car I-12.1
mettre le couvert to set the table, I-8
mettre fin à to put an end to
mettre une lettre à la poste to mail a letter, **1.1**
mettre en scène to direct (a play)
se mettre en forme to get in shape, I-11.1
se mettre au premier rang to get in the front row, **11.1**
se mettre à table to sit down for a meal, **2.1**
le **Mexique** Mexico, I-16
le **microbe** microbe, I
la **microbiologie** microbiology, I

le **microscope** microscope, I
midi (m.) noon, I-2.2
mieux better (adv.), **6**
le mieux (the) best (adv.), **6**
le **milieu** middle, **10.2**
le **militaire** soldier, I
militaire military
mille (one) thousand, I-6.2
les **milliers (m. pl.)** thousands, I
le **million** million
mi-long(ue) medium length, **5.1**
le **mimosa** mimosa
le **minaret** minaret, tower of a mosque, **14.1**
mince thin
le **minéral** mineral, I
le **ministère** ministry, I
minuit (m.) midnight, I-2.2
la **mise-en-plis** set (with hair curlers), **5.1**
miser sur to bet on
la **mission** mission, I
la **mi-temps** half (sporting event), I
moche terrible, ugly, I-2.2
le **modèle** model, I
moderne modern, I
moderniser to modernize, I
modeste modest, reasonably priced, I
moi me (sing. stress pron.), I-1.2, I-9
Moi de même. Likewise. (responding to an introduction), **13.2**
moi-même myself
le **moine** monk
moins less, I
à moins que (+ subjunc.) unless, **15**
au moins at least, I
Il est une heure moins dix. It's ten to one. (time), I-2
moins... que less . . . than, I
le **mois** month, I-4.1
la **moissonneuse-batteuse** combine harvester, **15.1**
les **moissons (f. pl.)** harvest
le **moment: en ce moment** right now, I
Un moment, s'il vous plaît. One moment, please., **3.2**
mon my (m. sing. poss. adj.), I-4
la **monarchie** monarchy, I
le **monastère** monastery
le **monde** world, I
beaucoup de monde a lot of people, I-13.1

un monde fou crowds of people
tout le monde everyone, everybody, I-BV
le **moniteur, la monitrice** instructor, I-9.1; camp counselor, I
la **monnaie** change; currency, I-18.1
faire de la monnaie to make change, I-18.1
Monsieur (M.) Mr., sir, I-BV
le **montagnard** mountain-dweller
la **montagne** mountain, I-14.1
à la montagne in the mountains, I
le **montant** amount
monter to go up, get on, get in, I-8.2; to take upstairs, I-17.1
monter une pièce to put on a play, I-16.1
monter en voiture to board (a train), **4.2**
montrer to show, I-17.1
moral(e) moral, I
le **morceau de craie** piece of chalk, I-BV
mordu(e) bitten, I
la **mort** death, I
mort(e) dead, I
mortel(le) fatal, I
Moscou Moscow, I
la **mosquée** mosque, **14.1**
le **mot** word, I
le mot apparenté cognate, I
le **motard** motorcycle cop, I-12.2
le **moteur** engine (car, etc.), I-12.1
la **moto(cyclette)** motorcycle, I-12.1
le **mouchoir** handkerchief, I-15.1
mouillé(e) wet, **5.2**
mourir to die, I-17
la **moutarde** mustard, I-6.2
le **mouton** sheep, **15.1**
le **mouvement** movement, I
mouvementé(e) eventful, I
moyen(ne) average, intermediate, I
le **Moyen-Âge** the Middle Ages
le **moyen de transport** mode of transportation, I
le **muezzin** in Muslim countries, the person who calls the faithful to prayer, **14.1**
municipal(e) municipal, I
le **mur** wall
musclé(e) muscular, I
le **musée** museum, I-16.2
le **musicien** musician, **11.1**
la **musique** music, I-2.2

musulman(e) Muslim
les **musulmans (m. pl.)** Muslims, **14.1**
le **mutilé de guerre** wounded veteran
la **mythologie** mythology, I

N

nager to swim, I-9.1
le **nageur**, la **nageuse** swimmer, I
la **naissance** birth
naître to be born, I-17
la **nappe** tablecloth, I-5.2
natal(e) where someone was born
la **natation** swimming, I-9.1
la **nation** nation, I
national(e) national, **11.1**
la **natte** braid, **5.1**
la **nature** nature, I
nature plain (adj.), I-5.1
la **navette: faire la navette** to go back and forth, I
ne... jamais never, I-12
ne... pas not, I-1.2
ne... personne no one, nobody, I-12.2
ne... plus no longer, **2**
ne... que only, **2.1**
ne... rien nothing, I-12.2
né: il est né he was born, I
nécessaire necessary, I
il est nécessaire de it's necessary to, **3.1**
il est nécessaire que (+ subjunc.) it's necessary that, **11**
négatif, négative negative, I
la **négritude** black pride
la **neige** snow, I-14.2
neige (inf. neiger): Il neige. It's snowing., I-14.2
nerveux, nerveuse nervous, I; emotional (illness)
les cellules nerveuses nerve cells, I
n'est-ce pas? isn't it?, doesn't it (he, she, etc.)?, I-1.2
le **nettoyage à sec** dry cleaning, **9.1**
nettoyer à sec: faire nettoyer à sec to dry-clean, **9.1**
neuf nine, I-BV
neutraliser to neutralize, I
le **neveu** nephew, I-4.1
le **nez** nose, I-15.1
avoir le nez qui coule to have a runny nose, I-15.1

ni... ni neither . . . nor, I
la **nièce** niece, I-4.1
le **niveau** level, I
vérifier les niveaux to check under the hood, I-12.1
les **noces (f. pl.)** nuptials
le voyage de noces honeymoon
Noël Christmas, **11.2**
Joyeux Noël! Merry Christmas!, **11.2**
noir(e) black, I-10.2
le tableau noir blackboard, I-3.1
le **nom** name, I-16.2; noun, I
le **nombre** number, I-5.2
nombreux, nombreuse numerous, **4.1**
nommer to name, mention, I
non no, I
non-fumeurs no smoking (section), I-7.1
non seulement not only, I
le **nord** north, I
normal(e) normal, I
normalement normally, usually, I
nos our (pl. poss. adj.), I-5
la **nostalgie** nostalgia, I
le **notable** dignitary, **11.1**
la **note** bill (currency), I-17.2; grade (on a test, etc.), **12.1**
recevoir de bonnes notes to get good grades, **12.1**
notre our (sing. poss. adj.), I-5
nourrir to feed, I
se **nourrir** to get food, nourishment
la **nourriture** food, nutrition, I
nous we, I-2; us (stress pron.), **9**; (to) us (dir. and ind. obj.), I-15
nouveau (nouvel) new (m.), I-4
nouvelle new (f.), I-4
la **nouvelle** short story
les **nouvelles (f. pl.)** news, I
novembre (m.) November, I-4.1
le **nuage** cloud, I-9.2
la **nuit** night, I
à la nuit tombante at nightfall
le **numéro** number, **1.2**; issue (of a magazine)
le bon (mauvais) numéro the right (wrong) number, **3.1**
le numéro de téléphone telephone number, **3.1**

Quel est le numéro de téléphone de... ? What is the phone number of . . . ?, I-5.2
numéroté(e) numbered, **4.1**
la **nuque** nape of the neck, **5.1**

O

l' **oasis (f.)** oasis, **14.2**
obéir (à) to obey, I-7
l' **objet (m.)** object, I
les objets en cuir leather goods, **14.1**
obligatoire mandatory, I; required, **12.2**
obligé(e) required
obliger to oblige, I
oblitérer to invalidate (a bus ticket), **10.2**
obtenir to obtain, **12.2**
l' **Occident (m.)** the West
occidental(e) western
occupé(e) busy, I-2.2
sonner occupé to be busy (telephone), **3.1**
occuper to occupy, I
l' **océan (m.)** ocean, I
octobre (m.) October, I-4.1
l' **odeur (f.)** scent, smell, I
l' **œil (m. pl. yeux)** eye, I
l' **œuf (m.)** egg, I-6.2
l'œuf sur le plat fried egg, I
l' **œuvre (f.)** work (of art), I-16
officiel(le) official, I
l' **officier (m.)** officer
offrir to offer, give I-15
l' **ogive (f.)** pointed Gothic arch
l' **oignon (m.)** onion, I-6.2
C'est pas tes oignons! None of your business!
l' **oiseau (m.)** bird, **15.2**
l' **omelette (f.)** omelette, I-5.1
l'omelette aux fines herbes omelette with herbs, I-5.1
l'omelette nature plain omelette, I-5.1
on we, they, people, I-3
On y va.(?) Let's go., Shall we go?, I-5
l' **oncle (m.)** uncle, I-4.1
l' **ongle (m.)** nail (finger, toe), **5.2**
onze eleven, I-BV
l' **opéra (m.)** opera, I-16.1
l' **opération (f.)** operation
opérer to operate, I
opposer to oppose, I-13.1
s' **opposer à** to be opposed to
l' **or (m.)** gold, I
l' **orage (m.)** storm

l' **orange** (f.)   orange (fruit), I-6.2
orange (inv.)   orange (color), I-10
l' **oranger** (m.)   orange tree
l' **Orangina** (m.)   orange soda, I-5.1
l' **orchestre** (m.)   orchestra, **11.1**
ordinaire   regular (gasoline), I-12.1
l' **ordinateur** (m.)   computer, I-BV
l' **ordonnance** (f.)   prescription, I-15.2
   faire une ordonnance   to write a prescription, I-15.2
l' **ordre** (m.): **en ordre**   in order
l' **oreille** (f.)   ear, I-15.1
   avoir mal aux oreilles   to have an earache, I-15
l' **oreiller** (m.)   pillow, I-17.2
les **oreillons** (m. pl.)   mumps, I
organisé(e)   organized, I
l' **organisme** (m.)   organism, I
original(e)   original, I
l' **origine** (f.): **à l'origine** originally, I
   d'origine américaine (française, etc.)   from the U.S. (France, etc.)
orner   to decorate, I
l' **os** (m.)   bone, **6.2**
ôter   to take off (clothing), I
ou   or, I-1.1
où   where, I-BV
oublier   to forget, **3.1**
l' **ouest** (m.)   west, I
oui   yes, I-1, I
l' **outil** (m.)   tool
ouvert(e)   open, I-16
l' **ouverture** (f.)   opening, I
l' **ouvrier**, l'**ouvrière**   worker, **2.2**
ouvrir   to open, I-15
ovale   oval, I
l' **oxygène** (m.)   oxygen, I

P

les **pages** (f. pl.) **jaunes**   yellow pages
le **pain**   bread, I-6.1
la **paire**   pair, I-10
le **palais**   palace, I
la **palmeraie**   palm grove, **14.2**
le **palmier**   palm tree, **14.2**
le **panier**   basket, I-13.2
paniquer   to panic
le **panneau**   backboard (basketball), I-13.2; road sign, **8.1**
   le panneau d'affichage   bulletin board, **12.1**

panoramique   panoramic, I
le **pansement**   bandage, **6.1**
le **pantalon**   pants, I-10.1
le **Pape**   Pope
la **papeterie**   stationery store, I
le **papier**   paper, I-6
   la feuille de papier   sheet of paper, I-BV
   le papier hygiénique   toilet paper, I-17.2
le **paquet**   package, I-6.2
par   by, through, I
   par avion   (by) airmail, **1.2**
   par dessus   over (prep.), I-13
   par exemple   for example, I
   par jour   a (per) day, I-3
   par semaine   a (per) week, I-3.2
le **paragraphe**   paragraph, I
paraît: il paraît   it appears; apparently, **14.1**
le **parallèle**   parallel, I
le **parc**   park, I-11.2
   le parc d'attractions   amusement park
parce que   because, I-9.1
parcourir   to travel, go through, I
pardon   excuse me, pardon me, I
le **parebrise**   windshield, I-12
le **parent**   relative
   les parents (m. pl.)   parents, I-4.1
parfait(e)   perfect, I
le **parfum**   perfume, **5.2**
parisien(ne)   Parisian, I-9
le **parking**   parking lot, I
le **parlement**   parliament, I
parler   to speak, talk, I-3.1
   parler au téléphone   to talk on the phone, I-3.2
parmi   among, I
partager   to share
   partager les frais   to "go dutch," to share expenses, **13.1**
participer (à)   to participate (in), I
particulièrement   particularly, I
la **partie**   game, match, I-9.2; part, I
   en partie   partly
   faire partie de   to be a part of, I
   la partie en simple (en double)   singles (doubles) match (tennis), I-9.2
partir   to leave, I-7.1

à partir de   from . . . on (date); based on
partout   everywhere, I
le **pas**   step
pas   not, I
   pas de (+ noun)   no (+ noun), I
   Pas de quoi.   You're welcome. (inform.), I-BV
   pas du tout   not at all, I
   Pas mal.   Not bad., I-BV
   pas mal de   quite a few, I
le **passage: être de passage**   to be passing through
   le passage pour piétons   pedestrian crossing, **8.2**
le **passager**, la **passagère** passenger, I-7.1
le **passé**   past, I
le **passeport**   passport, I-7.1
passer   to spend (time), I-3; to pass, go through, I-7.2
   passer à la douane   to go through customs, I-7.2
   passer à l'immigration   to go through immigration, I
   passer par le contrôle de sécurité   to go through security (airport), I-7
   passer un examen   to take an exam, I-3.1
   passer un film   to show a movie, I-16.1
se **passer**   to happen, I
passionné(e) de   excited by, I
passionner   to excite, I
le **pâté**   pâté, I-5.1
patient(e)   patient, I-1.1
le **patin**   skate, skating, I
   faire du patin   to skate, I-14.2
   faire du patin à glace   to ice-skate, I-14.2
   faire du patin à roulettes   to roller-skate, I
   le patin à glace   ice skate, I-14.2
le **patinage**   skating, I-14.2
le **patineur**, la **patineuse**   skater, I-14.2
la **patinoire**   skating rink, I-14.2
le **pâtre**   shepherd
le/la **patron(ne)**   boss
les **pattes** (f. pl.)   sideburns, **5.1**
le **pâturage**   pasture
le/la **pauvre**   poor thing, I-15.1
pauvre   poor, I-15.1
le **pavillon**   small house, bungalow, I
payer   to pay, I-6.1

payer en espèces to pay cash, I-17

le **pays** country, I-7.1

le **paysage** landscape, I

le **paysan** peasant

les **Pays-Bas (m. pl.)** the Netherlands, I-16

le **péage: l'autoroute à péage** toll road, I

la **pêche** fishing

  aller à la pêche to go fishing, I-9.1

  faire une belle pêche to catch a lot of fish, I

  le port de pêche fishing port, I

la **peau** skin

le **peigne** comb, 5.2

  donner un coup de peigne (à quelqu'un) to comb (someone's hair), 5.2

se **peigner** to comb (one's hair), I-11.1

  peindre to paint, I

la **peine: Ce n'est pas la peine.** It's not worth it. Don't bother.

le/la **peintre** painter, artist, I-16.2

la **peinture** painting, I-16.2

  péjoratif, péjorative pejorative, disparaging, I

le **pèlerinage** pilgrimage

le **penalty** penalty (soccer), I

  pendant during, for (time), I-3.2

  pendant que while, I

  pénétrer to penetrate

la **pénicilline** penicillin, I-15.2

  penser to think, I-10.1

le **penseur** thinker, I

la **pension** small hotel, I

  perdre to lose, I-8.2

  perdre des kilos to lose weight, I

  perdre patience to lose patience, I-8.2

le **père** father, I-4.1

  le Père Noël Santa Claus, 11.2

la **périphérie** outskirts, I

  périphérique: le boulevard périphérique beltway, ring road, 8.1

la **perle** pearl, I

la **permanente** permanent (hair), 5.1

  permettre to permit, allow, I-14

  Vous permettez? May I (sit here)?, 4.1

le **permis** license, I

le **permis de conduire** driver's license, I-12

le **personnage** character, I

la **personne** person, I

  ne... personne no one, nobody, I-12.2

  Personne ne (+ verb) No one (+ verb), 4

  personnel(le) personal, I

le **personnel de bord** flight attendants, I-7.2

  personnellement personally, I-16.2

la **perte** loss, I

  peser to weigh, 1.2

  petit(e) short, small, I-1.1

  le/la petit(e) ami(e) boyfriend (girlfriend)

  la petite annonce classified ad, 16.2

  le petit déjeuner breakfast, I-9

  prendre le petit déjeuner to eat breakfast, I-9

la **petite-fille** granddaughter, I-4.1

le **petit-fils** grandson, I-4.1

le **pétrolier** oil tanker, I

  peu (de) few, little, I-18, I

  à peu près about, 16.2

  un peu (de) a little, I

la **peur: avoir peur de** to be afraid of, 13.2

  de peur de for fear of

  faire peur à to frighten, I

la **pharmacie** pharmacy, I-15.2

le/la **pharmacien(ne)** pharmacist, I-15.2

la **photo** photograph, I

la **photosynthèse** photosynthesis

la **phrase** sentence, I

la **physique** physics, I-2.2

  physique physical, I

  la forme physique physical fitness, I-13

le **piano** piano, 11.1

la **pièce** room, I-4.2; play, I-16.1; coin, I-18.1

le **pied** foot, I-13.1

  à pied on foot, I-5.2

la **pierre** stone, I

le/la **piéton(ne)** pedestrian, I-12.2

le **pilier** pillar

  piller to pillage

le/la **pilote** pilot, 7.1

  le/la pilote de ligne airline pilot, I

  piloter to pilot, 7.1

  pincer to pinch

  piquant(e) spicy

la **sauce piquante** spicy sauce, 14.1

le **pique-nique: faire un pique-nique** to have a picnic, I-6

la **piqûre** injection, shot, 6.2

  faire une piqûre to give (someone) a shot, 6.2

la **piscine** pool, I-9.2

  la piscine couverte indoor pool, I

la **piste** track, I-13.2; ski trail, I-14.1

  la piste de course track (for running), 12.2

  pittoresque picturesque, I

le **placard** closet, I-17.2

la **place** seat (plane, etc.), I-7.1; parking space, I-12.2; place, I

  la place numérotée numbered seat, 4.1

la **plage** beach, I-9.1

la **plaine** plain, I

le **plan** map, I

  le plan du métro subway map, 10.2

  le plan de la ville street map, 8.1

la **planche à voile: faire de la planche à voile** to windsurf, I-9

la **plantation** grove, 14.2

la **plante** plant, I

la **plaque d'immatriculation** license plate

le **plastique: en plastique** plastic (adj.), I

le **plat** dish (food), I

le **plateau** plateau, I; tray, 7.1

la **platine** platinum

le **plâtre** cast (for broken arm, etc.), 6.2

  mettre (la jambe, etc.) dans le plâtre to put (someone's leg, etc.) in a cast, 6.2

  plein(e) full, I-13.1

  avoir plein de fric to have lots of money (slang), I-18.2

  faire le plein to fill up (a gas tank), I-12.1

  pleut (inf. pleuvoir): Il pleut. It's raining., I-9.2

  plier to bend; to fold, 9.1

la **plongée sous-marine: faire de la plongée sous-marine** to go deep-sea diving, I-9.1

  plonger to dive, I-9.1

la **pluie** rain, I

  les pluies acides acid rain, I

la **plupart (des)** most (of), I-8.2

le **pluriel** plural, I

plus more (comparative), I-10
 en plus de in addition to, I
 plus ou moins more or less
 plus tard later, I
plusieurs several, I-18
le **pneu** tire, I-12.1
 le pneu à plat flat tire,
 I-12.1
la **poche** pocket, I-18.1
le **poème** poem, I
la **poésie** poetry, I
le **poète** poet (m. and f.), I
le **poids** weight, **1.2**
le **poignet** wrist, **13.1**
poinçonner to punch (a hole
 in), **4.1**
le **point** point; period, I
 à point medium-rare (meat),
 I-5.2
 le point noir high-traffic
 area, **8.1**
 le point de suture (surgical)
 stitch, **6.2**
 le point de vue point of view
la **pointure** size (shoes), I-10.2
 Vous faites quelle pointure?
 What (shoe) size do you
 take?, I-10.2
le **poisson** fish, I-6.1
la **poissonnerie** fish store, I-6.1
le **pôle** pole, I
poli(e) polite, **13.1**
la **police secours** emergency aid,
 6.1
poliment politely
la **poliomyélite** polio, I
la **politique** politics
polluer to pollute, I
la **pollution** pollution, I
la **Polynésie française** French
 Polynesia
la **pomme** apple, I-6.2
la **pomme de terre** potato, I-6.2
le **pommier** apple tree
le/la **pompiste** gas station attendant,
 I-12.1
le **pont** bridge
populaire popular, I-1.2
la **porcelaine** porcelain, china, I
le **port** port, harbor, I
 le port de pêche fishing
 port, I
le **portail** doorway (church)
la **porte** gate (airport), I-7.1; door,
 I-17.1
le **portefeuille** wallet, I-18.1
le **porte-monnaie** change purse,
 I-18.1
porter to take (carry), **9.1**; to
 wear, I-10.1

porter un toast to toast,
 make a toast
le **porteur** porter, I-8.1
la **portière** door (of a vehicle),
 10.2
le **portrait** portrait, I
le **Portugal** Portugal, I-16
poser: poser sa candidature
 to apply for a position, **16.2**
 poser une question to ask a
 question, I-3.1
la **possibilité** possibility, I
possible: il est possible que
 (+ subjunc.) it's possible
 that, **11**
la **poste** post office, **1.1**
 mettre une lettre à la poste
 to mail a letter, **1.1**
le **poste** position (job), **16.2**
le **poste de péage** tollbooth, **8.1**
le **poste de pilotage** cockpit, **7.1**
le **poste de télévision** television
 (set), **2.1**
le **pot** jar, I-6.2
le **pot-au-feu** braised beef with
 vegetables, **2.1**
le **pouce** inch, I; thumb, **13.1**
la **poule** hen, chicken (animal),
 15.1
le **poulet** chicken (food), I-6.1
le **pouls** pulse, **6.2**
le **poumon** lung
la **poupée** doll, I
pour for; in order to, I-2
 pour que (+ subjunc.) so
 that, **15**
le **pourboire** tip (restaurant),
 I-5.2
 laisser un pourboire to leave
 a tip, I-5.2
le **pourcentage** percentage, I
pourquoi why, I-9.1
pourtant yet, still,
 nevertheless, I
pourvu que (+ subjunc.)
 provided that, **15.2**
pousser to grow, I; to push,
 10.2
pouvoir to be able to, I-6
 Pourrais-je parler à... ?
 May I speak to . . . ?, **3.2**
le **pouvoir** power
pratique practical
pratiquer un sport to play a
 sport, I-11.2
le **pré** meadow, **15.1**
précieux, précieuse precious, I
précis(e) precise, exact, I
 à l'heure précise right on
 time, I

la **prédiction** prediction
préférable: il est préférable que
 (+ subjunc.) it's preferable
 that, **11**
préféré(e) favorite, **2.1**
préférer to prefer, I-5
le **préfixe** prefix, I
prélever to deduct
prélevé(e) deducted
premier, première first, I-4.1
 en première in first class,
 I-8.1
 les tout (inv.) premiers
 (m. pl.) the very first, I
premièrement first of all, I
prendre to take, I-9.1; to buy;
 to eat (drink) (in café, restaurant, etc.)
 prendre un bain (une douche)
 to take a bath (shower),
 I-11.1
 prendre un bain de soleil
 to sunbathe, I-9.1
 prendre un billet to buy a
 ticket, I-9
 prendre conscience de
 to become aware of
 prendre la correspondance
 to change trains, **4.2**
 prendre des kilos to gain
 weight, I
 prendre part à to take part
 in, I
 prendre le petit déjeuner
 to eat breakfast, I-9
 prendre possession de
 to take possession of, I
 prendre un pot to have a
 drink, I
 prendre le pouls to take
 someone's pulse, **6.2**
 prendre rendez-vous
 to make an appointment, I
 prendre son temps to take
 one's time, **2.2**
 prendre la tension artérielle
 to take someone's blood
 pressure, **6.2**
 prendre le train (l'avion, etc.)
 to take the train (plane, etc.),
 I-9
préparé(e) prepared, **12.1**
préparer to prepare, I-4.2
près de near, I-4.2
prescrire to prescribe, I-15.2
les **présentations (f. pl.)**
 introductions, **13.2**
présenter to introduce, **13.2**; to
 present, I
la **préservation** preservation, I

presque almost, I
pressé(e) in a hurry, I
le **pressing** dry-cleaner's, **9.1**
la **pression artérielle** blood pressure, I
prêt(e) ready, I
prêt-à-porter ready-to-wear (adj.), I-10
  le **rayon prêt-à-porter** ready-to-wear department, I-10.1
prêter to lend, I-18.2
la **preuve** proof, I
la **prévision** prediction, I
prévoir to predict, I
prie: Je vous en prie. Please, I beg of you., I; You're welcome., I-BV
prier to pray, **14.1**
la **prière: en prière** at prayer, praying
primaire: l'école (f.) primaire elementary school, I
principal(e) main, principal
  le **professeur principal** homeroom teacher, **12.2**
la **principauté** principality
le **principe** principle
le **printemps** spring, I-13.2
pris(e) taken, I-5.1
le **prisonnier** prisoner
privé(e) private, I
le **prix** price, cost, I-10.1
  à prix fixe at a fixed price, I
probable: il est probable que it's probable, **14**
probablement probably, I
le **problème** problem, I-11.2
prochain(e) next, I-8.2
proche close, **10.1**
proclamer to proclaim
la **production** production, **15.1**
produire to produce
le **produit** product, I
  le **produit de beauté** cosmetic, **5.2**
  le **produit laitier** dairy product
le/la **prof** teacher (inform.), I-2.1
le **professeur** teacher (m. and f.), I-2.1
  le **professeur principal** homeroom teacher, **12.2**
la **profession** profession, **16.1**
professionnel(le) professional, I
profiter de to take advantage of, profit from, I
profond(e) deep, I
profondément profoundly, deeply

le **programme** TV program, I
le **progrès** progress, I
progressif, progressive progressive, I
le **projecteur** projector, **12.1**
le **projet** project, plan, I
la **promenade: faire une promenade** to take a walk, I-9.1
se **promener** to walk, I-11.2
proposer to suggest, I
propre clean, **9.1**; own (adj.), I
la **propriété** property
protéger to protect, I
la **protéine** protein, I
le **protestantisme** Protestantism
provenance: en provenance de arriving from (train, plane, etc.), I-7.1
provençal(e) from Provence, the south of France, I
la **Provence** region in the South of France
provenir to come from
le **proviseur** principal, **12.2**
les **provisions (f. pl.)** groceries, I
  muni de provisions with food
provisoire provisional
prudemment carefully, I-12.2
public, publique public, **3.1**
le **public** public (n.); audience, I
la **publicité** advertisement, I
les **puces: le marché aux puces** flea market, I
puisque since
puissant(e) powerful, I
le **pull** sweater, I-10.1
punir to punish, I-7
pur(e) pure, I
la **pureté** purity, I
la **pyramide** pyramid, I

Q

le **quai** platform (railroad), I-8.1
la **qualité** quality, I
quand when, I-3.1
quant à as for
quarante forty, I-BV
le **quart: et quart** a quarter past (time), I-2
  moins le quart a quarter to (time), I-2
le **quartier** neighborhood, district, I-4.2
quatorze fourteen, I-BV
quatre four, I-BV
quatre-vingt-dix ninety, I-5.2

quatre-vingts eighty, I-5.2
que that, which, whom, I
quel(le) which, what, I-7
  Quel est le numéro de téléphone de... ? What is the phone number of . . . ? I-5.2
  Quelle est la date aujour-d'hui? What is today's date?, I-4.1
  Quel temps fait-il? What's the weather like?, I-9.2
quelque some, I
  quelque chose à manger something to eat, I-5.1
quelquefois sometimes, I-5
quelques some, I-8.2
quelqu'un someone, I-12
qu'est-ce que what (interr. pron.), 6
  Qu'est-ce que c'est? What is it?, I-BV
  Qu'est-ce qu'il a? What's wrong with him?, I-15.1
qu'est-ce qui what (interr. pron.), 6
  Qu'est-ce qui arrive (se passe)? What's happening?, I
la **question: poser une question** to ask a question, I-3.1
la **queue: faire la queue** to wait in line, I-8.1
  la **queue de cheval** ponytail, **5.1**
qui who, I-BV; whom, I-11; which, that, I
  C'est de la part de qui? Who's calling?, **3.2**
  Qui ça? Who (do you mean)?, I-BV
  Qui est-ce? Who is it?, I-BV
quinze fifteen, I-BV
quitter to leave (a room, etc.), I-3.1
  Ne quittez pas. Hold on. (telephone), **3.2**
quoi what (after prep.), I-14
quotidien(ne) daily, everyday

R

raccrocher to hang up (telephone), **3.1**
racine root
raconter to tell (about), I
radicalement radically
la **radio** radio, I-3.2
la **radio(graphie)** X-ray, **6.2**

radioactif, radioactive
radioactive, I

la **rage** rabies, I

raide steep, I-14.2; straight
(hair), **5.1**

la **raie** part (in hair), **5.1**

le **raisin** grape(s)
les **raisins secs** raisins, **14.1**

la **raison** reason, I

ralentir to slow down, **8.1**

le **ralentissement** delay, **8.1**

ramasser to collect, **4.1**

la **randonnée pédestre**
backpacking
en **randonnée** backpacking,
hiking

le **randonneur**, la **randonneuse**
hiker, I

le **rang** row

rapide quick, fast, I

rapidement quickly, **2.2**

rappeler to call back, **2.2**

le **rapport** relationship; report, I

rapporter to report, I

le **rapprochement** reconciliation

la **raquette** racket, I-9.2

rare rare, I

rarement rarely

se **raser** to shave, I-11.1

le **rasoir** razor, shaver, **5.1**
la **coupe au rasoir** razor cut,
5.1

rassembler to collect, gather
together, I

rassurer to reassure

rater le train to miss the train,
4.2

le **rayon** department (in a store),
I-10.1; ray of light
les **rayons X** X-rays

la **réaction** reaction, I

réagir to react

réaliser to realize (an ambition),
achieve, I

la **réalité** reality, I

le **reboisement** reforestation

récemment recently

la **réception** front desk (hotel),
I-17.1

le/la **réceptionniste** desk clerk,
I-17.1

la **recette** recipe, I

recevoir to receive, I-18.1
recevoir de bonnes notes to
get good grades, **12.1**

la **recherche** research
faire de la recherche to do
research, I

rechercher to seek, I

réciproque reciprocal

la **récolte** harvest, **15.1**

récolter to harvest, **15.1**

recommandé(e)
recommended, I

la **réconciliation** reconciliation

reconnu(e) recognized, I

reconstruire to rebuild

la **récréation** recess, I

récrire to rewrite, I

récupérer to claim (luggage),
I-7.2

la **rédaction** paper, composition;
writing, **12.1**
faire une rédaction to write
a paper, **12.1**

redistribuer to redistribute,
pass (something) out again

réduire to reduce

refaire to do over, make over

réfléchi(e) reflexive

refléter to reflect, I

regarder to look at, watch I-3.1

se **regarder** to look at oneself, look
at one another, I

le **régime: faire un régime** to go
on a diet, I
le **régime alimentaire** diet, I

la **région** region, I

la **règle** rule, I

le **règlement** rule, I

régler to direct (traffic), I

le **règne** reign, I

régner to reign

regretter to be sorry, **13.2**
Je regrette. I'm sorry., **3.2**

régulier, régulière regular, I

régulièrement regularly, I

rejeter to give off

la **réjouissance** festivity

relativement relatively, I

le **relevé (de compte)** statement
(bank), I-18

se **relever** to get up

relié(e) connected, I

religieux, religieuse religious,
11.2

se **remarier** to remarry

remarquer to notice, I

rembourser to pay back,
reimburse, I-18.2

remédier to remedy

le **remembrement** regrouping

remettre: remettre en place to
reset (a bone), **6.2**
remettre sur pied to put
(someone) back on his/her
feet

les **remparts (m. pl.)** ramparts

remplir to fill out, I-7.2

renaître to be reborn

la **rencontre** meeting, I

rencontrer to meet, I

le **rendez-vous** meeting,
appointment
prendre rendez-vous to
make an appointment, I

rendre to give back, I-18.2; to
make

les **renseignements (m. pl.)**
information, I

la **rentrée des classes** beginning
of school year, **12.2**

rentrer to go home, I-3.1

renverser to overthrow

renvoyer to return (tennis ball),
I-9.2

la **répartition** distribution, I

le **repas** meal, **2.1**

le **repassage** ironing, **9.1**

repasser to iron, **9.1**

répéter to repeat, I

le **répondeur automatique**
answering machine, **2.1**

répondre to answer, I-8

la **réponse** answer, I

se **reposer** to rest, I

repoussé(e) pushed back, I

représenter to represent, I

la **reprise** reshowing, I

reproduire to reproduce, I

la **république** republic,
democracy, I

répudier to repudiate, cast off

le **réseau** system

la **réserve** resource, supply, I

réservé(e) reserved, I

réserver to reserve, **4.2**

le **réservoir** gas tank, I-12.1

résidentiel(le) residential, I

la **résistance** resistance, I

résoudre to solve

respecter to obey, **8.1**

la **respiration** breathing, I

respirer (à fond) to breathe
(deeply), I-15.2

responsable responsible

resquiller to cut ahead (in line),
13.1

ressembler à to resemble, I

ressentir to feel, I

le **ressortissant** citizen, national

le **restaurant** restaurant, I-5.2

la **restauration** food service, I
la **restauration rapide** fast
food

rester to stay, remain, I-17
rester en forme to stay in
shape, I-11.1

le **restoroute** roadside restaurant

le **retard** delay, **7.2**

en retard   late, I-8.2
se **retirer**   to retire
retomber   to fall back down, I
le **retour**   return, I
à votre retour   when you
return, I
la **retransmission**   rebroadcast, I
rétrécir   to shrink, **9.1**
se **retrouver**   to meet (again),
13.1
réunir   to bring together, I; to
reunite
réussir (à)   to succeed, to pass
(exam), I-7
le **rêve**   dream, I
se **réveiller**   to wake up, I-11.1
le **réveillon**   Christmas or New
Year's dinner, **11.2**
la **révélation**   revelation, I
revenir   to come back, I-16
rêver   to dream, I
revoir   to see again
la **révolution**   revolution, I
révolutionner   to
revolutionize, I
le **rez-de-chaussée**   ground floor,
I-4.2
le **rhume**   cold (illness), I-15.1
avoir un rhume   to have a
cold, I-15.1
riche   rich, I
la **richesse**   wealth, I
le **rideau**   curtain I-16.1
le lever du rideau   at curtain
time (theatre), I
rien   nothing, 2
Il n'en est rien.   Not so.;
Nothing could be further
from the truth.
ne... rien   nothing, anything,
I-12.2
Rien d'autre.   Nothing else.,
I-6.2
Rien ne (+ verb)   Nothing
(+ verb), 4
rien à voir avec   nothing to
do with
rigoler   to joke around, I-3.2
Tu veux rigoler?!   Are you
kidding?!, I
rigueur: de rigueur   necessary,
obligatory
rincer   to rinse, **2.1**
rire   to laugh, **12.1**
risquer   to risk
le **rite**   rite, ritual, I
la **rivière**   river, I
le **riz**   rice, I
la **robe**   dress, I-10.1; robe, I
Robin des Bois   Robin Hood

le **robinet**   faucet, **2.1**
le **rocher**   rock
le **roi**   king, I
le **rôle**   role, I
romain(e)   Roman
le **roman**   novel, I
le roman policier   detective
novel, mystery, I
roman(e)   Romanesque
le **romancier**, la **romancière**
novelist
rompre   to break, **13.1**
le **rond**   circle
rond(e)   round, I
rose   pink, I-10.2
la **rosée**   dew
le **rosier**   rosebush, I
la **roue**   wheel, I-12.1
la roue de secours   spare tire,
I-12.1
les deux roues   two-wheeled
vehicles, I
rouge   red, I-10.2
le **rouge à lèvres**   lipstick, **5.2**
la **rougeole**   measles, I
le **rouleau chauffant**   electric
roller, **5.2**
le **rouleau de papier hygiénique**
roll of toilet paper, I-17.2
rouler (vite)   to go, drive (fast),
I-12.1
la **route**   road, I-12.1
En route!   Let's go!, I
prendre la route   to take to
the road, I
routier   road (adj.), I
roux, rousse   redheaded, **5.1**
le **royaume**   kingdom
la **rubéole**   German measles, I
la **rue**   street, I-3.1
la **ruelle**   alley, **14.1**
le **rugby**   rugby, I
les **ruines (f. pl.)**   ruins
rural(e)   rural, I
le/la **Russe**   Russian (person), I
le **rythme**   rhythm, I

S

sa   his, her (f. sing. poss. adj.),
I-4
le **sable**   sand, I-9.1
le **sac**   bag, I-6.1; pocketbook,
purse, I-18.1
le sac à dos   backpack, I-BV
le sac de couchage   sleeping
bag
sacrer   to crown
le **safari**   safari

sage   good (child's behavior),
11.2
le **Sahara**   Sahara, **14.2**
saignant(e)   rare (meat), I-5.2
saigner   to bleed
saint(e)   holy
la **saison**   season, I
la belle saison   summer, I
la **salade**   salad, I-5.1
le **salaire**   salary, **16.2**
le **salarié**   full-time employee
sale   dirty, **9.1**
salé(e)   salt (adj.) **14.2**
le lac salé   salt lake, **14.2**
la **salle**   room, I
la salle à manger   dining
room, I-4.2
la salle d'attente   waiting
room, I-8.1
la salle de bains   bathroom,
I-4.2
la salle de cinéma   movie
theatre, I-16.1
la salle de classe   classroom,
I-2.1
la salle d'opération   operating
room, **6.2**
la salle de permanence   study
hall, **12.2**
la salle de séjour   living room,
I-4.2
la salle des urgences   emergency room, **6.1**
le **Salon**   official art show, I
le **salon de coiffure**   hair salon
saluer   to greet
Salut.   Hi., I-BV
samedi (m.)   Saturday, I-2.2
le **sandwich**   sandwich, I-5.1
le **sang**   blood
le **sang-froid**   calm
garder votre sang-froid   to
keep calm
sans   without, I-12.1
sans aucun doute   without a
doubt, I
Sans blague!   No kidding!, I
sans escale   non-stop (flight),
7.2
sans plomb   unleaded, I-12.1
sans que (+ subjunc.)   without (conj.) **15**
la **santé**   health, I-15.1
être en bonne (mauvaise)
santé   to be in good (poor)
health, I-15.1
le **sapin**   pine tree, **11.2**
le sapin de Noël   Christmas
tree, **11.2**
satisfait(e)   satisfied

la **sauce piquante** spicy sauce, **14.1**

la **saucisse de Francfort** hot dog, I-5.1

le **saucisson** salami, I-6.1

sauf except, I-16.2

sauvage wild

sauver to save, I

le **savant** scientist, I

savoir to know (information), I-16.2

le **savoir-vivre** good manners, **13**

le **savon** soap, I-11.1

le **saxophone** saxophone, **11.1**

scandalisé(e) scandalized, shocked, I

le **scarabée** beetle

la **scène** stage; scene, I-16.1

les **sciences (f. pl.)** science, I-2.2

    les **sciences humaines** social sciences, I

    les **sciences naturelles** natural sciences, I

scintiller to glitter

scolaire school (adj.), **12.1**

le **scorbut** scurvy, I

le **score** score, I-9.2

le **sculpteur** sculptor (m. and f.), I-16.2

la **sculpture** sculpture, I-16.2

la **séance** show (movie) I-16.1

sec, sèche dry, **5.2**

le **sèche-linge** clothes dryer, **9.1**

sécher to dry, **9.1**

    se **sécher** to dry (off), I-17.2

la **sécheresse** dryness, drought, I

le **séchoir** (hair) dryer, **5.2**

secondaire: l'école (f.)

    secondaire junior high, high school, I

la **seconde** second (time), I

seconde: en seconde in second class, I-8.1

le **secourisme** first aid

le/la **secouriste** certified first-aid practitioner

le/la **secrétaire** secretary, **16.1**

seize sixteen, I-BV

le **séjour** stay, I

le **sel: la croûte de sel** salt crust, **14.2**

    le **sel minéral** mineral salt

sélectif, sélective selective

la **selle** seat (bicycle, motorcycle)

selon according to, **1.2**

les **semailles (f. pl.)** sowing

la **semaine** week, I-2.2; allowance, I

    par semaine a (per) week, I-3.2

semblable similar, alike

sembler to seem, I

    il me (te, lui, etc.) semble que it seems to me (you, him, her, etc.) that, **14.1**

la **semoule de blé** semolina wheat, **14.1**

le **Sénégal** Senegal, I-16

le **sens** direction, **8.2**; meaning, I

    sens interdit wrong way (traffic sign), I

    sens unique one way (traffic sign), I

sensible sensitive

se **sentir** to feel (well, etc.), I-15.1

séparer to separate, I

sept seven, I-BV

septembre (m.) September, I-4.1

la **série** series, I

sérieusement seriously, **8**

sérieux, sérieuse serious, I-10

le **serpentin** streamer, **11.2**

serré(e) tight, I-10.2

serrer la main to shake hands, **13.1**

le **serveur, la serveuse** waiter, waitress, I-5.1

le **service** tip; service, I-5.2

    le **service du personnel** personnel department, **16.2**

    Le service est compris. The tip is included., I-5.2

la **serviette** napkin, I-5.2; towel, I-17.2

servir to serve (food), I-7.2; to serve (a ball in tennis, etc.), I-9.2

    servir à to be used for, **13.1**

se **servir de** to use, **2.2**

ses his, her (pl. poss. adj.), I-5.

seul(e) alone; single; only (adj.), I

    tout(e) seul(e) all alone, by himself/herself, I

seulement only (adv.), **2.1**

la **sève** sap

    la **sève brute** rising, crude sap

    tirer la sève to tap (maple sugar)

sévère strict, I

le **sexe** sex, I

le **shampooing** shampoo, **5.2**

le **shampooing-crème** shampoo-conditioner, **5.2**

le **short** shorts, I-9.2

si if, **9**; yes (after neg. question), I

le **SIDA (Syndrome Immuno-Déficitaire Acquis)** AIDS, I

le **siècle** century, I

le **siège** seat, I-7.1

    le **siège réglable** adjustable seat, **4.1**

le **sien, la sienne** his (pron.), hers

siffler to (blow a) whistle, I-13.1

le **signal** sign, I

signer to sign, I-18.1

la **signification** meaning

signifier to mean, I

s'il te plaît please (fam.), I-BV

s'il vous plaît please (form.), I-BV

simplement simply, I

sincère sincere, I-1.2

sinon otherwise, or else

le **sirop: le sirop d'érable** maple syrup, I

situé(e) located, I

six six, I-BV

le **ski** ski, skiing, I-14.1

    faire du ski to ski, I-14.1

    faire du ski nautique to water-ski, I-9.1

    le **ski alpin** downhill skiing, I-14.1

    le **ski de fond** cross-country skiing, I-14.1

le **skieur, la skieuse** skier, I-14.1

social(e) social, I

la **société** company, 16.2; society, I

    la **grosse société** large company, **16.2**

la **sociologie** sociology, I

la **sœur** sister, I-1.2

soi: chez soi home, I

    en soi in itself

la **soie** silk, **9.2**

    en soie silk (adj.), **9.2**

soigner to take care of, **6.1**

soigneusement carefully

le **soir** evening, in the evening, I-2

    ce soir tonight, **2.1**

    du soir P.M. (time), I-2

la **soirée** evening, I; evening party

    la **soirée théâtrale** evening at the theater

soit is, exists (subjunctive), I

soixante sixty, I-BV

soixante-dix seventy, I-5.2

le **sol** ground, I-13.2

le **soldat** soldier, **11.1**

le **solde** (bank) balance

les **soldes (f. pl.)** sale (in a store) I-10.2

le **soleil**   sun, **14.2**
   le **coucher du soleil**   sunset, **15.2**
   le **lever du soleil**   sunrise, **15.2**
   le **soleil levant**   rising sun, I
   Il fait du soleil.   It's sunny., I-9.2
   soluble dans l'eau   water-soluble, I
   soluble dans la graisse   fat-soluble, I
   sombre   dark, I
la **somme**   sum, I
le **sommeil**   sleep, I
le **sommet**   summit, mountaintop, I-14.1
   son   his, her (m. sing. poss. adj.), I-4
le **sondage**   (opinion) survey
   sonner   to ring, **3.1**; to sound
   sonner occupé   to be busy (telephone), **3.1**
la **sonnerie**   bell, **12.1**
la **sorte**   sort, kind, I
la **sortie**   exit, I-7.1
   la **sortie de secours**   emergency exit, **7.1**
   sortir   to go out, take out, I-7
   soudanien(ne)   from Sudan
   souffler   to blow
   souffrir   to suffer, I-15.2
   souhaiter   to wish, **12**
se **souhaiter**   to wish each other, **11.2**
le **souk**   Arab market, **14.1**
   soulager   to relieve
   soulever   to lift, **3.2**
se **soulever**   to rise up
les **souliers (m. pl.)**   shoes, **11.2**
   soumis(e)   submitted
la **soupe à l'oignon**   onion soup, I-5.1
le **souper**   supper
la **source**   source, I
   sourire   to smile, **12**
la **souris**   mouse
   sous   under, I
le **sous-marin**   submarine
les **sous-titres (m. pl.)**   subtitles, I-16.1
   soutenu(e)   supported
   souterrain(e)   underground, I
le **souvenir**   memory
se **souvenir de**   to remember, **3.1**
   souvent   often, I-5
   spatial(e)   space (adj.)
se **spécialiser**   to specialize, I
le **spectacle**   show, I
le **spectateur**   spectator, I-13.1

la **splendeur**   splendor, I
   splendide   splendid, I
le **sport: faire du sport**   to play sports, I
   pratiquer un sport   to play a sport, I
   le **sport collectif**   team sport, I
   le **sport d'équipe**   team sport, I
   les **sports d'hiver**   winter sports, skiing, I-14.1
   sport (inv.)   casual (clothes), I-10.1
   sportif, sportive   athletic, I
le **stade**   stadium, I-13.1; stage (of a process), I
le/la **standardiste**   telephone operator, **3.1**
la **station**   station; resort, I
   la **station balnéaire**   seaside resort, I-9.1
   la **station de métro**   subway station, I-4.2
   la **station de sports d'hiver**   ski resort, I-14.1
   la **station-service**   gas station, I-12.1
   la **station thermale**   spa
le **stationnement**   parking, I
   stationnement interdit   no parking (traffic sign), I
   stationner   to park, I-12.2
   Il est interdit de stationner.   No parking. (traffic sign), I-12.2
la **statue**   statue, I
le **steak frites**   steak and French fries, I-5.2
le **steward**   flight attendant (m.), I-7.2
   stop   stop (traffic sign), I
le **strapontin**   folding seat (on subway, etc.)
   strict(e)   strict, I
le **style**   style, **5.1**
le **stylo**   (ballpoint) pen, I-BV
le **stylo-bille**   ballpoint pen, **12.1**
   subventionner   to subsidize
se **succéder**   to follow one another, I
le **succès**   success, I
le **sucre**   sugar, I
   sucré(e)   sweet, with sugar, I
le **sud**   south, I
   sudaméricain(e)   South American
le **sud-est**   southeast, I
le **sud-ouest**   southwest, I
   suer: suer comme un bœuf   to sweat like a pig

   suffire   to suffice, be enough, I
la **Suisse**   Switzerland
   suisse   Swiss, I
   suivant(e)   following, I
   suivre   to follow, **6**
le **sujet**   subject, I
   super   terrific, super, I-2.2; super (gasoline), I-12.1
   superbe   superb, I
la **superficie**   area (geography), I
   supérieur(e)   upper
le **supermarché**   supermarket, I-6.1
   supersonique   supersonic, I
le **supplément**   surcharge (train fare), I
   payer un supplément   to pay a surcharge, I
   sur   on, I-BV
   sûr(e)   sure, I
   être sûr(e)   to be sure, **14.2**
   il est sûr que   it's sure that, **14**
la **surface**   surface, I
   surgelé(e)   frozen, I-6.2
   surpris(e)   surprised, **13.2**
   surtout   especially, above all, **3.2**
le **surveillant, la surveillante**   monitor, **12.2**
   surveiller   to watch, keep an eye on, I-12.2
le **survêtement**   warmup suit, I-11.2
   survivre   to survive
le **sweat-shirt**   sweatshirt, I-10.1
   sympa (inv.)   nice (abbreviation for **sympathique**), I-1.2
   sympathique   nice (person), I-1.2
le **symptôme**   symptom, I
le **syndicat d'initiative**   tourist office, I
le **synonyme**   synonym, I
le **système**   system, I

T

   ta   your (f. sing. poss. adj.), I-4
la **table**   table, I-BV
   la **table d'opération**   operating table, **6.2**
le **tableau**   blackboard, I-BV; painting, I-16.2
   le **tableau des arrivées**   arrival board, **4.2**
   le **tableau des départs**   departure board, **4.2**
   le **tableau des départs et des arrivées**   arrival and departure board, I

VOCABULAIRE FRANÇAIS-ANGLAIS   **483**

la **tablette rabattable**   pull-down tray, **4.1**
la **tache**   spot, stain, **9.2**
la **taille**   size (clothes), I-10.2
   la taille au-dessous   next smaller size, I-10.2
   la taille au-dessus   next larger size, I-10.2
   Vous faites quelle taille? What size do you take?, I-10.2
   tailler   to trim, **5.2**
le **tailleur**   suit (woman's), I-10.1; tailor, I
   le tailleur de pierre   stone cutter
le **talc**   talcum powder, **5.2**
le **talon**   heel, I-10.2
   à talons hauts (bas)   high- (low-)heeled (shoes), I
le **tambour**   drum, **11.1**
tant: en tant que   as
la **tante**   aunt, I-4.1
   taper à la machine   to type, **12.1**
le **tapis**   carpet, rug
   le tapis roulant   luggage carousel, **7.2**
   tard   late, I
   plus tard   later, I
le **tarif**   fare, I
   les tarifs aériens   airfares, I
la **tarte**   pie, tart, I-6.1
   la tarte aux fruits   fruit tart, pie, I
la **tartine**   slice of bread (with butter, jam, etc.), **2.1**
tas: des tas de   lots of, many
la **tasse**   cup, I-5.2
le **taureau**   bull
le **taux**   level, rate, I
le **taxi**   taxi, I-7.2
   te   (to) you (fam.) (dir. and ind. obj.), I-15.
le **technicien**, la **technicienne** technician, **16.1**
   technique   technical, I
   technologiquement technologically, I
le **tee-shirt**   T-shirt, I-9.2
la **teinturerie**   dry cleaner's, **9.1**
le **teinturier**   dry cleaner (person)
la **télé**   TV, I-3.2
   à la télé   on TV, I
la **télécarte**   prepaid telephone card, **3.1**
la **télécommande**   television remote control, **2.1**
le **télécopieur**   fax machine

le **téléphone**   telephone, I
   le téléphone à cadran   dial phone, **3.1**
   le téléphone sans fil   cordless telephone, **2.1**
   le téléphone à touches touch-tone phone, **3.1**
téléphoner   to telephone, **3.2**
téléphonique   telephone (adj.)
le **télésiège**   chairlift, I-14.1
le **téléviseur**   television (set), **2.1**
la **télévision**   television, **2.1**
tellement   so much
tel(le) que   as, such as
le **témoin**   witness (m. and f.)
la **température**   temperature, I-14.1
le **temps**   weather, I-9.2; time
   de temps en temps   from time to time, **4**
   il est temps que (+ subjunc.) it's time that, **11**
   Quel temps fait-il?   What's the weather like?, I-9.2
la **tendance: avoir tendance à** (+ inf.)   to tend (+ inf.), I
tendre à (+ **inf.**)   to tend (+ inf.)
se **tenir bien/mal**   to behave well/badly, **13.1**
le **tennis**   tennis, I-9.2
   les tennis (f. pl.)   sneakers, I
la **tension artérielle**   blood pressure, **6.2**
tenter   to tempt
le **terminal**   terminal (bus, etc.), **7.2**
terminale: en terminale   in the last year of school
terminer   to finish
se **terminer**   to end, finish
le **terminus**   last stop (of bus, train line), **10.2**
le **terrain**   field, ground, court
   le terrain de basket   basketball court, **12.2**
   le terrain de camping campground
   le terrain de football   soccer field, I-13.1
   le terrain de hand   handball court, **12.2**
   le terrain de sport   playing field
la **terrasse**   terrace, I-4.2
   la terrasse d'un café   sidewalk café, I-5.1
la **terre**   earth, soil, **15.1**
   la Terre   the Earth, I
   la terre cuite   terra cotta, earthenware

la **Terre-Neuve**   Newfoundland, I
   terrible   terrible; terrific (inform.), I-2.2
le **territoire**   territory, I
le **tétanos**   tetanus, I
la **tête**   head, I-13.1
   avoir mal à la tête   to have a headache, I-15.1
le **thé: le thé citron**   tea with lemon, I-5.1
   le thé à la menthe   mint tea, **14.2**
le **théâtre**   theater, I-16.1
la **théorie**   theory, I
le **ticket**   bus or subway ticket, **10.1**
le **ticket-restaurant**   restaurant voucher
   Tiens!   Hey!, Well!, Look!, I-10.1
le **tilleul**   linden tree, I
le **timbre**   stamp, **1.1**
   timide   timid, shy, I-1.2
   tirer des feux d'artifice   to shoot off fireworks, **11.1**
se **tirer d'une mauvaise situation** to get out of a bad situation, **8.1**
le **tissu**   fabric, **9.2**
le **titre**   title
   toi   you (sing. stress pron.), I-9
la **toilette: faire sa toilette**   to wash and groom oneself, I-11.1
les **toilettes** (f. pl.)   bathroom, I-4.2
le **toit**   roof
le **toit-terrasse**   rooftop-terrace, I
la **tomate**   tomato, I-6.2
   tomber   to fall, I-17
   tomber en panne   to break down (car), **8.2**
   ton   your (m. sing. poss. adj.), I-4
la **tonalité**   dial tone, **3.1**
   attendre la tonalité   to wait for the dial tone, **3.1**
la **tondeuse**   clipper
la **tonne**   ton, I
le **topographe**   topographer (m. and f.), I
se **tordre**   to twist (one's knee, etc.), **6.1**
   tôt   early, I
   total(e)   total, I
la **touche**   key (on a keyboard), **3.1**
   à touches   touch-tone (adj.), **3.1**
   toucher   to cash (a check), I-18.1; to touch, I
   toujours   always, I-5; still
la **tour**   tower
   la tour Eiffel   Eiffel Tower, I

le **tour: À votre tour.** (It's) your
   turn., I
   Le Tour du monde en quatre-
      vingts jours *Around the*
      World in Eighty Days
le/la **touriste** tourist, I
   tourner to turn, **8.2**
      sa chance tourne his luck
         changes
le **tournesol** sunflower
   tous, toutes all, every, I-7
      tous (toutes) les deux both, I
   tousser to cough, I-15.1
   tout(e) the whole, the entire,
      I-7; all, any
      À tout à l'heure. See you
         later., I-BV
      C'est tout? Is that all?, I-6.2
      en tout cas in any case, I
      les tout (inv.) premiers
         (m. pl.) the very first, I
      tout à fait exactly
      tout autour de all around
         (prep.), I
      tout de suite right away,
         I-11.2
      tout droit straight ahead,
         8.2
      tout le monde everyone,
         everybody, I-BV
      tout(e) seul(e) all alone, I-5.2
   toutefois still, nevertheless
la **toxicomanie** drug addiction
   toxique toxic, I
le **tracteur** tractor, **15.1**
la **tragédie** tragedy, I-16.1
le **train** train, I-8.1
   le train à grande vitesse
      (TGV) high-speed train, I
   traire to milk
le **traité** treaty
le **trajet** distance, I; trip, **10.2**
   transporter to transport, **6**
les **transports (m. pl.) en commun**
      public transportation, **10**
le **travail** work, **2.2**
      chercher du travail to look
         for work, **16.2**
   travailler to work, I-3.1
      travailler à mi-temps to work
         part-time, **16.2**
      travailler à plein temps to
         work full-time, **16.2**
le **travailleur** worker
   travailleur, travailleuse hard-
      working, I
les **travaux (m. pl.)** construction
      work, road work
   traverser to cross, I-12.2
   treize thirteen, I-BV

   trente thirty, I-BV
   très very, I-1.2
la **tribu** tribe
le **tribunal** court, **16.1**
la **tribune** grandstand, **11.1**
le **tricolore: le drapeau tricolore**
      French flag, I
le **tricot** knit, **9.2**
      en tricot knit (adj.), **9.2**
la **trigonométrie** trigonometry,
      I-2.2
   triste sad, **13.2**
   trois three, I-BV
   troisième third, I-4.2
le **trombone** trombone, **11.1**
se **tromper: Vous vous trompez.**
      You're mistaken., **4.1**
la **trompette** trumpet, **11.1**
le **tronc** trunk
   trop too (excessive), I-10.2
      trop de too many, too much, I
le **trophée** trophy, I
   tropical(e) tropical, I-9
le **trottoir** sidewalk, I-12.2
      le trottoir roulant moving
         sidewalk, **10.1**
le **trou** hole
le **trouble digestif** indigestion,
      upset stomach, I
le **troupeau** herd, **15.1**
   trouver to find, I-5.1; to think
      (opinion), I-10.2
se **trouver** to be located,
      found, I
   tu you (fam. subj. pron.), I-1
la **tuberculose** tuberculosis, I
   tuer to kill, I
la **Tunisie** Tunisia, I-16
le/la **Tunisien(ne)** Tunisian man,
      woman
   tunisien(ne) Tunisian, **14.2**
le **tutoiement** informal address
      using *tu*, **13.1**
se **tutoyer** to address (each other)
      as *tu*, **13.1**
le **type** guy (inform.), I
la **typhoïde** typhoide, I
   typique typical, I

U

   un, une a, one, I-BV
   unique: l'enfant unique only
      child, I
   unir to unite, I
   unisexe unisex, **5.2**
l' **unité (f.)** unit, I
l' **univers (m.)** universe
   universitaire university, I

l' **université (f.)** university, I
   urbain(e) urban
      l'appel inter-urbain long-
         distance call, **3.1**
l' **usine (f.)** factory, **2.2**
l' **ustensile (m.)** utensil, I
   utiliser to use, I
      en utilisant using, I

V

les **vacances (f. pl.)** vacation, I
      en vacances on vacation, I
le **vaccin** vaccination (shot), I
la **vaccination** vaccination, I
   vacciner to vaccinate, I
la **vache** cow, **15.1**
   vachement really (inform.), I
la **vague** wave, I-9.1
   vainement in vain
le **vaisseau** vessel
la **vaisselle** dishes, **2.1**
      faire la vaisselle to do the
         dishes, **2.1**
la **valeur** value, **1.2**
   valider to validate, **10.2**
la **valise** suitcase I-7.1
      faire les valises to pack, I-7.1
la **vallée** valley, I-14.1
   valoir to be worth
la **vanille: à la vanille** vanilla
      (adj.), I-5.1
la **vapeur d'eau** water vapor, I
la **variation** variation, I
   varié(e) varied, I
   varier to vary, I
la **variété** variety, I
   vaste vast, enormous, I
   vaut: il vaut mieux que (+ sub-
      junc.) it's better that, **11**
le **veau** calf, **15.1**
la **vedette** star (actor or actress),
      I-16.1
le **végétal** vegetable, plant, I
   végétarien(ne) vegetarian, I
la **veillée** evening gathering
le **vélo** bicycle, I-13.2
      à vélo by bicycle, I
      le vélo tout terrain (VTT)
         mountain bike, I
le **vélodrome** bicycle racing
      track, I
le **vélomoteur** moped, I-12.1
les **vendanges (f. pl.)** grape harvest
le **vendeur, la vendeuse**
      salesperson, I-10.1
   vendre to sell, I-8.1
   vendredi (m.) Friday, I-2.2
   venir to come, I-16

venir de (+ inf.) to have just (done something), **10.1**

le **vent** wind, I-14.2

    Il fait du vent. It's windy., I-9.2

la **vente** sale, I

le **ventre** abdomen, stomach, I-15.1

    avoir mal au ventre to have a stomachache, I-15.1

le **ver à soie** silkworm, I

le **verbe** verb, I

    vérifier to check, verify, I-7.1

    vérifier les niveaux to check under the hood, I-12.1

    véritable real, I

le **vernis à ongles** nail polish, **5.2**

le **verre** glass, I-5.2

le **verrier** glass-maker

    vers around (time); towards, I

le **versement** deposit, I

    verser to empty, pour (out); deposit

la **version originale** original language version (of a movie), I-16.1

    vert(e) green, I-10.2

    vertical(e) vertical, I

la **veste** (sport) jacket, I-10.1

    vestimentaire: normes vestimentaires dress code, I

le **veston** (suit) jacket, I

les **vêtements (m. pl.)** clothes, I-10.1

    Veuillez agréer, Madame (Mademoiselle, Monsieur), l'expression de mes sentiments distingués Sincerely yours (to close a letter)

la **veuve** widow

la **viande** meat, I-6.1

la **victoire** victory, I

le **vide** vacuum, space, I

    vide empty, I

la **vidéo(cassette)** videocassette, I-3.2

la **vie** life, I

    vieille old (f.), I-4.1

    vieux (vieil) old (m.), I-4.1

    vif, vive bright (color), I

    vigilant(e) vigilant, watchful, I

le **vignoble** vineyard, **15.1**

la **villa** house, I

le **village** village, small town, I

la **ville** city, town, **1.2**

le **vin (rouge, blanc)** (red, white) wine, I

    vingt twenty, I-BV

Vingt Mille Lieues sous les mers Twenty Thousand Leagues Under the Sea

    violent(e) violent, I

le **violon** violin

    viral(e) viral, I-15.1

la **virgule** comma, I

le **virus** virus, I

la **visite** visit, I

    visiter to visit (a place), I-16.2

la **vitamine** vitamin, I

    vite fast (adv.), I-12.2

la **vitesse** speed

    la limitation de vitesse speed limit, **8.1**

le **vitrail (pl. les vitraux)** stained-glass window

la **vitrine** (store) window, I

    Vive... ! Long live . . . !, Hooray for . . . !, I

    vivre to live, 6

    voici here is, here are, I-1.1

la **voie** track (railroad), I-8.1; lane (of a road), I-12.1

    voilà there is, there are (emphatic), I

le **voile** veil, **14.1**

    voilé(e) veiled, wearing a veil

    voir to see, I-10.1, I

    voir tout en rose to look at things through rose-colored glasses

    voire nay, even

le/la **voisin(e)** neighbor, I-4.2

la **voiture** car, I-4.2

    en voiture by car, I-5.2

    «En voiture!» "All aboard!", I-8

    la voiture à couloir central train car with central aisle, **4.1**

    la voiture de sport sports car, I-12.1

    la voiture gril-express train snack bar, **4.1**

    monter en voiture to board the train, I-8

la **voiture-lit** sleeping car, I-8.2

la **voiture-restaurant** dining car, I

le **vol** flight, I-7.1

    le vol intérieur domestic flight, I-7.1

    le vol international international flight, I-7.1

le **volley-ball** volleyball, I-13.2

le **volume** volume, I

    vos your (pl. poss. adj.), I-5

    voter to vote

    votre your (sing. poss. adj.), I-5

    voudrais: je voudrais I would like, I-5.1

    vouloir to want, I-6.1

    vous you (sing. form., pl.), I-2; you (stress pron.), I-9; (to) you (dir. and ind. obj.), I-15

la **voûte** vault, arch

le **vouvoiement** formal address as *vous*

se **vouvoyer** to address (each other) as *vous*

le **voyage** trip, I

    faire un voyage to take a trip I-7.1

    le voyage de noces honeymoon (trip)

    voyager to travel, I-8.1

le **voyageur, la voyageuse** passenger, I-8.1

    le voyageur à mobilité réduite handicapped traveler

    vrai(e) true, real, I

    vraiment really, I-2.1

la **vue** view, I

la **vulgarité** vulgarity, I

W

le **wagon à compartiments (à couloir latéral)** train car with compartments (with side aisle), **4.1**

le **walkman** Walkman, I-3.2

le **week-end** weekend, I-2.2

Y

    y there, I-5.2; I-18.2

le **yaourt** yogurt, I-6.1

les **yeux (m. pl; sing. œil)** eyes, I-15.1

    avoir les yeux qui piquent to have stinging eyes, I-15.1

Z

le **zappeur** television remote control, **2.1**

    zéro zero, I-BV

la **zone** area, zone, section, I-7.1

    en pleine zone tempérée right in the temperate zone, I

la **zoologie** zoology, I

    Zut! Darn!, I-12.2

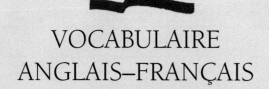

VOCABULAIRE
ANGLAIS–FRANÇAIS

The *Vocabulaire anglais–français* contains all productive vocabulary from Levels 1 and 2. The numbers following each entry indicate the chapter and vocabulary section in which the word is introduced. For example, **2.2** means that the word first appeared actively in Level 2, *Chapitre 2, Mots 2.* Boldface numbers without a *Mots* reference indicate vocabulary introduced in the grammar sections of the given chapter of Level 2. Numbers preceded by 1 indicate vocabulary introduced in Level 1; 1-BV refers to the Level 1 introductory *Bienvenue* chapter.

The following abbreviations are used in this glossary.

adj.	adjective
adv.	adverb
conj.	conjunction
dem. adj.	demonstrative adjective
dem. pron.	demonstrative pronoun
dir. obj.	direct object
f.	feminine
fam.	familiar
form.	formal
ind. obj.	indirect object
inf.	infinitive
inform.	informal
interr.	interrogative
interr. adj.	interrogative adjective
interr. pron.	interrogative pronoun
inv.	invariable
m.	masculine
n.	noun
past part.	past participle
pl.	plural
poss. adj.	possessive adjective
prep.	preposition
pron.	pronoun
sing.	singular
subj.	subject
subjunc.	subjunctive

A

a un, une, I-1.1
  a day (week) par jour
    (semaine), I-3.2
a lot beaucoup, I-3.1
abdomen le ventre, I-15.1
about à peu près, 16.2
to accelerate accélérer, 8.1
accident l'accident (m.), I-14.2
according to selon, 1.2
accountant le/la comptable,
  16.1
across from en face de, 4.1
act l'acte (m.), I-16.1
active actif, active, I-10
actor l'acteur (m.), I-16.1; le
  comédien, 16.1
actress l'actrice (f.), I-16.1; la
  comédienne, 16.1
address l'adresse, (f.), 1.2
to address (each other) as *tu*
  se tutoyer, 13.1
  informal address using *tu*
    le tutoiement, 13.1
addressee le/la destinataire, 1.2
advance: in advance à l'avance,
  4.2
advertisement: classified advertisement la petite annonce,
  16.2
aerobics: to do aerobics faire
  de l'aérobic, I-11.2
afraid: to be afraid avoir peur,
  13.2
Africa l'Afrique (f.), 14.2
after après, I-3.2
afternoon l'après-midi (m.), I-2
against contre, I-13.1
age l'âge (m.), I-4.1
agent (m. and f.) l'agent (m.),
  I-7.1
to agree être d'accord, I-2.1
air (adj.) aérien(ne), I-9
  air terminal l'aérogare (f.),
    I-7.1
airgram l'aérogramme (m.), 1.1
airline la compagnie aérienne,
  I-7.1
airmail par avion, 1.2
airplane l'avion (m.), I-7.1
airport l'aéroport (m.), I-7.1
aisle le couloir, I-8.2
  aisle seat (une place) côté
    couloir, I-7.1
algebra l'algèbre (f.), I-2.2
Algeria l'Algérie (f.), 14.1
all tous, toutes, I-7
  "All aboard!" «En voiture!»,
    4.1

all alone tout(e) seul(e), I-5.2
all right d'accord
  (agreement), I-3
  Is that all? C'est tout?, I-6.2
allergic allergique, I-15.1
allergy l'allergie (f.), I-15.1
alley la ruelle, 14.1
already déjà, I-14
also aussi, I-1.1
although bien que, 15
always toujours, I-5
ambulance l'ambulance (f.), 6.1
American (adj.) américain(e),
  I-1.1
among entre, I-9.2
and et, I-1
  and you? et toi? (fam.), I-BV
anesthesia: to give anesthesia
  faire une anesthésie, 6.2
anesthesiologist l'anesthésiste
  (m. et. f.), 6.2
angry fâché(e), I-12.2
ankle la cheville, 6.1
  to sprain one's ankle se
    fouler la cheville, 6.1
announcement l'annonce (f.),
  I-8.1
annually annuellement, 8
to answer répondre, I-8
answering machine le répondeur automatique, 2.1
antibiotic l'antibiotique (m.),
  I-15.1
Anything else? Autre chose?,
  I-6.2
apartment l'appartement (m.),
  I-4.2
apartment building l'immeuble
  (m.), I-4.2
apparently il paraît, 14.1
appear: it appears il paraît,
  14.1
application: job application
  la demande d'emploi, 16.2
to applaud applaudir, 11.1
apple la pomme, I-6.2
applicant (for a job) le/la
  candidat(e), 16.2
to apply for a position poser sa
  candidature, être candidat(e) à
  un poste, 16.2
appointment book l'agenda
  (m.), I-2.2
April avril (m.), I-4.1
area code l'indicatif (m.) de la
  ville, 3.1
arm le bras, 6.1
arrival l'arrivée (f.), I-7.2
  arrival board le tableau des
    arrivées, 4.2

to arrive arriver, I-3.1
arriving from (flight) en
  provenance de, I-7.1
arrow la flèche, 8.1
art l'art (m.), I-2.2
to ask (for) demander, I-5
  to ask a question poser une
    question, I-3.1
  to ask for directions
    demander son chemin, 8.2
aspirin l'aspirine (f.), I-15.1
astonished étonné(e), 13.2
at à, I-3.1
  at the à la, à l', au, aux, I-5
  at the home (business) of
    chez, I-5
  at what time? à quelle
    heure?, I-2
athletic sportif, sportive, I-10
August août, (m.), I-4.1
aunt la tante, I-4.1
autumn l'automne (m.), I-13.2
available disponible, 4.1
  to be available immediately
    être libre immédiatement,
    16.2

B

back (of an object) l'arrière
  (m.), 10.2
  back of the seat le dossier du
    siège, 7.1
  back (body) le dos
backboard (basketball) le
  panneau, I-13.2
backpack le sac à dos, I-BV
bacterial bactérien(ne), I-15.1
bag le sac, I-6.1
bakery la boulangerie-
  pâtisserie, I-6.1
balcony le balcon, I-4.2
ball (tennis, etc.) la balle,
  I-9.2; (soccer, etc.) le ballon,
  I-13.1
banana la banane, I-6.2
band: marching band la
  fanfare, 11.1
bandage le pansement, 6.1
bangs (hair) la frange, 5.1
bank la banque, I-18.1
to bargain marchander, 14.1
barn la grange, 15.1
baseball le base-ball, I-13.2
basket le panier, I-13.2
basketball le basket(-ball),
  I-13.2
  basketball court le terrain de
    basket, 12.2

bathing suit   le maillot (de bain), I-9.1

bathroom   la salle de bains (f.), les toilettes (f. pl.), I-4.2

to **be**   être, I-2.1
  to be able to   pouvoir, I-6
  to be afraid   avoir peur, 13.2
  to be better soon   être vite sur pied, I-15.2
  to be born   naître, I-17
  to be called   s'appeler, I-11.1
  to be careful   faire attention, I-9.1
  to be early   être en avance, I-8.1
  to be hungry   avoir faim, I-5.1
  to be in shape   être en forme, I-11.2
  to be late   être en retard, I-8.2
  to be on time   être à l'heure, I-8.1
  to be out of sorts   ne pas être dans son assiette, I-15.2
  to be thirsty   avoir soif, I-5.2
  to be used for   servir à, 13.1
  to be . . . years old   avoir... ans, I-4.1

beach   la plage, I-9.1

beautiful   beau (bel), belle, I-4

because   parce que, I-9.1

to **become**   devenir, I-16

bed   le lit, I-8.2
  to go to bed   se coucher, I-11.1

bedroom   la chambre à coucher, I-4.2

beef   le bœuf, I-6.1
  braised beef with vegetables   le pot-au-feu, 2.1

before   avant (prep.), I-7.1; avant que (+ subjunc.) (conj.), 15

beginner   le/la débutant(e), I-14.1

beginning of the school year   la rentrée, 12.1

to **behave well/badly**   se tenir bien/mal, 13.1

behind   derrière, I-BV

beige   beige (inv.), I-10.2

to **believe**   croire, I-10.2

bell   la sonnerie, 12.1

beltway   le boulevard périphérique, 8.1

beside   à côté de, I-5

best (adv.)   le mieux, 6
  the best (adj.)   le/la meilleur(e), 6
  best man   le garçon d'honneur, 11.2

better   meilleur(e), I-10 (adj.); mieux (adv.), 6
  it's better that   il vaut mieux que (+ subjunc.), 11; il est préférable que (+ subjunc.), 11

between   entre, I-9.2

beverage   la boisson, I-5.2

bicycle   le vélo, I-13.2; la bicyclette, I
  bicycle racer   le coureur cycliste, I-13.2
  by bicycle   à vélo, I-5.2

big   grand(e), I-1.1; gros, grosse, 8.1

bill   (currency)   le billet, I-18.1; **(invoice)** la facture, I-17.2

biology   la biologie, I-2.2

bird   l'oiseau (m.), 15.2

birthday   l'anniversaire (m.), I-4.1
  When is your birthday?   C'est quand, ton anniversaire? (fam.), I-4.1

black   noir(e), I-10.2

blackboard   le tableau, I-BV

blanket   la couverture, I-17.2

bleacher   le gradin, I-13.1

blond   blond(e), I-1.1

blood pressure: to take someone's blood pressure   prendre la tension artérielle, 6.2

blouse   le chemisier, I-10.1

to **blow a whistle**   siffler, I-13.1

to **blow-dry**   faire un brushing, 5.2

blue   bleu(e), I-10.2
  navy blue   bleu marine (inv.), I-10.2

board: arrival board   le tableau des arrivées, 4.2
  departure board   le tableau des départs, 4.2

to **board   (plane)**   embarquer, 7.2; **(train)** monter, I-8.2; monter en voiture, 4.2

boarding pass   la carte d'embarquement, I-7.1

bone   l'os (m.), 6.2

book   le livre, I-BV
  book of ten tickets (subway)   le carnet, 10.1

bookbag   le cartable, 12.1

born: to be born   naître, I-17

to **borrow**   emprunter, I-18.2

bottle   la bouteille, I-6.2

boundaries (on a tennis court)   les limites (f. pl.), I-9.2

box office   le guichet, I-16.1

boy   le garçon, I-BV

braid   la natte, 5.1

to **brake**   freiner, I-12.2

branch   la branche, 11.2

bread   le pain, I-6.1
  loaf of French bread   la baguette, I-6.1
  slice of bread (with butter, jam, etc.)   la tartine, 2.1

to **break**   casser, 9.2; rompre, 13.1; **(an arm, leg, etc.)** se casser, 6.1
  to break down (car)   tomber en panne, 8.2

breakfast   le petit déjeuner, 2.1

to **breathe (deeply)**   respirer (à fond), I-15.2

bride   la mariée, 11.2
  bride and groom   les mariés (m. pl.), 11.2

to **bring   (a person)**   emmener, 6.1; **(a thing)** emporter, 4.2

broke (slang)   fauché(e), I-18.2

brother   le frère, I-1.2

brown   (color)   brun(e), marron (inv.), I-10.2; **(hair)** châtain, 5.2

brunette   brun(e), I-1.1

to **brush (one's teeth, hair, etc.)**   se brosser (les dents, les cheveux, etc.), I-11.1
  brush cut   les cheveux en brosse, 5.1

building   le bâtiment, 15.1

bulletin board   le panneau d'affichage, 12.1

bun (of hair)   le chignon, 5.1

bunk (on a train)   la couchette, I-8.2

bus   l'autocar (m.) I-7.2; l'autobus (m.), 10.2; le bus, I-5.2
  bus station   le terminal; **(airport buses)** l'aérogare (f.) 7.2
  by bus   en bus, I-5.2

busy   occupé(e), I-2.2
  to be busy (telephone)   sonner occupé, 3.1

but   mais, I-1

butcher shop   la boucherie, I-6.1

butter   le beurre, I-6.2

button   le bouton, 9.2

to **buy**   acheter, I-6.1
  to buy a ticket   prendre un billet, I-7

C

cabin (plane)   la cabine, I-7.1
  business-class cabin   la cabine classe affaires, 7.1

coach-class cabin la cabine classe économique, **7.1**

first-class cabin la cabine première classe, **7.1**

café le café, I-5.1

cafeteria la cantine, **12.2**; la cafétéria, I

cake le gâteau, I-6.1

calculator la calculatrice, I-BV

calf le veau, **15.1**

call l'appel (m.), **3.1**; (long-distance) l'appel interurbain, **3.1**

to call appeler, **3.1**

to call back rappeler, **2.2**

to call on the telephone donner un coup de fil, **3.1**

Who's calling? C'est de la part de qui?, **3.2**

camel le chameau, **14.1**

on camel(back) à dos de chameau, **14.2**

can of food la boîte de conserve, I-6.2

Canadian canadien(ne), I-7

to cancel annuler, **7.2**

candelabra le chandelier, **11.2**

candle la bougie, **11.2**

cap (ski) le bonnet, I-14.1; (police officer's) la casquette, **8.2**

captain (on plane) le commandant de bord, **7.1**

car la voiture, I-4.2

sports car la voiture de sport, I-12.2

train car with central aisle la voiture à couloir central, **4.1**

train car with compartments (with side aisle) le wagon à compartiments (à couloir latéral), **4.1**

caravan la caravane, **14.2**

card la carte, **12.2**

credit card la carte de crédit, I-17.2

greeting card la carte de vœux, **11.2**

care (maintenance) l'entretien (m.), **15.1**

to take care of soigner, **6.1**

career la carrière, **16.2**

carefully prudemment, I-12.2

carrot la carotte, I-6.2

carry-on luggage les bagages (m. pl.) à main, I-7.1

cartoon le dessin animé, I-16.1

cash l'argent liquide (m.), I-18.1

cash register la caisse, I-6.2

to cash (a check) toucher (un chèque), I-18.1

cashier le caissier, la caissière, I

cassette la cassette, I-3.2

cast (for broken arm, etc.) le plâtre, **6.2**

castle le château, **4.2**

casual (clothes) sport (adj. inv.), I-10.1

cat le chat, I-4.1

to celebrate célébrer, **11.2**

ceremony la cérémonie, **11.2**

certain: to be certain être certain(e), **14**

it's certain il est certain, **14**

certainly certainement, **8**

chair la chaise, I-BV

chairlift le télésiège, I-14.1

chalk: piece of chalk le morceau de craie, I-BV

change la monnaie, I-18.1

change purse le porte-monnaie, I-18.1

to make change faire de la monnaie, I-18.1

to change changer (de), I-8.2

to change the channel changer de chaîne, **2.1**

to change lanes changer de voie, **8.1**

to change (subway) lines changer de ligne, prendre la correspondance, **10.1**

to change trains changer de train, prendre la correspondance, **4.2**

channel la chaîne, **2.1**

charcoal le charbon de bois, **14.1**

charcoal grill le braséro, **14.1**

to chat bavarder, I-4.2

to check vérifier, I-7.1; (luggage) faire enregistrer, I-7.1

to check under the hood vérifier les niveaux, I-12.2

to check out (of a hotel) libérer une chambre, I-17.2

check (in a restaurant) l'addition (f.), I-5.2; (bank) le chèque (bancaire), I-18.1

traveler's check le chèque de voyage, I-17.2

checkout counter la caisse, I-6.2

checkroom la consigne, I-8.1

cheek la joue, **13.1**

cheese le fromage, I-5.1

chemistry la chimie, I-2.2

chicken (animal) la poule, **15.2**; (food) le poulet, I-6.1

child l'enfant (m. and f.), I-4.1

chills (n.) les frissons (m. pl.), I-15.1

chocolate (adj.) au chocolat, I-5.1

to choose choisir, I-7.1

Christmas Noël, **11.2**

Christmas carol le chant de Noël, **11.2**

Christmas gift le cadeau de Noël, **11.2**

Christmas or New Year's dinner le réveillon, **11.2**

Christmas tree l'arbre (m.) de Noël, le sapin de Noël, **11.2**

Merry Christmas! Joyeux Noël!, **11.2**

church l'église (f.), **11.2**

city la ville, **1.2**

city hall la mairie, **16.1**

civil servant le/la fonctionnaire, **16.1**

to claim (luggage) récupérer, I-7.2

class (people) la classe, I-2.1; (course) le cours, I-2.2

classroom la salle de classe, I-2.1

clean propre, **9.1**

clean clothes le linge propre, **9.1**

to clear the table débarrasser la table, **2.1**

clerk: post office clerk l'employé(e) des postes, **1.1**

close proche, **10.1**

closed fermé(e), I-16.2

closet le placard, I-17.2

clothes les vêtements (m. pl.), I-10.1

clothing designer le grand couturier, I-10.1

cloud le nuage, I-9.2

Coca-Cola le coca, I-5.1

cockpit le poste de pilotage, **7.1**

coffee le café, I-5.1

black coffee l'express (m.), I-5.1

coffee with cream (in a café) le crème, I-5.1

coin la pièce, I-18.1

cold froid(e) (adj.), I-14.2; (illness) le rhume, I-15.1

to have a cold être enrhumé(e), I-15.1

It's cold (weather). Il fait froid., I-9.2

to collect ramasser, **4.1**

cologne l'eau (f.) de toilette, **5.2**

color la couleur, I-10.2

What color is . . . ? De quelle couleur est... ?, I-10.2

comb le peigne, **5.2**

to comb (hair) donner un coup de peigne, **5.2**; se peigner, I-11.1

combine harvester la moissonneuse-batteuse, **15.1**

to come venir, I-16
to come back revenir, I-16

comedy la comédie, I-16.1
musical comedy la comédie musicale, I-16.1

comic strip la bande dessinée, I-16

common courant(e), **13.1**

compact disc le compact disc, I-3.2

company l'entreprise (f.), la société, **16.2**
large company la grosse société, **16.2**

compartment: baggage compartment le comparti-ment, I-7.2; le coffre à bagages, **7.1**

complete complet, complète, **4.1**

completely complètement, **8**

computer l'ordinateur (m.), I-BV
computer science l'informatique (f.), I-2.2
computer scientist l'informaticien(ne), **16.1**

conductor (train) le contrôleur, I-8.2

confetti les confetti (m. pl.), **11.1**

confident confiant(e), I-1.1

congested (road, etc.) encombré(e), **8.2**

contents le contenu, **1.2**

convertible (car) la décapotable, I-12.2

to cook faire cuire, **14.1**; faire la cuisine, I-6

cordless: cordless telephone le téléphone sans fil, **2.1**

corn le maïs, **15.1**

corner le coin, **8.2**
at the corner of au coin de, **10.1**

corridor le couloir, I-8.2

cosmetic le produit de beauté, **5.2**

costume le costume, I-16.1

cotton (n.) le coton, **9.2**; en coton (adj.), **9.2**

to cough tousser, I-15.1

counter le comptoir, I-7.1

country le pays, I-7.1
country(side) la campagne, **15.1**
country code l'indicatif (m.) du pays, **3.1**

course le cours, I-2.2

court le tribunal, **16.1**; (basketball) le terrain de basket, **12.2**

courtyard la cour, I-4.2

couscous le couscous, **14.1**

cousin le/la cousin(e), I-4.1

to cover couvrir, I-15

cow la vache, **15.1**

cowshed l'étable (f.), **15.1**

crab le crabe, I-6.1

cream la crème, I-6.1
face cream la crème pour le visage, **5.2**

credit card la carte de crédit, I-17.2

crepe la crêpe, I-5.1

crew cut les cheveux en brosse, **5.1**

croissant le croissant, I-6.1

to cross (intersect) se croiser, **10.1**; (a street) traverser, I-12.2

crossroads le carrefour, I-12.2

crutches les béquilles (f. pl.), **6.1**

to cultivate cultiver, **15.1**

cup la tasse, I-5.2
winner's cup la coupe, I-13.2

curly frisé(e), **5.1**

currency la monnaie, **18.1**

curtain le rideau, I-16.1

customer le/la client(e), I-10.1

customs la douane, I-7.2
to go through customs passer à la douane, I-7.2

cut (on a person) la blessure, **6.1**

to cut couper, **5.2**
to cut (into a line) resquiller, **13.1**

cycling le cyclisme, I-13.2

cyclist (in a race) le coureur cycliste, I-13.2

cymbals les cymbales (f. pl.), **11.1**

D

dairy store la crémerie, I-6.1

to dance danser, I-3.2

dancer le danseur, la danseuse, **16.1**

Darn! Zut!, I-12.2

date (fruit) la datte, **14.2**; (day) la date, I-4.1
What is the date today? Quelle est la date aujourd'hui?, I-4.1

daughter la fille, I-4.1

day le jour, I-2.2
a (per) day par jour, I-3
What day is it? C'est quel jour?, I-2.2

dean of discipline le conseiller, la conseillère d'éducation, **12.2**

December décembre (m.), I-4.1

decorations les décorations (f. pl.), **11.2**

degree: It's . . . degrees Celsius. Il fait... degrés Celsius., I-14.2

delay le retard, **7.2**; le ralen-tissement, **8.1**

delicatessen la charcuterie, I-6.1

delicious délicieux, délicieuse, I-10

delighted enchanté(e), **13.2**

to deliver (mail) distribuer, **1.1**; (package) livrer

denim (adj.) en jean, **9.2**

deodorant le déodorant, I-11.1

department store le grand magasin, I-10.1

departure le départ, I-7.1
departure board le tableau des départs, **4.2**

deposit le versement

to deposit verser, I-18.1

to descend descendre, I-14.1

desert le désert, **14.2**

desk le bureau, I-BV
desk clerk le/la réceptionniste, I-17.1

detergent la lessive, **9.1**; le détergent

diagnosis: to make a diagnosis faire un diagnostic, I-15.2

dial le cadran, **3.1**
dial phone le téléphone à cadran, **3.1**

to dial (a telephone number) composer le numéro; faire le numéro, **3.1**

dictionary le dictionnaire, **12.1**

to die mourir, I-17

difficult difficile, I-2.1

dignitary le notable, **11.1**

dinar le dinar, **14.1**

dining car la voiture-restaurant, I-8.2

dining room la salle à manger, I-4.2

dinner le dîner, I-4.2

to eat dinner   dîner, I-4.2
diploma   le diplôme, **12.2**
direction   le sens, **8.2**
  to ask for directions   demander son chemin, **8.2**
directly   directement, **3.1**
dirty   sale, **9.1**
  dirty clothes   le linge sale, **9.1**
to discover   découvrir, I-15
dishes   la vaisselle, **2.1**
  to do the dishes   faire la vaisselle, **2.1**
dishwasher   le lave-vaisselle, **2.1**
to distribute   distribuer, **1.1**
district   le quartier, I-4.2; **(Paris)** l'arrondissement (m.), I
to dive   plonger, I-9.1
diving: to go deep-sea diving   faire de la plongée sous-marine, I-9.1
to do   faire, I-6.1
  to do the dishes   faire la vaisselle, **2.1**
  to do the laundry   faire la lessive, **9.1**
  to do the shopping   faire les courses, I-6.1
doctor   le médecin (m. et f.), I-15.2; **(woman)** la femme médecin
documentary   le documentaire, I-16.1
dog   le chien, I-4.1
dollar   le dollar, I-18.1
domestic (flight)   intérieur(e), I-7.1
donkey   l'âne (m.), **15.2**
door   la porte, I-17.1; **(of a vehicle)** la portière, **10.2**
doubt   le doute
  without a doubt   sans aucun doute, I
to doubt   douter, **14.2**
downtown   le centre-ville, **8.2**
dozen   la douzaine, I-6.2
drama   le drame, I-16.1
  drama club   le club d'art dramatique, I
dress   la robe, I-10.1
dressed: to get dressed   s'habiller, I-11.1
dressy   habillé(e), I-10.1
to dribble (a basketball)   dribbler, I-13.2
to drink   boire, **13**
  to have a drink   prendre un pot
to drive   conduire, I-12.2
driver   le conducteur, la conductrice, I-12.2

driver's license   le permis de conduire, I-12.2
driving lesson   la leçon de conduite, I-12.2
driving school   l'auto-école (f.), I-12.2
drum   le tambour, **11.1**
drums   la batterie, **11.1**
dry   sec, sèche, **5.2**
to dry   sécher, **9.1**
  to dry (off)   se sécher, I-17.2
to dry-clean   faire nettoyer à sec, **9.1**
dry cleaner (person)   le teinturier, la teinturière
dry cleaner's   le pressing, la teinturerie, **9.1**
dry cleaning   le nettoyage à sec, **9**
dryer (hair)   le séchoir, **5.2**
  clothes dryer   le sèche-linge, **9.1**
dubbed (movie)   doublé(e), I-16.1
duck   le canard, **15.2**
dune   la dune, **14.2**
during   pendant, I-3.2

E

each (adj.)   chaque, I-16.1
each (one) (n.)   chacun(e), **13.1**
ear   l'oreille (f.), I-15.1
earache: to have an earache   avoir mal aux oreilles, I-15.1
early   de bonne heure, **2.2**
  to be early   être en avance, I-8.1
to earn   gagner, I-3.2
earth   la terre, **15.1**
easy   facile, I-2.1
to eat   manger, I-5
  to eat breakfast   prendre le petit déjeuner, I-7
  to eat dinner   dîner, I-4.2
  to eat lunch   déjeuner, I-5.2
egg   l'œuf (m.), I-6.2
eggplant   l'aubergine (f.), **14.1**
eight   huit, I-BV
eighteen   dix-huit, I-BV
eighty   quatre-vingts, I-5.2
elbow   le coude, **13.1**
elective   le cours facultatif, **12.2**
elevator   l'ascenseur (m.), I-4.2
eleven   onze, I-BV
emergency: emergency aid   la police-secours, **6.1**

emergency exit   l'issue (f.) de secours, la sortie de secours, **7.1**
emergency room   la salle des urgences, **6.1**
employee   l'employé(e), **16.2**
  postal employee   l'employé(e) des postes, **1.2**
to employ   l'employeur, l'employeuse, **16.2**
employment agency   le bureau de placement, **16.2**
encyclopedia   l'encyclopédie (f.), **12.1**
energetic   énergique, I-1.2
engineer   l'ingénieur, la femme ingénieur, **16.1**
English (language)   l'anglais (m.), I-2.2
to enter   entrer, I-3.1
entire   entier, entière, I-10
entrance   l'entrée (f.), I-4.2
  entrance ramp   la bretelle d'accès, **8.1**
envelope   l'enveloppe (f.), **1.1**
to erase   effacer, **12.1**
eraser   **(pencil)** la gomme, **12.1**; **(blackboard)** la brosse, **12.1**
escalator   l'escalator (m.), l'escalier (m.) mécanique, **10.1**
especially   surtout, **3.2**
espresso   l'express (m.), I-5.1
European (adj.)   européen(ne), I-7
evening   le soir, I-2
  in the evening (P.M.)   du soir, I-2
every   tous, toutes, I-7; chaque, I-16.1
everybody/everyone   tout le monde, I-BV
everywhere   partout, I
exam   l'examen (m.), I-3.1
  French high school exam   le baccalauréat (bac, bachot), **12**
  to fail an exam   échouer à un examen, **12.1**
  to pass an exam   être reçu(e) à un examen, **12.1**; réussir à un examen, I-7
  to take an exam   passer un examen, I-3.1
to examine   examiner, I-15.2
except   sauf, I-16.2
to exchange (money)   changer, I-18.1
  exchange office (for foreign currency)   le bureau de change, I-18.1

exchange rate le cours du change, I-18.1

Excuse me. Excusez-moi., **4.1**

executive le cadre, la femme cadre, **16.1**

to **exercise** faire de l'exercice, I-11.2

exhibit l'exposition (f.), I-16.2

exit la sortie, I-7.1

expenses les frais (m. pl.), I-17.2

  to share expenses partager les frais, **13.1**

expensive cher, chère, I-10.1

eye l'œil (m., pl. yeux), I-15.1

  to have stinging eyes avoir les yeux qui piquent, **15.1**

eyelashes les cils (m. pl.), **5.2**

F

fabric le tissu, **9.2**

face la figure, I-11.1

  face cream la crème pour le visage, **5.2**

to **face** donner sur, I-17.1

  facing en direction de, **14.1**; (opposite) en face de

factory la fabrique, l'usine (f.), **2.2**

to **fail an exam** échouer à un examen, **12.1**

to **fall** faire une chute, I-14.2; tomber, I-17

  to fall asleep s'endormir, I-11.1

fall (season) l'automne (m.), I-13.2

family la famille, I-4.1

famous célèbre, I-1.2

fantastic fantastique, I-1.2

far from loin de, I-4.2

farm l'exploitation (f.) **15.2**; la ferme, **15.1**

  farm animal l'animal domestique, **15.1**

  farm equipment le matériel agricole, **15.1**

farmer l'agriculteur (m.), l'exploitant (m.), le fermier, **15.2**

farming (raising crops) la culture, **15.1**; (raising animals) l'élevage (m.), **15.1**

fast (adv.) vite, I-12.2; rapidement

father le père, I-4.1

faucet le robinet, **2.1**

favorite favori(te), I-10; préféré(e), **2.1**

February février (m.), I-4.1

to **feel (well, etc.)** se sentir, I-15.1

  to feel like (doing something) avoir envie de, **3.1**

  to feel out of sorts ne pas être dans son assiette, I-15.2

Festival of Lights (Hanukkah) la fête des Lumières, **11.2**

festivities les festivités (f. pl.), **11.1**

fever la fièvre, I-15.1

  to have a high fever avoir une fièvre de cheval, I-15.2

few peu (de), I-18

  a few quelques, I-8.2

field le champ, **15.1**

fifteen quinze, I-BV

fifty cinquante, I-BV

fig la figue, **14.2**

to **fill out** remplir, I-7.2

to **fill up (gas tank)** faire le plein, I-12.2

film le film, I-16.1

  adventure film/movie le film d'aventures, I-16.1

  foreign film/movie le film étranger, I-16.1

  horror film/movie le film d'horreur, I-16.1

  detective film/movie le film policier, I-16.1

  science fiction film/movie le film de science-fiction, I-16.1

finally enfin, I-11.1

to **find** trouver, I-5.1

fine l'amende (f.), **8.1**

Fine. Ça va.; Bien., I-BV

finger le doigt, **6.1**

to **finish** finir, I-7

fireplace la cheminée, **11.2**

fireworks le feu d'artifice, **11.1**

  to shoot off fireworks tirer des feux d'artifice, **11.1**

first premier, première (adj.), I-4.2; d'abord (adv.), I-11.1

  in first class en première, I-8.1

fish le poisson, I-6.1

  fish store la poissonnerie, I-6.1

fishing: to go fishing aller à la pêche, I-9.1

fitness (physical) la forme physique, I-11

five cinq, I-BV

to **fix one's hair** se coiffer, **5.1**

flag le drapeau, **11.1**

flight le vol, I-7.1

  flight attendant l'hôtesse (f.) de l'air, le steward, I-7.2

  flight attendants le personnel de bord, **7.1**

  flight crew l'équipage (m.), **7.1**

floor (of a building) l'étage (m.), I-4.2

flu la grippe, I-15.1

fluently couramment, 8

flute la flûte, **11.1**

to **fold** plier, **9.1**

to **follow** suivre, 6

foot le pied, I-13.1

  on foot à pied, I-5.2

for (time) depuis, I-8.2

forbidden interdit(e), I-12.2

forearm l'avant-bras (m.), **13.1**

forehead le front, **5.1**

foreign étranger, étrangère, I-16.1

foreman le contremaître, **2.2**

forewoman la contremaîtresse, **2.2**

to **forget** oublier, **3.1**

fork la fourchette, I-5.2

form le formulaire, **6.2**

forty quarante, I-BV

four quatre, I-BV

fourteen quatorze, I-BV

fracture la fracture, **6.2**

  multiple fracture la fracture compliquée, **6.2**

franc le franc, I-18.1

France la France, I-16

free libre, I-2.2

freezing: It's freezing. (weather) Il gèle., I-14.2

French français(e) (adj.), I-1.1; (language) le français, I-2.2

  French fries les frites (f. pl.), I-5.2

frequently fréquemment, 4

Friday vendredi (m.), I-2.2

friend l'ami(e), I-1.2; (pal) le copain, la copine, I-2.1

from de, I-1.1

  from the du, de la, de l', des, I-5

front (of an object) l'avant, **10.2**

  in front of devant, I-BV

frozen surgelé(e), I-6.2

fruit le fruit, I-6.2

full plein(e), I-13.1; (train car) complet, complète, **4.1**

full-time à plein temps, I-3.2

fun: to have fun s'amuser,
I-11.2
funny amusant(e), I-1.1;
comique, I-1.2
furious furieux, furieuse, **13.2**

G

to **gain weight** grossir, I-11.2
game le match, la partie, I-9.2
garage le garage, I-4.2
garden le jardin, I-4.2
garland la guirlande, **11.2**
gas(oline) l'essence (f.), I-12.1
  regular (gas) (de l'essence)
    ordinaire, I-12.1
  super (gas) (de l'essence)
    super, I-12.1
  unleaded (gas) (de l'essence)
    sans plomb, I-12.1
  gas station la station-service,
    I-12.2
  gas station attendant le/la
    pompiste, I-12.2
  gas tank le réservoir, I-12.2
gate (airport) la porte, I-7.1
gel le gel, **5.2**
geography la géographie, I-2.2
geometry la géométrie, I-2.2
to **get** obtenir, **12.2**
  to get a haircut se faire
    couper les cheveux, **5.2**
  to get a sunburn attraper un
    coup de soleil, I-9.1
  to get good (bad) grades
    recevoir de bonnes
    (mauvaises) notes
  to get in shape se mettre en
    forme, I-11.1
  to get in the front row
    se mettre au premier rang,
    11.1
  to get off (bus, train, etc.)
    descendre, I-8.2; **(plane)**
    débarquer, **7.2**
  to get on monter, I-8.2
  to get out of a bad situation
    se tirer d'une mauvaise
    situation, **8.1**
  to get up se lever, I-11.1
  getting off (a bus) la descente,
    10.2
gift le cadeau, I-10.2
girl la fille, I-BV
to **give** donner, I-3.2
  to give back rendre, I-18.2
glass le verre, I-5.2
glove le gant, I-14.1
to **go** aller, I-5.1

to go (in car, etc.) rouler,
I-12.2
to go deep-sea diving faire
  de la plongée sous-marine,
  I-9.1
to go down descendre, I-14.1
to go "dutch" partager les
  frais, **13.1**
to go fast rouler vite, I-12.2
to go fishing aller à la pêche,
  I-9.1
to go home rentrer, I-3.1
to go out sortir, I-7
to go through customs
  passer à la douane, I-7.2
to go to bed se coucher,
  I-11.1
to go up monter, I-17.1
to go windsurfing faire de la
  planche à voile, I-9.1
Shall we go? On y va?, I-5
goal le but, I-13.1
goalie le gardien de but, I-13.1
goggles (ski, etc.) les lunettes
  (f. pl.) I-14.1
good bon(ne), I-7; **(a child's
  behavior)** sage, **11.2**
  good manners le savoir-vivre,
    13
good-bye au revoir, ciao
  (inform.), I-BV
government worker le/la
  fonctionnaire, **16.1**
grade (on a test, etc.) la note,
  12.1
  to get good (bad) grades
    recevoir de bonnes
    (mauvaises) notes, **12.1**
grains les céréales (f. pl.), **15.1**
gram le gramme, I-6.2
granddaughter la petite-fille,
  I-4.1
grandfather le grand-père, I-4.1
grandmother la grand-mère,
  I-4.1
grandparents les grands-
  parents (m. pl.), I-4.1
grandson le petit-fils, I-4.1
grandstand la tribune, **11.1**
grass l'herbe (f.), **15.1**
gray gris(e), I-10.2
great chouette (inform.), I-2.2
green vert(e), I-10.2
  green beans les haricots
    (m. pl.) verts, I-6.2
**grilled ham and cheese
  sandwich** le croque-
  monsieur, I-5.1
grocery store l'épicerie (f.),
  I-6.1

groom le marié, **11.2**
ground le sol, I-13.2
ground floor le rez-de-chaussée,
  I-4.2
guidance counselor le
  conseiller, la conseillère
  d'orientation, **12.2**
guide(book) le guide, I-12.2
guitar la guitare, **11.1**
gym(nasium) le gymnase,
  I-11.2
gymnastics la gymnastique,
  I-2.2
  to do gymnastics faire de la
    gymnastique, I-11.2

H

hair les cheveux (m. pl.), I-11.1
  to fix one's hair se coiffer, **5.1**
  hair stylist le coiffeur, la
    coiffeuse, **5.2**
haircut: haircut with razor
  la coupe au rasoir, **5.2**
  haircut with scissors
    la coupe aux ciseaux, **5.2**
  to get a haircut se faire
    couper les cheveux
  to give a haircut faire une
    coupe, **5.2**
hairspray la laque, **5.2**
hairstyle la coiffure, **5.1**
half demi(e), I
  half past (time) et demie, I-2
ham le jambon, I-5.1
hand la main, I-11.1
handball court le terrain de
  hand, **12.2**
handkerchief le mouchoir,
  I-15.1
to **hang up (telephone)**
  raccrocher, **3.1**
hanger le cintre, I-17.2
Hanukkah Hanouka, **11.2**
happy content(e), I-1.1;
  heureux, heureuse, I-10.2
  Happy New Year! Bonne
    Année!, **11.2**
hard (adv.) fort, I-9.2
harvest la récolte, **15.1**
to **harvest** récolter, **15.1**
to **hate** détester, I-3.2
to **have** avoir, I-4.1
  to have a(n) . . . -ache avoir
    mal à... , I-15.2
  to have a cold être
    enrhumé(e), I-15.1
  to have a picnic faire un
    pique-nique, I-6

to have just (done something) venir de (+ inf.), **10.1**
to have to devoir, I-18.2
hay le foin, **15.1**
he il, I-1
head la tête, I-13.1
headache: to have a headache avoir mal à la tête, I-15.1
headphone l'écouteur (m.), **7.1**
health la santé, I-15.1
  to be in good (poor) health être en bonne (mauvaise) santé, **15.1**
  To your health! Bonne Santé!
health club le club de forme, I-11.2
to hear entendre, I-8.1
heel le talon, I-10.2
  high (low)-heeled (shoes) à talons hauts (bas), I-10.2
Hello. (when answering telephone) Allô., **3.2**; (greeting) Bonjour., I-BV
helmet le casque, **8.1**
her elle (stress pron.), I-9; la (dir. obj.), I-16; lui (ind. obj.), I-17.1; sa, son (poss. adj.), I-4
herd le troupeau, **15.1**
here is, here are voici, I-1.1
Hi. Salut., I-BV
high élevé(e), I-15; haut(e), I-10.2
  high school le lycée, I-1.2
  high school student le/la lycéen(ne), **12.2**
high-traffic area le point noir, **8.1**
highway l'autoroute (f.), I-12
  toll highway l'autoroute à péage, I-12.2
him le (dir. obj.), I-16.1; lui (stress pron.), I-9; lui (ind.obj.), I-17.1
his sa, son, I-4; ses, I-5
history l'histoire (f.), I-2.2
to hit frapper, I-9.2; (ball) envoyer, I-13.1
Hold on. (telephone) Ne quittez pas., **3.2**
holiday: national holiday la fête nationale, **11.1**
home: at the home of chez, **2.1**
homework (assignment) le devoir, I-BV
  to do homework faire les devoirs, I-6
horse le cheval, **15.1**
hospital l'hôpital (m.), **6.1**
hot: It's hot (weather). Il fait chaud., I-9.2

hot dog la saucisse de Francfort, I-5.1
hotel l'hôtel (m.), I-17.1
house la maison, I-3.1
how: How are you? Ça va? (inform.); Comment vas-tu? (fam.); Comment allez-vous (form.), I-BV
  How beautiful they are! Qu'elles (ils) sont belles (beaux)!, I
  how much combien, I-6.2
  How much is it? C'est combien?, I-6.2
  How much is that? Ça fait combien?, I-5.2
  How's it going? Ça va?, I-BV
hundred cent, I-5.2
to hurry se dépêcher, **2.2**
to hurt avoir mal à, I-15.1
  to hurt oneself se blesser, **6.1**
  It hurts. Ça fait mal., I-15.2
  Where does it hurt (you)? Où avez-vous mal?, I-15.2
husband le mari, I-4.1

I

I je, I-1
ice la glace, I-14.2
  ice cream la glace, I-5.1
  ice skate le patin à glace, I-14.2
  (ice) skating le patinage, I-14.2
  to (ice-)skate faire du patin (à glace), I-14.2
if si, 9
  if I were you (him, her, etc.) à ta (sa, votre, etc.) place, **9.2**
immigration l'immigration (f.), I-7.2
impatient impatient(e), I-1.1
impolite impoli(e), **13.1**
important: it's important that il est important que (+ subjunc.), **11**
impossible: it's impossible that il est impossible que (+ subjunc.), **11**
in dans, I-BV; à, I-3.1
  in back of derrière, I-BV
  in front of devant, I-BV
  in first (second) class en première (seconde), I-8.1
inexpensive bon marché (inv.), I-10.1
infection l'infection (f.), I-15.1
injection la piqûre, **6.2**

to give an injection faire une piqûre, **6.2**
to insist (that) insister (pour que + subjunc.), **12.1**
instructor le moniteur, la monitrice, I-9.1
to insure assurer, **1.2**
intelligent intelligent(e), I-1.1
interesting intéressant(e), I-1.1
intermission l'entracte (m.), I-16.1
international international(e), I-7.1
intersection le croisement, I-12.2
interview l'entretien (m.), **16.2**
to introduce présenter, **13.2**
introductions les présentations (f. pl.), **13.2**
to invite inviter, I-3.2
to iron repasser, **9.1**
ironing le repassage, **9.1**
it (dir. obj.) le, la, I-16.1
it is, it's . . . c'est... , I-BV
  It's expensive. Ça coûte cher., I-7.2
  it is necessary (+ inf.) il faut (+ inf.), I-9.1
  it is necessary that il faut que (+ subjunc.) **11.1**
Italian italien(ne), I-7
Italy l'Italie (f.), I-16

J

jacket le blouson, I-10.1
  (suit) jacket la veste, I-10.1
  ski jacket l'anorak (m.), I-14.1
January janvier (m.), I-4.1
jar le pot, I-6.2
jeans le jean, I-10.1
jeep la jeep, **8.1**
jersey le jersey **9.2**; en jersey (adj.), **9.2**
Jewish juif, juive, **11.2**
job l'emploi (m.), **16.2**
  job application la demande d'emploi, **16.2**
  job applicant le candidat, la candidate **16.2**
to jog faire du jogging, I-11.2
to joke around rigoler, I-3.2
judge le juge, **16.1**
July juillet (m.), I-4.1
  July 14 (French national holiday) le quatorze juillet, **11.1**
June juin (m.), I-4.1

K

key (to a room, etc.) la clé, I-12.2; (on a keyboard) la touche, 3.1
to kick donner un coup de pied, I-13.1
kilogram le kilo, I-6.2
kind le genre, I-16.1
to kiss (each other) s'embrasser, 13.1
kitchen la cuisine, I-4.2
kleenex le kleenex, I-15.1
knee le genou, 6.1
  to twist one's knee se tordre le genou, 6.1
knife le couteau, I-5.2
knit le tricot, 9.2; en tricot (adj.), 9.2
to know (be acquainted with) connaître; (information) savoir, I-16.2

L

lamb l'agneau (m.), 14.1
land la terre, 15.1
to land aterrir, I-7.1
landing (of plane) l'atterrissage (m.), 7.1
  landing card la carte de débarquement, I-7.2
lane (of a road) la voie, I-12.2
language la langue, I-2.2
last dernier, dernière, I-10
  last night hier soir, I-13
  last year l'année (f.) dernière, I-13
to last durer, 11.2
  late: to be late être en retard, I-8.2
Latin le latin, I-2.2
to laugh rire, 12.1
laundromat la laverie automatique, 9.1
laundry le linge, 9.1
  to do the laundry faire la lessive, 9.1
to learn (to) apprendre (à), I-9.1
  to learn one's lessons apprendre ses leçons, 12.1
lawyer l'avocat(e), 16.1
to lean (against) s'appuyer contre, 10.2
leather le cuir; en cuir (adj.), 9.2
  leather goods les objets (m. pl.) en cuir, 14.1

leather tanner le maroquinier, 14.1
to leave partir, I-7
  to leave (a room, etc.) quitter, I-3.1
  to leave (something behind) laisser, I-5.2
  to leave a message laisser un message, 3.2
  to leave a tip laisser un pourboire, I-5.2
left à gauche, 8.2
  to the left of à gauche de, I-5
  to turn left tourner à gauche, 8.2
leg la jambe, 6.1
  to break one's leg se casser la jambe, 6.1
lemonade le citron pressé, I-5.1
to lend prêter, I-18.2
lesson la leçon, I-9.1
letter la lettre, 1.1
lettuce la laitue, I-6.2
level le niveau, I-12.2
librarian (school) le/la documentaliste, 12.2
library (school) le Centre de Documentation et d'Information (CDI), 12.2
life vest le gilet de sauvetage, 7.1
to lift soulever, 3.2
to light allumer, 11.2
to like aimer, I-3.2
  I would like je voudrais, I-5.1
  Likewise. (responding to an introduction) Moi de même., 13.2
line (bus, train) la ligne, 3.1; (suburban train line) la ligne de banlieue, 4.2; (of people) la queue, I-8.1
  line of cars la file de voitures, 8.1
  to take the . . . line prendre la direction... , 10.1
  to wait in line faire la queue, I-8.1
lip la lèvre, 5.2
lipstick le rouge à lèvres, 5.2
to listen (to) écouter, I-3.2
  to listen with a stethoscope ausculter, I-15.2
liter le litre, I-6.2
literature la littérature, I-2.2
to live (in a city, house, etc.) habiter, I-3.1; vivre, 6
livestock le bétail, 15.1

living room la salle de séjour, I-4.2
lobby le hall, I-17.1
local local, 3.2
lock of hair la mèche, 5.1
locker la consigne automatique, I-8.1
long long(ue), I-10.2
long-distance (phone call) (l'appel) interurbain, 3.1
to look at regarder, I-3.1
to look for chercher, I-5.1
  to look for work chercher du travail, 16.2
to lose perdre, I-8.2
  to lose patience perdre patience, I-8.2
  to lose weight maigrir, I-11.2
lot: a lot of beaucoup de, I-10.1
  a lot of people beaucoup de monde, I-13.1
loudspeaker le haut-parleur, I-8.1
to love aimer, I-3.2
  love story (movie) le film d'amour, I-16.1
low bas(se), I-10
luggage les bagages (m. pl.), I-7.1
  carry-on luggage les bagages à main, I-7.1
  luggage carousel le tapis roulant, 7.2
  luggage cart le chariot à bagages, 7.2
  luggage compartment le coffre à bagages, 7.1
  luggage car (on a train) le fourgon à bagages, 4.2
lunch le déjeuner, 2
  to eat lunch déjeuner, I-5.2

M

ma'am madame, I-BV
machine l'appareil (m.), 7; la machine, 10.2
magazine le magazine, I-3.2
maid of honor la demoiselle d'honneur, 11.2
mail le courrier, 1.1
  mail carrier le facteur, 1.1
to mail a letter mettre une lettre à la poste, 1.1
mailbox la boîte aux lettres, 1.1
maitre d' le maître d'hôtel, I-5.2
to make faire, I-6.1
  make (of car) la marque, I-12.2
  makeup le maquillage, 5.2

man   l'homme (m.), I-10.1
manager   le directeur, la directrice, 16.1
map   la carte, 12.2
  road map   la carte routière, 8.1
  street map   le plan de la ville, 8.1
  subway map   le plan du métro, 10.1
March   mars (m.), I-4.1
to march   défiler
  to march in step   défiler au pas, 11.1
marching band   la fanfare, 11.1
market   le marché, I-6.2
  Arab market   le souk, 14.1
married: to get married   se marier, 11.2
marvelous   merveilleux, merveilleuse, I-10.2
mascara   le mascara, 5.2
match (singles, doubles) (tennis)   la partie (en simple, en double), I-9.2
material   la matière, 9.2
math   les maths (f. pl.), I-2.2
May   mai (m.), I-4.1
may: May I (sit here)?   Vous permettez?, 4.1
  May I speak to . . . ?   Pourrais-je parler à... ?, 3.2
mayor   le maire, 11.2
me   me (dir. and ind. obj.), I-15.2; moi (stress pron.), I-1.2
meadow   le pré, 15.1
meal   le repas, 2.1
meat   la viande, I-6.1
Mecca   la Mecque, 14.1
medicine   (medical profession) la médecine, I-15; (remedy) le médicament, I-15.2
medium: medium-length   mi-long(ue), 5.1
  medium-rare (meat)   à point, I-5.2
to meet (for the first time)   faire la connaissance de, 13.2
  to meet (again)   se retrouver, 13.1
menorah   la menorah, 11.2
menu   la carte, I-5.1
merchant   le/la commerçant(e), 16.1; le/la marchand(e), I-6.2
  produce merchant   le/la marchand(e) de fruits et légumes, I-6.2
message   le message, 3.2
  to leave a message   laisser un message, 3.2

meter maid   la contractuelle, I-12.2
middle   le milieu, 10.2
midnight   minuit (m.), I-2.2
  midnight mass   la messe de minuit, 11.2
military   militaire, 11.1
milk   le lait, I-6.1
minaret   le minaret, 14.1
mineral water   l'eau (f.) minérale, I-6.2
mirror   la glace, I-11.1
Miss (Ms.)   Mademoiselle (Mlle), I-BV
to miss (the train)   rater (le train), 4.2
missing: (noun) is missing   il manque (+ noun), 9.2
mistaken: You're mistaken.   Vous vous trompez., 4.1
mogul (skiing)   la bosse, I-14.1
moment: One moment, please.   Un moment, s'il vous plaît., 3.2
Monday   lundi (m.), I-2.2
money   l'argent (m.), I-3.2
  to have lots of money   avoir plein de fric (slang), I-18.2
monitor   le/la surveillant(e), 12.2
month   le mois, I-4.1
moped   le vélomoteur, I-12.2
morning   le matin, I-2
  in the morning (A.M.)   du matin, I-2
Morocco   le Maroc, I-16
mosque   la mosquée, 14.1
most (of)   la plupart (des), I-8.2
mother   la mère, I-4.1
motorcycle   la moto, I-12.2; la motocyclette, 8.1
  motorcycle cop   le motard, I-12.2
motorist   l'automobiliste (m. et f.), 8.1
mountain   la montagne, I-14.1
mouth   la bouche, I-15.1
movie   le film, I-16.1.
  movie theater   le cinéma, la salle de cinéma, I-16.1
moving sidewalk   le trottoir roulant, 7.2
Mr.   Monsieur (M.), I-BV
Mrs. (Ms.)   Madame (Mme), I-BV
museum   le musée, I-16.2
music   la musique, I-2.2
musician   le musicien, 11.1
Muslims   les Musulmans (m. pl.), 14.1

Muslim prayer leader   le muezzin, 14.1
must   devoir, I-18.2
mustard   la moutarde, I-6.2
my   ma, mon, I-4; mes, I-5

N

nail (finger, toe)   l'ongle (m.), 5.2
  nail polish   le vernis à ongles, 5.2
name   le nom, I-16.2
  What is your name?   Tu t'appelles comment? (fam.), I-11.1
nape (of the neck)   la nuque, 5.1
napkin   la serviette, I-5.2
narrow   étroit(e), I-10.2
national   national(e), 11.1
  national anthem   l'hymne (m.) national, 11.1
  national holiday   la fête nationale, 11.1
near   près de, I-4.2; proche, 10.1
necessary: it is necessary (+ inf.)   il faut (+ inf.), I-9.1; il est nécessaire de (+ inf.), 3.1
  it is necessary that   il faut que (+ subjunc.), il est nécessaire que (+ subjunc.), 11.1
to need   avoir besoin de, I-11.1
neighbor   le/la voisin(e), I-4.2
neighborhood   le quartier, I-4.2
nephew   le neveu, I-4.1
net   le filet, I-9.2
  net bag   le filet, I-6.1
never   ne... jamais, I-12
next   prochain(e), 4.2
new   nouveau (nouvel), nouvelle, I-4
  Happy New Year!   Bonne Année!, 11.2
  New Year's Day   le jour de l'An, 11.2
newspaper   le journal, I-8.1
newsstand   le kiosque, I-8.1
next   prochain(e), I-8.2
  next to   à côté de, I-5
nice (person)   aimable, sympa(thique), I-1.2; gentil(le), I-9
niece   la nièce, I-4.1
nine   neuf, I-BV
nineteen   dix-neuf, I-BV
ninety   quatre-vingt-dix, I-5.2

no one/nobody ne... personne, I-12.2; Personne ne... , **2**
No parking. Il est interdit de stationner., I-12.2; stationnement interdit, I
no smoking (section) (la zone) non-fumeurs, I-7.1
noise le bruit, **13.1**
noisy bruyant(e), **13.2**
non-stop (flight) sans escale, **7.2**
noon midi (m.), I-2.2
nose le nez, I-15.1
  to have a runny nose avoir le nez qui coule, I-15.1
not ne... pas, I-1
  Not bad. Pas mal., I-BV
notebook le cahier, I-BV
nothing ne... rien, I-12.2; Rien ne... , **2**
  Nothing else. Rien d'autre., I-6.2
novel le roman, I-16
November novembre (m.), I-4.1
now maintenant, I-2
number le numéro, I-5.2
  the right (wrong) number le bon (mauvais) numéro, **3.2**
  What is the phone number of . . . ? Quel est le numéro de téléphone de... ?, I-5.2
  You have the wrong number. C'est une erreur., **3.2**
numerous nombreux, nombreuse, **4.1**
nurse l'infirmier, l'infirmière, **6.1**

O

oasis l'oasis (f.), **14.2**
oats l'avoine (f.), **15.1**
to **obey** obéir (à), I-7; respecter, **8.1**
obvious: it's obvious that il est évident que, **14**
obviously évidemment, **8**
occasionally de temps en temps, **4**
o'clock: it's . . . o'clock il est... heure(s), I-2.2
October octobre (m.), I-4.1
of de, I-5
  of the du, de la, de l', des, I-5
to **offer** offrir, I-15
office le bureau, **2.2**
  school office le bureau de vie scolaire, **12.2**

often souvent, I-5
O.K. (health) Ça va.; (agreement) d'accord, I-BV
old vieux (vieil), vieille, I-4.1
  How old are you? Tu as quel âge? (fam.), I-4.1
omelette (with herbs/plain) l'omelette (f.) (aux fines herbes/nature), I-5.1
on sur, I-BV
  on board à bord de, I-7.2
  on foot à pied, I-5.2
  on time à l'heure, I-2
one un, une, I-1
  one-way ticket l'aller simple (m.), I-8.1
onion l'oignon (m.), I-6.2
  onion soup la soupe à l'oignon, I-5.1
only ne... que, seulement, **2.1**
on-ramp la bretelle d'accès, **8.1**
open ouvert(e), I-16.2
to **open** ouvrir, I-15.2
opera l'opéra (m.), I-16.1
operating room la salle d'opération, **6.2**
operating table la table d'opération, **6.2**
operator le/la standardiste, **3.1**
opinion: in my opinion à mon avis, I-10.2
to **oppose** opposer, I-13.1
opposing adverse, I-13.1
opposite (prep.) en face de, **4.1**
or ou, I-1.1
oral report l'exposé, **12.1**
  to give an oral report faire un exposé, **12.1**
orange (fruit) l'orange (f.), I-6.2; (color) orange (inv.), I-10.2
  orange soda l'Orangina (m.), I-5.1
orchestra l'orchestre (m.), **11.1**
to **order** commander, I-5.1
original language version (of a film) la version originale, I-16.1
other autre, I-BV
our notre, nos, I-5
out of bounds hors des limites, I-9.2
over (prep.) par dessus, I-13.2
  over there là-bas, I-BV
overcast (cloudy) couvert(e), I-14.2
to **overlook** donner sur, I-17.1
to **owe** devoir, I-18.2
  ox le bœuf, **15.1**

oxygen mask le masque à oxygène, **7.1**

P

to **pack (suitcases)** faire les valises, I-7.1
  package le paquet, I-6.2; le colis, **1.2**
packed (stadium) comble, I-13.1
painter le/la peintre, I-16.2
painting la peinture; le tableau, I-16.2
pair la paire, I-10.1
pal le copain, la copine, I-2.1
palm grove la palmeraie, **14.2**
palm tree le palmier, **14.2**
pancake la crêpe, I-5.1
pants le pantalon, I-10.1
pantyhose le collant, I-10.1
paper: sheet of paper la feuille de papier, I-BV
parade le défilé, **11.1**
parents les parents (m. pl.), I-4.1
Parisian parisien(ne), I-7
park le parc, I-11.2
to **park the car** garer la voiture, I-12.2
parking: No parking. Il est interdit de stationner., I-12.2
part (in hair) la raie, **5.1**
part-time à mi-temps, I-3.2
party la fête, I-3.2
to **pass (something to someone)** passer, I-7.2
  to pass (car) doubler, **8.1**
  to pass an exam être reçu(e) à un examen, **12.1**; réussir à un examen, I-7
passenger le passager, la passagère, I-7.1; (train) le voyageur, la voyageuse, I-8
passport le passeport, I-7.1
pâté le pâté, I-5.1
patient patient(e), I-1.1
to **pay** payer, I-6.1
  to pay attention faire attention, I-6
  to pay back rembourser, I-18.2
  to pay cash payer en espèces, I-17.2
pedestrian le/la piéton(ne), I-12.2
  pedestrian crossing les clous (m. pl.), I-12.2; le passage pour piétons, **8.2**

pen   le stylo, I-BV
   ballpoint pen   le stylo-bille,
      12.1
   felt-tip pen   le feutre, **12.1**
pencil   le crayon, I-BV
penicillin   la pénicilline, I-15.1
perfume   le parfum, **5.2**
permanent (hair)   la
   permanente, **5.1**
to permit   permettre, I-14
person   la personne, I-17.1
personally   personnellement,
   I-16.2
personnel department   le service du personnel, **16.2**
pharmacist   le/la
   pharmacien(ne), I-15.2
pharmacy   la pharmacie,
   I-15.2
physical education   l'éducation
   (f.) physique, I-2.2
physics   la physique, I-2.2
piano   le piano, **11.1**
to pick up (a telephone receiver)
   décrocher, **3.1**
picture   le tableau, I-16.1
pie   la tarte, I-6.1
pig   le cochon, **15.1**
pill   le comprimé, I-15.2
pillow   l'oreiller (m.), I-17.2
pilot   le pilote, **7.1**
to pilot   piloter, **7.1**
pine tree   le sapin, **11.1**
pink   rose, I-10.2
place   l'endroit (m.), **8.1**
   to take place   avoir lieu, **11.2**
to place   mettre, I-8.1
plain (adj.)   nature, I-5.1
plate   l'assiette (f.), I-5.2
platform (railroad)   le quai,
   I-8.1
to play (perform)   jouer, I-16
   to play (a sport)   jouer à,
      I-9.2; pratiquer un sport,
      I-11.2
   to play a musical instrument
      jouer d'un instrument de
      musique, **11.1**
play   la pièce, I-16.1
   to put on a play   monter une
      pièce, I-16.1
player   le joueur, la joueuse,
   I-9.2
please   s'il vous plaît (form.), s'il
   te plaît (fam.), I-BV
pocket   la poche, I-18.1
pocketbook, purse   le sac,
   I-18.1
police officer   l'agent (m.) de
   police, **8.2**; le gendarme, **8.1**

polite   poli(e), **13.1**
ponytail   la queue de cheval, **5.1**
pool   la piscine, I-9.2
poor   pauvre, I-15.1
   poor thing   le/la pauvre,
      I-15.2
popular   populaire, I-1.2
porter   le porteur, I-8.1
position (job)   le poste, **16.2**
possible: it's possible that
   il est possible que (+ subjunc.),
      11
postcard   la carte postale, **1.1**
post office   le bureau de poste,
   la poste, **1.1**
potato   la pomme de terre, I-6.2
pound   la livre, I-6.2
to pray   prier, **14.1**
preferable: it's preferable that
   il est préférable que (+ subjunc.); il vaut mieux que
   (+ subjunc.), **11**
to prepare   préparer, I-4.2
prepared   préparé(e), **12.1**
to prescribe   prescrire, I-15.2
prescription   l'ordonnance (f.),
   I-15.2
   to write a prescription   faire
      une ordonnance, I-15.2
to press   appuyer sur, **10.2**
pretty   joli(e), I-4.2
price   le prix, I-10.1
principal (n.)   la directrice, le
   proviseur, **12.2**
probable: it's probable that   il
   est probable que, **14**
problem   le problème, I-11.2
production   la production, **15.1**
profession   la profession, **16.1**
prohibited: . . . is prohibited
   il est interdit de... , **7.1**
projector   le projecteur, **12.1**
property   la propriété, **15.2**
provided that   pourvu que
   (+ subjunc.), **15.2**
public   public, publique, **3.1**
   public transportation   les
      transports (m. pl.) en
      commun, **10**
pulse: to take someone's pulse
   prendre le pouls, **6.2**
to punch (a ticket)   poinçonner,
   4.1
to punish   punir, I-7
to push   pousser, **10.2**
   to push the button   appuyer
      sur le bouton, **10.2**
to put (on)   mettre, I-8.1
   to put in (a coin)   introduire
      (une pièce), **3.1**

to put money aside   mettre
   de l'argent de côté, I-18.2
to put on makeup   se
   maquiller, I-11.1

Q

quarter: quarter after (time)
   et quart, I-2
   quarter to (time)   moins le
      quart, I-2
   Arab quarter   la médina, **14.1**
   Latin quarter   le Quartier
      latin, I
question: to ask a question
   poser une question, I-3.1
quickly   rapidement, **2.2**
quite   assez, I-1

R

rabbit   le lapin, **15.1**
race   la course, I-13.2
racket   la raquette, I-9.2
radio   la radio, I-3.2
raincoat   l'imper(méable), **9.2**
raining: It's raining.   Il pleut.,
   I-9.2
raisins   les raisins secs, **14.1**
rare (meat)   saignant(e), I-5.2
razor   le rasoir, **5.2**
   razor cut   la coupe au rasoir,
      5.2
to read   lire, I-12.2
ready-to-wear department
   le rayon prêt-à-porter, I-10.1
really   vraiment, I-2.1
to receive   recevoir, I-18.1
reception desk   la réception,
   I-17.1
record   le disque, I-3.2
to record   enregistrer, **2.1**
red   rouge, I-10.2
redheaded   roux, rousse, **5.1**
referee   l'arbitre (m.), I-13.1
registration card   (for automobile) la carte grise, **8**; (at hotel
   desk) la fiche d'enregistrement,
   I-17.1
regular (gasoline)   ordinaire,
   I-12.2
religious   religieux, religieuse,
   11.2
to remember   se souvenir de, **3.1**
remote control   le zappeur, la
   télécommande, **2.1**
to rent   louer, **4.2**

to **require** exiger, **12.1**
  required obligatoire, **12.2**
  reservations office le bureau de location, **4.2**
to **reserve (train seat)** louer, **4.2**; réserver, I-17
  restaurant le restaurant, I-5.2
  résumé le curriculum vitae (CV), **16.2**
to **return (tennis ball, etc.)** renvoyer, I-9.2
  right à droite, **8.2**
    to the right of à droite de, I-5
    to turn right tourner à droite, **8.2**
  right: it's right that il est juste que (+ subjunc.), **11**
  right away tout de suite, I-11.1
  ring: wedding ring l'alliance (f.), **11.2**
to **ring** sonner, **3.1**
to **rinse** rincer, **2.1**
  road la route, I-12.2
    road map la carte routière, **8.1**
    road sign le panneau (routier), **8.1**
  role le rôle, I-16
  roller (for hair) le rouleau, **5.2**
    electric roller le rouleau chauffant, **5.2**
  room (in house) la pièce, I-4.1; **(in hotel)** la chambre, I-17.1
    single room la chambre à un lit, I-17.1
    double room la chambre à deux lits, I-17.1
  rooster le coq, **15.2**
  round-trip ticket le billet aller-retour, I-8.1
  rude mal élevé(e), **13.1**
to **run** courir, **2.2**
  runner le coureur, I-13.2
  rush hour les heures (f. pl.) de pointe, les heures d'affluence, **8.1**

S

  sad triste, **13.2**
  Sahara le Sahara, **14.2**
  salad la salade, I-5.1
  salami le saucisson, I-6.1
  salary le salaire, **16.2**
  sales les soldes (f. pl.), I-10.2

  salesperson le vendeur, la vendeuse, I-10.1
  salt (adj.) salé(e), **14.2**
    saltcrust la croûte de sel, **14.2**
    salt lake le chott, le lac salé, **14.2**
  same même, I-2.1
  sand le sable, I-9.1
  sandwich le sandwich, I-5.1
    grilled ham and cheese sandwich le croque-monsieur, I-5.1
  Santa Claus le Père Noël, **11.2**
  Saturday samedi (m.), I-2.2
  sauce: spicy sauce la sauce piquante, **14.1**
to **save money** faire des économies, I-18.2
  savings account le compte d'épargne, I-18.1
to **say** dire, I-12.2
  scale la balance, **1.2**
  scarf l'écharpe (f.), I-14.1
  scene la scène, I-16.1
  schedule l'horaire (m.), I-8.1
  school l'école (f.), I-1.2
    high school le lycée, I-1.2
    school supplies le matériel scolaire, **12.1**
  school (adj.) scolaire, **12.1**
  science les sciences (f. pl.), I-2.2
  scissors les ciseaux (m. pl.), **5.2**
  score le score, I-9.2
to **score a goal** marquer un but, I-13.1
  screen l'écran (m.), I-7.1
  sculptor le sculpteur (m. and f.), I-16.2
  sculpture la sculpture, I-16.2
  sea la mer, I-9.1
    by the sea au bord de la mer, I-9.1
  seashore le bord de la mer, I-9.1
  seaside resort la station balnéaire, I-9.1
  seat le siège, I-7.1; **(on plane, at movies, etc.)** la place, I-7.1
    adjustable seat le siège réglable, **4.1**
    back of the seat le dossier du siège, **7.1**
    numbered seat la place numérotée, **4.1**
    seat belt la ceinture de sécurité, I-12.2
  seated assis(e), I-8.2
  second (adj.) deuxième, I-4.2; **(class)** seconde

  secretary le/la secrétaire, **16.1**
  section la zone, I-7.1
    smoking (no smoking) section la zone (non-)fumeurs, I-7.1
  security (airport) le contrôle de sécurité, I-7.1
to **see** voir, I-10.1
    See you later. À tout à l'heure., I-BV
    See you tomorrow. À demain., I-BV
to **seem** avoir l'air, **13.2**
    it seems to me (you, him, her, etc.) il me (te, lui, etc.) semble, **14.1**
  self-employed: to be self-employed être à son compte, **16.2**
to **sell** vendre, I-8.1
  semi-circle le demi-cercle, I-13.2
  semolina wheat la semoule de blé, **14.1**
to **send** envoyer, **1.1**
  sender l'expéditeur, l'expéditrice, **1.2**
  September septembre (m.), I-4.1
  seriously sérieusement, **8**
to **serve (transportation)** desservir, **4.2**; **(food, etc.)** servir, I-7.2
  service le service, I-5.2
    service station la station-service, I-12.2
    service station attendant le/la pompiste, I-12.2
  set (for a play) le décor, I-16.1; **(with hair curlers)** la mise-en-plis, **5.1**
    to set the table mettre le couvert, I-8
  seven sept, I-BV
  seventeen dix-sept, I-BV
  seventy soixante-dix, I-5.2
  several plusieurs, I-18.2
to **shake hands** se serrer la main, **13.1**
  Shall we go? On y va?, I-5
  shampoo le shampooing, **5.2**
to **shampoo** faire un shampooing, **5.2**
  shampoo-conditioner le shampooing-crème, **5.2**
to **share expenses** partager les frais, **13.1**
to **shave** se raser, I-11.1
  shawl le châle, **14.1**
  she elle, I-1
  shed (storage) le hangar, **15.1**

sheep le mouton, **15.1**
sheet le drap, I-17.2
  sheet of paper la feuille de
    papier, I-BV
shirt la chemise, I-10.1
shoes les chaussures (f. pl.),
  I-10.1; les souliers (m. pl.), **11.2**
shop la boutique, I-10.1
to **shop** faire des achats, I-10.1
short petit(e), I-1.1; court(e),
  I-10.2
shorts le short, I-9.2
to **shove** bousculer, **13.1**
show (movies) la séance,
  I-16.1; (TV) l'émission, **2.1**
to **show** montrer, I-17.1
  to show a movie passer un
    film, I-16.1
shrimp la crevette, I-6.1
to **shrink** rétrécir, **9.1**
shy timide, I-1.2
sick malade, I-15.1
  sick person le/la malade,
    I-15.2
side (in a sporting event) le
  camp, I-13.1; (of an object,
  person, etc.) le côté, **5.1**
sideburns les pattes (f. pl.),
  5.1
sidewalk le trottoir, I-12.2
  sidewalk café la terrasse (d'un
    café), I-5.1
to **sign** signer, I-18.1
silk la soie, **9.2**; en soie (adj.),
  9.2
since depuis, I-8.2
sincere sincère, I-1.2
to **sing** chanter, I-3.2
  singer le chanteur, la chanteuse,
    16.1
sink l'évier (m.), **2.1**
sir monsieur, I-BV
sister la sœur, I-1.2
to **sit (down)** s'asseoir, **2.1**
  to sit down for a meal
    se mettre à table, **2.1**
six six, I-BV
sixteen seize, I-BV
sixty soixante, I-BV
size (clothes) la taille; (shoes)
  la pointure, I-10.2
  the next larger size la taille
    au-dessus, I-10.2
  the next smaller size la taille
    au-dessous, I-10.2
  to take size (+ number) faire
    du (+ nombre), I-10.2
  What size do you take?
    Vous faites quelle pointure
    (taille)?, **10.2**

skate (ice) le patin à glace,
  I-14.2
  to (ice-)skate faire du patin
    (à glace), I-14.2
skater le patineur, la patineuse,
  I-14.2
skating le patinage, I-14.2
  skating rink la patinoire,
    I-14.2
ski le ski, I-14.1
  ski boot la chaussure de ski,
    I-14.1
  ski jacket l'anorak (m.),
    I-14.1
  ski pole le bâton, I-14.1
  ski resort la station de sports
    d'hiver, I-14.1
to **ski** faire du ski, I-14.1
skier le skieur, la skieuse,
  I-14.1
skiing le ski, I-14.1
  downhill skiing le ski alpin,
    I-14.1
  cross-country skiing le ski de
    fond, I-14.1
skirt la jupe, I-10.1
  tennis skirt la jupette, I-9.2
sky le ciel, I-14.2
to **sleep** dormir, I-7.2
sleeping car la voiture-lit, I-8.2
sleeve la manche, I-10.2
  long- (short-) sleeved à
    manches longues (courtes),
    I-10.2
slide (photo) la diapo(sitive),
  12.1
slot la fente, **3.1**
to **slow down** ralentir, **8.1**
  slowing le ralentissement, **8.1**
small petit(e), I-1.1
to **smile** sourire, **12**
smoking (section) (la zone)
  fumeurs, I-7.1
snack la collation, **7.1**
  snack bar (train) le gril-
    express, I-8, la voiture
    gril-express, **4.1**
sneakers les chaussures (f. pl.)
  de tennis, I-9.2
to **sneeze** éternuer, I-15.1
snowball la boule de neige,
  I-14.2
snowing: It's snowing. Il
  neige., I-14.2
so: so that pour que (+ subjunc.), **15**
soap le savon, I-11.1
soccer le foot(ball), I-13.1
  soccer field le terrain de
    football, I-13.1

social worker l'assistant(e)
  social(e), **16.1**
socks les chaussettes (f. pl.),
  I-10.1
soil la terre, **15.1**
soldier le soldat, **11.1**; le
  militaire
some quelques (pl.), I-8.2
somebody/someone
  quelqu'un, I-12.2
something to eat quelque
  chose à manger, I-5.1
sometimes quelquefois, I-5
son le fils, I-4.1
sore throat l'angine (f.), I-15.1
sorry désolé(e), **13.2**
  to be sorry être désolé(e),
    3.2, regretter, **13.2**
  I'm sorry. Excusez-moi., **4.1**;
    Je regrette., **3.2**
sound (of an animal) le cri,
  15.2
space (parking) la place,
  I-12.2
Spanish (language) l'espagnol
  (m.), I-2.2
to **speak** parler, I-3.1
  to speak on the telephone
    parler au téléphone, I-3.2
spectator le spectateur, I-13.1
speed limit la limitation de
  vitesse, I-12.2
to **speed up** accélérer, I-12.2
to **spend (money)** dépenser,
  I-10.1
spoon la cuillère, I-5.2
sporty (clothes) sport (adj.
  inv.), I-10.1
spot la tache, **9.2**
to **sprain** se fouler, **6.1**
spring (season) le printemps,
  I-13.2
stadium le stade, I-13.1
stage la scène, I-16.1
stain la tache, **9.2**
to **stain** faire une tache, **9.2**
staircase l'escalier (m.), I-17.1
stamp (postage) le timbre, **1.1**
  stamp machine le distributeur
    automatique, **1.1**
to **stamp (a ticket)** composter,
  I-8.1
standing debout, I-8.2
star (actor or actress) la
  vedette, I-16.1
starch l'amidon (m.), **9.1**
to **start the car** mettre le contact,
  I-12.2
station wagon le break, I-12.2
statue la statue, I-16.2

to **stay in shape** rester en forme, I-11.1

steak and French fries le steak frites, I-5.2

steep raide, I-14.1

stereo la chaîne stéréo, **2.1**

stitch le point de suture, **6.2**

  to give stitches faire des points de suture, **6.2**

stomach le ventre, I-15.1

  to have a stomachache avoir mal au ventre, I-15.1

stop l'arrêt (m.), **10.2**

to **stop (someone)** arrêter (quelqu'un), **8.1;** **(oneself)** s'arrêter, I-12.2

storage l'entreposage (m.), **15.2**

  storage shed le hangar **15.1**

store le magasin, I-3.2

to **store** entreposer, **15.2**

straight (hair) raide, **5.1**

  straight ahead tout droit, **8.2**

streamer le serpentin, **11.2**

street la rue, I-3.1

  street map le plan de la ville, **8.1**

stretcher le brancard, **6.1**

student l'élève (m. et f.), I-1.2

  high school student le/la lycéen(ne), **12.2**

to **study** étudier, I-3.1; faire des études, **7.2**

  to study French (math, etc.) faire du français (des maths, etc.), I-6

  study hall la salle de permanence, **12.2**

style le style, **5.1**

subject (school) la matière, I-2.2

subtitles les sous-titres (m. pl.), I-16.1

subway le métro, I-4.2

  by subway en métro, I-5.2

  subway station la station de métro, I-4.2

to **succeed** réussir (à), I-7

to **suffer** souffrir, I-15.2

suit (men's) le complet; **(women's)** le tailleur, I-10.1

  suit jacket la veste, I-10.1

suitcase la valise, I-7.1

summer l'été (m.), I-9.1

summit le sommet, I-14.1

sun le soleil, **14.2**

to **sunbathe** prendre un bain de soleil, I-9.1

Sunday dimanche (m.), I-2.2

sunglasses les lunettes (f. pl.) de soleil, I-9.1

sunny: It's sunny. Il fait du soleil., I-9.2

sunrise le lever du soleil, **15.2**

sunset le coucher du soleil, **15.2**

suntan lotion la crème solaire, I-9.1

super extra, super (inform.), I-2.2

  super (gasoline) (de l'essence) super, I-12.2

supermarket le supermarché, I-6.1

sure: to be sure être sur(e), **14.2**

  it's sure il est sûr, **14**

to **surf** faire du surf, I-9.1

surgeon le chirurgien, **6.2**

  orthopedic surgeon le chirurgien-orthopédiste, **6.2**

surprised surpris(e), **13.2**

  I would be very surprised ça m'étonnerait, **14**

to **surround** entourer, **8.1**

sweater le pull, I-10.1

sweatshirt le sweat-shirt, I-10.1

sweatsuit le survêtement, I-11.2

to **swim** nager, I-9.1

swimming la natation, I-9.1

T

table la table, I-BV

  table setting le couvert, I-5.2

  to clear the table débarrasser la table, **2.1**

  to set the table mettre le couvert, I-5.2

tablecloth la nappe, I-5.2

to **take** prendre, I-9.1; **(a person somewhere)** emmener, **6.1;** **(a thing somewhere)** emporter, **4.2**

  to take a bath (a shower) prendre un bain (une douche), I-11.1

  to take care of soigner, **6.1**

  to take an exam passer un examen, I-3.1

  to take off (plane) décoller, I-7.1

  to take place avoir lieu, **11.2**

  to take size (+ number) faire du (+ nombre), I-10.2

  to take something upstairs monter, I-17.1

  to take the train (plane, etc.) prendre le train (l'avion, etc.), I-7

  to take a trip faire un voyage, I-7.1

  to take a walk faire une promenade, I-9.1

taken pris(e), I-5.1

take-off (plane) le décollage, **7.1**

talcum powder le talc, **5.2**

to **talk** parler, I-3.1

  to talk on the phone parler au téléphone, I-3.1

to **tan** bronzer, I-9.1

tape recorder le magnétophone, **2.1**

tart la tarte, I-6.1

taxi le taxi, I-7.2

tea with lemon le thé citron, I-5.1

  mint tea le thé à la menthe, **14.2**

to **teach** enseigner, **12.2**

  to teach someone to do something apprendre à quelqu'un à faire quelque chose, I-14.1

teacher le professeur (m. and f.); le/la prof (inform.), I-2.1

  homeroom teacher le professeur principal, **12.2**

team l'équipe (f.), I-13.1

to **tear** déchirer, **9.2**

technician le/la technicien(ne), **16.1**

telephone le téléphone, **2.1**

  cordless telephone le téléphone sans fil, **2.1**

  telephone book l'annuaire (m.), **3.1**

  telephone booth la cabine téléphonique, **3.1**

  telephone card la télécarte, **3.1**

  telephone operator le/la standardiste, **3.1**

to **telephone** téléphoner, **3.2**

television la télé, I-3.2; **(programming)** la télévision, **2.1; (set)** le poste de télévision, le téléviseur, **2.1**

  television remote control la télécommande, le zappeur, **2.1**

to **tell** dire, I-12.2

temperature la température, I-15.1

ten dix, I-BV
tennis le tennis, I-9.2
 tennis court le court de tennis, I-9.2
 tennis game la partie de tennis, le match, I-9.2
 tennis shoes les chaussures (f. pl.) de tennis, I-9.2
 tennis skirt la jupette, I-9.2
terminal (with bus to airport) le terminal; l'aérogare (f.), **7.2**
terrace la terrasse, I-4.2
terrible terrible, I-2.2
test l'examen (m.), I-3.1
 to take a test passer un examen, I-3.1
 to pass a test réussir à un examen, I-7, être reçu(e) à un examen, **12.1**
textbook le livre scolaire, **12.1**
thank you merci, I-BV
that ce (cet) (m. sing. dem. adj.); cette (f. sing. dem. adj.), I-8; que (rel. pron., dir. obj.); qui (rel. pron., subj.), **1**
 That's expensive. Ça coûte cher., I-7.2
 that is to say c'est-à-dire, I-16.1
 that one celle (f. sing. dem. pron.); celui (m. sing. dem. pron.), **5**
the la, le, I-1; les, I-2
theater le théâtre, I-16.1
their leur, leurs, I-5
them elles, eux, (stress pron.), I-9; les (dir. obj.), I-16; leur (ind. obj.), I-17
then ensuite, I-11.1
there y, I-5; là, **5**
 there is, there are il y a, I-4.2; voilà (emphatic), I-BV
these ces (m. and f. pl., dem. adj.), I-8
they elles, ils, I-2
to **think** penser, I-10.2
third troisième, I-4.2
thirteen treize, I-BV
thirty trente, I-BV
this ce (cet), cette (m. and f. sing. dem. adj.), I-8
 this one celle (f. sing. dem. pron.); celui (m. sing. dem. pron.), **5**
those ces (m. and f. pl. dem. adj.), I-8; celles (f. pl. dem. pron.); ceux (m. pl. dem. pron.), **5**
thousand mille, I-6.2
three trois, I-BV

throat la gorge, I-15.1
 to have a frog in one's throat avoir un chat dans la gorge, I-15.2
 to have a scratchy throat avoir la gorge qui gratte, I-15.1
 to have a throat infection avoir une angine, I-15.1
to **throw** lancer, I-13.2
thumb le pouce, **13.1**
Thursday jeudi (m.), I-2.2
ticket (train, theater, etc.) le billet, I-7.1; **(bus, subway)** le ticket, **10.1**
 one-way ticket l'aller simple (m.), I-8.1
 round-trip ticket le billet aller-retour, I-8.1
 ticket machine le distributeur automatique, **10.1**
 ticket window le guichet, I-8.1
 traffic ticket la contravention, I-12.2
tie la cravate, I-10.1
tight serré(e); **(shoes)** étroit(e), I-10.2
time (of day) l'heure (f.), I-2
 at what time? à quelle heure?, I-2
 it is time that il est temps que (+ subjunc.), **11**
 to be on time être à l'heure, I-8.1
 What time is it? Il est quelle heure?, I-2
tip (restaurant) le pourboire, I-5.2
 to leave a tip laisser un pourboire, I-5.2
 The tip is included. Le service est compris., I-5.2
tire le pneu, I-12.2
 flat tire le pneu à plat, I-12.2
 spare tire la roue de secours, I-12.2
to à, I-3.1; **(flight, etc.)** à destination de, I-7.1
 to the à la, à l', au, aux, I-5
 to the left (of) à gauche (de), I-5
 to the right (of) à droite (de), I-5
today aujourd'hui, I-2.2
toe le doigt de pied, **6.1**
together ensemble, I-5.1
toilet (bathroom) les toilettes (f. pl.), I-4.2

toilet paper: roll of toilet paper le rouleau de papier hygiénique, I-17.2
token le jeton, **3.2**
tollbooth le poste de péage, **8.1**
toll highway l'autoroute (f.) à péage, I-12.2
tomato la tomate, I-6.2
tomorrow demain, I-2.2
 See you tomorrow. À demain., I-BV
tone (dial): to wait for the dial tone attendre la tonalité, **3.1**
tonight ce soir, **2.1**
too (also) aussi, I-1.1; **(excessively)** trop, I-10.2
tooth la dent, I-11.1
toothpaste le dentifrice, I-11.1
top le haut, **5.1**
touch-tone à touches, **3.1**
towel la serviette, I-17.2
town la ville, **1.2**
 town hall la mairie, **16.2**
tow truck la dépanneuse, **8.2**
toy le jouet, **2.2**
track la piste, I-13.2; **(for running)** la piste de course, **12.2**; **(train)** la voie, I-8.1
tractor le tracteur, **15.1**
trade le métier, **16.1**
traffic la circulation, I-12.2
 high-traffic area le point noir, **8.1**
 traffic jam le bouchon, **8.1**, l'embouteillage (m.), **8.2**
 traffic light le feu, I-12.2
 yellow (traffic) light le feu orange, I-12.2
tragedy la tragédie, I-16.1
trail la piste, I-14.1
 slalom trail la piste de slalom, I-14.1
trailer la caravane, **8.1**
train le train, I-8.1
 train station la gare, I-8.1
 station train arrives at la gare d'arrivée, **4.2**
 station train departs from la gare de départ, **4.2**
to **transfer (train, subway)** prendre la correspondance, **4.2**
to **transport** transporter, **6**
tray le plateau, **7.1**
 pull-down tray la tablette rabattable, **4.1**
tree: Christmas tree l'arbre de Noël (m.), **11.2**
trigonometry la trigonométrie, I-2.2

to **trim** tailler, **5.2**

trip le voyage, I; **(route)** le trajet, **10.2;**

trombone le trombone, **11.1**

truck le camion, **8.1**

tow truck la dépanneuse, **8.2**

trumpet la trompette, **11.1**

T-shirt le tee-shirt, I-9.2

Tuesday mardi (m.), I-2.2

Tunisia la Tunisie, **14.1**

Tunisian tunisien(ne), **14.2**

turkey (animal) le dindon, **15.2; (food)** la dinde

Turkish bath le bain turc, le hammam, **14.1**

to **turn** tourner, **8.2**

to turn off (the TV, etc.) éteindre (la télé, etc.), **2.1**

to turn on (the TV, etc.) allumer, mettre (la télé, etc.), **2.1**

TV la télé, I-3.2; **(set)** le poste de télévision, le téléviseur, **2.1**

twelve douze, I-BV

twenty vingt, I-BV

to **twist (one's knee, etc.)** se tordre, **6.1**

two deux, I-BV

type le genre, I-16.1

to **type** taper à la machine, **12.1**

typewriter la machine à écrire, **12.1**

U

uncle l'oncle (m.), I-4.1

under sous, I-BV

to **understand** comprendre, I-9.1

unemployed: to be unemployed être au chômage, **16.2**

unemployment le chômage, **16.2**

unfortunately malheureusement, **7.2**

unisex unisexe, **5.2**

United States les États-Unis (m. pl.), I-9.1

unleaded sans plomb, I-12.2

unless à moins que (+ subjunc.), **15**

unpleasant (person) désagréable, antipathique, I-1.2

until jusqu'à (prep.); jusqu'à ce que (+ subjunc.) (conj.), **15.2**

up to jusqu'à, I-13.2

us nous (stress pron.), I-9

to **use** employer, se servir de, **2.2**

U-turn: to make a U-turn faire demi-tour, **8.2**

V

to **vacate the room** libérer la chambre, I-17.2

to **validate (a bus ticket)** oblitérer, **10.2;** valider, **10.2**

valley la vallée, I-14.1

value la valeur, **1.2**

vanilla (adj.) à la vanille, I-5.1

vegetable le légume, I-6.2

veil le voile, **14.1**

vest: life vest le gilet de sauvetage, **7.1**

very très, I-1.1

vice-principal le censeur, **12.2**

videocassette la vidéo(cassette), I-3.2

video recorder (VCR) le magnétoscope, **2.1**

vineyard le vignoble, **15.1**

viral viral(e), I-15.1

volleyball le volley-ball, I-13.2

W

to **wait (for)** attendre, I-8.1

to wait in line faire la queue, I-8.1

waiter le serveur, I-5.1

waiting room la salle d'attente, I-8.1

waitress la serveuse, I-5.1

to **wake up** se réveiller, I-11.1

to **walk** se promener, I-11.2

walkman le Walkman, I-3.2

wallet le portefeuille, I-18.1

to **want** vouloir, I-6.1

warm-up suit le survêtement, I-11.2

to **wash** laver, **9.1; (one's face, hair, etc.)** se laver (la figure, les cheveux, etc.), I-11.1; **2.2**

to wash and groom oneself faire sa toilette, I-11.1

washcloth le gant de toilette, I-17.2

washing machine la machine à laver, **2.1**

to **watch** regarder, **2.1;** surveiller, I-12.2

Watch the closing doors! Attention à la fermeture des portes!, **4.1**

water l'eau (f.), I-6.2

to **water-ski** faire du ski nautique, I-9.1

wave la vague, I-9.1

wavy bouclé(e), **5.1**

we nous, I-2

to **wear** porter, I-10.1

weather le temps, I-9.2

It's bad weather. Il fait mauvais., I-9.2

It's nice weather. Il fait beau., I-9.2

What's the weather like? Quel temps fait-il?, I-9.2

wedding le mariage, **11.2**

wedding ring l'alliance (f.), **11.2**

Wednesday mercredi (m.), I-2.2

week la semaine, I-2.2

a (per) week par semaine, I-3.2

weekend le week-end, I-2.2

to **weigh** peser, **1.2**

weight le poids, **1.2**

to gain weight grossir, I-11.2

to lose weight maigrir, I-11.2

well bien, I-BV

well-done (meat) bien cuit(e), I-5.2

well-mannered bien élevé(e), **13.1**

wet mouillé(e), **5.2**

what quel(le), I-7; qu'est-ce que, I-13; quoi, **14**

What else? (shopping) Avec ça?, I-6.2

What is it? Qu'est-ce que c'est?, I-BV

What is . . . like? (description) Comment est... ?, I-1.1; (interr. pron.) qu'est-ce que (dir. obj.), **6;** qu'est-ce qui (subj.), **6**

wheat le blé, **15.1**

semolina wheat la semoule de blé, **14.1**

wheel la roue, I-12.2

wheelchair le fauteuil roulant, **6.1**

when quand, I-3.1

When is your birthday? C'est quand, ton anniversaire? (fam.), I-4.1

where où, I-BV

which quel(le) (interr. adj.), I-7; que (rel. pron., dir. obj.), qui (rel. pron., subj.), **1**

which one(s) laquelle (f. sing. interr. pron.); lequel (m. sing. interr. pron.); lesquelles (f. pl. interr. pron.); lesquels (m. pl. interr. pron.), **5**

to **whistle (blow a whistle)** siffler, I-13.1

white blanc, blanche, I-10.2
who qui, I-BV
  Who (do you mean)? Qui ça?, I-BV
  Who is it? Qui est-ce?, I-BV
  Who's calling? C'est de la part de qui?, 3.2
whom qui, I-14; que, 1
why pourquoi, I-9.1
wide large, I-10.2
wife la femme, I-4.1
to **win** gagner, I-9.2
wind le vent, I-14.2
window (in post office, bank, etc.) le guichet, 1.2
window (seat in plane) côté fenêtre, I-7.1
to **windsurf** faire de la planche à voile, I-9.1
windy: It's windy. Il fait du vent., I-9.2
wing l'aile (f.), 7.1
winner le/la gagnant(e), I-13.2
winter l'hiver (m.), I-14.1
to **wipe (one's hands, etc.)** s'essuyer, 13.1
to **wish** souhaiter, 12; (each other) se souhaiter, 11.2
with avec, I-5.1
without sans (prep.), I-12.2; sans que (conj.), 15
wool la laine, 9.2; en laine (adj.), 9.2
word processor la machine à traitement de texte, 12.1
work le travail, 16.1
  work (of art) l'œuvre, I-16.2
to **work** travailler, I-3.2
  to work full-time travailler à plein temps, I-3.2
  to work part-time travailler à mi-temps, I-3.2
worker l'ouvrier, l'ouvrière, 2.2
workplace le lieu de travail, 16.1
workshop l'atelier (m.), 14.1
worry: Don't worry about it. (after an apology) Ce n'est pas grave., 4.1
wound la blessure, 6.1
to **wrap (oneself up in)** s'envelopper dans, 14.1
wrinkled chiffonné(e), 9.1
wrist le poignet, 13.1
to **write** écrire, I-12.2
  to write a paper faire une rédaction, 12.1
wrong: What's wrong with him? Qu'est-ce qu'il a?, I-15.1

X

X-ray la radio(graphie), 6.2
  to do an X-ray faire une radio(graphie), 6.2

Y

year l'année (f.), I-4.1; l'an (m.), I-4
yellow jaune, I-10.2
yes oui, I-BV
yesterday hier, I-13.1
  the day before yesterday avant-hier, I-13
  yesterday morning hier matin, I-13
yogurt le yaourt, I-6.1
you te (dir. and ind. obj.), I-15; toi (stress pron.), I-9; tu, (subj. pron.) (fam.), I-1; vous (sing. form. and pl.), I-2
  You're welcome. De rien., Je t'en prie., Pas de quoi. (fam.); Ce n'est rien., Il n'y a pas de quoi., Je vous en prie. (form.), I-BV
young jeune, I-4.1
your ta, ton, tes (fam.), I-4; votre, vos (form.), I-5

Z

zero zéro, I-BV
zip code le code postal, 1.2
zipper la fermeture éclair, 9.2
zucchini la courgette, 14.1

INDEX GRAMMATICAL

adjectives comparative and superlative of *bon*, 151 (6); interrogative adjectives, 121 (5); plural with -*x*, 124 (5)

adverbs formation, 200 (8)

agreement of past participles with direct object, 12 (1); in reciprocal constructions, 37 (2); of reflexive verbs, 35 (2)

s'asseoir 34 (2)

boire 341 (13)

celui 122 (5)

ce que, ce qui 146 (6)

commands of *être, avoir,* and *savoir*, 412 (16); third-person commands, 412 (16); with object pronouns, 148 (6)

comparative of *bien* and *bon*, 151 (6)

conditional formation, 231 (9); in *si* clauses, 234 (9)

conjunctions with subjunctive, 388 (15)

demonstrative pronouns *celui,* 122 (5)

depuis 125 (5)

direct object pronouns agreement of past participles with, 12 (1); reflexive pronouns as, 35 (2); with indirect object pronoun in the same sentence, 175 (7), 199 (8)

employer 13 (1)

en in sentences with another pronoun, 256 (10); to refer to a person, 255 (10); vs. stress pronoun, 255 (10)

envoyer 13 (1)

faire with infinitive, 235 (9)

future in *quand* clauses, 198 (8); in *si* clauses, 234 (9); of *être, faire,* and *aller*, 174 (7); **of other irregular verbs, 196 (8)**; of regular verbs, 172 (7)

il me semble que 364 (14)

il paraît que 364 (14)

imperfect formation, 60 (3); in *si* clauses, 234 (9); use, 61 (3); vs. *passé composé*, 86 (4)

impersonal expressions with subjunctive, 282 (11)

indicative vs. subjunctive, 279 (11); with *il me semble que* and *il paraît que*, 364 (14)

indirect questions with *ce qui, ce que*, 146 (6)

infinitive with *faire*, 235 (9); with prepositions, 364 (14); of reflexive verbs, 65 (3); vs. subjunctive, 306 (12)

interrogative pronouns *lequel,* 121 (5); *qu'est-ce que* and *qu'est-ce qui,* 146 (6)

irregular verbs commands: *être, avoir,* and *savoir*, 412 (16); future: *être, faire,* and *aller*, 174 (7), other irregular verbs, 196 (8); imperfect, 61 (3); present indicative: *s'asseoir*, 34 (2), *boire*, 341 (13), *rire* and *sourire*, 307 (12), *suivre* and *vivre*, 147 (6); present subjunctive: 279 (11), *savoir, pouvoir,* and *vouloir*, 339 (13)

Photography

Front Cover: Charlie Waite/©Tony Stone Images; Abad, Charlie /La Photothèque SDP: 58, 93L, 211T, 286L, 289; Abeles/BSIP: 154R; Air France: 171L, 171R; Antman, M./Scribner: xR, xiiL, R-17T, R-17B, R-28T, R-29B, R-36B, R-45T, 34, 37B, 45R, 47/4, 63, 65T, 65B, 66, 69T, 70T, 86B, 89, 97R, 104T, 196, 210, 237, 250TR, 250BL, 255T, 259, 260C, 260B, 264T, 264B, 274T, 274B, 277, 281, 286R, 287T, 287B, 290–291/1, 290/2, 293, 302T, 307B, 308, 310, 311T, 321, 340, 408B, 411, 413T; Arbios, Roger/La Photothèque SDP: 423; Art Resource: 106T, 218L, 220L, 220R, 322, 323T; Ascani, M. Hoa-Qui: 161; Aurness, Craig/ Westlight: 357L, 370R; Autopresse: 203; Bajande/BSIP: 155B; Ball, David/DIAF: 93B; Barnes, David/La Photothèque SDP: R-6, 96; Barto, Gio/Image Bank: 367; Bear, Brent/Westlight: 320; Bellurget, Jean-Louis/La Photothèque SDP: 215; Bianco, Paul/La Photothèque SDP: 368; Billard, B./La Photothèque SDP: xivR, 361; Blanchard, M./Marco Polo: 238, 424; Blatty, Michael: R-24T, R-24B, 84; Boehm, M./La Photothèque SDP: 380, 396/2; Boucharlat/BSIP: 155T; Bouillot, F./Marco Polo: R-39, 11B, 60, 61, 86T, 93T, 94, 104B, 125B, 205B, 208/4, 233, 239, 278, 343; Bourret, J.P./Pitch: 370L; Boutin, G./Hoa-Qui: 130; Bouvet, Èric/Agence Ernoult Features: 182/2; Brown, Nancy/Image Bank: 120; BSIP: 157L; Bulloz: 98/2, 291/5, 327L, 327R, 338L, 338TC, 338BC, 338R; Carton/Pitch: 371B, 372/2; Chassagne, Georges/La Photothèque SDP: 183/4; Chemin, B./Hoa-Qui: 124; Ciné Plus: R-45B, 107TR, 107CR, 107BR; Croisile, H./DIAF: 242–243/1; Damm, J./Leo de Wys, Inc.: 352–353; Delacourt/Hoa-Qui: 241T; Delfino/Pitch: 365; Dewolf, Jean-Claude/La Photothèque SDP: 91, 132/3; Diaconesses, Tirot/BSIP: 151; Dunnell, Steve/Image Bank: 415; Durand, Guy/DIAF: 213; Fagot, Patrick/Explorer: R-36T; F.C.P.: R-32B; Fischer, Curt: viiTL, viiR, viiiBR, viiiTR, ixTR, ixBR, ixL, xiL, xiTR, xiiTR, xiiBR, xiiiL, xiiiTR, xivL, xvL, xvR, R-2T, R-2B, R-4, R-7T, R-7B, R-llT, R-12, R-16, R-20L, R-20R, R-22, R-23T, R-26–R-27, R-40, R-44, R-46, 4R, 5T, 5B, 11T, 15, 18B, 20–21/1, 23, 29T, 32T, 32B, 36, 37T, 40T, 41L, 41R, 42, 45L, 46–47/1, 47/5, 50–51, 54BR, 55, 70B, 72–73/2, 73/4, 74, 92, 93R, 97L, 98–99/1, 99/3, 116TL, 116TR, 116BL, 116BR, 126T, 131B, 133/4, 134T, 134B, 135, 136–137, 140, 146, 147, 149, 150, 152, 159/3, 159/4, 170T, 178, 194, 198L, 198R, 199L, 199R, 202, 204T, 206C, 206B, 207L, 207R, 208/2, 211B, 222–223, 232T, 232B, 236L, 241B, 243/3, 246–247, 250TL, 250BR, 258, 260T, 262, 263L, 263R, 265, 266–267/2, 266/1, 267/4, 269, 279, 282, 283, 284T, 284B, 294–295, 302B, 304, 311C, 311B, 312, 313T, 313B, 314–315/1, 314/2, 315/4, 318, 332, 336TL, 336TC, 336TR,

336BL, 336BC, 336BR, 339, 342B, 344, 347T, 347C, 347B, 348–349/1, 349/4, 366T, 373/5, 375, 381T, 381B, 384T, 384B, 386, 387, 388, 389, 390TL, 390TR, 390B, 392L, 392R, 393, 394T, 394B, 395T, 395B, 396–397/1, 396/3, 397/6, 398T, 398M, 399, 405T, 414, 417, 418–419/1, 418/2, 421, 425, 432–433; Fontaine, Benoit/La Photothèque SDP: 197; F. P. G. International: 314, 374; France TELECOM: 54C; Frazier, David R./Photolibrary: 8, 20/2, 21/5, 144T; Gauvreau, Vincent: viiBL, viiiL, xiBR, xiiiBR, R-32T, 4C, 4L, 10T, 10B, 11, 14, 15, 17T, 17B, 18T, 18C, 21/4, 40B, 43, 46/2, 54TL, 54TR, 54C, 59, 69C, 69B, 73/3, 119L, 119C, 119R, 121, 122, 125T, 126B, 133/6, 141, 144B, 154L, 176B, 201, 236R, 277, 299, 303, 316; Gaveau, Alain: R-5, R-14; Gely/Imapress: 430L; Gleizes, Pierre/Explorer: 270–271; Grandadam, S./Hoa-Qui: 205T, Grimberg, Marc/Image Bank: 48; Hallé/Marco Polo: 68, 99/4, 342T; Hervé, Frédéric/ Imapress: 158/2; Huteau, Michel/ANA: 123; Jeffrey, David/The Image Bank: R-3; Johnston, Greg/Photo 20-20; Jonathan/La Photothèque SDP: 357R, 362; Keystone/Sygma: 426L; Kirtley/ANA: 226; Krassovsky/ BSIP: 157R; La Vie du Rail: 95; Landau, Robert/ Westlight: 326R; Langeland, J.P./DIAF: R-30; Lavalette, Michèle/La Photothèque SDP: 181T; Le Bot, Alain/ DIAF: 29B, 81, 204C, 204B, 317, 408T; Legrand, Regis/La Photothèque SDP: 333; Madison, David/ Duomo: R-31T; Mahaux, J./Image Bank: 292; Marche, Guy/La Photothèque SDP: 371T; Marco Polo: 349/3; Mauritius/La Photothèque SDP: R-29T, 173; Mia and Klaus/Superstock: 62; Messerschmidt, J./Westlight: xL; NASA: 219R; Millet, Catherine: 431; Ozu, Kiki/La Photothèque SDP: 375; Panier, R./La Photothèque SDP: 397/4, 397/5; Philip, Charles/Westlight: 181B; Pierre, Georges/La Photothèque SDP: 372–373/1; Plailly, Philippe/CNRS: 405B; Plossu, Bernard/Marco Polo: 369T, 369B; Pratt-Pries/DIAF: 366B; Pysel, Czeslaw/La Photothèque SDP: 291/4; RATP: 253, Regine, M.:/ Image Bank: 145: Reynaud, M./France TELECOM: 73/5; Renaudeau, M./Hoa-Qui: 176T, 179, 208/3; Richer, X./Hoa-Qui: 208–209/1;Roger-Viollet: 64, 106B, 107L, 132/2, 219L, 221, 323B, 324, 325L, 325R, 326L, 426R, 427L, 427R, 430R; Romain, Jean-Marc/La Photothèque SDP: 90; Wayne Rowe: xvi–R-1, R-8–R-9, R-13, R-18–R-19, R-34–R-35, R-42–R-43, R-48–1, 14T, 22, 24–25, 67A, 67B, 76–77, 85, 87, 112–113, 158–159/1, 172, 177, 186–187, 190, 195, 200, 230, 234, 235, 254, 255, 256, 288, 307T, 315/3, 328–329, 345, 376–377, 398B, 400–401, 413B, 429; Santini, Pierre Jean/Agence Ernoult Features: 419/4; Sester, M./Pitch: 218R, 373/3; Simon/La Photothèque SDP: 182–183/1; SIRP-PTT: 72/1; SNCF: R-21T, R-21B, R-23B; Somelet, P./DIAF: 419/3; Vaisse, C./Hoa-

(continued on next page)

Qui: 242/2, 243/4; Valentin, E./Hoa-Qui: 132–133/1, 180B, 183/3; Valla, F/Pitch: 360, 373/4; Vance, David/Image Bank: 303; Villerot, Sylva/DIAF: 422; Wallet, P./Hoa-Qui: 131T, 133/5; Yamashita, Michael/ Westlight: 162–163, 170B, 174, 180T; Zurawik, J.F./La Photothèque SDP: 290/3.

Illustration

Becker, Neesa: 226; Collin, Marie-Marthe: 2–3, 164–165; Favre, Antoine: 350; Gregory, Lane: 117–118, 227–228, 275–276; Intesse, Yannick: 153; Kieffer, Christa: 378–379, 382–383; Kowalski, Mike: 216T, 216B, 217; Locoste-Laplace, Nathalie: 298; McCreary, Jane: 358–359, 406–407; Metivet, Henry: 26–27, 28, 166, 168–169; Miller, Lyle: R 25, 39, 56–57, 67, 82–83, 119, 160, 188–189, 248–249, 251–252, 272–273, 330–331; Nicholson, Norman: 111, 326, 354–355, 356, 402–403; Péron, Guy: 78–79, 80; Preston, Heather: 428R, 428L; Senée, Jean-Claude: 195; Spellman, Susan: 30–31, 114–115, 138–139; Taber, Ed: 108B, 108T, 109, 391; Tachiera, Andrea: 380; Taugourdeau, Sylvie: 52–53, 140, 192–193; Thewlis, Diana: R 10, R 37, 6–7, 127, 142–143, 224–225, 296–297, 300–301, 334–335; Torrisi, Gary: 245, 404.

Realia

Realia courtesy of the following: Air France: 167, 184; Boynton/Recycled Paper Products Inc.: 385; Compeed: 150; CARTCOM/Photo: E. Cuvillier, © Musée de la Poste; David, Jean-Louis: 128, 129; Éditions de Vecchi: 348; Éditions Les Quatre Zéphires: R-11; France TELE-COM: 54, 71, 74, 75, 152; Galeries Lafayette: 49; La Garantie Mutuelle Des Fonctionnaires (GMF), ©1987, LES ÉDITIONS ALBERT RENÉ/GOSCINNY-UDERZO: 191, 412; Gendarmerie Nationale: 141; Hôtel François 1er: 202; Institut Géographique National: 231; Inter-média Communication Consultants: 239; Laboratoire Conseil Oberlin: 156; © Michelin: 190, 207, 212; © 1991 Nathan, illustration Martine Heissat: 148; Orangina: 341; Parfum de Zagoras: 131; La Poste: 9, 19; RATP: 253, 254, 255B, 257, 268; La Redoute: 33, 229R; Roland-Garros: R-33; Saint-Laurent, Yves : 229L. SNCF: 45, 84, 97, 100, 101; Tunisair: 364; Voyages KUONI S.A.: 102.

Fabric designs by *Les Olivades*.

Maps

Eureka Cartography, Berkeley, CA.

In appreciation

Special thanks to the following people in France for their cordial assistance and participation in the photo illustration:

M. le Maire d'Ansouis; M. le Proviseur, les professeurs et les élèves du Lycée Henri IV; M. le Proviseur, les professeurs et les élèves du Lycée Val de Durance; Mme le Principal, les professeurs, en particulier Mlle Marie-Claude ÉBERLÉ, et les élèves du Collège Mignet; M. le Principal, les professeurs et les élèves du Collège du Pays d'Aigues; M. Jacques Lefèbvre et les élèves du Lycée du Parc Impérial; Groupe Scolaire Sainte-Anne.

Dr Christian Amat, Marie-Françoise, Camille, Emmanuel et Alexandre Amat/Jean-Pierre Antoine et Bébé le caniche/Helena Appel/La Famille Baud/Sonia Benaïs/La Famille Bérard/Jérôme Bernard/Sylvain Casteleiro/Adelaïde Chanal/Amy Chang/Andréa Clément/Émilie Cusset/La Famille Dandré et Josué/Michèle Descalis/Denise Deschamps/Mme Duclos/Élisabeth Éberlé/Jeanne Grisoli/Hélène Guion/David Hadida/Amelle Hafafsa, Amar et Riad/Thomas Hardy/Simone Kayem/Marie-France Lamy/Olivier Lucas/Harry Magdaléon/Dr Francis Maguet/Barbara Marone et Jessie le collie/Katy Martin/Jean Martinez/Dr Jean Mori/Claudette Mori/Elarif M'Ze/Magali Parola/Daniel Pauchon/Olivier Perrière/Élodie Perrin/Nelly Pouani/Estelle et Hélène Puigt/Claude Rivière/Nadège Rivière/Elzéar, Foulques et Amic de Sabran-Pontevès/Maître Frédéric Sanchez, avocat/Kalasea Sanchez/Martine Serbin/Michel Skwarczewski/Florence Vareilles/Maître Marie-Christine Viard-Vassiliev, avocate/Jonathan Viretto/Bernard et Jacqueline Vittorio

Air France (M. Philippe Boulze)/L'Art Glacier/Banque Marseillaise de Crédit/Boutique Frenchy's/Cabinet du Dr Amat/Cabinet du Dr Maguet/Charcuterie Guers/Compact Club/Complexe Sportif du Val de l'Arc/Fromagerie Gérard Paul/les Gendarmes de Beaumont/Grand Café Thomas/Le Grand Véfour (M. Guy Martin)/Hôtel Le Moulin de Lourmarin/ Pâtisserie Chambost/Pharmacie de l'Europe/Restaurant La Récréation/Restaurant Le Viêt-Nam/Salon de Coiffure Sylvie